Taxation of Loan Relationships and Derivative Contracts

GW00536389

Taxation of Loan Relationships and Derivative Contracts

Tenth Edition

David Southern QC
MA, DPhil, MPhil (Oxon), CTA (Fellow)
One of Her Majesty's Counsel
A Master of the Bench of Lincoln's Inn
A member of Temple Tax Chambers
Visiting Professor and Director of the School of Tax Law,
Queen Mary, University of London

Bloomsbury Professional

Bloomsbury Professional

An imprint of Bloomsbury Publishing Plc

Bloomsbury Professional Ltd	Bloomsbury Publishing Plc
41–43 Boltro Road	50 Bedford Square
Haywards Heath	London
RH16 1BJ	WC1B 3DP
UK	UK

www.bloomsbury.com

**BLOOMSBURY and the Diana logo are trademarks of
Bloomsbury Publishing Plc**

British Library Cataloguing-in-Publication Data
A catalogue record for this book is available from the British Library.

ISBN:	PB:	978-1-78043-891-7
	ePDF:	978-1-78451-136-4
	ePub:	978-1-78451-135-7

Typeset by Compuscript Ltd, Shannon

To find out more about our authors and books visit www.bloomsburyprofessional.com. Here you will find extracts, author information, details of forthcoming events and the option to sign up for our newsletters

Preface

For 20 years since the first edition of this book in 1996, I have endeavoured to follow each episode in the Homeric saga of loan relationships and derivative contracts. It would be a mistake, however, to seek to understand the current legislation in terms of what preceded it. To do so would be to miss the essential newness of developments. Legislators and tax authorities have to respond to multiple impulses, and the existing state of the law is only one factor amongst many.

Other fundamental changes have occurred. The decentralised system of tax administration based around that much respected figure, the District Inspector, has wholly disappeared. In the interpretation and application of tax law, the executive – in the form of HMRC – has to a considerable extent been substituted for the courts. In the courts there has grown up a tendency to bend the rules in order to get the bad guy.

Mr Justice Walton anticipated this state of affairs in 1982:

> 'It has been suggested that the whole of the law of taxation could be simplified and to a one-clause Act, "The taxpayer shall, after due enquiry and report by the Commissioners of Inland Revenue, be entitled to retain such portion of his income and assets as the Commissioners shall think fit", which would produce very much the same result as is produced today by the enormous mass of legislation which we have.'

(*Innocent v Whaddon Estates Ltd* [1982] STC 115 at 121)

At that time, the 'enormous mass of legislation' ran to two volumes of the Yellow and Orange Tax Handbooks, as compared with the current (2015/2016) eight volumes.

The writer of a book such as this is extremely dependent on criticism and conversation, if he is to avoid an undue proportion of errors and obscurity. I have depended on the advice and constructive criticism of Philip Ridgway and Rebecca Murray, colleagues in Temple Tax Chambers; Murray Clayton, of Freshfields Bruckhaus Deringer; Kiret Singh of Wilkins Kennedy; Bruce Hunter of Rotch; and Brian Lindsey of HW Fisher & Company, for crucial help with examples. The book would not have been written without the promptings, oversight and input of David Wright and his colleagues at Bloomsbury Professional.

The law is stated as at 31 October 2016.

David Southern QC
Temple Tax Chambers

While every care has been taken to ensure the accuracy of the contents of this work, no responsibility for loss occasioned to any person acting or refraining from action as a result of any statement in it can be accepted by the author or publisher.

The exchange rates used throughout the text for the purposes of the examples are not the particular exchange rates at the particular dates concerned but are sample rates used for illustrative purposes only.

Contents

Contents

Contents

Table of statutes

[*All references are to paragraph number*]

Table of statutory instruments

Table of cases

Abbreviations and references

ABS	=	asset-backed security
ADP	=	acceptable distribution policy
AfS	=	available for sale
AIM	=	Alternative Investment Market
AIT	=	approved investment trust
APB	=	Auditing Practices Board
ARC	=	Accounting Regulatory Committee
ASB	=	Accounting Standards Board
AUT	=	authorised unit trust
BEPS	=	Base Erosion and Profit Shifting
BIS	=	Bank for International Settlements
BLAGAB	=	basic life assurance and general annuity business
CA	=	Companies Act
CAA 2001	=	Capital Allowances Act 2001
CFC	=	controlled foreign company
CFM	=	Corporate Finance Manual
CGO	=	Central Gilts Office
CIS	=	collective investment scheme
CISX	=	Channel Islands Stock Exchange
COAP	=	change of accounting practice
CSA	=	collateral support agreement
CTA	=	Corporation Tax Act
CTSA	=	corporation tax self-assessment
CVA	=	counterparty valuation adjustment
DBV	=	delivery-by-value
DD	=	double deduction mismatch
DFI	=	derivative financial instrument
D/NI	=	deduction/non-inclusion mismatch
DPT	=	diverted profits tax

DTA	=	double taxation agreement
DVP	=	delivery versus payment
ECP	=	Eurocommercial paper
EEA	=	European Economic Area
EFRAG	=	European Financial Reporting Advisory Group
EIR		effective interest rate
ERSM	=	Employment Related Securities Manual
ESC	=	extra-statutory concession
FA	=	Finance Act
FCA	=	Financial Conduct Authority
FCPE	=	finance company partial exemption
FEOMA		Foreign Exchange and Options Master Agreement
FIE	=	financing income exemption
FOTRA	=	free of tax to residents abroad
FRA	=	forward rate agreement
FRC	=	Financial Reporting Council
FRR	=	Fixed Ratio Rule
FRS	=	Financial Reporting Standard
FRSSE	=	Financial Reporting Standard for Smaller Entities
FSA	=	Financial Services Authority
FSMA 2000	=	Financial Services and Markets Act 2000
FTT	=	First-tier Tribunal
FV	=	fair value
FVTPL	=	fair value through profit and loss
GAAP	=	generally accepted accounting practice
GEMM	=	Gilt Edged Market Maker
GMSLA	=	global master securities lending agreement
IDB	=	Inter Dealer Broker
HFT	=	held for trading
HMRC	=	Her Majesty's Commissioners for Revenue and Customs
HTM	=	held-to-maturity
IAS	=	International Accounting Standard
IASB	=	International Accounting Standards Board

IBCI	=	investment-based carried interest
ICAEW	=	Institute of Chartered Accountants in England and Wales
ICOM		International Currency Options Master Agreement
ICSD	=	international central securities depository
ICTA 1988	=	Income and Corporation Taxes Act 1988
IFEMA		International Foreign Exchange Master Agreement
IFRIC	=	International Financial Reporting Interpretation Committee
IFRS	=	International Financial Reporting Standard
IFRIC	=	International Financial Reporting Interpretations Committee
IMV	=	implied maturity value
IRR	=	internal rate of return
ISDA	=	International Swaps and Derivatives Association
ISMA	=	International Securities Market Association
ITA 2007	=	Income Tax Act 2007
ITEPA 2003	=	Income Tax (Earnings and Pensions) Act 2003
ITM	=	in the money
ITTOIA 2005	=	Income Tax (Trading and Other Income) Act 2005
L&R	=	loans and receivables
LIBOR	=	London inter-bank offered rate
LIFFE	=	London International Financial Futures and Options Exchange
LIFO	=	last in/first out
LLP	=	limited liability partnership
MNE	=	multi-national enterprise
MTN	=	medium-term note
NPV	=	net present value
OCI	=	other comprehensive income
OECD	=	Organisation for Economic Co-operation and Development
OEIC	=	open-ended investment company
OTC	=	over-the-counter, ie tailor-made and outside organised markets

OTM	=	out of the money
P2P	=	peer-to-peer
PE	=	permanent establishment
PFI	=	private finance initiative
PV	=	present value
QCB	=	qualifying corporate bond
RAAR	=	regime anti-avoidance rules
R&D	=	research and development
REIT	=	real estate investment trust
RNLR	=	relevant non-lending relationship
RPI	=	Retail Price Index
RTGS	=	real time gross settlement
RWA	=	risk-weighted asset
SDRT	=	stamp duty reserve tax
SE	=	Societas Europaea
SI	=	Statutory Instrument
SME	=	small and medium-sized enterprise
SOCIE	=	statement of changes in equity
SORP	=	Statement of Recommended Accounting Practice
SP	=	Statement of Practice
SPF	=	significant people function
SPV	=	special purpose vehicle
SSAP	=	Statement of Standard Accounting Practice
SSE	=	substantial shareholding exemption
STRGL	=	statement of total reported gains and losses
STC	=	Simon's Tax Cases
STI	=	Simon's Tax Intelligence
TCGA 1992	=	Taxation of Chargeable Gains Act 1992
TDA	=	total disallowed amount
TIA	=	tested income amount
TIOPA 2010	=	Taxation (International and Other Provisions) Act 2010
TMA 1970	=	Taxes Management Act 1970
UCITS	=	undertakings for collective investment in transferable securities

UITF	=	Urgent Issues Task Force
UT	=	Upper Tribunal
VCC	=	venture capital company
VCT	=	venture capital trust
ZC	=	zero coupon
ZCB	=	zero coupon bond

Glossary

(*Denotes that a term is defined.)

callable bond	=	a fixed interest bond which an issuer can retire before its scheduled maturity
cap	=	an agreement under which, in exchange for a one-off payment, the seller agrees to pay the buyer the difference (if positive) between the *strike rate and the current rate of interest at preset times on a specified notional amount of principal over the life of the cap, thus limiting the interest rate exposure of the buyer, who will typically be a borrower. The opposite of a *floor
carrying value	=	the amount required to pay off a liability (ie repayment of principal and finance costs incurred) at the time of measurement
closing out	=	action of off-setting a *long or *short position by entering into an equal and opposite risk
collar	=	a combination of a *cap and a *floor
contract for differences	=	a contract to pay the net differences between two sums calculated by reference to fluctuations in the value of an asset or in an index
conversion	=	turning of bonds into shares, so that bond holders become shareholders and loan capital becomes equity capital
conversion premium	=	difference between conversion price for shares and market price at time of issue of *convertibles
convertible	=	(deferred equity) bond issue, the terms of which allow the holder to exchange his bonds for another security, usually the equity of the issuer; a bond with an embedded *option

counterparty	=	the other party to a *non-synallagmatic contract
covered warrant	=	a *warrant issued by an entity other than the issuer of the shares or bonds which the warrant gives the right to acquire
credit	=	an accounting entry representing income, the incurring or increase of a liability or a reduction of an asset
credit derivative	=	a contract that transfers credit risk on loans and other assets from one party (the protection buyer) to another party (the protection seller)
cum div	=	shares or securities being sold with the rights to the next dividend or interest coupon
currency forward	=	OTC contract to sell or purchase a specified amount of foreign currency at a future date at a predetermined exchange rate
currency future	=	exchange-traded currency forward in standardised contract form
currency option	=	an *option to enter into a *currency forward or *currency future
currency swap	=	an *interest rate swap involving the exchange (physical or notional) of an amount of one currency for an amount of another currency with a subsequent re-exchange of currencies
curve	=	a plot of a rate or a value against time
cylinder option	=	a position *long on a put *option and *short on a call *option (or vice versa) with different *strike prices
debit	=	an accounting entry representing an expense, the acquisition or increase of an asset or a reduction of a liability
dirty price	=	(all-in price) the price of an interest-bearing security including accrued interest
effective interest rate	=	the constant rate of interest which takes a discounted sum to its redemption value

ex div	=	a security or share where the purchaser is not entitled to retain the dividend or interest shortly to be paid
fair value	=	an estimate of the price paid or payable if an asset is sold or a liability is discharged on the measurement date in an arm's length transaction
financial future	=	a *futures contract based on designated fixed interest financial instruments, interest rates, foreign currency or an index
floor	=	an agreement under which in exchange for a one-off payment the seller agrees to pay the buyer the difference (if negative) between the *strike rate and the current rate of interest at preset times on a specific notional amount of principal over the life of the floor, thus limiting the interest rate exposure of the buyer, who will typically be a lender. The opposite of a *cap
forward contract	=	OTC contract to sell or purchase a specified amount of a particular asset at a specific future date at a predetermined price
forward rate	=	an interest rate that will apply to a loan or deposit beginning on a future date and maturing on a second future date
forward rate agreement	=	an interest rate contract for differences under which one party agrees to pay another the difference between the actual interest rate and a specified fixed interest rate over an agreed period on a specified notional amount of principal
functional currency	=	currency of the primary economic environment in which the entity operates
futures contract	=	a standardised exchange-traded promise to buy or sell a given quantity of a particular asset at a specified future date at a pre-agreed price
gearing	=	the ratio between (a company's debt) and (market value of equity and debt)
grant price	=	the price of an *option

Glossary

hedge	=	(as noun) a contract entered into to reduce or counteract an opposite risk
implied forward premium (discount)	=	the difference in valuation of a *currency forward arising from the application of *spot rates and *forward rates
in the money	=	a contract which has *intrinsic value
initial margin	=	the *margin which is deposited with the exchange on entering into a *futures contract
interest cover	=	the ratio of profits to debt interest
interest rate swap	=	an agreement between two counterparties to exchange cash on a notional principal, usually a fixed-for-floating swap in which one counterparty agrees to pay a fixed rate over the term of the swap in exchange for a floating rate payment payable by the other counterparty
intrinsic value	=	the positive cashflow which the holder of an *option or option-related contract would realise if he could immediately exercise or sell his option
long	=	to hold an option, a forward contract or the underlying right on or of a particular item in the expectation that its price will rise
manufactured payment	=	a payment under a *stock lending or a *repo arrangement equal to the gross payment on the securities concerned representative of a real payment of dividend or interest and which the stock borrower or transferee is generally contractually obliged to the other party when the borrower or transferee receives a dividend or coupon on a security which passes its *ex-div date during the course of the arrangement
margin	=	collateral which traders in *futures contracts must deposit with the exchange to set against their positions and which comprises *initial margin and *variation margin
non-synallagmatic	=	a contract for payment of a sum of money, other than as consideration for a sale of property or supply of services

option	=	any contract under which one party (the holder) has purchased from a counterparty (the grantor) the right to require the grantor to sell (call option) or buy (put option) a specified asset at a specified date at a specified time
Perpetual	=	a bond not redeemable by an issuer except upon default or if a withholding tax is imposed or on the winding up of a company
Presentation currency	=	the currency in which the financial statements are presented
range forward	=	the equivalent in currency markets of a *collar
rebate	=	the return earned by a stock lender on a stock lending transaction when expressed as a margin in relation to the interest rate on cash collateral
repo	=	an agreement in which an institution or its counterparty transfers securities against payment subject to a commitment to repurchase them or substitute securities of the same description at a specified price on a future date specified or to be specified by the transferor, being a repurchase agreement for the transferor and a reverse repurchase agreement for the transferee
reset bond	=	one of a pair of bonds so linked that if the interest rate on one is increased (or decreased) the interest rate on the other will be correspondingly decreased (or increased)
reverse repo	=	a *repo from the point of view of the transfer of the securities
sell-buyback	=	a *repo by another name, ie a temporary disposal of a security, whereby the buyback price is reduced to reflect the dividend or interest which the temporary holder receives and does not pass back to the original owner
short	=	to sell an item which one does not own in the expectation that its price will fall

spot rate	=	in currency markets today's market exchange rate for an immediate transaction; in interest markets the rate at which a single future payment is discounted back to the present
stock borrowing	=	see *stock lending
stock lending	=	a transaction in which an institution or its counterparty transfers securities against appropriate collateral subject to a commitment that the borrower will return equivalent securities at some future date or when requested to do so, being stock lending for the institution transferring the securities and stock borrowing for the institution to which they are transferred
straddle	=	a combination of put and call *options in the same security with the same exercise price and date of expiry in which the gains on one set of options counterbalance the losses on the other
strike price/rate	=	the pre-determined level at which an *option can be exercised
swap	=	a *currency swap or an *interest rate swap
swaption	=	an *option to enter into a *swap
tick	=	the unit of price movement in the case of exchange-traded instruments
tick value	=	the cash value of one *tick
underlying	=	the ultimate deliverable asset on a *futures or *option contract; the price or index by reference to which payments under a derivative financial instrument are calculated
vanilla	=	a fixed versus a floating interest rate swap
variation margin	=	the *margin which a trader pays or receives when his futures positions are marked to market daily and the profit or loss on the previous day's position is realised
volatility	=	the randomness of an asset price
warrant	=	a securitised *option to purchase shares or bonds in the issuer at a stipulated price until the warrant's expiry date

yield to maturity	=	the average per period rate of interest which a discounted security or security repayable at a premium yields over its life
zero coupon	=	a security which pays no coupon until maturity
zero coupon	=	the *spot rate *curve of the *yield to maturity of risk-free zero coupon bonds plotted against maturity

Chapter 1

The Taxation of Finance

Overview

1.1   This chapter deals with:

- Corporate finance
- Law and accounting
- UK tax regime for financial instruments
- Debt/equity characterisation
- Corporate tax base
- Hybrids
- Derivatives
- Foreign exchange differences

Corporate finance

1.2   This book deals with the UK taxation of:

- loan relationships;
- derivative contracts; and
- foreign exchange differences.

In other words, it deals with the financing of business activity, other than through shareholders' funds. 'Shareholders' funds' comprise original equity + retained profits (reserves) + rights issues.

1.3   A company is a legal vehicle designed to enable funds to be raised and employed for the conduct of a business. The business must produce a rate of return which exceeds that available on the deposit of funds in a bank or in the holding of government bonds. The investor's purpose in investing in a business is to secure a higher rate of return than that offered by a bank deposit or government securities. If the business cannot achieve a superior return to that offered by these lower risk investments, then the business should be closed down so that the investor's funds can be put to alternative, more profitable and less risky use.

1.4   The price imposed by the nineteenth century legislation for the privilege of establishing a company by the simple act of entry on a register, whose members were protected from the company's debts by the principle of limited liability was the requirement that the company should produce annual accounts drawn up in accordance with the principles of double-entry bookkeeping. Hence corporate law regulates accounting matters, prescribes the format of accounts and the principles which they must observe.

1.5   Companies raise finance principally through shares (equity) and borrowing money (debt). Equity comprises retained earnings (reserves, profit and loss account) and the issue of new shares, either through an initial offering or rights issue to existing shareholders. Raising capital through equity is fundamentally different from debt. There are four fundamental distinctions between equity and debt:

1   The loan creditor has a legal entitlement to be repaid during the life of the company. The shareholder has no legal right to the return of his capital prior to the winding up of the company.

2   For accounting purposes interest on debt is an expense in earning profits, whereas dividends on shares are a distribution out of profits.

3   Debt is tax advantaged in that most tax systems follow the accounting treatment in regarding debt as a deductible expense in computing taxable profits.

4   Dividends and capital gains on shares are taxed on a realisations (cash) basis, whereas interest and value changes of debt are taxed on an accruals (accounts) basis.

1.6   The reason for the beneficial tax treatment of debt is this. If debt interest and dividends were alike non-deductible for tax purposes, this would significantly increase the rate of profit which a business would have to return in order to make investment in the business attractive to investors, as compared with bank deposits and government loans. Given the intensity of competition, the result would be that many businesses would become unviable and many business start-ups would never take place. Tax revenues would correspondingly be reduced rather than enhanced. The economy would fall back against competing economies by reason of lack of innovation, leading to social discontent and unrest. If on the other hand dividends and debt interest were alike deductible in computing taxable profits, no company need ever pay tax.

1.7   The profit which businesses earn over and above the risk-free rate of interest (the 'economic return') goes partly to the government in taxes and partly to investors. By this means a balance is sought between the public interest and the employees and owners of a particular concern.

1.8   Most businesses do not hold cash, because the purpose of most business in general is to use cash to earn higher returns that are obtained on cash investments. The exceptions are banks, insurance companies and certain investment businesses, all of which businesses consist in buying money (from depositors and policy-holders) and selling money to borrowers. The whole purpose of capital markets and bank intermediation is the matching of those with capital (lenders) with those who want capital (borrowers).

1.9   Most businesses are therefore loan debtors rather than loan creditors. However, within a group of companies it is common for a group company to raise funds from outside providers and then lend the money intra-group.

1.10   The largest borrowers of all are governments and public authorities, whose promises to repay are backed by the tax revenues of the political unit.

Law and accounting

1.11   Law is conservative. The economy is dynamic. Accounting seeks to reflect economic reality. Tax rules are form-based (based on rules) or substance-based (based on accounting). In general terms, in tax law will be used in an economic rather than a legal sense. Traditionally, it was said, law is prescriptive, but accounting is judgemental. However, accounting itself has become increasingly form-based, in the attempt to give it certainty and exclude subjective professional judgement. Tax rules seek to raise revenues in a fair and efficient way, without suffocating the economic activity on which the tax system is dependent. More specifically, tax law has the function of bringing company profits into charge to corporation tax. Company accounts, by contrast, are required to provide information for a wide range of users. The distinction between the different functions of accounts was illustrated in *GDF Suez Teeside Ltd v R & C Comrs* [2015] UKFTT 413 (TC). The Tribunal wrongly decided that generally accepted accounting practice (GAAP) -compliant accounts could not be accepted for tax purposes.

1.12   In the tax field, certainty is a component of the rule of law. It embodies the fundamental principle of legality to which the tax system should conform. Certainty in accounting does not have the same meaning as certainty in law, because they are operating in quite different spheres. Accounting has to mirror and reflect constantly changing economic and commercial circumstances. It necessarily lacks the fixity of law. Confusion arises from demanding the appearance of certainty where certainty cannot exist. Taxation law in general, and anti-avoidance rules in particular, rely for their operation and effect on open-textured concepts and terms, which in turn introduce other concepts which themselves require further clarification. Such provisions may lose the name of law and simply become enabling provisions to allow the executive to act on a pseudo-legal basis.

1.13 Legislation contains a range of alternatives and choices that can fundamentally and significantly affect the nature and extent of liability to taxation. Tax statutes attract different taxation consequences to different states of affairs. Typically, this arises in relation to the capital/income, debt/equity divide.

UK tax regime

1.14 Companies and governments have to raise finance. They do so in a variety of different ways. The principal means by which they do so is by the issue of securities. Securities may be shares (equity) or debt securities. Securities are essentially pieces of paper, or nowadays electronic entries, which the investor receives in return for his money, by which the borrower promises to repay money in the future. In the case of a company a different way of expressing the need to raise finance is to say that assets have to be financed, and this finance can be raised either by borrowing money from outsiders or by the provision of share capital by shareholders. Finance is a balance sheet liability, being money owed to creditors or belonging to shareholders. Debt instruments represent a contractual entitlement to benefits payable by an entity. Equity instruments represent a residual interest in the net assets of an entity.

1.15 Under a schedular tax system, income is classified under different types (schedules), and each schedule has its own computational rules, with losses under one schedule being carried forward against future profits under the same schedule rather than set against profits under other schedules. Under a generic tax system (all income theory), taxable profit includes capital gains and losses, so the income/capital distinction no longer applies. A fundamental issue for any tax system is whether unrealised capital increments should be taken into account in the computation of taxable income (pure or comprehensive income theory of taxation). The UK has given up the terminology of a schedular system while retaining it in substance. Hence, for example, Schedule E has become 'employment earnings', and Schedule D, Case 1 has become 'trade profits'.

1.16 The policy underlying the loan relationships legislation in *FA 1996* was to distinguish financial instruments which have an equity-linked return from financial instruments which have a debt-linked return. All changes in value which are recognised in the accounts are treated as income (or relievable expenditure). The same approach had been adopted in 1993 (for foreign exchange differences) and in 1994 (for derivative contracts). Equity instruments fall within corporation tax on capital gains, and are taxed on a realisations basis, because they are too remote from cash. Debt instruments come within the loan relationship rules and are taxed on an accounts basis, because they are considered sufficiently close to cash. The difference is accounted for on the basis that there is a legal obligation to pay interest and repay debt, whereas the payment of distributions is discretionary, and share capital is only in principle returned on a winding up.

1.17 The finance costs of debt are a cost of earning profits, not an application of profits. Finance costs are a price paid for the loan of the money. Hence, interest is deductible for tax purposes, and impairment losses may also be deductible. Interest is an expense incurred in earning profits, while distributions are an application of taxed profits. Interest is an above-the-line item, while dividends are a below-the-line item. Interest is deductible in computing the profits of the payer, and taxable as income in the hands of the lender. The cost of debt is the gross rate of return net of tax at the standard corporation tax rate. Dividends are non-deductible as regards the distributing company, but, because they are paid out of taxed profits, they may either be exempt or carry a tax credit in the hands of the shareholder.

1.18 The nature of the corporate tax base depends upon how finance costs are treated. If, and to the extent that, companies deduct the cost of finance as an interest expense, the return on that finance is not taxed at the level of the company obtaining the finance. Accounting profit reflects the business profit which finally belongs to shareholders. Accordingly, a tax based on accounting measures of profit draws a distinction between equity capital and debt. The costs of debt finance are deductible in computing profits, but the costs of equity finance are not. Dividends are paid out of profits and so are non-deductible. Hence, corporation tax falls on the income attributable to shareholders. In the case of cross-border investment and lending, equity finance is taxed on a source basis. The country where the company is resident taxes the profits attributable to equity finance, and the country where the investor is resident gives credit for that tax or exempts foreign dividends. The source country does not generally deduct tax from profits paid to providers of debt finance. In the absence of withholding tax, the return on international debt finance is taxed in the country where the lender is resident.

1.19 Returns on equity capital and returns on debt capital are treated differently for tax purposes (see **1.16**). The policy underlying the UK taxation of financial instruments is to keep within the capital gains tax regime gains on equity and equity-based products (other than distributions), while bringing within an income regime debt and debt-based products, and all derivative contracts. The capital gains regime taxes on a realisations basis, while the income regime taxes on an accounts basis. The reason for this distinction is that financial instruments other than equities are regarded as imposing obligations to transfer benefits to third parties. These liabilities give rise to expenses of the business, and so are deductible in computing profits. Hence, debt obligations are untaxed in the paying company, and profits and gains are taxed on an accounts basis in the hands of the recipient. Equity instruments confer a right to take what is left when third parties have been paid off. Benefits which are paid are non-deductible, and so paid out of taxed profits. There is no assurance that any benefits will be obtained. Therefore, gains on disposals of equity interests are taxed on a realisations basis, because such instruments carry equity risk. Furthermore, gains on equity derivatives, though measured on an accounting basis, are still taxed as capital gains: *CTA 2009, s 641*.

1.20   The UK has two accounts-driven regimes of taxation: for 'loan relationship'; and for 'derivative contracts'. Both have been profoundly affected by the introduction of International Accounting Standards (IAS) (called International Financial Reporting Standards (IFRS)) alongside UK GAAP (in the form of Statement of Standard Accounting Practices (SSAPs) and Financial Reporting Standards (FRSs)). For accounting periods beginning on or after 1 January 2015 UK GAAP now largely corresponds to IFRS. 'Old' UK GAAP only survives for foreign exchange differences (if the company so elects) and where the Financial Reporting Standard for Smaller Entities (FRSSE) can be used. For UK corporation tax purposes, corporate debt securities are termed 'loan relationships'. Debt may be expressed in a foreign currency, giving rise to exchange gains and losses (exchange differences). Currency contracts are classified for tax purposes as derivative contracts. Derivative contracts are taxed along the same lines as loan relationships, and are often entered into in conjunction with debt, eg a floating to fixed swap, to convert a floating rate security into a synthetic fixed rate security.

1.21   Under the 'true reflection' principle, companies are taxed on the resources available. Prior to 1 April 2016 amounts in respect of financial instruments going to the statement of total reported gains and losses (SOCIE) or equity (reserves) are treated as if they were going to the profit and loss account in computing tax liabilities, except where hedge accounting allows a different treatment. From 1 January 2016 only amounts recognised in the income statement (profit and loss account) are taken into account for loan relationship purposes: *CTA 2009, s 308(1)* (as amended).

1.22   'Financial instruments' are defined in both the Investment Services Directive of 10 May 1993 (93/22/EEC) and the Capital Adequacy Directive of 15 March 1993 (93/6/EEC) as comprising:

(a)   (i)   transferable securities;

     (ii)   units in collective investment undertakings;

(b)   money-market instruments;

(c)   financial futures, including equivalent cash-settled instruments;

(d)   forward interest-rate agreements;

(e)   interest-rate, currency and equity swaps; and

(f)   options to acquire or dispose of instruments listed in (a)–(e), including equivalent cash-settled instruments, options on currency and on interest rates (93/22/EEC Annex, Section B).

1.23   FRS 102 applies to all companies from 1 January 2015, and requires all financial liabilities that are not financial assets to be included in the balance sheet within one of the following categories:

- financial liability; or

- equity instrument.

See further **2.109**.

Equity

1.24   The distinction between equity and debt is a legal distinction, ultimately based on the issues of:

(a)   subordination, when things go wrong;

(b)   entitlement to surplus profits, when things go right; and

(c)   ability to withdraw money from a company, when an investor wants to change his investments.

There is no statutory definition of debt and equity, but there are accounting definitions, which are imported into corporate law via accounting standards: see **2.107–2.116**. A share creates a proprietary right in the company. A debt creates a liability.

1.25   The owners of the residual value in a company are the equity shareholders. The distinction between debt and equity is best expressed in the German terms *Fremdkapital* ('external finance') and *Eigenkapital* ('internal finance'). The distinction is between proprietors' capital and creditors' capital. Debt is capital provided by third party lenders, while equity is capital provided by shareholders. Share capital of a company is capital which has been subscribed by shareholders for shares, while loan capital is capital that has been borrowed. Equity does not have to be repaid, save on a winding up, and then only when all other debts and liabilities have been met. Share capital, by contrast, represents a liability of the business (the company) to its proprietors (shareholders). Retained earnings – called 'reserves' or 'profit and loss account' or simply 'equity' – belong to the equity shareholders.

Hence, in the standard format for company balance sheets contained in the *Small Companies and Groups (Accounts and Directors' Reports) Regulations 2008, SI 2008/409* and the *Large and Medium-sized Companies and Groups (Accounts and Reports) Regulations 2008, SI 2008/410*, debt appears in the top half of the balance sheet as a deduction from assets, while shares and profit and loss appear amongst shareholders' funds in the bottom half of the balance sheet, representing the company's liability to its proprietors.

1.26   By way of example, if a property company owns land bought for £1,000, which it has acquired by borrowings of £600 and own funds of £400, its balance sheet might show:

	£
Fixed assets	1,000
Liabilities	(600)
Net assets	400
Share capital	100
Share premium	100
Profit and loss (Reserves)	200
Shareholders' funds	400

This example shows that the original shareholders subscribed £1 of par value and £1 of premium for each share, and that the company has earned profits of £200, which have been retained in the company rather than distributed to shareholders. Profit and loss is the key item on a balance sheet. It expands and contracts like a concertina as the company's fortunes wax and wane, and as a company retains or distributes profits. It both enables the balance sheet to balance (by reflecting net increases and falls in net value of the business), and links the balance sheet to the income statement, which is the other primary accounting record of the company.

1.27   Equity is capital which a company owes to its shareholders. It represents the residual interest in the company. Equity is the residue of value left in a company when all creditors have been paid off. The origins of the term come from medieval land law. In the Middle Ages, land was wealth but illiquid wealth. To turn their asset into money, landowners had to mortgage their land. The lenders wanted security by way of mortgage for their loans. A mortgage is a transfer of ownership as security for a debt or other obligation, with an express or implied proviso for retransfer when the debt or obligation has been discharged (*Santley v Wilde* [1899] 2 Ch 474). The same mechanism is now used for the same reason in repo transactions (see **Chapter 19**).

1.28   The problem which arose was: what happened if the original landowner could only repay part of his debt? The lender had become the outright legal owner of the land. He was not obliged to reconvey it so long as any part of the debt was left outstanding. Hence the lender might lend £600, take a transfer of land worth £1,000, and receive back £550 of repayments. He was entitled to retain the land worth £1,000, and the repayments of £550, so long as the balance of £50 remained unpaid. That was the result in common law. However, in the Middle Ages there was a dualist legal system, with courts of equity competing for jurisdiction with the common law courts. The courts of equity said that the land was only conveyed to give security for the loan. The original landowner is entitled to the balance of the proceeds of sale after the mortgage on the land has been discharged. He holds the 'equity of redemption'. The debtor's continuing interest in the mortgaged property stems from the entitlement to require the property to be reconveyed on the discharge of the secured debt. This is a proprietary interest in the land itself, not simply a contractual right. Hence the interest which the courts of equity protected, the net balance after all external creditors have been paid off, came to be known *simpliciter* as equity.

1.29   UK companies have essentially evolved from large partnerships. When joint stock companies came to be formed in large numbers after 1844, the term 'joint stock' was taken over to refer to the interest of the ordinary shareholders in the capital of the company. The shareholders are residual claimants. They are the legal owners of the company. The holders of debt securities have only a contractual claim against the company, unless their debts are charged on assets of the company. The shareholders, by contrast, have rights which are in the nature of proprietary interests. An investment in the form of debt has a finite life. An investment in the form of a share continues until the company is wound up.

1.30   Non-derivative financial instruments may be accounted for as a financial asset, a financial liability or an equity instrument.

1.31   The boundary between shares (equity) and debt is essentially formal and legalistic rather than substantial and economic. In practice, debt and equity are often not two distinguishable classes of financial instruments, but rather two pieces of a common puzzle.

1.32   The dividing line between equity and debt is often unclear, and company law, accounting rules and tax rules locate the border in different places for different purposes. Company law adopts a form-based approach; accounting practice adopts a substance-based approach; and tax law has its own definitions, which sometimes follow company law and sometimes follow accounting practice.

1.33   Shares are securities which only give a right to economic benefits once all external claims on the company's resources have been met, and the balance of profit has been struck. Hence, dividends, which are a return on the shareholder's capital invested in the company, are only payable out of realised profits. The *Companies Act 2006* refers to 'distributions' rather than 'dividends', because the term 'dividends' is narrower in scope. *Section 829(1)* defines 'distributions' as every distribution of a company's assets to its members whether in cash or otherwise. *Section 829(2)* excludes:

(a)   a fully or partly paid issue of bonus shares;

(b)   the redemption or purchase of a company's own shares out of capital;

(c)   a court-approved reduction of capital;

(d)   a distribution of assets to members on a winding up.

1.34   Distributions can only be paid out of 'profits available for the purpose'. This fundamental rule of company law is contained in *CA 2006, s 830*, which provides:

'(1)   A company shall not make a distribution except out of profits available for the purpose.

(2)   A company's profits available for distribution are its accumulated realised profits, so far as not previously realised by distribution or capitalisation, less its accumulated, realised losses, so far as not previously written off in a reduction of capital or reorganisation of share capital duly made.'

1.35   Dividends are a distribution in respect of the share capital of a company, while interest is paid in respect of loan capital. Distributions are non-deductible for corporation tax purposes, because they are an application of profits, not an expense incurred in earning profits. It is fundamental to the taxation of companies that dividends and other qualifying distributions paid by UK resident companies are both left out of account in computing the income of the recipient company, and not deductible in computing the income of the paying company. The basic rule is stated in *CTA 2009, s 1305(1)*:

'In the calculation of a company's profits for corporation tax purposes, no deduction is allowed in respect of a dividend or other distribution.'

1.36   Every company limited by shares and registered under *CA 2006* must have ordinary shares. These are usually referred to as 'equities'. The term is an application of the 'equity of redemption', ie residual rights after discharge of prior commitments. Equity is the residue of value after deducting all the liabilities of the entity. The key test is this: if a company can be sued for non-payment of interest on an obligation, it is debt; if a company cannot be sued for non-payment, the item is equity. Unless and until they sell their shares, holders of equity capital are locked in. Their claims are postponed to those of loan creditors. Holders of preference shares occupy an intermediate position between loan creditors and shareholders, in that they receive a fixed return, like loan creditors and in preference to shareholders, but their claims rank after loan creditors.

1.37   The determination of distributable profits is essentially a matter of accountancy. ICAEW Tech/703 gives 'Guidance on the determination of realised profits and losses in the context of distributions under the Companies Act 1985'. This has been extensively supplemented by Tech 21/05, which gives guidance on fair value accounting, hedge accounting and issues arising from IAS 39 (IFRS 9).

1.38   The corollary of the rule that a company must only pay dividends from distributable profits is the rule that a company cannot return capital to its members, except on a winding up, a reduction of capital or a buy-back of shares. This classic principle of company law was expressed by Lord Russell in *Hill v Permanent Trustee Co of New South Wales Ltd* [1930] AC 720, at 731, in these terms:

> 'A limited company not in liquidation can make no payment by way of return of capital to its shareholders except as a step in an authorised reduction of capital. Any other payment made by it by means of which it parts with moneys to its shareholders must and can only be made by way of dividing profits. Whatever the payment is called … it still must remain a payment on division of profits.'

Hence, if a 100% subsidiary wants to transfer an asset to its parent, it is obliged to sell the asset for an amount at least equal to its carrying value, otherwise the subsidiary will make an unlawful distribution and the transaction will be ineffective.

1.39   It follows that equity is less flexible than debt, both in terms of the formalities for the creation of equity and when it comes to redemption. The power to borrow can be exercised by directors, but the power to issue shares has to be exercised by the company. Debt can be repaid at any time, but share capital can only be returned in accordance with a restricted number of company law procedures or on winding up. Hence the attraction of capitalising a company by debt rather than equity, because debt can be simply repaid, whereas any payment to shareholders in respect of shares will be a distribution, being either an income distribution payable out of realised profits or a capital distribution payable on a winding up. Further, shares are a more expensive means of raising finance, because dividends are not tax deductible; and, because shares carry a higher risk than debt, equity investors require a higher return, in terms of income and capital growth. While there are major legal limitations as to how much a company can pay out by way of dividends, a company can pay interest without legal limit. Also, the capital values of shares are more volatile than debt, because shares offer greater possibilities of gain and loss. Equity is a term wider than shares, because (a) many types of security have both debt and equity characteristics, and (b) debt may take the form of disguised equity.

1.40   A critical issue for corporate treasurers is to maintain the balance between equity and debt which optimises the company's finance costs and the returns to investors. This is called 'balance sheet efficiency'. This will include decisions on how much profit to distribute by way of dividend, and how much to retain as reserves. Equally, a critical issue for tax systems is to decide the nature and limits of what can be treated as debt; otherwise, a company could largely shield its revenue from tax by paying tax-deductible dividends.

1.41   Legally, the distinction between equity and debt is fundamental. In economic terms, it is relative. The difference relates essentially to relative priorities on winding up. Most securities are located on a broad spectrum, between pure share at one end, which ranks after all other obligations of a company, and pure debt on the other, which ranks ahead of all other claims on the company. Accounting and tax rules broadly follow the legal distinction, but in particular cases may adopt an economic rather than a legal distinction between debt and equity, so as to categorise debt as equity, or shares as debt, either as regards the whole instrument, or selectively in relation to particular aspects.

Debt

1.42   A company's capital = shareholders' funds [ie share capital + reserves] + long-term debt. It is money employed in the business which does not have to be repaid within 12 months. Debt is a liability on the balance sheet. Loan capital is borrowed capital, not subscribed capital. It is money borrowed from and owed to external providers. It constitutes a permanent (long-term) investment in the business, or deferred payment for assets purchased by a company.

1.43   Debt which arises from a lending of money to a company needs to be distinguished from trade debts, which arise from the supply of goods and services to a company, and obligations to pay taxes and public dues. Trade debt is a current liability which does not form part of the capital of the company. The essential characteristics of loan capital are:

● obligation to repay; and

● obligation to pay interest or equivalent until repayment.

1.44   Debt may be raised directly in capital markets, or through intermediaries (banks), or from investors such as private equity funds, VCTs and individuals. Repayment may be in a lump sum (bullet) or in instalments (amortised repayments). Non-bank investors may want debt (to reduce risk and accelerate returns) or shares (to give them a slice of longer-term equity gains). Given the high-risk nature of such investments, the difference between debt and equity may be marginal. The scenario has been dramatised in the BBC TV *Dragons' Den* programme.

1.45   Loans may be categorised according to:

- the purpose for which the loan is made, ie the activity which the lender is financing;

- the term of the loan, ie the maximum period which can elapse under the terms of the loan agreement between the advance of the loan and its repayment;

- whether interest is fixed rate (bonds) or floating rate (eg FRNs, overdraft);

- the circumstances in which the loan might become repayable.

1.46   Short-term debt is a current liability (repayable within 12 months). Debt repayable over a longer period is a long-term liability. Debt ranks above share capital on a liquidation. There are many degrees of subordination of debt. Subordination is a transaction whereby one creditor agrees not to be paid until a debtor on a higher rung of the ladder of subordination has been paid. The most deeply subordinated form of debt consists in perpetuals, ie debt only repayable on a liquidation. In such a case, the obligation to repay is contingent on the occurrence of a liquidation.

1.47   Gearing (leverage) is the ratio between share capital and debt, ie borrowing divided by shareholders' funds. 'Thin capitalisation' means a high ratio of debt to equity. A key decision for companies is what combination of share capital and debt capital to use. The higher the gearing, the higher the potential returns on share capital ('return on capital employed') because, once interest has been paid on debt, all additional profits arising from the use of the borrowed money belong to shareholders. The general idea behind gearing is to make a given sum of money go further, thereby improving the return on the investment.

1.48   Overdrafts are repayable on demand. 'On demand' means that time to effect repayment must be allowed: term loans are for a specific period and usually contain a penalty in the event of earlier repayment.

1.49   Securities issued by a company may be:

- securities issued pursuant to a facility,

- unlisted debt securities,

- listed debt securities.

1.50 Longer-term borrowing involves the issue of securities, ie debentures. The term 'debenture' has no hard and fast meaning, but it generally refers to any document which creates or acknowledges a debt. Domestic loan securities are loan stock. International loan securities are eurobonds or euronotes. 'Bonds' usually designates a maturity of more than five years, and paying interest at a fixed rate. 'Notes' denotes a maturity of less than five years. Eurobonds are internationally issued securities. 'Quoted eurobond' is defined in the *Income Tax Act 2007* (*ITA 2007*), *s 987* as any security that:

- is issued by a company;

- is listed on a recognised stock exchange; and

- carries a right to interest.

1.51 Domestic issues are frequently consolidated into 'stock', ie a single debt owed by the company to a trustee, who holds it and enforces the rights on behalf of the creditors as beneficiaries under the trust. Domestic stock is commonly secured by a fixed or floating charge. Loan notes will be guaranteed. Eurobonds are unsecured but may carry a guarantee. Interest-paying debt may be fixed rate or floating rate. If credit risk does not change, the value of floating rate debt stays constant, and the value of fixed rate debt fluctuates inversely to interest rates.

1.52 Debt may be repayable:

- on a contingency;

- at a fixed date; or

- on demand.

1.53 Fixed term debt is not repayable early, unless:

- the contract so provides;

- a tax grossing-up clause is activated; or

- a default occurs.

A company can only buy in its own listed debt if the debt contract so provides.

1.54 The concept of debt is inseparable from that of interest. Interest is called the 'coupon', because in the past it was represented by a strip at the bottom of a bond which was torn off and presented to the paying agent. A security which does not offer a rate of interest, but is instead issued at a discount to its par value, is called a 'zero coupon bond' (ZCB). In that case, the discount must be accrued and will be income (or expenditure) for both tax and accounting purposes. Interest is accumulated on a daily basis and debited on a periodic basis. Once it is debited, it is capitalised, ie treated as part of the principal debt: *Holder v CIR* 16 TC 540. Interest frequently requires the deduction of tax by the payer. International loans invariably require that interest is payable free of withholding tax, and contain a tax grossing-up clause should tax become deductible.

1.55 Debt assets are normally carried at historic cost and not revalued to fair values. Liabilities are classified as debt 'if they contain an obligation to transfer economic benefits'. Finance costs have to be charged to profit and loss account each year, eg accruals of discount. In that case, the discount must be accrued and will be income (or expenditure) for both tax and accounting purposes. Principles of conservatism point to creditor recognition of diminution in value of loans, ie to fair value at the end of each fixed period recognising changes in the value of the loan. In pragmatic terms, fair value accounting is impossible to apply to debtor liabilities, because it would mean that debtors could make profits by increasing insolvency risk.

1.56 For the investor, the disadvantages of debt as compared with equity are:

- the creditor has no 'voice', ie no right to vote and can control management only through covenants in the debt instrument;

- the creditor does not benefit from appreciation of capital value of the debtor's business.

Hybrid securities

1.57 There are many types of hybrid instrument, which combine characteristics of both debt and share capital. In classifying securities as equity, debt or a hybrid economic substance, accounting treatment and legal form all have to be considered. Preference shares may be participating or non-participating, cumulative or non-cumulative. Holders of non-voting redeemable, fixed-rate preference shares get a return which is indistinguishable from debt, but the shares remain equity. Subordinated debt mimics the repayment profile of equity, in that the holders obtain a higher reward for taking a greater risk. Nevertheless, it remains debt. Perpetuals are the most deeply subordinate form of debt. Holders of convertibles have the option of taking the higher risk and converting into shares. Thus, many instruments cluster at the debt/equity divide.

1.58 Convertibles are bonds which are convertible at the option of the holder into fully paid shares of the company at a fixed price. In the case of loan stock, this will be once a year for a one-month period after the company's results have been published. In the case of eurobonds, this is normally at any time from the start of the conversion period. Convertibles are contingent equity.

Hence, convertibles are 'relevant securities' and, therefore, the directors must be authorised to allot them. Because convertibles are treated as a share issue for company law purposes, the usual pre-emption rules will apply, unless disapplied. For accounting purposes, the loan element in convertibles is carried as debt until conversion. The expectation of the company and the investors is that the share price will rise during the life of the securities to a level which exceeds the conversion price.

1.59   Tax systems basically apply two alternative approaches on the taxation of hybrid instruments: bifurcation and integration. According to bifurcation, the instrument is divided into two or more separate parts and taxed in accordance with the tax treatment of the notional single instruments; the total tax is the sum of the different parts. Under the integration approach, the instrument is treated in its entirety as equity or debt.

1.60   An embedded derivative is a contractual term which, if it stood by itself, would be a derivative but which is buried in a larger contract. For example, a convertible is debt with an embedded derivative, ie a bond plus a call option to acquire shares, the price of the option being the difference between the value of the debt instrument with the conversion rights and the value of the debt instrument without the conversion rights. As a protection for investors, the convertible also gives investors a right (called a put option) to redeem the securities at a fixed date at a premium, the premium being calculated so that the investor gets the same return overall as he would have obtained on a straight (plain vanilla) bond with no conversion rights. Many conventional financial instruments contain an embedded derivative, eg a fixed rate mortgage is a floating rate mortgage plus an interest cap and collar.

1.61   Where the embedded derivative is classified as a derivative and is not closely related to the value of its host contract, IFRS requires it to be accounted for separately from the host contract and fair valued. In such cases, IFRS requires the issuer to decompose ('bifurcate') the instrument into two notional instruments, a derivative contract and a host contract. This is an expression of the basic tenet of IFRS that all derivative contracts must be brought on balance sheet and recorded at fair value, with changes in fair value going through the income statement.

1.62   Zero coupon shares are shares which carry no right to a dividend or any other participation in profits. *CTA 2009, s 476* defines 'shares' for the purposes of the loan relationship rules as,

> 'any share in the company under which an entitlement to distributions may arise'

If a zero coupon share carries the right to repayment of capital on a winding up, this would count as a distribution, be it a capital distribution, for the purposes of this provision.

1.63 However, a share may be so denuded of any economic value as not to constitute a share at all: see *Collector of Stamp Revenue v Arrowtown Assets Limited* FACV No 4 of 2003.

Quasi-equity

1.64 One reason why accounting and tax systems sometimes adopt an economic qualification of securities rather than a legal qualification is because of the phenomenon of disguised equity. An obvious categorisation problem arises if a shareholder lends money to a company, or a creditor holds an instrument which entitles him to an equity-type return and exposes him to an equity-type risk. The shareholder is then dealing with the company in two capacities: as a creditor and as a proprietor of the business. What he is doing is giving himself a right to extract capital prior to a winding up and a higher priority on a winding up. Debt owed to a shareholder or another related creditor ('connected party debt') is in general for tax purposes treated as disguised equity, if it is economically equivalent to equity capital. Third party debt has to be accepted as such for tax purposes, unless a related person provides a guarantee or another security for it.

1.65 Reclassification of debt as quasi-equity for tax purposes can take a number of forms:

1   Interest payments on disguised equity are treated as non-deductible for the borrower and as a receipt of dividends by the lender: *CTA 2010, ss 1000(1)E, 1005.*

2   Interest payments by the borrower may be disallowed in the borrower while continuing to be taxed as interest in the lender, subject to 'corresponding adjustments': *TIOPA 2010, s 147(3).*

3   An impairment loss, a waiver or release of quasi-equity may be disregarded for tax purposes: *CTA 2009, s 354.*

Derivatives

1.66 Derivatives are 'derived from' something outside themselves (such as currency, shares, an interest rate, a commodity, an index). Derivatives are tools for risk management, or rather the redistribution of risk. Thus, a forward or future is a common way to protect against the risk of volatile prices. For example, a farmer sells his crops forward, in order to be sure of obtaining a certain price. The merchant buys the contract forward, in order to ensure both availability and price. Both relinquish a possibility of future profit, in order to limit future loss or uncertainty. Either party can speculate in the contract, by assigning the benefit of the contract for its then market price. This is 'closing out' the contract. If there is no intention to take future delivery, or the subject matter of the contract is undeliverable (such as an interest rate), the essential subject matter of the contract is the difference between the strike price (K) and the market price of the underlying at the time of contractual performance (S2). If, at the time of performance (T2), the strike price is above the spot price, the seller makes a profit of (K – S2). If, at T2, S2 > K, the buyer makes a profit. There is much in common between insurance contracts and derivative contracts, but derivatives are assignable and tradeable. Derivatives are positioned halfway between risk reduction (insurance) and risk increase (trading).

1.67   A derivative is the sale of a promise, which is intended to be assignable, ie it may be settled in cash before it has reached its settlement date. Derivatives enable people to plan on a more flexible basis than fixed-rate, long-term contracts, which in any case will not be available when prices are volatile, eg airlines price tickets on the basis of anticipated aviation fuel prices. Derivatives enable future cash flows to be smoothed. Derivatives generate contingent income, ie income which is not clear at the time of the contract.

1.68   A derivative contract is then the sale of a promise. There are three kinds of such contract:

(a)   the sale of a promise solely to deliver a commodity at a date in the future for an agreed price, ie a forward contract;

(b)   the sale of a promise either to deliver a commodity or pay its value in the future for an agreed price, ie a futures contract;

(c)   the sale of a promise solely to pay the value of a commodity on a future date for an agreed price, ie a contract for differences, the difference being between the delivery price (K) and the spot price on the maturity of the contract (S2). In the case of derivative contracts, settlement is in general not by actual performance of the sale or option contract, but rather a difference payment derived from an actual asset and an actual price.

Promises can be exchanged (a swap), or a right to enter into a contract can be sold (an option).

1.69   The four basic building blocks of derivatives are forwards, futures, swaps and options:

●   'Forwards': a forward contract obliges the holder to buy a given asset on a specified date (T2) at the exercise price (K) fixed at the contract start date (T1).

●   'Futures': a futures contract is identical to a forward contract, but is exchange traded in the form of standardised contracts which are underwritten by the exchange.

- 'Swaps': a swap contract obliges two parties to exchange specified cash flows at specified intervals for a specified period.

- 'Options': the holder of an option contract has the right – but not the obligation – either to purchase a given asset at a specified future date (T2) at a specified price (K) agreed at the date of the contract (T1) (a call option), or to sell a given asset at a specified future date (T2) at a specified price (K) agreed at the date of the contract (T1) (a put option).

1.70   Hybrid derivatives are combinations of basic derivatives. Derivatives are accordingly classified into three groups:

Forward	<ul><li>Currency future</li><li>Commodity future</li><li>Interest rate future (forward rate agreement)</li></ul>
Swap	<ul><li>Interest rate swap</li><li>Currency swap</li><li>Forward rate swap</li><li>Off market swap</li><li>Quanto</li></ul>
Option	<ul><li>Currency option</li><li>Stock option</li><li>Stock index option</li><li>Interest rate cap</li><li>Interest rate floor</li><li>Interest rate collar (ie cap + floor)</li><li>Swap options (swaptions)</li><li>Warrants</li></ul>

1.71   'An option confers no more than a contractual right to acquire property on payment of a consideration' (*Vandervell v IRC* 43 TC 519 at 559). An option is neither an irrevocable offer nor a conditional contract but an asset in its own right:

> 'An offer is not strictly speaking either an offer or a conditional contract. It does not have all the incidents of the standard forms of either of these concepts. To that extent it is a relationship *sui generis*. But there are ways in which it resembles each of them. Each analogy is, in the proper context, a valid way of characterising the situation created by an option.' (*Spiro v Glencrown Properties Ltd* [1991] 1 All ER 600, per Hoffmann J at 606)

1.72 Caps and floors are something of an oddity. They are priced on the option theory. However, they are not options per se for tax and legal reasons, because there is no exercise mechanism or element of choice for the holder. The option is automatically triggered, as soon as the interest rate crosses the tripwire. This is similar to the type of option to acquire the goods under a hire-purchase contract which is normally exercised automatically on payment of the final hire charge. Such an option is not an option in the conventional sense.

1.73 It is inherent in the nature of derivatives that individual instruments may be broken down into their constituent parts. All reduce themselves into various combinations of forwards. A future is a series of sequentially written forwards: 'each day yesterday's contract is settled and today's contract is written'. A swap contract is a series or portfolio of forward contracts, all written at the origination date. An interest rate swap can be decomposed into two bonds, a long position in one bond being combined with a short position in another. An alternative decomposition of a swap is into a series of forward rate agreements, while a currency swap can be deconstructed into a series of currency forwards. A forward is itself a combination of put and call options. A company borrowing at a floating rate and swapping into a fixed rate constructs a synthetic fixed rate debt; a convertible is a bond with an embedded equity option. An option is a conditional forward. Each financial instrument is an aggregate of contractually created rights, the effect of which is to create a transfer or exchange of specified future cash flows at defined future points in time. The quantum of these cash flows is determined by reference to or derived from underlying cash, securities indices or physical markets. The tax treatment largely disaggregates instruments on an annual basis.

1.74 Thus, derivatives consist of a number of building blocks, which can be assembled, broken down and reassembled in a variety of ways. Each derivative can be analysed into its constituent parts, and reassembled as something different. The same economic result can be achieved by different combinations of instruments.

1.75 Derivatives are either bespoke or off-the-peg. Standardised products are exchange traded, and this makes the organisation of the market, control of risk and the calculation of cash flows much more straightforward. Non-standardised products are 'over the counter' (OTC). A future is an exchange-traded forward. Fundamental to the operation of exchange-traded products is the provision of security (a 'margin'). This serves as both a safeguard against insolvent counterparties, and a daily measure of profit and loss. As contracts go into the money and out of the money, ie have positive and negative values, the profit or loss realised in each managing period is computed.

1.76 The primary difference between forwards, futures, swaps and options is the amount of credit or default risk which they impose on counterparties to a contract. The aim of daily marking to market is to enable profits and losses to be recognised on a daily basis, so that potential exposures can be covered by providing additional margin, thereby minimising default risk. The value of the contract passes whenever it is marked to market.

1.77 Forwards, being largely OTC and lacking margin requirements, carry the greatest credit risk, because the value of the contract only passes on maturity or when it is closed out. Exchange-traded options are fair valued, and require margin payments, so that, as with futures, default risk is controlled. Swaps represent a halfway house as far as credit risk is concerned. Part of the value passes each time a periodic payment is due, but a residuum of value only passes when principal or notional principal is re-exchanged on the termination of the swap.

1.78 Delivery is the means of settling derivative contracts. Derivative contracts can be settled in one of five ways:

(a) by delivering cash ('cash-settled derivatives');

(b) by delivering the underlying, where this is possible ('physically settled derivatives');

(c) by delivering securities to the value of the amount payable;

(d) by closing out an exchange-traded contract (entering into an equal and opposite bargain); or

(e) by assigning the contract.

Broadly, the aim of the tax rules is to achieve the same economic result, regardless of the mode of settlement.

1.79 Cash-settled financial derivatives are essentially contracts for differences. 'Contract for differences' is defined in the *Financial Services and Markets Act 2000, Sch 2, para 19* as:

> 'a contract ... the purpose or pretended purpose of which is to secure a profit or avoid a loss by reference to fluctuations in the value or price of property of any description or in an index or other factor designated for the purpose of the contract.'

1.80 As with fixed-interest loan relationships (where the value of the principal varies inversely with interest rates), the profit or loss on a derivative transaction is a combination of payments and asset values. Payments receivable and payments due are aggregated for each contract for each accounting period. The balance is brought into the corporation tax computation, either as a trading or as a non-trading item.

Example 1.1

A borrows £10m at 7% floating on 1 January 2011. A pays B £50,000 for an interest rate cap at 7.5% for two years. On 1 April 2012 the interest rate rises to 8.25%, and remains at that level until 31 December 2012. If A's financial year ends on 31 December, and the cost of the instrument is spread, the entries in respect of the contract are:

Year	Qualifying payments received	Qualifying payments made	Net
	£	£	£
2011		(25,000)	(25,000)
2012	56,250*	(25,000)	31,250

$$* \, £10\text{m} \times (8.25 - 7.5\%) \times \frac{9}{12}$$

Example 1.2

An airline swaps 1,000 barrels of aviation fuel at an index price of $70 a barrel as the strike price for a period of one year. At the end of each month, an average spot price for the month will be calculated and compared with the strike price of $70. If spot price average is $80 per barrel, the airline will receive a payment of $10 × 1,000. If spot price average is $60, the airline will make a payment of the same amount. In either case, the airline will have fixed its fuel costs at $60 per barrel for a year, to the extent that the swap covers its actual consumption of fuel.

Example 1.3

X Ltd pays £50 for an option to buy 1,000 Y plc shares for £1.50 in six months' time. After three months, the Y shares stand at £1.60. The value of X's contract is:

$$[(1.60 - 1.50) \times 1000] - 5 = £95$$

This also illustrates the highly geared nature of derivatives. For an outlay of £5, X stands to gain £95.

Example 1.4 – Forward rate agreement

ABC plc borrows £1,000 at LIBOR + 1% for three years. It agrees to purchase three forward rate agreements (FRAs) from a bank. At the end of each year, ABC is to receive from the bank (or pay to the bank) £1,000 × (LIBOR – 7%). ABC (pays)/receives:

Year	LIBOR	ABC on loan	ABC on FRA	Net interest rate
1	6%	(70)	(10)	(8%)
2	7%	(80)	0	(8%)
3	8%	(90)	10	(8%)

1.81   FRAs are the building block of swaps. A vanilla swap (fixed to floating) is equivalent to a series of FRAs.

Structured instruments

1.82   All financial instruments embody a structure of reward and risk. Risk and reward are distributed by the terms of the instrument. In conventional financial instruments, the risk-reward structure is largely static. A structured instrument is produced by combining a conventional instrument with a derivative transaction. The risk and reward profile, and economic characteristics, of instruments can be altered by the use of derivatives. A currency contract can be used to convert a dollar floating rate liability into a sterling fixed rate liability. The sterling equivalent of the foreign currency proceeds of a sale or costs of a purchase can be fixed by means of a currency forward. Typically, there will be a series of redistributions of risk and reward producing a long chain of transactions. The net effect may be to minimise risk and reward (hedging) or maximise them (leverage). This process also produces new asset classes (eg credit derivatives).

1.83   Issuers of structured notes will normally command a high credit rating, so that credit and market risk can be separated. In some cases, however, the issuer of an instrument will have a lower credit rating, the purpose of the instrument being to reduce the funding costs which he would otherwise incur (eg convertibles, where the option premium is paid for by a reduction in the coupon). A structured instrument comprises a package of a number of distinct contracts.

Example 1.5

Transnational Bank issues a floating rate note repayable after five years denominated in dollars, which pays floating rate $ LIBOR, not to exceed 8% and not to fall below 4%. This constitutes three transactions:

- Purchase by the investor of a US$ floating rate security.

- Sale by the investor of an interest rate cap.

- Purchase by the investor of an interest rate floor.

1.84   Conventional financial instruments can normally be replicated by a derivative package. The issue then arises whether the conventional instrument and the synthetic instrument should be treated in the same way for accounting and tax purposes, or differently. Should economic equivalence or different legal substance prevail?

Example 1.6

1   A fixed rate borrowing with rolled-up interest only payable on maturity is equivalent to a zero coupon bond issued at a discount.

2   A forward sale of dollars for sterling is equivalent to borrowing dollars while depositing sterling, at fixed interest rates with the interest payable at delivery.

3   A cross-currency swap is equivalent to two back-to-back loans in the respective currencies.

Example 1.7

A UK company agrees to buy $100 for £60 in two years' time. A currency forward is an asset plus a liability. The asset is the dollar leg, ie the right to receive $100. The value of this right will fluctuate in accordance with changes in the ratio of exchange between sterling and the dollar. If sterling falls in value against the dollar (ie one gets fewer dollars per pound or more pounds per dollar), the value of the contract will correspondingly increase, and vice versa. The liability is the sterling leg, ie the obligation to pay £60. The value of this is constant.

Foreign exchange differences

1.85   Loan relationships and derivative contracts alike may produce gains and losses arising from the change in the ratio of exchange between the currency in which the company concerned prepares its accounts (reporting currency) and the currency in which contracts to which it is a party are denominated.

1.86   Foreign currency may be either a commodity or money. Foreign currency is a commodity where it serves as an object of commerce, and money where it serves monetary functions. Outside its national area, money functions as a commodity. This happens mainly in the market of foreign exchanges. Thus, money has a second use, to be purchased or exchanged. In this case it is, in the language of St Thomas Aquinas, 'measured, not a measure' (*mensuratum non mensura*). *TCGA 1992, s 21(1)(b)* says that 'any currency other than sterling' is an asset for capital gains tax purposes.

1.87   Foreign exchange differences enter into the loan relationship and derivative contracts legislation in a number of ways:

1   For the loan relationship rules, *CTA 2009, s 483(2)* states that 'any currency held by the company is treated as a money debt owed to the company', so that exchange gains and losses arising in respect of the currency are taxed or relieved.

2   Where there is a money debt which is not a loan relationship ('a relevant non-lending relationship' – *CTA 2009, ss 478–480*), then exchange gains and losses are will form part of loan relationship debits and credits.

3   Currency forwards and futures are derivative contracts, so gains and losses are taken into account on a fair value basis.

4   Foreign exchange risk will in many cases give rise to hedging relationships, in which case recognition of exchange gains and losses will be deferred.

See **Chapter 8**.

Chapter 2

The Accounting Framework

Overview

2.1   This chapter deals with:

- UK GAAP and IFRS
- Company law provisions
- Group accounts
- Accounts formats
- True and fair requirement
- Accounting regulators
- Adoption of IFRS in Europe
- UK convergence programme
- Accounting bases
- FRS 102
- Definition of financial instruments
- Classification of financial asset/liability
- Basic financial instruments
- Recognition and derecognition
- Non-basic financial instruments
- Debt/equity classification
- Taxable profits
- SMEs
- FRSSE
- Transition to FRS 102

Introduction

2.2 The development of the corporate tax base since 1965 has represented a gradual but quickening movement towards the measurement of corporate profits based on accrual and the taking of value changes through profit and loss account. These have been taken in response to the development of income recognition standards, notably in the form of FRS 5, Application Note G, 'Revenue Recognition'. This was issued in November 2003. It required recognition of income (and recognition of a corresponding asset) when the seller of goods or services obtained 'the right to consideration' for performance of his obligations, not in the legal sense of being able to invoice the customer, but in the economic sense of having an expectation of payment. This was only intended to codify existing good practice, but nevertheless was a shift from accounting based on the profit and loss account to balance sheet accounting. This in turn requires greater offset of profits and losses within a company and between related companies. Since the 1980s UK tax rules have been increasingly aligned with, and dependent on, accounting conventions and so it has been progressively more important for tax practitioners to understand the basis on which transactions and balances will be accounted for, and profits and losses recognised. The term 'UK accounting' has all but disappeared from the vocabulary of both practitioners and standard setters, to be overtaken by a new phrase 'accounting in the UK'. This apparently subtle change has a much deeper significance, one that perhaps hides the fact that things have become considerably more complicated for anyone trying to establish the accounting rules applicable to them and the basis on which their company will be taxed.

2.3 Accounting in the UK has been evolving for some time and no longer comprises only 'UK accounting' but also 'international accounting' in the form of International Financial Reporting Standards (IFRS). The term 'international accounting' could not, however, have simply been substituted for 'UK accounting'. UK-GAAP continues to exist alongside IFRS, though since 1 January 2015 with the application of FRS 102, the substantial differences have been considerably diminished.

2.4 *European Council Regulation of June 2002 (2002/1606/EC)* directed that, for periods beginning on or after 1 January 2005, all companies governed by the law of a member state should prepare their consolidated financial statements in accordance with those international standards adopted by the European Commission, if, at their balance sheet date, their securities are traded on a regulated market of any member state.

2.5 Under the Regulation, individual member states were given discretion as to whether to permit or require listed and/or unlisted companies to adopt international accounting standards. In the UK, it was decided that companies should be able to choose for themselves whether or not to adopt international standards when drawing up the annual accounts of single entities. Within certain constraints imposed by the Department of Business Innovation and Skills (see below), UK limited companies, including the subsidiaries of listed groups, therefore have some choice over the principles they will follow.

2.6 UK standards were also subject to transformation, with the primary aim of converging with IFRS. Initial changes to UK standards were imposed on the solus accounts of listed entities for periods beginning on or after 1 January 2005. More extensive changes have been imposed for accounting periods beginning on or after 1 January 2015.

2.7 To report under IFRS or converging UK standards is to walk on constantly shifting sands. The configuration of the standards and their interpretation do not remain still for long. Extra layers are being continually added, as a result of further amendments or the work of the International Financial Reporting Interpretation Committee (IFRIC). Consequently, even after a company has determined its basic formula, the outcome may still be unexpected.

2.8 Although consolidated accounts play little part in determining the tax treatment of individual items, understanding the particular basis of accounting being used by any single entity, the precise treatment afforded to individual items and the relationship between the entity and the consolidated accounts is critical in establishing an accurate picture of the tax base.

2.9 Being an accounts-based system, the loan relationships and derivative contracts rules have little to do with cash. In *Allchin v Coulthard* 25 TC 445, Lord Greene MR observed (at 496) that 'fund' had two meanings:

> 'The word "fund" may mean actual cash resources of a particular kind (eg money in a drawer or a bank) or it may be a mere accountancy expression used to describe a particular category which a person uses in making up his accounts.'

2.10 The rules in question are concerned with 'accountancy expressions'. As Lord Neuberger MR has observed (*Scottish Widows plc v R & C Comrs* [2011] STC 2171 at [128]):

> 'In connection with taxing business profits, the concept of a profit should normally be according its proper meaning, which will obviously depend on the specific context, but current accountancy practice is generally a good, and often the best, guide as to the precise quantification of any profit.'

Company law provisions

2.11   The requirement to produce company accounts, and the content and format of such accounts, all derive from corporate law. In the nineteenth century the incorporation of companies by entry on a register proved to be hugely convenient and fostered economic growth. The watershed in this development was the introduction of limited liability companies by the *Limited Liability Act 1855*. The price which companies had to pay for limited liability was much more intensive regulation and supervision. This meant accounts. The *Joint Stock Companies Act 1844, s XLII* required a balance sheet signed by the directors. The Joint Stock Companies Act 1856 required a balance sheet and an income and expenditure account. Such accounts were to be kept upon the principle of double-entry bookkeeping. It also gave directors power to create reserves. *Table B, reg 71* said:

> 'Every Item of Expenditure fairly chargeable against the year's Income shall be brought into Account, so that a just Balance of Profit and Loss may be laid before the Meeting, and in cases where any Item of Expenditure which may in fairness be distributed over several Years has been incurred in any One Year the whole Amount of such Item shall be stated, with the addition of Reasons why only a Portion of such Expenditure is charged against the Income of the Year.'

2.12   The *1856 Act* also contained an accounts format showing debt and reserves as clearly distinguished, with debt included in the liabilities of the company and reserves as part of shareholders' funds. The *Companies Act 1929* introduced the requirement for group accounts.

2.13   The accounting provisions of the *Companies Act 2006* came into force on 6 April 2008. The main legislation comprises *CA 2006, ss 380–539* and two sets of regulations, namely:

- the *Small Companies and Groups (Accounts and Directors' Reports) Regulations 2008, SI 2008/409*; and

- the *Large and Medium-sized Companies and Groups (Accounts and Reports) Regulations 2008, SI 2008/410*.

2.14   These two sets of regulations are substantially the same, and may be referred to together as the '*Accounts Regulations*'. *CA 2006* applies to 'UK-registered companies', as defined by *s 1158*, ie companies registered under the UK companies legislation.

2.15   In both sets of *Accounts Regulations*, *Sch 1, Part 2* deals with accounting principles. These are (*paras 11–15*):

- consistency,

- prudence,

- only profits realised at balance sheet date may be recognised,

- all liabilities must be recognised including those arising between the end of the accounting period and the signing of the accounts (post-balance sheet adjusting events),

- all income and charges relating to the financial year must be brought into account ('matching'),

- in determining individual items set-off is not allowed.

2.16 *Section B (paras 16–29) of Sch 1, Part 2 sets out historical cost accounting rules. Section C (paras 30–35) contains alternative accounting rules, providing for alternative valuation and depreciation rules. Section D (paras 36–41) contains rules for fair value accounting. While para 36(1) allows financial instruments to be fair valued, para 36(2) excludes fair value accounting for financial liabilities. Schedule 1, Part 3 deals with the notes to the accounts.*

2.17 The duty to prepare annual accounts applies to all UK-registered companies. Such company accounts are called 'individual accounts' (previously referred to as 'entity accounts'). The basic duty is set out in *CA 2006, s 394*:

> 'The directors of every company must prepare accounts for the company for each of the financial years. These accounts are referred to as the company's "individual accounts".'

2.18 Individual accounts can be 'Companies Act individual accounts' or 'IAS individual accounts': *CA 2006, s 395(1)*. A charity can only prepare Companies Act individual accounts (*s 395(2)*). Once IAS accounts are adopted, IAS must be retained, unless there is a 'relevant change of circumstance': *s 395(3)–(5)*. A relevant change of circumstance would occur if, for example, a company became a subsidiary of another company which did not prepare IAS individual accounts.

2.19 Companies Act individual accounts must comprise (*CA 2006, s 396*):

- a balance sheet which gives a true and fair view of the state of affairs of the company at the end of the financial year;

- a profit and loss account which gives a true and fair view of the profit or loss of the company for the financial year; and

- notes.

2.20 Accounting standards additionally require:

- a statement of total reported gains and losses (STRGL),

- a cash flow statement,

- reconciliation of movements in shareholders' funds,
- additional notes.

2.21   IAS individual accounts comprise (*CA 2006, ss 397, 474*):

- an income statement,
- statement of financial position,
- statement of (other) comprehensive income (OCI),
- statement of cash flows,
- a statement of changes in equity (SOCIE),
- notes.

Such accounts must state that they have been prepared in accordance with IAS.

2.22   The nature and extent of the accounts obligation depends upon the type of company. Where provisions do not apply to all companies, the legislation sets out the provisions in the order:

- small companies,
- public companies, and
- quoted companies.

2.23   All companies in a group have to produce individual accounts. Additionally, the principal company of the group must produce consolidated (group) accounts, unless exempt from this requirement.

2.24   *CA 2006* distinguishes between:

- micro entities, small, medium-sized and large companies,
- Companies Act individual accounts,
- Companies Act group accounts,
- IAS individual accounts, and
- IAS group accounts.

2.25   Accordingly, the UK rules allow individual companies to choose between IAS and UK GAAP. Unlisted groups and ordinary limited companies (except charities) may choose whether to adopt IFRS or continue with UK GAAP. In most cases, the choice, once made, cannot be reversed. Parent companies that are charities must use UK GAAP: *CA 2006, s 403(3).* IAS group accounts must state that they have been drawn up in accordance with IAS: *CA 2006, s 406.*

2.26   Financial reporting in a group should be made on a consistent basis, ie 'using the same financial reporting framework': *CA 2006, s 407(1)(a).* This does not apply if both the group and the individual accounts are prepared using IAS.

2.27   In summary, UK companies whose securities are publicly traded can choose to use IAS in their individual entity accounts. Non-listed companies and limited liability partnerships (LLPs) are permitted to use IAS in their entity and consolidated accounts. Parent companies are required to ensure consistency of choice within a group. However, where a parent company prepares both consolidated and individual accounts using IAS, it is not required to ensure that all its subsidiary undertakings use IAS.

Group accounts

2.28   In order to give a true and fair view, company accounts need to reflect the real economic situation of a company at the accounting reference date. The purpose of group accounts is to present the activities of related companies and undertakings as a single economic entity.

2.29   On consolidation, the assets, liabilities and turnover of all entities included in the consolidation will be amalgamated with intra-group payments, and intra-group assets, liabilities and payments will be eliminated.

2.30   *CA 2006, ss 380, 398* and *399* distinguish between the following situations:

(a)   companies subject to the small companies regime;

(b)   companies outside the small companies regime and not quoted;

(c)   companies outside the small companies regime and quoted;

(d)   companies subject to the small companies regime which are the parent companies of a group; and

(e)   companies outside the small companies regime which are the parent companies of a group.

2.31   Parent companies which are not subject to the small companies regime are required to prepare group accounts as well as individual accounts. A company which, at the end of the financial year, is a parent company must prepare consolidated accounts, unless (broadly speaking) it is itself a subsidiary undertaking: *CA 2006, s 399.*

2.32   The provisions in *CA 2006, ss 399–408, Sch 7* give effect to the requirements of the Seventh Company Law Directive on consolidated accounts (83/349/EEC) and the applicable accounting standards: FRS 102, Section 9 and IAS 27.

2.33   The obligation to prepare group accounts is laid down in *s 399. Section 404* sets out the scope of the obligation. Where a parent company prepares Companies Act group accounts, all the subsidiary undertakings of the company must be included in the consolidation, subject to limited exceptions. 'Subsidiary undertakings' means a body corporate, partnership or unincorporated association carrying on a trade or business, with or without a view to profit: *CA 2006, s 1161*.

2.34   All subsidiary undertakings must be included in the consolidation, unless such consolidation is not material for the purpose of giving a true and fair view, or the parent company is subject to long-term restrictions over the exercise of its powers: *CA 2006, s 405*.

2.35   The key issue in group accounts is what entities should be included within the scope of the consolidation. The UK, following EU law, takes a broad definition of subsidiary for this purpose, based on both legal control and economic control.

2.36   'Parent undertaking' and 'subsidiary undertaking' are defined in *CA 2006, s 1162* and *Sch 7*. An 'undertaking' is a parent undertaking in relation to a subsidiary undertaking if it:

(a)   holds the majority of voting rights;

(b)   has the right to appoint or remove directors;

(c)   has the right to exert dominant influence by virtue of the articles or a control contract;

(d)   controls a majority of voting rights;

(e)   has power to exercise, or actually exercises, a dominant influence; or

(f)   is managed on a unified basis with the subsidiary.

2.37   Criteria (e) and (f) are set out in *CA 2006, s 1162(4)* and *Sch 7, para 4*. The terms 'dominant influence' and 'managed on a unified basis' are also defined in FRS 102, Section 9 'Consolidated and Separate Financial Statements'. The test based on factual control is more important in practice than the tests based on legal control, because it restricts attempts to avoid the consolidation obligation.

2.38   There are three exemptions:

1   The first case is for companies whose accounting figures are included in the IAS group accounts of a European Economic Area (EEA) parent

undertaking, where the immediate parent company either (a) owns all the shares in the subsidiary, or (b) owns more than 50% of the shares and no notice requesting group accounts has been served by shareholders. The securities of the subsidiary must not be traded on an EEA exchange: *CA 2006, s 400.*

2   The second case is for companies whose accounting figures are included in the group accounts of a parent undertaking established outside the EEA, where the immediate parent company either (a) owns all the shares in the subsidiary, or (b) owns more than 50% of the shares and no notice requesting group accounts has been served by shareholders. The securities of the subsidiary must not be traded on an EEA exchange. The company must state in its individual accounts the name of the parent undertaking, and the fact that it is exempt from the requirement to draw up group accounts.

3   The third case is where a parent company prepares Companies Act group accounts and all the subsidiary undertakings of the parent are included in the consolidation: *CA 2006, ss 401, 405.*

2.39   The following table illustrates the variation that can apply between members of the same group of companies:

Indicative UK accounting permutations for periods of account beginning on/ after 1 January 2005

	Option 1	Option 2	Option 3	Option 4
Consolidated accounts	IFRS	IFRS	IFRS	IFRS
Solus plc	IFRS	IFRS	UK GAAP	UK GAAP
Limited company with listed securities	IFRS	UK GAAP	UK GAAP	UK GAAP
Non-listed company	IFRS	UK GAAP	UK GAAP	UK GAAP
Non-listed company using fair value override	IFRS	UK GAAP	UK GAAP	UK GAAP

Accounts formats

2.40   The *Accounts Regulations* prescribe the 'required formats for accounts', the notes which are to form part of the accounts, and the accounting policies to be followed. There are two sets of regulations, one governing small companies, the other governing medium-sized and large companies.

2.41 The accounting formats are:

Companies Act 2006	Type of company	Regulation	Type of accounts
ss 426–429	All companies	SI 2008/374	Summary financial statements
ss 394–396	General company (small company)	SI 2008/409, r 3, Sch 1, Part 1, Section B	Companies Act individual accounts
ss 396, 409, 410	General company (small company with related undertakings)	SI 2008/409, r 4, Sch 2	Companies Act or IAS individual accounts
ss 398, 404, 408	General company (small group)	SI 2008/409, r 8(1), 10, Sch 6	Companies Act small group accounts
s 444	General company (small company)	SI 2008/409, r 6(1), Sch 4	Companies Act abbreviated accounts
ss 394–396	General company (medium-sized or large)	SI 2008/410 rr 1, 2, Sch 1	Companies Act individual accounts
ss 394–396	Banking company	SI 2008/410, r 5, Sch 2. SI 2008/567	Companies Act individual accounts
ss 394–396	Insurance company	SI 2008/410, r 6, Sch 3; SI 2008/565	Companies Act individual accounts
s 399; 2002/1606/ EC	General company (medium-sized or large with related undertakings)	SI 2008/410, r 7, Sch 4	Companies Act or IAS individual or group accounts
ss 39, 403–406	General company (medium-sized or large group)	SI 2008/410, r 8, Sch 6, Part 1	Companies Act group accounts
ss 39, 403–406	Banking company (medium-sized or large group)	SI 2008/410, r 8, Sch 6, Part 2	Companies Act group accounts
ss 39, 403–406	Insurance company (medium-sized or large group)	SI 2008/410, r 8, Sch 6, Part 3	Companies Act group accounts
s 397	All companies	IAS 1	IAS individual accounts
ss 1210, 1242	Partnerships consisting solely of companies	SI 2008/569	Partnership accounts

The true and fair requirement

2.42   The overarching requirement of company accounts is that they should give a true and fair view of the company's profit and loss for an accounting period, and the company's assets and liabilities at the end of that period. The 'true and fair' requirement was introduced by *Companies Act 1948, s 147(2)*. This stated:

> 'proper books of account shall not be deemed to be kept … if there are not kept such books as are necessary to give a true and fair view of the state of the company's affairs and to explain its transactions.'

2.43   The cardinal principle is that all accounts prepared by all companies subject to *CA 2006* must give a 'true and fair view'. This is an EU requirement under *Directive 76/222/EC, art 2(3)*, which requires that:

> 'The annual accounts of a company shall give a true and fair view of the company's assets, liabilities, financial position and profit or loss.'

2.44   In UK law, this principle is set out in *CA 2006, s 393(1)*:

> '(1)   The directors of a company must not approve accounts … unless they are satisfied that they give a true and fair view of the assets, liabilities, financial position and profit or loss–
>
> (a)   in the case of the company's individual accounts, in the case of the company;
>
> (b)   in the case of the company's group accounts, of the undertakings included in the consolidation as a whole, so far as concerns members of the company;'

2.45   This principle is rearticulated for individual accounts in *CA 2006, s 396*, and for group accounts in *s 404*. Likewise, the auditor's report must state whether the accounts give a true and fair view: *CA 2006, s 495(3)*.

2.46   'True and fair' is not defined in the Directive or by statute. In 1983, 1984 and 1993, the opinion of counsel (Leonard Hoffmann QC and Mary Arden, as they then were) was sought on the significance of the concept. These opinions were updated by Martin Moore QC in an opinion of 21 April 2008. The view expressed was that:

(a)   'true and fair' was a statutory requirement;

(b)   in interpreting that concept, the courts would be unlikely to find that accounts would give a true and fair view unless they had been drawn up in accordance with the relevant accounting standards;

(c)   accordingly, while accounting standards had no direct legal effect as such, being simply rules of professional conduct for accountants, they were given indirect legal effect through the true and fair concept;

(d)   in short, 'true and fair' means 'drawn up in accordance with accounting standards'. Compliance with accounting standards is essential.

2.47   The Statement of Principles for Financial Reporting issued by the Accounting Standards Board (ASB) deals with the true and fair concept in paras 10–13, and says:

'The concept of a true and fair view lies at the heart of financial reporting in the UK … It is the ultimate test for financial statements.'

2.48   The form and content of accounts, the additional information to be provided, details of any departure from accounting standards in order to give a true and fair view ('the true and fair override') and reasons for such departure must accord with regulations to be issued by the Secretary of State: *CA 2006, s 396(3)–(5)*. The regulations governing the format of accounts are the two *Accounting Regulations*.

2.49   IFRS uses the term 'fair representation'. Martin Moore QC had advised that this means the same as 'true and fair'. The view that IFRS accounts can give a true and fair view has been questioned in certain opinions of George Bompas QC. However, this argument is unconvincing.

Accounting regulators

2.50   'Accounting standards' are defined in *CA 2006, s 464* as statements of standard accounting practice issued by a body prescribed by regulations. The current regulations are the *Accounting Standards (Prescribed Body) Regulations 2008, SI 2008/651*. The prescribed body is the ASB. The ASB was established on 1 August 1990, as the successor to the Accounting Standards Committee (ASC). The Financial Reporting Council (FRC) took over the role of the ASB on 2 July 2012. The FRC has oversight regulation of all accounting and audit matters in the UK. It issues Financial Reporting Standards (FRS). FRS in turn take the place of Statements of Standard Accounting Practice (SSAP) formerly issued by the ASC.

2.51   The FRC also oversees the Urgent Issues Task Force (UITF), which was established in March 1991, to produce abstracts on the interpretation of particular accounting standards, eg UITF 40 on income recognition for professional work in progress. Designated trade bodies produce Statements of Recommended Practice (SORP) for particular sectors, where the body in question is recognised by the ASB as a SORP-making body, eg the British

Banker's Association SORP on Advances; the Charities Commission's SORP 'Accounting by Charities'. Since 2004, the FRC regulates auditing activities through the Auditing Practices Board (APB).

2.52   Listed companies are required to observe the Listing Rules (FSA Sourcebook) and Guidance Manual issued by the Financial Services Authority (FSA). Companies whose shares are listed on the Alternative Investment Market (AIM) have to observe the AIM Rules issued by the Stock Exchange.

2.53   The International Accounting Standards Committee (IASC) issued International Accounting Standards (IASs). In 2001 the IASC was replaced by the International Accounting Standards Board (IASB), which issues International Financial Reporting Standards (IFRS), which are referred to generically as International Accounting Standards (IAS). The International Financial Reporting Standard Interpretations Committee (IFRSIC) plays much the same role as UITF in relation to UK accounting standards.

Adoption of IFRS within Europe

2.54   Under the terms of the Regulation, before an individual IFRS can fall within the scope of the IAS Directive it must be approved as suitable for use by the European Commission. Apart from the Commission, the endorsement mechanism includes an official Accounting Regulatory Committee (ARC) and a private sector body, the European Financial Reporting Advisory Group (EFRAG), which advises both the Commission and the ARC. The approval process, which takes about six months, has already operated to restrict the application of some standards, specifically IFRS 9 (replacing IAS 39) on financial instruments. This shows that the IASB – and business – should not presume automatic EU-endorsement of all its pronouncements. It is important to recognise that this system, while helping to ensure a full understanding of the proposals, introduces an element of delay and uncertainty, and is more than a little influenced by politics. By 31 December 2004, the Commission had adopted all existing international standards, including IAS 21 (Foreign Exchange) and revised versions of IAS 32 and IAS 39 (Financial Instruments) for use from 1 January 2005.

2.55   The key principle of IFRS is that all financial instruments be recognised on balance sheet, and all derivatives must be held on the balance sheet at fair value. This principle was introduced because, as derivatives have little or no initial cost, under accruals accounting they were generally held off balance sheet because there was no historic cost to record on balance sheet. IFRS 9 treats all derivatives as held for trading, and requires all derivatives and held for trading (HFT) financial assets to be measured at fair value, with all changes in those fair values recognised immediately in the profit and loss account. IFRS is a 'mixed measurement' model, in that some financial assets and liabilities are measured at amortised cost, and others – including all derivatives – are measured at fair value.

2.56   Continental GAAP had traditionally eschewed current value accounting, on the grounds that historic costs would be conservative and create hidden reserves, which would afford creditors a greater measure of security. Anglo-Saxon accounting, in an environment where businesses had a much greater dependence on public securities exchanges to raise finance, had always favoured transparency. The dominance of IFRS over traditional continental GAAP constitutes the resolution of this century-old dispute in favour of Anglo-Saxon accounting.

UK convergence programme

2.57   In a discussion paper of March 2004 entitled 'UK Accounting Standards – A Strategy for Convergence with IFRS', the ASB recognised the need to minimise the disruption of moving from UK to international accounting standards. It proposed a phased approach to convergence, with major changes over the following two years, and planned only to enhance existing UK financial reporting standards.

2.58   During 2005, the ASB chose to bring certain international standards into UK GAAP, more or less wholesale. IAS 32 was rebadged as FRS 25, and IAS 39 was rebadged as FRS 26. One of the most significant areas of change, under both international accounting and modified UK standards, and one that has certainly given rise to the greatest need for interpretation and guidance, is that of financing and hedging transactions.

2.59   The international standards must be adopted in the consolidated accounts of EU listed entities and may be adopted in the statutory accounts of the solus plc accounts or the statutory accounts of ordinary limited companies, including the subsidiaries of listed groups. The corresponding UK standards had to be adopted in any period of account beginning on or after 1 January 2005, if IFRS has not been adopted. However, FRS 25 [IAS 32] applied to the accounts of listed entities only, while FRS 26 [IAS 39] applied to the accounts of all UK companies.

2.60   IAS 32/FRS 25 covered both the presentation and the disclosure of financial instruments. The disclosure requirements were superseded by IFRS 7 for periods beginning on or after 1 January 2007; but, for tax purposes, the presentation requirements of this standard, in particular those governing the issue of compound financial instruments, are of primary importance.

2.61   In August 2009, the ASB issued a policy paper on 'The Future of UK GAAP'. The gravamen of this paper was that UK GAAP did not have a future.

The ASB proposed full convergence by 2013, with the IFRS for SMEs being used by all companies (ie instead of UK GAAP) other than those which use FRSSE. The FRC took over the role of the ASB on 2 July 2012. This did not mark any change of policy.

2.62 While global accounting harmonisation is still perceived to be an inherently good idea, there is an emerging sense that the intense detail prescribed both by national and by international standards is not necessarily suitable for the majority of organisations. Moreover, as the ongoing banking crisis since 2008 demonstrated, accounts drawn up on the same basis but in different jurisdictions vary hugely in terms of risk assessment, valuation, recognition and derecognition. The modern standards encourage the early recognition of income and this is further accelerated by the extensive use of fair value accounting. The financial crash of 2008–2010 caused a reconsideration of this approach, though this has not led to a revival of more conservative accounting policies.

FRS 100–FRS 103

2.63 The UK convergence programme has now culminated in the introduction of FRS 100, 101, 102 and 103. At a stroke these sweep away all existing UK accounting standards and replace them with a suite of four standards. These, combined with the FRSSE, govern financial reporting for all entities whose accounts are required to give a true and fair view.

2.64 FRS 100 – 'Application of Financial Reporting Standards' – sets out which framework is to be applied by which entities:

- those with publicly listed shares, or those whose regulators or markets require it, are required to report under EU-adopted IFRS in their consolidated financial statements;

- those which qualify as small (based on the Companies Act criteria) may use the Financial Reporting Standard for Smaller Entities (FRSSE);

- 'qualifying entities' may use the reduced disclosure framework set out in FRS 101 in their individual accounts;

- all other entities use FRS 102.

2.65 FRS 101 – 'Reduced Disclosure Framework – Disclosure exemptions from EU-adopted IFRS for qualifying entities' – permits 'qualifying entities' (broadly, members of a group where the parent prepares publicly available consolidated accounts including that company, which are intended to give a true and fair view) to prepare accounts using EU-adopted IFRS, but with exemptions from certain specified disclosures.

2.66 FRS 102 – 'The Financial Reporting Standard applicable in the UK and Republic of Ireland' – applies to financial statements that are intended to give a true and fair view and are not prepared under EU-adopted IFRS, FRS 101 or the FRSSE. It is effective for periods beginning on or after 1 January 2015. It is divided into sections, and each section is divided into paragraphs.

2.67 FRS 103 applies to insurance contracts, containing consolidated accounting and reporting requirements for insurance groups. FRS 105 is concerned with micro entities. Small companies can continue to use the FRSSE if they wish to do so.

Accounting bases

2.68 IFRS and FRS recognise two accounting bases: 'amortised cost' and 'fair value'. These are defined in IAS 39, Appendix A to IFRS 9 and the Glossary to FRS 102. Accounting may adopt a transaction-based approach or a balance sheet-based approach. A transaction-based approach works on the basis that there must be an event, a transaction with a third party, for a profit to be realised, a liability to be incurred, or an asset to be acquired. Accounting records the results of transactions. A balance sheet-based approach assumes that what goes on in the balance sheet is more important than whether transactions are completed or profits realised. IAS 39 is the mixed-measurement method. The accounting standards require many financial instruments to be measured in the accounts at fair value. It requires others to be measured at amortised cost.

2.69 Fair values are current market values, ie the amount a company would receive for an assignment of the asset or would have to pay to be relieved of a liability. Fair values represent a different kind of income recognition, reflecting how certain entities believe that they have already realised a profit. Fair value is the amount for which an asset could be exchanged, or a liability settled, between knowledgeable, willing parties in an arm's length transaction.

2.70 A balance sheet approach defines assets and liabilities, and derives profit and loss from change in value between two points in time. The basis of valuation is 'deprival value', ie the recompense that the owner of the asset would receive if he were deprived of it. The difference in the resultant measure of income is essentially that changes in the value of assets and liabilities not evidenced by realisation are now included as income. Gains and losses are recognised earlier in the balance sheet approach than under the traditional profit and loss approach, and gains and losses are recognised where none would previously have been recognised. Investment income and gains were traditionally calculated on a realisations rather than an accruals basis, without deduction of expenses. This was the essential reason why, prior to *FA 1996*, interest receivable and payable by companies was dealt with on a cash basis.

2.71   Fair value accounting goes further, and takes all value changes to profit and loss account as realised profits and losses. Accounting standards have now moved substantially away from historic cost accounting and towards annual remeasurement.

2.72   'Amortised cost' is the presence of accrual basis and historical cost. The amortised cost of a financial asset or financial liability is the amount at which the asset or liability is measured at initial recognition (usually 'cost') minus any repayments of principal, minus any reduction for impairment or uncollectibility, and plus or minus the cumulative amortisation using the effective interest method of the difference between that initial amount and the maturity amount. Amortisation is gradual redemption of a debt through a periodic repayment of principal. Thus, amortised cost basis is very close to accruals of historic cost, being historic cost plus accruals or minus write-downs.

2.73   As a rule an entity will prepare its financial statements, except for cash flow information, using the accruals basis of accounting. Accruals accounting (amortised cost basis) recognises a profit or loss when it is realised, ie when a transaction with a third party occurs, such as a sale or purchase. An event must occur for realisation to take place. A profit and loss approach measures annual profit and loss by matching revenues for an accounting period with the expenses incurred in earning it. As regards the balance sheet:

- unconditional receivables are recognised;

- firm commitments are not recognised; and

- planned future transactions are not recognised.

2.74   IFRS 9 provides that financial assets:

(i)   shall be recognised at FVTPL, unless

(ii)   measured at amortised cost because held to receive income, or

(iii) measured at fair value through other comprehensive income because held both for cash flows and with a view to sale.

2.75   For financial liabilities other than derivatives the default position is always amortised cost basis, with the following exceptions:

- there were initially recognised at FVTPL,

- financial guarantee contracts,

- commitments to provide a loan at below market rates.

FRS 102

2.76   For loan relationships and derivative contracts the main applicable sections are 11 and 12. These require separate treatment (see **2.82–2.100** and Chapter 11 below). However, numerous other sections are also relevant. The relationship of FRS 102 to IFRS and pre-1 January 2015 UK GAAP can be summarised as follows:

FRS 102 section	Topic	Former UK GAAP	IFRS
1	Scope		
1A	Small entities regime	FRSSE 2008/ 2015	
2	Concepts and pervasive principles		IASB Conceptual Framework
3	Financial statement presentation	FRS 3, FRS 18, FRS 28	IAS 1
4	Statement of financial position		IAS 1, IFRS 5
5	Statement of comprehensive income and income statement	FRS 3	IAS 1, IFRS 5
6	Statement of changes in equity, and statement of income and retained earnings	FRS 3	IAS 1
7	Statement of cash flows	FRS 1	IAS 7
8	Notes to the financial statements	FRS 18	IAS 1
9	Consolidated and separate financial statements	FRS 2, FRS 6, FRS 7	IFRS 3, IFRS 10, IAS 27
10	Accounting policies, estimates and errors	FRS 3, FRS 18	IAS 8
11	Basic financial instruments	FRS 4, FRS 25	IFRS 9, IAS 39
12	Other financial instruments issues		IFRS 9, IAS 39
13	Inventories	SSAP 9	IAS 2
14	Investments in associates	FRS 9	IAS 28
15	Investments in joint ventures	FRS 9	IAS 28, IFRS 11
16	Investment property	SSAP 19	IAS 40
17	Property, plant and equipment	FRS 15	IAS 16

FRS 102 section	Topic	Former UK GAAP	IFRS
18	Intangible assets other than goodwill	FRS 10, SSAP 13	IAS 38
19	Business combinations and goodwill	FRS 6, FRS 7	IFRS 3
20	Leases	SSAP 21, UITF 28	IAS 17, SIC-15
21	Provisions and contingencies	FRS 12	IAS 37
22	Liabilities and equity	FRS 25	IAS 32
23	Revenue	FRS 5, AN G, SSAP 9, UITF 216, UITF 40	IAS 18
24	Government grants	SSAP 4	IAS 20
25	Borrowing costs	FRS 15	IFRS 23
26	Share-based payment	FRS 20	IFRS 2
27	Impairment of assets	FRS 11	IAS 36
28	Employee benefits	FRS 17	IAS 19
29	Income tax	FRS 16, FRS 19	IAS 12
30	Foreign currency translation	SSAP 20	IAS 21
31	Hyperinflation	UITF 9	IAS 29
32	Events after the end of the reporting period	FRS 21	IAS 10
33	Related party disclosures	FRS 8	IAS 24
34	Specialised activities		
35	Transition to the FRS		
Glossary	Defined terms		IFRS 9, IAS 32, IAS 39

Section 1

2.77   Terms used are defined in the Glossary to FRS 102. The FRS applies to financial statements of companies and public benefit entities that are designed to give a true and fair view, as defined in the Companies Act: see **2.30–2.39**. Entities eligible to use the FRSSE may use that standard. A qualifying entity which is not a financial institution may take advantage of reduced disclosure requirements. The entity shall apply FRS 102 for accounting periods beginning on or after 1 January 2015.

Section 2

2.78   This sets out the qualitative requirements which financial statements must satisfy. Fundamental accounting concepts were concerned with measuring periodic profits, reflecting the primacy of the profit and loss account. The balance sheet essentially resulted from what was, and what was not, taken into account in the profit and loss account, and would reflect assets and liabilities at their transaction value (historic cost). Assets would appear at historic cost, meaning that part of the historic cost which had not previously been charged against revenues. The balance sheet reflects assets and liabilities at their historic cost, as reduced (or written down by amounts charged) against revenues.

2.79   Financial reporting now utilises a statement of comprehensive income to give a more comprehensive measure of income. Realised items go into the profit and loss account (income statement). Recognised but unrealised items go into the statement of comprehensive income. These include:

● revaluation gains,

● exchange gains and losses on retranslating net investments in foreign subsidiaries,

● tax on these items,

● changes in actuarial liabilities under a defined benefit pension scheme.

2.80   The statement of comprehensive income does not include transactions with shareholders. The statement of comprehensive income is in turn incorporated into the SOCIE. This shows the gains and losses from changes in ownership interest not arising from transactions with third parties or distributions to owners, where the ownership interest is measured as the difference between the assets and liabilities of the business. The 'true reflection' principle requires some items going through the SOCIE to be treated as realised for tax purposes. Gains and losses recognised in the SOCIE or taken to reserves have to be recognised subsequently in the profit and loss account ('recycling'). IFRS 9/ IAS 39 contain detailed requirements on when financial assets and liabilities should be shown on the balance sheet and in what form they should be shown (ie 'recognition') and when they should cease to be shown ('derecognition'). Thus the income statement deals with *realised* gains and losses, while the statement of comprehensive income takes in *recognised* gains and losses, and the balance sheet records both *recognised* and *realised* gains and losses.

2.81   For accounting purposes a substance over form approach is to be adopted. Paragraph 2.5 states:

'Transactions and other events and conditions should be accounted for and presented in accordance with their substance and not merely their legal form.'

2.82 Assets are an entitlement to receive future cash flows as a result of past events. Liabilities are obligations to pay cash in the future as a result of past events. Assets are deferred profits. Liabilities are deferred losses. Equity is the residual interest of shareholders in the form of shareholders' funds, ie the net worth of the entity, being (assets – liabilities).

2.83 Income is an increase in economic benefits arising from:

- inflows,
- enhancement in assets,
- decrease in liabilities.

2.84 Expenses are a decrease in economic benefits arising from:

- outflows,
- decrease in assets,
- increase in liabilities.

Expenses include depreciation.

2.85 In general assets and liabilities on recognition are measured at historic cost, unless there is a specific requirement to use fair value. Fair value will very seldom be used for non-derivative financial liabilities. Subsequent measurement will be on the basis of:

- amortised cost,
- fair value,
- revalaution model (property, plant and equipment, intangible property),
- lower of cost and net realisable value (inventory).

2.86 Performance is the relationship between income and expenses in a reporting period. An entity may present performance in a single financial statement (a statement of comprehensive income), or in two statements (an income statement and a statement of comprehensive income).

2.87 Income and expenses are recognised when it is probable that an economic benefit (asset) or economic detriment (liability) will arise, and the item, cost or value can be measured reliably. Any departure from this principle must be explained in notes. Contingent assets and contingent liabilities are not recognised until they become probable. Offsetting of assets and liabilities is in general not permitted.

2.88   Unlike IASB Conceptual Framework, Section 2 does not use the concept of 'discounted present value' of future cash inflows or outflows. However, this will be used in practice:

Example 2.1

Where a debt pays fixed interest of 5%:

(i)   present value (PV) of £1,000 to be received in one year's time is (1,000/1.05)

(ii)   PV of £5,000 to be received in two years' time is $(5,000/1.05^2)$

(iii)   PV of £20,000 to be received in three years' time is $(20,000/1.05^3)$

Section 3

2.89   An entity may depart from accounting standards in very exceptional circumstances, in order to give a true and fair view, and any such departure must be explained in notes.

2.90   A complete set of financial statements comprises:

- a statement of financial position–

  (a)   a statement of comprehensive income (with an 'other comprehensive income' section following the calculation of profit or loss for the period), or

  (b)   an income statement (showing the entity's profit or loss for the period) and a statement of other comprehensive income;

- SOCIE;
- cash flow statement;
- notes;
- comparative information for all amounts.

2.91   'Other comprehensive income' means:

(i)   items which may be reclassified to profit or loss. Hence, in the case of cash flow hedges under IAS 39 the portion of the profit or loss on the hedging instrument that is determined to be an effective hedge is recognised in other comprehensive income;

(ii)   items which cannot be reclassified to profit or loss, eg property revaluations.

The SOCIE comprises comprehensive income + changes in equity.

2.92   Financial statements are prepared on a going concern basis, unless (i) there is an intention to liquidate, or (ii) it has no realistic possibility of continuing for more than 12 months.

Section 4

2.93   The statement of financial position (formerly balance sheet) shows the entity's assts, liabilities and equity. Non-current and current assets, and non-current and current liabilities, are presented separately. 'Current' in general means expected to be realised (or to be settled) within 12 months after the end of the reporting period. Assets held for sale are separately disclosed in notes.

Section 5

2.94   Companies may adopt (a) a 'single-statement approach' (a statement of comprehensive income with an 'other comprehensive income' section following the calculation of profit or loss for the period) or (b) a 'Two-statement approach' (income statement showing the entity's profit or loss for the period plus a statement of other comprehensive income). Extraordinary items are items falling outside the entity's ordinary activities which are not expected to reoccur. This section also deals with discontinued operations.

Section 6

2.95   Changes in equity may be reported either in a SOCIE (reconciling movements of shareholders' funds with the income statement) or, if specified conditions are fulfilled, in a statement of income and retained earnings. The latter condition is fulfilled if the profit transferred to reserves in the income statement is the same as the increase in reserves in the balance sheet.

Section 7

2.96   Cash flows are divided into operating, investing and financing activities. Operating activities are the 'principal revenue-generating activities of the entity'. Investment activities are the acquisition and disposal of long-term assets and other investments. Financing activities are activities that result in changes in contributed equity and borrowings. Cash includes readily convertible to cash assets.

Section 8

2.97 Notes provide information about the basis of preparation of the financial statements, including accounting policies, judgments and estimations.

Section 9

2.98 A parent must in general prepare group (consolidated) accounts. A subsidiary is an entity controlled by its parent. Control is the power to govern the financial and operating policies of an entity so as to obtain benefits from its activities. On consolidation, intra-group transactions and balances are eliminated.

2.99 Payments to an intermediary such as an Employee Benefit Trust are assumed not to give rise to an expense unless the payer will receive no further economic benefits as a result of the payment.

Section 10

2.100 A change of accounting practice means (a) adoption of a different policy or standard, or (b) adoption of a different accounting framework. When accounting policies are changed, the balance sheet for the period in which the new policy is adopted must be restated, on the basis of the new policy. Resulting changes give rise to 'prior period adjustments'. Comparatives must be restated in the first accounting period in which the new basis is adopted.

Section 22

2.101 Financial instruments are classified as debt or equity. Equity is the residual interest in an entity's assets after deducting all of its liabilities. Debt is a contractual obligation to deliver cash or another financial asset.

2.102 Shares, options, rights and warrants that meet the definition of equity are measured at the fair value of the consideration received when they are issued, net of transaction costs.

2.103 When convertible debt is issued, the proceeds are allocated between the liability and equity components (bifurcation). The amount attributed to the liability is the fair value of a similar liability without the equity component, and the balance is allocated to the equity component.

Section 25

2.104   Borrowing costs are interest and other costs incurred in connection with the borrowing of funds. They include finance charges on finance leases and foreign exchange differences where these are treated as an adjustment to the interest cost.

2.105   An entity may, as a matter of accounting policy, adopt a policy of capitalising borrowing costs directly attributable to the acquisition, construction or production of a qualifying asset.

Section 30

2.106   An entity must recognise a functional currency (the currency of its primary operating environment) and its presentation currency (its reporting currency). Foreign currency transactions are translated at the spot rate on transaction date and retranslated on reporting dates, exchange differences on retranslation being recognised in profit. Exchange differences on non-monetary items are recorded in the same place as the gain or loss on the item itself.

Definition of financial instruments

2.107   Section 11 applies to basic financial instruments accounted for at amortised cost. Section 12 deals with non-basic financial instruments accounted for at fair value. Section 11 takes precedence of Section 12. Sections 11 and 12 correspond to the two main IFRSs addressing financial instruments, namely IAS 32 (Financial Instruments: Presentation) [FRS 25] and IAS 39 (Financial Instruments: Recognition and Measurement) [FRS 26]. IAS 32 specifies how financial instruments should be presented in financial statements. IAS 39 specifies when a financial instrument is to be recognised on the balance sheet and at what amount, and also when to remove a financial instrument from the balance sheet, and what to do with gains and losses.

2.108   IAS 32 and IAS 39 apply to all entities and to all financial instruments in financial statements intended to show *a true and fair view*. IAS 39 is to be replaced by IFRS 9 with effect from 1 January 2018. This has been adopted by EFRAG on 15 September 2015, but not yet endorsed by the EU. FRS 102 gives a choice to companies to use: (i) IAS 39; (ii) FRS 102, Sections 11 and 12; or (iii) IFRS 9, para 11.2. Prior to 1 January 2015, FRS 26 [IAS 39] was only mandatory for companies with listed securities, or using fair value measurement for financial instruments. FRS 25 [IAS 32] was mandatory except for companies using FRSSE.

2.109 IAS 39 applies to all types of financial instrument. IAS 32, para 11 has a series of accounting definitions which underlie the similar definitions used in tax legislation. In FRS 102 these removed to Section 22 and the Glossary:

• A financial instrument is any 'contract that gives rise to a financial asset of one entity and a financial liability or equity instrument of another entity'.

• A financial asset is 'any asset that is cash, an equity instrument of another entity, or a contractual right:

  (i) to receive cash or another financial asset from another entity, or

  (ii) to exchange financial assets or financial liabilities with another entity under conditions that are potentially favourable to the entity'.

• An equity instrument contains no obligation to transfer cash or another financial instrument on potentially unfavourable terms. An equity instrument is 'any contract that evidences a residual interest in the assets of an entity after deduction of all its liabilities'.

2.110 Contracts that are settled by delivery of a physical asset or a non-financial service are not financial instruments. For a contract to give rise to a financial instrument, both the entitlement and the performance obligation must be financial in nature.

2.111 Hence the standards extend the scope to certain contracts to buy or sell non-financial items only when those contracts can be settled in the same way as a financial instrument.

2.112 For example, a commodity contract that provides for settlement by receipt or delivery of a physical asset only is not a financial instrument, because it does not give rise to a financial asset of one party and financial liability in the other.

2.113 Often, such contracts are traded in much the same manner as some derivative financial instruments: for example, a commodity futures contract may be bought or sold for cash and may change hands many times. However, the parties buying and selling the contract are, in effect, trading the underlying commodity, and this does not alter the fundamental character of the contract in a way that creates a financial instrument. It remains a non-financial instrument, even though it is traded like a financial instrument. Nonetheless, even if many commodity-based contracts are not financial instruments, they are included within the scope of IAS 32 and 39, but only if they operate in the same manner as financial instruments.

2.114 A financial liability is any liability that is a contractual obligation to deliver cash or another financial asset to another entity, or a contractual obligation to exchange financial assets or financial liabilities with another entity under conditions that are potentially unfavourable. The definition states that a financial liability is any liability that is:

(a) a contractual obligation–

  (i) to deliver cash or another financial asset to another entity; or

  (ii) to exchange financial assets or financial liabilities with another entity under conditions that are potentially unfavourable to the entity; or

(b) a contract that will or may be settled in the entity's own equity instruments and is–

  (i) a non-derivative for which the entity is or may be obliged to deliver a variable number of its own equity instruments; or

  (ii) a derivative that will or may be settled other than by the exchange of a fixed number of the entity's own equity instruments.

2.115 All financial instruments that are *not financial assets* are to be included in the balance sheet within one of the following categories:

• financial liability, or

• equity instruments.

2.116 IFRS 9 largely reproduces IAS 39, but is more clearly laid out and expressed. It comprises:

• Chapters 1–7, divided into numbered sections and paragraphs (Section 1.1, etc, para 4.3.3, etc),

• Appendix A – Defined Terms,

• Appendix B – Application Guidance (so that B1 corresponds to Chapter 1, and B1 is also divided into sections and paragraphs).

Classification of financial asset/liability

2.117 In the recognition and measurement, IAS 39 categorises financial instruments into four types. These categories are defined:

• *A financial asset or financial liability at fair value through profit or loss (FVTPL).* The asset or liability classified in this category is measured at fair value on the balance sheet, with changes in fair value going through profit or loss in the period they arise. An item may fall into this category because it is held for trading (HFT). All derivatives, except hedges, fall into the HFT category.

Thus, all free-standing derivatives and embedded derivatives that are required to be separated from their host contract (except hedging instruments) are measured at fair value, and changes in fair value are taken to the income statement (ie profit or loss). However, in addition to the requirement for an item to be included in this category, a company may also, on initial recognition, designate a financial asset or financial liability as FVTPL, with (it is proposed) some restrictions.

- *Held-to-maturity ('HTM') investments.* This is a restricted category for only non-derivative financial assets with fixed maturity and fixed and determinable payments, which the company must intend to hold, and be able to hold, until maturity.

  HTM instruments are measured at amortised cost. If a company sells more than an insignificant proportion of its portfolio of HTM assets, other than because of a non-recurring and unpredictable circumstance, it must reclassify the remainder of its HTM assets as 'available for sale'. This 'tainting' expires at the end of the second year following the premature sales.

- *Loans and receivables (L&R).* L&R is defined as non-derivative financial assets with fixed and determinable payments that are unquoted in an active market. It is a sub-set of HTM which may be both repayable on the maturity (if any) or on demand. L&R, except those held for trading or designated as FVTPL, is measured at amortised cost basis.

  Also, a company may decide to classify any financial assets that meet the definition of L&R and HTM as at FVTPL or available for sale on initial recognition.

  In HTM, L&R categories, amortisation of premiums or discounts using the effective interest method, and losses due to impairment (impairment losses), are immediately included in current period profit and loss, as are most foreign exchange gains and losses (IAS 21). Other gains and losses are recognised only on removal of the instrument from balance sheet.

- *Available for sale (AfS).* Financial assets that do not fall into any of the three categories above are classified as AfS. A company may also designate a particular non-derivative financial asset as AfS.

  A financial asset classified as AfS is measured at fair value but gains and losses resulting from changes in fair value, rather than being included directly in profit or loss, are temporarily recognised in equity through the statement of change in equity.

2.118 IAS 39 recognises two classifications of financial liabilities. First, financial liabilities are measured at FVTPL. Second, others (mostly) are measured at amortised cost using the effective interest method.

2.119 As with financial assets, the first category is divided into two sub-categories:

- designated – a financial liability that is designated by the company as a liability at FVTPL upon initial recognition; and

- HFT – a financial liability classified as HFT, such as a derivative liability that is not a hedging instrument, eg a forward or swap contract whose value is unfavourable to the company at balance sheet date.

2.120 In largely the same manner as FRS 102, IFRS 9, Section 4 divides financial instruments into those held at amortised cost and those held at fair value. A financial asset is held at amortised cost if two conditions are satisfied:

(i) the asset is held to obtain income; and

(ii) the asset gives a contractual entitlement to specific payments of principal and interest on set dates.

2.121 IFRS 9 classifies all financial liabilities at amortised cost save in exceptional cases where the liability may be classified at FVTPL.

Basic financial instruments

2.122 A basic financial instrument which is accounted for in Section 11 is an instrument which satisfies the conditions in para 11.9. For a debt instrument to be basic, and so held at amortised cost, returns to the holder must be:

- a fixed amount;
- a fixed rate of return over the term of the instrument;
- a variable rate of return referenced to a quoted or observable interest rate; or
- a combination of fixed and variable rates where both are positive (eg LIBOR + 1%).

2.123 The instrument must carry a legal obligation to repay the debt and interest, and carry no contingent or variable repayment conditions save as to variable rate of interest. Financial instruments which do not satisfy these conditions are complex and fall under Section 12.

2.124 The definition of basic financial asset (or liability) is wide, and covers:

- cash,
- debt,

- bank accounts,

- trade receivables and payable, and

- cash settled commodity contracts.

2.125 Basic financial assets (liabilities) may include features such as:

- fixed or variable interest or both,

- links to an index,

- caps and floors,

- ratchets,

- non-contingent variations of interest rate,

- resets, and

- prepayment options and compensation for early repayments.

2.126 The return on discounted debt must be accounted for using the effective interest rate (IFRS 9, Section 5, B5.4). The effective interest rate is the rate which exactly discounts the estimated future cash flows over the expected life of the financial instrument to the net carrying value. The effective interest rate method for instruments issued at a discount means:

$$i = [(A^{(n-1)}/P) - 1]$$

where i = effective interest rate

A = amount payable on redemption

P = amount payable on subscription

N = term

Recognition and derecognition

2.127 A company is required to recognise all financial assets and liabilities, including derivatives, on its balance sheet at the time when it becomes a party to the contract concerned. IAS 39 is based on a 'mixed measurement model', whereby some financial instruments are included at fair value and others at amortised cost basis. Instruments meeting the definition of basic financial instruments within Section 11 will usually be held at amortised cost, except where an option to measure at fair value has been taken, or in the case of an investment in another entity's equity.

2.128 All financial assets and liabilities are initially measured at fair value, which usually equates to cost, ie the transaction price. Where the amortised cost basis is used, at each reporting date the initial carrying value is adjusted for:

- repayments of principal,

- plus or minus cumulative amortisation using the effective interest rate method,

- minus in the case of financial assets impairments.

2.129   Equity share investments are held at fair value, but only if there is a quoted market price or fair value can be reliably measured.

2.130   In the case of financial assets held at amortised cost basis, an impairment loss is recognised where there is objective evidence of an impairment. A financial liability is derecognised when one of the following happens:

- settlement, or

- transfer of risks and reward of ownership.

A financial liability is derecognised when it is discharged, cancelled or expires.

2.131   FRS 102, paras 11.33–11.35 [IFRS 9, Chapter 3] set out when a financial asset is derecognised. A financial liability is derecognised when it is extinguished, ie when the obligation specified in the contract is discharged or cancelled or expires. In broad terms, this depends on whether or not:

- it has transferred the contractual right to receive the cash flows from the asset;

- it has transferred substantially all the risks and rewards of ownership; and

- it has relinquished control of the asset.

Debt restructuring

2.132   Where the modification of restructuring of a financial instrument is considered substantial, the original debt is derecognised and the 'new' debt instrument recognised at its fair value. To the extent that the fair value of the new instrument differs from the carrying value of the old instruments, a gain or loss will be recognised in profit or loss: FRS 102, paras 11.36–11.38. Amending the terms of a loan does not constitute refinancing. A modification may be substantial or insubstantial. IAS 39 has a test that a change is substantial if it changes the carrying value by 10% or more. FRS 102 is more judgmental and has no specific measure.

Non-basic financial instruments

2.133   Section 12 deals with financial assets and liabilities which are not held at amortised cost, ie derivatives and financial assets recognised at fair value through profit and loss. It also deals with hedge accounting (see **Chapter 16**). All derivative financial instruments and non-financial derivatives falling within the scope of IAS 32, IAS 39, IFRS 9 and FRS 102 are recognised on the balance sheet. This is because IFRS require that all derivatives are required to be measured at fair value in the recognition on the balance sheet.

2.134   The cost of a derivative is often zero, yet a derivative can be settled or sold at any time for its fair value. Without measuring derivatives at fair value (as the historic cost model of old UK GAAP), they are invisible on the balance sheet. Also, gains and losses would be reported only when the derivative is settled or sold, rather than in the period in which the change in fair value occurred. It is important to recognise that, under IFRS and converging UK GAAP, all derivative contracts are recognised on the balance sheet and at fair value, with subsequent movements to profit or loss. This is a very significant change from the previous practice, under which most financial instruments were off balance sheet and recorded only as an integral part of the financial asset or liability they were hedging.

2.135   For example, the exchange rate inherent in a currency contract would be used to record the debtor or creditor which the contract was taken out to hedge, as and when that asset or liability was itself recognised in the accounts. No other element of the contract would appear on the face of the accounts. Similarly, the value of an interest rate contract would not appear anywhere on the balance sheet, but any periodic payments under the contract would be accounted for as part of net funding costs.

2.136   IAS 39, para 9 [IFRS 9, Appendix A] defines a derivative contract as a financial instrument which has three characteristics:

- its value depends upon a volatility (the 'underlying');

- it requires no initial investment or less than would be required for a non-derivative contract having similar exposure; and

- it is settled at a future date.

2.137   The full definition in para 9 states:

'A derivative is a financial instrument or other contract … with all three of the following characteristics:

(a)   its value changes in response to the change in a specified interest rate, financial instrument price, commodity price, foreign

57

exchange rate, index of prices or rates, credit rating or credit index, or other variable, provided in the case of a non-financial variable that the variable is not specific to a part to the contract (… the underlying;);

(b) it requires no initial net investment or an initial net investment that is smaller than would be required for other types of contract that would be expected to have a similar response to changes in market factors; and

(c) it is settled at a future date.'

This definition is taken into the Glossary to FRS 102.

2.138 Accordingly a derivatives is a financial instrument which has three characteristics:

(a) its value changes in respect of an underlying (eg a share, an interest rate, a currency, an index or any other variable);

(b) it requires no or minimal initial net investment;

(c) it is performed at a future date.

2.139 Financial instruments which come within Section 12 are recognised at fair value on acquisition, and thereafter at fair value, changes in fair value being taken to the income statement. This gives effect to the central principle of IFRS that all derivative financial instruments must be taken to balance sheet and fair valued.

2.140 FRS 102, Section 12 [IFRS 9, Chapter 6] also deals with hedge accounting. Hedging requires an 'economic relationship' between the hedged item and the hedging instrument. An economic relationship exists if the values of the hedged item and hedging instrument move in opposite directions in response to the hedged risk. If certain qualifying conditions are met, hedge accounting can be applied. Three types of hedging relationship are recognised:

- cash flow hedges (eg to reduce variable interest rate or foreign exchange rate risk);

- fair value hedges (eg to reduce fixed rate interest rate risk or change in share value risk); and

- net investment hedge (eg debt to finance investment in a foreign operation).

2.141 Hedge accounting allows recognition of the value movements on the hedged item to be deferred until its actual realisation. Hedging is dealt with in **Chapter 16**.

Summary

2.142   The accounting treatment prescribed is broadly:

Category	Measurement	Changes in carrying amount
Assets:		
Basic – FRS 102, Section 11	Amortised cost (except ordinary shares FVTPL)	Income – amortisation of premium or discount
Non-basic – FRS 102, Section 12	FVTPL	Income
FVTPL: HFT, including derivatives*	Fair value	Income
HTM	Amortised cost	
L&R	Amortised cost	Income – amortisation of premium or discount
AfS	Fair value	Equity (but interest, dividends, foreign exchange, etc to Income Statement)
Liabilities:		
In general	Amortised cost	Income – amortisation of premium of discount
FVTPL: HFT, including derivatives*	Fair value	Income

* Derivatives that are designated and effective hedging instruments are subject to different rules.

Debt/equity classification

2.143   IAS 32 deals with whether an instrument issued by an entity should be classified as debt or equity. The fundamental principle is that, on initial recognition, it is classified either as a financial liability or as an equity instrument. IAS 32, para 15 applies a 'substance over form' model to the debt/equity classification. Preference shares provide an example of the distinction between financial liabilities and equity made by IAS 32. The issuer must consider whether it has a contractual obligation to transfer cash or other financial assets to the holder of the share. In determining whether, on initial recognition, a preference share is a financial liability or equity instrument, IAS 32 requires an issuer to assess the particular rights attaching to the security. Preference shares which are mandatorily redeemable, or redeemable at the option of the holder (a 'puttable instrument'), contain a financial liability.

Such preference shares are treated as debt for accounting purposes: IAS 32, para 18(a), (b), Application Guidance AG25.

2.144 For example, if, under its terms of issue, a preference share is mandatorily redeemable on a certain date, the issuing company has such a contractual obligation. The preference share will therefore be a financial liability, not an equity instrument.

2.145 If the preference share is non-redeemable, but the company has a contractual obligation to pay a dividend, it will again be a financial liability. If, however, payment of a dividend is solely at the discretion of the directors (whether or not unpaid dividends accumulate), there is no contractual obligation to make a payment and the preference share will be classified as an equity instrument. The treatment of the coupon follows the treatment of the principal (IAS 32, para 35). So, if a preference share is classified as debt, its coupon will be shown as interest in the company's income statement. The coupon on an instrument that is classified as equity will be shown as a distribution.

2.146 This principle applies only for accounting, but not for company law or tax purposes. For tax purposes, dividends on preference shares remain dividends. This is because they are not considered as loan relationships for tax purposes.

Comparison of IFRS (FRS 101) and FRS 102

2.147 UK companies are thus left with a choice between:

- IFRS/FRS 101, and

- FRS 102.

2.148 The differences between the two are more presentational than substantive:

Area	FRS 102	IFRS
Profit and loss	Three measurement methods:	Four measurement methods:
	(i) amortised cost	(i) amortised cost
	(ii) FVTPL	(ii) FVTPL
	(iii) equity instruments – FVTPL unless FV cannot be measured reliably	(iii) fair value through OCI (for AfS)
		(iv) equity instruments – FVTPL unless unquoted equity instruments

Balance sheet	Basic financial instruments	FVTPL
	Non-basic (other) financial instruments	HTM
		L & R
		AfS
Hedging	IFRS 9/IAS 39	IFRS 9/IAS 39
	No quantified effectiveness measure	Effectiveness test

2.149 IAS 1 (and so FRS 101) permits an entity to prepare a single performance statement rather than a separate income statement and separate statement of comprehensive income.

Taxable profits

2.150 Tax law is concerned with bringing the 'profits' of a company into charge to corporation tax, by applying the law to the facts. 'Profits' are defined as 'income and chargeable gains': *CTA 2009, s 2*. Accounting is concerned with the provision of financial information generally, for a wide range of purposes. The accounts form the basis of computing taxable profits, but subject to numerous adjustments. Since 1990 there has been a policy to align taxable profits more closely with accounting profits. However, this policy is abandoned as soon as the accounting profit is less than putative taxable profit.

2.151 Profits have to be calculated according to accounting principles. Accounts have always formed the starting point for the computation of trading profits. *Income Tax Act 1803, s 84* provided that trading profits should be assessed to income tax under Schedule D, Case I on 'not less than the full amount of the profits or gains of such trade or manufacture', and this contained an implicit accounting requirement. Computation of profits in accordance with commercial accountancy goes back at least to 1894. In *Gresham Life Assurance Society Ltd v Styles* 3 TC 185, Lord Halsbury observed (at 188):

> 'Now to my mind it is very clear what is the intuitus both of the Enactment and the Rules under which the duties are to be ascertained. The thing to be taxed is the amount of profits and gains. The word "profits" I think is to be understood in its natural and proper sense – in a sense which no commercial man would misunderstand.'

2.152 In *Lothian Chemical Co Ltd v Rogers (Inspector of Taxes)* 11 TC 508, a company sought to claim as a deduction in computing its profits a payment of £4,000 which was the excess of the cost of building a new factory over the amount paid by the Ministry of Munitions. The payment was held to be non-deductible as a capital outlay. Lord Clyde said (at 520–521):

'My Lords, it has been said times without number ... that in considering what is the true balance of profits and gains in the Income Tax Acts ... you deal in the main with ordinary principles of commercial accounting. They do expressly exclude a number of deductions and allowances, some of which according to the ordinary principles of commercial accounting might be allowable. But where these ordinary principles are not invaded by statute they must be allowed to prevail.'

2.153   Profits are a matter of fact, to be established by accountancy evidence, except where and to the extent that either an express statutory direction applies or accountancy evidence leaves a gap. The classic statement of this principle was given by Lord Haldane in *Sun Insurance Office v Clark* 6 TC 59 at 78. In that case an insurance company charged 40% of its premium income to a reserve for unexpired risks. It was found as a fact that this was a reasonable and proper allowance to make. On a refusal to allow this as a deduction for income tax purposes, it was held that this item was properly allowable. Lord Haldane said:

'It is plain that the question of what is or is not profit or gain must primarily be one of fact to be ascertained by the tests applied in ordinary business. Questions of law can only arise when ... some express statutory direction applies and excludes ordinary commercial practice, or where, by reason of its being impracticable to ascertain the facts sufficiently, some presumption has to be invoked to fill the gap.'

2.154   The term 'ordinary principles of commercial accountancy' is a case-law term: see *Odeon Associated Theatres Ltd v Jones (Inspector of Taxes)* 48 TC 257 at 273. This case addressed the question of whether or not, when a company acquired cinemas in a commercially viable condition, but requiring expenditure on repairs and maintenance, the expenditure was deductible in its entirety as revenue expenditure, in accordance with the commercial accounts. At that time, the question asked was: what was correct and appropriate for (a) accounting and (b) tax purposes? 'Appropriate' is used where judgement has been applied. Since then, detailed rules have been developed in accounting standards designed to exclude professional judgement.

2.155   *Gallagher v Jones (Inspector of Taxes)* [1993] STC 537 concerned an unincorporated trader, who had no obligation to produce accounts in accordance with accounting standards. He acquired three canal boats on finance leases. As is normal, the rental period was divided into two periods:

- a primary period, in which the lessor recovers his outlay plus his turn on the finance; and

- a secondary period in which a reduced or nominal rental is payable.

2.156 Primary rental periods are often front loaded, as was the case here. Under each of the leases, £14,562 was payable on day 1, followed by 17 monthly payments of £2,080. Thereafter, there was a secondary rental period of 21 years, at an annual rent of £5. For the accounting period in which the narrow boats were acquired, the taxpayer's accounts showed a deduction for the lease expenditure on a cash basis of £77,200 (for each of three leases, the initial payments plus five monthly payments). SSAP 21 required the lease payments to be treated as a finance charge on a notional loan, the payments on which were to be spread over the term of the agreement in accordance with a recognised method of allocation. The Court of Appeal said that, for tax purposes, an unincorporated business had to produce accounts based on accounting standards. Lord Bingham MR stated (at 555–556):

> 'I find it hard to understand how any judge-made rule could override a generally accepted rule of commercial accountancy which (a) applied to the situation in question, (b) was not one or two or more rules applicable to the situation in question and (c) was not shown to be inconsistent with the true facts or otherwise inapt to determine the true profits or losses of the business.'

2.157 'Any adjustment required or authorised by law' is not confined to adjustments required by statute ('statutory overrides'), but may apply to adjustments authorised by case law. However, since the judgments in *Gallagher v Jones*, such non-statutory adjustments are unlikely to occur.

2.158 Adjustments required by law include adjustments under the loan relationships and derivative contracts rules, transfer pricing rules and capital allowances rules.

2.159 In the case of companies, the statutory requirement that accounts must give a true and fair view, introduced by *CA 1948, s 147(2)*, effectively displaced the common law rule. *CA 1985, s 236* made provision for statements of accounting practice to be prepared by professional bodies. *Section 226(3)* required accounts to comply with *Sch 4*. *Schedule 4, para 36A* required the accounts to say whether or not they had been compiled in accordance with applicable accounting standards so as to give a true and fair view.

2.160 In the case of trades in general, *FA 1998, s 46(1)* provided:

'(1) In the provisions of the Tax Acts relating to the computation of the profits of a trade, profession or vocation references to receipts and expenses are (except where otherwise expressly provided) to any items brought into account as credits and debits in computing such profits.'

2.161   This was important because it required taxable profits to be computed by reference to the profit and loss account, not by reference to the balance sheet. The profit and loss account and the balance sheet articulate with each other. Whatever goes through the profit and loss account must also go through the balance sheet. However, the converse is not true. *FA 1998, s 46* said that items which go through the balance sheet, but do not enter the profit and loss account, are not included in taxable profits, because these relate to realised profits. To that extent, *s 46* was out of step with accounting developments, which gave the balance sheet priority over the profit and loss account.

2.162   *FA 2002, s 103(2)* introduced a statutory definition of GAAP with effect from 24 July 2002. It also substituted 'generally accepted accounting practice' for all references to 'normal accounting' and the like. The common law rule in *Odeon Theatres* and *Gallagher v Jones* was thus generally replaced by a statutory rule that, for tax purposes, profits had to be computed in accordance with GAAP-compliant accounts.

2.163   For tax purposes, companies must use accounts drawn up in accordance with either IFRS or UK GAAP. *CTA 2010, s 1127* says:

'(1)   In the Corporation Tax Acts "generally accepted accounting practice" means UK generally accepted accounting practice. This is subject to subsection (3).

(2)   In the Corporation Tax Acts "UK generally accepted accounting practice"–

(a)   means generally accepted accounting practice in relation to UK companies (other than IAS accounts) that are intended to give a true and fair view, ...

(3)   In relation to the affairs of a company or other entity that prepares IAS accounts, in the Corporation Tax Acts "generally accepted accounting practice" means generally accepted accounting practice in relation to IAS accounts.'

2.164   Unincorporated traders (individuals and partnerships) are required to use an accounts basis. *ITTOIA 2005, s 25* in turn codifies the basic rule for the computation of trade profits:

'(1)   The profits of a trade must be calculated in accordance with generally accepted accounting practice, subject to any adjustment required or authorised by law in calculating profits for income tax purposes.'

2.165 *ITTOIA 2005, s 27(1)* requires the profits to be derived from the profit and loss account:

'(1) … in the calculation of the profits of a trade, references to receipts and expenses are to any items brought into account as credits or debits in calculating the profits.'

2.166 For corporation tax purposes, *CTA 2009, s 46(1)* has the corresponding rule to *ITTOIA 2005, s 25*:

'(1) The profits of a trade must be calculated in accordance with generally accepted accounting practice, subject to any adjustment required or authorised by law in calculating profits for corporation tax purposes.'

2.167 The corresponding rule to *ITTOIA 2005, s 27* for corporation tax is in *CTA 2009, s 48(1)*:

'(1) In the Corporation Tax Acts in the context of the calculation of the profits of a trade, references to receipts and expenses are to any items brought into account as credits or debits in calculating the profits.'

SMEs

2.168 In its accounting and auditing requirements, the companies legislation imposes a simplified and lighter regime for micro entities, small and medium-sized enterprises (SMEs). For accounting purposes, the distinction is between small companies on one hand, and medium-sized and large companies on the other. For auditing purposes, small, medium-sized and large companies are distinguished.

2.169 The definitions of a 'small company' and 'small groups' are set out in *CA 2006, ss 381–384*. The definitions of 'medium-sized company' and 'medium-sized group' are found in *ss 465–467*. For accounting periods beginning on or after 31 December 2006, a small company remains eligible for the small companies regime whether its individual accounts are in accordance with Companies Act or IAS. A company qualifies as a small or medium-sized company if, for the financial year in question and the previous financial year, it meets two out of three criteria relating to maximum:

- turnover,
- assets, and
- number of employees.

2.170   With effect from 1 January 2016, the maximum figures are:

Maximum (two out of three)	Micro	Small companies	Medium-sized companies
Turnover	≤ €2m	≤ €10m	≤ €50m
Assets	≤ €2m	≤ €10m	≤ €43m
Employees	<10	<50	<250

2.171   Depending upon the accounting format used, the balance sheet for these purposes comprises either:

- called up share capital not paid;
- fixed assets;
- current assets;
- prepayments and accrued income;
- or simply assets.

2.172   'Quoted companies' are companies whose securities are listed on an EEA recognised exchange, the New York Stock Exchange or Nasdaq (*CA 2006, s 385*). An unquoted company is a company whose securities are not so listed.

2.173   These definitions are derived from Commission Recommendation of 6 May 2003 (2003/361/EC). To provide guidance the EU Commission publishes 'The new SME definition: Users guide and model declaration' ('the Guide'). EU law defines 'enterprise' or 'undertaking' by reference to the reality of the economic unit rather than relying on the technical boundaries of legal entities. EU law is concerned with the reality of control, rather than the precise legal structure: see para 9 of the Preamble to 2003/361/EC.

2.174   As noted in the previous paragraph, whether or not an enterprise is a micro, small or medium-sized enterprise is to be determined by its headcount, turnover and balance sheet. In the case of an autonomous enterprise, its data for this purpose are to be determined exclusively by reference to its accounts: *Art 6(1)*.

2.175   An enterprise will not be an autonomous enterprise if it is a linked enterprise or partner enterprise: *Art 3(1)*. If an enterprise is a 'linked' or 'partner' enterprise, the data are calculated on a proportional or consolidated basis: *Art 6(2)–(4)*.

2.176   An enterprise will be a linked enterprise if it has a relationship with another enterprise which falls within *Art 3(a), (b), (c)* or *(d)*. In particular, two enterprises are both linked enterprises if one enterprise has the right to exercise a dominant influence over another enterprise, either pursuant to a contract entered into with that enterprise or pursuant to its memorandum or articles of association: *Art 3(c)*.

2.177 The term 'dominant influence' refers to situations where the enterprise subject to the dominant influence:

'has no real freedom to determine its course of action on the market, and if the agreements or practices are concerned merely with the internal allocation of tasks as between undertakings.' (*Centratherm BV v Sterling Drug Inc* (Case 15/74) [1974] ECR 1147)

2.178 A shareholders' agreement would fall within *Art 3(d)*: see *Steele v EVC International NV* [1996] STC 785.

2.179 While *Art 3(3)(c)* refers to a contract or provisions of the memorandum and articles, the competition law cases suggest that the relationship between two enterprises does not need to be formalised for a dominant position to exist.

2.180 There is a presumption of no dominant influence where the investors listed in *Art 2(2)* (which include venture capital companies) do not involve themselves directly or indirectly in the management of the enterprise in question. *Art 2(2)(a)* (which includes venture capital companies) only applies if the investment does not exceed €1.25m.

2.181 A 'partner enterprise' is an enterprise which is not a linked enterprise, and whose share capital is owned as to 25% by another enterprise (upstream enterprise) or which owns 25% of the share capital of another enterprise (downstream enterprise). An exception exists for shares owned by public investment funds and certain other categories of public sector shareholders: *Art 3(2)*.

2.182 The meaning of 'small or medium-sized enterprise' was considered by the First-tier Tribunal (FTT) in *Pyreos Ltd v R & C Comrs* [2015] SFTD 517. A venture capital company (VCC) held a 25%–50% shareholding in a company P Ltd which was claiming research and development (R&D) allowances on the basis that it was an SME. *Art 3, para 2* of the Recommendation would normally exclude such a company from the category of SME, unless the shareholding was held by a VCC, in which case the company in which the VCC held shares could be regarded as 'autonomous'. The Tribunal held that:

(i)   the company holding the shareholding in the claimant company was a VCC; and

(ii) 'may' in *Art 3* was mandatory, so that, once it was established that the shareholding was a VCC, its shareholding could not exclude P Ltd from the SME category.

2.183 In *Monitor Audio Ltd v R & C Comrs* [2016] SFTD 1 a company in the Royal Bank of Scotland group, WR, held 25%+ of the capital of Monitor Audio. Monitor claimed R&D allowances under *CTA 2009, s 1004*. Its entitlement depended upon whether or not it was an SME. *Art 3* of the Recommendation provided that a partner enterprise included an upstream company which held more than 25% of the capital or voting rights of another enterprise, unless it was an institutional investor or VCC. Neither term was defined. It was held that WR had little day-to-day involvement in the business, and should be regarded as an institutional investor, not as a partner enterprise.

FRSSE

2.184 Small companies and small groups may use the FRSSE. Unincorporated businesses which would be classified as small if incorporated may also use the FRSSE. Businesses using the FRSSE are exempt from other accounting standards and UITF Abstracts, except in relation to consolidated accounts, in which case certain accounting standards apply: FRSSE, para 16. It is a mandatory requirement that, if the FRSSE is used, this must be stated in a prominent position on the balance sheet, above the signature of the balance sheet approving the accounts by a director or the proprietor: *CA 2006, s 414(3)*; FRSSE, para 2.36. Prior to 1 January 2016 a company may use FRSSE if it satisfies the requirement of *CA 2006, s 382* and is not excluded by *s 384*.

2.185 The FRSSE is withdrawn from 1 January 2016. Instead small companies can use the small entities regime in FRS 102, Section 1A.

Transition to FRS 102

2.186 Section 35 deals with the transition to FRS 102. Essentially this involves three changes:

• Assets and liabilities as at the end of the last pre-FRS 102 are recognised and measured as if FRS 102 had applied for that period.

• Adjustments are taken to the opening profit and loss reserves for the first FRS 102 accounting period.

• Section 12 is applied to hedging relationships which exist at the date of transition.

2.187   Off-balance sheet hedging is not allowed under FRS 102. Hence where hedging was not recognised prior to the adoption of FRS 102, it is necessary to bring the hedging instrument on to balance sheet, and restate the hedged item accordingly.

2.188   The taxation of change of basis adjustments is governed by the *Loan Relationships and Derivative Contracts (Change of Accounting Practice) Regulations, SI 2004/3271* (COAP). These regulations apply to most transitional adjustments arising in respect of loan relationships and derivative contracts from change in accounting practice. The effect of COAP is to defer or exclude for tax purposes adjustments which are brought into account on the transition to the new accounting policy.

2.189   The general rule is that in most cases the effect of the regulations is to spread such adjustments over ten years beginning with the first accounting period in which the new accounting policy is adopted (*reg 3A*). Debits and credits are accelerated if the company ceases to be within the charge to UK corporation tax unless there is a 'qualifying transfer', ie a transfer of 75% ownership of the trade or business to a UK resident company, in which case spreading continues in the transferee. Where amounts relate to own credit risk, debits and credits are spread over five years, on a sliding scale of 40% to 10%.

2.190   Certain adjustments are excluded:

(i)   debits or credits which arise in the same period as that in which the asset or liability falls to be discharged: *reg 4(3)*;

(ii)   debits or credits in circumstances where the company is treated as a party to the contract is treated as holding an embedded derivative: *CTA 2009, s 585(2)* and the corresponding notional loan relationship is one to which *reg 4(3)* applies: *reg 4(4)(a)*;

(iii) debits and credits not covered by the *Loan Relationships and Derivative Contracts (Disregard and Bringing into Account of Profits and Losses) Regulations 2004, SI 2004/3256* (the 'Disregard Regulations') but which hedge loan relationships to which *reg 4(3)* applies: *reg 4(4)(b)*.

Other adjustments are dealt with under the Disregard Regulations: *reg 3C*.

2.191   A major change introduced by FRS 102 is that non-commercial loans, ie loans at less than a market rate of interest or interest free loans, are classified as 'financing transactions'. They have to be accounted for on initial recognition or on the adoption of FRS 102 on a discounted basis (fair value) rather than at cost (transaction price): para 11.13. Under FRS 102, loans at non-market rate must be initially recognised as fair value, ie the present value of the cash receivables discounted at the market value of interest for similar debt instruments. The difference to transaction price on initial recognition is treated as an investment or capital contribution in the debtor. The transitional adjustment produces a loan relationship credit in the borrower and debit in the lender. To the extent that the loan is restated at a new carrying value, it will for accounting purposes accrete back up to the par value over the remaining term of the loan.

2.192   If the loan is repayable on demand it is recognised at transaction price (face value). The same applies for connected company non-commercial loans (which will be the normal situation).

Chapter 3

The Scheme of the Legislation

Overview

3.1   This chapter deals with:

- Corporation tax legislation
- Key provisions
- Distributable profits
- History of the legislation
- Profits available for distribution
- Non-corporates

Introduction

3.2   UK tax legislation has a common structure:

- *First* it identifies an event or transaction which gives rise to a charge to tax.
- *Secondly* it identifies a person on whom to visit the charge.
- *Thirdly* it prescribes the amount, computation and conditions of the charge.

3.3   The development of Parliament's constitutional power in the political system was based on the principle that taxes could not be raised by the executive without the consent of Parliament expressed in legislation granting 'supplies' to the Crown. The Bill of Rights 1688 laid down the principle that taxes could only be raised with the consent of Parliament, and were only imposed for one year at a time. Hence direct taxes are imposed by annual Finance Acts, which regularly make substantial changes to the tax system.

3.4   Until 2014 it was taken for granted that, as a result of the evolution of the tax system since 1799, a state official fixes the amount of tax which a person has to pay, subject to a right of appeal to an independent tribunal.

3.5   In recent years, both these principles – the levying of tax by Parliament subject to an independent appeal – have been extensively suspended and the powers of the executive in the form of HMRC correspondingly enlarged. Much tax legislation now takes the form of enabling legislation, which simply transfers taxing powers to HMRC. This in turn leaves the courts, which historically had the function of standing between the citizen and the state, without reliable guidance as to what is and what is not lawful taxation. This was graphically demonstrated by the accelerated payments legislation in *FA 2014*, which empowers the Revenue to impose tax-like payments by executive fiat, with no right of appeal. The courts have hitherto chosen to ratify rather than regulate the operation of this legislation, notwithstanding the wholesale exclusion of judicial process which it entails, and thereby overlooking the truth that institutions which do not use the power they have will find that they have no power to use: *R (on the application of Rowe) v R & C Comrs* [2015] EWHC 2293.

Direct taxes

3.6   Income tax was first introduced in 1799. The *Income Tax Act 1803* was replaced by the *Income Tax Act 1806*. The *Income Tax Act 1842* largely followed the provisions of the *1806 Act*, and income tax has been continuously on the statute books since 1842. The *1842 Act* was supplemented by the *Income Tax Act 1853*. The *1842* and *1853 Acts* (and much subsequent legislation) were consolidated in the *Income Tax Act 1918*. This was replaced by the *Income Tax Act 1952*. That in turn was consolidated 18 years later into the *Income and Corporation Taxes Act 1970*. That also lasted for 18 years, until it was replaced by the *Income and Corporation Taxes Act 1988*.

3.7   As the changing title of the consolidation Act shows, a separate corporation tax was introduced alongside income tax in *FA 1965*. The same Act also introduced a separate capital gains tax, which was really a form of reserve income tax. Capital gains tax was put into a separate Act by the *Capital Gains Tax Act 1979*, which was replaced by the *Taxation of Chargeable Gains Act 1992*.

3.8   Corporation tax was intended to be levied on the same basis as income and capital gains tax for individuals, but paid by companies rather than individuals and charged at a different rate. It was assessed in accordance with income tax and capital gains tax principles: *ICTA 1988, s 9(1)*; *TCGA 1992, s 8(3)*. Corporation tax applies *instead* of income tax or capital gains tax. If corporation tax does not apply, the charge to income tax or capital gains tax is reinstated. For example, a non-UK resident investment company pays income tax, not corporation tax, on its UK source income. However, the development of accounting standards from the 1980s onwards, and the increasing dominance of the accounting results for corporation tax purposes, led the development of corporation tax to take a separate path from income tax, as a distinct tax in its own right.

3.9   Hence, when the Tax Law Rewrite was set up to rewrite a substantial body of existing tax legislation on a clearer and more transparent basis, the decision was taken to separate corporation tax from income tax. Hence the income tax legislation is now contained in:

- *Income Tax (Earnings and Pensions) Act 2003 (ITEPA 2003)*

- *Income Tax (Trading and Other Income) Act 2005 (ITTOIA 2005)*

- *Income Tax Act 2007 (ITA 2007)*

3.10   The corporation tax legislation is to be found in

- *Corporation Tax Act 2009 (CTA 2009)*

- *Corporation Tax Act 2010 (CTA 2010)*

- *Taxation (International and Other Provisions) Act 2010 (TIOPA 2010)*

3.11   There is no distinction in principle between *CTA 2009* and *CTA 2010* – some topics are found in one, other topics in the other. The capital gains legislation for both individuals and companies remains in *TCGA 1992*. The capital allowances legislation for incorporated and unincorporated businesses alike is to be found in the *Capital Allowances Act 2001*. Law forming part of the corporation tax code is also found in individual Finance Acts, eg diverted profits tax is contained in *FA 2015*.

3.12   A major change made by the Tax Law Rewrite was to substitute for the former schedules of different categories of income a verbal description of different types of income. Hence Schedule A income became property income charged to tax under *ITTOIA 2005, Part 3* and *CTA 2009, Part 4*. Schedule D, Case 1 income became 'trading income'.

3.13   The old schedules were recast as follows:

Former Schedule	New type of income
Schedule A	Property Income
Schedule D, Case I	Trading income
Schedule D, Case II	Trading income
Schedule D, Case III(a)	Non-trading credits and debits
Schedule D, Case V	Trading income/ Non-trading credits and debits
Schedule D, Case VI	Miscellaneous income
Schedule E	Employment income
Schedule F	Distributions

Scope and administration

3.14   The first tax separate administration act was the *Taxes Management Act 1880*. This is the predecessor of the *Taxes Management Act 1970*, which – extensively amended – is still in force. The administrative provisions governing corporation tax are now largely set out separately in *FA 1998, Schedule 18*.

3.15   As legal persons, companies are liable to taxation by analogy with the taxation of individuals. Individuals pay income tax and capital gains tax. Companies are liable to corporation tax on their 'profits'. 'Profits' comprise two components: income; and chargeable gains (*CTA 2009, s 2(2)*). 'Company' means 'any body corporate or unincorporated association'. However, a 'company' does not include 'a partnership, a local authority or a local authority association' (*CTA 2010, s 1121*).

3.16   For corporation tax purposes, a 'company' includes:

(a)   all UK resident companies;

(b)   non-resident companies;

(c)   unincorporated associations; and

(d)   authorised unit trusts.

'Company' does not include partnerships (ie general partnerships, LPs and LLPs).

3.17   Authorised unit trusts are treated as companies for corporation tax purposes. Unit trusts do not borrow money, but are not within the loan relationship rules as regards creditor relationships. Special rules apply to approved investment trusts, authorised unit trusts, venture capital trusts, OEICs and insurance companies. The tax treatment of collective investment schemes is intended to reflect the tax treatment of individuals.

Structure of the legislation

3.18   The legislation imposing corporation tax has a number of elements:

1   Corporation tax is an annual tax, which is renewed at the rates set by annual Finance Acts.

2   *CTA 2009* imposes a charge to corporation tax on companies which have profits or losses arising from–

   (a)   trading income;

(b)   property income;

(c)   loan relationships,

(d)   derivative contracts;

(e)   intangible fixed assets;

(f)   know-how and patents;

(g)   distributions; and

(h)   miscellaneous income.

These categories replaced the various schedules and cases which formerly appertained to income tax.

3   *CTA 2009* also has rules relating to accounting periods, company residence, various special forms of relief (such as research and development expenditure) and investment companies.

4   Rules on exempt distributions appear in *CTA 2009*.

5   *CTA 2010* deals with losses, group relief, community investment tax relief, oil activities, leasing, real estate investment trusts, special types of company, reconstructions without a change of ownership, transactions in securities, manufactured payments and repos, transactions in land, and distributions.

6   *TIOPA 2010* deals with double taxation relief, transfer pricing, tax arbitrage, the worldwide debt cap and offshore funds.

7   *TCGA 1992* contains the rules for the computation of capital gains, which in the case of a UK resident company are charged to corporation tax on capital gains. The Act deals with reorganisations, share exchanges, conversion of securities and reconstructions.

8   The *Capital Allowances Act 2001 (CAA 2001)* contains the rules governing capital allowances, which take the place for tax purposes of the depreciation charge which has to be included in the commercial accounts. This equally applies to unincorporated businesses.

9   The administrative provisions for corporation tax are set out in *FA 1998, Sch 18* and the *Taxes Management Act 1970 (TMA 1970)*. These also contain the rules for tax appeals.

10   *FA 2015* contains the diverted profits tax.

11   As noted in **Chapter 2**, Financial Reporting Standards (FRSs) are issued by the FRC, while International Financial Reporting Standards (IFRSs) are issued by the IASB. While not legislation, they are given statutory recognition by *CA 2006, s 464*.

3.19   Where an 'all income' treatment applies, profits are ascertained in accordance with the commercial accounts, in the usual way. The taxable profit is then regarded solely as income and not as gains. The areas where the all income treatment applies are:

1   *Loan relationships*: 'Loan relationships' are types of corporate debt defined in *CTA 2009, s 302*. Profits and gains on loan relationships include interest, capital accruals, expenses, fluctuations in capital values, foreign exchange differences and losses.

2   *Derivative contracts:* 'Derivative contracts' are defined in *CTA 2009, ss 576–583*, and are contracts for differences, futures and options. However, gains on certain notional derivative contracts are treated as capital gains for corporation tax purposes: *CTA 2009, ss 639–673*.

3   *Intangible fixed assets:* 'Intangibles' are defined in *CTA 2009, s 713*. The definition follows the accounting definition in FRS 102 but expressly includes intellectual property. Patents, copyrights, trademarks, registered design, design rights and goodwill all fall under this concept.

3.20   The primary legislation is supplemented by numerous statutory instruments relating to corporation tax, such as the *Corporation Tax (Instalment Payments) Regulations 1998, SI 1998/3175*.

3.21   The hedge accounting rules are contained for tax purposes in the *Loan Relationships and Derivative Contracts (Disregard and Bringing into Account of Profits and Losses) Regulations 2004, SI 2004/3256* (the 'Disregard Regulations'). These have been frequently amended, and operate on a different basis from 1 January 2016 onwards.

3.22   The change of accounting basis or policy produces transitional adjustments. These are dealt with for tax purposes in the *Loan Relationships and Derivative Contracts (Change of Accounting Practice) Regulations 2004, SI 2004/3271*.

3.23   *CTA 2009, s 35* says: 'The charge to corporation tax on income applies to the profits of a trade'. A trading company is a company whose business consists wholly or mainly in carrying on a trade. A trade is an activity carried on on a systematic basis with a view to making a profit. Investment companies derive the bulk of their income from activities other than trading, and in particular from holding investments, ie companies whose business consists wholly or partly of making investments (*CTA 2009, s 1218(1)*). Non-trade profits will be taxable under the various other heads of charge in *CTA 2009*. From total profits received from those sources and capital gains, a company with investment business deducts expenses of management, by reference to the accounting period in which they are charged against profits (*CTA 2009,* *ss 1219–1231)*. These will include reasonable directors' fees, interest, office and administrative expenses. Capital expenditure is excluded.

3.24   Gains on capital assets are taxed and computed under *TCGA 1992*. Capital gains for companies are computed by deducting the base cost of the asset from the proceeds of sale. The base cost is increased by index-linking (*TCGA 1992, s 53*). Realised capital losses can only be set against capital gains. Rules to counter the buying of losses and gains are contained in *TCGA 1992, ss 184A–184I, Sch 7A*. 'Chargeable assets' are very broadly defined, but do not include any asset held as trading assets. Qualifying corporate bonds (QCBs) are not chargeable assets, but in the case of companies they are loan relationships, so all gains and losses are income items. There is a wide-ranging exemption for capital gains on substantial shareholders: 'substantial shareholding exemption' (SSE) (*TCGA 1992, Sch 7A*).

3.25   Companies resident in the UK have unlimited liability to tax, ie they are taxable on their income and capital gains, wherever arising. Companies not resident in the UK are only liable to UK corporation tax if they (i) carry on a trade in the UK through a permanent establishment, or (ii) carry on a trade of dealing in or developing land in the UK: *CTA 2009, s 5(2), (2A)*. In the former case, their liability to corporation tax is restricted to (a) the chargeable profits of the permanent establishment, and (b) gains arising from the disposal of assets used by the permanent establishment for its purposes or the purposes of its trade. *CTA 2009, ss 21–32* apply for the purposes of determining the profits attributable to a permanent establishment for corporation tax purposes. These attribution rules chiefly apply to banks. This is because banks, in order to use capital efficiently, generally carry on international operations through permanent establishments rather than subsidiaries.

3.26   The rules on repos and stock lending are contained in *CTA 2009, ss 542–559*, as part of the loan relationship provisions.

Key statutory provisions

3.27   The key statutory provisions on corporation tax are located as follows:

TCGA 1992	*s 116*	Reorganisations involving QCBs
	s 117	QCBs
	ss 126–139	Reorganisations and reconstructions involving shares and non-QCBs
	ss 170–179B	Capital gains groups
	Sch 5AA	Definition of 'scheme of reconstruction'
	Sch 7AC	Substantial shareholding exemption
FA 1998	*Sch 18*	Administration and appeals

CAA 2001		Capital allowances
ITTOIA 2005	*ss 409–414*	Purchase of own shares
	ss 427–460	Deeply discounted securities
ITA 2007	*ss 564A–564Y*	Alternative finance arrangements
	ss 565–614	Manufactured payments, repos, stock lending
CTA 2009	*ss 1–12*	Charge to corporation tax and accounting periods
	ss 13–33	Company residence and PEs
	ss 34–200	Trading income
	ss 180–187	Change of basis adjustments
	ss 202–291	Property income
	ss 292–569	Loan relationships
	ss 570–710	Derivative contracts
	ss 711–931	Intangible fixed assets
	ss 931A–931W	Exempt distributions
CTA 2010	*ss 5–17*	Foreign currency rules
	ss 35–96	Loss relief
	ss 97–188	Group and consortium relief
	ss 269A–269CN	Banking companies
	ss 438–465	Close companies
	ss 731–751	Transactions in securities
	ss 780–814	Manufactured payments, repos and stock lending
	ss 997–1028	Company distributions
	s 1030	Distributions on winding up
	s 1032	Payment of interest on special securities held by companies
	ss 1033–1048	Purchase of own shares
	ss 1049–1053	Stock dividends
TIOPA 2010	*ss 2–145*	Double taxation relief
	ss 146–230	Transfer pricing
	ss 231–259	Arbitrage rules
	ss 260–363	Worldwide debt cap
FA 2015	*ss 77–116*	Diverted profits tax (DPT)

3.28   The loan relationship rules apply to:

- sterling denominated loan relationships;

- interest payable in sterling;

- foreign currency denominated loan relationships including interest, premiums and discounts;

- money debts due under a cash-settled derivative contract where a security is issued in respect of the money debt;

- foreign exchange differences on money debts not arising from a transaction for the lending of money; and

- deeply discounted securities.

3.29   The derivative contracts rules apply to:

- currency contracts (spots, forwards, futures, cylinders, currency exchanges under forward contracts, cross currency swaps);

- currency options (including swaptions);

- interest rate contracts (swaps, forward rate agreements, financial futures);

- interest rate options (caps, collars, floors, swaptions);

- debt contracts and options;

- property and equity derivatives; and

- most credit derivatives.

3.30   Capital gains tax applies to:
- foreign currency equity not held on trading account;

- contingent liabilities other than options;

- units of currency;

- foreign currency-denominated shares held as investments; and

- certain deemed relevant contracts which arise from bifurcation.

Foreign currency rules

3.31   The rules on reporting amounts recorded in non-sterling currencies and conversion rates are contained in *CTA 2010, ss 5–17. Section 5* requires profits for corporation tax purposes to be computed in sterling. There are then a series of special rules for companies operating in one currency, and preparing accounts in another. Where an amount in one currency is translated into sterling for tax purposes, the 'average exchange rate' must be used, ie the average rate for the accounting period or the appropriate spot rate at the date of translation (*s 11*). Where foreign currency-denominated loan relationships and derivative contracts are fair valued, the *Loan Relationships and Derivative Contract (Exchange Gains and Losses using Fair Value Accounting) Regulations 2005, SI 2005/3422*, set out the necessary calculations.

3.32 Where a company, in accordance with normal accountancy practice, keeps its accounts (or accounts relating to a non-UK branch or, being non-resident, keeps the accounts of its UK branch) in a foreign currency, exchange differences will be calculated using the local currency as the reference currency, and the net result translated into sterling at the appropriate exchange rate for UK corporation tax purposes.

3.33 Profits of a foreign branch (or a foreign subsidiary in consolidated accounts) which operates as a separate or quasi-independent entity are to be reported using the 'closing rate/net investment method'. What is translated is the balance sheet total ('the net investment'), not the elements which go into that total. The profit and loss are translated at the closing rate ('closing rate method') or, if more suitable, using average rates.

Distributable profits

3.34 *CA 2006, s 830(1), (2)* contain the basic rule that distributions to shareholders can only be made out of 'profits available for distribution':

'(1) A company may only make a distribution out of profits available for the purpose.

(2) A company's profits available for distribution are its accumulated, realised profits, so far as not previously utilised by distribution or capitalisation, less its accumulated, realised losses, so far as not previously written off in a reduction or reorganisation of capital duly made.'

3.35 'Realised profits' and 'realised losses' are defined in *s 853(4)*:

'References to "realised profits" and "realised losses", in relation to a company's accounts, are to such profits or losses of the company as fall to be treated as realised in accordance with principles generally accepted at the time when the accounts are prepared, with respect to the determination for accounting purposes of realised profits or losses.'

This thus recognises that income recognition principles change over time.

3.36   ICAEW Tech 02/10 'Guidance on the determination of realised profits and losses in the context of distributions under the Companies Act 1985' gives guidance on what constitutes 'realised' profits and losses, for the purpose of determining the amount of distributable profits. This guidance has no legal status, but in practice is binding. This is to be replaced by new guidance, an exposure draft of which was issued on 9 March 2016.

3.37   'Realised profits' are those arising from:

- 'qualifying consideration';

- fair value accounting, where this is normal practice; or

- exchange movements on monetary items.

3.38   Fair value profits and exchange gains will be realised profits, but will only constitute 'qualifying consideration' so as to be distributable to the extent that they can be converted into cash. An in-the-money derivative contract will not give rise to distributable profits. An out-of-the-money derivative contract will give rise to a realised loss. The bedrock of whether something is distributable is whether a company has cash, which is not subject to payment liability (eg a tax liability, pension liability or other creditor claim).

3.39   The ICAEW Guidance refers to 'qualifying consideration'. 'Qualifying consideration' is:

- cash;

- assets readily convertible to cash, ie 'other assets the cash realisation of which can be assessed with reasonable certainty'; or

- release of a liability, where the asset originally received was qualifying consideration.

3.40   A company may reduce or cancel (a) its share capital, and (b) its share premium account in accordance with the prescribed company law procedures. There is little difference between the rules for share capital and the rules for share premium account. Save for specified purposes, sums in share premium account must be treated as if they were part of paid up share capital: *Companies Act 2006, s 610*.

3.41   There are two ways in which share capital can be reduced. Which method is used depends upon the resolutions passed by the company:

1   Return of capital: share capital is reduced and the amount by which it is reduced repaid to shareholders. The accounting entries are–

      DR share capital   CR Cash

2   Credit to reserves: share capital is reduced and the amount of the reduction is credited to a general or special reserve. The accounting entries are–

      DR share capital   CR reserves

3.42   Method 2 is commonly used to cancel a deficit on profit and loss account, to enable payment of dividends to be resumed: *Archibald Thomas Black & Co Ltd v Batty* 7 TC 158; *Quayle Munro Ltd, Petitioners* 1992 SC 24 at 26. Equally it can be used to create distributable reserves. In *Quayle Munro* the Court of Session observed at 27:

    'We see no reason to doubt that the funds held in the special reserve which it is proposed to create may be treated by the company as profits available for distribution, and thus as distributable profits'

3.43   This statement accords with accounting guidance given before the introduction of *Companies Act 2006* in TECH 07/03 (March 2003). *Companies Act 2006* states that a reserve arising from a reduction of share capital is not distributable subject to any provision made by order: *s 654(1)*. However, this prohibition does not apply in relation to a reserve arising both from a court-approved reduction of capital and from the solvency statement procedure: *Companies (Reduction of Share Capital) Order, SI 2008/1915, reg 3*. Such an addition to reserves is to be treated for the purposes of *Part 23* (distributions) as a realised profit except where the order of the court provides otherwise.

3.44   If an unlimited company cancels its share capital, the reserve so created is only realised if the company issued the share capital for qualifying consideration. If the return of capital method of capital reduction is used, there will be a part disposal of the shares in return for a capital distribution: *TCGA s 122(1)*. If a preference dividend is reclassified as interest under IAS 32, that does not affect the quantum of distributable profits. Where hedge accounting is used, and changes in value are taken to equity rather than income, that will not give rise to realised profits.

History of the loan relationships and derivative contracts legislation

3.45   A debt generally comprises two elements:

(a)   principal, ie the nominal value of the debt; and

(b)   interest, ie 'payment by time for the use of money' (*Bennett v Ogston (Inspector of Taxes)* 15 TC 374). Interest is consideration paid by the borrower for the use of the principal.

The value of a fixed interest security issued or acquired at a discount or at a premium converges towards its par value at maturity. If the value of money falls or rises, this also alters the value of the security. The value of a fixed rate security issued for a fixed term fluctuates with interest rates. If interest rates fall, the value of the debt will rise. If interest rates rise, the value of the debt will fall. Bond prices are inversely related to interest rates. Inflation decreases the real value of debt, while deflation increases it. The value of all debts also fluctuates because of credit risk. If the likelihood of repayment is reduced, the value of the debt will fall.

3.46   Whether these alterations in value were capital items, or simply interest in another guise, was a question which had long vexed the courts. In *National Provident Institution v Brown* (1921) 8 TC 57, it was held that all differences between the acquisition price of a security and its realisation price were taxable as income under the charge in Schedule D, Case III on 'all discounts'.

3.47   In *Lomax (Inspector of Taxes) v Peter Dixon & Son Ltd* (1943) 25 TC 353, it was held that, where debentures paid a reasonable commercial rate of interest, a premium payable on redemption was a capital receipt because it constituted compensation for capital risk, not deferred interest.

3.48   In *Lomax*, it was concluded that discount on bonds did not constitute interest. However, it is difficult to separate out pure time value of money costs from rewards for assuming non-interest based risk, such as credit risk. Where six-year loan notes were issued at par, with a premium of 30% payable on redemption, the premium was held to be income (*Davies (Inspector of Taxes) v Premier Investment Co Ltd* (1945) 27 TC 27).

3.49   Historically, tax rules for investment income and gains adopted a receipts rather than an accruals basis. This was linked to the principle of deduction of tax at source (*IRC v Whitworth Park Coal Co Ltd* (1959) 38 TC 531 at 575). *Income Tax Act 1803, s 208* provided that no assessment to tax should be made in respect of any annuity, yearly interest of money or other annual payment. Instead, the fund from which the payments were made was to bear tax without any deduction for such payment. The payer was entitled to deduct tax from the payment and to retain it against the liability of the fund. In the hands of the payee, it was 'pure profit income' on which no further liability to tax arose. The obligation of the payer to deduct income tax from interest, and account for this as tax paid by the lender, underlay the rule until 1996 that interest expense was disallowed as a deduction for tax purposes and then added back on a cash basis and treated as charge on income, ie a liability incurred before and not as an expense incurred in carrying on the business.

3.50   Interest was regarded as investment income, taxation of which was borne by the fund from which the interest was paid. This approach was encapsulated in the comment of Rowlatt J in *Leigh v IRC* 11 TC 590 at 595: 'receivability without receipt is nothing'. This approach never made sense when applied to banks, whose income derives from the margin between interest paid by borrowers and interest paid to depositors, so that a bank clearly has an expense to set against its income. As has been observed: 'It appears to me that the doctrine that "receivability without receipt is nothing" is a doctrine which can be pressed too far' (*Dunmore v McGowan (Inspector of Taxes)* (1978) 52 TC 307, per Stamp LJ at 316).

3.51   Accordingly, prior to the introduction of the *FA 1996* rules, interest was taxed and relieved on a paid basis (rather than an accruals basis); debt assets and liabilities were carried at historic cost; discounts were taxed on realisation or regarded as capital items. This led the commercial accounts and tax accounts of a company to diverge markedly. In the accounts of a company, the liability for interest is treated as accruing from day to day and, at the end of the period of account, interest accrued up to the end of the period will be shown as an expense, even though it may only be payable in the following period. The Case I computation gave effect to this treatment, to give symmetry in matching earnings with the costs incurred in the same period to achieve those earnings. In some trades, interest is both paid and received, so the accruals treatment was normally allowed for tax purposes, even when the strict rule pre-1996 was that payment of interest was disallowed as a Schedule D, Case I deduction and only allowed as a charge on income.

3.52   From the 1990s onwards, the nature of accounting underwent a profound transformation. Judgement-based accounting was held to rely to an undue extent on subjective accounting judgement, which offered insufficient guidance and safeguards in complex financial transactions. There was a shift in favour of highly detailed accounting standards, whose correct application would produce a single, correct, mathematical solution. Accounting standards multiplied and were replaced at a regularly increasing tempo. Where accounting led, taxation followed, and the mantra 'tax follows the accounts' was adopted.

3.53   This shift was of major importance. The taxable profit had always been determined by the accounting profit. However, tax law contained numerous cases where tax was assessed on a hypothetical basis. In the case of transactions in securities, rules introduced by *FA 1960, ss 28–43* authorised the Revenue to reconstruct an alternative and hypothetical state of affairs by reference to which the liability to tax could be determined. These rules are now contained in *ITA 2007, ss 682–713*. Once it was established that business tax follows the accounts, commercial reality increasingly took the place of legislative hypothesis.

3.54   In the period 1993–96, a number of new codes of tax rules for companies and capital market activities were introduced. It has been said that the three Finance Acts of 1993, 1994 and 1996:

> 'effected a revolution … [They] abolished a cornerstone of UK tax law – the distinction between capital and revenue – in taxing profits from these instruments. It started the trend … of tying the tax result much more closely to the profit figure revealed in a company's accounts.' (Inland Revenue Technical Note, 8 November 2000)

3.55   The codes in question were:

(a)   the 'foreign exchange rules' (*FA 1993, ss 60, 92–96, 125–170, Schs 15–18*; *SI 1994/3226–3232*);

(b)   the 'financial instruments rules' (*FA 1994, ss 147–177, Sch 18*; *SI 1994/3233*); and

(c)   the 'loan relationships rules' (*FA 1996, ss 80–105, Schs 8–15*).

3.56   The codes shared significant common features, seeking to tax and relieve real, economic gains and losses. In all these rules, accounting was king. However, the approach adopted to the computation of profits for tax purposes differs significantly. The *FA 1993* foreign exchange rules were highly prescriptive, the loan relationship rules moderately so, and the financial instruments rules non-prescriptive. The process was continued with the intangible fixed assets code in *FA 2002, Sch 29*, which introduced an 'all income' treatment for intellectual property assets and goodwill.

3.57   Any measure of income requires that capital be maintained. Capital, as such, has to be recognised and measured, as happens under an accounts-based approach. To abolish the capital/income divide is to move the tax base to an expenditure tax, as is used for VAT. This is why the 'all income' approach applies only to monetary assets, and not to non-monetary assets, shares being regarded as non-monetary assets.

3.58   The legislation both reflected and accelerated the trend for tax authorities and the courts to rely more heavily on accounts and accountancy evidence for the determination of profits and income for tax purposes. While this is reasonable, there are risks. Law and accounting differ fundamentally. Law is essentially prescriptive; accounting is inherently judgemental. Accounting extensively requires the application of skill and judgement to facts and situations where there is room for conflicting views. Accounting methods will always give way to the express words of the statute, and the legislation includes numerous specific statutory overrides of wide impact.

3.59   The foreign exchange and financial instrument rules applied from the beginning of the first accounting period commencing on or after 23 March 1995: *FA 1993, s 165(7)(b)*; *FA 1994, s 147(4)*; *SIs 1995/3224* and *1995/3225*. The loan relationship rules applied to interest for the whole of the first accounting period which ended after 31 March 1996: *FA 1996, Sch 15, paras 1(2), 3(2)* and *(3)*. With regard to other profits, gains, expenses and losses on loan relationships, the rules applied from 1 April 1996: *FA 1996, s 105* and *Sch 15, para 3(2)*.

3.60   Prior to 1995, the Inland Revenue had long been promising a review of the rules on the taxation of interest, because of the asymmetry which the tax treatment of interest produced between commercial accounts and tax accounts. The need for a recasting of the legislation became more urgent once QCBs became exempt from capital gains tax. Numerous schemes were developed for re-characterising taxable income gains as non-taxable QCB gains. The government's wish to establish a gilt strips market required certain tax changes. The Inland Revenue's consultative document was published on 25 May 1995. The final scheme was enacted in *FA 1996*. In its original form, it was a masterpiece of drafting by a parliamentary counsel, aptly named Mr Laws. The new scheme was confined to companies, because it is based on accruals, which requires the keeping of accounts. Non-corporate businesses are outside the rules, notwithstanding that they too must keep accounts which give a true and fair view.

3.61   The original loan relationship rules took effect from 1 April 1996 or, rather, in relation to accounting periods ended after 31 March 1996: *FA 1996, s 105*. Where a company's accounting period straddled 31 March 1996 (transitional accounting period), the new provisions applied through the transitional rules in *Sch 15*. Interest fell within the new rules for the whole of the transitional accounting period.

3.62   As far as companies are concerned, from 1 April 1996 foreign exchange rules in *FA 1993*, the financial instruments rules in *FA 1994* and the loan relationships rules in *FA 1996* all applied for corporation tax purposes, displacing a large body of older legislation and case-law, which remained applicable for income tax and capital gains tax purposes. However, the 'tax follows the accounts' mantra was always more honoured in theory than in practice, because HMRC claimed a right to override the accounting result, if it did not produce the 'correct' tax result.

3.63   The whole corpus of the UK legislation was substantially recast by *FA 2002*. For accounting periods beginning on or after 1 October 2002, this restructuring produced two sets of rules:

1   The loan relationship rules in *FA 1996*, which deal with all forms of on balance sheet debt, interest and interest equivalents, including foreign

exchange gains and losses in respect of loan relationships, money debts and foreign currency. The rules also deal with debtor loan relationships used for hedging purposes, where the effect of the hedge is recognised for accounting purposes. *FA 1993* and the foreign exchange transitional rules are largely repealed.

2   The derivative contracts rules in *FA 2002, Sch 26*, which applied to:

(a)   options;

(b)   futures; and

(c)   contracts for differences.

These categories include currency contracts and all forms of off balance sheet derivative contracts, ie contracts which classified as non-basic financial instruments under FRS 102, Section 12. They are items which are quantitatively recognised as derivative financial instruments or financial assets under FRS 102 and whose financial results are recorded in the accounts. Derivatives used for matching purposes also fall in part under these rules. From 16 March 2005, the rules applied to all derivatives, including property and equity derivatives.

3.64   Further extensive changes were made for accounting periods beginning on or after 1 January 2005, to take account of the impact of IAS and, in particular, of the bifurcation of certain hybrid securities, and the extension of the derivative contracts rules to take in both equity and property derivatives.

3.65   *FA 2009* introduced the 'wordwide debt cap' which was designed to prevent debt finance from being used to reduce UK profits in two situations (see **Chapter 20**):

1   *Debt push-down*: loans are put into the UK to strip out earnings. This was directed at highly geared takeovers of UK companies.

2   *Upstream loans*: loan interest is taken out of the UK and profits returned to the UK by exempt dividends.

3.66   The UK sought to introduce one system to deal with both issues. This was done by limiting the deduction of finance costs in cases where the borrowings of the UK resident group of companies exceeded 75% of the borrowings of the worldwide group of companies. *FA 2009, Sch 17* also introduced new notification obligations in respect of international movements of capital of over £100m.

3.67   In 2013 the government launched an extensive consultation on the revision of the legislation in 'Modernising the taxation of corporate debt and derivative contracts' (6 June 2013). Because the adoption of FRS 102 for accounting periods beginning on or after 1 January 2015 would cause extensive accounting changes, it was decided to postpone the new loan relationships legislation for accounting periods beginning on or after 1 January 2016. However, some preliminary changes were brought in by *FA 2014*.

1   *FA 2014, ss 27*: changes were made to the rules affecting corporate investors with holdings in OEICs, units trusts and bond funds which are treated as loan relationships under *CTA 2009, ss 487–497* (the 'bond fund rules').

2   *FA 2014, s 26*: it was provided that the release of debtor loan relationships of a bank under the stabilisation powers in the *Banking Act 2009* would not give rise to a loan relationship credit: new *CTA 2009, s 322(5A)*.

3   *FA 2014, s 28*: the notional disposal of loan relationships and derivative contracts on degrouping was extended to include losses.

4   *FA 2014, ss 28–29*: new anti-avoidance rules were introduced from 5 December 2013 in the form of *CTA 2009, ss 695A, 1305A* derecognising for tax purposes intra-group derivative contracts designed to transfer profit from one group company to another.

3.68   The legislation was substantially recast by *F(No 2)A 2015, Sch 7* with effect from accounting periods beginning on or after 1 January 2016. However, certain changes took effect from 1 January 2015 and 18 November 2015:

1   Profits and losses on loan relationships and related transactions are confined to those going through the income statement. Amounts carried to other comprehensive income are only taxed when released to profit and loss: *CTA 2009, ss 308(1), 308(1A)* as amended.

2   The 'fairly represents' override to the commercial accounts is replaced by a wide anti-avoidance rule: *CTA 2009, ss 455B–455D*.

3   The definitions of 'amortised cost basis' and 'fair value' in *CTA 2009, s 313* are amended to accord with accounting definitions, as set out in the amended *CTA 2009, s 476*.

4   With effect from 15 November 2015 the deemed release rules were modified. *CTA 2009, ss 361A, 361B* were repealed. A revised corporate rescue exemption was introduced as *ss 361D, 362A*.

5   For accounting periods beginning on or after 1 January 2015 relief from a charge to tax on debt release was also granted in cases of debt restructuring, where–

(a)   but for the release there is a material risk that within 12 months the debtor company would not be able to pay its debts: new *CTA 2009, s 322(5B)*; and

(b)   in cases of substantial modification of a debt, there was a material risk that but for the restructuring the debtor company would have been unable to pay its debts: new *CTA 2009, s 323A*.

6   A new *CTA 2009, s 328(2B)* provides that exchange gains and losses of an investment company are not omitted from a company's profit and loss under *s 328(2A)* if a designated currency election has effect at the relevant time.

7   The Disregard Regulations are substantially revised (see below).

3.69   The Disregard Regulations are dealt with in **Chapter 16**. They seek to limit tax volatility by enabling companies to defer recognition of gains and losses, where:

(a)   a 'hedging relationship' (as defined by *CTA 2009, s 475A*) exists between a hedged item and a hedging instrument;

(b)   gains and losses on the hedging instrument are intended to be equal and opposite to gains and losses on the hedged item.

3.70   Prior to FRS 102 hedging could be carried out off balance using SSAP 20. The introduction of FRS 102, and associated tax changes, required the Disregard Regulations to be fundamentally recast with effect from accounting periods beginning on or after 1 January 2016.

3.71   The required amendments were made by:

- *Exchange Gains and Losses (Bringing into Account Gains or Losses) (Amendment) Regulations, SI 2015/1960*;

- *Loan Relationships and Derivative Contacts (Disregard and Bringing into Account of Profits and Losses) (Amendment) Regulations, SI 2015/1961*; and

- *Loan Relationships and Derivative Contacts (Exchange Gains and Losses using Fair Value Accounting) (Amendment) Regulations, SI 2015/1963*.

3.72   Because FRS 102 (following IAS 39) does not allow off balance sheet hedging, the Disregard Regulations were amended from an election-in to an election-out approach. In other words, if the company wishes to disregard its commercial accounts for tax purposes, it must now elect to do so (rather than, as previously, elect out of the Disregard Regulations and into the commercial accounts for tax purposes). In particular it is still possible to adopt hedge accounting for net investment in a foreign operation, which is no longer possible for accounting purposes.

BEPS Project

3.73   The Organisation for Economic Co-operation and Development's (OECD) Base Erosion and Profit Shifting (BEPS) Project is designed to counter measures by multi-national enterprises (MNEs) to reduce their tax costs in developed countries (which are by definition high tax jurisdictions, with high tax to GNP ratios). As developing countries depend on MNEs for up to 70% of their tax revenues, these measures can only be at the expense of developing countries. The proposals include a number of recommendations affecting loan relationships. In particular Action 4 deals with 'Limit base erosion via interest deductions and other financial payments' and Action 9 is concerned with 'Risks and capital'. This proposes to limit net deductions for interest by reference to a fixed ratio rule or a group ratio rule. The fixed ratio rule would limit interest deductibility to a percentage of a company's earnings before interest, taxes, depreciation and amortisation (EBITDA). The percentage is to be in a 'corridor' from 10% to 30%.

3.74   States may instead as a supplement to the fixed ratio opt for a group ratio. A group ratio rule may be adopted, limiting the interest deduction in a given jurisdiction to a percentage of the net interest/EBITDA ratio of the worldwide group. Under this approach only net interest expense which takes an entity's net interest to EBITDA ratio above the higher of fixed ratio and group ratio is disallowed. Action 2 is also relevant, which is concerned with hybrid mismatches.

3.75   The UK has already introduced a group ratio rule in the form of the worldwide debt cap (see **Chapter 20**). The government proposes to introduce with effect from 1 April 2017 a fixed ratio of 30% where the annual interest expense of a UK group exceeds £2m. Hybrid mismatches will be the subject of legislation to apply from 1 January 2017.

3.76   Tax systems constantly pursue the will-o'-the-wisp of a consistent taxation of debt and equity. If the risk factor exceeds a certain level, investors will only be prepared to make debt investments. In that case the choice is not between equity finance and debt finance (as the BEPS approach fondly imagines) but between debt finance and no finance.

Non-corporates

3.77   The pre-1 April 1996 rules on interest received and paid, and gains and losses on debt assets, still largely apply to individuals, trustees and partnerships which do not include a company.

3.78   In brief, the rules for individuals, trustees and partnerships not involving companies are:

(a)   Profits of a trade must be calculated in accordance with GAAP: *ITTOIA 2005, s 25*.

(b)   Premiums and discounts are taxed on realisation, subject to special rules for relevant discounted securities and gilt strips set out in *ITTOIA 2005, ss 430–460*.

(c)   Tax at source has to be deducted from yearly interest unless paid by or to a bank carrying on a *bona fide* banking business in the UK: *ITA 2007, s 874*. Banks and other deposit-takers deduct income tax from interest paid to UK-resident individuals under a separate scheme: *ITA 2007, s 851*.

(d)   Interest is deductible in computing trade profits or property income.

(e)   'Debts on a security' are assets for capital gains tax purposes. Otherwise, gilts and most forms of corporate debt (QCBs) are exempt from capital gains tax.

(f)   Where a security is transferred with the benefit of accrued interest, an additional charge to tax under the accrued income scheme is imposed: *ITA 2007, ss 615–681*.

(g)   Relief for bad debt for traders is confined to bad debts proved to be such; debts released as part of a *CA 2006, s 895* or *Insolvency Act 1986, s 110* arrangement; and debts irrecoverable on insolvency: *ITTOIA 2005, s 35*.

Chapter 4

Loan Relationships: Scope and Definition

Overview

4.1   This chapter deals with:

- Scope of application

- Trading/non-trading

- Definition of loan relationship

- Actual loan relationships

- Legal substance

- Meaning of loan

- Deemed loan relationships

- Relevant non-lending relationships

Scope of application

4.2   All loan relationships constitute monetary debts owed by or to companies. There are three types of loan relationship:

- **Type 1**: Actual loan relationships (where there is a loan).

- **Type 2**: Deemed loan relationships (where there is no loan but a company issues an instrument, usually to pay for acquisitions.

- **Type 3**: Relevant non-lending relationships ('RNLRs') (debts arising from the supply of goods and services).

Types 1 and 2 come within the loan relationship rules for all purposes. Type 3 only comes within the loan relationship rules for limited purposes.

4.3   All loan relationships are either 'creditor loan relationships' (*CTA 2009, s 302(5)*), ie assets, or 'debtor loan relationships' (*s 302(6)*), ie liabilities. A debtor loan relationship is a liability which obliges a company to transfer financial benefits, whereas a creditor loan relationship is an asset which entitles a company to receive financial benefits. In general, only companies carrying on a financial trade (eg banks) will have creditor loan relationships, while other types of business will have debtor loan relationships, because they raise money through loans in order to carry on their business. However, in practice there are many departures from this scheme.

4.4   Only companies have loan relationships, because corporation tax, and so the loan relationship rules, apply to 'companies': *CTA 2009, s 2(1)*. Corporation tax is charged on the 'profits' of companies, which means 'income' and 'chargeable gains': *s 2(2)*. All profits and losses on loan relationships are regarded as income: *ss 2(3), 295(1)*. 'Company' means any body corporate or unincorporated association, but not a local authority or partnership. An authorised unit trust is treated as a company under *CTA 2010, s 1121*. An LLP is not a company for corporation tax purposes (*CTA 2009, s 1273*), although an LLP is treated as transparent for tax purposes. Accordingly, if a company is a member of an LLP, and the LLP had a loan, the company will have a loan relationship to the extent of its interest in the LLP.

Example 4.1

Georgian LLP is a 50/50 LLP with two members, A Ltd and Mr B. It is a body corporate, but not a company. The bank lends 1,000 to Georgian LLP. A Ltd has a debtor loan relationship of 500.

4.5   The loan relationship rules depend on a legal definition of what is a loan relationship. The term solely exists for tax purposes. It has no meaning in company law or accounting. Accounting standards are of limited relevance in determining what is and what is not a loan relationship. Hence, where IAS 32 requires redeemable preference shares to be treated as liabilities for accounting purposes, such instruments remain shares for tax purposes. On the other hand, where IAS 39 requires a convertible bond to be bifurcated into a notional debt instrument and a notional equity instrument or derivative contract, the notional bond is a loan relationship.

4.6   By contrast, the derivative contracts rules depend upon an accounting definition of a derivative contract, based on accounting rules.

The exclusivity and interaction rules

4.7   The loan relationships legislation rested on a basic policy decision that profits and losses on debt were to fall within the loan relationships rules, but distributions on shares would fall outside the rules and gains and losses on shares would remain within the capital gains tax rules.

4.8   There are detailed priority rules at *CTA 2009, ss 464–465*. The transfer pricing rules and distributions rules take precedence over the loan relationship rules. Subject to those rules, the loan relationships rules provide an exclusive code of taxation for corporation tax purposes and take priority over any other rules relating to corporation tax, and in particular over the derivative contracts rules: *CTA 2009, s 464*. General income tax and capital gains tax rules apply to matters falling outside the above rules. The broad hierarchy is:

1   transfer pricing rules,

2   distributions rules and capital gains rules on shares,

3   loan relationship rules,

4   derivative contracts rules,

5   general corporation tax and capital gains tax rules.

4.9   The scheme of taxation in *CTA 2009* is both comprehensive (*'all* profits ...') and exclusive. *CTA 2009, s 464(1)* (formerly *FA 1996, s 80(5)*) contains the 'exclusivity rule', namely that the amounts taxable and deductible under the loan relationship rules take precedence for corporation tax purposes over all other taxing rules, save as prescribed by *ss 464(2), (3), 465*.

> '(1)   The amounts which are brought into account in accordance with this Part [*CTA 2009, Part 5*] in respect of any matter are the only amounts which may be brought into account for corporation tax purposes in respect of it.'

4.10   *Section 464(2)* then says that *s 464(1)* is 'subject to any express provision to the contrary'. *CTA 2009, s 699* contains a similar rule for derivative contracts within *Part 7* of *CTA 2009*.

4.11   In *DCC Holdings (UK) Ltd v R & C Comrs* [2010] STC 80 at [7], Moses LJ observed that the loan relationship rules are:

> 'a discrete and exclusive code for the taxation of all of the profits and gains of a company a rising from its loan relationships.'

4.12   This means that, where the loan relationship rules apply to any 'matter', no other legislation applies. It is the combination of rules in *CTA 2009, ss 295(1)* and *296* which assigns profits on loan relationships to the 'income' side of corporation tax and establishes the 'all income' treatment. 'Profits' always refers to a net balance, struck after deducting expenditure from income. It is this net figure which constitutes the 'profits' which are brought into charge to tax.

4.13   In *Versteegh Ltd v R & C Comrs* [2014] SFTD 547, Group Co (Lender) lent money to a subsidiary Borrower Co (Borrower). The Borrower became liable to pay rolled up interest to the Lender. The liability was discharged by issuing irredeemable preference shares to a 100% subsidiary of the Lender (the Share Recipient). Tax asymmetry was claimed, ie loan relationship debit in Borrower but no corresponding credit in any other group company.

4.14   The Revenue accepted that a separate tax charge under the transfer of income stream rules (*TA 1988, s 786; ITA 2007, s 809AZA; CTA 2010, ss 777–779*) was not an 'express provision to the contrary' within *s 464(2)* and so was not outside the exclusivity principle. This case went on appeal to the Upper Tribunal under the name *Spritebeam*.

4.15   In *Spritebeam Ltd v R & C Comrs* [2015] STC 1222, the Upper Tribunal held that:

(a)   the value of the shares was not income of the Lender within *TA 1988, s 786(5)*;

(b)   the exclusivity principle under *FA 1996, ss 80(5), 84* precluded a charge on the lender under any other provision;

(c)   there was a sufficient connection between the issue of the shares and the Share Recipient for the value of the share to be taxable as 'other income' of the Share Recipient under Schedule D, Case VI.

4.16   *Section 303(4)* provides that a debt shall not be taken to arise from the lending of money to the extent that it is a debt arising from rights conferred by shares in a company. *Section 465* excludes distributions from the loan relationships rules, except to the extent that credits rise in connection with an 'avoidance arrangement, ie an arrangement the main purpose or one of the main purposes of which is to secure a tax advantage.

4.17   The loan relationship rules do not apply to:

• shares (*CTA 2009, ss 303(4), 476(1)*);

• distributions (*s 465(1)*);

- trade debts, except for 'relevant matters' (*ss 479(2), 481*); and

- embedded derivatives (*s 415*).

'Equity instrument' is defined as for accounting purposes: *s 476(1)*.

4.18   The legislation applies to:

- capital fluctuations in the value of debt instruments, as these are reflected in the accounts;

- interest and interest equivalents (discounts and premiums);

- charges and expenses connected with debt instruments;

- 'related transactions', ie profits and losses on acquisition and disposal of loan relationships;

- hybrid instruments pending conversion; and

- exchange differences other than those on derivative contracts.

Shares and distributions

4.19   Shares are a liability to shareholders which company law only allows to be returned to shareholders on a winding up, a reduction of capital or a purchase of owns shares. The characteristic of shareholders' funds is that the company can never be obliged to make an outflow of financial benefits to shareholders. Redeemable shares can only be redeemed out of profits. Cumulative preferential dividends are required to be shown as appropriations, even if not paid.

4.20   For company law purposes a distribution is a payment by a company to shareholders in respect of shares: *CA 2006, s 829(1)*. As regards tax law, income distributions are defined in *CTA 2010, s 1000(1)*. These do not include a return of capital on a winding up. A return of capital on a winding up is described as a capital distribution under *TCGA 1992, s 122*. However, *CTA 2010, s 1030* says that a return of capital on a winding up is not a distribution for the purposes of the Corporation Tax Acts. *CTA 2009, s 476(1)* says that 'shares' for the purposes of the loan relationship rules means shares on which distributions may be payable:

> 'In this Part–
>
>   …
>
> "share", in relation to a company, means any share in the company under which an entitlement to receive distributions may arise'

4.21   The purpose of the definition in *s 476* is to distinguish debt instruments from equity instruments for the purposes of the Act. It demarcates the two categories for tax purposes. What *s 476* is designed to do is to exclude from the loan relationship rules capital contributions, which carry no right to dividends or repayment on winding up. It follows from this that zero coupon shares, ie shares with no entitlement to dividends, will not be 'shares'.

4.22   For the general purposes of corporation tax 'ordinary share capital' is defined in *CTA 2010, s 1119* as meaning all the company's shares other than fixed rate preference shares carrying no other rights:

> '"ordinary share capital", in relation to a company, means all the company's issued share capital (however described), other than capital the holders of which have a right to a dividend at a fixed rate but have no other right to share in the company's profits.'

4.23   The definition in *ITA 2007, s 989* is in the same terms. Hence zero coupon shares have to be taken into account in deciding whether shares held by a shareholder constitute a 5% interest so as to qualify for entrepreneurs' relief from capital gains tax: *Castledine v R & C Comrs* [2016] UKFTT 145 (TC).

4.24   If debt is exchanged for 'ordinary shares' in the debtor company, no tax charge on the derecognition of debt by the debtor company will arise. This is provided for by *CTA 2009, s 322(4)*:

> '322 **Release of debts: cases where credits not required to be brought into account**
>
> (1)   This section applies if–
>
> > (a)   a liability to pay an amount under a company's debtor relationship is released, and
> >
> > (b)   the release takes place in an accounting period for which an amortised cost basis of accounting is used in respect of that relationship.
>
> (2)   The company is not required to bring into account a credit in respect of the release for the purposes of this Part if any of conditions A to E is met.
>
> (3)   …
>
> (4)   Condition B is that the release is not a release of relevant rights and is–
>
> > (a)   in consideration of shares forming part of the ordinary share capital of the debtor company, or
> >
> > (b)   in consideration of any entitlement to such shares.'

4.25   Given that the definition of 'ordinary share capital' in *CTA 2010, s 1119* differs from the definition of 'shares' in *CTA 2009, s 476*, the question arises whether 'shares' in *s 322(4)(a)* have to be 'shares' within *s 476*, or simply have to be 'ordinary share capital' within *CTA 2010, s 1119*. Zero coupon shares come within the *s 1119* definition but fall outside the *s 476* definition, whereas fixed rate preference shares carrying no other rights would come within *s 476* but not meet the definition in *s 1119*. Either the *s 476* definition limits the scope of *s 322(4)*, or it is irrelevant in the context of *s 322(4)*. Having regard to the context, *s 322(4)* imports the *CTA 2010, s 1119* definition, and this excludes the *CTA 2009, s 476* definition.

4.26   An exception to the rule that shares are not caught occurs where the shares amount to a material interest in a unit trust scheme or in an offshore fund which has more than 60% debt assets ('the bond fund rules'). In that case, such an asset is treated as a loan relationship, with compulsory fair value accounting: *CTA 2009, ss 490, 493*.

Three categories of loan relationship

4.27   The term 'loan relationship' has three meanings:

- Actual loans: *CTA 2009, s 302(1)*.

- Deemed loans: *CTA 2009, s 303(3)*.

- Debts which are treated as loan relationships for particular purposes ('relevant non-lending relationships'): *CTA 2009, ss 479–480*.

4.28   In all cases, there must be a debt for a loan relationship to exist. A debt is a necessary, but not a sufficient, condition for the existence of a loan relationship.

- An actual loan exists where there has been a transaction for the lending of money.

- A deemed loan exists where there is no transaction of money, but the debtor has issued a security instrument to the creditor.

- A relevant non-lending relationship exists where there is a debt owed by or to a company which does not come within the first two categories.

4.29   Actual loans and deemed loans come within the loan relationship rules for all purposes. Relevant non-lending loan relationships come within the rules as regards particular matters, eg interest, debt write-backs and foreign exchange differences.

Money debts

4.30   In order for there to be a loan relationship, there must be a 'money debt'. 'Money debt' means the same as 'debt', because all debts have to be capable of being expressed in money. 'Money debt' is defined in *CTA 2009, s 303(1)*:

'(1)   For the purposes of this Part a money debt is a debt which–

    (a)   falls to be settled–

        (i)   by the payment of money,

        (ii)   by the transfer of a right to settlement under a debt, which is itself a money debt, or

        (iii)   by the issue or transfer of any share in any company,

    (b)   has at any time fallen to be so settled,

    (c)   may at the option of the debtor or creditor fall to be so settled.'

4.31   If the debt can at any time be settled by the payment of money, it is immaterial that it can also be discharged in other ways: *s 303(2)*. The definition is extended to the issue or transfer of any shares in a company in order to bring in mandatorily convertible or exchangeable debt within the loan relationship rules.

4.32   A contingent right to receive an unascertainable amount of money at an unknown date is not a debt (*O'Driscoll v Manchester Insurance Committee* [1915] 3 KB 499). Contingent liabilities, such as a liability arising under a guarantee or an earn-out agreement, will not be debts, and so cannot give rise to loan relationships. This also applies to the assets created under the sort of agreement for a purchase of shares which was the subject of *Marren v Ingles* (1980) 54 TC 76. That case was concerned with the right to receive additional consideration on a sale of shares, where it was uncertain whether the additional consideration would be payable at all, or, if it did prove to be payable, in what amount. The right to receive contingent deferred consideration was held to be a capital gains tax asset. Thus, an earn-out is part consideration for a sale, to which part of the acquisition cost must be attributed.

4.33   A debt may arise from:

(a)   a transaction for the lending of money;

(b)   the issue of a security, regardless of the origin of the liability;

(c)   the sale of a promise to pay a sum of money at a future date;

(d)   the sale of goods, services or assets on credit;

(e)   a court judgment; or

(f)   a statutory provision.

4.34   Transactions under (a) and (b) fall wholly within the loan relationship rules. Transactions under (c) come within the derivative contracts rules. Anything else gives rise to a relevant non-lending relationship. This third category is very wide in scope because it includes all impairments of debts, whatever their origin.

Type 1: Actual loan relationships

4.35   The definition of 'loan relationship' is broad because of the breadth of the definition of 'money debt'. *CTA 2009, s 303* defines money debt and says that it includes a debt which falls to be settled by payment of money or by the issue of securities, pursuant to a right which may be vested or contingent, eg convertibles or perpetuals.

4.36   'Loan' is defined in *CTA 2009, s 476* as including 'any advance or money'. The usual meaning of the term 'loan' is that it is an advance of money on terms providing for repayment: *Chow Yoong Hong Choong Fah Rubber Manufactory* [1962] AC 209 at 216; *CIR v De Vigier* 42 TC 24 at 41; *Champagne-Perrier SA v HH Finch Ltd* [1982] 3 All ER 713 at 717; *Potts Executors v IRC* 32 TC 211 at 235.

4.37   'Loan relationship' includes 'any advance of money': *s 476(1)*. In the first place, a loan relationship is a money debt arising from a transaction for the lending of money. *Section 302(1)* says:

> '(1)   for the purposes of the Corporation Tax Acts a company has a loan relationship if–
>
> > (a)   the company stands in the position of a creditor or debtor as respects (whether by reference to a security or otherwise), and
> >
> > (b)   the debt arises from a transaction of the lending of money.'

The two requirements of *s 302(1)* are cumulative.

4.38   A loan of money has three aspects:

(a)   a deposit or transfer of money which creates a debtor/creditor relationship;

(b)   the obligation of the debtor to pay interest or an interest-equivalent, though the creditor may forgo his right to interest; and

(c)   the promise of repayment.

4.39 *Chitty on Contracts* (31st ed, Sweet & Maxwell, 2012), Vol 2, para 38-238 says:

> 'A contract of loan of money is a contract whereby one person lends or agrees to lend a sum of money to another, in consideration of a promise express or implied to repay that sum on demand, or at a fixed or determinable future time, or conditionally upon an event which is bound to happen, with or without interest.'

4.40 The *Financial Services and Markets Act 2000, Sch 2, para 22* defines 'deposit' as:

> 'Rights under any contract under which a sum of money (whether or not denominated in a currency) is paid on terms under which it will be repaid, with or without interest or a premium, and either on demand or at a time and in circumstances agreed by or on behalf of the person making the payment and the person receiving it.'

Again, it is difficult to understand how there can be a sum of money which is not denominated in a currency.

4.41 For a loan, there must be a lending of money and a promise to repay. These are two separate promises, which do not depend for their validity on a connection (*synallagma*) between them. A synallagmatic contract consists of two promises, each of which is the equivalent of the other. If X promises to cut someone's hair for £10, the sum of £10 is the equivalent of a haircut. By contrast, a loan agreement comprises two distinct promises. X pays Y £100 by way of loan. Y agrees to repay £100 plus interest of £10. The contract is non-synallagmatic. With a synallagmatic contract, the two claims *come into existence at the same moment when the contract is concluded.* For this reason, civil law has the concept of a 'consensual contract', because the consensus is sufficient to establish the mutual rights and obligations. Such contracts are to be distinguished from 'real contracts', such as loan contracts. Real contracts are also concerned with performance and counter-performance. However, in contrast to the position under a consensual contract, the obligations do not stand in a relationship of mutuality, because the creation of the mutual obligations depends upon a 'real' act, ie a factual event. In the case of a contract of loan, the repayment obligation (and any obligation to pay interest) arise only when the lender advances the amount of the loan to the borrower. The contract itself does not give rise to a payment obligation. In addition to the agreement of the parties, a factual circumstance is required for the conclusion of the contract.

4.42 Where a bank allows a customer to overdraw an account, the customer is regarded as having borrowed from the bank to the extent of the overdraft: *Cunliffe Brooks & Co v Blackburn Benefit Society* (1884) 9 App Cas 857 at 868. This is a special rule for banks. In *Potts' Executors v CIR* 32 TC 211 a director had a running account with a company. The company paid tax bills on his behalf. A debit balance was outstanding until he paid it off. The question was whether the payments to third parties constituted a loan by the company to the director, for the purposes of the income settlements legislation. It was held that there was not a loan 'according to the ordinary fair meaning of the words'.

4.43   A vendor selling property to a purchaser does not make a loan if part of the purchase price is left unpaid (*IRC v Port of London Authority* 12 TC 122; *Champagne Perrier-Jouet SA v HH Finch Ltd* [1982] 3 All ER 713). 'A vendor selling property to a purchaser cannot be said to lend him the unpaid portion of his purchase price' (*Ramsden v IRC* 37 TC 619, per Harman J at 625). See *Chitty on Contracts* (31st edn, Sweet & Maxwell, 2012), Vol 2, paras 38-241 and 38-242. Nor does a company which issues a loan or debenture as consideration for the acquisition of property borrow money. Where a company supplies goods on terms that payment will not be required for a certain period, this will be an agreement to leave the purchase price outstanding. If property is sold, and one price applies if there is immediate payment, and a higher price if payment is deferred, the difference is treated as interest: *CTA 2009, s 480(5)*.

Intra-group balances

4.44   Inter-company loan accounts and directors' loan accounts will be loan relationships, if there is a lending of money. If the loan account is simply a running account to pay for supplies, the balance will be a trade debt, not a loan relationship. Interest will in all cases be within the loan relationship rules. If the debts are loan relationships, the 'connected persons' rules will apply. Where the inter-company debt represents both a loan and outstanding payment for goods and services, it will be necessary to analyse the account into its two component parts.

4.45   A common borderline case arises where company A supplies goods or services to company B, and company A leaves the price outstanding. Has A agreed to supply credit to buy the goods, or to supply the goods on credit? What matters is the legal nature of the transaction. In any case, it is always open to B to issue a security for the debt to A, thus bringing the arrangement under notional loans, if it was not already an actual loan. If it is a trade debt, it will be a notional non-lending relationship.

Example 4.2

X Ltd owes Y Ltd £100 for stationery. X Ltd issues a debenture for £100 to Y Ltd. The original debt has been discharged by a new contractual relationship. It has been replaced by a different debt.

4.46   In *MJP Media Services Ltd v R & C Comrs* [2011] STC 2290, the structure was alleged to be an upstream payment by MJP to its parent Carat, which MJP then waived.

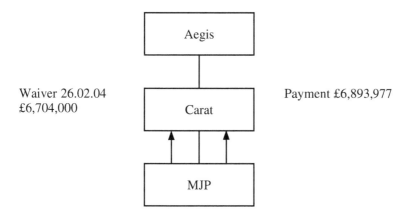

Waiver 26.02.04
£6,704,000

Payment £6,893,977

4.47   The Tribunal decided that there was insufficient evidence of money passing, let alone a lending of money, so the debt, if any, could not be a loan relationship. Basic documentation to explain the transactions was not available. No instrument had been issued representing security for the rights of the creditor. There was no evidence that debts arose from the transaction for the lending of money: 'lending of money is a question of fact to be determined by the Tribunal' ([95]). The Upper Tribunal, affirming these findings, agreed that the documents submitted to the Tribunal were 'incomplete evidence because the results of the transactions rather than the nature of these transactions' ([27]). The Upper Tribunal observed at [39] that:

> 'parties cannot make a transaction answer a description which it does not otherwise answer by saying that it does.'

This, however, begs the question, because it assumes the answer before asking the question.

4.48   The Tribunal also suggested that money has to be transferred to constitute a loan; and (on the authority of *Potts Exors v IRC* 32 TC 211) that a payment by A to C of B's debt to C cannot be an advance of money by A to B, and so constitute a loan. That is doubtful. An advance can be in the form of creating a credit. For a loan, either cash must be passed or credit must be made available, in either case accompanied by an obligation to repay. This is because a loan is a 'real contract'. Equally, there is no reason why a payment by A to C with the agreement of B cannot constitute a loan by A to B. The Upper Tribunal did not deal with these points.

4.49   The issue which arose in the case was, where the creditor and debtor are connected, and the creditor makes a partial release of the debt, could the creditor obtain a tax deduction in respect of the amount released under the law as it stood until 1 January 2005. This question arises because the requirements of an 'authorised accounting method' under the loan relationship rules (prior to the amendments in *FA 2004*) conflicted with normal accounting practice. *FA 1996, s 85(3)(c)* made the assumption that all amounts due would be paid in full. The law changed with effect from 1 January 2005 with the introduction of IAS, and the simple requirement for correct accounts rather than use of an 'authorised accounting basis'. The Tribunal rejected the argument on the grounds that the 'paid in full as due' assumption, otherwise disapplied by *FA 1996, Sch 9*, was, in the case of connected companies, reinstated by *FA 1996, Sch 5, para 6(3)*. This assumed that the waived amount was still payable.

Finance leases

4.50   FRS 102, Section 20 recognises a distinction between rentals under finance leases ('finance leases') and rentals under contracts of simple hire ('operating leases'). The economic substance of a finance lease is a secured loan for the purchase of an asset, residual value at the end of the lease passing to the lessee, and the lessor having no intention of retaining the asset. Accordingly, rentals under finance leases are to be accounted for as payments for the acquisition of a chattel, and apportioned for accounting purposes between a finance charge and a reduction of the outstanding obligation for future amounts payable (FRS 102, para 20.17). The same applies to hire purchase contracts. For tax purposes, leases are classified as 'long funding leases', which is a more extensive category than finance leases. In the case of a long funding lease, capital allowances go to the lessee. Finance leases, long funding leases and hire purchase agreements are not loan relationships. The IASB is proposing to abolish the distinction between finance leases and operating leases, which will produce consequent changes to the UK legislation.

4.51   The acquisition of receivables under a factoring agreement will not create a money debt between the purchaser and the seller, so the loan relationship rules will not apply. The position is to be distinguished from securitisation, where loan relationships are either transferred or created by the transaction.

Hybrids

4.52   Hybrids share the characteristics of both equity and debt. Quasi-equity is equity with debt features, eg redeemable fixed rate preference shares. Under IAS 32, all redeemable preference shares are classified as liabilities rather than as shareholders' funds for accounting purposes, so that dividends on such shares will be reported as interest in the accounts, thereby reducing profits. Such shares (and the dividends on them) will still be treated as shares for legal and tax purposes.

4.53   Quasi-debt is debt with equity features. Quasi-debt is a means whereby companies can reduce the cost of borrowing, by issuing debt securities which carry the right to convert into shares at a later date, perhaps with premium put options, and interest enhancements. If, when that date arrives, the share price has risen above the conversion price, the investor can make a profit, which compensates for the lower rate of interest received prior to conversion.

4.54   Convertibles are corporate loan stock that can be converted into the issuer's ordinary or preferred stock at an agreed price over a specific time period. Under IAS 32 and IAS 39, a convertible may have to be bifurcated, ie it has to be treated as two separate instruments: a discounted bond (loan relationship) and an equity option. Wherever bifurcation applies for accounting purposes, it also has to be adopted for tax purposes. Hence, the tax and accounting treatment of convertibles will largely follow that of debt with warrants, ie debt issued with a securitised warrant enabling the holder to buy shares of the issuer at an agreed price at a specified future date.

Guarantees

4.55   Loan guarantees involve a lender (B), a primary debtor (D) and a secondary debtor (G), who is guarantor of D's obligation to B. Loan guarantees are commonly taken in dealings with groups of companies, from other companies in the group. A guarantee, unless supported by a charge over a deposit, merely creates a personal obligation between the lender and the guarantor. It is a collateral entitlement of the lender. Unless the guarantee is called, the guarantor does not stand in the position of a debtor or creditor. So long as the guarantor only has a secondary liability, the issue of a guarantee will not create a loan relationship. A guarantee given to a related company will have transfer pricing implications, if the guarantee is not on arm's-length terms.

Example 4.3

G plc guarantees a loan of £1m owed by its connected company D to B bank. Arrears of interest of £200,000 accumulate, but D claims a deduction for this amount. B calls on G's guarantee. G pays B £1.2m. G acquires by subrogation B's loan asset. As G and D are connected, G obtains no impairment relief.

4.56   In *Hendy (Inspector of Taxes) v Hadley* 53 TC 353 at 356, the High Court held that a guarantor who discharged an obligation was not a borrower, and had not paid interest. The General Commissioners' conclusion to the contrary was 'an impossible conclusion' (but see, *per contra, Westminster Bank Executor and Trustee Co (Channel Islands) Ltd v National Bank of Greece SA* 46 TC 472 at 485).

4.57   In *Holder v IRC* 16 TC 540, some individuals had to pay £64,482 to Midland Bank under a guarantee which they had given of the borrowings of a company in which they were interested. The bank had debited interest to the company every six months, and then added the sum to principal. The guarantors wanted to analyse the payment to the bank as comprising interest arrears of £17,861 16s 5d, with the balance as capital, so that they could claim the interest element as a deduction from income. Romer LJ observed (at 558):

'The relations between the company and the bank were regulated not by any special agreement, but by the ordinary usage prevailing between bankers and their customers as to the method of keeping accounts. In accordance with this usage the balance of principal and interest was struck at the end of each half-year and the aggregate sum was introduced as the first item in the subsequent half-yearly account and interest calculated upon it'

4.58   The position of the guarantor was explained by Viscount Dunedin in these words:

'The guarantor does not pay on an advance made to him, but pays under his guarantee. It is true that he pays a sum which pays all interest due by the person to whom the advance is made, but his debt is his debt under the guarantee, not a debt in respect of the advance made to him.'

4.59   Lord Macmillan said (at 569):

'The short answer ... is that the Appellants received no advance from the bank and owed no interest to the bank.'

4.60   When the arrears of interest are paid, this will be a receipt of interest by the bank (*Pretoria-Pietersburg Rly Co Ltd v Elgood (or Elwood) (Surveyor of Taxes)* 6 TC 508). The arrears of interest will be debited to the suspense account and credited to interest income. There will not be a payment of interest by G, the guarantor, because G has never borrowed any money from B.

4.61   However, under the general law or under specific terms of the guarantee, a guarantor may step into the shoes of the party whose obligation he has guaranteed. Subrogation is a doctrine of equity. When one person (B) has a claim against another (D), which a third person (G) discharges, G has in certain circumstances the right to have the benefit of the claim and the remedy for enforcing it, even though it has not been assigned to him. In these circumstances, G is said to be subrogated to the rights of B. G replaces B in the transaction, to the extent that he discharges D's liabilities. Subrogation will act as an assignment by operation of law of B's rights against D to G. G will thus become a creditor of D under a loan relationship. G also has an independent right to indemnification by the primary debtor, express or implied. This will be a money debt, but not a loan relationship.

4.62 Payment under a guarantee is therefore a 'related transaction'. It is an acquisition of rights under a loan relationship, for payment of the amount which G pays to B. However, G will have to bring in as a credit the full value of the loan relationship. Hence, G gets no debit for its payment to B. In accounting terms, the effect of the transaction is neutral.

4.63 If G and D are connected, G will have to bring in credits under the loan relationship as they fall due, regardless of whether they are paid or not. The guarantor will get no impairment relief for the asset which he is treated as acquiring. As far as D is concerned, its debtor loan relationship continues, though it may now be a connected party loan relationship. Thus, D would not bring in any credit, and would not have to bring in a credit for any subsequent release.

4.64 If the guarantor is a trading company (but not a bank), it might be able to claim a deduction as a trading expense. *Lawson v Johnson Matthey plc* [1992] STC 466 concerned a case where a parent (JM) agreed to sell its insolvent subsidiary (JMB) for £1, undertaking as part of the transaction to capitalise it with £50m. If the parent had not agreed to this transaction, it would itself have become insolvent. It successfully claimed a revenue deduction in respect of the £50m, on the grounds that it would not have been able to carry on its business but for the payment. The payment was therefore laid out 'wholly and exclusively for the purposes of the trade' within *ICTA 1988, s 74(1)(a)*. Lord Templeman said (at 472):

> 'if the £50 million were paid to procure the transfer of the shares in JMB to the Bank of England, the payment is attributable to capital. If, on the other hand, the £50 million were paid to remove the threat posed by the insolvency of JMB to the continuation in business of the taxpayer company, it seems to me that the payment is attributable to revenue ... I have come to the conclusion that the £50 million was paid, and paid solely, to enable the taxpayer company to be able to continue in business.'

4.65   In *Redkite Ltd v Inspector of Taxes* [1996] STC (SCD) 501, a company guaranteed the borrowings of its subsidiary, and had to pay £1.67m under that guarantee. It was held that the guarantee had not been given for the purposes of that company's trade. Accordingly, a payment under the guarantee was not deductible as a revenue item.

4.66   However, in *Vodafone Cellular Ltd v Shaw (Inspector of Taxes)* [1997] STC 734, a parent company successfully claimed as a revenue deduction a payment made to free it of an onerous contract, the benefit of which contract was enjoyed by two subsidiaries who reimbursed the parent for the charges which it paid under the contract. It was held, first, that the payment was a *revenue payment* because it did not go to the heart of the company's profit-generation operation. Secondly, because the liability was that of the parent, it was held that the payment was made 'wholly and exclusively' for the purpose of the parent's trade. The cancellation of the contract led to the release by the parent of the charges made to the subsidiaries. The benefit which the subsidiaries thereby obtained was a consequence, not a purpose, of the parent company's action. The crucial observation was made by Millett LJ at 742:

'The object of the taxpayer in making the payment must be distinguished from the effect of the payment.'

4.67   The judgment of Millett LJ is the leading authority both on (a) the capital/revenue distinction, and (b) the 'wholly and exclusively' requirement for deductibility of trading expenses.

4.68   As regards loans which become irrecoverable, or guarantees of such loans, the lender or guarantor may obtain relief by way of a loss for capital gains tax purposes, but only to the extent that he does not obtain a debit under the loan relationship rules (*TCGA 1992, s 253(3), (12), (15)*). A 'qualifying loan' is a loan to a UK resident borrower used by him wholly for the purposes of a trade, profession or vocation (not being a trade which consists of or includes the lending of money) (*s 253(1)*). A lender may claim a capital loss for part of a loan which becomes irrecoverable, and the same relief is extended to a guarantor of a qualifying loan who makes a claim for this purpose (*s 253(4)*).

4.69   Where the guarantee is given by a related company to the borrower, no payment for the guarantee is made; but, if such a payment would have been made in an arm's length situation, the guarantor will have to bring in additional income in the form of the notional guarantee fee, while the borrower may be able to claim a 'compensating adjustment'. Any guarantee fee paid by the debtor will be deductible as an expense of entering into a loan relationship.

Summary – actual loans

4.70   Actual loans include the following:

- overdrafts granted by a bank;

- bank loans and other borrowings;

- deposits;

- loan notes, loan stock and debentures issued to raise funds;

- gilts (subject to two exclusions);

- some intra-group balances;

- gilt strips;

- bills of exchange drawn or made in payment of interest;

- funding bonds;

- perpetual debt; and

- notional bonds arising on the bifurcation of a convertible.

4.71   Accordingly, the following will not be actual loan relationships:

- an invoice, being merely a creditor's demand for what is claimed to be owing;

- a promissory note;

- debts arising from leasing, the supply of goods and services, hire purchase;

- rentcharges and payments under wayleave agreements;

- bills of exchange drawn or made in payment of dividends;

- money debts arising from the sale of assets;

- paying off someone else's liabilities;

- judgment debts;

- payments under a guarantee, subject to subrogation rights and/or the terms of the agreement.

Type 2: Deemed loan relationships

4.72   Deemed loans are defined by reference to the existence of a debt plus an instrument creating or evidencing it, namely 'an instrument … issued … for the purpose of representing security ... or the rights of a creditor in respect of, any money debt'. *CTA 2009, s 303(3)* provides that:

> 'A money debt is a debt arising from a transaction for the lending of money for the purposes of this Part if an instrument is issued by any person for the purpose of representing–
>
> (a) security for the debt, or
>
> (b) the rights of a creditor in respect of the debt.'

4.73   The key phrase is 'instrument ... issued ... for the purpose of representing security'. The issue of a security will give an independent right of action arising from the terms of the security, without the need to examine the underlying transaction. Notional loans may be regarded as simply an extension of actual loans. While many actual loans will be accompanied by the issuing of an instrument, the essence of notional loans is that an instrument is issued, but there is no lending of money, so the requisite underlying debt arises from a transaction other than the lending of money.

4.74   This is a major extension of the concept of loan relationship. The main example of a deemed loan will be the issue by a company of loan notes or other debt securities in consideration for the acquisition of other assets, such as shares in a company or land. The issue of loan stock by way of acquisition consideration on purchase of an asset is not a loan in law, but is treated as a loan for tax purposes (*IRC v Port of London Authority* 12 TC 122). Amongst other common transactions, this rule is intended to cover loan notes issued by a company in payment for shares on a share exchange within *TCGA 1992, s 135*, eg:

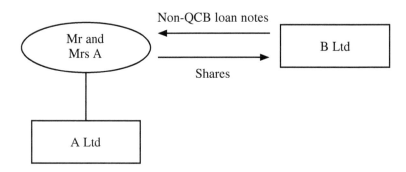

4.75   The non-QCB loan notes issued by B Ltd to Mr and Mrs A in exchange for their A Ltd shares are loan relationships of B Ltd. They will ordinarily be interest-bearing, guaranteed and redeemable in tranches over a period of years.

Loan notes are, for tax purposes, deferred payments of cash. All QCBs held by companies are loan relationships, but corporate bonds and loan notes held by individuals may be QCBs or non-QCBs.

4.76   An 'issue' is not confined to physically delivering an instrument to a person, but covers conferring rights which are 'represented by' the instrument (*National Westminster Bank plc v IRC* [1994] STC 580). An issue involves a unilateral act by one party, putting the thing issued into circulation to the public or a section of the public. An 'instrument' is any written document (*Stamp Act 1891, s 122(1)*; *Taylor v Holt* 3 H & C 452; *London, Chatham and Dover Rly Co v South Eastern Rly Co* [1893] AC 429).

4.77   The mere acceptance of money on loan, creating the relationship of debtor and creditor, does not in itself constitute an 'issue' (*Agricultural Mortgage Corpn Ltd v IRC* [1978] STC 11). In that case, Goff LJ observed (at 21) that there was a 'distinction between money raised and security for the loan', and continued (at 23):

> 'the mere acceptance of money on loan, albeit it creates the relationship of debtor and creditor and gives the latter a chose in action, is not enough … there must be something recognisable as a thing which is or can be issued … there must be something emanating from the company, being either (i) a document which in itself constitutes security for loan capital, or (ii) some act on the part of the company, such as registration or a letter of acceptance or possibly both, or the issue of a certificate whereby the company recognises the rights of and perfects the title of the lender.'

4.78   A subsidy, which may be repayable in certain circumstances, is a business receipt and not a loan, notwithstanding that, in the legislation authorising the payment, it may be called 'an advance' (*Smart (Inspector of Taxes) v Lincolnshire Sugar Co Ltd* 20 TC 643 at 664). Overdrafts are loans (*Cunliffe Brooks & Co v Blackburn and District Benefit Building Society* (1884) 9 App Cas 857).

Conversion of money debt into loan relationship

4.79   It is possible for a money debt to be converted into a loan relationship through the issuing of an instrument to represent the creditor's rights or a security for the creditor's rights. It is also possible to covert the money debt into a loan relationship through making a loan to repay the debt. There is nothing to prevent a loan from being created through book entries. Balances of contractual debts can be readily converted into loan relationships if the debtor issues a debenture. Where the debtor issues a security in respect of a money debt, there will be a loan relationship, regardless of whether there has been a lending of money. For a debt which is not a loan relationship to be converted into a loan relationship, it is necessary to be able to point to a new agreement which effects this change. This point is brought out in the HMRC's Corporate Finance Manual (CFM).

4.80   Paragraph CFM31040 states:

> **'31040. Money debts: Do they arise from the lending of money?**
>
> ...
>
> **Trade debts**
>
> A company may be a debtor because it has not paid for goods and services it has received. There is a money debt, but it did not arise from lending money. So trade debts are not loan relationships.
>
> A trade debt does not become a loan just because it has been outstanding for a long time. But if the creditor company lends money to the debtor company so that it has the funds to repay the debt (by book entry, or by cash changing hands), there will be a new agreement between the parties (not necessarily in writing), which is separate from the trade debt. This is a loan relationship because it is a debt for lending money.
>
> ...
>
> **Inter-company accounts**
>
> Balances on inter-company accounts may arise from the lending of money where one group company has borrowed money from another. These are loan relationships.
>
> Where the balances represent unpaid amounts for goods and services supplied by one group company to another, they are trade debts, which are not loan relationships.'

4.81

In the House of Commons, Standing Committee E (19th sitting, 29 February 1996, at 613), it was stated:

> 'Loan relationship ... does not extend to invoices or payments under guarantees, but it does extend to tradeable loan notes, for example, when taken in exchange for a take-over bid. Whether promissory notes are covered by the new rules depends on whether there is a loan of money. If there is, the promissory note is covered; if there is not, then it is not.'

Type 3: Relevant non-lending relationships

4.82 Relevant non-lending relationships (RNLRs) are defined in *CTA 2009, ss 478–480*. There are two types: RNLRs not involving a discount; and RNLRs involving a discount. These rules are very broad in scope, and can have a major effect by unexpectedly catapulting a company into the loan relationship rules. Broadly these provisions have two effects:

1   They make simple contract debts at interest or denominated in a foreign currency into loan relationships, but only for the purposes of taxing or relieving the interest or exchange fluctuations. If a debenture is issued to represent the debt, it will be a deemed loan relationship (Type 2).

2   All debts which are released or impaired are treated as loan relationships.

4.83 An RNLR not involving a discount (see *s 479*) is a money debt in relation to which a company stands as debtor or creditor with the following characteristics:

1   it is not an actual or notional loan relationship; and

2   it has one of the following features–

(a)   interest on the debt is payable by or to the company, or

(b)   it may give rise to foreign exchange gains or losses (as defined by *s 475*), or

(c)   it may give rise to an impairment loss, a reverse debit or reversal of a previous impairment in relation to a 'business payment', ie a trading expense, or

(d)   it has given rise to an allowable deduction which is released.

4.84 An RNLR involving a discount (see *s 480*) is a money debt in relation to which a company stands in the position of creditor with the following characteristics:

1   it is not an actual or notional loan relationship;

2   it gives rise to a discount;

3   the discount would not be a trading receipt;

4   the discount does not fall within the alternative finance arrangements in *ss 503–520*; and

5   if the debt assets arises from the disposal of property, the transaction in question was not an intra-group transfer of an insurance business within *ss 340–341* or intra-group transfer of a derivative contract within *s 625*.

4.85   The purpose of this category is to bring within the loan relationship rules interest, discounts foreign exchange differences, releases and impairments on debts owed or held by companies which are not actual or deemed loan relationships. Thus, an RNLR is only a loan relationship for limited purposes, namely, 'relevant matters' (*s 481*). The RNLR rules bring within the loan relationship rules the release of trade debts. The effect of bringing RNLRs into the loan relationship rules is to import into trade debts, and debts of a UK property business, the full panoply of the 'connected companies' rules which apply to Type 1 and Type 2 loan relationships. Hence, releases and impairment of trade debts and of a deemed trade come within the scope of the loan relationship rules.

4.86   'Relevant matters' are:

- interest;
- discounts;
- exchange gains and losses;
- where interest is payable, profits arising from a related transaction in respect of the right to receive interest or discount;
- impairment or release of trade debts;
- reversals of impairment or release of trade debts; and
- impairment, or reversal of impairment, of discounts.

4.87   Two categories are of particular importance:

1   *Section 479(2)(c)* says that RNLRs include cases where there is a loss by reason of an unpaid business payment (or reversal of previous impairment):

> '(c) a debit in relation to which an impairment loss (or credit in respect of the reversal of an impairment loss) or release debit arises to the company in respect of an unpaid (or previously unpaid) business payment.'

Section 479(3) says that 'business payment' means:

> 'a payment which, if it were paid, would fall to be brought into account for corporation tax purposes as the receipt of a trade, UK property business or overseas property business carried on by the company.'

2   *Section 479(2)(d)* says that RNLRs include 'a debt in relation to which a relevant deduction has been allowed to the company and which is

released'. 'Relevant deduction' means an amount which has been allowed as a deduction in calculating the profits of a trade or a deemed trade: *s 479(3)(c)*. 'Release' is not defined. However, its general legal meaning is that of a gratuitous act, ie a giving up of a claim against someone against whom it could have been enforced.

4.88   Where a debt is an RNLR, the loan relationships rules apply to all 'relevant matters': *CTA 2009, s 481(1), (3)*. 'Relevant matters' include the impairment or release of trade debts (*s 481(3)(d)*):

> '(d)   in the case of a debt in relation to which an impairment loss or release debit arises to the company in respect of unpaid business payment, the impairment or release.'

4.89   As a result of these provisions all impairments and release of trade debts are brought within the loan relationship rules. In general this only makes a difference where debtor and creditor are connected companies. The consequences of coming within the RNLR rules in the case of *connected* companies are that:

(a)   as regards the creditor company, a release or impairment debit will not be deductible for tax purposes: *CTA 2009, s 354*;

(b)   as regards the debtor, the release of the debt will not be taxable, except in the case of a deemed release: *s 358*.

4.90   In short, in the case of debt impairment or release between connected companies, whatever the nature or source of the debt, the creditor's loss cannot be claimed, and the debtor's profit cannot be taxed under the normal provisions for trading profits or the loan relationship rules.

4.91   Debits or credits in respect of late paid or overpaid corporation tax are non-trading debits and credits on RNLRs: *FA 2009, ss 101, 102*; *CTA 2009, s 482(1)*. Interest payable on tax under *TMA 1970, ss 86, 87A* and *88* is not a debt under the loan relationship rules, and is non-deductible: *TMA 1970, s 90*.

4.92   Transfer pricing adjustments which give rise to interest liabilities or receipts constitute 'interest' on RNLRs: *CTA 2009, s 484*. Foreign currency and provisions for liabilities made in a foreign currency are treated as money debts, with special rules for insurance companies: *s 483*. Exchange differences on foreign tax debts are ignored.

4.93   Exchange differences on items which are 'money debts' but not loan relationships are brought within the loan relationship rules by *s 481(3)(b)*. Hence, if a company orders machinery to be paid for in euros on delivery in two years' time, exchange differences on the liability will be taxed or relieved as income. Foreign currency is treated as a money debt under *s 483(2)*.

Characterisation of legal obligations

4.94   In practice questions may frequently arise as to whether a legal obligation is truly a loan, and if so to what extent it truly constitutes indebtedness. This question has arisen with circular loan arrangements ('round-tripping') in circumstances where:

- expenditure for a particular purpose qualifies for tax relief;

- a loan is taken out to acquire qualifying assets, eg software, the original master version of a film;

- the loan is secured on the asset and only repayable from that asset;

- the purchase price exceeds the true value;

- the loan makes possible the higher asset cost;

- the vendor of the asset takes a lease back of the asset for annual payments which will repay the loan over a fixed period;

- the proceeds of the loan are deposited by the vendor as security for repayment of the loan via the annual instalments;

- the effect of the loan is to gear up the tax relief on the initial expenditure.

In other words money travels in a closed loop back to its starting point.

4.95   The courts apply three principles:

1   There is a basic presumption that legislation refers to the legal nature of a transaction and not to its economic effect.

2   The legal nature of a transaction means its legal substance, objectively determined. Parties cannot alter the nature of a transaction by mislabelling it or disguising it as something else.

3   Tax legislation is concerned less with legal substance than with the economic and financial outcome of arrangements.

4.96   The issue can be analysed in a number of ways:

(a)   legal substance,

(b)   sham,

(c)   mislabelling,

(d)   substance over form,

(e)   effect of tax avoidance motive.

Legal substance

4.97   It is the legal substance, rather than the accounting treatment or underlying economic characteristics of the transaction, which will be determinative of its legal categorisation. If the legal substance does not correspond to what the parties have done, this will be characterised as mislabelling. In *Chow Yoong Hong v Choong Fah Rubber Manufactory* [1961] 3 All ER 1163, Lord Devlin observed at 1167:

> 'There are many ways of raising cash besides borrowing. One is by selling book debts and another by selling unmatured bills, in each case for less than their face value. Another might be to buy goods on credit or against a post-dated cheque and immediately sell them in the market for cash … The task of the court in such cases is clear. It must first look at the nature of the transaction which the parties have agreed. If in form it is not a loan, it is not to the point to say that its object was to raise money for one of them or that the parties could have produced the same result more conveniently by borrowing and lending money.'

4.98   In *Welsh Development Agency v Export Finance Co Ltd* [1992] BCLC 148, the question which arose was whether a transaction constituted a sale of goods, or a charge or mortgage secured on the goods, ie a loan. Dillon LJ observed at 160:

> 'in determining the legal categorisation of an agreement and its legal consequences the court looks at the substance of the transactions and not at the labels which the parties have chosen to put on it.'

4.99   At 178 he stated that legal classification must be based on 'some objective criterion', which can be the factual circumstances and the legal definition of a concept:

> 'But the question can also arise where, without any question of sham, there is some objective criterion in law by which the court can test whether the agreement which the parties have made does or does not fall into the legal category in which the parties have sought to place their agreement.'

4.100   The *locus classicus* on the definition of legal substance is the judgment of Staughton LJ at 185–186, where he observed:

> 'One can start from the position that statute law in this country, when it enacts rules to be applied to particular transactions, is in general referring to the legal nature of a transaction and not to its economic effect ... There are ... two routes by which this principle can be overcome. The first, which I will call the external route, is to show that the written document does not represent the agreement of the parties. It may, if one wishes, then be called a sham, a cloak, or a device. The second is the internal route, when one looks only at the written agreement, in order to ascertain from its terms whether it amounts to a transaction of the legal nature which the parties ascribe to it.'

4.101   In evaluating the legal nature of facts, the courts will seek to establish the reality of the matter. For example in a film scheme case, where a partnership had acquired a 20-year licence (with all instalments paid up-front) to exploit and distribute films, and then granted similar rights for 20 years for the same payments to a subsidiary of the vendor, the First-tier Tribunal held that the partnership was not engaged in a trade. As the Court of Appeal put it:

> 'The FTT further held that, although the acquisition of the Rights by licence and sub-licence were not sham transactions, Eclipse 35 cannot be considered on any realistic basis to have a customer or to offer to provide any goods or services by way of business.' (*Eclipse Film Partners No 35 LLP v R & C Comrs* [2015] STC 1429 at [68])

4.102   A payment of £503m by Eclipse 35 (for the purchase of the licence of film rights) was to be repaid (as consideration for the sub-lease back of film rights) with interest over 20 years. The Tribunal held this was of the nature of an investment.

Mislabelling

4.103   Parties may categorise their transactions in a particular way, because they hope thereby to gain a particular tax or other advantage. Where parties call an arrangement by one name, but its true legal character belongs in a different category, that is 'mislabelling' and the courts will adopt the true legal classification. A letting agreement may be called a licence rather than a lease. However, if its terms confer exclusive possession of a property or part of a property for a period of time, it is a lease. Hence a lease remains a tenancy, even if it is called a licence. As Lord Templeman stated in *Street v Mountford* [1985] AC 809 at 819:

> 'if the agreement satisfied all the requirements of a tenancy, then the agreement produced a tenancy and the parties cannot alter the effect of the agreement by insisting that they only executed a licence. The manufacture of a five pronged implement for manual digging results in a fork even if the manufacturer, unfamiliar with the English language, insists that he intended to make and has made a spade.'

4.104   There is thus a tension between freedom of contract and freedom to classify one's transactions in a particular way, and the objective determination of the true legal nature of what is done. The courts have determined that a two-stage process has to be adopted:

1   ascertainment of the substantive rights and obligations;

2   attribution of the correct legal label to those rights and obligations.

4.105   For example, fixed and floating charges are both consensual securities created by agreement between the parties. The parties can choose what rights and obligations to create. Whether the package of rights and obligations amounts to a floating charge is a question of law. The label attached by the parties is not determinative. As Lord Millett (who disliked floating charges) observed:

> 'The question is not merely one of construction. In deciding whether a charge is a fixed charge or a floating charge, the court is engaged in a two-stage process. At the first stage it must construe the instrument of charge and seek to gather the intentions of the parties from the language they have used … Once these have been ascertained, the court can embark on the second stage of the process, which is one of categorisation. This is a matter of law. (*Agnew v Commissioners of Inland Revenue* [2001] 2 AC 710 at 725)

4.106   A second type of mislabelling occurs when a payment is given one description, or stated to be consideration for X, but the court holds that the true character of the payment is different, or the attribution of consideration is incorrect.

4.107   In *Fitzleet Estates Ltd v Cherry* 51 TC 708, under the law as it then stood (*Income Tax Act 1952, ss 169, 170*), if interest was not payable out of profits brought into charge to tax, the payer of the interest has to deduct income tax from the income and account for the tax to the Inland Revenue. Capitalised interest was not charged to revenue and so not paid out of profits.

A number of property companies recognised future profits on a development as income, transferred a corresponding sum to balance sheet as an increase in the value of properties in course of development, and claimed that this was not a capitalisation of interest. Templeman J (as he then was) observed that this constituted a capitalisation of interest, however, so-called, and one could not convert a bottle of claret into burgundy by changing the label on the bottle (at 716):

> 'The company justify the capitalisation of interest by pointing to a capital gain, but cannot pretend that they were charging interest to revenue just because there was an unrealised capital profit equal to the interest and available to be transferred to revenue. It is not possible to substitute claret for burgundy by changing the label on the bottle.'

4.108 Under *FA 1994* the profit on a 'financial instrument' (ie a derivative contract) was the excess of amounts of 'qualifying payments' received (Amount A) over qualifying payments made (Amount B). If B > A, there was a deductible loss. In *Prudential plc v R & C Comrs* [2009] STC 2459, the question was whether front-end payments of £105m made in two foreign exchange swaps, were 'qualifying payments' under *FA 1996, s 151(1)(b)*, and so deductible, as being payments to the counterparty as inducements to enter into the contract (deductible) or a pre-payment of the final currency leg which Prudential was obliged to pay to the counterparty. The court held (at 2464) that calling these front-end payments 'Additional payments … for entering into the transaction' was simply a case of mislabelling.

4.109 In *Tower MCashback LLP 1 v R & C Comrs* [2011] STC 1143 the partnership claimed capital allowances of £27.5m for the purchase of licences for computer software. 75% of the price was obtained by means of a bank loan, which was interest free and only repayable from the exploitation of the software rights. The Supreme Court held that 75% of the expenditure was incurred on acquiring finance rather than software. In more detail:

1   Computer software qualifying for 100% first year allowances (FYAs) under *CAA 2001* was valued on the basis of predicted income, as per a business plan.

2   A bank lent £20.6m on interest-free non-recourse terms to individual members of a limited partnership (Tower) for the purchase of the software.

3   The members of Tower added £6.9m of their own funds and paid £27.5m to a software house (MCashback) for a licence to exploit *part of* the software, which gave a right to receive clearing fees.

4   MCashback deposited £22.5m (82%) with the bank, which would be repaid from the clearing fees received by Tower.

5   Tower was only liable to repay the loan out of the clearing fees received.

6   The members of the LLP claimed 100% FYAs of £27.5m on the basis that they had incurred expenditure of £27.5m on the purchase of software rights, being 25% paid directly and the other 75% being provided from the interest-free non-recourse loans: see [25]. For 40% taxpayers, the value of the capital allowances (a) of £27.5m would be £11m, and (b) of £6.9m would be £2.75m.

4.110   The Supreme Court held (at [71]) that the division of software rights was unrealistic. This cast doubt on the 'commercial soundness' of the transaction and the valuation of the rights acquired (see [72]). There had been a loan of £20.6m but the issue was 'whether there was real expenditure on the acquisition of software rights' (see [76]). The issue was whether the expenditure incurred was £27.5m (including the loan) was limited to £6.9m. As Lord Walker said at [75]:

'In this case there was a loan but there was not, in any meaningful sense, an incurring of expenditure of the borrowed money in the acquisition of software rights. It went into a loop in order to enable the LLPs to indulge in a tax avoidance scheme'

4.111   Furthermore, he considered that:

'The transfer of ownership (or at least of rights) indicated the reality of some expenditure on acquiring those rights, but was not conclusive of the whole of the expenditure having been for that purpose.'

4.112   Lord Hope said at [89]:

'A significant part of the money which was passing from one party to another in this case was returned to its source immediately … This suggests that it is, to say the least questionable, whether it was expended in their acquisition at all.'

Sham

4.113   If arrangements are called by the wrong name with the aim of misleading third parties, that is 'sham'. The classic description is by Diplock LJ in *Snook v London & West Riding Investments Ltd* [1967] 2 QB 786 at 802:

'If it has any meaning in law, it means acts done or documents executed by the parties to the "sham" which are intended by them to give to third parties or to the court the appearance of creating between the parties legal rights or obligations different from the actual legal rights or obligations (if any) which the parties intend to create.'

4.114   In effect, this requires proof of fraud. The evidential standard is high, and for this reason this allegation will be rarely adopted. There is a definitive account of mislabelling and sham in Rebecca Murray, *Tax Avoidance* (3rd ed, Sweet & Maxwell, 2016), Chapter 8.

Round tripping

4.115   Many of these arrangements involve money going round in a circle (a 'loop' or 'round tripping'). 'Round tripping' (where money leaves the lender and then returns to him so as to reduce his commercial exposure) creates a loan. This is the basis of sale and leasebacks. Where a tax advantage arises from deferral of payment arrangements, or loans financed by the vendor, a different analysis may be appropriate.

4.116   Many tax-planning arrangements depend upon the principle that a transfer of property with the purchase price left outstanding is a sale and not a gift. If there is no intention that the money should be paid to the transferor, or there is no realistic possibility that it could be paid or demanded, the transaction may be a sham or analysed on the basis that its true legal substance is different from the label attached to it by the parties, ie mislabelling.

4.117   As an alternative to leaving the purchase price or part of the purchase price outstanding, the transferor may return the proceeds of sale directly or indirectly to the bank which has loaned the purchaser the wherewithal to effect the transaction. In a range of circumstances, loans may be returned to the lender not at the end of the transaction but at the start of the transaction. In other cases, a loan will be repayable not by the borrower but by the vendor, who in turn will receive the return on the project financed. Non-interest non-recourse (or limited recourse) loans all raise particular questions. For a loan to exist as a matter of law, there must as a matter of fact be (a) a transfer of credit to the borrower, accompanied by (b) a *bona fide* intention by the borrower to repay, and (c) a genuine possibility that the loan may be repaid.

4.118   In a limited recourse finance transaction, a bank will lend money to a project company, but the bank's security is limited to the assets and revenues of the project itself. In such cases, the bank will require income streams or contracts to which the project company is party to be assigned to it, in order to service and repay the debt, and enable the bank to take over the project, if the company defaults.

4.119   In *Ensign Tankers (Leasing) Ltd v Stokes* [1992] STC 226:

1   A limited partnership (VP, of which Ensign was a member) raised $3.25m, which it contributed to a film company (LPI) to meet production costs of a planned film.

2   LPI sold the negative to VP.

3   LPI raised a production loan from a bank. It paid the money into a VP bank account and described the payment as a loan to VP. VP then paid the money back to LP1, and accounted for the payments as production expenditure, qualifying for first-year allowances.

4   The VP loan was to be repaid out of the net profits, payable as to 75% to LPI and 25% to VP.

5   VP claimed first-year allowances on expenditure of $14m.

4.120   The House of Lords held that VP had been trading, but there had been no loan, simply a payment of $3.25m by VP for the negative: per Lord Goff at 426.

4.121   In a tax avoidance context, the principle in *WT Ramsay Ltd v IRC* [1981] STC 174 must be considered. Lord Wilberforce famously observed at 180:

'If it can be seen that a document or transaction was intended to have effect as part of a nexus or series of transactions, or as an ingredient of a wider transaction intended as a whole, there is nothing in the doctrine to prevent it being so regarded; to do so is not to prefer form to substance, or substance to form. It is the task of the court to ascertain the legal nature of any transaction to which it is sought to attach a tax or a tax consequence and if that emerges from a series or combination of transactions, intended to operate as such, it is that series or combination which may be regarded.'

4.122   Etherton Ch has stated:

'Ramsay ... marked the end of an unduly literal interpretative approach to tax statutes and a formalistic insistence in examining steps in a composite scheme separately.' (*Eclipse Film Partners No 35 LLP v R & C Comrs* [2015] STC 1429 at [110])

4.123   As explained by Lord Nicholls in *BMBF* (**4.132**) there are two elements:

●   to adopt a purposive construction of the statute;

●   appying it to a realistic view of the facts.

4.124 In *MacNiven (Inspector of Taxes) v Westmoreland Investments Ltd* [2001] STC 237, M had a property-investment subsidiary, W. By 1987, W owed M £42m in accrued interest. To crystallise tax losses through payment of accrued interest, M lent additional sums of £124m to W, so that W could:

(a) replace former zero-coupon loans with interest-bearing loans;

(b) make repayments of principal owed to M; and

(c) make payments of £73m interest (including interest on the new and refinanced borrowings).

4.125 The question was, had W made a payment of interest? The Revenue wanted to rely on the *Ramsay* principle to treat the circular movement of money as a fiscal nullity. The House of Lords decided that W had made a payment. The debt, in respect of which the interest was paid, was *pro tanto* extinguished.

4.126 The court said that the *Ramsay* principle is a question of the application of the particular taxing provision to the particular facts, and these equally applied to the Revenue (at 255). As Lord Nicholls put it (at 243):

'The paramount question always is one of interpretation of the particular statutory provision and its application to the facts of the case.'

4.127 Secondly, the court said that the *Ramsay* approach is a principle of interpretation, subject to statute. It is not a broad, overriding principle to which all statutes are subject, as it would be if it were a principle of Community law.

4.128 Thirdly, the court said that statutory requirements could be formulated in commercial or in legal terms. If the statute imposing the tax adopts a legal reference to elements of a transaction by reference to their legal nature, it makes no difference that parts of the transaction do not have a commercial purpose. As Lord Hoffmann put it (at 250):

'If the legal position is that tax is imposed by reference to a legally defined concept ... the court cannot tax a transaction [by reference to] the economic effect.'

4.129 In this case, payment was a legal concept and did not have some other commercial meaning (at 260). Where a term in a statute has a clear and well-understood meaning, Parliament is taken to have intended that it should have that meaning. As Lord Hoffmann said (at 256):

'If a transaction falls within the legal description, it makes no difference that it has no commercial purpose.'

4.130 Finally, even if a word is used in a commercial sense, that does not of itself establish that the *Ramsay* principle is applicable:

'Even if a statutory expression refers to a business or economic concept, one cannot disregard a transaction which comes within the statutory language, construed in the correct commercial sense, simply on the ground that it was entered into solely for tax reasons. Business concepts have their boundaries no less than legal ones.' (at 256)

4.131 The House of Lords concluded that there had been a loan and a payment of interest for tax purposes. There was circularity of cash flow combined with the fact that the transaction took place entirely for tax purposes: see [68] at 258. Nevertheless, this was not relevant to the conclusion.

4.132 In *Barclays Mercantile Business Finance Ltd v Mawson* [2005] STC 1 (*BMBF*):

1   a bank bought a gas pipeline from BGE for £91m; there was a transfer of ownership to the bank; and then the bank leased the pipeline back to BGE;

2   BGE deposited the £91m with the bank;

3   the lease rentals were reduced by the capital allowances which the bank obtained by reason of the purchase of the pipeline; and

4   on that basis, the lease rentals paid by BGE matched the deposit receipts received by BGE.

4.133 The House of Lords held that the bank had incurred expenditure of £91m, and what the vendor did with the money received was irrelevant.

4.134 The central principle was stated by Lord Nicholls in these terms:

'[32] The essence of the new approach [*Ramsay*] was to give the statutory provision a purposive construction in order to determine the nature of the transaction to which it was intended to apply and then to decide whether the actual transaction (which might involve considering the overall effect of a number of elements intended to operate together) answered to the statutory description ... however one approaches the matter, the question is always whether the relevant provision of statute, upon its true construction, applies to the facts as found ...

[39] The present case, like *MacNiven*, illustrates the need for a close analysis of what, on a purposive construction, the statute actually requires'

4.135   In *Tower MCashback LLP 1 v R & C Comrs* Lord Walker observed of *BMBF*:

> '[77] One of the lessons of *BMBF* is that it is not enough for HMRC, in attacking a scheme of this sort, to point to the money going round in a circle. Closer analysis is required.'

Of the relationship between *BMBF* and *Ensign Tankers*, Lord Walker stated (at [80]): 'both are good law'.

4.136   In *Strategic Value Master Fund Ltd v Ideal Standard International Acquisition SARL* [2011] EWHC 171 (Ch), a debtor sought to cure a breach of its loan covenants by:

(a)   borrowing €75m from a subsidiary;

(b)   advancing it to its parent ('Topco');

(c)   borrowing the money back from Topco; and

(d)   lending the money back to the subsidiary.

All these transactions took place on the same day, 29 October 2009, and were pre-planned.

4.137   It was held that these steps were sufficient to cure the breach of lending covenants because: (a) the economic effect of the transactions was irrelevant; and (b) the transactions did change the situation of the parties. As Lewison J said at [41]:

> 'The financial position of the Company had indeed changed … The debt that the Company owed to Topco was "additional" debt because (i) the debt did not exist before 29 October 2009, and (ii) the amount of the Company's debt to Topco was greater than its previous debt.'

4.138   What these cases establish is that the circular movement of funds does not matter if the transaction which they effect accords with the statutory description and is not of itself productive of the tax saving claimed.

Synthetic loans

4.139   The priority of legal substance over economic substance is illustrated by the local authority swaps cases.

4.140   Transactions which have the economic structure of a loan can be given the legal form of an interest rate swap. In the 1980s, UK local authorities were subject to restrictions imposed by central government on the amount of money which they could borrow on capital account. They sought to get round these restrictions by raising money off balance sheet through front-loaded interest rate swaps.

4.141 The local authority would make a fixed to floating swap with a bank. The interest rates would be so calculated that the bank would pay less than the commercial rate on its side of the swap. To compensate the local authorities for this, the bank made an up-front payment, so that the subsequent payments by local authorities were made up of repayments of the up-front payment (economically, a loan) and the interest payments under the swap.

Example 4.4

Notional amount of loan £25m for ten years

X pays 5% on £25m fixed and £2.5m up-front. The arm's-length interest rate would have been 7%.

Y pays LIBOR + 2% on the notional principal of £25m.

X and Y set off the periodic payments.

Y has borrowed £2.5m for [(LIBOR + 1%) – 5%] (LIBOR + 2%> 5%)

4.142 Because interest rates rose, local authorities began to make enormous losses under these contracts. The district auditor obtained a declaration that the contracts were unlawful and so not binding on the local authorities, because they had no power to enter into them under *Local Government Act 1972, s 111(1)*. The capital market transactions could not be brought within the councils' borrowing functions: *Hazell v Hammersmith and Fulham LBC* [1991] 1 AC 521.

Economic equivalence

4.143 There is no doctrine of 'economic equivalence', so that transactions which have the economic substance but not the legal form of loans are not treated as lending transactions: 'the mere economic equivalence of a transaction to a loan does not show that it is a loan' (*HSBC Life v Stubbs* [2006] STC (SCD) 9, para 71).

4.144 The Revenue sought to extend the application of the term 'loan relationship' to synthetic debt, ie transactions which have the economic but not legal characteristics of lending. However, these attempts were rejected by the courts: *Griffin (Inspector of Taxes) v Citibank Investments Ltd* [2000] STC 1010 at 1032 (para [20]). Where a floating rate loan is matched by a fixed-to-floating interest rate swap, to produce synthetic fixed rate debt, the derivative will come within the derivative contract rules, but subject to the hedge accounting rules, when recognised for tax purposes.

Trading/non-trading

4.145 The UK tax system distinguishes between profits and losses made from normal trading activities and between profits and losses from non-trading activities. As noted above, all loan relationships are trading or non-trading loan relationships. Trading loan relationships give rise to trading debits and credits, whereas non-trading loan relationships give rise to non-trading debits and credits. The distinction matters, because debits and credits on trading loan relationships simply go into the general computation of trading profits as income or expenses: *CTA 2009, s 297(2), (3)*. The general rules for the relief of trading losses apply. Non-trading debits and credits are separately computed: *s 299*. If they produce a loss (a 'non-trading deficit'), a special scheme of loss relief applies: *ss 300, 456–463*.

Example 4.5

A bank lends money to Company 1 at 8% interest, which Company 1 (a manufacturer) on-lends to Company 2 at 10%. Company 2 requires the money to finance its trade. Company 2 has a trading debit, and has to deduct income tax from the interest it pays to Company 1. Company 1 has a non-trading credit (interest received) and non-trading debit (interest paid to bank). The bank receives interest gross and has a trading credit.

4.146 There is a basic distinction between investment holding companies (non-trading) and investment dealing companies (trading) (see *Rangatira Ltd v New Zealand Comr of Inland Revenue* [1997] STC 47). Interest paid or received under provisions of the Tax Acts (eg interest on tax paid late or underpaid) are non-trading credits and debits on relevant non-lending relationships. All profits and losses from loan relationships arising from mutual trading and mutual insurance business (other than life assurance business) are deemed to be non-trading: *CTA 2009, s 298(3)*.

4.147 It is thus necessary to determine whether a company is party to a relationship:

(a)   wholly for the purposes of a trade;

(b)   wholly other than for the purposes of a trade; or

(c)   partly for the purposes of a trade and partly for other purposes.

The test applies on a loan-by-loan, not a company-by-company, basis.

4.148   A trading company is a company whose business consists wholly or mainly in carrying on a trade or trades. Loan relationship credits will in general only be trading credits if the company is carrying on a financial trade. *Section 298(1)* imposes a narrow test to determine whether creditor loan relationships are trading loan relationships. It says:

> 'For the purposes of this Part, a company is taken to be a party to a creditor relationship for the purposes of a trade it carries on only if it is a party to the relationship in the course of activities forming an integral part of the trade.'

4.149   Only companies carrying on a financial trade are likely to satisfy this test. 'Integral' means 'central to' or 'as its main purpose'. A trading company which also finances subsidiaries is not lending money as an integral part of its trade.

4.150   In *Euroceanica (UK) Ltd v R & C Comrs* [2013] SFTD 1052, a shipping company received interest on two bank deposits it was required to make as part of the financing arrangements for the purchase of new vessels. The question was whether the interest received formed part of the company's 'relevant shipping profits' for the purpose of tonnage tax. The answer to that question depended upon whether the company was party to a creditor loan relationship 'in the course of activities forming an integral part of its trade' within *CTA 2009, s 298(1)* (ex-*FA 1996, s 103(2)*). The Tribunal observed:

> '[57] … It is clearly not the case that only financial traders can treat interest income as trading income …
>
> [58] Our view is that, on the basis of the reasoning in the *Bank Line* case, whatever the nature of the taxpayer's trade (from solicitor, to ship owner, to utilities company), a fund and its related income can be treated as a part of a taxpayer's trading activities to the extent that it is currently actively supporting that trade.'

4.151   On that basis the Tribunal concluded that the interest receipt arose from activities integral to the shipping company's trade. On *Bank Line* see **4.153** below.

4.152   For debtor loan relationships, the test is more general. Interest paid and debtor relationships are regarded as trading items if the obligations under which they are payable are contracted for the purposes of a trade, such as a currency future bought to hedge a specific trading transaction, where hedge accounting is not used.

4.153 Hence, if a company is carrying on a trade (eg insurance) and has to make investments as part of that trade, the income from the investments constitutes trade gains (*Norwich Union Fire Insurance Co v Magee (Surveyor of Taxes)* 3 TC 457 at 460). Income from investments may be included in 'trading income' (*IRC v Imperial Tobacco Co (of Great Britain and Ireland) Ltd* 29 TC 1). In *Bank Line Ltd v IRC* 49 TC 307, Lord Avonside said (at 333):

> 'Income becomes a trading receipt when it arises from capital actively employed and at risk in the business, capital which is employed in the business because it is required for its support or, perhaps, to attract customers looking to the credit of the business. Trading income is "the fruit" of the capital employed in the business in a present and active sense.'

4.154 In the case of insurance companies, investments are not set aside but have to be available at any time to meet the requirements of the business. Hence, such assets are 'capital employed in the business'. In *Liverpool and London and Globe Insurance Co v Bennett* 6 TC 327, it was held that interest on reserve funds of an insurance company invested overseas was not foreign income taxable on a remittance basis but was properly assessable under Schedule D, Case I. This was because it was a fund 'employed and risked in the business'. Fletcher Moulton LJ observed (at 371):

> 'The formation of reserve funds out of the accumulations of premiums or otherwise so as to meet the demands made upon it under its policies is an essential part of the business of such a company, and the dividends from such investments form an integral part of its business profits.'

4.155 Buckley LJ formulated the 'employed and risked in the business' test in these terms (at 374):

> 'The question ... here ... is ... whether the interest and dividends are profits of the business as fruits derived from a fund employed and risked in the business.'

4.156 In *Owen (Inspector of Taxes) v Sassoon* 32 TC 101, a non-resident member of Lloyd's claimed exemption from tax on the income of securities in his Lloyd's trust fund, but this income was held to form part of the profits of his underwriting trade, which was carried on in the UK. Where a trading company keeps money at a bank as working capital, the funds remain circulating capital, and interest on that deposit will be a trading item. However, if it makes a fixed-term deposit, or keeps a deposit on an indefinite basis, or in excess of its working capital requirements, that deposit is likely to be regarded as having been withdrawn from the business.

4.157   The time-honoured 'wholly and exclusively' test of deductibility of trading expenses (*CTA 2009, s 54*) is excluded for loan relationship purposes. Instead, the 'unallowable purposes' rule applies: see **6.153– 6.183**. Apportionment of items between trading/non-trading is permitted. In *Consolidated Investment and Enterprise Ltd v Income Tax Comr* [1996] STC 288, the Privy Council considered the correct way of allocating interest charges between trading and non-trading income. In a composite business, interest expenses and income will be pooled, and then allocated *pro rata* to the various types of expense or receipt.

4.158   The distinction between trading and non-trading is a mixed question of fact and law:

'These questions between capital and income, trading profits and non-trading profits, are questions which, though they may depend to a very great extent on the particular facts of each case, do involve a conclusion of law to be drawn from those facts.' (*Davies (Inspector of Taxes) v Shell Co of China Ltd* (1951) 32 TC 133, per Jenkins LJ at 151)

4.159   The essential questions to answer, in deciding whether an item falls on the trading or non-trading side of the line, are:

(a)   what type of company is involved?

(b)   if a loan relationship is involved, is it a debtor or a creditor relationship?

(c)   what is the object of the expenditure: trade finance or investment?

(d)   by virtue of what entitlement is interest paid or receivable?

(e)   where applicable, is the transaction a hedging transaction, and what is the item hedged?

4.160   In order to be 'in the nature of trade', a transaction has to have the 'badges of trade'. These were familiarly identified in para 116 of the Final Report of the Royal Commission on the Taxation of Income and Profits (1955) as:

(a)   the subject matter of realisation;

(b)   length of period of ownership;

(c)   frequency or number of similar transactions;

(d)   supplementary work on or in connection with the property realised;

(e)   the circumstances responsible for the realisation; and

(f)   motive.

4.161   In *Marson (Inspector of Taxes) v Morton* (1986) 59 TC 381, at 391–392, these were alternatively summarised as:

(a)   whether or not a one-off transaction;

(b)   transaction related to a trade which the taxpayer otherwise carries on;

(c)   nature of the subject matter;

(d)   way in which the transaction was carried on;

(e)   source of finance;

(f)   enhancement work;

(g)   whether or not broken down into lots;

(h)   intentions at the time of purchase; and

(i)   did the item purchased provide enjoyment for the purchaser?

4.162   In the leading case on trading/non-trading, it was held that:

> '"Trade" cannot be precisely defined, but certain characteristics can be identified which trade normally has ... Sometimes the question ... becomes a matter of degree, of frequency, of organisation, even of intention, and in such cases it is for the fact-finding body to decide on the evidence whether a line is passed.' (*Ransom (Inspector of Taxes) v Higgs* [1974] STC 539 at 554)

4.163   Where there is any element of ambiguity, motivation will be relevant (*Iswera v IRC (Ceylon)* [1965] 1 WLR 663).

4.164   The trading/non-trading distinction has been reviewed in *Clarke (Inspector of Taxes) v British Telecom Pension Scheme* [2000] STC 222, where the transactions in question (sub-underwriting undertaken by pension schemes trustees) were held to have been 'habitual, organised, for reward, extensive and business-like'. These characteristics would normally have established the character of the transactions as trading. However, the finding of the Special Commissioners that the sub-underwriting 'formed an integral part of the investment process and took its colour therefrom' was upheld by the Court of Appeal.

4.165   For an investment company, all loan relationship items will be non-trading. Investment companies receive the bulk of their income from holding investments. Holding companies are investment companies, and they are not regarded as holding the shares in subsidiaries as trading stock. Indeed, it is not possible to have any group (or consortium) where shares are held on trading account.

4.166   To determine whether a company is a trading or investment company, its business has to be examined over a reasonable period of time. In *FPH Finance Trust Ltd v IRC* 26 TC 131, a company carried on a general financial business as a trader. It had income from investments and from its trade. It suffered losses and, after 15 months, was put into liquidation. The question was whether it was a trading or an investment company in the period preceding the liquidation. The House of Lords held that the question must be answered by looking at the nature of the company's activities by reference to its yearly results over a period of years. Lord Atkin (at 151) observed:

'The opposite view that a company, while still continuing its ordinary trading, may be an investment company one year and a non-investment company the next, popping in and out of the Inland Revenue pigeon-holes as trade was bad or good, seems to me inconsistent with the language used and from a business point of view to be deprecated.'

4.167   The trading/non-trading issue becomes problematic:

(a)   where a trading company makes non-trade investments;

(b)   where a trading company receives income from non-trade investments;

(c)   where a trading company borrows for a purpose not connected with its trade, eg as a means of financing a subsidiary; or

(d)   in the case of hybrid companies, such as a trading company with foreign subsidiaries, which will be considered as both a trading and an investment company. As companies maintain a general pool of borrowing, which is retired and refreshed for a combination of reasons, it is often difficult to identify borrowing with a specific purpose.

4.168   Normally, there will be little advantage in having interest chargeable as trading rather than investment income. However, where there are unrelieved trading losses, *CTA 2010, s 46* allows 'interest or dividends on investments which would fall to be taken into account as trading receipts in computing ... trading income but for the fact that they have been subjected to tax under other provisions' to be set against the trading loss. In *Bank Line v IRC* 49 TC 307, a shipping company established a replacement fund to meet the costs of replacement of its ships, and claimed that the interest on these funds was trading income. The claim was rejected for reasons explained by Lord Cameron (at 325):

> 'there is ... a material difference between such investments and the investment of funds which are or can be at call to meet the current demands of the trading activity carried on by the Company. In the latter case the fruit of the investment may fairly be categorised as a trading receipt – a receipt arising out of the use of the capital held as available in the relevant period to meet the fluctuating demands of the trade or business.'

4.169 In *Nuclear Electric plc v Bradley (Inspector of Taxes)* [1996] STC 405, Nuclear Electric's business was generating electricity. Each year, an accrual was made in respect of back-end costs (storing and reprocessing of fuel for reuse and disposal of radioactive waste). The amounts accrued were an allowable deduction in computing trading profits. The sums so accrued were invested and the investments produced income. The question was whether the investment income was trading income. In the Court of Appeal Millett LJ said that 'the nature of the trade must be such that it can fairly be said that the making and holding of investments at interest is an integral part of the trade' ([1995] STC 1125 at 1139–1140). The House of Lords held that the investment income was not trading income, because the investments arose from a voluntary decision of the company to withdraw the sums from the business, and the investments were not actively employed in the trade. It was a 'segregated reserve fund'. Lord Jauncey stated (at 411):

> 'Although NE [Nuclear Electric] had incurred a liability to make future payment it was no more obliged to set up a fund to meet this liability than were the shipowners [in *Bank Line* 49 TC 307]. However, having done so, NE during the year of assessment neither used the fund for this purpose nor employed it in any other way in the business of generating electricity. Whether income from investments held by a business is trading income must ultimately depend upon the nature of the business and the purpose for which the fund is held. At one end of the scale are insurance companies and banks part of whose business is the making and holding of investments to meet current liabilities ... At the other end of the scale are businesses of which the making and holding of investments form no part ... the business of NE [Nuclear Electric] was to produce and supply electricity. The making of investments was neither an integral nor any part of its business. Furthermore the investments ... were in no sense employed in the business of producing electricity during the year of assessment.'

4.170 By contrast, the income which a travel agent obtains by investing funds received from customers until payment is made to suppliers (airlines, hotels, etc) will be trading income, because the earnings of such income are an essential part of the business of a travel agent. The same applies to commission paid to traders by finance companies when goods are sold under credit arrangements provided by the finance company. It also applies to interest received by jewellers on cash deposits held by them to enable them to purchase stock.

4.171   In BIM40805 HMRC states that in the case of ordinary trading companies interest on an investment may be treated as trading income if:

(a)   the investment is short term,

(b)   it is an integral feature of the trading activity to make and hold such an investment,

(c)   the funds remain employed in the business in the year of assessment and are not withdrawn from the business.

Trading in a tax avoidance context

4.172   The test of trading is objective. In the dividend-stripping cases, the Revenue argued that a transaction of this type (1) did not form part of the company's trade of dealing in shares; and (2) did not produce a trading loss. The question was, could you look through the transaction to find that it had a fiscal (non-trading) purpose? In *JP Harrison (Watford) Ltd v Griffiths (Inspector of Taxes)* 40 TC 281, it was held that you could not. In *Harrison*, Lord Guest said (at 304):

> 'The test is an objective one. The question to be asked is not quo animo was the transaction entered into, but what in fact was done by the Company … one has to look at the transaction by itself irrespective of the object, irrespective of the fiscal consequences'

4.173   In *Finsbury Securities Ltd v Bishop (Inspector of Taxes)* 43 TC 591 and *Lupton (Inspector of Taxes) v FA and AB Ltd* 47 TC 580, the opposite conclusion was reached.

4.174   In *Lupton*, Megarry J observed in a classic formulation that a transaction which was solely designed to achieve a tax advantage could not be trading (at 597–598):

> 'A trading transaction … is not deprived of its trading nature merely by the presence of a fiscal motive for carrying it out, nor by the fact that as a trading transaction it makes a loss and not a profit … At the other extreme lies the transaction that is far removed from trading, designed to secure a tax advantage … The question is whether, viewed as a whole, the transaction is one which can fairly be regarded as a trading

transaction. If it is, then it will not be denatured merely because it was entered into with motives of reaping a fiscal advantage.'

4.175 Lord Morris said at 625 that one had to consider 'the reality of the matter':

'My Lords, the various arrangements are not to be regarded as sham transactions. They were as real as they were elaborate. But I cannot think that there is room for doubt that they were no more than devices which were planned and contrived to effect the avowed purpose of tax avoidance. ... That was the reality of the matter.'

4.176 In *Lupton* 47 TC 580 Lord Denning distinguished at 605 in the Court of Appeal between a 'trade' and a 'tax recovery device':

'If the transaction is in truth a transaction in the nature of trade, it does not cease to be so simply because the trader had in mind a tax advantage. But if it is in truth a tax-recovery device and nothing else, then it remains a tax-recovery device notwithstanding that it is clothed in the trappings of a trade.

4.177 Lord Morris echoed this in the House of Lords at 620:

'It is manifest that some transactions may be so affected or inspired by fiscal considerations that the shape and character of the transaction is no longer that of a trading transaction. The result will be, not that a trading transaction with unusual features is revealed, but that there is an arrangement or scheme which cannot fairly be regarded as being a transaction in the trade of dealing in shares.'

Chapter 5

Loan Relationships: General Computational Provisions

Overview

5.1 This chapter deals with:

- Debits and credits

- Related transactions

- Computation of taxable profits

- Amortised cost basis

- Fair value basis

- Adjustments of change of accounting basis

Debits and credits

5.2 The central structural principle of the loan relationship rules is that of symmetry. In other words, every debit of 100 in the debtor should be matched by a credit of 100 in the creditor, and vice versa. To that end the distinction between income and capital was abolished, and an all-income accruals approach adopted. This resulted in the costs of debt finance being wholly untaxed in the borrower and wholly taxed in the lender. The widespread use of SSAP 20 hedging extended the symmetry concept into derivative contracts.

5.3 This principle gives rise to three general rules which apply for the loan relationship rules:

(a) 'all income treatment', ie all items which come within these rules are treated as arising on revenue account, not capital account;

(b) tax follows the accounts, ie the taxable profit is based on the accounting profit; and

(c) the loan relationship rules constitute an exclusive and self-contained code for the taxation of items falling within their scope.

5.4 *Finance (No 2) Act 2015, Sch 7* introduced wide-ranging changes which took effect for accounting periods beginning on or after 1 January 2016. *Finance Act 2016* made further changes, which mostly took effect from 1 April 2016, but in some cases took effect from an earlier date.

5.5 Hence, the loan relationship rules in *CTA 2009, Parts 5 (Loan Relationships) and 6 (Relationships treated as loan relationships)* are an accounting-based regime whereby the GAAP-compliant commercial accounts of the individual company are the basis for determining the amounts to be brought into account for tax purposes. The scheme of the computational provisions is to aggregate credits and debits as trading profits or non-trading income. The aggregation of non-trading items takes in non-trading foreign exchange and financial instruments losses. The scheme is:

	Trading	*Non-trading*
Aggregate credits	Trading income	Non-trading income
Aggregate debits	Trading expenses	Non-trading deficit

5.6 For accounting purposes a debit is an expense or an asset; a credit is a receipt or a liability. The loan relationship rules only use the terms in the meaning which they have in income statements. Hence a credit is income, an increase in an asset or a decrease in a liability; a debit is an expense, a decrease in an asset or an increase in a liability. For accounting periods beginning on or after 1 January 2016 only debits and credits which appear in profit or loss account are taken into account for tax purposes. Items which are recognised only in the Other Comprehensive Income (OCI) are only taken into account for tax purposes when either (i) they are recycled to the income statement (reclassified to profit or loss, IAS 1, eg a revaluation surplus), or (ii) the loan relationship is derecognised: *CTA 2009, s 320A*. The same applies to items which only appear in the SOCIE (which includes total comprehensive income) or the balance sheet. This corresponds with the tax principle that all profits and losses on loan relationships and related transactions are treated as income items ('all income' approach). Examples of items taken to OCI which may later be recycled to profit and loss are:

- investments classified as available for sale,

- cash flow hedges,

- own credit spread under IFRS 9.

5.7 All profits and losses on loan relationships which go through the income statement come within the corporation tax rules. The legislation does not distinguish between capital and income, but instead an 'all income' treatment is adopted. This includes 'profits or losses of a capital nature', eg profits on certain types of discount and debt write-offs. *CTA 2009, s 295(1)* says:

> 'The general rule for corporation tax purposes is that all profits arising to a company from its loan relationships are chargeable to tax as income'

5.8 This is elaborated in *s 293(3)*, which states that:

> '(3) Except where the context indicates otherwise, in this Part references to profits or losses from loan relationships include references to profits or losses of a capital nature.'

Hence the loan relationship rules exclude the rule on the non-deductibility of capital expenses: *CTA 2009, s 297(4)*.

5.9 The loan relationship rules bring into account 'debits' and 'credits', which include exchange differences. All income and profits on loan relationships are 'credits'. All expenses and losses on loan relationships are 'debits'. *CTA 2009, s 296* says:

> 'Profits and deficits arising to a company from its loan relationships are to be calculated using the credits and debits given by this Part.'

5.10 In the application of the loan relationship rules, the following terminology is adopted:

	Term	*Meaning*	*CTA 2009*
(a)	Credits	Receipts of trade	*s 297(2)*
		Non-trading credits	*s 301(2)(a)*
(b)	Debits	Expenses of trade	*s 297(3)*
		Non-trading debits	*s 301(2)(b)*
(c)	Non-trading deficit	Excess of non-trading debits over non-trading credits	*s 300(1)*
(d)	Deficit period	Accounting period in which non-trading deficit is incurred	*s 456(2)*
(e)	Creditor relationship	Asset	*s 302(5)*
(f)	Debtor relationship	Liability	*s 302(6)*
(g)	Exchange gains or exchange losses	Profits or gains which arise as a result of comparing at different times the expression in one currency of the whole or some part of the valuation put by the company in another currency of an asset or liability of the company, or losses which so arise	*s 475*

Example 5.1

A Ltd receives interest of 100 on a loan to B Ltd.

A's accounting entries are:

DR Cash   100   CR Interest   100

B's accounting entries are:

DR Interest   100   CR Cash   100

These are the same items which go into the tax computation.

Accountings periods beginning on or after 1 January 2016

5.11   For accounting periods beginning on or after 1 January 2016, *CTA 2009, s 306A* defines the amounts which are brought into charge to tax ('the s 306A amounts'). These are income (*s 306A(1)*) and expenses (*s 306A(2)*):

> '(1)   The matters in respect of which amounts are to be brought into account for the purposes of this Part in respect of a company's loan relationships are –
>
> > (a)   profits and losses of the company that arise to it from its loan relationships and related transactions (excluding interest or expenses),
> >
> > (b)   interest under those relationships, and
> >
> > (c)   expenses incurred by the company under or for the purpose of those relationships and transactions.'

5.12   Profits and losses on loan relationships include profits and losses arising on the acquisition and disposal of loan relationships, which are called 'related transactions' in the legislation. *Section 293* says:

> '(1)   In this Part references to profits or losses from loan relationships include references to profits or losses from related transactions.'

5.13   'Related transaction' in relation to a loan relationship is defined in *s 304* as the acquisition, transfer or disposal of a loan relationship:

> '(1)   In this Part "related transactions", in relation to a loan relationship, means any disposal or acquisition (in whole or in part) of rights or liabilities under the relationship.

(2) For this purpose the cases where there is taken to be such a disposal and acquisition include those where rights or liabilities under the loan relationship are transferred or extinguished by any sale, gift, exchange, surrender, redemption or release.'

5.14 Hence, the novation, assignment or release of a loan relationship will be a 'related transaction'. The definition of related transaction does not cover the case where a company becomes party to a loan relationship. When a contract is novated, the original agreement is discharged and replaced by a new agreement between different parties. Novation is a mechanism whereby the burden of a contract can be transferred to another party. This is in contrast to assignment, which can be used to transfer rights but not liabilities.

5.15 Expenses incurred when entering into or disposing of loan relationships are deductible as debits, if they are incurred directly (*s 306A(2)*):

'(a) in bringing any of the loan relationships into existence,

(b) in entering into or giving effect to any of the related transactions,

(c) in making payments under any of those relationships or as a result of any of those transactions, or

(d) in taking steps to ensure the receipt of payments under any of those relationships or in accordance with any of those transactions.'

5.16 The former requirement (in *CTA 2009, s 307(3)* (repealed)) that the credits and debits brought into account should 'fairly represent' the profits and losses on loan relationships is removed, so strengthening the importance of the commercial accounts for tax purposes (see **5.29–5.35**).

5.17 *Section 308* changes the law by providing that amounts recognised in determining a company's profit or loss on loan relationships are limited to those items which pass through profit and loss account ('recognised in the company's accounts for the period as an item of profit or loss': *s 308(1)*). Hence items taken to OCI, which would previously have been taken into account for computing profits and losses on loan relationships, do not now affect the tax computation. *Section 321* (amounts directly recognised in equity) is accordingly repealed.

5.18 Amounts recognised as items of OCI are recognised for tax purposes in two situations:

(a) when subsequently transferred ('recycled') to profit and loss account: *s 308(1A)*;

(b) where in an accounting period beginning on or after 1 January 2016 an amount is recognised in OCI but not transferred to profit and loss, and

141

that amount is later derecognised without having been recycled to profit and loss, or there is no expectation that it will be transferred to profit and loss, it is recognised as a debit or credit for tax purposes at the time of derecognition or deemed derecognition by virtue of a recapture rule: *s 320A*.

5.19   Legal costs, issue costs, commitment fees to banks for keeping open a line of credit, guarantee fees and termination costs will be deductible. Thus, the expense of obtaining a guarantee from a parent for the issue of loan stock is deductible. In *Hoechst Finance Ltd v Gumbrell (Inspector of Taxes)* [1985] STC 150, such a cost was held not to be an expense of management. However, legal fees are a borderline category. If, in accounting for fixed-term debt, expenses are deducted from the money borrowed, effectively relief on an accruals basis will be obtained for the expenses of raising the finance. The Inland Revenue's views on the scope of 'expenses' were set out in *Tax Bulletin*, Issue 25, October 1996, 356–357. It is there suggested that only charges and expenses directly incurred will be deductible, and those costs will have to be spread over the period of the loan relationship, rather than taken up-front.

Example 5.2

A company issues £1 shares for £20, the subscription price is to be satisfied by (a) a payment of £1, and (b) an undertaking by the subscriber to guarantee a bank loan to the company of £19. The company charges £19 to the profit and loss account as the cost of the guarantee. This is a loan relationship debit.

5.20   As far as investment companies are concerned, the loan relationships deductions take precedence over 'management expenses'.

5.21   In *Sun Life Assurance Society v Davidson (Inspector of Taxes)* 37 TC 330, it was held that stamp duties and brokerage charges incurred on the acquisition of investments formed part of the acquisition costs and were not therefore deductible as management expenses. The 'severability' test of deductibility was formulated by Lord Reid (at 360):

'It seems to me more reasonable to ask, with regard to a payment, whether it should be regarded as part of the cost of acquisition, on the one hand, or, on the other hand, something severable from the cost of acquisition which can only properly be regarded as an expense of management.'

5.22   In *Camas plc v Atkinson (Inspector of Taxes)* [2004] STC 860, an investment company incurred professional costs of £583,495 in investigating a merger which did not take place. It claimed a revenue deduction for the expenditure as an expense of management. The Court of Appeal held that: (1) the costs of investigating an acquisition were deductible expenses of management, because they formed part of the decision-making process as to whether or not to make an acquisition; and (2) the distinction between revenue and capital expenditure was not relevant in this context.

5.23   Expenses incurred on transactions which do not reach fulfilment ('abortive expenditure') are deductible: *CTA 2009, s 329*.

Commercial accounts and statutory overrides

5.24   The 'general rule' that tax follows the accounts is stated in *CTA 2009, s 313(1)* in these terms:

'(1)   The general rule is that the amounts to be brought into account by a company as credits and debits for any period for the purposes of this Part may be determined on any basis of accounts that is in accordance with generally accepted accounting practice.'

5.25   This is largely repeated in *s 307(2)*, which says that the amounts to be taken into account are those which go into the computation of the company's annual profit or loss:

'(2)   The general rule is that the amounts to be brought into account by a company as credits and debits for any period of account for the purposes of this Part in respect of the matters mentioned in section 306A(1) are those which are recognised in determining the company's profit or loss for the period in accordance with generally accepted accounting practice.'

5.26   The amounts recognised are restricted to those which enter the profit and loss account. *Section 308(1)* says:

'(1)   References in this Part to an amount recognised in determining a company's profit or loss for a period are references to an amount that is recognised in the company's accounts for the period as an item of profit or loss.'

5.27   Amounts recognised in OCI and later recycled to profit and loss are brought into charge when reclassified. This is provided for by *ss 308(1A), (1B)*:

'(1A) The references in subsection (1) to an amount recognised in the company's accounts for the period as an item of profit or loss includes a reference to an amount that–

(a)   was previously recognised as an amount of other comprehensive income, and

> (b) is transferred to become an item of profit or loss in determining the company's profit or loss for the period.'

Under *s 310*, the Treasury has power by regulation to modify the effect of *s 308(1)*.

5.28 *CTA 2009, s 313(1)* is subject to *s 313(2)*. *Section 313(2)* contains an extensive list of statutory overrides, ie departures from the commercial accounts. The list comprises:

(a) *ss 311, 312* (derecognition rules);

(b) *s 349(2)* (connected party loan relationships);

(c) *s 382(2)* (company partners using fair value accounting);

(d) *s 399(2)* (fair valued index-linked gilts);

(e), (f) [repealed]

(g) *s 482(3)* (discounts from a relevant non-lending relationship (RNLR)); and

(h) *s 490(3)* (holdings in collective investment schemes (CISs)).

Thus the principle that 'tax follows the accounts' is heavily qualified.

5.29 Prior to its repeal for accounting periods beginning on or after 1 January 2016, *CTA 2009, s 307(3)* referred to the amounts to be taxed as those which 'fairly represent' the profits and losses of the company. HMRC regarded the word 'fairly' as authorising a departure from the commercial accounts, when this is necessary to secure the 'correct' tax result. In *DCC Holdings (UK) Ltd v R & C Comrs* [2011] STC 326, the meaning of the words 'fairly represent' was considered by the courts. The facts of that case are as follows:

1 A repo is a sale of security by the original holder to an interim holder. The original holder receives cash, and the interim holder becomes owner of the securities. The arrangement constitutes a secured loan. When the loan is due for repayment, cash (repurchase price) is paid by the original holder to the interim holder and the securities are transferred by the interim holder to the original holder. In net-paying repo, the interim holder is entitled to retain interest received on the securities while the arrangement subsists and the repurchase price is adjusted to take account of this.

2 DCC entered into net-paying repos. It bought gilts for £812.2m, received a coupon of £28.8m and resold the gilts after 18.5 days for £785.2m.

3 *ICTA 1988, s 737A(5)* said that, on a net-paying repo, the difference between the purchase price and the repurchase price was to be treated as a payment (or receipt) of manufactured interest and added (or subtracted)

from the repurchase price. Thus, the repurchase price was increased to (785.2 + 28.8m) = £814m.

4   The difference of (814 – 812.2m =) 1.8m was treated by *s 730A* as interest received.

5   *FA 1997, s 97* said that a payment of manufactured interest was to be treated as a payment of real interest.

6   The accounting treatment under FRS 5, Application Note B treated the repo as a secured loan for 18.5 days. DCC argued that under the repo rules it had a credit of £1.8m, and under the loan relationship rules it had a debit of £28.8m.

5.30   In the Supreme Court, Lord Walker identified the key issue at [25] as being whether the words 'fairly represent' could be stretched, or needed to be stretched, 'in order to avoid the absurd result of DCC's deemed income receipt in respect of the coupon being different from its deemed interest payment as a borrower which is party to a loan relationship'. He deplored 'the absurdity of that asymmetrical result'.

5.31   He continued:

'[26] In my opinion the need for a symmetrical solution lies at the heart of this appeal … the deemed income flows … are intended to have a self-cancelling effect'

5.32   Having regard to the accountancy evidence, he pointed out that only a small part of the interest would have accrued during the period of repo (£2.9m). The deemed payment only related to that element, not the entirety of the coupon actually received:

'[43] If the credit from an actual relationship under which DCC is a creditor is a time-apportioned sum, the debit under a hypothetical relationship under which DCC is a debtor making a payment representative of interest must also be a time-apportioned sum … The language of *s 84(1)* [*FA 1996, CTA 2009, s 307(3)*] is in my view amply wide enough to enable this to be done, and unless it is done, the subsection's requirements of fair representation cannot be satisfied … on the accruals basis mandated by *s 84(1)* … both the credit and the debit should be £2.9m'

Thus the 'fairly represent' requirement was held impliedly to override the repo legislation which had been enacted earlier.

5.33   A remarkable example of the disregard of GAAP-compliant accounts for tax purposes was provided by *GDF Suez Teeside Ltd v R & C Comrs* [2015] UKFTT 413 (TC). It was held that a profit which was not recognised for accounting purposes should be recognised for tax purposes. The circumstances were:

1   Teeside Power Limited (TPL) built, owned and operated an electricity generating plant. It entered into long-term contracts with ENRON for the supply of electricity. ENRON became insolvent, leaving TPL as an unsecured creditor. The value of TP's claims in the administration ('the Claims') was estimated at £200m.

2   The administrator of ENRON issued letters which constituted an instrument representing a monetary debt in the form of TPL's Claims. The debt constituted a deemed loan relationship.

3   TPL assigned the Claims to a Jersey subsidiary TRAIL in consideration of the issue of new shares in TRAIL. TPL did not recognise a profit, because where assets are exchanged for shares in a subsidiary there is no real gain. TRAIL did not recognise an asset because the Claims were a contingent asset.

4   TPL was assessed to corporation tax on the basis that it has disposed of a loan relationship for a profit of £200m.

5.34   The First-tier Tribunal (Tax Chamber) held that TPL's accounts were GAAP-compliant ([134]) and HMRC's proposed accounting treatment was not GAAP-compliant ([140]). Notwithstanding this, the Tribunal held that the 'fairly represents' override allowed the Revenue to tax a profit which was not recognised in the accounts:

> '153. Following this logic we have concluded that the £200m of profit should be recognised by TPL in the accounting period when the Claims were transferred to TRAIL despite the fact that no profit was recognised for accounting purposes ... It was accepted by Mr Wild [TPL] that the gains would be recognised by TPL when payments were made in respect of the Claims through the revaluation of the TRAIL shares, [or] when TRAIL distributed its profits or when TPL disposed of the TRAIL shares.'

It is very difficult to understand how any process of 'logic' can lead to this conclusion.

5.35   For accounting periods beginning on or after 1 January 2016, the 'fairly represents' override was repealed and replaced by a new, targeted, anti-avoidance rule in *CTA 2009, ss 455B–455D*.

Derecognition

5.36   In certain circumstances where assets and liabilities are matched, GAAP may permit or require the whole or part of those assets and liabilitites to be derecognised, eg an interest receipt may be matched with a dividend payment.

5.37 In certain cases, amounts not recognised for accounting purposes are recognised for tax purposes. Where credits on a creditor relationship are not brought into account, or not fully brought into account, for accounting purposes, they must be brought into account for tax purposes under *CTA 2009, ss 311, 312. Section 311* reads:

'(1) Section 312 applies for the purpose of determining the credits and debits which a company is to bring into account for a period for the purposes of this Part in the following case.

(2) The case is where–

(a) the company is, or is treated as, a party to a creditor relationship in the period, and

(b) as a result of tax avoidance arrangements to which the company is at any time a party, an amount is (in accordance with generally accepted accounting practice) not fully recognised for the period in respect of the creditor relationship.

...

(6) For the purposes of this section and section 312 an amount is not fully recognised for a period in respect of a relationship of a company, if–

(a) no amount in respect of the relationship is recognised in determining its profit or loss for the period, or

(b) an amount is so recognised in respect of only part of the relationship.

(7) For the purpose of this section arrangements are "tax avoidance arrangements" if the main purpose, or one of the main purposes, of any party to the arrangement, in entering into them, is to obtain a tax advantage.

(8) In subsection (7) "arrangements" includes any arrangements, scheme or understanding of any kind, whether or not legally enforceable, involving a single transaction, or two or more transactions'

5.38 The rule is that credits in respect of the creditor relationship which would otherwise not be brought into account must be brought into account for tax purposes. Additional credits are computed under *s 311(1)* on the basis that full credits and debits under the creditor and debtor relationship are brought into account, but the additional debits must not exceed the additional credits. In other words, *ss 311* and *312* operate as a snake but not as a ladder.

5.39 'Tax avoidance arrangements' are defined as arrangements whose 'main purpose or one of the main purposes' of which is the avoidance of tax. If a transaction with a non-fiscal purpose also saves tax, it is not a tax avoidance arrangement.

5.40 The same rule applies for debits on loan relationships, provided that the debit recognised for tax purposes does not exceed the credit recognised for tax purposes in respect of the same loan relationship: *CTA 2009, s 312(1A), (1B)*.

Example 5.3

Parent Ltd subscribes 1,000 for 10% preference shares in its subsidiary, S Ltd. S Ltd lends P Ltd 1,000 at 10%. Under IAS 32 the preference shares are classified as liabilities. For accounts purposes, S Ltd's payment and receipt of 100 are offset. For tax purposes, P Ltd must bring in a credit of 100.

Loan relationships in wrappers

5.41 In general, a company must be legally a party to a loan relationship to be taxable in respect of it. Where *CTA 2009, ss 330A, 607A* apply, a company may be subject to tax in respect of a loan relationship (or derivative contract) to which it is not in law a party. *Section 330A* applies where a company is exposed to the risks and rewards of a loan relationship, though not formally a party to it. *Section 330A* is unusual in that (i) it looks through connected companies, and (ii) it is the sole situation in which an individual may hold a loan relationship.

5.42 The situations where this may apply are:

(a) repo and stock lending transactions (hence *CTA 2009, ss 331, 332* are repealed);

(b) securitisations, where beneficial ownership is transferred by the originator but legal title is retained (as in mortgage securitisations);

(c) structured finance arrangements.

5.43 In all these situations there are parallel provisions which apply to the same subject matter:

(a) the repo legislation in *CTA 2009, ss 542–559*;

(b) the special regime for securitisations in *CTA 2010, s 623* and the *Taxation of Securities Companies Regulations 2006, SI 2006/3296*;

(c) the structured finance arrangements in *CTA 2010, ss 752–774*.

Sections 330A–330C are intended to be a fall-back, where these more specialised provisions do not apply.

Debt releases

5.44   Debt contracts will ordinarily be wholly executed on the creditor's side and remain executory on the part of the debtor. In that case in order to be released from further obligations the debtor will have to prove release by deed or some consideration agreed by the other party ('accord and satisfaction') in place of his existing obligation or in addition to it. A release not by deed which is executed on one side only will operate as a discharge if the other party agrees to accept some other or additional consideration in return for the right which he gives up. If a bank agrees to accept a payment of 500 to discharge a loan of 1,000, the debtor provides consideration for this purpose.

5.45   It is an absolute principle that a debtor records a liability until there is a formal waiver of the debt. If the lender writes off the receivable in its own books, this does not lead to a release of liability in the books of the debtor. If the creditor goes further and releases the debtor from the whole or part of his obligation to repay the loan, the debtor has to bring in a corresponding credit in the profit and loss account. IAS 39, paras 39, 41 say, with regard to derecognition of a financial liability:

> '39. An entity shall remove a financial liability (or a part of a financial liability) from its balance sheet when, and only when, it is extinguished – ie when the obligation specified in the contract is discharged or cancelled or expires.
>
> 41. The difference between the carrying amount of a financial liability (or part of a financial liability) extinguished or transferred to another party and the consideration paid, including any non-cash assets transferred to liability assumed, shall be recognised in the profit and loss.'

5.46   The terms 'release' and 'waiver' relate to circumstances where a company relinquishes, or forbears to enforce, rights that it has against another party. The variation of a bilateral contract by mutual agreement is often described as 'waiver'. The essence of release (waiver) of a debt is that it is a gratuitous transaction: in accounts terms, the creditor gains nothing in return. It is the opposite of 'discharge', whereby the debtor performs an act which in law constitutes payment of the debt.

5.47   'Release', properly defined, is simply one form of impairment loss. The effect of a release is to reduce the liabilities of the debtor, without any corresponding performance by the debtor. Accordingly, 'release' is used in the legislation in the legal sense of a transaction which exonerates a debtor, without payment, from the whole or part of his liability.

5.48   In the legislation, 'release' is used as a portmanteau term to cover a number of concepts:

1   A *variation* of a contract is an agreed alteration of the terms of an existing contract, falling short of the repeal of the existing contract and substitution of a new one (*Morris v Baron & Co* [1918] AC 1 at 25–26; *British and Beningtons Ltd v North Western Cachar Tea Co Ltd* [1923] AC 48 at 62; *IRC v Eurocopy* [1991] STC 707).

2   A *waiver* is the abandonment of a legal right. In *Banning v Wright* 48 TC 421, Lord Hailsham LC stated (at 450):

   'The primary meaning of the word "waiver" is the abandonment of a right in such a way that the other party is entitled to plead the abandonment by way of confession and avoidance if the right is thereafter asserted.'

   In the same case, Lord Simon said (at 460) that:

   '"waiver" signifies the relinquishment of anything which one has the right to expect.'

   If a company agrees to accept a smaller amount in discharge of a debt due to a company, this will also not be binding, unless an element of consideration can be found, or the waiver is binding in equity, eg as a 'promissory estoppel' (*Central London Property Trust Ltd v High Trees House Ltd* [1956] 1 All ER 256n).

3   A *release* is the discharge or renunciation of a claim, which may take a number of forms: *Chitty on Contracts* (31st edn, Sweet & Maxwell, 2012) Vol 1, paras 22-001–22-012. A voluntary release by a company of a debt, or part of a debt, by deed will be a rare occurrence. A waiver is not binding as such, because it is not supported by consideration. It has been said that 'a compromise is a release of claims for valuable consideration and in the case of a release there is no such consideration' (*Bank of Credit and Commerce International SA v Ali* [1999] 2 All ER 1005 per Lightman J).

4   In *Collins v Addies* [1991] STC 445, [1992] STC 746 it was held that, in the case of a novation of a debt, full payment could constitute release. Nourse LJ observed (at 749):

   '"release" does not include any transaction which either consists of or amounts to a repayment of the loan, even if the transaction, when viewed in isolation, might be said to have the effect of releasing the debtor from his obligation to repay the loan ... The limitation ... is not one which excludes a novation, being a transaction which does not enable the company to recover the money.'

5   An *accord and satisfaction* is an agreement between two persons, one of whom has a right of action against the other that the right will be satisfied by a stipulated action of the other. A debt-equity swap is an example of an accord and satisfaction. Confession and avoidance is a pleading which admits the truth of a fact alleged in the preceding pleadings, but seeks to avoid its effect by alleging some new matter.

6   A bad debt is a debt which is due but which the creditor recognises is unpayable or unenforceable.

7   An impairment is a recognition in accounts that a debt is or may become bad.

Example 5.4

A Ltd lends B Ltd £50,000 for ten years at 6%.

1   At the end of Year 2, interest rates have risen, and B agrees to pay 8%. This is a variation.

2   In Year 4, B only pays interest at 7%, and A indicates that he will not sue for the balance of interest. This is a waiver.

3   In Year 8, A agrees in writing that £10,000 of the debt may be treated as discharged. This is a release.

4   In Year 9, A concludes that B is unlikely to pay the debt in full and he writes it down by £10,000.

5   At the end of Year 10, B fails to pay, and A has to write off arrears of interest and £10,000 of the loan. This is a bad debt.

6   Alternatively, B issues A shares in satisfaction of A's debt. This is accord and satisfaction.

5.49   Accordingly, in the case of the debtor, if a contractual obligation to pay a liability is extinguished, eg by release, the liability must be derecognised and a corresponding amount recognised in the income statement. The amount recognised in the income statement will accordingly enter into the loan relationship credits of the debtor, except in the case of connected company debt.

5.50   It is central to the operation of the loan relationship rules that release credits and release debits are not recognised for tax purposes in the case of connected companies' loan relationships. This is considered in **Chapter 6**.

Accounting bases

5.51   The two accounting methods recognised by IFRS and FRS are 'amortised cost basis of accounting' and 'fair value accounting', both of which are defined in *CTA 2009, s 313.*

5.52   *Section 313(4)* says:

> 'In this Part "amortised cost basis of accounting" in relation to a company's loan relationships means a basis of accounting under which an asset or liability representing the loan relationship is measured in the company's balance sheet at its amortised cost using the effective interest rate method, but with that amortised cost being adjusted as necessary where the loan relationship is the hedged item under a designated fair value hedge.'

5.53   *Section 313(4A), (7)* provide that 'amortised cost', 'effective interest method', 'hedged item' and 'designated fair value hedge' are defined as in accounting standards.

5.54   Furthermore, *s 313(5)* says:

> 'In this Part "fair value accounting" means a basis of accounting under which–

> (a)   assets and liabilities are shown in the company's balance sheet at their fair value, and

> (b)   changes in the fair value of assets and liabilities are recognised as items of profit or loss'

5.55   'Fair value' is then defined in *s 313(6)* by reference to its definition, in *s 476(1)*, namely 'the meaning it has for accounting purposes'.

5.56   Thus for accounting periods beginning on or after 1 January 2016 'amortised cost' and 'fair value' accounting are both defined as in accounting standards. While the definition of fair value formerly set out in the legislation was the same as the accounting definition, the legislative definition of 'amortised cost' in part differed from the accounting definition.

5.57   The tax definition in *CTA 2009, s 313(4)* (for accounting periods beginning before 1 January 2016) stated:

> '(4) In this Part "amortised cost basis of accounting", in relation to a company's loan relationship, means a basis of accounting under which an asset or liability representing the loan relationship is shown in the

company's accounts at cost adjusted for cumulative amortisation and any impairment, repayment or release.'

5.58   The definition in FRS 102, Appendix I (imported for tax purposes by *s 313(4A)*) states:

'amortised cost (of a financial asset or financial liability)

The amount at which the financial asset or financial liability is measured at initial recognition minus principal repayments, plus or minus cumulative amortisation using the effective interest method of any difference between that initial amount and the maturity amount, and minus any reduction (directly or through the use of an allowance account) for impairment or uncollectability.'

5.59   The difference between the two definitions is that the former tax definition only provides for recognition 'at cost' (ie transaction price), whereas the accounting definition allows for initial recognition at fair value.

5.60   In the case of complex financial instruments FRS 102, para 12.7 says that a financial asset or liability must be initially recognised at the fair value, which will 'normally' be the transaction price (ie cost). 'Normally' allows for exceptions, as in the case of non-commercial loans.

5.61   These definitions are largely derived from IAS 39, para 9. The 'knowledgeable and willing party dealing at arm's length' is the same hypothetical person as the 'prudent prospective purchaser' standard in *TCGA 1992, s 273(3)*. No possibility is entertained that an independent person would not have entered into the transaction at all. Where securities are listed, the fair value will normally be market price, unless that is distorted by exceptional factors.

5.62   Amortised cost basis will accrue gains and losses over the period to which they relate. Fair value accounting will measure the market value of an asset on acquisition, at set intervals and on disposal, and changes in fair value will be realised gains or losses in the income statement. As the court observed in *Kleinwort Benson Ltd v South Tyneside Metropolitan Borough Council* [1994] 4 All ER 972 at 984:

'It is possible to assess the positive and negative value of any given contract at any given time by reference to the current market levels ("mark to market"). This facility can be used merely to value the contract for internal or accounting purposes or it can be used in relation to a sale or close out of the contract … This underlines the dynamic character of any party's portfolio of contracts.'

As this extract shows, fair value accounting was previously described as 'mark to market'.

Amortised cost basis

5.63 Accruals accounting is about recognising events when they occur, ie it requires a transaction with a third party to give rise to an accounting event.

5.64 All financial assets and liabilities not classified as 'fair value through profit and loss' fall into the category entitled 'Financial liabilities (carried) at amortised cost' under IAS 39, paras 47 and 56. This includes:

- Trade receivables.

- Bank loans.

- Bonds and debentures.

5.65 These items are initially recognised at fair value at the time of acquisition, which will normally be the cost of the asset or the amount of the liability: IAS 39, Application Guidance 64. Fair value at inception is the present value of the future cash flows discounted at the implicit interest rate. Directly attributable transaction costs are deducted from the amount at which the liability is booked. Finance costs must thereafter be calculated using the effective interest method: IAS 39, para 9. The effective rate of interest is the rate of interest which takes the opening debt to zero on maturity (as regards the borrower) and to the amount payable on redemption (as regards the lender).

When a company buys another company, it consolidates the accounts on a fair value basis.

5.66 The 'effective interest method' is the constant rate of interest which takes a discounted debt from its initial value to its value on maturity. Finance costs goes to the profit and loss account as a debit, and finance income to profit and loss as a credit. Finance costs are allocated to periods over the term of the debt at a constant rate on the carrying amount. In the case of zero coupon bonds (ZCBs), it is necessary to work out the implied yield to maturity ('effective interest rate'), using the formula:

$$i = \frac{A}{P}^{i/n} - 1$$

where:

- i = implied rate of interest

- A = amount payable on maturity

- P = principal
- n = term.

Example 5.5

Borrow £700; repay £1,100 after four years.

Finance charge £1,100 – £700 = £400 (spread over four years)

Implicit rate of interest = 0.12

Year	Loan	Finance charge	C/f
1	700	84	784
2	784	94	878
3	878	105	983
4	983	117	1,100
		400	

5.67   More complicated mathematics are required where the borrower makes fixed instalment repayments over the term of the loan, because the balance on which interest is charged is constantly declining, so that the interest element in each instalment declines as the principal element increases. Each instalment has to be divided into a finance element (treated as interest) and principal (repayment of loan). More accurately, once the finance charge has been computed, the balance goes to reduce capital outstanding, with the result that, on the next payment, the finance charge will be reduced because the effective rate of interest is applied to a smaller balance outstanding.

Example 5.6

On day 1 of its accounting period, Bank Ltd lends Trader Ltd £95,514, nominal amount £100,000, repayable after six years and bearing interest at 8%. The effective rate of interest is 9%.

Year	Opening value	Finance cost	Payment	Closing value
1	95,514	8,596	(8,000)	96,110
2	96,110	8,650	(8,000)	96,760
3	96,760	8,708	(8,000)	97,468
4	97,468	8,772	(8,000)	98,240

5	98,240	8,842	(8,000)	99,082
6	99,082	8,918	(8,000)	100,000

Example 5.7

Accounting period (AP) to 31/12

Zero coupon bond bought at £80, 1 July 2015

Redeemable at £100, 31 December 2017

Effective interest rate 9%

		Profit
1	Hold to maturity	£
	AP to 31/12/15	3.60
	AP to 31/12/16	7.50
	AP to 31/12/17	8.90
2	Hold until disposal ('related transaction')	
	AP to 31/12/15	3.60
	AP to 31/12/16	7.50
Sell for £95, 01/01/17: 95 – (80 + 3.60 + 7.50) =		3.90

Example 5.8

A zero coupon bond is issued for £81 on 1 January 2015 and is sold for £102 on 30 June 2016. Par value is £100, redeemable 31 December 2017.

Accounting by issuer (amortised cost basis)	*Debit*
	£
AP to 31/12/15	9
AP to 31/12/16 (102 – (81 + 9))	12

In all the above examples, the tax treatment follows the accounting treatment.

Example 5.9

A company borrows £100, repayable in ten annual instalments of £13. The effective interest rate is 5%. The finance cost and movement on the carrying amount is:

Year	Opening balance	Finance cost	Payment	Closing balance
1	100	5	13	92
2	92	5	13	84
3	84	4	13	75
4	75	4	13	66
5	66	3	13	56
6	56	3	13	46
7	46	2	13	35
8	35	2	13	24
9	24	1	13	12
10	12	1	13	0

5.68   Where an amortised cost basis is used, loan relationships cannot be revalued, unless the liability is released. The essential objection to such revaluation is that it is an unacceptable mixture of amortised cost and fair values. As is explained in *R v IRC, ex p S G Warburg* [1994] STC 518 at 526:

'it is axiomatic that to take a value that is lower of cost and market will be to recognise a loss on any stock which has lost value since purchase, while omitting to include any increase in value of a stock which has risen since its purchase.'

5.69   If a financial trader wishes to obtain immediate recognition of downward movements in the value of his trading stock of debt securities, he must use fair values.

5.70   Within an amortised cost basis, companies must normally use economic accrual (actuarial method) to accrue finance costs which relate to more than one accounting period. As a simplified alternative, the 'rule of 78 (sum of digits) method' may still be used (see below).

5.71   *Economic accrual (actuarial) method.* Where repayment is by way of fixed instalments, interest is charged at the prescribed rate and deducted from the instalment, the balance going to reduce the outstanding capital.

Example 5.10

£100,000 borrowed at 8%, repayable in four equal annual instalments.

Year	Capital £	Interest £	Repayment £	Balance £
1	100,000	8,000	30,200	77,800
2	77,800	6,224	30,200	53,824
3	53,824	4,306	30,200	27,930
4	27,930	2,234	30,200	(36)
		20,764		

Example 5.11

X agrees to lend Newco £500 repayable after five years with a premium of £500 (amounting to £1,000 in total).

For accounting purposes, Newco must accrue the premium of £500 at a constant rate of return on the carrying amount.

The effective rate of interest is 14.87%.

Year	Carrying amount £	Finance costs £	Balance c/f £
1	500.00	74.35	574.35
2	574.35	85.40	659.75
3	659.75	98.11	757.86
4	757.86	112.69	870.55
5	870.55	129.45	1,000.00
Total		500.00	

5.72 *Rule of 78 (sum of digits) method.* This formula is still used in consumer credit legislation and in apportioning lease payments between the financial charge element (CR in OCI) and the amount which reduces the outstanding notional liability (DR liabilities). Add together the number of interest periods, weight them in inverse order, and apportion the interest amongst the interest periods according to the weighting.

Example 5.12

Loan of £100,000 to be paid in four equal amounts of £30,200.

Year	Weighting	Apportionment	Interest £
1	4	4/10 × 20,800	8,320
2	3	3/10 × 20,800	6,240
3	2	2/10 × 20,800	4,160
4	1	1/10 × 20,800	2,080
	10		20,800

Comparison

Year	Straight-line £	Economic £	Rule of 78 £
1	5,200	8,000	8,320
2	5,200	6,224	6,240
3	5,200	4,306	4,160
4	5,200	2,234	2,080

5.73   Instalments have to be broken down into a payment of interest, any surplus going to reduce the loan outstanding.

Example 5.13

X Ltd borrows £500, repayable in four annual instalments of £150. The implicit interest rate is 7.71%. The movement on carrying amount and interest charge is:

Year	Opening balance	Payment	Interest	Closing balance
1	500	150	38.55	388.55
2	388.55	150	29.96	268.51
3	268.51	150	20.70	139.21
4	139.21	150	10.79	0
		600	100.00	

The interest is charged to profit and loss and is a debit for tax purposes. The closing balance will appear as a creditor in the balance sheet. At any given time, the NPV of the cash flows equals the loan outstanding.

5.74 As interest rates change, the fair value of fixed rate loans changes. Where amortised cost basis is used, the carrying value will not change. However, early settlement fees will be calculated by reference to current interest rates. Where a company ceases to be a party to a loan relationship, but continues to accrue amounts in relation to it in subsequent accounting periods ('post-cessation receipts'), the company will continue to be regarded as being party to the loan relationship in those periods: *CTA 2009, ss 188–195*.

Fair value accounting

5.75 A company can assign financial liabilities to the category 'fair value through profit or loss', so long as this category is adopted on initial recognition: IAS 39, paras 9, 39, 50.

5.76 Where fair value accounting is used, a discount is usually applied to reflect transactional and administrative costs, and counterparty credit risk. Resultant valuations may then be:

(a)   carried to balance sheet as 'Other assets'; or

(b)   carried to balance sheet as 'Other liabilities'.

When cash is received, it will be off-set from these items.

5.77 Where the company is the creditor in a loan relationship, the fair value is the amount which the company would obtain for all of the rights under the relationship in respect of future payments. Where the company is the debtor in the loan relationship, the fair value is the amount it would have to pay to an independent person to assume the liabilities for future payments under the loan relationship. There are many different ways of applying fair values, the key being how the discount factor to obtain NPVs is calculated. Fair value cash flows also take into account credit risk in establishing NPVs. The essence of amortised cost basis is spreading expenditure or income forwards. The essence of fair value accounting is discounting future income or expenditure back to NPV. The normal discount factor will be:

$$\frac{1}{(1 + i)^n}$$

where:

- i = rate of interest
- n = term of years.

5.78   The effect of applying fair values to fixed-rate debt liabilities would be that, if interest rates fell, the company would be treated as incurring extra borrowing; while, if interest rates rose, the company would be treated as having repaid debt.

Example 5.14

A company lends £1,000 for three years at 10% fixed, the principal being repayable in a bullet payment at the end of the term. The NPV of the future cash flows is:

Year	Amount	Discount factor	NPV
1	100	$\dfrac{1}{1.10}$	91
2	100	$\dfrac{1}{1.10^2}$	83
3	1,100	$\dfrac{1}{1.10^3}$	826
Total	1,300		1,000

After one year, interest rates rise to 12%:

Year	Amount	Discount factor	NPV
1	100	$\dfrac{1}{1.10}$	91
2	100	$\dfrac{1}{1.10^2}$	80
3	1,100	$\dfrac{1}{1.10^3}$	783
Total	1,300		954

Fair value loss = (1,000 – 954) = 46. However, the company will still receive £1,000 at the end of Year 3. Accordingly, the loss will have to be unwound over Years 2 and 3.

Example 5.15

A company borrows £1,000 at a rate of 10% for five years. Interest is payable in arrears, and the whole loan is repayable by one bullet payment at the end of

Year 5. At the end of Year 1, interest rates fall to 7% and remain at that level. Under IAS 39, the company takes fair value adjustments through the reserves. The fair value of the loan is increased at the end of Year 1 from £1,000 to £1,102 (1,192 – 90), to reflect the amount which could have been borrowed over a four-year period at 7%. The additional cost is taken in Year 1 and the discount unwound in Years 2 to 5. The finance cost is adjusted to the carrying value of the loan.

Present value calculation (of remaining cash flows at end of Year 1)

Year	Pay	Discount factor @10%	NPV	Discount factor @7%	NPV
1	100	0.90	90		90
2	100	0.83	83	0.93	93
3	100	0.75	75	0.88	88
4	100	0.68	68	0.81	81
5	1,100	0.62	684	0.76	840
Total	1,500		1,000		1,192

Fair value adjustments

Year	Opening balance	Interest	P & L	Revaluation	Total charge	Closing balance
1	1,000	100	100	102	202	1,102
2	1,102	100	77	(23)	54	1,079
3	1,079	100	76	(24)	52	1,055
4	1,055	100	74	(26)	48	1,029
5	1,029	100	71	(29)	42	1,000
Total			398	0	398	

Example 5.16

A company borrows £1,000 at a fixed rate of 12% for five years. At the end of Year 1, interest rates fall to 8% and remain at that level for the remaining four years. Under IAS 39, para 9 the entity chooses to take the fair value adjustment to equity. The income statement shows the finance cost of £1,200, whereas the balance sheet shows the liability at each year end represented by the remaining cash flows discounted at 8%. The additional cost in Year 1 is unwound over the remainder of the term:

Year	Finance cost	Equity	Total charge	Opening balance	Closing balance
1	120	132	252	1,000	1,132
2	120	(29)	91	1,132	1,103
3	120	(32)	88	1,103	1,071
4	120	(34)	86	1,071	1,037
5	120	(37)	83	1,037	1,000
	600	0	600		

Example 5.17

A company acquires a ZCB at the beginning of 2016 for £760, its fair value. The bond matures at the end of 2018 at £1,000. It is classified as available for sale, with fair value gains and losses being reported in equity. The effective interest rate is 9.6%. At the end of 2016, 2017 and 2018, its fair value is £850, £950 and £1,000 respectively.

Year	Amortised cost	Interest – income statement	Fair value changes – equity	Fair value	Taxable amount
2016	760	73	17	850	90
2017	833	80	20	950	100
2018	913	87	(37)	1,000	50
		240	0		240

Thus, the fair value changes have to be unwound on redemption.

5.79   It is very unusual for companies to fair value their own liabilities to market. If this were the case, every time a company suffered a downgrading of its credit rating, it would have to mark down its liabilities, producing a large credit for loan relationship purposes. If a debtor relationship was revalued every time a company's creditworthiness fell, the debtor company would make larger profits in proportion to its inability to pay its debts.

Difference between amortised cost and fair value

5.80   As appears from these examples, the differences between amortised cost and fair value accounting for debt securities are broadly as follows:

- Amortised cost basis:

    - Debt security is recorded at fair value at inception.

    - Coupon is accrued and premium/discount amortised over the life of the security.

    - Interest accrued prior to purchase ('dirty' interest) held on balance sheet until interest is settled.

- Fair value:

    - Debt security is valued to its current market price.

    - Premiums/discounts are incorporated into fair value.

    - Coupon is accrued.

Revaluations

5.81 Investment companies will use amortised cost basis accounting for assets, but under FRS 102 are required to revalue listed securities – shares and bonds – to fair value on the accounting reference date, producing a credit to income and expenditure. No impairment relief is available on falls in value, or tax payable on upwards revaluations: *CTA 2009, s 324*. The reason is that this does not give rise to a *s 306A(1)* matter for tax purposes: *s 307(2)*. Exchange gains and losses are recognised under *s 324(4)*, and *s 325* adds that, if fair value accounting is used, revaluations are recognised.

5.82 Under the Association of British Insurers' SORP 'Accounting for Insurance Business' of December 2006, insurance companies are required to account for assets on a fair value basis. For tax purposes, in the case of non-life insurance business, a company may elect to continue to use a realisations basis rather than a fair value basis.

5.83 A bank changed its basis of valuation of stock in trade from lower of cost and market value to mark to market (fair values) with effect from 1 April 1986. The change in the basis of stock valuation threw up an increase of £4.1m. This was treated as a prior year adjustment to reserves (ie without going through the profit and loss account). The inspector raised an additional assessment to tax in this amount. The bank claimed that this was inconsistent with a previously announced Revenue practice, that a change of basis of stock valuation from one valid basis to another valid basis would not be taken into account in determining income for tax purposes. The court held that:

(a) whether or not mark to market was a valid basis was a matter of fact, to be determined on a substantive tax appeal, rather than on judicial review; and

(b)   the action of the inspector in treating the revaluation gain as income was not so unreasonable as to be justiciable under public law.

(*R v IRC, ex p S G Warburg & Co Ltd* [1994] STC 518)

5.84   In *Pearce (Inspector of Taxes) v Woodall-Duckham Ltd* 51 TC 271, a company changed its method of valuing work-in-progress from an on-cost basis to an accrued profit basis (ie direct cost plus part of the anticipated profit). The closing value of work-in-progress as at 31 December 1968 was £22,702,538 (prime cost). This figure was carried forward as the opening value as at 1 January 1969, and to this figure was added a separate item of £579,874: 'Surplus arising on change in valuation of contract work in progress at 31st December 1968.' This in turn increased the closing valuation of work-in-progress on 31 December 1969. It did not alter the profits earned in 1969 as such. The Revenue added the upwards adjustment to the value of work-in-progress to the taxable profits for 1969. The resultant accounting figure was held to be a 'profit' for tax purposes. Templeman J said (at 285):

'The anticipated profit for work carried out prior to 1969 falls to be taxed in the year 1969, when it is first revealed and first brought into account; just as the anticipated profit for the work carried out during 1969 falls to be taxed in the year 1969, when it is first revealed and first brought into account.'

5.85   Furthermore, Stamp LJ said (at 291):

'The £579,874, being the difference between the value put upon work-in-progress at the end of 1968 and the valuation at the opening of the 1969 account, appears to me to be an artificial and unreal figure not representing a profit. The true profit is arrived at by comparing the value put upon work-in-progress at the end of 1968 and the value put upon it at the end of 1969, and it is a trading not a casual or non-trading profit. True, you are not comparing like with like, but that must always be so when for good commercial reasons and without infringing any principle of income tax law – I refer in particular to the rule that you must not anticipate a profit – trading stock or work-in-progress falls to be written up or written down.'

Non-compliant accounts

5.86   If a company does not have GAAP-compliant accounts, its taxable profits are computed as if it did. This is provided for in *CTA 2009, s 309*:

'(1)   If a company–

> (a)   draws up accounts which are not GAAP-compliant accounts, or
>
> (b)   does not draw up accounts at all,
>
> this Part applies as if GAAP-compliant accounts had been drawn up.'

5.87   If accounts do not comply with GAAP, they will not apply for tax purposes. The question whether accounts are GAAP-compliant is a question of fact, on which the decision of the fact-finding tribunal is final unless:

(a)   the decision is inadequately reasoned or not based on, or inconsistent with the evidence;

(b)   the appellate tribunal does not like the conclusion, in which case the fact-finding tribunal will have made an error of law.

5.88   The notion of being 'GAAP-compliant' has thus become much more prescriptive. The assumption is that GAAP requires a single mandatory method of accounting in any given case. Whereas it would formerly have been possible to have permissible alternatives to accounting for a transaction, all of which would have been in accordance with the correct principles of commercial accountancy, nowadays the assumption is that there is a single correct method of accounting for any transaction. Any heretic is to be burned at the stake on fires stoked by accounting regulators. This also shows the danger of making the tax result over-dependent on the accounting result. When tax enjoyed a greater measure of autonomy, accounting choices were less crucial and accounting disputes could safely be left to the innocent enjoyment of accounting anoraks, who would not have been equipped to earn a living in professional practice.

5.89   In *Greene King plc v R & C Comrs* [2016] EWCA Civ 782:

1   The group holding company (HoldCo) held an interest-bearing debt of £300m owed by a subsidiary (Sub 1). HoldCo assigned the right to receive interest (NPV £20.5m) to a second subsidiary (Sub 2), in consideration of the issue of preference shares with a nominal value of £1.5m by Sub 2 to HoldCo. This was an interest strip. Sub 2 credited £1.5m to share capital. The balance of £19m was credited by Sub 2 to share premium account. HoldCo continued to recognise the creditor loan relationship at £300m.

2   HoldCo argued that–

(a)   Sub 1 continued to obtain a loan relationship debit for the interest;

(b)   dividends on the preference shares were not liable to corporation tax;

(c)   the loss of interest entitlement of (20.5) did not have to be derecognised, because there was a corresponding increase in the value of its Sub 2 shares;

(d) Sub 2 was not liable to tax on the interest which it received from Sub 1 (except in so far as the actual amounts received exceeded the NPV of these payments) because *FA 1996, s 84(2)(a)* excluded from charge amounts taken to share premium account;

(e) the economic and commercial substance of the transaction (which is what the accounts had to reflect) was reflected by leaving the whole of the loan recognised. Even if there should be a partial derecognition of the Sub 1 debt, accreting back would not constitute a realised profit. It should be offset against the carrying value of the investment in the subsidiary.

3   The Revenue argued that the Sub 1 loan should be derecognised as to £20.5m. This amount would be accreted back over the period to redemption (15 months), so producing a loan relationship credit equivalent to Sub 1's debit and a flat tax result.

4   The issues were therefore–

(a) whether GAAP required partial derecognition of HoldCo's interest entitlement;

(b) if so, whether that amount should be taken to profit and loss as it accrued; and

(c) whether there was a loan relationship between Sub 1 and Sub 2, so bringing the payments within *FA 1996, s 84(2)(a)*.

5.90   The FTT held that HoldCo's accounts were not GAAP-compliant. This was affirmed by the Upper Tribunal. Mann J stated at [2014] STC 2439 at [64]:

'What happened in the present case is that, as a matter of substance, the rights to interest to the end of the loan were disposed of. What also happened, as a matter of substance, was that PLC [HoldCo] acquired preference shares in its subsidiary. The commercial substance of the transaction was plainly, in my view, a transaction with those two separate albeit commercially connected limbs. It is true that the economic effect of the transaction, at one level, is to leave PLC in the same position because the decrease in value of the loan might be said to be reflected by an increase in value of its shareholding in the subsidiary. However, *in relation to the loan the real substance of the transaction was that the loan had become less valuable ... the correct reflection in the accounts of the company, in order to present a true and fair view, is to reflect the change in assets in the manner proposed by Mr Chandler (derecognition)*' [emphasis added]

5.91   Mann J also held that:

(a) at [95], by reference to ICAEW Tech 07/30, the accretion back was a 'realised profit', so the increase was to be taken to profit and loss under *FA 1996, s 84(1)(a)*; and

(b)   at [145], the assignment of the right to receive interest did not without more (the issue of an instrument) create a loan relationship;

(c)   for that reason, *FA 1996, s 84(2)(a)* (exclusion from loan relationship profits of amounts credited to share premium account) did not apply.

The Court of Appeal overturned (b) and (c). Importantly, the Court held that the interest received by Sub 2 following the assignment of interest strip to it by HoldCo arose from a loan relationship of Sub 2, and came within *s 84(2)(a)*. Hence there was no double charge to tax in the group as a result of the scheme. Critically, Etherton C held:

'[40] … from the moment of the assignment to [Sub 2] of the interest strip [Sub 2] and [Sub 1] stood in a position of creditor and debtor as respects the money debt represented by the future instalments of interest …

[46] … It is consistent with the intention apparent from [*FA 1996*] section 81(3) that the loan relationship code embraced a wide category of corporate debt, which would not in ordinary legal or trade terms be characterised as a loan.'

Change of accounting basis

5.92   The general 'change of basis' rules are contained in *CTA 2009, ss 180–187*. Where, in computing the profits of a trade, there is a change of basis from one correct accounting method to another, the rules for tax adjustments seek to align the tax charge with the accounting change, so that:

(a)   amounts do not drop out of charge; and

(b)   amounts are not charged twice to tax.

5.93   The adjustment falls to be made in the period in which the change of basis is adopted. First, a positive adjustment has to be calculated, then a negative adjustment. The positive adjustment is found by adding up:

(a)   receipts brought into account on the new basis which were not brought into account on the basis used in the previous accounting period;

(b)   expenses taken into account on the new basis to the extent that they have already been taken into account before the change; and

(c)   deductions in respect of opening trading stock or work in progress to the extent not matched by credits in respect of closing trading stock or work in progress in the last period before the change.

5.94   The negative adjustment is the mirror image of the positive adjustment. The net result of the adjustments is, for corporation tax purposes, treated as a receipt or expenditure for the last day of the accounting period in which the change occurs.

5.95   Accordingly, under the change of basis rules, a company is required:

(a)   to calculate its profits for the accounting period prior to that in which the change of basis occurred using the new method;

(b)   to calculate the prior year adjustment; and

(c)   to add the prior year adjustment to the profits for the accounting period in which the change of basis occurs.

Example 5.18

● A company's accounting period is the calendar year.

● The company decides to accelerate recognition of profits.

● The profits for the year ended 31 December 2016 were £100,000 (old basis) and £120,000 (new basis).

● Accordingly, the prior year adjustment is £20,000.

● The profits for the year ended 31 December 2017 are £180,000.

● To this must be added the prior year adjustment (£20,000).

● So the company's profits for the accounting period ending 31 December 2015 are £180,000 + £20,000 = £200,000.

5.96   The change of basis rules are overridden where a deduction has been allowed in the previous period under the old basis where, on the new basis, such expenditure would be spread into more than one period after the change. In such a case, no deduction is allowed after the change.

Example 5.19

In the accounting period ended 31 December 2017, X plc incurs fees of £100 in relation to a five-year swap, which it expenses in their entirety. On 1 January 2018, X decides to spread the fees over the period of the swap. For tax purposes, no further deduction is allowed.

5.97   Where a company changes from amortised cost basis to fair values, the prior year adjustment arising on the fair value adjustment is deferred for tax purposes until the assets are disposed of, unless the company opts to spread the adjustment over six years: *CTA 2009, ss 185, 186.*

Example 5.20

X plc holds as an investment a £1m fixed rate bond acquired on 2 January 2014 at par. Amortised cost basis is used.

At 31 December 2017 (X's year end) the bond is worth £1.25m.

On 2 January 2018, X decides that it may sell the bond, and switches to fair value.

At 31 December 2018 the bond is worth £1.15m. The economic profit on the bond over the two years is £0.15m, and an adjustment will be made in Year 2 to reflect this.

Year	Unadjusted £	Adjusted £
1	–	250,000
2	(100,000)	(100,000)
	Adjustment in Year 2	150,000

5.98   'Change of accounting basis' includes 'change of accounting policy'. Where there is a change in accounting policy, *CTA 2009, ss 315 – 318* require a debit or credit to be brought into account in the accounting period in which the change is recognised. Prior period adjustments arising from a change of accounting basis are brought in for tax purposes under *s 316*. These bring into account a change in the 'tax adjusted carrying value' as defined in *s 465B* of a loan relationship between the end of the earlier and the beginning of the following accounting period, the credit or debit being in the later period. Examples of a change of basis would be:

- a change from UK GAAP to IFRS, or from amortised cost basis to fair value;

- a change from pre-1 January 2015 UK GAAP to FRS 102;

- a change in the method of accrual used for a loan relationship over its term;

- a change in a company's yield curve used to establish PV, where a company uses fair values; or

- a change in valuation formulae.

5.99   Under self-assessment the obligation is on the taxpayer to operate a consistent basis for the calculation of his profits, and make correcting adjustments where changes are made within an accounting period or between accounting periods.

5.100   Special rules apply for accounting adjustments arising on the adoption of IAS for accounting periods beginning on or after 1 January 2005, and FRS 102 for accounting periods beginning on or after 1 January 2015. In the case of adjustments prescribed by *reg 4*, recognition of these changes for tax purposes is deferred to the accounting period beginning on or after 1 January 2006: *Loan Relationships and Derivative Contracts (Change of Accounting Practice) Regulations 2004, SI 2004/3271, reg 3*. These Regulations require transitional adjustments to be deferred until a period beginning on or after 1 January 2006, and spread over a period of ten years, with minor exceptions.

5.101   The ten-year spreading is accelerated if the company ceases to be within the charge to corporation tax. A transitional adjustment may be transferred where there is a reconstruction of a trade or business without change of ownership, within *CTA 2010, ss 938–953*.

5.102   Under *CTA 2010, s 996*, where two companies are in the same CGT group, and one uses UK GAAP and the other uses IAS, and a tax advantage arises as a result of differences between the accounting standards, both must compute profits, for tax purposes, using UK GAAP.

5.103   *CTA 2009, s 463A* gives the Treasury power to amend by regulation the corporation tax legislation when there is a relevant change of an accounting standard.

Non-commercial loans

5.104   An area in which the adoption of FRS 102 caused particular difficulties was that of non-commercial loans. This in turn led to provisions in *Finance Act 2016, Sch 7* designed to remove asymmetries in tax accounting for deemed finance charges, ie cases where a notional finance charge is incurred, and deductible loan relationship debit of 100 in the debtor company is not matched by a corresponding credit of 100 in a creditor company.

5.105   The *Finance Act 2016* changes take effect from 1 April 2016. Where an accounting period straddles 1 April 2016, the period is divided into two periods: *FA 2016, Sch 7, para 12(2)*.

5.106   Non-commercial loans are loans made to a company on terms more favourable than market terms (as to interest, duration or amount). They are usually found in the form of a loan made by an individual shareholder or a parent company shareholder to a company in which the provider of funds holds shares. They are common in SMEs (where the transfer pricing rules do not apply) and in group situations (where they may do). Under old UK GAAP such loans were recognised at cost. Modern standard-setters take the view that it is misleading to describe such loans as having a nil or reduced financing cost. The finance cost has simply been wrapped up in the amount lent. Accordingly, non-commercial loans should be regarded as discounted debt. In consequence FRS 102 requires a company to recognise interest-free and non-market rate loans at the present value of future payments, discounted at the putative market rate of interest for a similar debt. The loan then accretes back to the redemption amount over its term. The borrower company has an initial credit to equity and subsequent notional finance charges of the same amount, taking the loan from its discounted amount to the repayment amount.

5.107   This gives rise to notional finance costs, ie finance costs which do not involve any transfer of benefits to a third party, but which are deemed to do so. It is important to note that, if the loan is repayable on demand, it can be recognised at transaction value, and there is no requirement to discount the amount repayable on redemption under FRS 102. In that case the loan should be included amongst short-term creditors.

Example 5.21

Mr Brown and his family own all the shares in Brown Engineering Ltd (an SME). The accounting reference date is 31 March. Mr Brown lends the company 1,000 interest free on 1 April 2014, repayable after four years. The company adopts FRS 102 on 1 April 2015. For accounting purposes we have to assume that a bank has made a fixed rate loan at, say, 8% for four years.

On 1 April 2015, on first adoption of FRS 102, it will make the following adjustments to its accounts:

DR Liabilities   206   CR Equity   206

The credit to equity will be unwound over the next three years, as shown below. Brown Engineering Ltd will be deemed to incur notional finance costs, and restate the loan balance as follows, taking the discount on adoption of FRS 102 to OCI:

Loan balance

Year	Notes	Opening amount	Finance cost	Closing amount	OCI
To 31 March 2015	Original	1,000	0	1,000	
To 31 March 2015 – comparative	Comparative, treating loan as ZCB with EIR of 8%	735	59	794	206
To 31 March 2016	FRS 102 first year	794	63	857	
To 31 March 2017		857	68	925	
To 31 March 2018		925	75	1,000	

5.108   For tax purposes two sets of rules are of significance:

1   In the case of non-commercial transactions ('provision not at arm's length') the transfer pricing rules in *TIOPA 2010, Part 4* require a company to make transfer pricing adjustments in respect of its loan relationships or derivative contracts, but only if the adjustment would produce an increased charge to UK tax. In that case, those adjusted debits and credits are used to calculate its profits on loan relationships and derivative contracts in priority to the loan relationships and derivative contracts rules: *CTA 2009, ss 446, 693*. These rules apply to UK to UK and UK to non-UK transactions.

2   Where the transfer pricing rules are not in issue (eg SMEs), the loan relationships and derivative contracts rules apply. These are (up to a point) based on commercial accounts, not an arm's length standard.

5.109   A number of situations need to be distinguished with regard to non-commercial loans:

(i)   loans in existence prior to adoption of FRS 102 on or after 1 January 2015;

(ii)   Category (i) loans in existence at the start of an accounting beginning on or after 1 January 2016;

(iii)   new loans coming into existence after 1 April 2016.

Category (i)

5.110   Under *CTA 2009, ss 315–317* if a change in accounting policy led to a change in the carrying value of a loan relationship, the change in value had to be brought into account for tax purposes (as for accounting purposes) in the first period in which the new accounting policy was adopted. On that basis Brown Engineering Ltd would have (as noted above) a loan relationship credit of 206 in its accounting period beginning on 1 April 2015.

5.111   The *Loan Relationships and Derivative Contracts (Change of Accounting Practice) Regulations 2004, SI 2004/3271, regs 3, 3A* say that debits and credits prescribed by *reg 4* ('the applicable amounts') shall be brought into account over the 'prescribed period', which is ten years. Prior period adjustments and adjustments on change of accounting policy come within *reg 4*. Hence the credit of 206 will be spread over ten years.

Category (ii)

5.112   The *F(No 2)A 2015, Sch 7* changes apply for accounting periods beginning on or after 1 January 2006: *para 103*. For such accounting periods amounts that are included in OCI are not taken into account in computing a company's loan relationships and derivative contracts profits, until recycled to profit and loss: *CTA 2009, s 308(1)(1A)* as amended by *F(No 2)A 2015, Sch 7, para 5*.

5.113   In the case of Brown Engineering Ltd, the credit of 206 went to OCI under the previous accounts, and was taken into account as a credit under the loan relationship rules. Under *F(No 2)A 2015, Sch 7, paras 115, 116* there are transitional provisions in relation to amounts that:

(i)   were recognised in the company's accounts as other items of OCI;

(ii)   have not been recycled to profit and loss in an accounting period beginning before 1 January 2016;

(iii)   have been brought into account as credits or debits under the loan relationship rules in an accounting period beginning before 1 January 2016;

(iv)   would be taxable under *CTA 2009, s 308(1A)* (or *s 597(1A)* in the case of derivative contracts) on being transferred to profit and loss.

5.114   Debits reversing the credit will be brought into account over a five-year period. Under *para 116(5)* this is on a sliding scale (first year, 40%; second year, 25%; third year, 15%; fourth and fifth years, 10%).

Category (iii)

5.115   The credit on recognition to the borrower is no longer taxable: *CTA 2009, s 308(1)* as amended.

5.116   Brown Engineering Ltd would get a double debit (finance cost + transitional adjustment). That would not offend the symmetry principle, provided someone else had a corresponding credit. However, as the lender is an individual, he will only be taxed on interest or discounts received in cash. An individual is not liable to tax on deemed finance charges. There will be no matching UK tax liability.

5.117   To cater for this situation, with effect from 1 April 2016 a new section, *CTA 2009, s 446A*, is introduced by *FA 2016, Sch 7, para 2*. This section applies where a loan liability is initially, or on change of accounting basis, recognised in the borrower's company's accounts at a discounted amount. To the extent that there is no corresponding credit, the 'relevant discount amount' is not to be included in the borrower's loan relationship debits for corporation tax purposes. The 'relevant discount amount' (deemed finance cost, ordinarily deductible as a loan relationship debit) will be eliminated by *CTA 2009, s 446A* in two situations, the rationale being that the lender would not be chargeable to UK tax on the notional finance receipt, so that there would be a debit but no corresponding taxable income:

(a)   where the creditor is an individual;

(b)   where the creditor is a company resident in a non-qualifying territory, or a company effectively managed in a non-taxing non-qualifying territory.

5.118   'Non-qualifying territory' means a territory other than one with which the UK has a double taxation agreement containing an appropriate non-discrimination provision: *TIOPA 2010, s 173*. 'Non-taxing' means having no corporate taxation.

Example 5.22

In the case of Brown Engineering:

(i)   the company obtains a debit of 206 for the deemed finance cost (spread over three years);

(ii)   it has to bring in a corresponding credit as that amount is recycled from OCI (spread over ten years) (*s 306(1A)*);

(iii) 63 of the debit enters into the tax computation for the year to 31 March 2016;

(iv)   the balance of the credit (143) is eliminated by the debit under *para 116(5)* (spread over five years);

(v)   as the creditor is an individual, there is no tax charge on the corresponding credit of 143, so the notional finance cost in the company is eliminated by a charge under *CTA 2009, s 446A* (over the two remaining years of the debt).

Hence for Brown Engineering Ltd the result would be:

Year	Debit finance cost (see *5.106*)	Credit (spread over ten years)	Para 116(5)	Notes	S 446A – 'relevant discount amount'	Net effect
To 31 March 2016	(63)	20.60		Unwinding of credit		(42.40)
To 31 March 2017	(68)	20.60	(57.20)	40% of unrelieved credit	68	(36.60)
To 31 March 2018	(75)	20.60	(35.75)	25%	75	(15.15)
To 31 March 2019		20.60	(21.45)	15%		(0.85)
To 31 March 2020		20.60	(14.30)	10%		6.30
To 31 March 2021		20.60	(14.30)	10%		6.30
To 31 March 2022		20.60				20.60
To 31 March 2023		20.60	(143.00)			20.60
To 31 March 2024		20.60				20.60
To 31 March 2025		20.60				20.60
	(206.00)	206.00	(206.00)	(143.00)	143.00	0.00

5.119   *Finance Act 2016, Sch 7, para 3* provides that there is to be no loan relationship credit unless it reverses a preceding debit under the transfer pricing rules. In other words, where a transfer pricing adjustment has been made in respect of a loan, a company is not required to bring in as a credit a discount on inception of the loan. The same rule applies to derivative contracts: *Finance Act 2016, Sch 7, para 4*, amending *CTA 2009, s 693*.

Example 5.23

Global plc, resident in the UK, has a wholly owned subsidiary Local Co, resident in State B. Global lends Local Co £10m interest free for ten years. Under the transfer pricing rules, interest of 7% a year is attributed to Global. Under FRS 102 the loan is accounted for as a loan asset of £6m and a capital contribution of £4m. There is no debit for this under the transfer pricing rules (because it would reduce Global's UK profits). When Global records a notional financial receipt unwinding the discount, that is not taken into account under the loan relationship rules.

5.120 As regards transfer pricing and foreign exchange matching, if a UK borrower has a foreign currency loan from a connected non-resident lender, and part of the loan is ignored for transfer pricing purposes (because a third party lender would only have lent a smaller sum), the foreign exchange gains and losses on any unrecognised part of the loan will also be disregarded fort UK tax purposes: *CTA 2009, s 447(1)–(4)*. A difficulty arises if the loan in question is matching an asset expressed in a foreign currency, ie the loan functions in a hedging relationship, because foreign exchange gains on the disregarded part of the loan will be left out of account, but not exchange differences on the matched asset. *Finance Act 2016, Sch 7, para 5* confines the disregard to the unmatched part of the loan, by introducing *CTA 2009, s 447(4A)*. This is accompanied by a series of further amendments, relating to:

(i)   debtor relationships that are 'equity notes' (*CTA 2009, s 448; CTA 2010, s 1015(6)*);

(ii)   creditor relationships not at arm's length (*CTA 2009, ss 449, 451*);

(iii)   derivative contracts (*CTA 2009, s 694*).

In turn a definition of 'matched' is introduced: *CTA 2009, s 475B*.

5.121 As regards connected company loan relationships, prior to accounting periods beginning on or after 1 January 2016, connected company loan relationships had to be recognised at cost (not fair value): *CTA 2009, ss 313(4), 348, 349* (prior to amendment). Under the new *s 313(4A)* 'amortised cost basis' has the same meaning for tax as it has for accounting purposes. This will extend the tax consequences of notional finance charges.

Summary of computational provisions

5.122   The outline of the computational provisions is:

1   For the purposes of corporation tax, all profits and gains arising to a company from its loan relationships and related transactions are chargeable to tax as income, in accordance with its GAAP-compliant commercial accounts.

2   If the company is party to a loan relationship for the purposes of a trade, profits and gains arising from the loan relationship are included in the computation of trading profit as receipts or expenses of that trade.

3   If the company is party to a loan relationship other than for the purposes of a trade, profits and gains arising from the loan relationship are separately computed as non-trading credits and non-trading debits, unless the company is carrying on a property business.

4   The amounts to be taxed or relieved are determined by accounting methods, subject to numerous statutory overrides.

5   Only credits and debits which go through the income statement are taken into account under the loan relationship rules.

6   Interest payments are, as a rule, taxed or relieved as they accrue, not when they are paid.

7   Foreign exchange differences are included in credits and debits.

5.123   The following items are treated as receipts and expenses, credits and debits:

(a)   interest;

(b)   discounts and premiums;

(c)   expenses directly incurred in bringing the loan relationship into being or enforcing obligations under it, or carrying out a related transaction;

(d)   exchange differences;

(e)   impairment losses;

(f)   releases of debts between unconnected parties;

(g)   capitalised interest which is treated as 'capital expenditure on a fixed capital project';

(h)   reversals of impairments;

(i)   imputed interest pursuant to transfer-pricing adjustments; and

(j)   price differentials on stock-lending and repo transactions.

Chapter 6

Loan Relationships: Special Computational Provisions

Overview

6.1   This chapter covers:

- Tests of connection
- Connected company relationships
- Releases
- Deemed releases
- Late payment of interest
- Deeply discounted securities
- Non-arm's length transactions
- Capitalised interest
- Group continuity rules
- Deduction schemes
- Receipts cases
- Mezzanine financing
- Unallowable purposes
- Regime anti-avoidance rule

Tests of connection

6.2   A variety of special rules for the taxation of loan relationships apply where:

- two companies are connected;
- two companies become connected;

- two companies cease to be connected; or

- a company is connected with a participator.

This is because the legislation treats shareholder debt as quasi-equity, on the grounds that, where the lender is a related party, the economic significance of the debt-equity distinction does not correspond to the legal distinction. The approach of the legislation is to try to reconstruct, in relation to a related party transaction, what the tax consequences for the related party would be, if it were not related. In other words, the question is always: what would the arm's length situation be? Related party situations are deemed to be abusive, as regards the arm's length principle. However, the importance of the affiliation principle in transfer pricing renders this assumption doubtful.

6.3 The connected companies rules apply in the case of actual loan relationships (Type 1), deemed loan relationships (Type 2) and 'relevant matters' pertaining to relevant non-lending relationships (Type 3): see HMRC's Corporate Finance Manual at CFM41070.

6.4 A 'connected companies relationship' exists if there is a 'connection' between the company and another company standing in the position of a debtor, as stated in *CTA 2009, s 348(4)*. Connection may be direct or indirect, ie through a series of loan relationships: *s 348(5)*. Connection takes effect from the beginning of the accounting period in which the connection arises. If companies are connected for one day in an accounting period, they are connected for the whole of the accounting period: *s 348(6)*.

6.5 A connection may be established in in one of four ways, which apply for different purposes:

(a) through control (*CTA 2009, s 472*);

(b) through a major interest (*s 473*);

(c) through participation in a close company (*ss 375(2), 409, 410*);

(d) through a controlling corporate partner of a partnership which is debtor or creditor under a loan relationship (*ss 383, 467*).

6.6 In tabular form, these may be summarised:

	Type of connection	Definition	Transactions affected
1	Control	s 472	Impaired loans, releases, deemed releases
2	Major interest	s 473	Discounted securities

3	Participation in close company	ss 375, 409, 410	Late interest, discounted securities
4	Controlling corporate partner	ss 383, 467	Impaired loans, releases
5	Trustees of occupational pension scheme	s 378	Late interest

Control in general

6.7   Connection is largely defined in terms of control. The loan relationship rules have their own definitions of 'connection' and 'control'. They are derived from tax and companies legislation more generally. The corporation tax legislation has two definitions of 'control':

(a)   a narrow test in *CTA 2010, s 1124*; and

(b)   a wide test in *CTA 2010, s 450*.

6.8   The narrow test is a formal test, based on voting power. The wide test adds to this a series of economic tests. As Lord Hoffmann observed, in the *s 450* test the ordinary meaning of 'control' 'is enormously widened by subsequent subsections': *R v IRC, ex p Newfields Developments Ltd* [2001] STC 901 at [10].

6.9   Companies are managed by the directors, subject to the terms of the memorandum and articles: *Companies Act 1985, Table A, art 70*; *Companies Act 2006, Model Articles, Clause 3*. The ultimate constitutional authority, subject to the law, is the general meeting.

6.10   The narrow test looks at control by the shareholders at the board level: *Irving v Tesco Stores (Holdings)* [1982] STC 881 at 910.

6.11   The broad test additionally looks to control and economic entitlement at the shareholder level: *Steele (Inspector of Taxes) v European Vinyls Corpn (Holdings) BV* [1996] STC 785 at 795.

6.12   The narrow test contained in *CTA 2009, s 472* applies for loan relationship purposes. This only looks to the voting power test of control and does not include the economic tests of entitlement to profits available for distribution or assets on a notional winding up.

Test 1: Control

6.13   The main test is the narrow 'control' test in *CTA 2009, s 466*, which states:

> '(2)   There is a connection between a company ("A") and another company ("B") for an accounting period if ... –
>
> (a)   A controls B,
>
> (b)   B controls A, or
>
> (c)   A and B are both controlled by the same person.'

6.14   Thus, 'connection' is defined by reference to:

● 'control' of one company by another company; or

● control of two companies by 'the same person', who may be a natural person (an individual) or a juristic person (a company).

Thus it is clear that, while only companies can have connected loan relationships, connection can be traced through an individual.

6.15   This narrow test is used for loan relationships by virtue of *CTA 2009, s 472*, which says:

> '(2)   For those purposes "control", in relation to a company, means the power of a person to secure that the affairs of the company are conducted in accordance with the person's wishes–
>
> (a)   by means of the holding of shares or the possession of voting power in or in relation to the company or any other company, or
>
> (b)   by virtue of any power conferred by the articles of association or other document regulating the company or any other company.'

'Connection' is therefore defined in terms of voting control or an agreement which gives voting control.

6.16   *Interpretation Act 1978, s 6(1)* says that: 'In any Act, unless the contrary intention appears ... (c) words in the singular include the plural and words in the plural include the singular'. In *Floor v Davis (Inspector of Taxes)* [1975] STC 476 the question was whether 'person' in *FA 1965, Sch 7, para 15(2)* included 'persons', where it said: 'If a person having control of a company exercises his control so that value passes out of shares'. The House of Lords decided by 3:2 that the *Interpretation Act* applied. The only majority opinion was that of Viscount Dilhorne, who said (at 641) that the test was whether reading words into the singular to include the plural had the effect of rendering the provision in question 'unworkable or to produce a result which Parliament cannot have intended'. Lord Wilberforce (dissenting) said (at 639) that to read the singular as including the plural 'would involve an uncertain and indefinite extension of the paragraph'.

6.17 Tests of connection between companies by reference to control are found throughout the tax legislation. The legislation normally defines the scope of such provisions. It does this by stating whether the rights and powers of one person or a plurality of persons apply for this purpose, and whether the rights and powers of associates are to be attributed to a person. If a taxing statute refers to 'person' without any words defining the scope of the term 'person', the legislative context suggests that the term simply means 'person' in the singular. Accordingly, in a situation where two shareholders each hold 50% of the voting power in two companies, the companies are not connected under this test.

Example 6.1

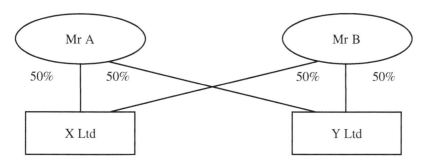

X Ltd and Y Ltd are not connected under the control test, but are connected under the 'major interest' test. Under the 'voting power' test of control in *CTA 2009, s 472*, only one person can control a company.

Example 6.2

In a situation where Mr A and Mr B each own 50% of A Ltd and B Ltd:

● A Ltd has distributable reserves of 1,000

● B Ltd has a deficit on profit and loss of (1,000)

● B Ltd owes 500 to A Ltd

● A Ltd releases the debt.

The accounting entries are:

- B Ltd: DR liabilities 500, CR P/L 500
- A Ltd: DR P/L 500, CR assets 500.

Is the reduction in P/L in A Ltd attributable to a loss, or to a payment to shareholders?

There is no distribution by A Ltd because there is no transfer of assets to shareholders, who are in the same position financially. Their shares in A Ltd will have fallen in value; their shares in B Ltd will have risen in value. See *CTA 2010, ss 1020, 1021*.

There can be no distribution by B Ltd because it has a deficit on P/L.

A Ltd gets an impairment loss, because 'person' in *CTA 2009, s 363(3)* does not include the plural. The definition of 'persons' is confined to persons acting together. This is right, because B Ltd has a taxable credit.

Example 6.3

A Ltd owns 75% of B Ltd, which owns 51% of C Ltd. A, B and C are all connected.

Example 6.4

A Ltd owns 10 'A' shares in C Ltd which carry one vote and the ability to appoint all the directors. B Ltd owns 90 voting shares in C Ltd. Both A Ltd and B Ltd are connected to C Ltd.

Example 6.5

L Bank has lent £1,000 to Z plc. In the event of default, L Bank has the right to appoint the majority of directors. Until default occurs, L Bank is not connected with Z plc.

6.18   Shares held by partnerships, including company partners, are directly attributed to those company partners, according to their profit share entitlement.

There is an exclusion for the general partner of a limited liability partnership which is a collective investment scheme within *FSMA 2000, s 235*.

Example 6.6

The Cesso Partnership consists of A Ltd, B Ltd and Mr T. Their respective profit share entitlements are 60:20:20. The partnership owns 85% of the ordinary shares in Z Ltd, and has lent £1,000 to Z Ltd. A Ltd is regarded as holding 60% of 85% of the shares in Z, ie 51%. A Ltd controls Z Ltd. If Z Ltd cannot repay the debt, A Ltd will get no bad debt relief, whereas B Ltd will.

Test 2: Major interest

6.19   'Major interest' is defined in *CTA 2009, s 473* in the same terms as in the controlled foreign company (CFC) and transfer pricing legislation. Three conditions need to be satisfied for a major interest to exist:

● Company A and another person [C] control company B.

● A and C each hold 40% of the voting power in B.

● Both A and C (or a company connected with A or C) has either lent money to B or borrowed money from B.

6.20   In determining whether A and C have control of B, or whether each of A and C has a 40% interest in B, the interest, rights and powers of any company connected with A or C respectively is attributed to each of them under *s 474*. Options are treated as having been exercised. 'Connection' and 'control' are defined by reference to *CTA 2009, ss 466, 472* (ie the narrower test). The 'major interest' test is of particular relevance in relation to consortiums.

6.21   The 'major interest' test means that two 50:50 deadlock companies will each have a major interest in the company in which they hold shares, provided that each has lent money to or borrowed money from that company. This test is of particular importance in relation to joint ventures. In *Steele (Inspector of Taxes) v European Vinyls Corpn (Holdings) BV* [1996] STC 785, it was held that two companies, each owning 50% of the shares in a third company, were connected within *ICTA 1988, s 839(7)* by virtue of a shareholders' agreement on the management of the company, and as such together controlled it within *ICTA 1988, s 416(2), (3)*. As a result, a Dutch resident company was unable, by reason of *article 10* of the *1980 UK-Netherlands double tax convention*, to secure repayment of the tax credit attaching to a dividend paid by a UK subsidiary. *FA 1997, s 68* was designed to ensure that consortium relief would not be lost if a voting agreement existed between members, thereby making them connected persons and breaching the rule that no person (whether alone or with connected persons) should control more than 75% of the voting rights in a company controlled by a consortium. The current rule is in *CTA 2010, s 155*. This provides that arrangements entered into by a joint venture company (as defined) are 'arrangements' so as to preclude group relief or consortium relief where one of the companies (the claimant company or surrendering company) could leave the group or consortium.

Test 3: Participation

6.22   The 'participator' test applies in relation to deeply discounted securities issued by close companies to participators and associates of participators. It also applies where interest is paid late by a close company to a participator, as provided in *CTA 2009, s 375*. 'Participator' is defined in terms of *CTA 2009, s 841, CTA 2010, s 454*, but that definition is modified to exclude a pure loan creditor from 'participator' for the purposes of the loan relationship rules under *CTA 2009, s 411*. A person is a 'participator' if he:

(a)   owns or is entitled to acquire share capital in the company;

(b)   owns or is entitled to acquire voting rights in the company;

(c)   has a right to receive distributions or amounts payable to loan creditors by way of a premium on redemption of a loan; or

(d)   is entitled to secure that income or assets of the company, whether present or future, will be applied directly or indirectly for his benefit.

A holder of a convertible is always a participator, because he has a right to acquire shares.

6.23   An 'associate' is a close relative or partner of a participator, the trustee of a settlement created by the participator, or the trustees of a testator whose estate contains shares in which the participator has an interest. The powers of an associate or any number of associates may be added to those of the participator.

Example 6.7

N Ltd was controlled by the trustees of the W Will Trust. L Ltd was controlled by the trustees of the W Discretionary Trust. Mrs W had a life interest under the Will Trust. She was a participator in N Ltd under *ICTA 1988, s 417(1)(c)*. Therefore, the trustees of the Will Trust were her 'associates' under *s 417(3) (c)(i)*, and the trustees of the Discretionary Trust were her 'associates' under *s 417(3)(b)* (*R v IRC, ex p Newfields Developments Ltd* [2001] STC 901).

Loan creditor

6.24   'Loan creditor' is defined in *CTA 2010, s 453* as meaning a creditor (other than a bank acting in the ordinary course of its business) in respect of any redeemable loan capital issued by a company or any debt incurred by the company:

(a)   for any money borrowed or capital assets acquired by the company;

(b)   for any right to receive income created in favour of the company; or

(c)   for consideration the value of which to the company was (at the time when the debt was incurred) substantially less than the amount of the debt (including any premium thereon).

6.25   Thus the expression 'loan creditor' extends to a person who has not lent money to a company, but it simply means the unpaid vendor of a capital asset. Under *CTA 2010, s 453(4)* a person carrying on a business of banking is not deemed to be a loan creditor in respect of loan capital or debt issued to him for money lent in the ordinary course of banking business.

6.26   Because, under *CTA 2009, s 454*, a 'loan creditor' is a 'participator', amounts due to participators as loan creditors are taken into account in determining that participator's entitlement to assets of the company available for distribution on a winding up.

6.27   Where a company can be wound up in a solvent liquidation, the loan creditor who is also a shareholder will be paid in full, before receiving his residual entitlement as shareholder. The existence of pre-emption rights to shares or debt will not be added to actual rights held until they become exercisable. The existence of option rights will be added to other existing rights.

Test 4: Controlling corporate partner

6.28   A partnership trade is carried on by the partners collectively, ie the firm. For tax purposes the concept of a notional separate trade carried on by each partner is introduced: *R & C Comrs v Vaines* [2016] STC 1201. The general rule is that a partnership is transparent for tax purposes, so that, in the case of a partnership which is carrying on a trade, the company partner's share of the firm profits is treated as arising directly to and taxable on the corporate partner: *CTA 2009, ss 380(3), 467(2), 1259*. This rule applies to LLPs, notwithstanding the fact that an LLP has entity status under *s 1257*. 'Company' means any body corporate or unincorporated association, but not a local authority or partnership: *CTA 2010, s 1121*. Partnership is not defined for corporation tax purposes. An LLP is a corporate body. However, this point does not matter because an LLP is treated as transparent for tax purposes. *CTA 2009, s 380(3)* deems that actions taken by the partnership in relation to a money debt are regarded for a company partner as having been undertaken by the company. This is in accordance with the general transparency rule in relation to taxation of partnerships.

6.29   A company partner's share of debits and credits comprises its 'appropriate share of the total credits and debits', ie as apportioned in accordance with the profit-sharing arrangements: *CTA 2009, ss 383, 467(4), 474(8)*.

6.30   A corporate member of a partnership who has a controlling interest in the partnership is 'connected' with any other corporate partners: *CTA 2009, s 383(3)*. If one company partner is connected with another company, and they together control the partnership, there will be a controlling partner: *s 383(7)*. 'Control' is defined in accordance with *s 472: s 383(8)*.

6.31   Where a 'company partner' (ie a company which is a member of a partnership) is treated as a creditor or debtor of a loan relationship incurred by the firm, and that company partner (or that company partner and a connected company partner) controls the partnership, there will be a deemed connection between the company partner and each other company partner. 'Control' of a partnership means 'the right to a share of more than one half of the assets, or more than one half of the income of the partnership'.

Disregarded connection

6.32   There are two sets of 'exempt circumstances' in which a company does not have to account on an amortised cost basis for debt assets which it holds in a connected company. These are set out in *CTA 2009, ss 468–471*. Subject to numerous conditions, companies trading in marketable debt (eg listed debt or commercial paper) of their parent are not treated as connected in relation to that debt. Where the creditor is a financial trader using fair values, who buys and sells creditor relationships as an integral part of his trade, connection is ignored. The loan relationships of the company with which the trader is connected must either be listed, or the period between issue and redemption must be less than 12 months. At least 70% of assets of the same kind must be in the beneficial ownership of non-connected persons, but this condition can be breached for up to three months in aggregate in any accounting period, to allow the trader to accept placements of new issues prior to onwards sale. Financial traders are accordingly able to hold and deal in listed debt and commercial paper issued by affiliates without either having to use accruals accounting or losing impairment.

6.33   The second set of exempt circumstances in which a creditor relationship may be held applies to insurance companies, when certain creditor loan relationships are being held for the purposes of its basic life assurance and general annuity business (BLAGAB).

6.34   Shares that are held as trading assets are ignored, under *CTA 2009, s 472(3)*. *Sections 363(6)* and *466(3)* exclude control by common ownership through:

● the Crown;

● a Minister of the Crown;

● a government department;

● a Northern Ireland department;

● a foreign sovereign power; or

● an international organisation.

Circumstances and consequences of connection

6.35   The circumstances in which a connection arises, and the consequences of that connection, may be summarised as follows:

Statutory provision	Nature of connection	Circumstance	Consequence
CTA 2009, s 349	Control	Loan relationship between connected companies	Amortised cost basis mandatory
CTA 2009, s 453	Control	Loan relationship at less than a commercial return with benefit to company connected with creditor (P)	Loan relationship fair valued including benefit to P
CTA 2009, s 361	Control	Creditor becomes connected with debtor and debt acquired at undervalue	Deemed release chargeable to tax

Statutory provision	Nature of connection	Circumstance	Consequence
CTA 2009, s 362	Control	Creditor becomes connected with debtor and pre-connection debt is impaired	Deemed release chargeable to tax
CTA 2009, s 358	Control/ controlling corporate partner	Release credit	No credit for debt releases
CTA 2009, s 354	Control/ controlling corporate partner	Release debit/ impairment	No relief for release/ impairment
CTA 2009, s 352	Control	Debt disposal	Debits and credits limited to what would have been due, had relationship continued
CTA 2009, s 355	Control	Companies have ceased to be connected	No debits disallowed in connected period allowed in non-connected period
CTA 2009, ss 409–411	Participation	Issue of deeply discounted security by close company to participator	Issuer obtains no debit prior to redemption but investor taxed on accruals
ITTOIA 2005, ss 440, 441	'Connection' as defined in *ITA 2007, s 993*	Disposal of deeply discounted security to connected person	Market value disposal and acquisition
CTA 2009, s 695	Control	Abandoned options and connected companies	Company making transfer of value incurs credit
TIOPA 2010, s 241	Control as defined in *CTA 2010, s 1122*	Arbitrage transaction	Disallowance of debit

Amortised cost basis

6.36   The use of an amortised cost basis of accounting for connected companies relationships by creditor and debtor is mandatory under *CTA 2009, s 349(1), (2)*. By way of exception, under *s 349(3)*, reset bonds within *s 454* are fair valued. These are bonds whose terms may be varied to alter the fair value of the bond by more than 5% ('bull and bear notes'). These are paired notes, such that, on reset, one produces a profit and the other a loss. The loss-producing note is then disposed of, so that the loss could (but for the statutory provision) be set against a profit realised elsewhere.

Impairment losses where connected companies relationship exists

6.37   Forgiveness of loan by a parent company is a capital contribution – a dividend paid downwards. Therefore, a revenue deduction is not allowed for the release. Equally, a gift is not a profit. Hence, the debtor company does not have to bring in a credit for the release of a connected companies relationship. In other words, there is an automatic matching rule in connected company relationships, and the treatment is approximated to an arm's length situation. If debt waiver is disregarded for tax purposes, it is equivalent to a capital contribution. The accounting entries in the debtor company will be:

DR Liabilities   CR Capital contribution

6.38   The principal rule is that, where there is a loan relationship, and the debtor and creditor are connected under the control test, no impairment relief is available. The reason for the general rule is to stop the duplication or cascading of bad debt relief amongst corporate groups, and because connected party debt is regarded as disguised equity. This rule and the related rules only apply where companies are connected through the control and controlling corporate partner tests.

Example 6.8

(a)   A lends £1m to its subsidiary B. B lends £1m to an unconnected company, C, which becomes insolvent, so that the whole loan is lost. In the absence of a restriction, both A and B could claim bad debt relief, amounting to £2m of relief for £1m of loss.

(b)   A owns B and C. B has losses of £1m, and debts of £2m owed to A. C has profits of £2m. B can surrender £1m of losses to C. C lends B £1m, which B cannot repay. If C could claim bad debt relief, its remaining profits would be free of tax, but the group would not have suffered any financial loss.

6.39   The specific rules are:

(a)   both companies must use amortised cost basis for the debt (*CTA 2009, s 349*);

(b)   no impairment relief or release debit is available to the creditor company (*s 354*);

(c)   no release credit arises in the debtor (*s 358*); and

(d)   related transactions concerned with connected companies debt are disregarded (*s 352*).

6.40   As very few debtors will fair value liabilities, *s 349* will only bite on creditor relationships. Amongst creditors, only financial traders will use fair value. However, there is an excepting provision for such companies in *s 46*. Connected companies are unlikely to hold debt in each other as trading stock. Hence, the rule in *s 349* is of very limited application. The purpose of the rule is, where fair value might unusually be used, to prevent bad debt relief being obtained between connected parties by a revaluation of debt.

6.41   The general rule is stated in *s 354(1)*:

'(1)   The general rule is that no impairment loss or release debit in respect of a company's creditor relationship is to be brought into account for the purposes of this Part for an accounting period if section 349 (application of amortised cost basis to connected company relationships) applies to the relationship for the period.'

6.42   *Section 354(2)* then provides an exception for (a) debt-equity swaps (*s 356*) and (b) insolvent creditors (*s 357*). *Section 354(2A)* provides that where a loan relationship has been revalued as a result of its being the hedged item under a designated fair value hedge, any debit or credit on the loan relationship that represents the reversal of such adjustment shall be brought into account in computing the company's loan relationship profits, notwithstanding the existence of a connected companies' loan relationship.

6.43   If the impairment is subsequently reversed, the creditor is not required to bring in a credit, having been originally denied a debit: *s 360*.

6.44   If creditor and debtor only become connected as a result of a debt-swap which gives the creditor control of the debtor, the creditor can obtain impairment relief in respect of all the loans which he treats as discharged by reason of the debt-equity swap: *s 356*. If he does not write off all his loans to the debtor at this point, he will not obtain relief for any subsequent impairments.

6.45   Intra-group accounts will often comprise a mixture of pure lending and amounts owed for intra-group supplies and recharges. In that case, the debt must be broken down into two parts, only one of which will constitute an actual loan relationship. A trade debt is a relevant non-lending relationship (RNLR). The release of a debt for which a trading deduction has been given is treated as a non-trading profit on a loan relationship. There is a proviso which exempts, from treatment as a receipt, a release of debt formerly allowed as a trading expense where the release is part of a 'relevant arrangement or compromise', ie a voluntary arrangement under the *Insolvency Act 1986*, or a compromise or arrangement under *CA 2006, s 895*.

6.46   In practice, trade debt can be converted into a loan relationship by issuing a debenture, to represent the debt, which then falls within the loan relationship rules. If the debt is then released, no credit arises in the debtor, provided the necessary connection exists, and the debt is accounted for on an amortised cost basis.

Partnership loans

6.47   Just as companies are financed by debt and equity, so partners finance a partnership through capital contributions and member loans. The question is whether a purported loan by an investor to a partnership of which he is a member is treated as a debt for tax purposes. This depends upon the extent to which a partnership is treated as a separate entity for tax purposes. A partner may supply goods or services to a partnership other than in his capacity as a partner. For example, an accountant who owns office premises may rent them to a partnership of which he is a member, and the rent payable is properly deductible as an expense of the partnership in earning the firm's profits. Equally, a partner may lend money to a partnership of which he is a member, and the interest payable to him is deductible as a partnership expense, in the same way as interest payable to a bank would be: *Heastie v Veitch & Co* 18 TC 306 at 319. See *MacKinlay v Arthur Young McLelland Moores & Co* [1989] STC 898 at 903.

6.48   Where a partner lends money to a partnership of which he is a member, he is on both sides of the transaction, as creditor and debtor, unless the partnership is treated as if it were an opaque entity. UK tax law has proceeded in the opposite direction. The general rule is that a partnership is transparent for tax purposes, so that, in the case of a partnership which is carrying on a trade, the company partner's share of the firm profits is treated as arising directly to and taxable on the corporate partner: *CTA 2009, s 1259*. This rule applies to LLPs, notwithstanding the fact that an LLP has entity status: *s 1257*. By way of exception, for the purposes of the transactions in land rules (*CTA 2010, ss 356OA–356OT*), a partnership may be regarded as 'another person' distinct from the members of the partnership: *s 356OO(2)*.

6.49 *CTA 2009, s 380* deems debits and credits of the partnership in relation to a money debt or loan relationship to have been undertaken by the company partner in relation to his appropriate share. This is in accordance with the general transparency rule in relation to partnerships. Accordingly, if a company is a member of an LLP, and the LLP had a loan liability, the company member will have a loan relationship to the extent of its interest in the LLP.

Example 6.9

Georgian LLP is a 50/50 LLP with two members, A Ltd and Mr B. It is a body corporate, but not a company. The bank lends 1,000 to Georgian LLP. A Ltd has a debtor loan relationship of 500.

6.50 A corporate member of a partnership who has a controlling interest in the partnership is 'connected' with any other corporate partners: *CTA 2009, s 383*. Where there is a connected companies loan relationship: (a) no impairment relief is available to the company which waives the debt (*s 354*), and (b) no taxable release debit arises in the debtor company (*s 360*). Thus, to the extent that a controlling partner releases other corporate partners from liability to repay a loan made to the partnership, the other company partners are not required for tax purposes to bring into account any profits arising in respect of the transaction. Where a connected companies relationship is disposed of in a related transaction, the related transaction is disregarded for tax purposes: *s 352*.

Unconnected to connected

6.51 If two unconnected companies become connected through the control test, this only produces an immediate tax consequence where the carrying value of the obligation differs as between creditor and debtor company, in which case the deemed release rules may apply.

Connected to unconnected

6.52 Where a connected party loan relationship ceases, because the creditor company ceases through redemption, disposal or release to be a party to the loan relationship, *CTA 2009, s 352(1)–(3)* provide that, in the accounting period in which the connected loan relationship ceases:

(a) No account is to be taken of amounts which would have accrued subsequently.

(b)   The debits to be brought into account for that period in respect of the loan relationship shall not be more than they would have been, had the loan relationship continued.

(c)   The credits to be brought into account shall not be less that they would have been on the same assumption.

(d)   Exchange gains and losses are unaffected.

6.53   This is designed to prevent a circumvention of the exclusion of impairment relief by a related transaction, and means that intra-group debt waivers will not be recognised for tax. This means that, if a group company is sold, and the parent waives debts owed by the company being sold while debtor and creditor are still connected, there will be no charge to tax on the debtor or deduction for the vendor. Sales agreements need to take account of this factor. In either case, the solution is for the seller to waive the debt in its entirety on sale. This will, however, increase the sale consideration attributable to the shares. Moreover, an undertaking to procure repayment of outstanding group debt owed by the target may increase stamp duty payable.

Example 6.10

A Ltd loans £100 to its wholly owned subsidiary, B Ltd. B cannot repay the loan. A assigns the debt to P (an unconnected party) for £50. A is not entitled to bring in a debit of £50. The accounting entries for the creditor are:

DR Cash   50   CR Loan asset   100
DR P/L   50

6.54   Where *s 355* applies:

●   an impairment loss occurs in an accounting period during which companies are connected;

●   the companies cease to be connected in that period; and

●   the loan relationship continues to exist after connection has ceased,

CTA 2009, *s 355* restricts the subsequent availability of tax relief in respect of the impairment loss or release debit disallowed under *s 354*.

6.55   This prevents a company from claiming during a later accounting period later relief which was disallowable during the connection period. It does not prevent a subsequent claim for impairment not excluded by *s 354*.

Example 6.11

A Ltd has an accounting period ending 31 December.

It lends 100 to its subsidiary B Ltd.

In the accounting period ending 31 December 2010, A Ltd writes the debt down to 50.

In the accounting period ending 31 December 2011, A Ltd sells its B Ltd shares but retains the B debt.

In the accounting period ending 31 December 2012, A Ltd writes off the balance of the debt.

The results are:

Year-end	Impairment	Written-down value	Debit
31.12.10	50	50	0
31.12.12	50	50	50

6.56   If, after the connection has ceased, the creditor fair values the loan asset, there will be a catch up adjustment by reference to the difference between the carrying value of the loan relationship, determined on an amortised cost basis at the end of the preceding period, and the fair value.

6.57   The effect of *CTA 2009, ss 352(1)–(3)* is modified by *s 352(3A)–(3C), 352A*. If a loss on the disposal of the asset is caused by changes in the market rate of interest between acquisition and disposal, the seller can obtain release for the loss, notwithstanding that this is a connected companies loan relationship at the time of disposal. This remains subject to *s 354*, which excludes debits for the release of impairment of connected companies debts.

Debt release

6.58   *CTA 2009, s 322* allows a departure from the general rule concerning release credits in cases where an amortised cost basis is used. No credit for the release needs to be recognised by the debtor if any one of the five conditions set out in *s 322(3)–(5B)* is met.

6.59   The five conditions are:

- *s 322(3)*: Condition A – the release is part of a 'statutory insolvency arrangement';

- *s 322(4)*: Condition B – the release 'is in consideration of, or of any entitlement to, shares forming part of the ordinary share capital of the debtor company';

- *s 322(5)*: Condition C – the debtor company meets one of the 'insolvency conditions', and the creditor is not connected with the debtor;

- *s 322(5A)*: Condition D – the release is under stabilisation powers exercised under the *Banking Act 2009*, where a debtor bank is in financial difficulties; and

- *s 322(5B)*: Condition E – the release is part of a corporate rescue.

6.60   *Section 322(4)* overlaps with *s 356*. *Section 322(4)* applies to unconnected debtors to prevent a charge on the release of a debt where the debt is used to pay up new shares.

6.61   *Section 356* applies to creditors who become connected with the debtor company as a result of a debt-equity swap, to preserve impairment relief in the creditor.

6.62   These two provisions are considered in the section on debt-equity swaps in **Chapter 11**.

6.63   Where the release takes place as part of a statutory insolvency arrangement, there is no taxable credit in respect of the release in the debtor under *CTA 2009, s 322(3)*. For the purposes of this provision, a statutory insolvency arrangement is defined in *CTA 2009, s 1319* as meaning:

(a)   a company voluntary arrangement under the *Insolvency Act 1986*;

(b)   a compromise or arrangement under *Companies Act 2006, s 895*; or

(c)   a compromise or arrangement governed by a foreign law similar to (a) or (b).

Example 6.12

H Bank has lent Property Ltd £5m. The Bank decides to write off the loan, to remove non-performing loans from its balance sheet. It also releases the loan, so that Property Ltd can recapitalise. Property Ltd enters a company voluntary arrangement. There is no release credit in Property Ltd.

6.64   *CTA 2009, s 322(5)* provides that, where the debtor meets 'the insolvency condition', there is no taxable credit in respect of the release in the debtor. Under this provision, a company meets 'the insolvency condition' if (*ss 322(6), (7), 323*):

- it is in insolvent liquidation;

- it is in insolvent administration;

- it is in insolvent administrative receivership;

- an appointment of a provisional liquidation is in force; or

- it is subject to an equivalent foreign legal procedure.

6.65   To prevent a credit arising in the company which obtains the release, the creditor may instead assign the loan to an unrelated party. The debt will remain in existence, so there is no loan relationship credit. The lender will make a loss on a 'related transaction', namely the assignment of the debt, and the loss will be a loan relationship debit. If the assignee is an individual, the debt would be a QCB within *TCGA 1992, s 117*. If the debtor is subsequently able to make payments on the debt, the creditor will receive money tax-free, a gain on a QCB in the hands of an individual being tax-free.

Debt restructurings

6.66   The modification of the terms of debt may be a variation of the existing debt or the rescission of the existing debt and its replacement by a new obligation: *Morris v Barron & Co* [1918] AC 1 at 25–26. A rescission will be a 'related transaction' and so may trigger a tax charge. When the terms of a debt are significantly modified, the existing debt is treated as discharged and replaced by a new debt. IFRS requires a substantial modification of terms to alter the value of the obligation by at least 10%. FRS 102 is less prescriptive and does not specify any threshold. FRS 102, para 11.37 states:

> 'If an existing borrower and lender exchange financial instruments with substantially different terms, the entities shall account for the transaction as an extinguishment of the original financial liability and the recognition of a new financial liability. Similarly, an entity shall account for a substantial modification of the terms of an existing financial liability or a part of it (whether or not attributable to the financial difficulty of the debtor) as an extinguishment of the original financial liability and the recognition of a new financial liability.'

6.67   In the case of a release of part of a debt, in essence, the old loan has been replaced by a new loan, and the credit is the difference between the amount that would have been accrued in respect of the old loan and the amount to be accrued in respect of the new loan. This is not a variation of the existing contract but a new contract.

6.68   The credit in the debtor's accounts will relate not only to the absolute reduction in indebtedness, but also to the reduction in finance costs for the remainder of the term. If liabilities and finance costs for the term of the new loan are to be accurately reflected in the accounts, the whole of the gain should be recognised in the period in which the renegotiation is concluded. The alternative is to leave the debts on the original loan unaltered, but to bring in an interest subsidy as a credit for the remainder of the term. HMRC regard the former view as correct, ie recognition of the whole gain in the year in which it arises.

6.69   A debtor faced with a loan relationship credit following a debt renegotiation can, in the first instance, set available losses against that credit. For example, an investment company can carry forward excess management expenses to set against the debt released.

Corporate rescue/substantial modification exemptions

6.70   In non-connected situations, for accounting periods beginning on or after 1 January 2015, two new corporate rescue exemptions were introduced. By virtue of *CTA 2009, ss 322(5B), 323A* (introduced by *F(No 2)Act 2015, Sch 7, paras 16–18, 107*) a debtor does not have to bring in a credit for a release or part release of a debt, where:

(a)   it is reasonable to assume that, without the release and associated arrangements, the debtor company would have been unable to pay its debts within 12 months;

(b)   the debtor company would have been unable to pay its debts by reason of going concern or balance sheet insolvency: *s 323(A1)*.

HMRC regard the phrase 'unable to pay its debts' as having the same meaning as in *s 123* of the *Insolvency Act 1986*.

6.71   Circumstances coming within the relief include:

● likely breach of financial covenants,

● enforcement action by creditors,

● adverse trading conditions,

● cash flow shortfalls,

● balance sheet deficit,

● qualified audit reports.

6.72   Under *CTA 2009, s 323A*, where a debt obligation is 'significantly modified' (as defined for accounting purposes) and without the modification there would be a material risk that the company would not be able to pay its debts within 12 months, the debtor does not have to bring in a credit for the modification or replacement.

Insolvent liquidation

6.73   If a creditor is connected with a debtor, and the creditor goes into insolvent liquidation, impairment relief becomes available in respect of amounts owed by the debtor from the date that insolvency proceedings commence: *CTA 2009, s 357*. The proceedings in question are:

(a)   the creditor goes into insolvent liquidation;

(b)   an administration order is in force in relation to the creditor;

(c)   a provisional liquidator is appointed under *IA 1986, s 135*; or

(d)   a foreign legal proceeding equivalent to (a)–(c) commences.

6.74   This change is made to reverse the result in *Toshoku Finance UK plc v IRC* [2002] STC 368. In that case, the structure was:

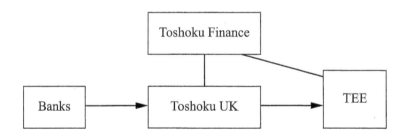

6.75   Banks lent money to Toshoku UK, which in turn lent it to TEE. All the Toshoku companies were insolvent. On 26 January 1998, Toshoku UK went into a creditors' voluntary liquidation. As at that date, TEE owed $156m to Toshoku UK. Of the available assets of TEE, Toshoku UK was entitled to receive $23m. Under the law as it stood, no bad debt relief was available (*FA 1996, s 87(2), (3)(b), Sch 9, paras 5(1), 6(3)*). Toshoku UK was assessed to corporation tax on the whole of the $23m as interest contractually payable on the loan of $156m, no departure from the assumption of payment in full being allowed. The question was whether corporation tax payable by the liquidator of the company fell within the words 'any necessary disbursements by the liquidator in the course of his administration' (*Insolvency Rules 1986, SI 1986/1925, r 4.218(1)(m)*), so as to take priority over provable debts of creditors (ie the banks), whose claims ranked lower. It was held that the payment of the tax on post-liquidation profits was an expense of winding up, taking priority over the claims of creditors proving in the winding up.

6.76 If a release occurs as a result of the creditor's insolvency and the debtor was connected with the creditor before it became insolvent, but is not connected thereafter, the debtor company is not required to bring in a credit for the release: *CTA 2009, s 359*.

6.77 The commencement of administration or receivership will mark the start of a new accounting period, but the accounting reference date does not change (*CTA 2009, ss 10, 11(1), (2)*). The assets of the company remain in the legal and beneficial ownership of the company. Accordingly, any group relationships and connected party loan relationships continue during the administration or receivership.

6.78 A company entering into liquidation ceases to be the beneficial owner of its assets, though legal ownership of the assets remains vested in the company: *Ayerst v C & K (Construction) Ltd* [1976] AC 167.

6.79 Under *FA 1954, s 17(6)(a)* a successor company could claim use of trading losses and capital allowances of a company previously carrying on trade, if the predecessor owned beneficially 75% of shares of the successor. Legal ownership of assets of a company in winding up remains with that company, but control and custody passes to the liquidator, who is an officer of the court, acting on behalf of contributories (solvent winding up) or creditors (insolvent winding up). Lord Diplock said at 179 that the company in winding up had thereby divested itself of beneficial ownership of its assets:

> 'I do not see how it can make any relevant difference that the legal ownership remains in the person in whom the full ownership was previously vested instead of being transferred to a new legal owner. Retention of the legal ownership does not prevent a full owner from divesting himself the beneficial ownership of the property by declaring that he holds it in trust for other persons. I see no reason why it should be otherwise where an event occurs which by virtue of a statute leaves him with the legal ownership of property but deprives him of all possibility of enjoying the fruits of it or disposing of it for his own benefit.'

6.80 Loan relationships use the concept of 'control' rather than 'beneficial ownership': *CTA 2009, s 466*. This raises the question: does loss of beneficial ownership of shares mean loss of control? When a company goes into liquidation, this brings an accounting period to an end, such that a connected company creditor relationship would cease to be a connected company relationship for the new accounting period. However, where the statutory concept is 'control' rather than beneficial ownership, the commencement of the liquidation of a company should not lead to the loss of control of shares vested in the company. This contrasts with provisions such as *CTA 2010, s 1154(6)* (which applies for defining a group for group relief) and says:

> '(6) In this Chapter references to ownership are to be read as references to beneficial ownership.'

6.81 This is a point which has not yet received a definitive answer. In many situations where the question will arise, one of the exceptions from the connected party rules for debt-equity swaps or an insolvency situation will apply.

6.82 Where a government investment in a company is written off, no loan relationship credit need be brought in, and instead the amount written off is deducted from losses carried forward: *CTA 2009, s 326*; *CTA 2010, s 92*.

Deemed releases

6.83 'Deemed releases' are releases which do not take place in legal or accountancy terms but are treated as taking place for corporation tax purposes when a creditor becomes connected with a debtor company.

1   *Section 361* applies where a company is or becomes connected with the debtor and acquires impaired debt of the debtor company.

2   *Section 362* applies where a company *already* holds impaired debt of an unconnected company and then *becomes* connected with the debtor company.

6.84 Where a creditor relationship is acquired at a discount, or stands at a discount, and the creditor becomes connected with the debtor, the debtor is required to bring in as a loan relationship credit the difference between the nominal value and the discounted value of the loan relationship. By this means (the thinking appears to be, though there is no discernible policy), any impairment debit which the creditor has obtained in the pre-connection period will be recaptured.

6.85 In the case of connected companies, the general rule is in *s 358(1)*. *CTA 2009, s 358(1)* says that if connected company debt is released, no release credit is recognised for tax purposes in the debtor. It is thus the other side of the coin of *s 354*. Section *358(2)* says that *s 358(1)* does not apply to 'deemed releases' or releases of 'relevant rights'. Thus, the exemption from charge in *CTA 2009, s 358(1)* does not apply to 'deemed releases' or 'a release of relevant rights': *s 358(2)*. 'Relevant rights' are defined in *s 358(4)* as rights acquired before 18 November 2015 in circumstances where there was no deemed release under *CTA 2009, s 361* by reason of the former corporate rescue exemption (*s 361A*) and debt for debt exception (*s 361B*), which were repealed with effect from the same date.

For this purpose only, the control test of connection applies: *s 363*.

6.86 When debt becomes impaired, restructuring often leads to a connection between the creditor and the borrower. The deemed release rules apply in four situations:

(a)   a company acquires debt owed by a subsidiary to a third party;

(b)   a company acquires control of another company and at the same time acquires debt owed by that company;

(c)   a company holds debt of a company and then acquires control of the debtor company;

(d)   a company unconnected with a debtor buys in its listed debt at a discount, and then becomes connected with the debtor.

6.87 The main statutory provisions are in *CTA 2009, ss 361–363A*. These were subject to major change with retrospective effect under *Finance Act 2012, s 23*, inserting *s 363A*. The situations were particularly directed at situation (d) above.

6.88 The first case (*CTA 2009, s 361*) is where the identity of the creditor changes, and the new creditor is or becomes connected with the debtor. The paragraph applies where:

1   Parent Ltd lender (or an unconnected creditor) holds impaired debt owed by Target Ltd.

2   There has been no corresponding release by the creditor of Target's debt.

3   Shares in Target are sold together with the loan owed by Target to an acquiring company ('Acquirer Ltd').

4   Immediately after the acquisition of shares and debt Acquirer becomes connected with Target.

5   Target owes more than Acquirer pays to obtain the debt asset.

6.89 At that point, there is a deemed release by the new creditor of the difference between the nominal amount of the loan ('the pre-acquisition carrying value' in the debtor's accounts) and the consideration which he has given to acquire it. That does not give rise to an impairment loss. The debtor has to bring in a corresponding credit, which is chargeable to tax. Accrued interest (ie interest owed but unpaid by the debtor) is left out of account and so excluded from the tax charge: *s 361(5), (6)*.

6.90 The second case (*CTA 2009, s 362*) applies where the identity of the creditor does not change but he becomes connected with the debtor. The section applies where:

(a) the identity of the creditor (C) does not change;

(b) the creditor is originally not connected with the debtor company (D), but becomes connected with the debtor company;

(c) the pre-connection carrying value (PCCV) in D's accounts exceeds the PCCV in C's accounts

6.91 D's PCCV is the liability on D's accounts if its accounting period had ended immediately before C and D became connected. If C is a party to the loan relationship on the last day of the period of account preceding that in which C and D become connected, C's PCCV is the cost of the asset on an amortised cost basis at the end of the accounting period accounts value at that date. In any other case it is the consideration given by C for the asset.

6.92 When C and D become connected, there is a deemed release by the creditor of the difference between D's PCCV and C's PCCV. The creditor has no additional impairment loss. The debtor has to bring in a credit for the deemed release: *CTA 2009, s 362*. Hence, any accrued impairment relief is recaptured.

6.93 *CTA 2009, s 363A* applies to:

(a) any arrangement entered into before 27 February 2012 where the deemed release would have occurred on or after that date; and

(b) arrangements made on or after 27 February 2012.

6.94 This is an anti-avoidance rule. It provides that where arrangements are entered into, the main purpose of which or one of the main purposes of which is to avoid a deemed release under *s 361* or *362*, such arrangements are 'not to achieve that effect'.

Example 6.13: Case 1 – *s 361*

1   Vendor Ltd lends its subsidiary Target Ltd £500. Target Ltd gets into difficulties, and Vendor Ltd writes down the debt in its books to £200. Purchaser Ltd acquires the Target Ltd shares for £1 and the X Ltd debt for £200.

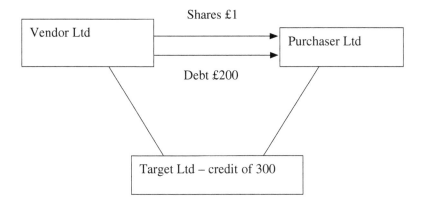

When Purchaser Ltd acquires the Target Ltd shares, Purchaser is deemed to release 300 of the debt, and Target Ltd must bring in a loan relationship credit of 300.

2   Holding plc (H) owns all the shares in Target Ltd (T). T owes H 50, which is repayable on demand. T's debt has been written down to 20 in the books of H. H's acquisition cost for T is 40. H sells to Acquirer plc (A) for 100 all the T shares plus the debt owed by T to H. Of the purchase consideration, 20 is allocated to the debt, and 80 to the shares. H makes a gain of 40 (80 − 40) on the shares. A's base cost is 80. A makes a deemed release of 30, and T has to bring in a credit of this amount.

3   As in (a) but 50 of the purchaser consideration is attributed to the debt. H makes a gain of 10 (50 − 40) on the shares, and has to bring in a loan relationship credit of 30 (50 − 20) on the debt (total gain remains 40). A's carrying value for the debt is 50. There is no deemed release.

4   As in (1) but H releases the debt and the whole purchase consideration is allocated to the shares. H makes a gain of 60 (100 − 40) on the shares. A's base cost for the shares is 100.

Example 6.14: Case 2 – *s 363*

C Ltd lends 1,000 to D Ltd, an unconnected company. C Ltd impairs the debt to 600. This is the carrying value in C's accounts at the end of its accounting period on 31 December 2012. In February 2013, C Ltd acquires a 60% shareholding in D Ltd. D Ltd has to bring in a credit for a deemed release of 400.

6.95   There are two 'relevant exceptions' to the deemed release charge under *s 361*, namely:

- equity-for-debt exception: *s 361C*; and
- corporate rescue exception: *s 361D*.

6.96   The equity-for-debt exception applies where the debt is exchanged in an arm's length transaction for ordinary shares in the purchaser or a company connected with the purchaser.

6.97   The corporate rescue exception in *s 361D* applies where:

(a)   within 60 days of C's becoming connected with D, the debt is released; and

(b)   the corporate rescue conditions are satisfied, ie–

    (i)   C acquires its rights under the loan relationship in an arm's length transaction;

    (ii)   it is reasonable to assume that, but for the release, D would have been unable to pay its debts (as defined): *s 361D(4)*.

6.98   There is one exception to *s 362*, namely the corporate rescue exception in *s 362A*. The conditions are the same as for the *s 361D* corporate rescue exception.

Example 6.15

C Ltd has lent 1,000 to D Ltd, an unconnected company. C Ltd only expects to recover 400 of the loan, and has written the debt down to 400 in its books, obtaining impairment loss relief on 600. The pre-connection value of the loan relationship is 400. C Ltd then purchases all the shares in D Ltd. C Ltd is deemed to release 600 of the debt, and D Ltd brings in a credit of 600, which is taxable. The release is equal to the difference between the carrying value of the loan relationship in the creditor's accounts at the time when the parties become connected (determined without taking into account previous impairment losses) and the market value of the loan. The deemed release takes place when the companies become connected.

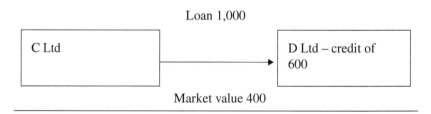

Loan 1,000

| C Ltd | | D Ltd – credit of 600 |

Market value 400

6.99 *CTA 2009, s 322(4)* takes precedence over *CTA 2009, s 362*. So where a creditor company treats a creditor relationship as wholly or partially discharged in return for the issue of ordinary shares in the debtor, there is no deemed release in the debtor company, even if:

(a) the creditor company would have made an impairment provision in respect of the debt if an accounting period had ended immediately before the debt for equity swap takes place; and

(b) as a result of the debt for equity exchange the creditor company were to obtain control of the debtor company.

6.100 In short, *s 322(4)* trumps both *ss 362* and *363A*. The point here is that the equity-for-debt exception (*s 361C*) only applies for the purposes of *s 361*, not *s 362*.

6.101 Given these rules, if the parent company sells both shares and debt of a subsidiary to a purchaser, the parent company should release the debt prior to disposal down to its acquisition price. The release of trade debt (being an RNLR) prior to disposal will not produce a credit in the debtor under *CTA 2009, ss 358, 479(2)(d), 481(3)(f)*. If the target company has available losses, they can be set against any credit arising on a deemed release.

6.102 The deemed release rules invent a transaction which does not exist and tax it as if it did. The policy underlying these rules – other than simply to raise tax – has always been unclear.

6.103 In situation (1), the debtor company has to bring in a credit, whether or not the prior creditor was connected. The unconnected lender will have obtained impairment relief, but the connected lender will not. The white knight who acquires both the shares of an ailing company from its existing parent, and the debt of the same company from an unconnected bank, takes the impaired debt on to its balance sheet at its acquisition cost, for both accounting and tax purposes.

6.104 In situation (2), where creditor and debtor are not connected in the accounting period in which the write-down occurs (so that impairment loss relief can be obtained), HMRC's concern is that there will be a loss of tax once the creditor and debtor become connected, because the debtor company will not be chargeable to tax on a subsequent debt release. There is, therefore, perceived to be a 'gap' in the taxation provisions. To ensure tax neutrality where both distressed debt is held or acquired and the parties become connected, the charge is intended to catch the credit on the release, which would cease to be taxable once debtor and creditor had become connected.

6.105   In both cases, the result is to tax paper profits. In most cases the exemption from charge on a debt release for companies in an insolvency situation will also apply.

Late or unpaid interest

6.106   Interest is allowed as a debit when an amortised cost basis applies, regardless of whether it is paid or not. This is subject to two exceptions in *CTA 2009, s 373*. These apply if:

(a)   interest is not paid within 12 months of the end of the accounting period in which it falls due; and

(b)   the creditor does not bring in a credit corresponding to the borrower's debit for interest.

6.107   If these conditions are fulfilled, and the case falls within the two exceptions, the taxation of the interest reverts to the cash basis.

6.108   This occurs in two situations:

(a)   where there is a loan to a participator in a close company and neither the CIS-based close company or CIS limited partnership are met: *s 375*;

(b)   where the loan is by the trustees of an occupational pension scheme to a debtor company (D), and D is the employer company, or connected to the employer company (control or major interest tests): *s 378*.

6.109   A person is a 'participator' in a close company if he:

- holds shares;
- has options for shares;
- has the right to receive distributions;
- has entitlement to acquire the right to distributions; or
- has the ability to secure that the income or assets of the company are applied for his benefit.

6.110   However, a person is not a participator if he is only a loan creditor, having no other rights or interest.

6.111   A person is an 'associate' of a 'participator' if he is a:

- partner;

- relative (spouse, parent, grandparent, child, grandchild, sibling);

- trustee of a settlement made by the participator or by a relative, living or dead, of the participator; or

- trustee of a settlement or personal representative of a deceased where the participator has an interest in the shares or obligations of the shares held by the trustees or personal representative respectively.

6.112 In the case of MBOs and private equity-backed acquisitions, interest on subordinated debt will be rolled up and added to the principal until the senior debt is paid off. Accordingly, there is an exclusion if the borrower is a close company by reason of being controlled by a limited partnership which is a collective investment scheme (CIS) within *FSMA 2000, s 235*. The 'CIS-based close company' and 'CIS limited partnership' conditions are that:

(a) the lender is a limited partnership which is a CIS, or would be a CIS but for the lack of corporate status;

(b) the lender is not resident in a 'non-qualifying territory' (as defined in *TIOPA 2010, s 172*, ie a territory with which the UK has an ordinary DTA and which has been designated by the Treasury as 'qualifying';

(c) the borrower is an SME (as defined in *TIOPA 2010, s 172*); and

(d) the borrower would not be a close company, but for the attribution to one partner of the rights of another partner under *CTA 2010, ss 448, 451(4)(c)*.

6.113 This exclusion is chiefly of application to private equity-backed acquisitions. Such transactions are usually highly geared. This keeps the absolute equity cash element to be funded by the investors to a minimum. Greater leverage enables the investors to maximise the internal rate of return (IRR) on the equity if a successful exit (sale or flotation) is achieved. It reduces the potential loss should the target fail, by giving the investors an enhanced priority. It eliminates or reduces the potential tax charge in the target. It is common for the interest accruing on investor debt to remain outstanding, either throughout the life of the loan notes or, at the very least, for an initial period. It is not unusual for interest to continue to roll up until redemption of the loan notes. Moreover, the inter-creditor agreement will always provide that interest is only to be payable when all payments due on senior debt have been made, and payment of interest will not lead to breach of banking covenants.

6.114 To avoid interest being recharacterised as a distribution, it is common to employ a double Newco structure, so that one company holds investor debt and another company holds investor shares.

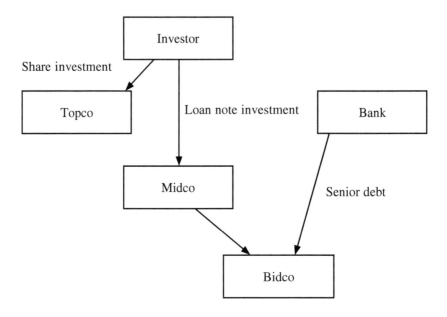

Close companies' deeply discounted securities

6.115 Under *CTA 2009, ss 409–412* where, for any accounting period:

(a) the debtor is a close company which has issued a deeply discounted security (as defined in *ITTOIA 2005, s 430*), and

(b) the creditor is a participator or associate of a participator or a company controlled by a participator,

the issuer will only obtain relief for the discount on redemption (rather than on an accruals basis).

6.116 This rule will not apply if the creditor is a company and brings in credits for the discount on an amortised cost basis: see *s 410(2)* ('the corresponding creditor relationship condition'). There is also an exclusion where the debt is issued to the general partner of a limited liability partnership which is a collective investment scheme within *FSMA 2000, s 235 (CTA 2009, s 410(3)–(6A))*. The issuer must be a company which is only close because it is controlled by the general partner, to whom the rights of other partners are attributed. It must also be an SME. The general partner must be the general partner of a limited partnership which is a CIS, or would be but for its lack of corporate status. None of the partners must be resident in a non-qualifying territory.

6.117 Only the 'participation' test of connection applies for this purpose. 'Participator' is defined in accordance with *CTA 2010, s 454*. A person is not regarded as a participator in a company '"just because" he is a loan creditor of the company': *s 411(3)*. The operative words are 'just because'. If a person both lends money to and owns shares in a company, the 'loan creditor only' exemption will not apply. Thus, where a loan creditor has any shareholding in the debtor company, or rights which would make him a participator in the debtor, the loan relationship will be taken into account in determining whether the creditor is connected with the debtor.

Example 6.16

Materials Ltd, a close company, issues to Mr Jones, who holds 10 of the 100 issued ordinary shares in the company, a loan note for £1,000, repayable at £1,500 in five years' time. After four years, the loan note is repaid early. The premium payable on redemption can only be treated as a loan relationship debit for Materials Ltd when the loan is repaid.

6.118 If one close company (A) and one non-close company (B) have equal stakes in a third company (C), C will be treated as a close company. This is because it is not controlled by a non-close company, and – in order to treat it as close – it is not necessary to include a non-close company as a participator. Hence, C will be connected with A and B.

Non-arm's length transactions

6.119 Where a transaction involving loan relationships is not a transaction at arm's length, an arm's length standard is imposed: *CTA 2009, s 444*. This rule does not apply where transfer pricing adjustments are made, because the transfer pricing rules take precedence over the loan relationship rules, except as regards foreign exchange gains and losses. 'Not at arm's length' is not defined, but is likely to have the same meaning as 'otherwise than by way of a bargain made at arm's length' within *TCGA 1992, s 17(1)(a)*. Where an arm's length standard is imposed, the debits and credits are to be found by taking the terms which would have been entered into between 'independent persons'. The practical importance of this provision is limited, because it does not apply if the transaction itself would never have taken place between independent persons.

6.120 The arm's length rule does not apply:

(a)   to transactions within capital gains tax groups; and

(b)   to debits arising from the acquisition of rights under a loan relationship where these rights are acquired for less than market value. The rule only applies to the acquisition of a debt asset at an overvaluation.

6.121   Hence, where a link between companies falls short of the capital gains tax group standard, all transfers or rescheduling of loan relationships between them may be liable to the substitution of arm's length prices. Where a transaction is not a transaction at arm's length, credits and debits at market value must be substituted for any values which do not correspond to arm's length terms.

Capitalisation of finance costs

6.122   For accounts purposes, companies may, instead of expensing finance costs when they are incurred, capitalise them as part of the value of fixed capital asset or project, when prescribed conditions are met (FRS 102, Section 13).

6.123   Property developers keep the cost of developments on revenue account, capitalise interest as part of work in progress, and release it as expenses to match sales. In such cases, relief for interest will only be available when the cost of work-in-progress is debited to the profit and loss account on the sale of the development, either on an accruals or on a paid basis.

6.124   Historically, payments that are treated as paid out of capital in the books of a company have not been allowed as a Schedule D, Case I deduction (*Chancery Lane Safe Deposit and Offices Co Ltd v IRC* 43 TC 83; *Fitzleet Estates Ltd v Cherry (Inspector of Taxes)* 51 TC 708).

6.125   For tax purposes, special rules apply where a loan is taken out to fund a capital project, and a normal accounting method allows interest and other expenses to be carried to a fixed capital account rather than to be expensed to the profit and loss account. A company is allowed to treat the deduction as a debit for tax purposes on an accruals basis: *CTA 2009, s 320(1), (2)*. Where this rule applies, capitalised interest can be brought into account as though it were not being capitalised. Where capitalised interest is included in development costs in this way, it must be excluded from any debit arising from the writing down or depreciation of the asset: *s 320(4)–(6)*. This treatment is only available for:

(a)   a fixed capital asset; or

(b)   a project.

Example 6.17

A company includes in the cost of a 'fixed capital asset' interest of £500,000 in year ended 30 April 2016. The interest does not pass through the profit and loss account but is added to the asset value. The interest expense will be deductible for tax purposes in the year ended 30 April 2016.

6.126   If shares in a company are purchased as a long-term investment and are shown as an investment in the company's accounts, such shares will be treated as a fixed capital asset. If the costs of obtaining loan finance are capitalised as part of the cost of the shares, relief will be available for such costs as if the expenditure had not been capitalised.

6.127   In the case of private finance initiative (PFI) projects, in cases where the project is 'off' the operator's books for tax purposes (composite trade treatment), a tax deduction can still be claimed for capitalised interest as it is accrued, if the operator carries the project as a fixed asset in his books and chooses to capitalise finance costs.

The group continuity rules

6.128   The group rules constitute a major departure from the solo entity rules, which generally prevail for tax purposes. The group transfer rules, which exist for chargeable assets, loan relationships and derivative contracts, are part of the rules designed to prevent the recognition at entity level of profits and losses which would disappear on consolidation. From the tax point of view, the company does not want to be taxed at entity level on profits on intra-group transactions, while HMRC do not want losses on intra-group transactions to be recognised at entity level.

6.129   The rules derive from the capital gains tax group rules. The starting point is the definition of capital gains tax group: *CTA 2009, s 335(6)*. This comprises a principal company, its 75% subsidiaries, and their 75% subsidiaries, provided that every company in the group is an effective 51% subsidiary of the principal company (*TCGA 1992, s 170(3)*). For the purposes of both the 75% and 51% subsidiary qualification, the three tests of voting power, entitlement to profits on a distribution, and entitlement to assets on a winding up, apply (*TCGA 1992, s 170(6)–(8)*). A UK permanent establishment of a non-resident company can be a member of a capital gains tax group. Both companies (or any permanent establishment) must be within the charge to UK corporation tax.

6.130   A company cannot belong to more than one group. Nor can a company be a principal company if it is a 75% subsidiary, unless it is the principal company of a group which includes its own effective 51% subsidiaries, which would not be effective 51% subsidiaries of the company above their 75% parent (*TCGA 1992, s 170(5)*). A group remains the same group as long as the principal company does not change. When the principal company of one group is taken over by another UK resident company, the rules applying to chargeable gains will treat the old group and the resultant new group as the same group (*TCGA 1992, s 171(10)*).

Example 6.18

X holds 75% of the shares in X1, which holds 75% of the shares in XX1. Y plc acquires 75% of the shares in X. Y is the principal company of a group comprising the Y group, X and X1. X1 is the principal company of a group comprising itself and XX1.

6.131   *CTA 2009, s 340* treats creditor loan relationships as continuing where they are transferred between group companies. As with capital gains assets, the base cost of the original assets is carried across to the transferee company. This allows gains and losses to be realised in the company which makes optimum use of them. The rule applies equally to connected party debt. It is a condition of the continuity rule that the transferee '"directly or indirectly" replaces the other ("the transferor") as a party to a loan relationship' (*s 336(1)(b)*). As one party to a loan relationship must be 'replaced' by another, the whole relationship must be transferred. No debits or credits will accrue to the transferor by virtue of the transfer, but future debits or credits in respect of that loan relationship will be recognised by the transferee, who will take over the transferor's book value. If the debt is acquired intra-group at a discount, it may give rise to a tax charge on repayment of the debt.

6.132   The same rule also applies to transfers of debtor relationships intra-group. Debtor relationships can only be transferred by novation, in other words by entering into a new contract which is substituted for the existing contract:

> 'A debtor cannot relieve himself of his liability to his creditor by assigning the burden of the obligation to somebody else; this can only be brought about by the consent of all three, and involves the release of the original debtor.'

(*Tolhurst v Associated Portland Cement Manufacturers (1900) Ltd* [1902] 2 KB 660 at 668)

6.133   The basic 'disregard' rule is in *CTA 2009, s 340(3)–(6)*. Where this section applies, the loan relationship will be deemed to be transferred at its 'tax-adjusted carrying value'. This is the value at which the loan relationship would be treated as being carried for the purposes of the loan relationships legislation, ie if the transferor's accounting period had ended immediately before the transfer. All payments, other than those related to the transaction, are brought into account, taking the transfer into effect. Thus, interest and discounts will be taxable in the company to which they accrue. *Section 340* takes precedence over the transfer pricing rules: *s 340(7)*.

6.134   The rule also has effect in relation to transfers between insurance companies which have effect as an insurance business transfer scheme: *s 337*. If the contract is held for long-term insurance business, the no gain/no loss treatment does not apply on a related transaction between group companies: *s 336(4)*. The rule does not apply where an insurance company switches an asset from one category of business to another, or removes an asset from long-term life insurance business.

6.135   The group continuity rule does not apply if the transferor company 'is regarded as using fair value accounting as regards the loan relationship': *CTA 2009, s 341(1)*. The transferor is 'regarded as using fair value accounting' if: (a) it uses fair values; (b) without using fair value accounting it brings in credits and debits for the relationship on a fair value basis; or (c) the security is of a type which has to be accounted for on a fair value basis, ie index-linked gilt-edged securities: *CTA 2009, s 399*. In this case, the transferee has to bring into account the fair value of the asset, and, if he uses an amortised cost basis, make an accounting adjustment. Both transferor and transferee are required to use the same fair value: *s 341(3)*. If a discount arises in respect of the transaction, the amount to be brought into account by the transferee must be increased by the discount: *s 341(4)*.

6.136   In the case of an issue of new securities in exchange for loan relationships in intra-EU cross-border reorganisations, which constitutes a reorganisation within *TCGA 1992, ss 127–130* (or would constitute such a reorganisation but for the use of QCBs), the loan relationship will also be disposed of for its notional carrying value: *CTA 2009, ss 339, 342*. Again, there is an exception if the transferor uses fair value accounting: *s 343*.

6.137   If the transferee company leaves the group within six years of the transfer while still party to the transferred loan relationship, there is a degrouping charge: *ss 344–346*. The degrouping charge brings into the taxable profits the gain held over on the intra-group transfer. Losses will also be recognised. The transferee is deemed to dispose of the loan relationship at that time for a consideration equal to the fair value and immediately reacquired it. If the deemed disposal would give rise to a loss, the loss is only recognised in the case of a creditor relationship hedged by a derivative, and a corresponding credit would arise under the derivative contracts rules: *s 345(2)–(5)*.

6.138   There is no degrouping charge if:

(a)   the principal company of the group becomes a member of another group of companies;

(b)   the transferee company leaves the group by reason of an exempt distribution within *CTA 2010, ss 1075–1078*; or

(c)   the transferee company leaves the group as part of a European cross-border transfer of business or merger.

There is an anti-avoidance rule in *s 347*.

Intra-group financing arrangements

6.139   A large number of intra-group financing arrangements have been adopted, which seek to achieve tax asymmetry, in the form of a deduction for finance costs in the borrower company without a corresponding credit for finance receipts in the creditor company.

Vocalspruce Ltd v R & C Comrs [2015] STC 861

6.140   Parent Co (B) subscribed for zero coupon bonds (ZCBs) issued by subsidiaries. The ZCBs had a redemption price of 100 and issue price of 80. B also subscribed for shares in V with a nominal value of 80 and share premium of 20. To pay the subscription moneys B transferred the ZCBs to V. As the discount accrued, V credited the amount of the accrual to share premium account. The assignment from B to V was held to be a related transaction, which did not of itself give rise to a tax charge because of the 'single company' fiction for intra-group transfers.

6.141   The aim of the arrangement was to obtain a debit for the discount in the debtor companies, without a corresponding taxable credit in V. V sought to take advantage of *FA 1996, s 84(2)(a)* which excluded from loan relationship profits amounts to be taken to share premium account.

6.142   The Court of Appeal held that the credit to share premium account in V involved two transactions:

(a)   the accrual of the discount; and

(b)   the crediting of the discount to share premium.

6.143   If the discount was first credited to profit and loss, and then transferred to share premium, the profit at (a) was within the loan relationship rules.

Greene King plc v Rev & C Comrs [2014] STC 2439

6.144   A similar scheme also failed to achieve its objective in *Greene King plc v R & C Comrs* [2016] EWCA Civ 782: see **5.89–5.91**.

Mezzanine financing

6.145   Mezzanine financing comprises highly subordinated debt, which may be given an equity wrapper, to give it the legal characteristics of shares. In such cases, (a) the debt-like shares (*CTA 2009, Part 6, Chapter 6A*) and (b) the disguised interest rules (*CTA 2009, Part 6, Chapter 2A*) apply to bring the return on the securities within the loan relationship rules. These rules disapply the dividend override in *CTA 2009, s 465*, which says that the distribution rules in general take precedence over the loan relationship rules.

6.146   Where shares are held by a bank or other financial trader, dividends are treated as taxable (*CTA 2009, s 130*). This rule is intended to prevent banks from gaining a tax advantage by funding borrowers by subscribing for preference shares, rather than lending money at interest.

6.147   Similar rules are applied to investors in *CTA 2009, ss 521A–521F*, where shares offer a guaranteed return. Some legal shares will be classified in the balance sheet under IAS 32 as financial liabilities. This will generally be confined to issues of automatically redeemable fixed rate preference shares. In general, debt-like shares remain shares for tax purposes. Otherwise, the issuer could strip out his taxable profits by deducting dividends on the preference shares. However, in the case of the investor holding debt-like shares, the dividends or other financial return on the instruments may be treated as interest for tax purposes, and so taxable, rather than as dividends or capital gains. The disguised debt rules are capable of applying in the same circumstances as the 'receipts case' rules, but take precedence. The tax position of the issuing company is unaffected.

6.148 *CTA 2009, s 521C* applies where:

- a company holds shares in another company;

- the shares are accounted for as a liability in the issuing company;

- the share produces a return which is 'economically equivalent to interest';

- the issuer and investor are not connected; and

- the shares are held for an unallowable purpose as defined by *s 521E*.

6.149 Where *s 521C* applies, then under *s 521B*:

- the share is treated as a creditor loan relationship;

- any distribution is treated as interest; and

- no debits may be brought into account in relation to the shares, eg in relation to unpaid subscription monies.

6.150 The rule does not apply to shares held on trading account, because in that case there is a *CTA 2009, s 130* charge. The rule also does not apply to 'excepted shares' within *s 521D*, ie a qualifying publicly issued share, or a share which mirrors a public issue.

6.151 'Unallowable purpose' means being held for the main purpose, or a main purpose, of securing a tax advantage.

Disguised interest

6.152 'Disguised interest' can also be taxed as such under *CTA 2009, ss 486A–486G*. Under *s 468B*, a return is 'economically equivalent to interest' if:

- it is reasonable to assume that the return relates to the time value of money;

- the return is reasonably comparable with commercial rates of interest; and

- there is no practical likelihood that it will cease.

Unallowable purposes

6.153 Under the rules for calculating the taxable profits of a trade, no deduction is allowed 'for expenses not incurred wholly and exclusively for the purposes of the trade': *CTA 2009, s 54(1)(a)*. This rule does not apply for computing profits of loan relationships. Instead, there is a general prohibition on deductions where the loan relationship has an unallowable purpose. *CTA 2009, s 441(3)* says that, where a loan relationship has an unallowable purpose, no debit in respect of the loan relationship shall be brought into account 'as on a just and reasonable basis is attributable to the unallowable purpose'.

6.154   Under *s 442(1)*, a loan has an unallowable purpose if its purposes include a purpose which 'is not amongst the business or other commercial purposes of the company'. Under *s 442(2)*, the 'business or other commercial purposes' of the company do not include any part of its activities in respect of which it is not within the charge to corporation tax. *Section 442(3)* says that *s 442(4)* applies if a loan relationship has a tax avoidance purpose. Under *s 442(4)*, a 'tax avoidance purpose' is only regarded as not being amongst the 'business or other commercial purposes' of the company if the securing of a tax advantage is 'the main purpose or one of the main purposes' for which the company entered into the loan relationship or related transaction.

6.155   The reference to 'tax avoidance purpose' is extended by *s 442(5)*, which states:

'(5)   The references … to a tax avoidance purpose are references to any purpose that consists in securing a tax advantage (whether for the company or any other person).'

6.156   Thus, a payment which does not itself have an unallowable purpose will be tainted, if it is intended to secure a tax advantage for another company or individual.

6.157   A tax avoidance purpose is defined by reference to *CTA 2010, s 1139* as being 'a relief or increased relief from, or repayment or increased repayment of, tax, or the avoidance or reduction of a charge to tax or an assessment to tax or the avoidance of a possible assessment thereto, whether the avoidance or reduction is effected by receipts accruing in such a way that the recipient does not pay or bear tax on them, or by a deduction in computing profits or gains.'

6.158   'Tax advantage' has been given a wide construction (*Emery v IRC* 54 TC 607). However, in *IRC v Kleinwort Benson Ltd* 45 TC 369, a financial trader bought a security which could only yield a profit on resale if the company obtained repayment of a tax credit. Although the gaining of a tax advantage was essential to the profitability of the transaction, it was not held to be the 'main object'. While the borrower will be denied a full deduction, the lender will still be taxed on the whole sum.

6.159 'Main purpose' tests were introduced in *FA 1960* and began to proliferate (in the form of 'main purpose' or 'main object' clauses) after 1996, when the 'unallowable purpose' rule for loan relationships was introduced by *FA 1996, Sch 9, para 13*. The nature of such tests, and the difference between 'main object' and 'main benefit' tests was considered by the Court of Appeal in *Lloyds TSB Equipment Leasing (No 1) Ltd v R & C Comrs* [2014] STC 2770 at [47]–[64].

6.160 In applying a main purpose (object) provision:

(a) the test is subjective;

(b) application of the test requires a full factual enquiry;

(c) the conclusion (that the test does not, or does, apply) must be reasoned;

(d) the test is solely statutory;

(e) the object of the transaction must be identified, which will ordinarily be a baseline amount of profit + a tax benefit;

(f) the relative importance of the objects must be established (similar to the 'main benefit' test, where the test is objective and can often be mathematically determined);

(g) the question whether the whole transaction was driven by the tax advantage must be considered.

6.161 The notion of tax advantage is taken from the transactions in securities rules introduced in 1960, and now to be found in *ITA 2007, ss 682–713*. These rules are irrelevant to the unallowable purpose rules for two reasons:

1   The loan relationship rules are an exclusive code.

2   The transactions in securities rules require a comparison between the actual transaction into which a person entered, and a hypothetical transaction which he would – in the court's view – otherwise have entered into. The central principle of the loan relationship rules is that a company is taxed on what it has done, not what it might have done: tax follows the accounts. As the FTT said in *Iliffe News and Media Ltd v R & C Comrs* [2013] SFTD 309 at [263]:

'the Tribunal is not concerned to compare the actual transactions by "hypothesising some perfect transaction", but instead must ascertain whether the transactions were undertaken with the object of obtaining or increasing a tax benefit'

6.162 As Lightman J observed in *IRC v Trustees of the Sema Group Pension Scheme* [2002] STC 276 at [53]:

'Obviously if the tax advantage is mere "icing on the cake" it will not constitute a main object. Nor will it necessarily do so merely because it is a feature of the transaction or a relevant factor in the decision to buy or sell. The statutory criterion is that the tax advantage shall be more than relevant or indeed an object; it must be a main object. The question whether it is so is a question of fact for the commissioners [fact-finding appeal tribunal] in every case.'

6.163   In *IRC v Brebner* 43 TC 705, Lord Pearce observed that the test of motive was subjective, and had to be looked at in the context of the transaction as a whole (at 715):

'The "object" which has to be considered is a subjective matter of intention ... that which had to be ascertained was the object (not the effect) of each interrelated transaction in its actual context, and not the isolated object of each part regardless of the others.'

6.164   Lord Upjohn (at 718) confirmed that a taxpayer will not be denied 'the choice of the least taxed route':

'when the question of carrying out a genuine commercial transaction ... is considered, the fact that there are two ways of carrying it out – one by paying the maximum amount of tax, the other by paying no, or much less, tax – it would be quite wrong as a necessary consequence to draw the inference that in adopting the latter course one of the main objects is ... avoidance of tax.'

6.165   The loan relationship debit is an essential part of the transaction, if it is to be commercial. Provided that the transaction is part of the normal business of the company, and not part of an activity whose sole rationale is fiscal, the unallowable purposes rule has no application. It is helpful in this context to consider the *Lupton* principle and, in particular, Megarry J's observation (*Lupton (Inspector of Taxes) v FA and AB Ltd* 47 TC 580 at 597–598):

'A trading transaction ... is not deprived of its trading nature merely by the presence of a fiscal motive for carrying it out, nor by the fact that as a trading transaction it makes a loss and not a profit ... At the other extreme lies the transaction that is far removed from trading, designed to secure a tax advantage ... The question is whether, viewed as a whole, the transaction is one which can fairly be regarded as a trading transaction. If it is, then it will not be denatured merely because it was entered into with motives of reaping a fiscal advantage.'

6.166 A tax avoidance purpose is only unallowable if it is the main purpose, or one of the main purposes, for which the company is a party to the loan relationship or has entered into a related transaction by reference to it. A statement on the scope of this provision was made by the Economic Secretary to the Treasury (Mrs Angela Knight MP) during the report stage of the Finance Bill (*Hansard,* 28 March 1996, col 1192–1193). The thrust of the statement was expressed in this passage:

> 'Where a company is choosing between different ways of arranging its commercial affairs, it is acceptable for it to choose the course that gives a favourable tax outcome. Where paragraph 13 comes into play is where tax avoidance is the object, or one of the main objects, of the exercise.'

6.167 Guidance on the non-application and application of the unallowable purpose test is published in HMRC's Corporate Finance Manual at paras CFM38180 (non-application) and CFM38190 (application). The circumstances where the rule would not apply are limited. Paragraph CFM38190 states:

> 'SS441–442 would normally apply to loan relationship debits:
>
> - which, subject to the comments at CFM38180 (fourth and fifth bullets), relate to the write-off of loans where the purpose of the loans was not amongst the business or other commercial purposes of a company. An example of a loan of this nature would be an interest-free loan made by a company, whose business consists in operating a widgets retail outlet, which had lent the money to a football club supported by one of the directors of the company for the purpose of providing financial support to the football club. Furthermore, if the company borrowed to make the loan to the football club, then SS441–442 would normally also apply to disallow the loan relationship debits relating to the interest or other finance costs on that borrowing. If, however, the purpose of the loan included a commercial or other business purpose such as advertising, then this would be taken into account in arriving at the amount attributable to the unallowable purpose on a just and reasonable basis (S441(1)–(3));
>
> - which, subject to the comments at CFM38180 (fourth and fifth bullets), relate to a borrowing the proceeds of which are used in such a way that the company cannot or does not expect to make an overall pre-tax profit. An example would be where a company borrows at interest and on-lends at a rate of interest that is less than the rate of interest on the borrowings; or
>
> - where a company or a group of companies enters into one or more transactions or arrangements which have the main purpose or

one of the main purposes of securing loan relationship debits for repayments of loan principal, in addition to payments of interest, on the true economic commercial borrowing to the company or group. An example of this would be where one group company undertakes a borrowing of £20m at 8.4% for 5 years from a third party and at the same time a second group company pays that third party £13m for preference shares of £20m in the first group company to be delivered 5 years later. The effect of this is that, economically, the group borrows £7m on an amortising basis at 8.4% but for tax purposes the group claims relief as loan relationship debits for both the interest of £1.4m on the group amortised borrowing of £7m and the repayment of the £7m loan principal. In such circumstances SS429–430 are likely to apply to disallow the amounts equivalent to repayments of principal.

6.168 So far, HMRC have attacked a number of types of transaction by using the unallowable purpose rule:

(a)   interest on funding costs on share buy-backs;

(b)   borrowing by a UK resident company from its non-resident (tax haven) parent in order to fund the purchase of assets from the parent;

(c)   the making of loans by a subsidiary to a parent, where the effect of the loan interest is to give the parent interest income to set off against losses;

(d)   borrowing for a non-business purpose;

(e)   borrowing where a company on-lends at a loss; and

(f)   borrowing to enter into a tax avoidance arrangement.

6.169   In *AH Field (Holdings) Ltd v R & C Comrs* [2012] UKFTT 104 (TC), a company had substantial distributable reserves but little available cash, all its funds being invested in property assets. The company wanted to increase its cash flow to enhance investor returns, without borrowing from the bank to fund distributions.

6.170   Instead it entered into the following transactions:

(a)   the company borrowed £2m from the bank;

(b)   it used the £2m to pay a dividend to the shareholders;

(c)   the shareholders lent the £2m back to the company in the form of a deeply discounted security redeemable after 363 days;

(d)   the bank loan was paid off after three days;

(e)   when the loan note became due for repayment, the company borrowed £2m from the bank to redeem the loan, and the proceeds of redemption were then lent back to the company on similar terms;

(f)   the arrangement was repeated annually.

6.171   The Revenue refused to allow a deduction from profits for the loan note discount, on the grounds that the loan had an unallowable purpose.

6.172   The taxpayer argued that the loan relationship debits were a consequence, not the purpose of the transaction. The transaction as such had a business (non-fiscal) purpose, namely remunerating investors by income distributions rather than capital appreciation. To this end the company had substituted a liability for distributable reserves, debt for equity.

6.173   The Tribunal concluded that the main purpose of the transaction was to reduce the company's UK corporation tax liability, and that this was an unallowable purpose.

6.174   The Tribunal did not make findings of fact adequate to support the inferences which the Tribunal drew. Indeed, the inference was contrary to the Tribunal's findings of fact. All the funds raised by the loan were used for the purposes of the business. That is a commercial loan. What the Tribunal decided was that the unallowable purpose test can catch not only solely tax-motivated transactions, but also transactions which are so influenced by their tax effect that the tax effect must be taken to be one of the main purposes of the transaction. That extends the scope of the statutory wording far beyond what can be justified by the wording of the legislation. The key error of the Tribunal was at [126]:

> 'the test applied by para 13 [*FA 1996, Sch 9*] is not distinguishing simply between transactions which are solely motivated by tax and transactions which are carried out for business purposes. It is directed at transactions which have some business purpose, but which nevertheless are so influenced by their tax effect, that it is reasonable to assume that the tax effect must have been one of the main purposes for entering into the transaction.'

In this case the funding had a commercial purpose and all that the company was doing was changing the funding mix to get a better tax result.

6.175   In *Fidex Ltd v R & C Comrs* [2016] STC 1920, a company held bonds with a value of 100. In its last UK GAAP period it issued preference shares transferring 95% of the value of the bonds. In the following year it adopted IAS. IAS required the derecognition of the accounting value both of the bond asset of 95 and the preference share liability of 95. The company claimed a loan relationship debit (change of basis adjustment) of 95 for the later period.

6.176   The accounting evidence was that under FRS 4 the preference shares were 'non-equity shares'. Shares could not be classified as liabilities. Applying IAS 39 derecognition rules to the opening value at the start of the later accounting period, because the preference shares transferred the risks and rewards of the bonds to the holder of the preference shares, 95% of the asset value would have to be derecognised. The preference shares would be reclassified as liabilities under FRS 32. This led to a corresponding derecognition of 95% of the obligation represented by the shares.

The preference shares, however, remained shares for UK tax purposes.

6.177   HMRC raised the argument at the FTT hearing (not previously advanced) that the loan relationship whose derecognition gave rise to the debit has an unallowable purpose, ie tax avoidance was a main purpose or one of the main purposes of having entered into the loan relationship.

6.178   The FTT held that the *para 19A* debits crystallised at 31 December 2004. Accordingly, the bonds had an unallowable purpose in the earlier period but not in the later period: *Fidex Ltd v R & C Comrs* [2013] SFTD 964 at [190].

6.179   The Upper Tribunal (UT) and the Court of Appeal held that, by reference to the wording of *Sch 9, para 19A(3)(b)*, the unallowable purpose carried over into the following accounting period. Accordingly, the debit was disallowable because the loan relationship, ie the bonds held by the company, had an 'unallowable purpose' within *CTA 2009, ss 441–442: FA 1996, Sch 9, para 13*. The UT also held that a purpose held only for a single moment of time may be an unallowable purpose ([147]). The UT also rejected an apportionment argument.

6.180   This conclusion is open to question. The debit in question arose not from the holding of the loan relationship, but was a consequence of the accounting practice. So long as the change of accounting practice was legitimate, and correctly implemented, the debit in question was simply the consequence of that change and had nothing to do with any purposes for which the loan relationship was entered into.

6.181   In *Iliffe News and Media Ltd v R & C Comrs* [2013] SFTD 309, four subsidiaries assigned to their parent unregistered trademarks for a nominal sum. The parent then leased back the trademarks to the subsidiaries for a payment of £50m. The parent lent the subsidiaries £50m to fund this transaction. The Revenue argued that the debits of the subsidiaries for interest on the loans had an unallowable purpose. The Tribunal held that the loans had as one of their main purposes a tax avoidance purpose, but that there was no evidence before the Tribunal any part of the loan relationship debit could be attributed to that purpose.

6.182 In *Travel Document Services v R & C Comrs* [2016] SFTD 186 the unallowable purpose rule was held to apply to notional loan relationships ('non-qualifying shares' treated as rights under a creditor relationship under *CTA 2009, s 522(1)*, formerly *FA 1996, s 91B*) in the same way as it applies to actual loan relationships.

1 TDS held shares in LGI valued at £272m.

2 TDS entered into a total return swap with its parent (P), which had the effect of converting the LGI shares into a deemed creditor loan relationship: *FA 1996, s 91B*. P agreed to pay TDS interest on its deemed creditor loan relationship of £272m. TDS agreed to pay P an amount equal to changes in the fair value of the deemed loan relationship.

3 Another group company transferred to LGI liabilities under loan relationships of £243m, thereby reducing the fair value of TDS's shares in LGI.

4 TDS became liable to pay P £253m, and claimed a non-trading loan relationship debit of this amount.

6.183 The FTT held that TDS's main purpose of entering into the total return swap was a tax avoidance purpose, and that on a just and reasonable basis the whole of the debit should be disallowed.

Regime anti-avoidance rules

6.184 From 18 November 2015 new regime anti-avoidance rules (RAAR) are introduced: *CTA 2009, ss 455B–455D*. The RAAR apply where arrangements are entered into with a main purpose of enabling a company to obtain a loan or derivative-related tax advantage. By way of filter an arrangement will only be within the RAAR where the tax advantage sought cannot be reasonably regarded as consistent with the principles and policy objectives of the legislation. Where the RAAR applies, any loan related tax advantage will be counteracted by adjustments to debits and credits 'on a just and reasonable basis'.

Chapter 7

Impairment Losses

Overview

7.1   This chapter deals with:

- Impairment

- Trading losses

- Non-trading deficits

- Pre-trading loans

- Sideways relief

- Carry-back claims

- Carry-forward relief

- Group and consortium relief

Impairment

7.2   Losses are not assessed to tax. Only profits are charged and therefore assessed to tax. Unutilised trading losses are automatically carried forward to set off against profits of later accounting periods arising from the same trade: *CTA 2010, s 45*. Except in the case of banking companies, this provides an automatic set-off of earlier period trading losses against later period trading income: *Sun Life Assurance Company of Canada (UK) Ltd v R & C Comrs* [2010] STC 1173. Companies may make claims to utilise trading losses at an earlier date: *s 37*. However, the requirement to make a claim for a trading loss to be carried forward was removed by *FA 1990, s 39*. Deficits on trading loan relationships are taken into the calculation of trading profits and losses for an accounting period. Deficits on non-trading loan relationships are the subject of separate statutory provisions, which largely follow the rules for utilisation of trading losses.

7.3   Where amortised cost basis accounting is used, no debits arising from the revaluation of a loan relationship can be brought in except (i) impairment losses, and (ii) debits arising from releases: *CTA 2009, s 324.* 'Impairment loss' is defined in *s 476(1)* as a 'debit in respect of the impairment of a financial asset', including uncollectability.

7.4   The loan relationship rules are based on the principle that amounts taxed and relived as debits and credits are the profits and losses arising in accounts drawn up in accordance with GAAP. When a debt is impaired or written off by a creditor company, its expense will normally be allowable as a loan relationship debit. The main exception is in relation to connected company debts.

7.5   An impairment may arise if there is non-payment either of interest or of principal, which is written off or written down in the accounts. Once interest becomes overdue, it becomes an 'accrued amount': *CTA 2009, ss 361(6), 465B(3)(a).* When a bank credits doubtful interest to an interest suspense account, rather than profit and loss, impairment relief equivalent to the interest credited to the suspense account is given immediately.

7.6   An impairment loss is the amount by which the carrying amount of an asset exceeds its recoverable amount. Impairment was an essential element of the IASB's strategy of moving financial reporting from historic cost to a current cost, accruals to a fair value basis. IAS takes the view that, if a hole in a road opens in front of you, you do not have to wait until you have fallen into it in order to record the event. This requires regular review of the carrying amount of assets. Value reductions revealed by impairment reviews will be deductible in computing profits both for accounts and for tax purposes. The applicable accounting standards are FRS 102, Sections 21, 27 [IAS 36, 37, 39].

7.7   The profits of debtor and creditor are measured differently. It is right for the creditor, for purposes of conservatism, to take account of impairment of loans, but it is equally right to treat the debtor as still on the hook. The creditor should revalue the loan asset at the end of each accounting period and recognise diminutions in value. Accordingly, there is an asymmetry between the granting of relief for impairment, and the taxation of releases. The creditor normally gets relief before the debtor suffers any charge. On the debtor side, debt write-offs are treated as ordinary income: IAS 39, paras 39, 41.

7.8   The view was formerly taken that, for tax purposes, profits and losses could not be anticipated (*BSC Footwear Ltd (formerly Freeman, Hardy and Willis Ltd) v Ridgway (Inspector of Taxes)* 47 TC 495 at 535). There was one long-established exception to this rule, which involves stock-in-trade (*Ostime (Inspector of Taxes) v Duple Motor Bodies Ltd* 39 TC 537).

7.9 With regard to onerous contracts, FRS 102, para 21.11A (supplemented by Example 2 in the Appendix) states:

'If an entity has an onerous contract, the present obligation under the contract shall be recognised and measured as a provision.'

7.10 *Herbert Smith (a firm) v Honour (Inspector of Taxes)* [1999] STC 173 confirms that such a provision is deductible for tax purposes when made. In that case, a firm made a provision of £4.8m in respect of rent for premises which would no longer be required for the business, and only re-lettable at a lower rent, after the firm had moved to new premises on 31 December 1990. The provision was made for the accounting period ending on 30 April 1990. The provision was, on the evidence, in accordance with the principles of commercial accountancy. The expenditure was certain to be incurred; there was no benefit which would arise from the expenditure in future years; therefore the expenditure had to be recognised in full when it became pure loss. The Revenue disallowed the provision, and the Special Commissioners upheld the disallowance on the grounds that there was a free-standing rule against non-anticipation of profits or losses. The High Court held that there was no evidence on the basis of which the Special Commissioners could reject the accounts. Where the accounts are in accordance with accepted principles of commercial accountancy, it follows that there is no independent rule against anticipation of liabilities or profits. Lloyd J said (at 204):

'Such a rule would be inconsistent with resort to generally accepted principles of commercial accounting in very many cases, since it would disallow any provision made in accordance with the concept of prudence.'

However, the case was really about accruals, not about prudence.

7.11 Where expenditure produces no income, the amount of the expenditure will normally give rise to a loss at that point. Where a company using amortised cost basis continues to make 'provision' for a loan relationship, after the accounting period in which the company ceased to be a party to the loan relationship, the provision is regarded as being made in the post-cessation accounting period.

7.12 The holder of a creditor loan relationship, as a general rule, can obtain tax relief for any impairment of that asset which is recognised in his accounts. The major exception is where creditor and debtor are connected companies: see **6.37–6.46**. IAS 39 imposes prescriptive rules about recognition of impairment. If, at balance sheet date, there is objective evidence of impairment, the carrying amount of the asset must be reduced by the impairment loss, which is recognised in profit and loss account: IAS 39, paras 63–68.

Trading losses

7.13   The importance of the distinction between trading and non-trading losses on loan relationships lies principally in terms of the flexibility with which losses may be used. The use of trading losses on loan relationships is governed by the general provisions of *CTA 2010*. There are special rules for the use of non-trading deficits on loan relationships.

7.14   Trading losses arising from loan relationships will be available in the normal way, ie:

(a)   for set-off against the profits (including chargeable gains) of the same accounting period;

(b)   to carry back against the profits (including chargeable gains) of the previous 12-month period;

(c)   carried forward against trading income from the same trade; or

(d)   made available for group relief.

(*CTA 2010, ss 37, 45, 130*)

Carry-forward of trading losses under *CTA 2010, s 45* (which, as noted at **7.2** is automatic) applies where no current year claim can be made.

7.15   'Banking company' is defined in *CTA 2010, s 269B* as a UK resident company, or UK PE of a non-resident company, carrying on specified regulated activities. For accounting periods beginning on or after 1 April 2015, the proportion of a banking company's taxable profits (ignoring pre-1 April 2015 trading losses and non-trading loan relationship deficits) which may be offset by carried-forward losses is 50%: *CTA 2010, s 269CA*. For accounting periods beginning on or after 1 April 2016, this is reduced to 25%. The restriction applies alike to trading profits *(s 45)*, non-trading loan relationship deficits *(s 457)* and management expenses *(CTA 2009, ss 63, 1223)*. Losses which would have been available for offset but for this restriction continue to be available for carry forward.

Non-trading deficits

7.16   Non-trading losses on loan relationships ('non-trading deficits') are subject to special rules. First, they are pooled with non-trading derivative contracts losses to form a 'non-trading deficit' (under *CTA 2009, s 574*, non-trading derivative contracts debits and credits being treated as non-trading loan relationship debits and credits). Such pooled losses may be group relieved as non-trading losses against the claimant company's total profits for the period, ie excluding carried-forward debits. One of the outstanding positive features of the loan relationship rules is the ability to treat deficits on non-trading loan relationships as trading losses, so as to be available for surrender by way of group relief. Where non-trading deficits are utilised for group relief, they are treated in the same way as trading losses. Losses on trading loan relationships are trading losses in any event.

7.17   Relief for non-trading loan relationship losses (which includes non-trading derivatives contracts losses) can be obtained in one or more of four ways. The loss is called a 'non-trading deficit', and the accounting period in which it arises is called the 'deficit period': *CTA 2009, s 456(2)*. Relief may be claimed selectively, ie 'for the whole or any part of the deficit'. The four modes of relief are:

(a)   surrender by way of group relief, for which purpose the non-trading deficit is treated as a trading loss (*CTA 2010, s 99(1)(c)*);

(b)   set-off against any total profits of the company for the deficit period (*CTA 2009, s 459(1)(a)*);

(c)   carry-back to be set off against profits for the preceding year (*s 459(1) (b)*); and

(d)   automatic carry-forward as a non-trading deficit for succeeding accounting periods (*s 457(1)* – 'the basic rule').

7.18   Where a non-trading deficit is carried forward under *CTA 2009, s 457*, the set-off must normally occur in the first subsequent accounting period in which there are non-trading loan relationship profits available for set-off ('the next accounting period'): *s 457(3)*. Under *s 458*, a company may opt to postpone the set-off of a carried-forward deficit against non-trading credits of the next following period. Such a claim must be made within two years of the later accounting period. The purpose of this option is to prevent loss of foreign tax credits. If, in the next accounting period, a company has foreign source interest which carries a foreign tax credit, postponement of set-off allows the company to benefit from the foreign tax credit, which would otherwise be lost.

7.19   The effect of these rules is that a non-trading deficit cannot be carried forward and set off against trading profits, nor be surrendered by way of group relief in a succeeding period. It can only be carried forward against non-trading profits. 'Non-trading profits' means (*s 457(5)*):

'So much of the profits of a company (of whatever description) as do not consist in trading income'

Accordingly, a carried-forward deficit can be set against chargeable gains, as well as property income.

7.20   Separate claims are not required for group relief or to carry forward a deficit. While sideways and carry-back relief require a claim, in the absence of any such claim, a brought-forward non-trading deficit will be automatically set against non-trading profits of the next accounting period. A claim to relieve a non-trading deficit under *s 459* must normally be made within two years following the deficit period (*s 460(1)(a)*)). A claim in any deficit period is restricted to the non-trading deficit for that period and cannot be augmented by a carried-forward deficit.

Example 7.1

Year	Non-trading deficit	Non-trading profits	Set-off
1	200		
2		100	100
3		Foreign dividend of 75 plus tax credit of 25	Elect not to set off
4		100	100

Pre-trading loans

7.21   Where a loan is entered into prior to trading, this is a 'non-trading' loan relationship. However, a company may elect for the expenditure on the loan relationship to be treated as pre-trading expenditure. When this occurs, the expenditure is brought into account as a trade expense in the period in which the company's trade commences (*CTA 2009, ss 329–330*). The company must commence a trade within seven years of the end of the accounting period in which the non-trading debit arises. The election must be made within two years of the end of the accounting period in which the expenditure is incurred. In *Khan v Miah* [2001] 1 WLR 2123, it was held that partners preparing to trade were carrying on a trade when they prepared premises for the opening of a restaurant.

Set-off against profits of the deficit period

7.22   Where a claim is made under *s 459(1)(a)* to set a non-trading deficit against profits of any description for the deficit period, the profits against which the deficit is to be set off must be identified in the claim. On such a claim, relief is given after trading losses carried forward from earlier accounting periods but before:

(a)   trading losses of the deficit period;

(b)   trading losses carried back; and

(c)   a loan relationship deficit carried back.

(*CTA 2009, s 461(6)*)

7.23 The non-trading deficits of the deficit period may then be set against other profits of the same accounting period. After that claim, relief may be given:

(a) for trading losses; or

(b) for a carried-back deficit from a later accounting period.

7.24 For investment companies, management expenses for the current year and unrelieved management expenses carried forward from previous years take precedence over a loan relationship deficit (*CTA 2009, s 1219*).

7.25 Ring fence profits of oil companies cannot be reduced by non-trading deficits on loan relationships (*CTA 2010, ss 286, 287*).

Carry-back claims

7.26 Where a carry-back claim is made under *CTA 2009, s 459(1)(b)*, relief is given against profits of a later period before profits of an earlier period: *s 462(5)*. Under *ss 462, 463*, carry-back relief is given after:

(a) relief in respect of losses incurred in earlier periods for which relief is given in priority to *s 462*;

(b) relief in respect of trade charges;

(c) where the company is an investment company:

   (i) any deduction for capital allowances under *CAA 2001, s 208*;

   (ii) any deduction for management expenses under *CTA 2009, s 1219*;

   (iii) any relief for business charges; and

   (iv) any current year relief under *CTA 2009, s 459(1)(a)* for that accounting period.

No current year or carry-back claims may be made insofar as the deficit includes a carried-forward deficit.

7.27 A carry-back claim can only be made in respect of a sum which is the smaller of:

(a) the non-trading deficit for the deficit period less any carried-forward debit, and any current year and group relief claims; and

(b) the total profits available for relief under *CTA 2009, ss 462, 463* (*s 462(2)*).

7.28 'The permitted period', ie the periods to which non-trading deficits can be carried back, means 'the period of twelve months immediately preceding the beginning of the deficit period': *s 462(2)*.

Example 7.2

Accounting period ends 31 December. Non-trading loan relationship deficit for 2016 is carried back against profits on loan relationships for 2015. The losses in 2016 arise evenly over the year.

Year end	Profits	Adjustment	Adjusted profits/deficit
	£000	*£000*	*£000*
31/12/2015	48	(48)	–
31/12/2016	(80)	48	(32)

Carried-forward deficit (32)

Carry-forward relief

7.29   A carried-forward deficit may only be set against non-trading profits, ie profits which do not consist of trading income: *CTA 2009, s 458(1)*.

Special rules for banks

Surrender by way of group relief and consortium relief

7.30   Where non-trading deficits are utilised for group relief, they are treated in the same way as trading losses. Unlike other cases of surrender of losses by way of group relief, such as management expenses and property business losses, the loss is not restricted to the excess over profits of the company for the accounting period. Carried-forward deficits cannot be surrendered by way of group relief and can only be set against non-trading profits for succeeding accounting periods (*CTA 2009, s 457(1)–(3)*).

7.31   In the case of consortium relief, *CTA 2010, ss 132, 133* say that consortium relief is only available where one company is a member of a consortium and the other is:

(a)   a trading company owned by the consortium and which is not a 75% subsidiary of any company;

(b)   a trading company which is a 90% subsidiary of a holding company owned by the consortium and is not a 75% subsidiary of a company other than the holding company; or

(c)   a holding company owned by the consortium and which is not a 75% subsidiary of any company.

7.32   For these purposes, a holding company is defined in *CTA 2010, s 185(2)*. In broad terms, a holding company means a company which holds shares or securities in trading subsidiaries which are its 90% subsidiaries. Thus, in the case of direct ownership by the consortium, the consortium-owned company must be a trading company; whereas, in the case of a holding company owned by a consortium, the holding company must own a 90% interest in trading companies in the relevant period.

7.33   Consortium relief is a by-product of and supplementary to group relief, available in circumstances where group relief is inapplicable because the 75% common ownership test is not achieved. Consortium relief revolves around a number of definitions. The key definition is 'company owned by a consortium', which implies a definition of 'consortium' and 'member of a consortium'. To be 'a company owned by a consortium', a company must first be either a 'trading company' or 'holding company' of 90% subsidiaries which are all trading companies. The 90% test must satisfy the 'voting rights', 'profits' and 'assets' tests (see below). A company will be owned by a consortium if 75% or more of its ordinary share capital is owned by other companies, each of which holds at least 5% of the shares. The members of the consortium must be 'equity holders', and an equity holder is a person who holds ordinary share capital in a company or loan creditor in respect of a loan which is not a normal commercial loan.

Link companies and group/consortium companies

7.34   A link company is a member of a group and a consortium. For example, S2 is a link company:

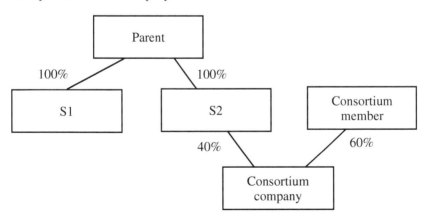

7.35   Consortium companies can surrender losses to S2, and S2 can in turn group relieve losses. A link company is a member of a group and a member of a consortium. Thus, in the following structure, S2 is a link company:

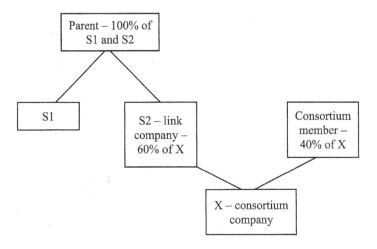

7.36   The link company can transmit losses of the consortium company to other group companies. Equally, losses of the link company's group can be surrendered to the consortium company. If S1 has losses of 100, and S2 and X each have profits of 200, S1 can surrender 100 of its losses to S2, which can in turn surrender 60 of those losses down to X. The link company must either be UK resident or have a UK trade.

7.37   A 'group/consortium company' is a company which is both a consortium company and a member of a group, as in this structure:

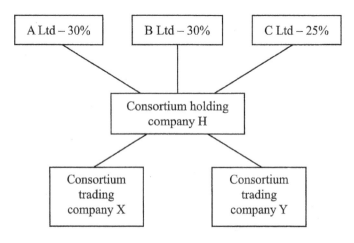

7.38   The three consortium companies are group/consortium companies. Group relief must be claimed before consortium relief. If X has no profits, and H has profits of 70, a loss of 100 in Y can be surrendered up to H as to 70 under group relief, and 9 of that loss can be surrendered up to A, 9 to B and 7.50 to C. Because H is not wholly owned by members of a consortium, only 85% of any loss can be consortium relieved. Thus, in this situation, group relief is more valuable than consortium relief.

Consortium conditions

7.39   For consortium relief to be available, consortium condition 1, 2 or 3 must be met.

Consortium condition 1 is satisfied (*CTA 2010, s 132*) if:

- where a company owned by a consortium is a trading company or holding company, it surrenders losses upwards to a claimant company which is a member of a consortium; or

- where a member of a consortium is a trading company or holding company, it surrenders losses downwards to a company owned by a consortium, and both companies are 'UK related'.

7.40   Consortium condition 2 is satisfied (*s 133(1)*) if:

- where a company owned by a consortium is a trading company or holding company, it surrenders losses upwards to a claimant company which is not a member of a consortium;

- the claimant company belongs to the same group as a link company which is a member of a consortium; and

- the surrendering company, claimant company and link company are all 'UK related'.

7.41   Consortium condition 3 is satisfied (*s 133(2)*) if:

- the surrendering company is not a company owned by a consortium but is a member of the same group as a link company;

- the link company is a member of a consortium;

- the claimant company is a company owned by a consortium and is a trading company or holding company; and

- the surrendering company, claimant company and link company are all 'UK related'.

7.42   'UK related' means a UK resident company or the UK permanent establishment of a non-resident company: *s 134*. The members of the consortium can be resident anywhere in the world, and so may comprise resident and non-resident companies. A UK resident company can be treated as a consortium company so long as it is at least 75% owned by two or more companies, wherever those companies are resident. If a consortium company is a holding company of a trading group, it need not be UK resident, nor need the majority of its trading subsidiaries be UK or EU resident.

7.43   Where one of the conditions for relief is fulfilled, both the consortium and the company owned by the consortium are treated as tax transparent. The consortium company can surrender up losses to a consortium member proportionate to that member's shareholding in the consortium company, while the consortium member can surrender down to the consortium company a similar amount of its own losses. In either case, the claim is a 'consortium claim'.

7.44   Hence, the following structure will be a consortium and, if X has losses of 100, it can surrender 60 to A and 40 to B:

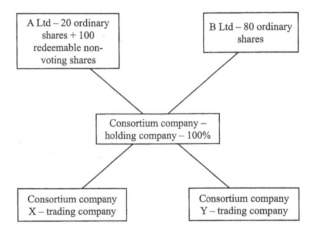

7.45   If the claimant company and surrendering company do not have co-terminous accounting periods ('overlapping period'), relief will be restricted accordingly (*CTA 2010, ss 139, 142*). A member's share in a consortium is determined by reference to his accounting period.

7.46   A consortium member's share of a consortium, in relation to the accounting period of the surrendering company, is limited to 'the ownership proportion of the surrenderable amount': *s 143(2)*. This is the lowest of (*s 143(3)*):

- the percentage of ordinary share capital beneficially owned by that member ('voting test');

- the percentage of profits available for distribution to equity holders to which it is entitled ('profits test'); and

- the percentage of assets available for distribution to equity holders on a notional winding up ('assets test').

'Ordinary share capital' means all shares other than fixed rate preference shares (*CTA 2010, s 1119*).

7.47   Fixed rate preference shares:

- are issued for consideration which is or includes new consideration;

- do not carry any right to conversion into shares or securities or to the acquisition of any additional shares or securities;

- do not carry any right to dividends other than dividends which are of a fixed amount or fixed rate percentage of nominal value, and represent no more than a reasonable commercial return on the new consideration received in respect of the issue of shares; and

- do not carry, on repayment, any rights to an amount exceeding the new consideration received.

7.48   In establishing whether a company has a sufficient participation in the consortium company to count as a member of a consortium, equity returned to that company will be ignored. This is what *CTA 2010, s 166(6)(c)* calls 'the returned amount'. This provision is primarily directed at loan backs from the consortium company to a member of the consortium.

7.49   Consortium relief will also be denied where there are option arrangements in force which, if implemented, would deprive a member of the consortium of the requisite level of beneficial ownership of shares in the consortium company. 'Option arrangements' under *CTA 2010, s 173* means arrangements by which there could, as a result of the exercise of a right (the option right) to acquire shares or securities in the consortium company or to require a person to acquire shares or securities in the consortium company, be a variation in the percentage of:

- profits available to equity holders; or

- assets to which any of the equity holders is entitled on a notional winding up.

7.50   The impact of these provisions is limited by SP 3/93 and ESC C10. ESC C10 says that the special rules will not be applied where there is a joint venture agreement which provides for certain 'triggering events', and the triggering event has not occurred. A triggering event will be an event which leads one member to leave the joint venture and make over his participation to the other members, eg the voluntary departure of a member or the liquidation of a member. SP 3/93 is concerned with the same provisions as ESC C10, and operates in conjunction with it. SP 3/93 provides that negotiations for disposal of a participation will not, so long as they remain subject to contract, activate the anti-avoidance rule.

Consortium and impairment relief

7.51   To prevent double use of the same losses, a lender's rights to impairment relief will be restricted where impairment relief has been claimed by the company or any other group company in the same or any preceding accounting period. The aim of these provisions is to prevent double relief both under the loan relationship and under the consortium rules. The claim for bad debt relief will be reduced by any amount surrendered by way of group relief (the 'relevant reduction').

7.52   Where a member of a consortium, or another member of its group, makes a loan to a consortium holding company or to a 90% subsidiary of a consortium holding company, debt relief for loan relationships is limited to the greater of the claim for bad debt relief and the claim to consortium relief.

7.53   Where there is a 'relevant consortium creditor relationship', special rules apply. A 'relevant consortium creditor relationship' is a loan by a member of a consortium to a consortium company: *CTA 2009, s 364(2)*. If the holder of the relevant consortium creditor relationship impairs or releases the debt, he has a 'net consortium debit' (*s 365(3)*). If the consortium company surrenders a loss for group relief purposes, the group relief claim will be restricted to the excess of that amount over the net consortium debit: *s 365(5), (6)*.

7.54   The rules are set out in *CTA 2009, ss 364–371*, and apply where:

(a)   bad debt relief is claimed by a member of a consortium or, where the member of a consortium is a link company, a company in the same group as the link company;

(b)   the debit is in respect of a debt owed by a consortium company or, if there is a consortium holding company, a subsidiary of the consortium holding company; and

(c)   the claim is made in a group accounting period, ie the claimant's accounting period or, where a link company is involved, an accounting period of the link company and claimant company which coincides or overlaps as to more than six months.

Imported losses

7.55 There are provisions to prevent a non-resident company which comes within the charge to corporation tax from claiming a deduction for any loss on a loan which arose prior to the time when the company came within the charge to corporation tax: *CTA 2009, s 327*. A loss is 'referable to a time when a relationship is not subject to United Kingdom taxation so far as, at the time to which the loss is referable, the chargeable company would not have been chargeable to tax in the United Kingdom on any profits arising from the relationship'. Hence the provision is only likely to apply where a non-resident company becomes UK resident, not when a non-resident company establishes a UK branch. This provision only applies if amortised cost accounting is used, as fair value accounting will produce an opening value of the asset at its fair value. *Section 327(4)* applies to cancel the loss where the loan relationship is transferred to another person to realise the imported loss.

Example 7.3

A (non-resident) company holds as an asset 10% loan stock with a nominal value of £100. On 1 April 2016, it becomes UK resident. In its accounts to 31 March 2017, it makes a 20% doubtful debt provision for the loan stock. This is regarded as 80% attributable to the pre-immigration period, and the balance is regarded as due to deterioration in credit-rating in the post-immigration period. On 31 March 2018, it sells the loan stock for £40. Its tax accounts are:

		£
Year to 31/3/2017	Interest	10
	Provision	(20)
	Add back	16
	Net Profit	6
Year to 31/3/2018	Interest	10
	Loss (80 – 40)	(40)
	Add back	32
	Net Profit	2

Chapter 8

Securities

Overview

8.1   This chapter deals with:

- Meaning of security
- Debt
- Dematerialised securities
- Regulatory capital (perpetuals)
- Securitisation
- Private finance initiative
- Structured finance arrangements
- QCBs (*TCGA 1992, s 117*)
- Non-QCBs
- Deeply discounted securities (*ITTOIA 2005, ss 427–442*)
- Excluded indexed securities (*ITTOIA 2005, s 433*)
- Euro commercial paper
- Warrants
- Capital contributions
- Gilts
- Stripped securities (*ITTOIA 2005, ss 443–452G*)
- Stamp duty

Introduction

8.2   Instruments or transactions which give rise to loan relationships or deemed loan relationships give rise to a 'money debt': *CTA 2009, s 303*. Debt instruments give rise to a money debt. Equity instruments do not. Interest payable on debt instruments is deductible in computing profits for accounting and tax purposes. Distributions on equity instruments are non-deductible. That is the key distinction. In practice, financial instruments have to be placed on a broad spectrum, running from pure debt to pure equity, with instruments between the two poles having the characteristics of both in varying proportions.

8.3   Debt involves a legal obligation to repay. In other contexts, the question has arisen whether a remote contingency of repayment indicates that an obligation should not be classified as a loan at all. Thus it may be argued that a loan connected with employment is simply earnings by another name, or a loan made in connection with a tax planning scheme does not create any economic obligation for the investor. The question is, at what point in a particular statutory context does a loan have such non-commercial features as to deprive it of the legal characterisation as a loan? In *Sempra Metals Ltd v R & Comrs* [2008] STC (SCD) 1062 at [143] the Special Commissioners held that loans made by an employee benefit trust to employees on favourable terms and with little prospect of repayment were nevertheless loans:

'As to the loans, albeit that they were on terms which reflected the employee benefit nature of the arrangements rather than an arm's length commercial arrangement between trustee/lender and beneficiary/borrower, they were nevertheless real loans on which interest was paid, and in respect of which, in some cases, principal was repaid.'

8.4   The key question here is, what the Special Commissioners meant by '*real* loans'. Later cases have adopted a 'commercial', substance-over-form approach, and dismissed arguments based on legal, statutory considerations as unreal: *Ingenious Games LLP v R & C Comrs* [2016] UKFTT 521 (TC), [213]–[225].

8.5   In a commercial context where securities are issued for the purpose of raising funds, and the question is, in what way for company law, accounting and tax purposes, funds have been raised, the legal nature of the obligation is paramount.

Meaning of security

8.6   A security is a commercial document. In most cases, an 'instrument representing security' will itself be a 'security'. The prime legal meaning is a secured debt claim:

'"Security" … denotes a debt or claim, the payment of which is in some way secured. The security would generally consist of a right to resort to some fund or property for payment … some form of secured liability is postulated.' (*Singer v Williams (Surveyor of Taxes)* 7 TC 419, per Viscount Cave at 431)

8.7   In the same case, it was said that the meaning of the term derives from its context:

> 'The word "securities" has no legal signification which necessarily attaches to it on all occasion of the use of the term. It is an ordinary English word used in a variety of collocations: and it is to be interpreted without the embarrassment of a legal definition and simply according to the best conclusion one can make as to the real meaning of the term as it is employed in, say, a testament, an agreement or a taxing or other statute as the case may be. The attempt to transfer legal definitions from one collocation to another leads to confusion and sometimes to a defeat of true intention.'

8.8   Debentures are corporate bonds which in the UK are generally backed by security, eg a charge over land and buildings. For company law purposes, there is a general definition of 'debentures', which includes 'Debenture stock, bonds or other securities of a company, whether or not constituting a charge on the assets of the company': *CA 2006, s 738.* A debenture 'is a document which either creates a debt or acknowledges it': *Levy v Abercorris Slate and Slab Co* (1887) 37 Ch D 260 at 264.

8.9   There are many statutory definitions of 'securities' for particular purposes, eg *ITEPA 2003, s 420(1)* contains a definition of securities for the purposes of the employment-related securities rules. This definition extends to shares as well as debentures. There is an important definition in *TCGA 1992, s 132(3)(b)*:

> '(b)   "Security" includes any loan stock or similar security whether of the United Kingdom or any other government, or of any public or local authority in the United Kingdom or elsewhere, or of any company, and whether secured or unsecured.'

8.10   This definition suggests that a security must be issued by a company or body corporate, so that a security constituting a loan relationship, a deeply discounted security or an exempt indexed security could not be issued by an individual or trustees. *TCGA 1992, Sch 4B, para 2(1)(c)* refers to the issuing of a security by trustees, but this is in a particular context.

8.11   *TCGA 1992, s 251(6)* says that any debenture issued after 16 March 1993 whose issue falls within the reorganisation rules is to be a security within *s 132*. However, this expanded definition applies only 'for the purposes of' that section. Under *TCGA 1992, ss 116(4A), 117(A1)*, all creditor loan relationships are securities within *s 132(3)(b)*. *Section 251(7), (8)* deems all loan relationships and relevant discounted securities to be securities within *s 132*, if they would otherwise not be. The legal structure of debt securities determines their character for tax purposes.

8.12   'Debts on a security' are chargeable assets: *TCGA 1992, s 251(1)*. The majority of debts on a security are taken out of the charge to capital gains tax, because qualifying corporate bonds (QCBs) are exempt assets by virtue of *s 115(1)(a). Section 251* says:

'(1)   Where a person incurs a debt to another, whether in sterling or in some other currency, no chargeable gain shall accrue to that (that is the original) creditor ... on a disposal of the debt, except in the case of a debt on a security (as defined in section 132).

...

(6)   For the purposes of this section a debenture issued by any company on or after 16th March 1993 shall be deemed to be a security (as defined in section 132) if –

(a)   it is issued on a reorganisation (as defined in section 126(1)) or in pursuance of an allotment on any such reorganisation;

(b)   it is issued in exchange for shares in or debentures of another company ...

(c)   ...

(d)   it is issued in pursuance of rights attached to any debenture issued on or after 16th March 1993 and falling within paragraph (a), (b) or (c) above.'.

8.13   *Section 115* says:

'(1)   A gain which accrues on the disposal by any person of –

(a)   gilt-edged securities or qualifying corporate bonds ...

shall not be a chargeable gain.'

8.14   For companies, the exemption from capital gains tax in *TCGA 1992, s 115(1)* has little significance, as all returns on these assets are taxed as income under the loan relationship rules.

8.15   There are effectively four definitions of 'qualifying corporate bond':

●   one in *TCGA 1992, s 117(A1)* for the purposes of corporation tax on capital gains (ie for company holders);

- a second main definition in *s 117(1)* for capital gains tax purposes (ie for holders not liable to corporation tax, such as individuals and trustees);

- a special definition for insurance companies in *s 117A*; and

- a special definition for authorised unit trusts and offshore funds in *s 117B*.

Debt

8.16 Essentially, all company finance is either equity (internal capital, provided by the shareholders) or debt (external capital, provided by third parties). Quasi-equity is debt provided by shareholders. A company can borrow from banks or other lenders (indirect financing), or tap the capital markets by issuing debt securities to investors (direct financing). The issue of 'debt securities' by a company, for the purposes of obtaining finance from institutions and other types of investor, can be structured in many different ways. Debt securities represent a written acknowledgement of indebtedness under which the debtor (the 'issuer') raises finance from holders of the security in exchange for a benefit, such as interest, or the option to acquire a different type of instrument. There are many different types of debt security, eg commercial paper (short-term), bonds (long-term). A secured bond is ordinarily called a debenture (although the legal definition is wider); an unsecured bond is called loan stock. Types of corporate debt within the loan relationship rules include:

1   *Short-term finance* by means of bank advances under overdraft arrangements.

2   *Term loans* for a period of normally up to five years.

3   *Syndicated loans.* A syndicated loan arises when a number of lenders jointly fund a loan, each providing a specified proportion called a 'participation'. Syndicated loans are an alternative to public offerings or international placement of bonds and are normally for a term of three to seven years, for amounts ranging from £10m to £5bn (Eurotunnel involved a syndicate of some 140 banks). While the borrower obtains a separate loan from each syndicate member, one member acts as agent for the other lenders ('lead bank'), for which he receives an additional fee.

4   *Commercial paper.* Commercial paper means bills of exchange issued by companies with a maturity date of less than a year for a minimum of £150,000. A bill of exchange is an order by A (the drawer) to B (the drawee) to pay a sum of money to C (the payee). The drawee of the bill only incurs liability under the bill if he 'accepts' it (*Bills of Exchange Act 1882, ss 17(1), 53(1), 54(1)*). 'Finance' or 'bank' bills are bills drawn on a bank in pursuance of an acceptance credit facility. A holding company will normally enter into a commercial paper programme on behalf of its subsidiaries.

Once a bill has been accepted, it may be used as a means of raising finance, either by using it as security for a loan or by being discounted.

A commercial paper programme takes one of three forms:

(i)   direct issue of paper to the market, arranged by a group of banks;

(ii)   note issuance facilities, whereby paper is issued through banks; and

(iii)   revolving underwriting facilities, whereby the issue is underwritten by a group of banks.

The interest on commercial paper is normally not yearly interest, and so can be paid without deduction of tax, even when none of the exemptions in *ITA 2007, ss 875–888* applies.

5   *Multi-option facilities*. Multi-option facilities are an uncommitted facility offered by a group of banks to a company, to provide financing for a period from a few days to a year. Normally, the arrangement includes a back-up minimum committed facility. Like syndicated loans, they are administered by a lead bank. Multi-option facilities operate through a tender principle. When the borrower requires funds, the participating banks may tender to provide them. Multi-option facilities will contain a grossing-up clause for interest.

6   Bonds are long-term debt securities which may be unsecured (loan stock) or secured (debentures). 'Long-term' simply means having a term of over one year, ie not repayable in the current accounting period.

8.17   Most forms of borrowing other than bank borrowing involve the issue of debt securities, either commercial paper or bonds. Under the *Financial Services and Markets Act 2000 (FSMA 2000), s 19*, it is a criminal offence for a person who is not an 'authorised person' to carry on a 'regulated activity'. 'Regulated activities' include 'accepting deposits' (*Sch 2, para 4*). 'Accepting deposits' is defined in *FSMA 2000 (Regulated Activities) Order 2001, SI 2001/544, reg 5* to include the issue of debt securities. Accordingly, *reg 9* provides that a sum is not a deposit if it is received in consideration for the issue of debt securities. Commercial paper can only be issued to persons who acquire, hold, manage or dispose of investments as part of their ordinary business. Borrowing from authorised institutions is outside the regulations.

8.18   Any unsecured or secured loan note is, in law, a debenture. Debenture loan stock is loan securities divided into units. Debenture/loan stock will generally be issued through the medium of a trust, with the lenders becoming entitled to a beneficial interest in the rights under the contract of the loan to which the company and the trustee are parties.

8.19   It is common practice for a subsidiary (special purpose vehicle, SPV) to issue bonds, which the parent (P) guarantees, and use the proceeds of the bond issue to refinance and develop the parent's business. The on-lending constitutes a separate debt between P and SPV (*Re Polly Peck International plc (in administration)* [1996] 2 All ER 433). Repayment of the loans made by SPV cannot be on an on-demand basis, and SPV needs to make a small profit, otherwise SPV might be regarded as an agent for P. If P guarantees the bonds and subsequently becomes insolvent, SPV can prove in the liquidation for the funds on-lent. If, as is inevitable, SPV then defaults, the bond-holders can also prove in P's liquidation on the basis of P's guarantee. If the solvency of the guarantor is in doubt, the guarantee may be an unlawful preference or a transaction at an undervalue (*Insolvency Act 1986, ss 238–241*; *Re M C Bacon Ltd* [1990] BCLC 324).

8.20   An issue of debt securities may take effect either as a simple one-off issue, or pursuant to a shelf programme, such as a medium-term note (MTN) programme. Under an MTN programme the issuer can issue several different tranches of debt securities at different periods of time. The issuer under an MTN programme will agree to a series of terms under which it can issue debt securities of, inter alia, different maturities and currency; and the programme will stipulate the total amount which can be issued.

8.21   A callable bond is a fixed rate loan which can be repaid early at the option of the borrower. Accordingly, it is a bond plus a series of options on the price of the bond granted by the investor to the issuer.

Example 8.1

- Amount £1,000

- Term 5 years

- Coupon 10%

- Call protected period – years 1–2

- Callable – after three years at 106%; after four years at 104%.

8.22   The qualitative nature of the debt securities which are offered to investors will depend on the issuer's perception of marketability for that particular note. For instance, the issue of convertible notes offers investors a rate of return which is secured on the issuer's assets. However, such notes have the added attraction of enabling investors to obtain, at a future date, a share in the profits of the issuer. Alternatively, an issuer may decide to issue a zero coupon exchangeable bond, which could be exchangeable into shares. An issuer also needs to consider whether the debt securities should be issued at par, at a premium, or discount to par. If a coupon is payable, the issuer will also need to consider whether it is payable at a fixed rate, or floating rate. Once an issuer determines the nature of the debt securities which will be issued, it becomes necessary to consider the structuring aspects of the transaction. The issuer must ensure that the debt offering is structured in such a way that the marketability of the debt is not impaired. For practical purposes, the issuer will need to enter into arrangements for enabling the debt securities to be traded on a relevant stock exchange. The finance structure will additionally need to comply with any corporate and regulatory obligations imposed in jurisdictions in which the issuer and investors will be located. The way in which offerings of debt securities are structured will typically be motivated by investor protection requirements, and the need to facilitate the marketability of the securities. However, many of the intermediaries used for the purposes of structured finance may have tax consequences for the debt issue.

8.23   The role of lead manager is normally performed by an investment bank, which is responsible for managing the issue of the debt securities. The lead manager will advise upon the structure and timing of the debt issue. If the debt securities are to be issued on a stock exchange, the lead manager will normally deal with the relevant regulatory body for the relevant stock exchange. For tax purposes, it will often be necessary to ensure that the securities are listed on a recognised stock exchange, to ensure that interest payments can be made under the Eurobond exemption without deduction for, or on account of, UK tax.

8.24   Underwriters are essentially a group of investment banks who agree to underwrite the issue of the debt securities. Consequently, they bear the risk of the debt offering not being fully subscribed and would, in such an event, be required to buy all of the unsold debt securities. The underwriters will be consulted on all aspects of the debt offering and will seek to ensure that nothing is contained in the terms and conditions of the issue which affect marketability.

8.25   A trustee is often appointed in respect of the debt securities. The terms of the appointment are governed by what is known as an 'indenture'. The role of a trustee is to represent the interests of bondholders. The trustee will typically act as the common depositary for the purposes of holding the debt securities. In contrast, an issuer may appoint a fiscal agent who is an agent of the issuer. A fiscal agent will owe no obligations to the bondholders.

8.26   The role of the paying agent is to receive from the issuer payments of capital and interest on the debt securities and distribute such amounts to the investors. The issuer may appoint paying agents in one or several jurisdictions.

8.27   The typical structure for the issue of debt securities is for them to be issued under an indenture between the issuer, together with any guarantor of the issuer, and a bank, such as the Bank of New York or Citicorp, which will act as a trustee of the debt securities representing the interests of investors. The terms of the indenture may be governed by English law, or foreign law such as, in the United States, the *Trust Indenture Act of 1939*. The indenture is a document which contains a list of promises or what are known as covenants by the issuer, such as the circumstances in which security, like a mortgage, will be granted over the issuer's property. The function of the trustee is principally to appoint an intermediary to enforce the rights of bondholders against the issuer, and to perform administrative duties for the issuer, such as possibly sending interest payments to bondholders.

Dematerialised securities

8.28   An issuer in offering debt could issue definitive bonds, ie a certificate representing each bond to every investor. The definitive bond might either be bearer or registered. In the case of registered securities, the physical certificate issued merely evidences, and does not constitute, the security. In the case of bearer securities, the physical certificate constitutes, and does not merely evidence, the claims on the issuer.

8.29   The significant disadvantage of issuing debt in this way is that the debt becomes difficult to transfer, and consequently marketability is affected. Dematerialisation replaces physical instruments with electronic records and, in the case of bearer securities, a tangible asset with an intangible asset.

8.30   The typical nature of a debt offering is for the issuer to use the services of a clearing system, which eliminates the physical movement or holding of certificates. Ownership is then transferred by book transfer.

8.31   Where a clearing system is used for a debt offering, the issuer will create a permanent global debt security (representing a 100% interest in the debt securities) which is lodged with a depositary, such as a bank. The purpose of the depositary is to preserve the security of the global debt security. The global security is held by the depositary under the terms of a deposit agreement entered into between the depositary and the issuer. The global security may either be in bearer or registered form. If in bearer form, title to the securities will pass by delivery.

8.32   The deposit agreement will provide for the depositary to issue dematerialised depositary interests which represent 100% of the underlying global security. The certificate less depositary interests are then traded through the book-entry system of a clearing system, such as Euroclear or Clearstream. The book-entry interests are held by persons who have accounts with the clearing system, known as 'direct participants', or through persons who are direct participants, in which case the beneficial owners are 'indirect participants'.

8.33   Ownership of book-entry interests is shown on, and transferred through, records maintained by each clearing system. Under the terms of the indenture, the depositary is regarded as the sole holder of the global security. Except as provided for in the indenture, no other person will be regarded as being entitled to have any debt securities registered in their name. Any person owning a book-entry interest is obliged to rely on the procedures of the intermediary for the purposes of exercising any rights and obligations of a holder under the indenture or deposit agreement. In certain circumstances, the deposit agreement will enable the owner of book-entry interests to exchange them for definitive registered bonds evidencing interests in the permanent global security, for example where the depositary has discontinued providing its services and the issuer fails to appoint a successor. The bondholders are required to look to their intermediary for payments on the debt securities. The rules of the depositary will determine payments and transfers in respect of a bondholder's interest in the global security.

8.34 The operators of book-entry systems are principally Euroclear and Clearstream which enable their account holders to settle securities transactions by electronic book-entry transfers. Essentially, an investor who wishes to hold a debt security will do so indirectly through an account with a bank or other financial intermediary that in turn has an account with the depositary.

The diagram below shows the typical structure for a debt offering:

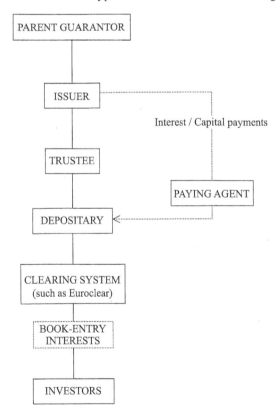

8.35   If an issuer intends to make returns of income or capital on the debt securities, it will generally make such payments through a paying agent to the depositary, as the holder of the permanent global security. The depositary, under the terms of the depositary agreement, is then obliged to pass such payments down the chain, such as to Euroclear or Clearstream, and thence to the ultimate beneficial owners. If definitive securities are issued, the issuer will maintain a paying agent and a transfer agent through which the registration of transfer of bonds can be effected. Since the holder of the permanent global bond is deemed to be the legal owner, the depositary is consequently the legal owner of all interest and capital payments made in respect of the debt securities. The issuer accordingly has no liability to the owners of the book-entry interests in respect of such payments. An owner of a book-entry interest must enforce his or her rights against the clearing systems.

Debts on a security

8.36   *TCGA 1992, s 251(1)* took 'debts on a security' out of the simple debt regime and taxed them as chargeable assets in the hands of individuals. A 'debt on a security' must be a 'security' within *TCGA 1992, s 132(3)(b)*. For companies, debts on a security are, in most cases, loan relationships. The courts have criticised the statutory provisions in this area as 'meagre and confusing' (*Aberdeen Construction Group Ltd v IRC* 52 TC 281 at 298–299). The Inland Revenue originally intended to draw the boundary between debts which were in the loan relationship rules and debts which were outside the new rules, along the line of the debt on a security/simple debt boundary of capital gains tax: *TCGA 1992, ss 132(3)(b), 251(1)*; Consultative Document, para 45. For the purpose of capital gains tax, debts are not assets (therefore not attracting loss relief from capital gains) unless they are 'debts on a security'.

8.37   In order to constitute a security, it will normally be necessary for there to be a significant chronological interval between the time when an instrument is issued and the time it can be redeemed. Something intended to enure for a nominal period will not constitute a security.

8.38   There are four cases on the meaning of 'debt on a security': *Cleveleys Investment Trust Co v IRC* 47 TC 300; *Aberdeen Construction Group Ltd v IRC* 52 TC 281; *W T Ramsay Ltd v IRC* 54 TC 101; and *Taylor Clark International Ltd v Lewis (Inspector of Taxes)* [1997] STC 499; affd [1998] STC 1259.

8.39   In *Cleveleys*, an investment company (C) loaned £25,000 to a trading company (F), on the understanding that it would ultimately obtain a 51% interest in F. F drew a bill of exchange for £25,000 in favour of C, and undertook to carry through a scheme of capital reconstruction to give C the agreed shareholding. C in turn guaranteed F's overdraft, and advanced a further £10,000. F became insolvent and the £35,000 was lost. C claimed:

(a) that the £25,000 was advanced as part of a composite transaction, which created an asset and gave rise to an allowable loss; and

(b) that the bill of exchange was a 'debt on a security' and so a chargeable asset for capital gains tax purposes.

8.40 C succeeded on the first point (by a majority), but failed on the second point (by a different majority). This was on the ground that the document was a mere acknowledgment of the debt. As Lord Migdale said:

> 'The written acknowledgment of the loan and the bill of exchange may make it quicker for the Appellants to get repayment of their advance, but neither documents helps them to get it or affords them any right against Falkirk over and above its obligation to repay, and neither document would enable Falkirk to go against any third party for payment.'

8.41 A 'debt on a security' is not a secured debt (*Cleveleys* at 318), ie not a debenture in the conventional sense. In *Ramsay*, Lord Fraser said (at 194) that a 'debt on a security' is a debt in the nature of an investment which can be dealt in and purchased with a view to being held as an investment. Lord Wilberforce distinguished between 'mere debts' and 'debts with added characteristics' (at 189). 'A debt on a security', he said, 'had to have a structure of permanence'. In *Taylor Clark International*, the taxpayer company sought to claim a currency loss on a promissory note issued by a subsidiary as a loss on a 'debt on a security' (not being a QCB). Robert Walker J concluded that a 'debt on a security' must:

(a) be capable of assignment;

(b) carry interest; and

(c) have a structure of permanence, ie have a fixed term and not be capable of being repaid early without a penalty.

Regulatory capital

8.42 Capital adequacy rules (a) define what counts as capital or 'own funds', and (b) prescribe the minimum solvency ratio which banks must maintain. Banks are required to maintain regulatory capital which constitutes a prescribed proportion of their risk-weighted assets. Capital adequacy standards for international banks are laid down by the Basel Committee on Banking Supervision of the Bank for International Settlements (BIS). These are given legislative force within the UK by EU and UK legislation. In particular, *FSMA 2000* requires all authorised institutions to conduct their business in a prudent manner, which includes complying with capital adequacy requirements.

8.43 Under the *Second Capital Adequacy Directive (93/6/EEC)* a bank's assets are divided into 'trading book' and 'banking book'. On the banking side, to each risk-weighted lending balance a specified amount of capital has to be allocated.

Example 8.2

A bank lends £1m to a company. The asset is risk-weighted at 100% (= 1). If the bank's solvency ratio is 10%, capital of £100,000 will have to be allocated to the loan. The bank's gross profit will be (interest + fees received) – (cost of capital + cost of funds).

8.44 Capital comprises Tier 1, Tier 2 and Tier 3 capital. There are no limits on Tier 1 capital. Tier 2 capital cannot exceed Tier 1, so that surplus Tier 2 capital will not be 'capital' for capital adequacy purposes. Tier 3 capital can only be used to meet trading book requirements.

8.45 Tier 1 comprises 'core capital', ie share capital (ordinary shares [equity] plus preference shares), reserves and published interim retained profits. Tier 1 debt is a contradiction in terms, in that Tier 1 capital should have no 'cost of carry', ie be deeply subordinated as share capital and not be subject to any legal obligation to pay interest. Tier 2 comprises 'supplementary capital', ie semi-permanent resources such as hybrid instruments and long-term subordinated debt. Subordinated term debt must not exceed one-half of Tier 1. It also includes revaluation reserves, general provisions (not to exceed 1.25% of risk-weighted assets). Tier 3 capital comprises 'ancillary capital', ie short-term subordinated, unsecured debt with a term of at least two years (Supervisory and Surveillance Department (Bank of England), 1995/2).

8.46 The solvency ratio (minimum of 8% and, in practice, 10–15%) is the ratio of capital to total assets which a bank must maintain. For banking book assets, the minimum ratio required is 8%, of which a minimum of 4% must be Tier 1 capital. Because of the short-term nature of trading book assets, the Tier 1 capital adequacy requirement for trading book assets is only 2%. Tier 1 capital is expensive to maintain because dividends are non-deductible for tax purposes. Moreover, the need to maintain, at best, equal amounts of Tier 1 (share) and Tier 2 (long-term debt) capital restricts the ability of banks to increase their gearing. By the same token, an increase in Tier 1 capital increases the capacity to raise Tier 2 capital.

8.47   The adequacy of banks' regulatory capital is assessed at two levels:

- solo consolidated ratio, ie the authorised entity plus the capital of certain subsidiaries which pass regulatory tests; and

- group consolidated ratio, ie the authorised entity plus the capital of all the financial companies in which the parent or its subsidiaries have a 20% participation or more. Minority interests of a reporting bank in other financial entities will be included in that bank's capital resources.

8.48   If an SPV is used to raise capital, capital invested in it needs to be included as minority interest in Tier 1 capital. Accounting rules are based on control. If the bank controls the SPV, it can be consolidated without any adjustments. Everyone other than the bank holds a 'minority' interest. 'Minority' here means 'external'.

Example 8.3

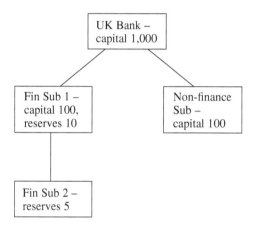

Consolidated capital of UK bank is 915 (1,000 – 100 + (10 + 5)).

8.49   The latest guidelines are in the Basel III accord (Capital Requirement Directive III), which was implemented from 2013. This divides regulatory capital into:

- Tier 1 common equity (CET1);

- Additional Tier 1 (AT1);

- Tier 2; and

- Tier 3.

8.50 *Securities*

8.50   CET1 must be accounted for as equity. AT1 must meet 14 criteria to be accounted for as equity, such as:

- callable only by issuer with consent of regulator;
- perpetual (ie no fixed redemption date);
- any dividend or coupon must be discretionary and non-cumulative;
- automatically convertible into common equity if trigger event occurs.

8.51   Additional Tier 1 capital features as part of equity accounting, as opposed to liability accounting. Innovative Tier 1 capital is a finance structure designed to provide tax-deductible funding costs in respect of hybrid securities which count as Additional Tier 1 regulatory capital (equity) for banks. Such securities are referred to as 'preferred securities' or 'perpetuals'.

8.52   If all these requirements are met, the preferred securities will be debt for tax purposes, allowing interest to be tax deductible, but count as shares for regulatory purposes. Accordingly, the finance cost of Additional Tier 1 capital will be lower than that of common equity, ie share capital. Preferred securities are thus a special category of hybrid instrument.

8.53   Under Basel III, such securities will be contingent convertibles (Co-cos). Additional Tier 1 capital will have a trigger point above the non-viability point, so that they will have potential for loss absorption. Conversion is likely to constitute a release of debt. In that case, liability write-down will produce a taxable profit. It is unlikely that the issuer would be required to bifurcate the bond into a loan relationship and an equity instrument under IAS 39, because there is no way in which a premium or discount on redemption can be derived from the instrument. Co-cos will be Eurobonds, to take advantage of the gross payment facility.

8.54   The issuer of a perpetual has a contingent obligation to repay the principal. Perpetuals are accordingly loan relationships: *CTA 2009, ss 303(1)(a), 476(1); Reed International Ltd v IRC* [1975] STC 427. Interest payable on such securities are not 'results dependent' within *CTA 2010, s 1015(4)*, so cannot be recharacterised as a distribution. The 'equity notes' rules in *CTA 2010, ss 1015(6), 1016* apply because interest on such securities is only liable to tax recharacterisation if held by a person funding or associated with the issuer.

8.55   Tier 2 capital (T2) is going concern capital. It must be unsecured, wholly subordinated to the claims of all non-subordinated creditors. If a trigger event occurs, T2 capital converts into CET1 capital. Hence T2 capital may be accounted for as a convertible.

8.56   In a technical note issued in September 2010 HMRC provided guidance as to whether the return on an instrument was 'results dependent' so as to attract distribution treatment under *CTA 2010, s 1015(4)*. HMRC draws a distinction between statutory bail-in (not results dependent) and contractual bail-in (results dependent). *CTA 2010, s 1023A* provides that a payment made in respect of 'tier two capital' is not a distribution.

8.57   *The Taxation of Regulatory Capital Securities Regulations 2013, SI 2013/3209,* provide that a 'regulatory capital security' (ie a security which qualifies as AT1 or T2) is to be treated as a loan relationship from 1 January 2014. No credit or debit is to be allowed for tax purposes on conversion or write down in the case of the issuer or a connected creditor. For group relief purposes the security is treated as a 'normal commercial loan'. There is no duty to deduct withholding tax on interest under *ITA 2007, ss 874, 889.*

8.58   INTM 267776 gives guidance on the allocation of AT1 capital to the UK permanent establishment of a foreign bank.

8.59   CRD 3 is to be replaced by CRD 4. HMRC has issued a document: 'The Current Tax Treatment of Instrument Designed to be Compliant with Capital Requirements Directive 4.'

Securitisation

8.60   Asset securitisation is the process of converting receivables and other assets which are not readily marketable into securities – so-called 'asset-backed securities' (ABSs) – which can be placed and traded in the capital markets. All that is required is a pool of homogeneous assets, eg mortgages, credit cards, telephone bills, property rentals). Securitisation means the re-packaging of loan relationships (typically mortgages or credit card receivables) into securities, which are then sold to outside investors. A securitisation involves four parties: the originator; the special purpose vehicle (SPV); the investors; and a rating agency. The originator is the original creditor, who sells his debt assets to an SPV. The SPV will issue Eurobonds and use the proceeds to pay the purchase price to the originator. The interest payments will be debits under the loan relationship rules, and will match the interest receipts on the debt assets. The SPV now owns the portfolio of debt assets, but appoints the originator to administer the loan portfolio on his behalf. The originator (or SPV) pays a rating agency to provide a credit rating for the securities issued by the SPV, without which investors will not subscribe for these instruments. The fallibility of rating agencies in this regard contributed to both the expansion of credit up to 2007 and the financial crisis which began in 2008.

8.61   There are three models of securitisation: (a) sale; (b) loan; and (c) synthetic. A true sale will be off balance sheet. The aim will normally be that the disposal should generate neither a profit nor a loss. One form of credit enhancement for the investors is 'over-collateralisation', ie more assets are sold to the SPV than the SPV securitises, thus giving it a reserve. If the originator sells the assets at a loss in order to achieve over-collateralisation, that loss is unlikely to be recognised. This is because, in all cases of non-arm's length transactions, the loan relationship rules impose an arm's length standard. General rules can also substitute for a non-trade disposal 'the market realisable value at the time' (*Petrotim Securities Ltd (formerly Gresham Trust Ltd) v Ayres (Inspector of Taxes)* 41 TC 389 at 407; *Stanton (Inspector of Taxes) v Drayton Commercial Investment Co Ltd* 55 TC 286).

8.62 In the loan structure, the originator retains the asset portfolio in its balance sheet ('covered bonds'). The SPV grants a loan to the originator. This will be on balance sheet, secured financing. The originator retires existing funding and meets the loan expense from the asset receivables. In a synthetic structure, the originator retains legal ownership of the assets, but transfers the risk and rewards of ownership to the SPV. Thus, the synthetic structure is a credit derivative. The protection buyer is the originator and the protection seller is the SPV. As in the other two models, the SPV will issue securities to meet its liabilities, which bonds themselves bear a credit risk, which is thereby transferred to the investor.

8.63 In the sale and debt models, the securities issued by the SPV are secured only on the assets securitised. Accordingly, the SPV is thinly capitalised. By covering the associated risks with some form of credit enhancement, the asset-backed debt offers a high level of security.

8.64 The accounting treatment is crucial to securitisation, because the originator will normally wish to remove the securitised assets from his balance sheet. Derecognition is only possible if no significant benefits or risks are retained.

8.65 Where derecognition applies, a profit will be recognised on the disposal to the SPV, which will – in the case of a sale transaction – normally be a disposal in the course of a trade. The SPV will normally not only pay an immediate price, but also undertake to transfer back to the originator any profit on the transferred loans. This is, in most cases, achieved by means of notional loans between the SPV and the originator, whereby the interest margin is calculated so as to transfer any surplus to the originator. The SPV will have to offer investors some form of credit enhancement in order to persuade them to invest in the SPV's securities. This is because the SPV is interposed between the investors and the underlying borrowers, and the SPV itself will only have limited capital.

8.66 Under IFRS, an asset is an entitlement to future cash flows. An entity may transfer the contractual rights to cash flows in respect of an asset, or it may retain the contractual right to cash flows but assume a contractual obligation to pass them on (a 'pass-through' arrangement). For derecognition to occur under

IAS 39, in the case of a pass-through arrangement, three conditions have to be fulfilled (IAS 39, para 19):

(a)   the originator has no obligation to pay amounts to the creditors of the SPV, unless it collects equivalent amounts from the original asset;

(b)   the originator has no power of disposal over the original asset, other than to pledge it as security for the creditors of the SPV; and

(c)   there is no material delay in the transfer of cash flows.

8.67   The main imperative in the tax treatment of securitisations is that there should be no tax leakage in the form of additional tax burdens which would not have arisen if the assets had been retained by the originator. Securisation SPVs are normally set up on the basis that expenditure will match income, so there will be a very small margin of profit. Under IAS 39, however, unrealised profits in the SPV will be recognised under IAS 39 on the adoption of IAS. Accordingly, *CTA 2010, ss 623–625* allow securitisation companies to compute their profits for tax purposes on a basis set out in regulations. The regulations are the *Taxation of Securitisation Companies Regulations 2006, SI 2006/3296*. Under *reg 14*, securitisation companies are taxed by reference to the greater of:

(a)   nil;

(b)   the retained profit (*reg 10*) less amounts received from other securitisation companies plus dividends (as adjusted) paid to investors; and

(c)   any credit which would be brought into account for loan relationship purposes where a loan relationship was transferred intra-group and the transferee company then left the group.

8.68   'Securitisation company' is extremely broadly defined in *reg 4* as:

*   a note-issuing company,

*   an asset-holding company,

*   an intermediate borrowing company,

*   a warehousing company,

*   a commercial paper funded company.

All these terms are separately defined.

8.69   If the assets transferred by the originator to the SPV are not trading assets (eg debt receivables), but capital assets (eg property investments), a capital gain may arise, which can be avoided if the SPV is a member of the originator's capital gains tax group. As far as the SPV is concerned, the aim is that income and expenditure should be in equilibrium, ie payments to investors, and the return of excess profits to the originator should equal income receipts, so that no tax is payable in the SPV. Where this is not possible, a receivables trust may be used to intercept the payments to the SPV. The receivables trust will transfer to the SPV payments up to the amount of its tax-deductible expenditure, the balance being paid to the issuer. However, this is simply a securitisation within a securitisation, and may simply move the problems back a stage.

8.70   Securitisations are a species of collateralised loan obligation (CLO) transactions. Asset pools are tranched according to credit risk. CLO securities are issued via SPVs with varying risk/return and maturity profiles.

Private finance initiative

8.71   Under the private finance initiative (PFI), public sector bodies entered into long-term contracts with the private sector for the supply of goods, services and a series of income payments. Under long-term partnerships between public authorities and private providers, the private sector partner ('the operator') agrees to build, maintain and operate the facility (the hospital, the health care centre, the school, the motorway, the prison) at its own cost, which it recovers by a series of annual payments ('unitary payments') from the public sector body ('the purchaser'). The property is acquired by the operator, with the public sector body having a lesser interest or licence.

8.72   This is similar to finance leasing. The broad accounting principle is to convert what would be a physical asset of the lessor into a financial asset, with a corresponding financial liability and physical asset of the lessee. Accordingly, the rental payments by the lessee have to be split into a finance charge and a capital element, on a basis which gives a constant yield on the amount of the notional loan outstanding.

8.73   PFI projects have four distinct characteristics:

(a)   the public sector purchaser cannot claim capital allowances;

(b)   PFI is not based on statute but on HMRC practice;

(c)   the structure of legal agreements is distinctive; and

(d)   in particular, the process is set in a public law framework.

8.74   The question is, therefore, whether for tax purposes the purchaser should be regarded as owning an asset which he does not hold for accounting purposes. If, for tax purposes, the operator is regarded as holding a physical asset ('an asset of the property'), he will incur capital expenditure but can claim capital allowances. In most cases, however, it will be of advantage for the operator if all his expenditure is treated as revenue expenditure in the course of a financial trade, consisting primarily in the making of a notional loan to the purchaser ('composite trade' or 'contract debtor' treatment). This in turn produces cost savings for the purchaser, and saves pointless recycling of tax moneys (payment of additional tax by operator, which goes to fund higher costs of purchaser).

8.75   Under the 'composite trade' treatment, ownership of the property remains vested in the purchaser, even if property risk has been transferred for accounting purposes.

8.76   The choice is thus between a 'lease and capital allowance' and 'composite trade' tax treatment of the operator. The anticipated tax treatment crucially influences the prices which he can quote in the competitive tendering process. Official guidance is contained in *Tax Bulletin*, Issue 40, April 1999, 640; *Tax Bulletin*, Issue 60, August 2000, 950; and Customs Business Brief 18/2003 of 30 September 2003.

Structured finance arrangements

8.77   In *IRC v John Lewis Properties plc* [2001] STC 1118 (High Court), [2003] STC 117 (CA), a property holding company was paid rents under leases by subsidiaries. The holding company sold the right to receive the rents for five years (rents totalling £27.6m) to a bank for a lump sum payment of £25.5m. For accounting purposes under FRS 5, the holding company was required to treat the £25.5m as a loan, and the balance of £2.1m as a finance cost. To further replicate the loan treatment, the holding company entered into a vanilla swap, so that it was paying commercial floating rate interest on a loan of £25.5m. For tax purposes, it was held that the receipt was a capital receipt, arising from a part disposal of the leasehold interests, ie sale of an interest in land. The company was then able to reinvest the proceeds of disposal and claim roll-over relief.

8.78   In the High Court, Lightman J said (at 1140):

'There is no broad "economic equivalent" test entitling the court to treat a capital item as income because it is the economic equivalent of income.'

8.79   In the Court of Appeal, Arden LJ (dissenting) held (at 139) that the 'commercial reality of what JL [John Lewis] received was discounted rents and hence income'. Dyson LJ suggested that there were five indicia of a capital sum:

(a)   duration;

(b)   the value of the asset assigned;

(c) whether the payment causes a diminution in the value of the assignor's interest;

(d) whether the payment is a single lump sum or a series of recurrent payments; and

(e) if the disposal of the asset is accompanied by a transfer of risk.

8.80 With effect from 6 June 2007, such transactions are likely to fall under either:

(a) 'transfer of income stream': *CTA 2010, ss 752–757*; a payment for the transfer of an income stream is treated as income; or

(b) the 'finance arrangement code': *ss 758–774*; such arrangements give rise to a deemed loan relationship, with relief for payment of the finance charge but not for the repayment of principal.

The 'transfer of income stream' charge only arises if the transaction does not constitute a finance arrangement: *s 755*.

8.81 'Finance arrangements' are of three types:

- Type 1 (*s 758*);
- Type 2 (*s 763*); and
- Type 3 (*s 767*).

8.82 In a Type 1 arrangement:

(a) a 'borrower' receives an 'advance' from a 'lender';

(b) the borrower records a financial obligation in respect of the advance;

(c) the borrower assigns an income-producing asset (a 'security') to the lender; and

(d) the payments in respect of the security reduce the liability, the excess being a finance charge.

Example 8.4

The rules apply where:

(a) A Ltd has predictable income of 20 a year for five years (total 100).

(b) A Ltd assigns the right to the income to B Ltd for five years for 80, which is the NPV of the assigned income. B Ltd becomes entitled to the income for the next five years.

(c)   The accounting entries are:

DR Cash 80   CR Liabilities 80

The transaction creates a liability because A Ltd has to make payments to B Ltd (the assigned income).

(d)   A Ltd treats the payments to B Ltd as being applied first in payment of a finance charge on the liability, with the balance going to reduce the indebtedness (in other words, treating the advance as a loan of 80 and finance charge of 20, spread over five years).

(e)   A Ltd does not bring into charge to tax the receipt of 80, because 80 is a capital sum derived from an asset, but A Ltd has brought forward capital losses to set against it.

(f)   Absent special rules, A Ltd would get a tax deduction for the sums assigned to B.

8.83   The absence of a tax charge in A Ltd which would otherwise have arisen is classified as a 'relevant effect' under *CTA 2010, s 759*. Where the arrangement would have had the 'relevant effect', the arrangement does not have the relevant effect but instead the borrower is taxed on the otherwise untaxed income (100), but obtains a deduction for the finance charge (20). The advance is treated as a loan relationship, and the finance charge as a loan relationship debit: *s 761*. In other words, the income diverted to the lender is taxed as income of the borrower.

8.84   Hence, under these rules, A Ltd is taxed on 80, so A is taxed and the tax authority receives the benefit of the NPV of tax on income of 20 a year for five years. A Ltd's otherwise unrelievable losses are restored.

8.85   In Type 2 and Type 3 arrangements, a partnership is involved. In complex schemes:

(a)   the borrower owns an income-producing asset worth 100, which produces income of 5 a year;

(b)   the borrower sets up a limited partnership and transfers the asset to the partnership by way of capital contribution of 100;

(c)   the lender becomes a member of the partnership, making a contribution of 20 to the capital of the partnership (the 'loan');

(d)   the lender is entitled to 99.99% of all profits of the partnership until the loan is repaid plus interest, and thereafter to 0.01% of the profits;

(e)   the partnership lends 20 to the borrower;

(f)   when, after five years, the borrower has received 99.99% of 25, the lender's partnership share is bought for a nominal amount by an associate of the borrower; and

(g)   the borrower withdraws his capital of 100.

The economic effect of the arrangement is that the borrower has applied income of 25 on which it would otherwise have been taxable to repay a loan of 20 plus interest of 5.

8.86   Where an arrangement is a structured finance arrangement in relation to a borrower partnership, and where a change in the membership of the borrower partnership relating to the lender would have had the 'following effect', namely, that a member of the borrower partnership is not taxed on income which would otherwise have been taxable, then:

* the loan is treated as a loan relationship of the borrower;

* the borrower is taxed on the income which he has not received;

* the borrower obtains a loan relationship debit for the amounts treated as deemed interest on the loan; and

* there is no disposal of the security for capital gains tax purposes.

8.87   The net effect of the rules is that the loan relationship rules apply as if the borrower and the lender had entered into a loan relationship at the date of the transaction. The transfer of the asset, or the right to income from the asset, is treated as a realisation of income, not as producing a capital gain. The factored income or receipts are still treated as arising to the borrower.

8.88   The 'transfer of income stream' rules in *CTA 2010, ss 752–757* are intended to impose a generic charge in cases which are similar to the finance arrangement rules but do not fall within the definition of Type 1, 2 or 3. They apply where a company transfers a right to income ('relevant receipts') for a payment (normally the NPV of the transferred income) without transferring the asset giving rise to the right to income. The amount received for the transfer ('the relevant amount') is taxed as income of the transferor.

Qualifying corporate bonds

8.89   In the case of a company, all loan relationships are qualifying corporate bonds (QCBs): *TCGA 1992, s 117(A1)*.

8.90   In the case of an individual, a QCB is a loan note which does not have any equity features and which does not give rise to a foreign exchange gain or loss. *TCGA 1992, s 117(1)* defines a corporate bond as a bond which has two characteristics: (1) it is and has been 'at all times' a 'normal commercial loan' (*s 117(1)(a)*); and (2) it is expressed in and only redeemable in sterling (*s 117(1)(b)*). 'Normal commercial loan' is defined in *CTA 2010, s 162*, but the definition is adapted for the purpose of defining QCB. In the case of an individual, a debt security is a QCB under *TCGA 1992, s 117(1)* if:

(a)   it is a security within *TCGA 1992, s 132(3)(b)*;

(b)   it is a normal commercial loan;

(c)   it is expressed in sterling;

(d)   there is no provision for redemption in foreign currency (a provision for redemption at the exchange rate ruling at the date of redemption to be ignored);

(e)   (not being a corporate bond within (a)–(c)) it is a deeply discounted security. All zero coupon bonds securities of various kinds are classified as 'deeply discounted securities', and all deeply discounted securities are also QCBs (*TCGA 1992, s 117(2AA)*); and

(f)   it was issued after 13 March 1984.

8.91   Section 117(1) provides:

'(1)   For the purposes of this section, a "corporate bond" is a security, as defined in section 132(3)(b)–

(a)   the debt on which represents and has at all times represented a normal commercial loan, and

(b)   which is expressed in sterling and in respect of which no provision is made for conversion into, or redemption in, a currency other than sterling,

and in paragraph (a) above "normal commercial loan" has the meaning which would be given by section 162 of CTA 2010 if in paragraphs (a) to (c) of subsection (2) of that section there were substituted the words "corporate bonds (within the meaning of section 117 of TCGA 1992)".

For the purposes of subsection (1)(b) above–

(a)   a security shall not be regarded as expressed in sterling if the amount of sterling falls to be determined by reference to the value at any time of any other currency or asset; and

(b)   a provision for redemption in a currency other than sterling but at the rate of exchange prevailing at redemption shall be disregarded.

(7) … a corporate bond–

(a) is a "qualifying" corporate bond if it is issued after 13 March 1984'

8.92   There is nothing in the definition of 'normal commercial loan' that requires payment of interest. It will not be a normal commercial loan if it pays interest above a commercial rate. The tests of what constitutes a 'normal commercial loan' are stated in *CTA 2010, ss 162–164* as follows:

(a) non-convertible, subject to three exceptions for convertibility into:

(i)   fixed rate preference shares which, if convertible, convert only into shares or securities in the subsidiary's listed parent;

(ii)   shares or securities in the subsidiary's listed 75% parent;

(iii) securities offering a reasonable commercial return not dependent on the results of the company's business which if convertible, convert only into shares or securities in the company's listed parent;

(b) does not give an entitlement to interest which varies with the debtor company's results or the value of its assets or which exceeds a reasonable commercial return;

(c) does not carry an entitlement on repayment to an amount exceeding the consideration lent or which is not reasonably comparable with the amount repayable on listed securities;

(d) does not carry any right to the acquisition of additional shares or securities; and

(e) on redemption, does not repay either more than the amount lent or more than is reasonable in comparison with the issue terms of securities listed in the Official List of the Stock Exchange.

8.93   Where a QCB loan note is issued to individuals in exchange for shares, the hypothetical capital gain arising on the sale of the shares is calculated at the time of the exchange, and brought into charge when the loan notes are disposed of: *TCGA 1992, s 116(10)*. Prior to 16 March 1993, it was possible to exchange shares for loan notes which were exempt simple debts, ie not 'securities' within *TCGA 1992, s 132(3)(b)* and so not QCBs within *s 116*. This meant that the loan notes could be disposed of free of tax (not being debts on a security), and the capital gain on the shares was never brought into charge. *TCGA 1992, s 251(6)* deems any debenture issued on or after 16 March 1993, whose issue falls within *TCGA 1992, ss 126(1), 135, 136*, to be a security within *s 132*. Hence, it will also be a QCB (*s 117(6A)*). Consequently, a gain deferred on exchange for shares will be chargeable under *s 116(10)* on disposal of the QCB.

8.94   A loan note will always be a QCB if it is a deeply discounted security within the definition in *ITTOIA 2005, s 430*, even if it is redeemable in a foreign currency or is not a normal commercial loan: *TCGA 1992, s 117(2AA)*.

Non-QCBs

8.95   A debt security which does not meet the statutory definition of a QCB is, in the hands of an individual, a non-QCB and is a chargeable asset. A non-QCB is a loan note which, when held by an individual, is not a QCB for tax purposes but treated as a share.

8.96   It follows from the definition of QCB, in the case of non-corporates, that there are a number of ways in which securities which would otherwise be QCBs can be given non-QCB status:

(a)   denominate the bond in a foreign currency rather than sterling;

(b)   denominate the loan note in sterling, but draft it in terms which ensure that it is not a sterling bond, by including a provision for redemption in a currency other than sterling at a rate other than the spot rate on the date of redemption (so that *s 117(1)(b)* is not satisfied);

(c)   denominate the loan note in sterling, but draft it in terms which ensure that it does not constitute a normal commercial loan by attaching to the loan note the right to subscribe for further loan notes (so that *s 117(1)(a)* is not satisfied); or

(d)   construct the loan note so that it is not a commercial loan, by making part of the interest referable to the subsequent profits of the target company (so that *s 117(1)(a)* is not satisfied).

8.97   These methods are not exclusive and may be used in combination. There are also more exotic possibilities, such as providing that the bond will be redeemable in euros if the UK (or what is left of the UK following Brexit) joins the third stage of EMU. In practice, a variant of (b) is by far the most common method.

8.98   Where an individual wishes to ensure that a loan note is a non-QCB, it is normal practice to insert a foreign exchange redemption clause (usually in US dollars), exercisable at the option of the holder some 30 days prior to redemption. This is to make the bond into a non-sterling bond, so that *TCGA 1992, s 117(1)(b)* is not satisfied. The bond may be expressed in sterling, but a provision may be included to allow the bond to be redesignated into or made redeemable in a foreign currency – normally US dollars – provided that the ratio of exchange between sterling and dollars is not that prevailing at the date of redemption. The details of the non-sterling loan note are normally as follows:

1   The holder has the right to elect (say) 30 days before redemption that the loan note should be redesignated in a foreign currency ('the foreign currency equivalent') at the exchange rate prevailing at the date of the election.

2   To (a) remove the foreign exchange exposure and (b) ensure that the bond cannot be regarded as a deeply discounted security (and so automatically rank as a QCB (*TCGA 1992, s 117(2AA)*)), there is a further provision limiting the foreign currency equivalent to not less than 99.5% and not more than 100.5% of the amount of foreign currency which would be payable if sterling were converted into the foreign currency at the spot rate prevailing on the date of redemption.

8.99   While periods of less than 30 days occur (eg seven days), there is a possibility that a shorter period would be regarded as bringing the bond within *s 117(2)(b)*, which says that 'a provision for redemption in a currency other than sterling but at the rate of exchange prevailing at redemption shall be disregarded'. The use of an upwards cap and downwards floor in turn may lead HMRC to argue that the possibility of redeeming in a foreign currency is not a real option, because there is no significant foreign exchange exposure, but this is unlikely.

8.100   If a subsidiary issues a loan other than in the form of a normal commercial loan (because it carries the right to acquire additional shares or securities), the effect will be to reduce the share of profits and assets which the parent is entitled to receive for the purposes of the tests in *CTA 2010, ss 165, 166* and so lead to possible de-grouping.

Conversion/exchange of non-QCBs for QCBs

8.101   *TCGA 1992, s 115* provides that a gain that accrues on the disposal of a QCB is not a chargeable gain. *Section 116* then provides that where a reorganisation (including a conversion within *TCGA 1992, s 132*) involves a QCB, a 'modified reorganisation' treatment applies:

(a)   the ordinary reorganisation treatment is disapplied: *s 116(5)*;

(b)   where chargeable assets (non-QCB) are exchanged for or converted into exempt assets (QCBs) a special tax regime applies under *s 116(10)*;

(c)   the QCBs are acquired at their market value. The built-in gain is calculated at that point and frozen until the QCB is redeemed: *s 116(10)*.

Example 8.5

An individual holds a sterling-denominated security, which contains an option for redemption in a foreign currency. It is a non-QCB. The option for conversion lapses. The instrument becomes a QCB at that time. To deal with such a situation, *TCGA 1992, s 132(3)(a), (ia), (ib)* provides that the term 'conversion of securities' includes the conversion of a non-QCB into a QCB, or of a QCB into a non-QCB. The purpose of this provision is to apply the 'reorganisation' rules in *TCGA 1992, ss 126–128* to such events. The consequence is that:

(a) in the case where a non-QCB becomes a QCB, any gain rolled over into the non-QCB is computed at that point and becomes chargeable under *s 116(10)(c)* when the QCB is redeemed or otherwise disposed of;

(b) if a QCB is converted into a non-QCB, any gain held over on acquisition of the QCB will become chargeable under *s 116(9)*.

8.102 In *Weston v Garnett (Inspector of Taxes)* [2005] STC 1134 the question arose whether a loan note which was indirectly convertible into shares was a 'normal commercial loan' within *ICTA 1988, Sch 18, para 1(5),* and so a QCB, and accordingly exempt from capital gains tax for individuals:

1 Individuals owned the shares in W Ltd.

2 The individuals created a settlement of which they were the beneficiaries, and so liable to tax on capital gains realised by the trustees under *TCGA 1992, s 77(1)*.

3 The trustees established C Ltd, and subscribed for loan notes (first loan notes) issued by C Ltd which were convertible into deeply discounted securities (second loan notes); the second loan notes were in turn convertible into shares in C Ltd. The loan notes carried the bulk of value in C Ltd (and so W Ltd) because, on conversion, they would swamp the existing shares in C Ltd.

4 The individuals then gifted their W Ltd shares to C Ltd, holding over the capital gain under *TCGA 1992, s 165*.

5 A third party purchased the C Ltd shares and loan notes from the trustees.

6 It was argued that the first loan notes were QCBs because, although convertible into securities which could be converted into shares (and so not a 'normal commercial loan'), the second loan notes were also QCBs because a deeply discounted security was a QCB.

8.103 The court held that the right to convert the first loan notes into the second loan notes carried with it the right to convert the underlying loan into shares, and that this prevented the first loan notes from being a normal commercial loan. The trustees disposed of non-QCBs and were taxable on the capital gain realised.

8.104   Chadwick LJ said at [31] (at 1144):

'The right to convert the loan into shares ... was an essential term of the bargain between lender and borrower ... The whole object of the loan was to ensure that the value of the existing Carraldo shares was diluted ... That object could only be achieved conferring on the holders of the first loan notes a present right ... to require the conversion of the loan into shares.'

8.105   Buxton LJ noted at [44] (at 1146) that it was the nature of the debt which determined the nature of the bond:

'The argument ... was confused by being focused on whether it was right to say that the original bonds carried a right to conversion into shares ... But the statutory test for whether that end has been achieved does not turn on the nature of the bond but on the nature of the debt or loan relationship that the bond represents.'

8.106   When *TCGA 1992, s 117(1)(b)* talks about a 'security', it is referring to a formal document. The status of a bond as a non-QCB is fixed on issue by its terms, even where its terms permit its subsequent 'transmogrification' (per Briggs J) into an instrument which is a QCB: *Harding v R & C Comrs* [2008] STC 3499. In that case:

1   Mr H owned B shares in a highly successful company, FDL, together with two other individual shareholders.

2   By the subscription agreement of 5 April 1990, a German company, C2000 AG, agreed to provide capital to FDL for new A and C ordinary shares.

3   The subscription agreement also contained call options whereby C2000 AG could buy, and put options whereby the holders could sell, all the B ordinary shares in FDL for non-QCB loan notes.

4   On 13 January 1995:

- the options to sell the B shares to C2000 AG were exercised; and

- C2000 AG sterling-denominated loan notes were issued in payment, which were redeemable on 1 July 1995.

5   The loan notes were redeemable in foreign currency, if notice to this effect was given by 23 January 1995. Two B shareholders gave notice by

23 January that they wanted redemption in a foreign currency. Mr H gave no such notice, so his loan note became redeemable in sterling only.

6   Prior to 25 November 1996, the frozen gain treatment under *TCGA 1992, s 116* depended upon the occurrence of a transaction. With effect from 25 November 1996, *FA 1997, s 88(4)* amended *s 116(2)* by adding the words:

'references to a transaction include references to any conversion of securities (whether or not effected by a transaction) within the meaning of section 132'

7   It was argued that–

(a)   the loan notes changed from non-QCBs to QCBs on 24 January 1995;

(b)   this did not occur in a transaction but under the terms of the instrument; and

(c)   accordingly, on redemption, Mr H's loan notes were QCBs, with the result that the capital gain rolled into the loan notes on 13 January 1995 dropped out of assessment.

8.107   The Court of Appeal held that, having regard to *TCGA 1992, s 117(1)(c)*, if the loan note contained a provision on issue for redemption in a currency other than sterling, it was a non-QCB and the subsequent lapsing of that provision did not alter its legal status.

8.108   In *Klincke v R & C Comrs* [2010] STC 2032, shares were exchanged for non-QCB loan notes, so that the gain on the shares was rolled over into the non-QCBs. The terms of non-QCB loan notes were amended by means of an extraordinary general meeting of noteholders to remove a currency conversion clause. The loan notes were then redeemed.

8.109   The Upper Tribunal held that:

1   The amendment of a non-QCB (as opposed to the lapsing of a term) made the instrument into a QCB.

2   This was a 'conversion of securities' within *TCGA 1992, s 132* and so benefitted from the reorganisation treatment in *s 127*.

3   The modified reorganisation treatment under *s 116(10)* then applied to freeze the gain rolled into the non-QCB, which became chargeable on redemption.

8.110   In *Blumenthal v R & C Comrs* [2012] SFTD 1264, shares were exchanged for non-QCB loan notes. The terms of the loan notes were amended to depress their value for a short period (loan notes could be redeemed for

3% of par if held by non-relevant holder) and to convert them into QCBs (by removing the option to redeem in a foreign currency). During the period when the value was depressed, the loan notes were redeemed. It was argued that this created a loss, rather than bringing the frozen gain into charge. The FTT held that the reduction of value clause was ineffective (because of drafting errors) and the frozen gain became chargeable on conversion into a QCB.

8.111   In *Hancock v R & C Comrs* [2014] SFTD 1163, taxpayers sold their shares in B Ltd (the 'original shares') to L Ltd, in return for various loan notes (the 'new holding'):

(a)   non-QCB loan notes (B loan notes 2004);

(b)   additional loan notes which were amended to become QCB loan notes (revised B loan notes 2004);

(c)   the B loan notes 2004 and revised B loan notes 2004 were exchanged for discounted QCB loan notes ('mixed conversion');

(d)   the discounted notes were redeemed.

8.112   The purpose of *TCGA 1992, s 116* is to freeze a gain which arises when shares are exchanged for QCBs, so that the held over gain is taxed when the QCBs are redeemed.

8.113   The taxpayer argued that *s 116* did not apply, because *s 116(1)(b)* requires that either:

(i)   the original shares were or included a QCB and the new holding does not; or

(ii)   the original shares were not or did not include a QCB and the new holding was or included a QCB.

8.114   The relevant conversion was at (c). The original shares and new holding both included a QCB. Therefore *s 116* could not apply and there was no tax charge on the deferred gain under *s 116(10)*. Hence the gain deferred at (a) and (b) vanished at (d).

8.115   The Upper Tribunal held that the conversion at (c) should be regarded as two separate conversions, so that the frozen gain on both sets of loan notes became chargeable on redemption at (d).

Deeply discounted securities

8.116   A deeply discounted security is a security which, at the time of its issue, carries the right to a deep discount for the investor. Strips are also regarded as a deeply discounted security, because the security produced by the decomposition of the stripped instrument necessarily carries a discount (*ITTOIA 2005, s 443(1)*). A deeply discounted security which pays no interest is a zero coupon bond (ZCB). The bifurcation of a convertible bond into a notional loan relationship and derivative contract necessarily produces a ZCB. For companies, deeply discounted securities are loan relationships. For individuals, special taxing provisions apply. Other than for strips, individuals and trustees are taxed on a realisations basis: *s 439*. Individuals may set losses against other income. Trustees may set losses against other income from deeply discounted securities. Gilts (but not gilt strips) are specifically excluded from the deeply discounted securities rules: *s 432(1)(b)*.

8.117 The use of discounted securities is intended to convert an income receipt in the hands of the lender (interest) into a capital receipt (discount). Tax rules, broadly speaking, seek to reclassify the discount as income. However, except in the case of financial traders, not every discount is so affected, only discounts which are 'deep'.

'Discount yield' means:

$$\frac{\text{Discount}}{\text{Par value}} \times \frac{365}{n}$$

where n = number of days to maturity.

8.118 In order to establish whether or not a discount is deep, it is necessary to compare the issue price with the amount payable on redemption. If there is one finite maturity date which is known at the outset, this is unproblematic. Where there are a number of possible occasions when the bond can be redeemed, the security will be deeply discounted if the amount payable on any occasion of redemption exceeds the prescribed rate.

8.119 *ITTOIA 2005, ss 427–442* deal with gains on 'deeply discounted securities'. Gains on such securities are 'charged to income tax' as savings and investment income. 'Deeply discounted security' is defined in *s 430* as follows:

'(1) … a security is a "deeply discounted security" … if, as at the time it is issued, the amount payable on maturity or any other possible occasion of redemption ("A") exceeds or may exceed the issue price by more than A × 0.5% × Y, where Y is the number of years in the redemption period or 30, whichever is the lower.'

8.120 *Securities*

8.120 A security is a deeply discounted security if the discount, expressed as a percentage of the amount payable on redemption, is greater than $(0.5\% \times n)$, where n = number of years to redemption, where the instrument has a duration of less than 30 years. If the instrument has a life of more than 30 years, the discount must not exceed 15%, if the instrument is to escape classification as deeply discounted. Interest is disregarded in determining whether the security is issued at a deep discount. If the term is six months, the relevant percentage is 0.25%. If the term is nine months, the relevant percentage is 0.375%. If the term is four years, the relevant percentage is 2%. In other words, there is a deep gain if:

$$\frac{(A - P)*100}{A} > \min\,(15,\, 0.5 \times n)$$

where:

- P = issue price
- A = amount payable on redemption
- n = term in years

8.121 Where a company issues a ZCB to a corporate investor, both borrower and investor will bring in the finance charge as a loan relationship debit (credit). The finance charge is the effective interest rate under IAS 39.

8.122 In the case of bonds which have a bullet repayment of principal and interest at the end of the term, the implied yield to maturity must be less than 0.5% per annum, using the formula:

$$i = \left(\frac{A}{P}\right)^{1/n} - 1$$

where:

- i = effective interest rate
- A = amount payable on maturity
- P = amount payable on issue
- n = term

The effective interest rate is the constant rate which takes the issue amount to the redemption amount at maturity.

Example 8.6

Loan note		2,000
Term		4 years
Amount payable on maturity		4,000
Discount	$\dfrac{2,000 \times 100}{4,000}$	= 50%
Relevant percentage	0.5% × 4	= 2%
Effective rate of interest		= 18.92%

Year	Opening amount	Finance cost	Carried forward
1	2,000	379	2,379
2	2,379	450	2,829
3	2,829	535	3,364
4	3,364	636	4,000
		4,000	

Thus, the finance cost of £2,000 is attributed to the four years in accordance with the amount outstanding at the year end.

Example 8.7

A bond is issued for 95 repayable at 100 after (a) two years, or (b) 12 years. The discount is 5%. In (a), the relevant percentage is 1%. As 5% >1%, the bond is deeply discounted. In case (b), the relevant percentage is ½ × 12 = 6%. As 5% <6%, the bond is not deeply discounted. It follows that everything except a minimal discount yield will be 'deep'.

8.123   Redemption at the option of any person other than the holder will be disregarded, if either the 'third party option conditions' or 'commercial protection conditions' are met, and the occasion to which these conditions apply does not coincide with redemption on some other ground: *ITTOIA 2005, s 431(1), (4)*. The 'third party option conditions' are that:

(i)   the issuer and the holder are not connected, and

(ii)   the main benefit or one of the main benefits to be derived from the redemption is 'the obtaining of a tax advantage by any person': *s 431(2)*.

'Tax advantage' has the same meaning as in *CTA 2010, s 1139: ITTOIA 2005, s 460(2)*.

8.124 The 'commercial protection conditions' are that the option to redeem is exercisable:

(i) only on the occurrence of an event adversely affecting the holder;

(ii) only on the occurrence of a default by any person: *ITTOIA 2005, s 431(3)*; or

(iii) if, at the time when the security was issued, it seemed unlikely that the option would be exercisable.

8.125 The test of connection is the narrower control test. Companies are connected if one controls the other, or if they are under common control. Two or more persons acting together to secure or exercise control of a company are connected with each other in relation to that company (*Floor v Davis (Inspector of Taxes)* 52 TC 609; *Steele (Inspector of Taxes) v European Vinyls Corpn (Holdings) BV* [1996] STC 785).

8.126 If not otherwise 'securities' within *TCGA 1992, s 132*, deeply discounted securities are deemed to be securities by *TCGA 1992, s 251(7), (8)*, which reads:

'(7) Where an instrument specified in subsection (8) below is not a security (as defined in section 132), that instrument shall be deemed to be such a security for the purposes of this section ...

(8) The instruments mentioned in subsection (7) above are –

(a) ...

(b) any instrument which ... is not a loan relationship of a company but which would be a deeply discounted security for the purposes of Chapter 8 of Part 4 of ITTOIA 2005 if section 432(2) of that Act (excluded indexed securities) were omitted.'

8.127 No income tax loss will arise to an individual where (*ITTOIA 2005, ss 440–444*):

(a) a deeply discounted security issued by a close company is transferred to a person (the transferee);

(b) the transferor (the relevant person) is the person to whom the security was first issued and is connected with the transferee; and

(c)   the relevant person paid for the security an amount exceeding its market value at the date of issue.

See *Campbell v IRC* [2004] STC (SCD) 396.

8.128   Where a deeply discounted security is issued to an individual to satisfy an earn-out right within *TCGA 1992, s 138A*, the individual will only be charged to income tax on the discount; he will not also be charged to capital gains tax: *ITTOIA 2005, s 442*.

8.129   *ITTOIA 2005, ss 435–436* apply where securities are issued in tranches under the same prospectus and, when looked at individually:

(a)   some of the securities are deeply discounted securities, and

(b)   others are not.

8.130   In such a case, if the aggregate nominal value of (b) is greater than the aggregate nominal value of (a), none of the securities are relevant discounted securities. If a security is only a deeply discounted security because it is issued to or held by a connected person, it will be a deeply discounted security for the purposes of applying *s 435(2)*.

8.131   Without specific provision, it would be possible to obtain a timing advantage by issuing deeply discounted securities to connected parties. Where a deeply discounted security is held, or has previously been held by a connected company, the issuer will only be able to obtain relief for the discount on a paid basis, ie on redemption, while the investor will remain liable to tax on an accruals basis. In most cases, this rule only applies if the beneficiary company is non-resident or, if UK resident, is not subject to corporation tax.

Excluded indexed securities

8.132   An excluded indexed security is a security where the amount payable to discharge the debt (on redemption or otherwise) is geared to the change in value of a chargeable asset. Such securities are outside the deeply discounted security regime ('excluded'), because their value is 'indexed' to the value of chargeable assets. Hence, gains are taxed under the capital gains tax rules if held by non-corporates.

8.133   'Excluded indexed security' is defined in *ITTOIA 2005, s 433(1)* as follows:

'(1)   … "excluded indexed security" means under the terms of which the amount payable on redemption is determined by applying to the amount for which the security was issued the percentage change (if any) over the security's redemption period in –

(a)   the value of chargeable assets of a particular description, or

(b)   an index of the value of such assets.'

Quoted Eurobonds

8.134   Bonds are frequently raised in London (but Brexit will remove this business from London) by companies, syndicates of banks, states and public bodies in dollars, yen, euros and other major currencies. They are called 'Eurobonds' but more correctly 'international bonds'.

8.135   International debt invariably requires interest to be paid without any withholding tax. Interest on quoted Eurobonds may be paid gross: *ITA 2007, s 882*. 'Quoted Eurobond' is defined in *s 987*. The definition encompasses three requirements. The security must:

(a)   be issued by a company;

(b)   be listed on a recognised stock exchange; and

(c)   carry a right to interest.

8.136   'Recognised stock exchange' is defined in *ITA 2007, s 1005*. An exchange must be designated as such by HMRC, who may designate exchanges set up outside the UK, as well as UK exchanges which have the status of a 'recognised investment exchange' within *FSMA 2000, s 285*. HMRC give their view of the scope of the exemption in Revenue Brief 21/08.

8.137   Admission to listing is distinct from admission to trading. The type of listing includes 'technical listing', ie where the debt is held by related parties and there is no intention for the security to be offered to the public or actively traded on the stock exchange. The Channel Islands Stock Exchange (CISX) has been particularly favoured for this purpose. Existing intercompany debt, which may often be undocumented and only reflected in intra-group balances, must be converted into the form of a listable security. This will normally be done by means of a bond listing agreement between the borrower and the lender.

8.138   The documentation for a listed Eurobond will normally include all or some of the following:

(a)   listing memorandum, setting out the terms of the issue;

(b)   subscription agreement, setting out the terms on which investors agree to subscribe for the issue;

(c)   deed of covenant, whereby the issuer undertakes to issue definitive bonds, should the permanent global bond become void or in other specified circumstances;

(d)   fiscal agency agreement, whereby a fiscal agent agrees to act as custodian of the permanent global bond and any definitive bonds, and to make payments due under them;

(e)   payment agent agreement, whereby the fiscal agent appoints paying agents in different jurisdictions;

(f)   security agreement, whereby the issuer undertakes to create a fixed and floating charge over its assets for the benefit of the bond-holders;

(g)   security trust agreement, whereby a trustee agrees to hold the security interests created under the security agreement on trust for the bond-holders;

(h)   inter-creditor agreement, whereby the security trustee agrees to the priorities for distribution of any sums received; and

(i)   trustee agreement, whereby a trustee agrees to exercise rights on behalf of bond-holders, eg to consent to an early redemption for tax reasons.

Eurocommercial paper

8.139   A Eurocommercial paper (ECP) programme is a means of borrowing money, whereby the issuer raises money by issuing at short notice short-term debt securities ('notes' with a term of up to one year) to dealers. 'Commercial paper' means notes issued pursuant to a facility under which the programme is 'uncommitted'. The issuer has no contractual obligation to issue, and the dealers have no contractual obligation to subscribe. Terms are agreed in the light of prevailing conditions. The notes may be interest-bearing, discounted and index-linked. ECP programmes are usually set up on a multi-currency, multi-dealer, basis, thereby allowing the issuer maximum flexibility. Typically, notes are issued within two days after the issuer and the dealers agree terms. Euronotes are unlisted and issued in large denominations for maturities of (as stated) up to one year. As with Eurobonds, 'Euro' means that the notes are issued outside the issuer's country (so that they are not domestic securities) and sold in countries beyond that of its currency denomination. Because the notes are not underwritten, they have to be placed by the dealer. A programme is characteristically set up to provide the issuer with a war chest to draw on as needed, to finance possible future acquisitions or investments.

8.140   The Euronote Association issues standard documentation for an ECP programme. The normal documents for such a programme are:

(a)   the notes;

(b)   dealer agreement;

(c)   issuing and paying agency agreement;

(d)   deed of covenant;

(e)   information memorandum;

(f)   in the case of a guaranteed programme, a deed of guarantee.

8.141   If the issuer is not an authorised institution or authorised European institution under the *Second Banking Co-ordination Directive (77/780/EEC)*, it would be an offence under *FSMA 2000, s 19* if the notes were issued in the UK, unless he can rely on an exemption under *SI 2001/544, reg 9*. The Regulations create an exemption for, inter alia, 'commercial paper', ie debt securities which must be redeemed before the first anniversary of the date of issue.

8.142   The covenants and protections which are normally found for longer-term debt securities are not included, as the short-term nature of the borrowing lowers the holder's credit risk. The notes invariably contain a tax grossing-up clause. The notes comprise a covenant to bearer to pay the principal amount of the note at maturity, and (where applicable) a covenant to pay the interest and the index-linked amount. There are also provisions dealing with particular currencies, eg sterling (where certain wording is required on the face of the note).

8.143   As with Eurobonds, Euronotes are initially issued as global notes delivered straight into the Euromarket clearing system, where the notes remain until maturity. The issuer will deliver a single word-processed global note, representing all the notes to be issued at a given time, to a representative of the common depositary of the clearing system, which will hold the note until maturity. Transfers of notes during their lifetime are made by book entry in the records of the clearing system. Payment at maturity is also made direct to the clearing systems which credit the accounts of their respective account-holders.

8.144   The programme notionally comprises definitive bearer notes in specified denominations. Normally, the holder has no right as such to require the issue of definitive notes in partial replacement of the global note. The issuer is only obliged to replace global notes with definitive notes if default is made by the issuer. Thus the holders, while in theory holding a proprietary security, in practice simply have a contractual claim against the clearing system.

8.145   The dealer agreement provides the legal framework for the issue, once the issuer and the dealers have agreed the terms of an issue. It has four elements:

1   It gives the timetable for any new issue.

2   It contains the usual representations, warranties and indemnities of the issuer, repeated whenever notes are issued under the programme.

3   It contains the conditions precedent which have to be satisfied before the first issue of notes under the programme.

4   It contains selling restrictions designed to ensure that dealers only sell notes in conformity with applicable securities legislation.

8.146   The issuer appoints an agent to whom it delivers pre-signed global notes. The notes are then available for issue and delivery against payment of the purchase price. The terms of the agent's appointment specify that, once it receives confirmation that a bargain has been struck between the issuer and the dealer, the agent completes the note with the requisite details, authenticates it and delivers it to the depositary for the clearing system. The agent is also responsible for receiving purchase moneys, and for paying interest and amounts due on maturity.

8.147   If the notes are permanently represented only by a single global note which is held within the clearing system, the only party with a contractual relationship with the issuer is the bearer of the global note, ie the depositary. The holders have no direct claim against the issuer. Likewise, even though there is an obligation to issue definitive notes on default by the issuer, only the depositary can enforce this. Accordingly, the issuer enters into a deed poll which provides that, should the issuer fail to issue a definitive note in replacement of a global note, the issuer is obliged to pay the amounts due in respect of the notes directly to the account-holders of the clearing system, in substitution for the issuer's obligations under the global note. As the deed of covenant effectively replaces the global note in prescribed circumstances, it normally contains the same gross-up provision in respect of payments made under it as the notes themselves.

8.148   The information memorandum is the market document by which the dealers sell notes to investors. This is regularly updated in the course of the programme. Under the dealer agreement, the issuer will be expected to represent and warrant the accuracy of the information memorandum and confirm that there has been no material change to the financial condition of the issuer or its subsidiaries since the most recently published financial statements.

Warrants

8.149   Bonds may be issued with a warrant to subscribe for further bonds at par at a specified interest rate and of a specified maturity. In such a package, three securities are involved:

(a)   the original bond;

(b)   the warrant; and

(c)   the new bond.

8.150   A global warrant is a warrant deposited with a depositary, to avoid public issue. Warrants for bonds are debt options within the derivative contracts rules, when held by companies. Bonds are often issued with share warrants, which will be quoted options within *TCGA 1992, s 144(8)(a)*. When the warrant is detached, it will be treated as a separate asset. The original bond will be a loan relationship, but separating the separate acquisition costs of the different elements in the package is difficult. Securities (equity or debt) may also be issued with equity warrants, enabling the holder to subscribe for new shares or debt in the issuer (or an associated company) at a fixed price. Warrants are akin to long-term, securitised, call options.

8.151   Warrant issues take one of two forms:

(a)   a money-raising exercise, where an option premium is charged; or

(b)   a bonus issue of warrants, where the holders do not have to pay anything for the option.

8.152   Investment trusts commonly make such issues, to overcome the discount of share value to assets. An ordinary option is written by someone who does not own any securities, so he has to obtain existing shares should the option be exercised. A warrant, by contrast, leads to a new issue of shares. Share issues are not within capital gains tax, because capital gains tax is limited to disposals of chargeable assets (*TCGA 1992, s 1*). While the release of an onerous liability may produce a gain, it does not lead to a capital gains tax charge. A company issuing its own shares is not making a disposal, nor is it a transaction on revenue account: it is a tax nothing.

8.153   The tax system has to deal with the possibility that the option may not be exercised. Hence, *TCGA 1992, s 144(1)* provides that the grant of an option is the disposal of an asset. This tax treatment is only provisional. If the option is exercised, the grant and the exercise are treated as a single transaction (*s 144(2)*). In that case, the grant of the option is treated as part of a larger transaction, and is a tax nothing. On the other hand, capital gains tax will arise if the option is granted but abandoned. If the option relates to debt securities, the option will be a derivative contract, and taxation will fall under *CTA 2009*.

Example 8.8

Z plc, whose shares stand at 50, issues for 10 a warrant exercisable in two years' time to buy new shares at 100. Z will be subject to corporation tax on capital gains of 10, the balance going to profit and loss account, and cash going to balance sheet. If, in two years' time, the shares trade at 80, the option will be abandoned and the provisional tax treatment will become definitive. If, in two years' time, the spot price of the shares is 110, the option will be exercised.

The issue of the warrant and issue of the shares is a single transaction, with 110 being credited to share capital and share premium account.

8.154   A debt with warrants issue gives rise to two traded instruments. This constitutes a debt and equity issue, with the proceeds having to be apportioned between liabilities and shareholders' funds ('split accounting'). The warrant proceeds constitute part payment for the share capital that will be issued should the warrant be exercised. As the proceeds relating to the debt will be less than the par value, the debt will necessarily be issued at a discount.

8.155   There are two methods of apportioning cost between warrants and the other securities with which they are issued in a package.

Method A – Cost apportionment on issue

8.156   A company issues bonds and warrants in units of 5 bonds plus 1 warrant, at a cost of £5 per unit:

First market value of one bond	=	97p
First market value of one warrant	=	25p
Thus, first market value of one unit	=	510p

Cost apportionment:

Bond	=	97p × ($^{500}/_{510}$)	=	95.1p
Warrant	=	25p × ($^{500}/_{510}$)	=	24.5p
Unit	=	(95.1p × 5) + 24.5p	=	500p

Method B – Cost apportionment on disposal

8.157   A company issues bonds and warrants in units of 5 bonds plus 1 warrant, at a cost of £5 per unit. An investor buys 1,000 units at a cost of £5,000. Some time later, he sells the warrants for £970 net. If on the date of sale the market prices were:

Bonds	=	180p		
Warrants	=	100p		
Value of 5,000 bonds	=	5,000 × 180p	=	£9,000
Value of 1,000 warrants	=	1,000 × 100p	=	£1,000
Value of 5,000 units	=	£10,000		

Cost apportionment:

Bonds	=	£5,000 × ($^{9,000}/_{10,000}$)	=	£4,500
Warrants	=	£5,000 × ($^{1,000}/_{10,000}$)	=	£500

Chargeable gain on sale of 1,000 warrants: £970 less £500 indexed to date of sale.

8.158   Under *FA 1996, Sch 9, para 3*, where an amortised cost basis is used, if the amount of credits or debits in respect of a loan relationship to be brought in depends upon the exercise of an option or other contingent right under the control of a party to that loan relationship, it will be assumed that the party in question will exercise the option 'in the manner which appears ... as at the end of the accounting period in question, to be the most advantageous to that party'.

Capital contributions

8.159   Capital contributions are sums placed at the disposal of a company by shareholders for which no shares are issued and which, accordingly, do not form part of share capital. A capital contribution is an 'advance', but not a debt and so not a loan relationship. As Lord Neuberger has said, a capital contribution is effectively a gift: *R & C Comrs v Alan Blackburn Sports Ltd* [2009] STC 188 at [30]. Capital contributions are commonly made where there is a deficit on profit and loss account, and the purpose of the payment is to enable the company to resume payment of dividends. Capital contributions normally go straight to reserves without passing through the profit and loss account. They are non-distributable. The essence of a capital contribution is that there is no finance cost and no obligation to repay. Accordingly, it does not contain an obligation to transfer economic benefits, and is accounted for as equity, not a liability. If the shares in the company which receives the benefit are disposed of, it may be possible to treat the capital contribution as 'enhancement expenditure' within *TCGA 1992, s 38(1)(b)*, so as to be deductible from the proceeds of sale in computing the capital gain or loss. In other words, a capital contribution may be regarded as a form of share premium.

8.160   In *Trustees of F D Fenston Will Trusts v R & C Comrs* [2007] STC (SCD) 316, trustees sought to use capital contributions to a Delaware company to establish a loss on the disposal of their shares in the company, on the basis that these payments were enhancement expenditure. The Special Commissioners held that the expenditure was not 'expenditure reflected in the state and nature of the asset at the time of the disposal', so as to be deductible within *s 38(1)(b)*.

8.161 It has been stated (in *Kellar v Williams* [2000] 2 BCLC 390 at 392) that a capital contribution is:

'a payment made to enhance the capital of a company ... The making of such "contribution" ... creates no obligation on the company to repay the money nor can the payer recover it from the company whether as a debt or in any other way.'

8.162 When paid to the company, the capital contribution will not be an income receipt if it is marked with a capital purpose (*Ryan (Inspector of Taxes) v Crabtree Denims Ltd* [1987] STC 402). If returned to the contributor, the payment will be regarded as a dividend.

8.163 If the capital contribution arises by way of a reclassification of debt as a capital contribution, the question arises whether this will constitute a release of debt in respect of which the company will have to bring in a corresponding loan relationship credit. However, as the item is not removed from the balance sheet, but transferred from liabilities to shareholders' funds, this should not be required. The legal documentation should be drawn so as to counter an argument that the transaction constitutes a release.

Example 8.9

The Union of Cotton Mill Operatives has established a trading company to provide services to its members. The Union holds the one £1 issued share and has lent the company £1,000. The company has a deficit as follows:

Balance sheet

Assets

Assets	500	
Liabilities	(1,000)	
Net assets		(500)

Shareholders' funds

Called up share capital	1	
Profit and loss account	(501)	
		(500)

The loan is reclassified as a capital contribution:

Balance sheet

Assets

Net assets	500

Shareholders' funds

Called up share capital	1
Profit and loss account	(501)
Capital contribution	1,000
	500

Once the profit and loss account is positive, the capital contribution can be treated as an accretion to distributable reserves.

Gilts

8.164   Gilts are stocks where repayment of capital and payment of interest are guaranteed by the UK government. Gilt-edged securities are defined in *TCGA 1992, s 288, Sch 9* and *CTA 2009, s 476* as UK government securities which are either:

(a)   listed in *TCGA 1992, Sch 9, Part II*; or

(b)   issued under *s 12* of the *National Loans Act 1968* and specified by Treasury order.

8.165   The National Loans Fund was established on 1 April 1968 as a separate vehicle for all central government borrowing operations and most domestic lending transactions previously met from the Consolidated Fund. It is an account of the Treasury at the Bank of England (*National Loans Act 1968, s 1*). Under *s 12*, the Treasury may, in order to raise money, issue such securities on such terms as it thinks fit.

8.166   There are three basic types:

- conventional;
- floating rate; and
- index-linked.

Conventional stock and floating rate are dated (fixed date of redemption) and undated (no fixed date of redemption). Convertibles give the holder the right to convert into a different stock.

8.167   Index-linked gilts were introduced in 1981. Both the capital repayment and interest payments rise in line with the Retail Price Index (RPI).

Index-linked pay a fixed coupon and pay their nominal value on maturity; but, in addition to the coupon and payment of nominal value:

(a) each payment of interest is varied by reference to the change in the RPI; and

(b) the amount payable on redemption is varied by reference to the change in RPI between the date of issue and the date of redemption. Assuming that the RPI rises over this period (ie inflation), the increase in the interest payable is the 'interest uplift', and the increase in the amount payable on redemption is the 'capital uplift'.

8.168 The capital uplift is found by taking the RPI eight months prior to the date of issue and eight months prior to the date of redemption:

R_0 = RPI 8 months prior to date of issue (base RPI)

R_n = RPI 8 months prior to date of maturity

P = nominal value

V = value at maturity

$$\text{Then } V = \frac{R_n \times P}{R_0}$$

Capital uplift = V – P

8.169 Interest uplifts are calculated on the same lines. In the usual case of twice-yearly interest:

R1 = RPI 8 months prior to payment date

I = coupon

then each interest payment is:

$$\frac{R_1 \times I}{R_0 \times 2}$$

This methodology is familiar from *TCGA 1992, s 54*.

8.170 Indexation of the capital repayment has the result that, for short-dated gilts, the bulk of the investment return derives from the capital element. The value of an index-linked gilt at maturity is its 'implied maturity value' (IMV). Whereas a conventional gilt has a fixed maturity value (par), the maturity value of an index-linked gilt depends upon the change of RPI between the two dates of measurement.

IMV = the maturity value taking into account accruals of discount and the known inflation uplift:

$$\frac{R_n}{R_0} \times 100$$

where

R_n = latest published RPI number

R_0 = base RPI eight months prior to the issue of the stock.

8.171   *CTA 2009, s 399* requires index-linked accounts to be brought into account for tax purposes using fair value accounting. Under *ss 399(3), 400*, in calculating profits on an index-linked gilt in any accounting period, an 'adjustment' is to be made. The adjustment is to be made where:

(a)   the accounting method gives credits or debits by reference to the carrying value of the gilts at two different times; and

(b)   there is a change in the RPI over this period.

8.172   The adjustment is the change in the book value of the gilt between the two dates of measurement attributable to the change in the RPI. If the gilt is held over the whole of an accounting period, the two dates of measurement will be the start and end of the accounting period. Otherwise, the two dates will be the date of acquisition and the end of the accounting period, or the start of the accounting period and disposal, or acquisition and disposal if both occur in the same accounting period.

8.173   The amount of the adjustment is deducted from loan relationship credits. In other words, changes in value due to the convergence towards par value on redemption are taxable, but capital uplifts caused by inflation are not taxable.

8.174   The indexation relief is to be calculated by reference to changes in the investor's carrying value. An upwards adjustment is added to the carrying value at the earlier time. A downwards adjustment is deducted from the carrying value at the earlier time.

8.175 The two main methods of calculating the opening value (book value) are:

(a) conventional net yield method; and

(b) straight line method.

8.176 Using the conventional method, no uplift in value is brought into the commercial accounts prior to redemption or disposal, but the adjustment may be deducted each year for tax purposes, producing a tax credit.

8.177 Using the straight line method, the book value will be increased each year as the bond converges towards its IMV. Deductions for the capital uplift will fall year by year, because the same fraction will be applied to a larger sum. Hence, annual profits will be more (because the deduction is smaller) but the profit on maturity will be less (because it will already have been largely accrued through additions to the book value).

8.178 Neither method is acceptable for tax purposes, because of the requirement for fair value accounting, although, in practice, the straight line method will approximate to a fair value method.

8.179 Provisions may be introduced allowing the Treasury to exclude adjustments, or that a different method of calculating the indexation adjustment is to be used: *CTA 2009, s 400(4).*

8.180 Gilts cannot give rise to chargeable gains: *TCGA 1992, s 115.* Where a company holds 5.5% Treasury Stock 2008–12, only interest is taxable: *CTA 2009, Sch 2, para 9.*

8.181 Inflation-linked adjustments to the value of index-linked gilts are brought into charge for tax purposes to the extent that the company (or an associated company) is a party to a 'relevant hedging scheme': *CTA 2009, ss 400A–400C.* This involves consideration of the 'economic profit or loss made by the relevant group or company': *ss 400A(8), 400B.* The aim is to prevent the company from obtaining a deduction for a loss on the hedging contract, while not being taxed on the index-linked gain. It is only upwards adjustments to the capital value of the index-linked gilt which are brought into charge.

8.182 'Associated company' is defined in *s 400C* by reference to: (a) companies included in consolidated accounts; (b) connection, using the 'control' test (*CTA 2009, s 466*); or (c) connection, using the 'major interest' test.

8.183 The Central Gilts Office (CGO) is a book entry transfer and settlement system run by the Bank of England. This service is available for professional dealers, eg Gilt Edged Market Makers (GEMMs), Inter Dealer Brokers (IDBs), custodians and investment institutions. The CGO keeps a computer record of all members' holdings, and is, therefore, able to arrange the simultaneous transfer of stock and money between accounts. As it is a book entry system, there are no certificates used and no transfer forms.

8.184   The essentials of the CGO are:

- gilts are dematerialised, ie held in uncertificated, electronic form;

- gilts are transferred within the system, by making transfers between accounts;

- trades are settled within the system;

- each CGO member has a settlement bank which gives an unlimited guarantee of the member's obligations; and

- gilts held within CGO are identified as being for principal only, for principal and clients, or for clients only.

Stripped securities

8.185   Stripping is the process of separating a standard coupon bond into its constituent interest and principal payments, so that they can be separately held or traded as ZCBs, eg a ten-year coupon bond can be separated into 21 ZCBs, one from the principal payment and 20 from the semi-annual coupons. The coupons would mature at six-monthly intervals. Because all returns are taxed as income, it is a matter of indifference to companies whether a gilt is held in its stripped or unstripped form. Thus, a gilt strip is a repackaged bond.

8.186   *CTA 2009, s 403* defines 'strip' as a security issued under the *National Loans Act 1968* which represents a right to a payment of interest or principal under the gilt-edged security.

8.187   'Strips' are also defined in *ITTOIA 2005, s 444* in similar terms. A 'strip' is a security:

(a)   issued for the purposes of representing a payment of interest or principal;

(b)   issued in conjunction with an underlying security;

(c)   where the underlying security is not itself a strip;

(d)   if issued after 26 March 2003, issued by the government of any territory; and

(e)   if issued on or before that date, issued under the *National Loans Act 1968* in a case where the underlying security was itself a gilt.

8.188   Strips enable the principal gilt and the coupons both to trade separately in their own right as 'zeros'. This is of assistance to pension funds wishing to fund deferred pensions. When the Bank of England strips a gilt, the particular holding of the gilt that is stripped will cease to exist, the strips being exchanged for it. No intermediary or special purpose vehicle (SPV) is involved. Accordingly, coupon strips (like principal strips) will be ZCBs, and will no longer have the character of coupon interest. Gilts are stripped and reconstituted via a facility provided by the CGO system. The process of stripping and reconstitution is done via GEMMs. Index-linked gilts cannot be stripped.

8.189   Gilt strips are loan relationships, and all strips are deeply discounted securities (but gilt-edged securities that are not strips are not deeply discounted securities): *ITTOIA 2005, s 443*. For individuals and trustees, there is a notional disposal and reinvestment each year on 5 April, with income tax being payable on any increase in value (*s 445*). In the case of companies, *CTA 2009, s 401* provides that the decomposing and reconstituting of a strippable gilt is regarded as a redemption, either of the gilt being decomposed or of the strips being reassembled.

FOTRA securities

8.190   Some gilts are issued with free of tax to residents abroad (FOTRA) conditions. No liability to corporation tax arises in respect of FOTRA securities beneficially owned by non-residents: *CTA 2009, ss 404, 1279, 1280*.

8.191   A surety is a person who assumes legal responsibility for the fulfilment of the whole or part of another person's debt by putting up security as a guarantee that the debt will be repaid should the debtor default. The obligation of a surety is thus necessarily a collateral obligation, taking for granted the principal liability of another, the principal debtor.

8.192   The provision of a surety will not be the issue of a security as such, for the purposes of loan relationships, because the surety's liability is only contingent.

Stamp duty and SDRT

8.193   Where a UK company issues debt, or there is a transfer of debt, such transactions are not subject to stamp duty or stamp duty reserve tax (SDRT), provided the securities constitute 'loan capital' within the meaning of *FA 1986, s 78*. The term 'loan capital' is defined under *ss 78(7)* and *79(12)* as:

> '(a)   any debenture stock, corporation or funded debt, by whatever name known, issued by a corporate or other body of persons …;

    (b)   any capital raised by such a body if the capital is borrowed or has the character of borrowed money, and whether it is in the form of stock or any other form;

    (c)   stock or marketable securities issued by the government of any country or territory outside the United Kingdom.'

8.194   However, under *s 79(5), (6)*, the exemption will not apply where:

(a)   the instrument transferring loan capital carries a right of conversion into shares or other securities; or

(b)   the instrument transferring loan capital carries:

    (i)   a right to interest exceeding a reasonable commercial rate of return on the nominal amount of capital;

    (ii)   a right to interest which is determined by reference to the results of a business, or the value of property; or

    (iii)   a right on repayment to an amount which exceeds the nominal amount of the capital and is not reasonably comparable with what is generally repayable on loan capital listed on the London Stock Exchange.

8.195   The definition thus excludes loan stock which, inter alia, carries a right of conversion. In such circumstances, it is necessary to structure the debt offering by using a tax-neutral intermediate SPV located in a jurisdiction which will not trigger any local transfer taxes. For instance, if a UK issuer wishes to offer a right of conversion, it could establish an SPV to act as the issuer in a jurisdiction such as Jersey. The UK company would offer the SPV a debt security, listed on a recognised stock exchange (for the purposes of the quoted Eurobond exemption), which would be subscribed for with the proceeds of the debt offering made by the SPV to investors. The benefit of such a structure is that the proceeds of the debt offering are transferred to the UK company, interest payments on the debt securities by the UK company are free of withholding taxes, and the issue of the convertible debt is free of stamp duty in Jersey. Additionally, the issue of the plain vanilla debt security in the UK to the SPV is free of stamp duty.

8.196   The issue of debt securities to a depositary could be subject to stamp duty or stamp duty reserve tax (SDRT) (*FA 1986, ss 70, 96*). Where debt securities are transferred to a depositary receipt or clearance service, no SDRT should be payable. This is because the 1.5% SDRT charge that applies in those circumstances only applies in respect of 'chargeable securities' as defined for the purposes of the principal charge to SDRT under *FA 1986, s 87*, which does not extend to exempt loan capital (*s 95(5)(a)*). However, as indicated, the issue of convertible debt will cause structuring difficulties which may need to be resolved by the creation of an SPV in a tax-neutral jurisdiction for the purposes of making the debt offering.

8.197 It is possible that, in some circumstances, the transfer of non-UK securities may attract a charge to stamp duty or SDRT. A stamp duty charge may arise in respect of non-UK property where an agreement or transfer is executed in the UK, or wherever executed, which relates to anything done or to be done in the UK (*Stamp Act 1891, s 14(4)*). The UK imposes an SDRT charge on the transfer of 'chargeable securities' for consideration in money or money's worth (*FA 1986, s 87*). The definition of 'chargeable securities' includes loan capital, interests in or other rights arising out of loan capital, and rights to allotments of or to subscribe for loan capital (*FA 1986, s 99(3)*). However, expressly excluded from the definition are securities which are issued by a body corporate not incorporated in the UK (*FA 1986, s 99(4)*). It is important for registers relating to such securities to be kept outside the UK, otherwise transfers will potentially be subject to SDRT. This is because the definition of 'chargeable securities' includes securities which, whilst issued by a body corporate not incorporated in the UK, are registered in a register kept in the UK by or on behalf of the body corporate by which they are issued or raised. The definition includes a register kept in the UK by the relevant body corporate, and also one maintained on its behalf (*FA 1986, s 99(4)(a)*).

Chapter 9

Interest

Overview

9.1   This chapter deals with:

- Interest
- Discounts
- Interest recharacterised as a distribution
- Withholding tax on interest
- Location of source of interest
- Double taxation agreements
- Grossing up clauses
- EU Savings Directive
- Quoted Eurobond exemption
- Banking privilege
- Interest payments to companies
- Public revenue dividends
- Funding bonds
- Accrued interest

Interest

9.2   The debt/equity distinction is fundamental. Both at domestic level and internationally, the choice of medium produces a different tax outcome. Because the finance cost of debt is fully deductible, the return on debt is not taxed at the level of the company paying the interest. The return on equity capital is, by contrast, taxed at the company level. Internationally, equity finance is taxed on a source basis. The source country takes the profits attributable to equity finance, and the country of residence of the investor either exempts the source or gives credit for source country tax. The return on international debt is normally paid free of withholding tax and taxed on a residence basis.

9.3   No deduction is to be made in respect of interest in computing a company's income, except in accordance with the loan relationship rules. Likewise, interest receipts are to be calculated exclusively by reference to these rules.

9.4   There is no statutory definition of interest in the Taxes Acts. It is a concept of common and contract law. It is commonly defined as a return for the use or retention by one person of a sum of money belonging to or owed to another. 'Interest … is payment by time for the use of money' (*Bennett v Ogston* 15 TC 374, per Rowlatt J at 379). 'Interest is compensation for delay in payment' (*Bond v Barrow Haematite Steel Company* [1902] 1 Ch 353 at 363). Interest is 'just recompense to the creditors for being deprived of the use of his money' (*Schulze v Bensted* 7 TC 30 at 33). The concept of interest is something payable in money, at a rate, by reference to a principal, with set rests and which is compulsorily payable (*Re Euro Hotel (Belgravia) Ltd* 51 TC 293 at 301–302). A rate of interest is the amount payable at the end of one unit interval of time for each unit of capital borrowed.

9.5   Under case law:

(a)   there must be a principal amount, by reference to which interest is calculated – this is why interest on swaps of notional principal is not interest in the strict sense; and

(b)   interest accrues by reference to time intervals ('rests') which may be continuous, hourly, daily, weekly, monthly, or at other intervals (see *Wigmore v Summerson* 9 TC 577; *Bennett v Ogston* 15 TC 374; *Westminster Bank v Riches* 28 TC 159).

9.6   In *Chevron Petroleum (UK) Ltd v BP Petroleum Developments Ltd* [1981] STC 689 two oil exploration companies held separate exploitation rights of two separate but adjacent oil fields. They shared the costs of developing the two adjacent oil fields, in proportion to the oil extracted from the respective fields. It was held that, where a variable sum contingently payable by one co-venturer to another on certain adjustment dates became payable, and included an amount calculated and described as 'interest', that amount was interest for tax purposes. The court said (at 694):

'In its nature a sum is "interest of money", … it retains that nature even if the parties to a contract provide for it to be wrapped up with some other sum and the whole paid in form of a single indivisible sum.'

9.7   Thus, the fact that a sum is only contingently payable, and is not separately identified in a payment, does not prevent it from having the nature of interest. In this case, the sum which was regarded as interest was calculated by applying an interest factor to a sum for a period of time.

9.8   Under para 36 of the SORP on Advances, a bank should credit doubtful interest to an interest suspense account rather than to profit and loss. Interest so dealt with is not a payment of interest.

9.9   If, under the banker's right of set-off, a debt owed by a customer (ie an asset) is used to pay off *pro tanto* a debt owed to a customer, there will be payment: *Re Harmony and Montague Tin and Copper Mining Co (Spargo's Case)* (1873) 8 Ch App 407 at 414.

9.10   When a bank, expecting to be paid, adds unpaid interest to the principal of a loan, eg when calling in a guarantee, the bank is treated as receiving a payment of interest when the debt is added to the loan as an additional advance. The debtor company does not pay interest, the interest being in effect capitalised (*IRC v Holder* 16 TC 540 at 560; *Paton (Fenton's Trustee) v IRC* 21 TC 626; *Minsham Properties Ltd v Price (Inspector of Taxes)* 63 TC 570).

9.11   The term 'set-off' may be used in a strict legal sense (using an asset to pay a liability *pro tanto*) or in the sense of effecting a calculation of an amount due (*Cooker v Foss (Inspector of Taxes)* [1998] STC (SCD) 189). A company held accounts in credit and overdrawn accounts. The bank agreed to set off debtor interest against creditor interest. The company argued that it did not receive interest, but that its obligation to pay interest was reduced. Even if the arrangements did provide for a figure equivalent to interest on the creditor balances to be taken into account in computing the interest payable to the bank, they did not provide for interest to be payable or to accrue to the company. It was held that the nature of the agreement was to reduce the company's interest payments, so it was not regarded as both receiving creditor interest and paying a larger amount of interest.

9.12   Under corporation tax self-assessment for companies, interest paid by HMRC on over-payments of tax is taxable, and interest payable to HMRC for under-payments of tax is deductible, under the loan relationship rules (*FA 1998, ss 33, 34; TMA 1970, s 90*).

9.13   The courts may analyse lump sum payments into an interest and a principal element. In *Lord Howard de Walden v Beck (Inspector of Taxes)* 23 TC 384, the taxpayer paid a capital sum for a series of promissory notes of fixed amounts repayable over 20 years. The return on the promissory notes was equivalent to a return of 4% on the sums paid for them. It was held that the return on the promissory notes was deferred interest. Here again, there were: (a) a fixed overall amount payable; (b) periodic payments to discharge it; and (c) a reliable basis upon which the implicit rate of interest could be calculated.

9.14 In *Scoble v Secretary of State for India* 4 TC 478, the predecessor of the Secretary of State leased land to a railway company for 99 years. After 50 years the Secretary of State had an option to purchase the shares of a railway company for a gross sum, and a further option to convert the capital sum into an annuity payable for the duration of the term. The amount of the annuity was calculated by charging interest at 2.85% on the capital sum. The question was: was this an annuity or a capital sum payable by instalments? The court held that each payment had to be disintegrated into a repayment of capital, and a payment of interest on the balance outstanding, divided into fixed amounts of capital and interest.

9.15 Book entries may, in limited circumstances, constitute a loan and payment of interest if, as a result, there is an effective transfer of benefits to the payee. Where book entries constitute payment of interest, payment is regarded as made at the date of the book entry, ie when it is debited in the books of the payer. Normally, the question of payments by book entries will only arise in dealings between connected companies.

Discounts

9.16 Where a note or bond which becomes payable at a future date is acquired at a discount, either on issue or on an intermediate transaction, a profit on its disposal may be a capital or an income profit, depending upon the function which the discount performs.

9.17 In *Leeming v Jones* 15 TC 333 at 357, Lord Buckmaster observed that 'discount is in reality only interest in another form'. Where a bond redeemable at 100 is bought for 90 and sold at 95, the difference between the price paid for the instrument and the amount received on sale represents:

(a) how much interest or discount has accrued as the bond converges with its maturity value;

(b) in the case of a fixed rate or zero-coupon bond how much the value of the promise to pay has altered as a result of changes in interest rates;

(c) whether the discount is compensation for capital risk.

9.18 In *National Provident Institution v Brown* 8 TC 57, all profits on discounting transactions were held to be taxable as income, and not the profit on the realisation of an investment.

9.19 In *Willingale (Inspector of Taxes) v International Commercial Bank Ltd* 52 TC 242, a consortium of banks discounted bills of exchange for periods of up to ten years, bringing in the discounts on an accruals basis over the term of the bill in their own accounts. Evidence was given that an acceptable alternative accounting treatment would be only to recognise the discounts on redemption. It was held that, for tax purposes, the profit on the bill at maturity, ie the discount, could be taxed at maturity, if this could accord with correct commercial accounting. The income did not exist until the bills were sold or they matured. What this case establishes is that, if there is a choice of correct accountancy methods, a company may use one for tax purposes, even if it uses a different method for its commercial accounts.

9.20   The leading case on discounts is *Lomax (Inspector of Taxes) v Peter Dixon & Son Ltd* 25 TC 353. The facts were as follows:

1   A UK company made shareholder loans of £317,000 to a Finnish company.

2   As security for the loans, the Finnish company issued 680 loan notes with a face value of £500 (total £340,000). The loan notes were redeemable over a period of 20 years.

3   The loan notes bore a commercial rate of interest.

4   The loan notes were redeemable at a premium of 20% of their face value.

9.21   The tax issue was how the premium on redemption was to be taxed. Lord Greene observed: 'There can be no general rule that any sum which a lender receives over and above the amount which he has lent ought to be treated as income.' The court concluded that the premium was intended to reflect credit risk, was a capital receipt and so (as capital gains tax did not exist at the time) was not taxable. The applicable tax principles were stated by Lord Greene at 367 in these terms:

'(1) Where a loan is made at or above such a reasonable commercial rate of interest as is applicable to a reasonably sound security, there is no presumption that a "discount" at which the loan is made or a premium at which it is payable is in the nature of interest.

(2) The true nature of the "discount" or premium, in so far as it is not conclusively determined by the contract, will fall to be determined as a matter of fact by Commissioners.

(3) In deciding the true nature of the "discount" or premium, in so far as it is not conclusively determined by the contract, the following matters together with any other relevant circumstances are important to be considered, viz. the terms of the loan, the rate of interest expressly stipulated for, the nature of the capital risk, the extent to which, if at all, the parties took or may reasonably be supposed to have taken the capital risk into account in fixing the terms of the contract.'

Where no interest is payable, a discount or premium will normally be an interest-equivalent.

9.22 The distinction between (a) a deep discount, and (b) an interest-bearing security with rolled-up interest, is essentially one of drafting. However, the two types of security are quite distinct: *Willingale v International Commercial Bank Ltd* [1978] AC 834 at 842; *Schulze v Benstead* 7 TC 30.

9.23 In *Pike v R & C Comrs* [2011] UKFTT 289 (TC), Mr P claimed relief for a loss of £3,463,563 on a disposal of a security for the tax year 1999/2000.

9.24 Mr P subscribed to loan stock in a company of which he was the 99% shareholder. The loan stock was drafted as (a) issued for £6m and (b) redeemable after 13 years for £6m plus interest accruing on a daily basis at £7.25% per annum. The Tribunal report gives the amount payable on redemption as £11,780,974, but it is not clear how this sum was calculated. Mr P transferred the loan stock to a trust, claiming a loss of £3,463,563 under *FA 1996, Sch 13, para 2*.

9.25 As a matter of drafting, this was an interest-bearing security with rolled-up interest. It was never a deeply discounted security.

9.26 In *Healey v R & C Comrs* [2015] STC 1749, an individual subscribed for an instrument at a discount. Some of the interest coupons were stripped out and held by KB. KB then bought back the instruments at a price which reflected the accrued interest. The price difference was held to be taxable as income as a discount under *ITTOIA 2005, s 381*. This provides:

'381(1) All discounts, other than discounts in deeply discounted securities, are treated as interest for the purposes of the Act.'

9.27 No part of the discount was held to be attributable to capital risk, because the borrower was a blue chip company.

Interest recharacterised as dividends

9.28 Many jurisdictions attack 'participating loans', ie loans which give an equity-like return. In such cases, interest is treated as a disguised distribution, and a deduction for that element of the interest is disallowed. There are a number of circumstances in which an item otherwise deductible as a loan relationship debit (interest or discount) can be recharacterised as a non-deductible distribution. Interest payable on loans which have equity characteristics is not deductible as interest, or may not be deductible in full. Interest is essentially calculated by reference to the principal in respect of which it is paid. If the amount of the payment is linked to something else, it is not interest. A payment by reference to the profits of a business is not interest but 'giving the lenders a share of the profits *eo nomine*' (*AW Walker & Co v IRC* 12 TC 297 at 302).

(a)　Non-commercial securities

9.29　The deeming of interest as dividends principally occurs in relation to securities which are classified as 'non-commercial securities' under *CTA 2010, ss 1000(1)E, 1005.*

9.30　'Securities' are defined by *s 1117(1)* as 'including securities not creating or evidencing a charge on assets'.

9.31　*Section 1005* defines 'non-commercial securities' as securities which pay a rate of return which is in excess of 'a reasonable commercial return':

'securities of a company are non-commercial securities if the consideration given by the company for the use of the principal secured by them represents more than a reasonable commercial return for the use of the principal.'

9.32　Where a security is a non-commercial security, then as regards both issuer and investor, that part of the return which exceeds a reasonable commercial return is treated as a distribution. This treatment applies to interest-bearing and discounted securities alike. The recharacterisation is achieved by *s 1000(1)E* which provides:

'In the Corporation Tax Acts "distribution", in relation to any company, means anything falling within any of the following paragraphs.

...

E. Any interest or other distribution out of the assets of the company in respect of securities of the company which are non-commercial securities ... except:

(a) however much (if any) of the distribution represents the principal secured by the securities, and

(b) however much (if any) of the distribution represents a reasonable commercial return for the use of the principal.'

9.33　'In respect of securities' is defined in *s 1114(1)*. *Section 1114(3)* says 'interest paid by a company on money advanced without the issue of a security for the advance' is treated as done in respect of securities.

9.34　Hence, the return of the 'principal secured' (ie the amount of capital which the investor is guaranteed to receive on redemption) does not constitute a distribution. 'Principal secured' includes an issue premium paid by the investor which constitutes 'new consideration' (*s 1007*). Hence, in determining whether the security carries a reasonable commercial rate of return for the use of the principal, the principal and the premium are aggregated.

9.35 The test of whether a return is excessive falls to be applied at the time the security is issued. What is a 'reasonable commercial return' is a question of fact, taking into account market rates on comparable securities, the credit rating of the issuer, the degree of risk, whether the loan note is secured, the quality of the covenants, the marketability of the security and similar factors. A legal point also arises. Does the phrase 'the principal thereby secured' refer to the amount raised by the issue, or the amount payable on redemption? In other words, where securities are issued at a discount, does the 'principal secured' include the discount (assuming that the securities are listed or issued on terms reasonably comparable with listed securities)? This point is not settled, but there is an argument that it means the amount payable on redemption: that is the amount *thereby secured*. If there is provision for early redemption, the result may be to give a return in excess of the effective rate of interest. A normal commercial penalty payable on early redemption will not trigger *s 1000(1)E*.

9.36 Subject to this uncertainty, where debt securities are issued at a deep discount as defined by *ITTOIA 2005, s 430(1)*, the securities will be a 'deeply discounted security' as defined by that section, and *CTA 2010, s 1000(1)E* is also capable of recharacterising part of the accrued discount as a distribution.

Example 9.1

Mr A lends £1,000 to X Ltd on terms that he will be repaid £1,500 after two years. The effective rate of interest is 22.47%. The commercial rate of interest would have been 15%. The discount is analysed as follows:

Year	B/f	Discount	Distribution	Total	C/f
1	1,000	150.00	74.70	224.70	1,150
2	1,150	172.50	102.80	275.30	
Total		322.50	177.50	500.00	

(b) Special securities

9.37 *CTA 2010, s 1000(1)F* applies to interest in excess of a reasonable commercial return in respect of 'special securities'. A special security is a security which meets any one of five conditions set out in *s 1015*:

- Condition A – securities issued otherwise than for new consideration.

- Condition B – securities convertible into shares, not being listed securities and not being issued on terms comparable with listed securities, or carrying a right to receive shares in or securities of a company.

- Condition C – securities the return on which is linked to the results of the business or part of the business.

- Condition D – securities linked with shares in the company as defined in *s 1017(2)*, ie where it is necessary or advantageous for a person who acquires, holds or disposes of the securities also to acquire, hold or dispose of a linked holding of shares.

- Condition E – the securities are equity notes issued by an associated or funded company.

9.38   What Condition B is referring to is the right to receive bonus shares or securities in the company. A further refinement is to provide that the right to acquire additional loan notes is in a company other than the purchaser, eg the right to acquire additional securities in the parent or a subsidiary of the acquiring company.

9.39   Where the amount to be repaid is linked to the value of particular assets, the guaranteed amount to be repaid on maturity could be very small, with the result that any interest paid would be 'excessive'. In such cases, the 'excessive interest' test applies to payments made by reference to the amount of the new consideration received by the company, rather than the 'principal secured'. Where the company receives new consideration of 100, but only undertakes to repay a guaranteed amount of 10, 'the principal so secured' will be regarded as 100. Where the interest payments are not excessive applying this test, the company and investors will be able to treat the security as a normal loan. Any excessive amount on this test will continue to be treated as a distribution: *CTA 2010, ss 1008–1011*.

9.40   This special test of what constitutes the 'principal secured' may in turn be disapplied by *s 1009* or *s 1012*. If this happens, the normal definition of 'principal secured', as the minimum amount of capital guaranteed to be repaid on redemption, is reinstated. The first situation where the *s 1008* definition is excluded is where the value of the security is linked to dividends paid by, or to fluctuations in the value of shares in, the issuing company or an associated company of the issuing company: *s 1009*. The second situation is where there are hedging arrangements in place relating to all or some of the issuing company's liabilities under the security: *ss 1012–1014*. These disapplying rules are themselves disapplied (so reinstating *s 1008*) if, in the first case, the security is issued by a bank or securities house and its value is linked to a qualifying share index: *ss 1009(2), (3), 1010*. This is important in relation to securities issued by banks and finance houses. The second situation is where the hedging arrangements meet four conditions: *s 1013*. The main requirement is that debits in respect of the securities should be matched by credits in respect of the hedging arrangements.

9.41 As regards the 'results of the business' test, *CTA 2010, s 1000(1)F* provides that, where consideration for the use of money owed by a company is 'to any extent dependent on the result of the company's business', the payment is a dividend and not interest. This does not apply to any part of a distribution to which *CTA 2010, s 1000(1)E* applies, ie to the extent that the consideration represents 'a reasonable commercial return for the use of that principal'.

9.42 Under *s 1017*, consideration on a loan shall not be treated as dependent on the results of the company business where the terms of the security provide for the rate of interest to be reduced if the company's results improve, or to be increased if the company's results deteriorate. It is not clear whether the arithmetic relationship has to be directly inverse.

9.43 With regard to Condition E ('equity notes'), interest payable on a bond which has an unspecified maturity, or a maturity in excess of 50 years, and is held by an associated company ('equity notes') constitutes a distribution. Distribution treatment is also prescribed where the securities in respect of which the interest is paid are 'connected with' shares, ie a debt security is held with a share and the two have to be disposed of together.

Example 9.2

A company borrows £1,000 from a group of investors to buy a property, on terms that the loan will only be repaid from the proceeds of sale, and the investors will receive 80% of any profit, according to their respective contributions. After two years, the property is sold for £3,000. It is held that a commercial rate of interest for a loan of this type would have been 25%. The investors will receive a profit of 80% × 2,000 = 1,600. Of this sum, £500 will be deductible as interest when paid by the company. The balance of £1,100 will be a non-deductible notional dividend. The debt claim of the investors will be a 'security' within *CTA 2010, s 1117(1)*.

9.44 *CTA 2010, s 1032(1)* limits the impact of the 'special securities' rules by providing that the recharacterisation of interest as dividends under *ss 1000(1)F, 1015* in respect of special securities will not apply where the amounts in question are paid to another company within the charge to UK corporation tax. It is important to note that the non-commercial securities rules are expressly excluded from the ambit of this provision.

Withholding tax on interest

9.45   Withholding tax is tax on a payment which is collected by the payer, eg when an employer deducts and accounts for income tax on wages and salaries under PAYE. Withholding tax arises when a person who is obliged to make a payment to another person is required:

(a)   to deduct an amount from the payment which represents tax paid by the payee;

(b)   is obliged to account to the tax authority for the amount deducted as tax paid by the payee;

(c)   is only obliged to pay the payee the net amount after deduction of the tax withholding; and

(d)   is liable for any failure to deduct the correct amount, rather than the payee who will be treated as having paid the tax which should have been deducted.

9.46   Withholding tax is a tax on the fund out of which the interest is paid, collected by the payer. Withholding tax 'typically forms the counterpart to the principle of worldwide taxation. It designates the imposition of local taxes on the local income of non-residents': *Athinaïki Zythopoiia AE v Greece* Case C-294/99 [2002] STC 559 at 564 (para 25 of Advocate General).

9.47   With effect from 6 April 2016 a £5,000 dividend nil rate band and £5,000 savings nil rate band are introduced for income tax purposes: *ITA 2007, ss 4, 12A, 13A*. To allow for the payment of interest free of tax the obligation for banks, building societies and other deposit takers to deduct income tax at source from interest is removed from 6 April 2016: *FA 2016, s 39, Sch 6*.

9.48   *ITA 2007, s 874(2)* requires the deduction of income tax at basic rate (20%) from annual interest. The main rule in *s 874(1), (2)* states:

'(1)   This section applies if a payment of yearly interest arising in the United Kingdom is made–

(a)   by a company,

(b)   by a local authority,

(c)   by or on behalf of a partnership of which a company is a member, or

(d)   by any person to another person whose usual place of abode is outside the United Kingdom.

(2)   The person by or through whom the payment is made must, on making the payment, deduct from it income tax on it at the basic rate in force for the tax year in which it is made.'

9.49 *Section 874* is a free-standing provision, outside the self-assessment system, and the tax payable under it is not allocated to any specific category.

9.50 No obligation to deduct tax arises in respect of interest paid under the *Late Payment of Commercial Debts (Interest) Act 1998*, because interest payable under the *Act* is not an 'annual payment' (*Tax Bulletin*, Issue 42, August 1999, 685–687).

However, there are numerous exceptions.

9.51 Under the loan relationship rules, both 'short' and 'yearly' interest are deductible as debits and taxable as credits. Yearly interest is interest calculated by reference to a period of a year or more, whereas short interest is calculated by reference to a shorter period (*Cairns v MacDiarmid (Inspector of Taxes)* 56 TC 556). The distinction is only relevant to the deduction of withholding tax under *ITA 2007, s 874*, which only applies to a payment of 'yearly interest'. It does not and cannot apply to discounts. Hence, when interest is payable to a lender resident in a jurisdiction (eg Jersey) with which the UK does not have a double taxation agreement providing for interest to be taxable only in the country of residence of the recipient, the borrower will invariably issue discounted loan notes rather than interest-bearing securities. Zero coupon discounted notes will not be subject to deduction of tax at source because the 'discount' does not represent an interest payment. Capital repayments on debt securities will not be subject to source taxation in the UK.

The obligation to withhold tax on interest applies where the interest is rolled up.

Location of source

9.52 For the withholding obligation to apply the interest must arise from a UK source.

ITTOIA 2005, ss 369–381 charge to income tax 'interest' which has a UK source. Interest always falls within *s 369(1)*, even if the interest is brought into charge under *ITTOIA 2005, s 5* as trade profits, so that expenses can be deducted from the interest which is not then 'pure profit' income. *Section 368(2)* says:

> '(2) Income arising to a non-UK resident is chargeable to tax under this Part only if it is from a source in the United Kingdom.'

9.53 The combined effect of this provision and *ITA 2007, s 874(1)* makes the distinction between 'UK source interest' and 'non-UK source interest' important, because this determines whether or not withholding tax has to be deducted. By 'source' is meant the legal obligation which gives rise to the obligation to pay and the entitlement to receive interest.

9.54   The leading case is *Westminster Bank Executor and Trustee Co (Channel Islands) Ltd v National Bank of Greece SA* 46 TC 472. The National Bank of Greece, which had a UK permanent establishment, paid interest as guarantor on bonds issued by a Greek bank in 1927 and 1930. Interest was payable in London and the governing law was English law. The bank deducted income tax at the standard rate (7s 9p in the pound) from interest payments. The Executor and Trustee Co (a non-resident company) sued for payment of the sums deducted. The House of Lords held that the interest had a non-UK source. Lord Hailsham said (at 495):

'Once the location of the source of the income is held to be situated outside the United Kingdom, it is therefore not taxable in the hands of the present Respondents [the Executor and Trustee Co] under Case III, or indeed under Schedule D or the Income Tax Acts at all … Once it is decided that the source of the income is an obligation outside the United Kingdom, the Appellants' claim to deduct income tax must fail against the present Respondents.'

9.55   The criteria for ascertaining the source of interest are as follows:

(a)   residence and place of business of the borrower;

(b)   *situs* of the debt;

(c)   where the interest will be paid;

(d)   the place where the debt can be enforced; and

(e)   the location of the resources out of which the interest is paid.

These factors are set out in the cases, and summarised in *Tax Bulletin*, Issue 9, November 1993.

9.56   Applying these factors in *National Bank of Greece*, the court held that the following indications pointed to a non-UK source, as outlined at 493–494:

'The obligation was undertaken by a principal debtor which was a foreign corporation. That obligation was guaranteed by another foreign corporation which … had at the time no place of business in the United Kingdom. It was secured by lands and public revenues in Greece … Whatever method of payment was selected … the discharge of the principal debtor's obligation would have involved … a remittance from Greece'

9.57   In *Ardmore Construction Ltd v R & C Comrs* [2016] STC 1044:

1   A UK company (A Ltd) and Gibraltar trusts were in the same beneficial ownership.

2   A Ltd subscribed 1,000 for shares in two non-resident companies owned by the Gibraltar trustees.

3   The non-resident companies lent 1,000 to the Gibraltar trusts, which in turn lent 1,000 to A Ltd.

4   A Ltd paid interest to the Gibraltar trustees from its UK bank account but failed to deduct withholding tax.

9.58   The Upper Tribunal held that a multi-factorial test had to be followed to determine the source of interest ([42]). The legal situs of a debt was held not to be a relevant factor for income tax purposes ([46]). However, the place where the debt could be enforced, and so the residence of the debtor, was a relevant factor ([52]). Applying the multi-factorial test the interest was held to arise in the UK.

Double taxation agreements

9.59   The withholding tax does not apply where a UK double taxation agreement (DTA) so provides or the interest is payable to a person in another EU Member State (though this is likely to change if and when the UK leaves the EU, unless the UK (or English, if that is then the case) government is able to find means of protecting UK/English economic interests).

9.60   Interest may be paid to a non-resident who is resident in a country having a double taxation agreement with the UK containing an interest article which either (a) limits the UK withholding rate, or (b) makes interest taxable only in the country of residence of the payee. In the case of cross-border payments, double taxation agreements commonly provide for the payment of interest free of tax or at a reduced rate of withholding.

9.61   Where a DTA does apply, it is necessary to comply with various administrative requirements. A UK borrower cannot apply the treaty rate to interest paid to an overseas lender without authority from HMRC to do so.

9.62   Provisional Treaty Relief (PTR) was introduced in 1999. Since 1 September 2010, a new passport system has been in operation: 'DT Treaty Passport Scheme – Operational Overview' (HMRC, May 2010). The lender submits DTTP1 to HMRC, in order to become an approved passport holder. Within 30 days of entering into a loan with a passport holder, the UK borrower notifies HMRC on form DTTP2. HMRC then grant authority from the date of the loan to apply the treaty rate of withholding tax, which will usually be nil.

9.63   DTAs in general:

(a)   provide that the exemption is not available if the loan is made through ('effectively connected with') a UK PE of the lender;

307

(b)   require that the lender must be beneficially entitled to the interest ('beneficial owner') if the exemption is to apply;

(c)   may not apply the exemption in cases of thin capitalisation.

Grossing-up clauses

9.64   In order to minimise the cost of funds, an issuer must ensure that the qualitative nature of the debt, and the structure adopted for the debt offering, does not cause tax consequences which make the holding of the debt disadvantageous for investors. It is market practice, in a debt offering, for an issuer to undertake to make 'additional payments' in specified circumstances. The issuer will normally undertake to make all payments in respect of principal and interest without any withholding or deduction of any taxes, duties, levies, imposts, assessments or other charges, unless required to do so by law. If any such deduction or withholding is required, the issuer undertakes to pay such additional amounts to ensure that the net amount paid to any investor after deduction will be equal to the amount stated in the debt securities.

9.65   It is accepted market practice for the issuer to carve out the circumstances in which additional amounts are paid. The circumstances in which additional payments will be made are specified in the indenture agreement. The issuer will not normally pay additional amounts arising in respect of:

(a)   tax imposed because of the existence of any connection (present or former) between the holder of the debt securities and the relevant taxing jurisdiction other than the holding of bonds or the collection of principal/ interest on the debt securities;

(b)   tax imposed because of where presentation is required, eg the presentation of the bond for payment in the UK;

(c)   tax imposed because of the failure of the holder/beneficial owner of the debt securities to comply with a request of the issuer, such as a request relating to a claim for relief under any double tax treaty to provide information concerning the residence in a taxing jurisdiction of the holder/beneficial owner, or to make any declaration for the purposes of satisfying an exchange of information requirement which is imposed by legislation of the taxing jurisdiction as a precondition to exemption from withholding tax;

(d)   any tax which would not have been withheld if presentation for payment had been made to a paying agent in another jurisdiction;

(e)   any tax relating to inheritance, gift, sale, transfer, wealth, state or similar tax charge; or

(f)   any withholding or deduction imposed on a payment to an individual pursuant to the *EU Savings Directive*.

9.66   An issuer will normally seek to protect itself from the obligation to make payments of additional amounts by including an option to redeem the debt securities ('optional tax redemption'). There is usually a tax redemption provision which enables the issuer to redeem where the obligation to pay additional amounts arises as a result of any change in law of the taxing jurisdiction, such as in respect of any statute, regulations or rulings, or change in official position regarding the application of such statute, regulations or rulings which becomes effective after the offering date of the debt securities. However, the option to redeem is usually subject to the issuer taking reasonable commercial steps to avoid the obligation to pay additional amounts.

9.67   As an agreement providing for non-deduction of interest is void (*TMA 1970, s 106(2)*), the loan documentation will provide for a grossing-up clause, should tax become deductible from interest. Three conditions will normally be attached:

(a)   if the lender ceases to be a bank, there is no requirement for grossing up;

(b)   the lender will be required to take the benefit of the interest article in an applicable double taxation treaty; and

(c)   if the borrower is required to gross up, he has the right to pay off the loan.

9.68   International debt agreements invariably contain grossing up clauses, which require the debtor to pay additional amounts, should withholding tax become deductible from the interest (or if the rate of withholding tax is increased), to ensure that the lender still receives the same amount post-tax. If the grossing-up clause is triggered, the debtor will in turn obtain the right to redeem early. In turn, the issuer's right to redeem may be restricted by a restructuring clause, to prevent opportunistic redemptions when interest rates move against the borrower.

9.69   The case of *Indofood International Finance Ltd v JP Morgan Chase Bank* [2006] STC 1195 involved an on-loan arrangement. An Indonesian company wanted to borrow on international capital markets. To do so, it had to raise money in a way which avoided the 15/20% Indonesian withholding tax. It set up a Mauritius finance company to issue bonds and on-lend the proceeds to the parent company. The rate of withholding was reduced to 10% under the Indonesia-Mauritius DTA. The finance company charged its loan asset in favour of the noteholders, and agreed to restrict its activities. The bonds were held by a trustee. The structure was thus:

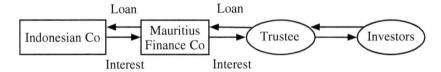

9.70   The Finance Co, as issuer, reserved the right to redeem the issue at par for 'tax reasons', ie in the event that there were changes to the Indonesian/ Mauritius double taxation agreement, which made it more expensive to service the loan from the Mauritius company. While the bonds were outstanding, on 24 June 2004 Indonesia gave notice to terminate its double taxation agreement with Mauritius, with the result that the rate of withholding tax paid by Indonesian Co to the Mauritius Finance Co would increase from 10% to 20%, increasing the grossed-up rate from 11.53% to 12.97%. Accordingly, the issuer sought to redeem, but the trustee refused to agree to the redemption notice.

9.71   The right to redeem was only exercisable if the gross-up obligation could not be avoided by the issuer's taking measures reasonably available to it. Accordingly, the issuer was required to restructure the loan (if possible) to circumvent problems arising from treaty changes, in preference to redeeming the loan.

9.72   The High Court upheld the bondholders' claim that the loan could have been restructured by the assignment by the Mauritius company of its debt asset to a Netherlands company. The Court of Appeal reversed this on the grounds that, in the circumstances envisaged, the Dutch company would not be the beneficial owner of the interest payable on the on-loan, and so would not have been entitled to treaty benefits. In that case, it would not have been able to take advantage of the freedom from withholding tax on interest payable by the Indonesian company under the Netherlands-Indonesia double taxation agreement.

9.73   A finance company will, in general, need to be the beneficial owner of income which it receives, in order to obtain treaty relief, notwithstanding that it has charged its assets to the noteholders and uses the interest received to pay its own interest liability to the investors. The effect of giving this broad meaning to 'beneficial ownership' would be to deny treaty relief in a wide range of circumstances where 'treaty shopping' may be alleged. HMRC have listed a number of safe harbours, where they will not seek to invoke an 'international fiscal meaning' of beneficial ownership.

Banking privilege

9.74   The exemptions from the obligation to deduct income tax from yearly interest of money are set out in *ITA 2007, ss 875–888*. The most important exclusion (*ss 878, 879*) relates to the 'banking privilege', ie payments of interest to and by banks. 'Bank' is defined in *ITA 2007, s 991*. A bank is a person authorised under *FSMA 2000, s 42* to carry on a business of 'accepting deposits', as defined in *FSMA 2000 (Regulated Activities) Order 2001, SI 2001/544, reg 5*. A bank is also a 'European authorised institution' under the *Second Banking Coordination Directive* of 15 December 1989 (77/780/EEC). This introduced the 'banking passport' for EU credit institutions authorised in their home state. Interest payable to a bank is payable without deduction of tax if the bank is beneficially entitled to the interest and within the charge to corporation tax as respects the interest. Interest paid by a bank in the ordinary course of its business may be paid without withholding tax. If a bank assigns a loan to a non-bank, interest can no longer be paid gross.

9.75   Besides banks, other persons authorised under *Part 4* of *FSMA 2000* who pay interest in the ordinary course of their business may pay interest gross where the business consists wholly or mainly in dealing in financial instruments as principal. 'Financial instruments' includes money, shares and securities, derivatives and credit derivatives: *ITA 2007, s 876*.

9.76   A 'qualifying certificate of deposit' is a transferable certificate issued by a deposit-taker recognising an obligation to pay a stated sum of money under *ITA 2007, s 985*, under which:

(a)   the amount payable at maturity exclusive of interest is not less than £50,000 (or its equivalent in foreign currency at the time of issue);

(b)   the obligation to pay that amount arises after a period of not more than five years; and

(c)   interest may or may not be payable.

9.77   As provided for in the Bank of England Notice of 1 November 1996, the minimum denomination for certificates of deposit issued in the UK is £100,000 or its currency equivalent. Accordingly, a certificate can only fail these tests by having a maturity of more than five years (as provided for in para 6(ii) of the Notice).

9.78   If a certificate of deposit does have a maturity of more than five years, but is issued by a bank in the ordinary course of its business, there is no general requirement to deduct tax from interest.

Interest payments by companies

9.79   A company (defined as including a partnership in which one of the partners is a company) can pay annual interest without deducting UK tax to a wide range of bodies listed in *ITA 2007, ss 930, 936*. These bodies include local authorities, charities, health service bodies, pension schemes and managers of certain investment plans. The test is both subjective (the company must believe a state of affairs exists) and objective (the belief must be reasonable). The condition subject to which a UK resident company can make gross payments is that the payee is either:

(a)   UK resident;

(b)   a partnership, each member of which is a UK resident company; or

(c)   a non-resident company carrying on a trade in the UK through a branch or agency to which the payment is made. The Treasury has power to extend the list of exempt bodies.

9.80   Provided that one of these conditions is satisfied, the payments which can be made without a withholding obligation are:

- annuities or other annual payments;

- royalties or other sums paid in respect of the use of a patent;

- UK source interest;

- dividends and interest paid in respect of a security issued by a UK building society listed, or capable of being listed, on a recognised stock exchange; and

- the proceeds of sale of UK patent rights by a non-resident company to which the payments are due.

9.81   If a loan is assigned by a lender within the charge to corporation tax, to a non-UK resident company which does not carry on a trade in the UK through a permanent establishment and so is not within the charge to UK corporation tax, income tax will have to be deducted from the interest payments. If a loan is transferred by a UK branch of a non-resident company to a part of that company outside the UK, it would seem that 'the person' means 'the UK branch', so tax would also become deductible in these circumstances.

9.82   A corporate borrower who incorrectly pays interest gross will be liable for the non-deducted income tax plus a penalty of up to £3,000. Tax indemnities are essential in the loan documentation, because the payer could be liable to pay tax which he failed to withhold as well as a penalty.

Example 9.3

Property Investor UK Ltd (UK resident) and Property Investor Jersey Ltd (Jersey resident) lend £1,000 at 15% to Property Developer Ltd (UK resident). The borrower will have to split the interest payments, and pay half gross and the other half net of tax.

Public revenue dividends

9.83   'Gilt-edged securities' are defined in *ITA 2007, s 1024* as securities so designated under *TCGA 1992*, ie securities issued by the UK government. 'Public revenue dividends' are defined as interest on gilt-edged securities: *ITA 2007, s 891*. 'Gross-paying government securities' are those securities designated as such by the Treasury: *ss 893–894*. There is a general exemption from the obligation to deduct withholding tax from interest on gilt-edged securities: *s 877*. However, the holder of the securities elects to receive interest net of tax ('self-withholding' – *s 895*).

Funding bonds

9.84   The issue of bonds (funding bonds) in lieu of interest is treated as a payment of interest up to the market value of the bonds: *ITA 2007, ss 939, 940*. This was the treatment adopted in *Scottish and Canadian General Investment Co Ltd v Easson (Surveyor of Taxes)* 8 TC 265, and overrules *Cross (Inspector of Taxes) v London and Provincial Trust Ltd* 21 TC 705. *CTA 2009, ss 413–414* provide that the issue of a funding bond is a payment of interest, but the redemption of a funding bond is not a payment of interest, provided that the issue was such a payment.

Accrued income scheme

9.85   Accrued interest is an adjustment to the quoted price which compensates a seller for a portion of the coupon that would have been received, had the stock been held until payment date. The amount of accrued interest received is in proportion to the period from the previous payment date to the settlement date (normally the next business day). If the stock is ex-dividend, accrued interest is calculated from the next payment date and is therefore usually negative. It will remain negative until the business day before the payment day (ie when the settlement day is the same as the payment date), when the accrued interest will be zero. It will then continue to accrue as normal.

9.86   Accrued interest is calculated by taking the actual number of days from the last dividend date (the next dividend date in the case of ex div stocks) to the settlement date, and assumes a 365-day year.

9.87 *Interest*

Days accrued = number of days between previous payment date and settlement date.

Accrued interest = coupon × days accrued ÷ 365.

Example 9.4

8% Treasury 2009 on 19 February 2013

Previous payment date	18 November 2012
Settlement date	20 February 2002
Days accrued	20 Feb – 18 Nov = 94 days
Coupon	8%
Accrued interest	$\dfrac{8 \times 94}{365} = 2.0602$ per 100

9.87   Accordingly, when securities are purchased with the right to future income, including income accrued but not paid up to the date of purchase, the amount paid by the investor includes an element attributable to the accrued and accruing income. Accrued interest forms part of the price of the security. The whole sum paid is a capital payment, as regards both the seller and the purchaser (*Wigmore (Inspector of Taxes) v Thomas Summerson & Sons Ltd* 9 TC 577 at 581; *Schaffer v Cattermole (Inspector of Taxes)* 53 TC 499 at 507). This gave rise to 'bond-washing', ie converting income into capital by selling a security cum div. This was described by Rowlatt J as follows (*IRC v Sir John Oakley* 9 TC 577 at 585):

> 'The result is that nobody on the Super-tax level … will ever buy a security that is full of dividend, because he is buying Super-tax; and if a man wants to sell a security, if he is on Super-tax, he had better sell it when it is full of dividend, because then he is selling Super-tax.'

9.88   This, in turn, led to legislation treating the sale of securities cum div or the sale of income rights as producing a charge to income tax (*FA 1927, ss 33, 35*). In the case of individuals, the accrued income scheme under *ITA 2007, ss 615–681* applies where securities are acquired with a right to accrued interest (cum div) or without a right to accrued interest (ex div). In the case of a cum div transfer, the transferor is taxable under the special provisions on the full amount of the accrued income profits: *s 617(1)*. The transferee is entitled to deduct, from the amount received on payment date, the accrued interest. In the case of an ex div transfer, the opposite treatment applies.

Quoted Eurobond exemption

9.89 Interest on quoted Eurobonds can be paid without deduction of withholding tax: *ITA 2009, ss 882, 987.*

The EU Savings Directive

9.90 The Savings Directive (2003/48/EC) applied to paying agents who, in the course of a business or profession, make or secure payments of savings income to payees in EU Member States and dependent and associated territories. It extended the definition of interest to include payments of many kinds. Its application was confined to amounts payable to individuals. It was repealed with effect from 1 January 2016, as it had been superseded by the Council Directive on exchange of information (2014/107/UE).

Private placements/Peer-to-peer lending

9.91 Qualifying private placements are exempt from withholding tax obligations: *ITA 2007, s 888A.* A qualifying private placement is an unlisted debt security, which is a loan relationship of the issuer, and meets the conditions set out in the *Qualifying Private Placement Regulations 2015, SI 2015/2002.* These specify a minimum aggregate value of £10m, and that the issuer should have a certificate from each non-resident lender that he is resident in a country which has a DTA with the UK containing a non-discrimination clause, and beneficially entitled to the interest for commercial reasons.

9.92 Peer-to-peer (P2P) lending consists of loans made on a P2P website by investors to individual or small businesses. On a non-statutory basis withholding tax is not required where loans are intermediated from one lender to a borrower by means of an intermediary registered with the Financial Conduct Authority (FCA). Where a P2P loan becomes irrecoverable, the loss may be set against interest receivable on other P2P loans: *ITA 2007, ss 412A–412J.*

Deductibility of corporate interest expense

9.93 As a general principle all corporate interest expenses are deductible in computing taxable profits. However, the UK has a large number of rules restricting the deductibility of financing costs:

- transfer pricing rules;
- the unallowable purpose rule and regime anti-avoidance rule for loan relationship and derivative contracts;
- the distribution rules;
- the tax arbitrage (anti-hybrid) rules;

9.94 *Interest*

- group mismatch rules;
- worldwide debt cap.

9.94   The UK also has regimes which work in the opposite direction and are regarded as constituting unfair tax completion:

- research and development allowances;
- patent box.

9.95   The OECD Base Erosion and Profit-Shifting (BEPS) plan advocates in Action 4 the introduction of general restrictions on corporate interest deductions. The aim is to ensure that financing costs are deductible in the jurisdiction in which the corresponding profits are earned. In two consultation papers HMRC has announced that it will seek to introduce these proposals by 1 April 2017.

9.96   The BEPS Final Report recommends the introduction of interest deduction restriction rules in three cross-border intra-group situations:

(a)   where debt and borrowing costs are placed in high tax jurisdictions;

(b)   where the shares for intra-group financing exceed third party borrowing costs;

(c)   where tax-deductible borrowing costs are used to fund tax exempt income.

9.97   In these situations BEPS Action 4 makes two recommendations:

(a)   a Fixed Ratio Rule (FRR) restricting relief for net financing costs to 30% of EBITDA;

(b)   an optional group ratio rule, whereby a company is allowed to deduct finance costs in addition to the FRR up to a company's share of the net third party financing costs of the group.

EBITDA refers to profits chargeable to corporation tax excluding tax interest, tax depreciation, tax amortisation, loss relief and group relief.

9.98   Given political uncertainty in the UK, the conflicting aim of enhancing the attractions of the UK to international business, besides the difficulty of integrating the new rules into the existing corporate tax system, the declared aim of introducing the new rules by 1 April 2017 appears over-ambitious, even if the new government adopts the same plan. A question therefore arises whether the UK, or indeed anyone, will implement Action 4.

Chapter 10

Foreign Exchange Gains and Losses

Overview

10.1   This chapter deals with:

- Bretton Woods system

- Pre-1993 case law

- Taxation of non-corporates

- New system for corporates introduced in 2005

- Functional and presentation currencies

Accruals basis

10.2   The collapse in the rate of exchange between sterling and the US dollar of 13–20% following the vote on Brexit, and comparable falls against other currencies, highlighted the vulnerability of UK business to currency fluctuations. Companies will generally seek to reduce this risks by hedging (see **Chapter 16**), but hedging covers a wider range of risks than exchange gains and losses. The risks are concentrated in the areas of:

(a)   borrowing and lending;

(b)   contracts for the provision of goods and services denominated in a foreign currency;

(c)   investments denominated in a foreign currency.

10.3   Currency gains and losses under (a) will be recognised on an annual basis; currency gain and losses under (b) will be recognised when the profit is recognised; gains and losses under (c) fall within the capital gains rules and are recognised on a realisations basis.

Example 10.1

On 1 June 2016, when £1 = US$1.50 [0.67/1], a UK company with a 31 December year end borrows $1,500 repayable after eight months (repayable 1 March 2017). The sterling equivalent of the loan is £1,000.

On 31 December 2016, when £1 = $1.10 [0.90/1] the company records the liability in its accounts at £1,350. The company has a foreign currency loss of £350.

10.4   Historically, exchange rates were largely fixed, and exchange gains and losses seldom troubled accounting or tax systems. Under the Bretton Woods system (1944), the par value of currencies was fixed by reference to a certain number of grammes of fine gold or a certain number of US dollars (gold parity standard). The dollar itself was theoretically convertible into gold. Periodically, currencies were revalued or devalued against the dollar. Under the system of fixed exchange rates, exchange differences were not a common problem in the accounts of UK companies. There had only been two major devaluations of sterling: that by Stafford Cripps in September 1949, which took the value of the pound down from $4.03 to $2.80, and the Wilson government devaluation of November 1967 which reduced the value from $2.80 to $2.40.

10.5   The accounting and tax system distinguished between gains and losses on revenue account (income or expenses) and gains and losses on capital account (tax nothings). *Firestone Tyre and Rubber Co Ltd v Evans (Inspector of Taxes)* 51 TC 615 related to a currency loss on a long-term debt in 1965. The question was considered on the basis of capital versus revenue distinctions in a current account between the UK subsidiary and its US parent. It concluded that a single account could be regarded as split between capital and revenue balances and that only the exchange losses on the revenue part were tax deductible.

10.6   The Bretton Woods system broke down on 15 August 1971 when the convertibility of dollars into gold was suspended. Thereafter, currencies floated freely against each other. The volatility thereby caused was mitigated by the concept of matching. For the UK the crux of the exchange rate problem throughout the twentieth century was the maintenance of an adequate supply of US dollars at a reasonable price. This is because the UK has through most of this period run a balance of payments deficit. Most imports are priced directly or indirectly in dollars. If foreign creditors hold more claims on sterling than UK creditors hold claims on dollars, the exchange rate £:$ falls. As long as the UK remains a member of the EU, the problem is eclipsed by the larger issue of the €:$ exchange rate. Hence the prospective economic catastrophe of Brexit. The apparently preferred solution of worldwide free trade would be inconsistent with the World Trade Organisation's rules on most favoured nation treatment.

10.7 In *Pattison (Inspector of Taxes) v Marine Midland Ltd* 57 TC 219 matching was recognised for tax purposes. A bank borrowed in dollars by way of subordinated loan stock to the value of $15m, did not convert the dollars into sterling, and lent them on in the course of its business. Because sterling depreciated against the dollar, the sterling equivalent of the bank's dollar liabilities increased, while the sterling equivalent of its dollar lending assets also increased by a corresponding amount. The Revenue argued that the losses on capital account should be disregarded, but the gains on revenue account were taxable. For accounts purposes, the monetary assets and liabilities denominated in dollars were valued in sterling at the year-end exchange rate, but to the extent that liabilities were matched by assets, no profit or loss was shown. Only the profit or loss on the unmatched dollars was taken to income. The Court of Appeal and the House of Lords held that, where there was matching, no profit or loss arose for tax purposes. The unmatched position was always on current account and thus was taxable or tax allowable depending on whether it was a profit or a loss. This 'matching' concept thus departed from the Inland Revenue view of the law, which would have looked separately at the capital account and the revenue account items, and would thus have disallowed the losses on capital account borrowing, but taxed the profits on current account assets. The Commissioners and the High Court considered the capital versus revenue definition and found in favour of the Inland Revenue. However, this point was not considered in the Court of Appeal or House of Lords.

10.8 In response to this decision, on 25 January 1985 the Inland Revenue issued a provisional Statement of Practice setting out the way in which it would aim to deal with the exchange gains and losses for tax purposes. The Statement of Practice made it clear that it did not apply to non-trading companies, nor could groups of companies be regarded as a single entity for matching purposes. It had no application to capital gains.

10.9 The circumstances in *Whittles (Inspector of Taxes) v Uniholdings Ltd (No 3)* [1995] STC 185 were considered to give rise to an extension of the *Marine Midland* matching principle, so that the two sides of the transaction should be taken together to establish the tax result. These two sides were a dollar loan (the proceeds of which had been converted into sterling) and a dollar forward contract to fund the loan repayment. After much dispute on the nature of the facts, the court held that the loan and forward contract were part of a single composite transaction, so that the effect of the two combined should be the basis for computing the tax liability of the company. The case was overturned (with no further right of appeal granted) in the Court of Appeal.

10.10 *Beauchamp (HM Inspector of Taxes) v F W Woolworth plc* 61 TC 542 concerned borrowing by a UK company in Swiss francs. In 1971, F W Woolworth, although a UK publicly quoted company, was 52.7% owned by the US Woolworth corporation. Under the Exchange Control Regulations in force at that time, such a UK company was required to raise a pro rata proportion of its loan finance outside the UK, such foreign currency borrowing had to be for a minimum period of five years, and contracts for the forward purchase of foreign currency could only be made with a maturity date of no more than six months.

10.11 Thus, when the company wished to extend its general credit facilities to finance the cash flows arising from the steady expansion of its trading activity, it had no option but to raise five-year loans from overseas. It did this by taking out two Swiss franc loans each of SF50m, each with a five-year term. They were at fixed interest rates, one of them at 6% and one at 7%. Each loan could be repaid early at the option of the borrower, although a premium was payable in the event of this option being exercised. One of the loans was, in fact, repaid early. The loan proceeds were converted into sterling immediately upon receipt and then used for the general business purposes of the company. The loans were repaid out of general funds. As a result of the repayment, the company suffered exchange losses totalling £11.4m.

10.12 The taxpayer company claimed that these exchange losses were allowable deductions for tax purposes, given that the loans were to deal with short-term cash flow problems and thus represented temporary facilities rather than part of the structure of the capital account borrowing of the company. The Special Commissioners agreed with this view and found in favour of Woolworth. The House of Lords gave judgment in favour of the Revenue. The basis of the decision was that the question as to whether a loan transaction entered into by the taxpayer was of a revenue or capital nature was a question of law, to be determined in the light of the facts found by the Commissioners. A loan was a revenue transaction only if it was temporary and fluctuating and incurred in meeting the ordinary running of the business. The nature of the loans involved in this case, being fixed in amount for a definite period of greater than one year, was sufficient to determine that in law they should be regarded as transactions of a capital nature. This meant that the exchange differences on them were regarded as 'nothings' for tax purposes – exchange losses failing to achieve tax relief, but any exchange gains on such items similarly being tax free.

10.13 The response of UK accounting was SSAP 20 (introduced in April 1983). The accounting system adapted to these fluctuations by requiring foreign currency differences to be measured at accounting reporting dates, with foreign currency gains accounted for as income, and losses accounted for as expenses. Hence, if a company held foreign currency debt as an asset, the changes in value relative to the reporting currency (sterling) between the date when the asset was acquired and the date when the asset was disposed of would be accrued over the period of ownership. SSAP 20 did away with the distinction between revenue and capital accounts, and recognised all foreign exchange gains and losses as income and expenses. It both required currency gains and losses to be recognised on an accruals basis and taken to revenue, but allowed deferral of recognition where risks were hedged.

10.14 For tax purposes, *FA 1993* finally replaced the outdated and confused system of taxing exchange gains and losses by following the accounting treatment in SSAP 20, but with significant modifications. SSAP 20 survived as part of old UK GAAP until the adoption of:

(a) IAS 21 for companies using IFRS;

(b) FRS 23 for companies using new UK GAAP; and

(c) FRS 102, Section 30 for accounting periods beginning on or after 1 January 2015 for all entities except those to which it does not apply.

10.15 For accounting purposes the main issues arise on the incorporation of the results of subsidiaries into consolidated accounts. For tax purposes the main issues arise in computing the sterling equivalent or the taxable profit or allowable losses of a given entity.

10.16 Where a company lends or borrows in a foreign currency, has a loss or profits measured in a foreign currency, enters into transactions priced in a foreign currency and carries forward or carries back a foreign currency loss, it is necessary to translate the resultant foreign currency gain or loss.

10.17 If a person gets more foreign currency per £ the sterling exchange rate rises. So if the ratio of exchange between £:$ moves from 1:1.50 to 1:2. the rate of exchange relative to the dollar has risen. If a person gets less foreign currency per pound, the sterling exchange rate falls. So if the ratio exchange £:€ moves from 1:1.30 to 1:1.10, the rate of exchange sterling relative to the euro has fallen.

10.18 The general rule is that exchange differences on the settlement or translation of monetary items are recognised as in the profit or loss account in the period in which they arise. On initial recognition, foreign currency transactions are translated into the functional currency using the exchange rate between the foreign currency and the functional currency on the date of the transaction. If the transaction is settled in the same accounting period as that in which it occurred, all the exchange differences are recognised in that period. When the transaction is settled in a subsequent accounting period, or a loss computed in a foreign currency is carried forward or back, then exchange differences recognised in each period between initial recognition and the date of settlement is determined by the exchange rates during each period.

The translation date will be:

(a) the transaction date;

(b) the balance sheet date; or

(c) the valuation date (if different from the balance sheet date).

10.19   There are a number of possible exchange rates:

- closing rate;

- spot rate for a transaction;

- average rate–

  - historical (transaction) rate,

  - forward contracted rate.

10.20   At each balance sheet date:

(a)   foreign currency monetary items are translated using the closing rate;

(b)   non-monetary items are measured at historic cost;

(c)   non-monetary items measured at fair value are revalued.

Realisations basis

10.21   Foreign currency is an asset for capital gains tax purposes: *TCGA 1992, s 21(1)(b)*. That is because its value can be measured in sterling. If, however, foreign currency is held as a means of exchange, its value cannot be measured, and it is not an asset for capital gains tax purposes. However, the distinction between money as a means of exchange and money as a commodity was doubted in *Camdex International Ltd v Bank of Zambia* [1997] CLC 714.

10.22   The decision in *Bentley v Pike* 53 TC 590 established that a gain or loss on an asset should be computed by comparing the sterling value at the date of sale of the consideration received with the sterling value at the date of acquisition of the acquisition cost. Accordingly, recognition of currency fluctuations was postponed until disposal. In that case:

1   In October 1967 the taxpayer became entitled to German property worth DM132,780, which had a sterling equivalent of £11,446 at the then prevailing exchange rate of 1:11.5.

2   In July 1973 the property was sold for DM152,241 which had a sterling equivalent of £23,175 at the then prevailing exchange rate of 1:6.6.

10.23   The question was whether the taxable gain was (a) DM(152,241 – 132,780) = DM19,461 calculated at the July 1973 exchange rate (£2,948), or (b) £(23,175 – 11,446) = £11,729, being the difference between the sterling equivalent of the disposal proceeds and the sterling equivalent of the acquisition cost, largely arising from the devaluation of sterling in November 1967. It was held that the latter was the correct approach.

10.24   This decision was subsequently upheld in *Capcount Trading v Evans (Inspector of Taxes)* [1993] STC 11. In that case, a company bought Canadian shares which it later sold, realising a substantial loss. If the sterling equivalent of the sale price were compared with the sterling equivalent of the purchase price using the spot rate at the date of sale, the capital loss was £16m. If the dollar price was translated into sterling using the spot rates prevailing at the time of purchase and the time of sale respectively, the capital loss was £3m. This was because, during the period of ownership, sterling had fallen sharply against the Canadian dollar, so that the dollars used to purchase the shares were worth much less in sterling terms than the dollars received on the disposal. The court held that, for capital gains tax purposes, the currency was not money but 'money's worth', which fell to be valued in sterling terms at the date of the transaction in question. Nolan LJ observed (at 25):

'the capital gains tax provisions are essentially concerned with gains or losses on the acquisition and disposal of a single asset. By way of contrast the income tax legislation dealing with the profits of traders is concerned with the results shown over a given period by what will commonly be a large number of operations and transactions of different types, some of them still in progress when the period comes to an end.'

10.25   In a subsequent case, *Poseidon Inc v Inspector of Taxes* [1996] STC (SCD) 273, the Special Commissioners did not apply the *Bentley v Pike* principle. It was held that, when consideration for a chargeable asset disposal was received in instalments, exchange losses arising (due to spot rates changing from the rate on the contracted date of disposal) were deductible as irrecoverable consideration under *TCGA 1992, s 40(2)*.

10.26   The decision in *Poseidon* was overturned by the decision in *Goodbrand v Loffland Bros North Sea Inc* [1997] STC 102. In that case, the taxpayer disposed of four drilling rigs for US$38.6m (= £33.3m). The whole gain (£6.7m) was taxable in one year, but the dollar proceeds were payable in monthly instalments over nine years. The issue was whether, in capital gains computations, a taxpayer could claim relief under *TCGA 1992, s 48* for an exchange loss that arises on deferred consideration (ie when consideration actually received in currency and translated into sterling at the spot rate on receipt is less than the sterling equivalent of the deferred consideration calculated at the time of disposal in accordance with *TCGA 1992, s 48*). The Inland Revenue won the case on appeal to the Chancery Division, with the result that the consideration must be calculated as the sterling equivalent of the currency amount at the date of disposal, and no claim is possible under *TCGA 1992, s 48* for any exchange loss. It was held that the capital gain was fixed on the disposal, and subsequent variations in the exchange rate were irrelevant. In consequence, the company paid more capital gains tax on the disposal than was justified by the overall sterling equivalent of the gain, converting the monthly instalments into sterling at the then prevailing spot rate (£23.8m).

10.27   *CTA 2010, s 9C* permits a company to compute its chargeable gains arising in respect of ships, aircraft and shares in its functional currency, or in the case of an investment company which has so elected its designated currency. The gain is then translated into sterling at the spot rate at the time of disposal. Hence foreign exchange gains and losses do not enter into the calculation of capital gains. *Section 9C(10)* applies to no gain/no loss transfers, eg intra-group transfer of assets. 'Functional currency' and 'designated currency' are explained at **10.30** below.

Tax treatment of exchange gains – non-corporates

10.28   The tax treatment of exchange gains and losses under the old rules continues to apply to sole traders and partnerships of individuals. The rules may be summarised as follows, insofar as they apply to traders:

	Type of transaction	*Tax treatment of exchange difference*
1	Ordinary trade debtors	Trading profit – accruals basis
2	Ordinary trade creditors	Trading profit – accruals basis
3	Foreign currency bank current accounts (assets)	Trading profit – accruals basis if held for trade purposes. Otherwise, capital gain
4	Foreign currency overdrafts	Trading profit – accruals basis
5	Interest payable or receivable	Follows the tax treatment of the interest itself – convert at spot rate on the payable/ receivable date
6	Currency swaps	If for trading transactions, then follows trading treatment of swap. Otherwise taxed as a part of the capital gain on the settlement of the swap
7	Borrowing of over one year and not entirely of an 'overdraft' nature	Nothings – no tax relief for losses – gains tax free
8	Loans which are 'debts on security', including debentures	Capital gain/loss on realisation
9	Simple loans – not 'debts on security'	Nothings
10	Foreign currency denominated share capital of the taxpayer	Nothings

Type of transaction	Tax treatment of exchange difference
11 Investment in foreign currency denominated shares	Capital gain/loss on realisation
12 Foreign currency denominated shares held by a share dealer	Trading income – probably on a realisation basis – treatment varies depending on accounting treatment and other factors
13 Currency options	If for trading transactions then follow trading treatment for option. Otherwise taxed as part of capital gain or under *TCGA 1992, s 143*
14 Matched transactions	*Marine Midland*

Accounting rules

10.29   IAS 21 must be adopted in the consolidated accounts of EU listed groups and may be adopted in the statutory accounts of the solus plc accounts or the statutory accounts of ordinary limited companies, including the subsidiaries of listed groups. FRS 102, Section 30 follows IAS 21.

Hedge accounting requirements are set out in FRS 102, Section 12: see **Chapter 16**.

10.30   The general rule, for accounting purposes, is that profits should be calculated by reference to a company's functional currency. IAS 21 allows a company to have twin currencies – its 'presentation currency' and its 'functional currency'. IAS 21 distinguishes between 'functional currency' ('currency of the primary economic environment in which the company operates') and 'presentation currency' (currency in which financial statements are presented). This distinction is key to the tax treatment of an entity.

10.31   The starting point for determining the functional currency under IAS 21 is that it should be the currency of the primary economic environment of the entity. While the criteria used to determine a company's 'presentation currency' (ie the currency in which the accounts may be drawn up) may not be significantly different, IAS 21 requires a company to determine its 'functional currency' (ie the currency in which it predominately operates). If the functional currency is different from the presentation currency, the accounts must disclose this, together with certain additional financial information.

10.32   The normal presentation currency (currency of account) will be sterling. However, companies may draw up accounts which also give the accounts figures in euros (*CA 2006, s 469*). In *Re Scandinavian Bank Corp* *plc* [1987] BCLC 220, it was held that a company may have a multi-currency share capital, provided that, in the case of a public company, it has allotted share capital of not less than the authorised minimum denomination in sterling.

10.33   Accordingly, IAS 21 allows the functional currency and presentation currency to differ. If the presentation currency differs from the entity's functional currency, it needs to translate its transactions, results and financial position into the presentation currency. For accounting purposes, the main issues arise on the incorporation of the results of subsidiaries into consolidated accounts. Under IAS 21, for a subsidiary company to have a functional currency different from that of its parent, it has to be classed as a 'foreign entity' rather than a 'foreign operation'. To be a foreign entity, the following characteristics are required:

- activities carried out with autonomy;

- sales predominantly in other than parent's reporting currency;

- activities financed from own operations or local borrowings;

- low volume of transactions with parent;

- costs settled in local currency.

This means that subsidiaries will generally need to use the functional currency of their parent.

10.34   All transactions entered into in currencies other than the functional currency are treated as transactions in a foreign currency. Such transactions are translated into the functional currency, normally at the spot rate. Foreign currency monetary assets and liabilities are translated at the closing rate. Non-monetary assets are reported at historic cost or fair value.

10.35   Exchange differences on monetary items are recognised in profit and loss for the period. In consolidated financial statements differences arising on a monetary item that forms part of the entity's net investment in a foreign operation are recognised initially in OCI and are reclassified from equity on disposal of the foreign operation.

Functional v presentation currency

10.36   As noted earlier, *FA 1993* introduced a separate accounts-based system for taxing foreign exchange gains and losses based on SSAP 20 with effect from 23 March 1995. This was replaced in 2002. The tax treatment of foreign exchange gains and losses is now largely dealt with in the same way as other credits and debits arising under the derivative contracts and loan relationship rules in *CTA 2009*. The general rule, for tax purposes, is that a company's taxable profits 'must be calculated and expressed in sterling': *CTA 2010, s 5(1)*.

10.37   For tax purposes, the main issues arise in computing the sterling equivalent of the taxable profit or allowable losses of a given entity. There are a series of rules:

1   If a UK resident company, other than an investment company, has a non-sterling presentation currency but a sterling functional currency, profits and losses (but not chargeable gains or allowable losses) must be recalculated as if the company prepared its accounts in sterling: *CTA 2010, s 6(1), (2)*.

2   If a UK resident investment company has a non-sterling presentation currency, but has sterling as a 'designated currency' or, failing such designation, as a functional currency, its profits and losses (but not chargeable gains or allowable losses) must be recalculated as if the company prepared its accounts in sterling: *s 6(1A), (2)*.

3   If a UK resident company, other than an investment company, has different presentation and functional currencies, and the functional currency is not sterling, profits and losses (but not chargeable gains or allowable losses) must be calculated in the functional currency and translated into sterling: *s 7(1), (2)*.

4   If a UK resident investment company has different presentation and designated or functional currencies, and the designated currency or, failing such designation, functional currency is not sterling, profits and losses (but not chargeable gains or allowable losses) must be calculated in the functional currency and translated into sterling: *s 7(1A), (2)*.

5   If a UK resident company has a non-sterling presentation currency, and the case does not fall within (1)–(4), its taxable profits are the sterling equivalent: *s 8*.

6   If a non-resident company carries on a trade in the UK through a permanent establishment (PE), and the presentation currency of the company is not sterling, the profits of the PE are the sterling equivalent amount: *s 9*.

10.38   As noted, functional currency (F) is the currency of the primary economic environment in which the entity operates: IAS 21, para 4. Presentation currency (P) is the currency in which the financial statements are presented.

The special provisions cover the tax treatment of companies with the following scenarios:

Presentation (ie accounts) currency	*Functional currency*	*Computation*	*CTA 2010*
Foreign currency	Sterling	Sterling	*s 6*
Foreign currency	Same foreign currency as presentation currency or The accounts are neither IFRS nor 'new' GAAP accounts, and so no functional currency concept	Foreign currency	*s 7*
Foreign currency or sterling (FX1)	Different non-sterling currency (FX2)	FX1	*s 8*

10.39   These rules take account of the fact that a company following IAS 21 or FRS 102, Section 30 is permitted to draw up accounts in a currency other than its functional currency, referred to as its 'presentation currency'.

10.40   The system is largely successful in ensuring that companies can prepare their corporation tax computations in their functional currency, thereby simplifying a group's ability to enter into tax-efficient hedging arrangements, and minimising the occasions when corporation tax is likely to arise on fictitious profits.

Company with a foreign functional currency that prepares accounts in the same currency

10.41   Where a company uses a foreign currency as both its functional and its presentation currency, such a company is required to compute, in sterling, profits or losses that fall to be computed for corporation tax purposes in accordance with GAAP by:

(a)   computing the profits or losses in the accounts (ie functional) currency; and

(b)   taking the sterling equivalent of those profits or losses.

10.42   The sterling equivalent is found by translating the foreign currency amount into sterling at the 'appropriate exchange rate' (*CTA 2010, s 11*), which is defined as either:

(a)   the average exchange rate for the current accounting period; or

(b)   the appropriate spot rate of exchange for the transaction in question.

Companies with a foreign functional currency that prepare accounts in a different foreign currency

10.43 *CTA 2010, s 7(1)* requires such a company to compute, in sterling, profits or losses that fall to be computed for corporation tax purposes in accordance with GAAP by:

(a) computing the profits or losses in the *functional* currency as if the company prepared accounts in that currency; and

(b) taking the sterling equivalent of those profits or losses.

10.44 The sterling equivalent is found by translating the foreign currency amount into sterling at the 'appropriate exchange rate', which is defined as either:

(a) the average exchange rate for the current accounting period; or

(b) the appropriate spot rate of exchange for the transaction in question.

10.45 Such a company would normally be following IAS 21 or FRS 102, so it would have first prepared accounts in the functional currency and then translated them into the foreign presentational currency, with exchange movements arising from that translation going directly to equity. Given that none of the exchange movements taken to equity as a result of the translation into the presentation currency would have arisen had the company prepared functional currency accounts, they are ignored for tax purposes. It is likely that a practical approach to the tax computations will be to prepare parallel functional currency accounts for tax purposes, based on the functional currency figures from which the foreign presentation currency accounts were derived.

Companies with a foreign functional currency that prepare accounts in sterling

10.46 *CTA 2010, s 7* requires such a company to compute, in sterling, profits or losses that fall to be computed for corporation tax purposes in accordance with GAAP by:

(a) computing the profits or losses in the *functional* currency as if the company prepared accounts in that currency; and

(b) taking the sterling equivalent of those profits or losses.

10.47   The sterling equivalent is found by translating the foreign currency amount into sterling at the 'appropriate exchange rate', which is defined as either:

(a)   the average exchange rate for the current accounting period; or

(b)   the appropriate spot rate of exchange for the transaction in question.

10.48   Such a company would normally be following IAS 21 or FRS 103, so it would have first prepared accounts in the functional currency and then translated them into the sterling presentational currency, with exchange movements arising from that translation going directly to equity. Given that none of the exchange movements taken to equity as a result of the translation into the presentation currency would have arisen had the company prepared functional currency accounts, they are ignored for tax purposes.

10.49   Because IAS 21 and FRS 102 require translation of the income and expense items at the transaction date exchange rate, but permit the use of an average rate for the period except where exchange rates fluctuate significantly, the rate(s) used to translate the functional currency results into the sterling presentation currency are acceptable for tax purposes. Therefore, in practice it should be possible to base the tax computation on the sterling accounts, but ignoring exchange movements taken to equity and recorded in the statement of changes in equity rather than in the profit and loss account.

Non-UK incorporated, UK resident company that prepares foreign currency accounts which are neither IFRS nor UK GAAP

10.50   A company incorporated outside the UK (and hence subject to GAAP appropriate to the country of incorporation) that is tax resident in the UK will need to prepare a UK corporation tax return in accordance with UK rules. For 'accounts-based' income (trading profits and losses, loan relationships, derivative contracts and intangible fixed assets), the starting point is accounts drawn up in accordance with generally accepted accounting practice.

10.51   As neither IFRS nor UK GAAP will have been used to prepare the foreign currency accounts, the question arises whether the accounts have been drawn up in accordance with 'generally accepted accounting practice' and thus represent 'correct accounts' for the purposes of the specific requirements of the loan relationships and the derivative contracts tax regimes, and for the rules applying to trading profits and intangibles. HMRC interpret the requirement for 'correct accounts' to mean that the accounts have been drawn up disclosing profits and losses computed in accordance with GAAP 'as would have applied to a UK incorporated company' in the same circumstances as the foreign company in question. The consequences of HMRC's approach are that, if either IFRS or 'new' UK GAAP would have been mandatory for such a notional UK incorporated company, HMRC will require the company to calculate its UK taxable result from notional accounts that are either presented in, or disclose, the functional currency of the company as determined according to the tests in IAS 21/FRS 102.

Company with a sterling functional (or local) currency and a sterling presentation currency that has a foreign branch

10.52 If the foreign branch has a sterling functional currency, the branch results will not be distinguishable in the company's statutory accounts from other transactions undertaken in the UK and no issues arise in relation to exchange gains and losses (although there may need to be special computational work undertaken to deal with double taxation relief for foreign tax on branch profits).

(a) If the foreign operation is deemed to be an integral part of the investing company (ie the affairs of a foreign entity are so closely interlinked with those of the investing company that its results are regarded as being more dependent on the economic environment of the investing company's currency than on that of its own currency), it would be regarded as having a sterling functional currency under IAS 21/FRS 102. Each branch transaction is translated into sterling at the exchange rate for the relevant day and all exchange movements are taken to profit and loss account.

(b) Under IAS 21/FRS 102, the closing rate/net investment method is used for 'free-standing' branches. The balance sheet is translated into sterling at the closing rate and the results for the period are translated at either the closing or the average rate for the accounting period. Exchange movements arising from retranslation of opening balance sheet figures, and restating at closing rate the assets and liabilities representing the results of the period that had been translated at average rate, are both taken to equity, ie exchange movements resulting from consolidating the branch results and balance sheet into the entity accounts are taken directly to equity.

Designated currency

10.53 With effect from 1 April 2011, a UK resident investment company can elect for their taxable profits and losses to be calculated in a currency that is different from their functional currency, in which case the 'designated currency' takes the place of the functional currency: *CTA 2010, s 9A*; *CTA 2009, s 328(3C)*; *FA 2011, Sch 7*. An election can only be made where:

(a)   a significant proportion of the company's assets or liabilities are denominated in the designated currency; or

(b)   the designated currency is the functional currency of the ultimate parent.

An election takes effect from the day specified in the election.

10.54   'Investment company' is defined in *CTA 2010, s 17(3A)* as:

'a company whose business consists wholly or mainly in the making of investments and the principal part of whose income is derived from those investments.'

10.55   The main purpose of the rule is to allow an investment company to adopt the functional currency of its ultimate parent for tax purposes.

Example 10.2

An investment company has a sterling functional currency and significant dollar receivables. It can elect for US $ to be the designated currency for tax purposes.

Permanent establishments

10.56   *CTA 2010, s 8* also applies to a UK permanent establishment of a non-resident company that prepares branch accounts in a currency other than sterling in support of its corporation tax self-assessment (CTSA) return. There is no specific provision for branches of UK resident companies whose accounts are prepared in a currency that is different from that of the company's presentation or functional currency and whose results are consolidated into the entity accounts using IAS 21/FRS 102 equivalent (IAS 21, paras 38–47).

10.57   In the case of a UK permanent establishment of a non-resident company that prepares branch accounts in a foreign currency, the accounts in question are those required by HMRC in support of the CTSA return. *CTA 2010, s 8* requires such a company to compute in sterling the profits or losses of the permanent establishment that fall to be computed for corporation tax purposes in accordance with GAAP (ie trading profits attributable to the permanent establishment) by:

(a)   computing the profits or losses in the branch accounts currency; and

(b)   taking the sterling equivalent of those profits or losses.

10.58   As the UK taxable result of a permanent establishment carrying on a trade must be computed from accounts prepared in accordance with GAAP, it is necessary to establish what GAAP is for a UK permanent establishment of a non-UK resident company.

10.59   In relation to UK branches of non-UK resident companies, GAAP means:

●   *The non-UK company prepares IFRS accounts using EU adopted IAS –* the UK permanent establishment tax computation should be based on branch accounts prepared in accordance with the same IFRS as adopted by the non-UK company.

●   *The non-UK company prepares IFRS accounts using locally adopted versions of IAS that are different to the EU adopted versions –* the UK permanent establishment computation should be based on UK GAAP.

●   *The non-UK company prepares UK GAAP accounts –* the UK permanent establishment computation should be based on branch accounts prepared in accordance with same version of UK GAAP as adopted in the company's accounts.

●   *The non-UK company prepares accounts in accordance with local GAAP which is neither EU adopted IAS, locally adopted IAS nor UK GAAP and does not have securities listed on an EU exchange which are attributed to the UK permanent establishment for regulatory purposes –* the UK permanent establishment computation should be based on branch accounts prepared in accordance with UK GAAP appropriate to an unlisted UK company (to be consistent with the 'stand-alone entity' approach).

●   *The non-UK company prepares accounts in accordance with local GAAP which is neither EU adopted IAS, locally adopted IAS nor UK GAAP and does have securities listed on an EU exchange which are attributed to the UK permanent establishment for regulatory purposes –* the UK permanent establishment computation should be based on branch accounts prepared in accordance with UK GAAP appropriate to a listed UK company: FRS 102.

10.60   It follows that the UK taxable profits or losses of the UK permanent establishment must be computed from branch accounts drawn up in either the functional currency or the local currency of the PE as determined by IFRS/ UK GAAP principles, as appropriate. The sterling equivalent is found by translating the foreign currency amount into sterling at the 'appropriate exchange rate', which is defined as either:

- the average exchange rate for the current accounting period; or

- the appropriate spot rate of exchange for the transaction in question.

10.61   Since we are dealing here with the translation of the results for an entire accounting period, and not a specific transaction, it is reasonable to infer that the foreign currency taxable profit must be translated at the average exchange rate for the period.

Tax rules

10.62   The basic rule is in *CTA 2009, s 328(1)*, which says that all exchange gains and losses on loan relationships, RNLRs, interest, and interest on overpaid or underpaid UK tax are taxable or relievable under the loan relationship rules. As *CTA 2009, s 328(1)* says:

'The reference in section 306A(1) to the profits and losses arising to a company from its loan relationships and related transactions includes a reference to exchange gains and losses so arising.'

10.63   'Exchange gains and losses' are defined in *s 475* as profits or losses arising from the comparison at different times of an amount expressed in one currency with the valuation of the same item in a different currency:

'(1)   References in this part to exchange gains or exchange losses, in relation to a company, are references respectively to–

(a)   profits or gains which arise as a result of comparing at different times of the expression in one currency of the whole or some part of the valuation put by the company in another currency of an asset or liability of the company, or

(b)   losses which so arise.'

10.64   *Section 328(3)–(7)* then has a series of exceptions to the general rule, so that *s 328(1)* does not apply to:

(a)   gains and losses arising to an investment company from adopting a designated currency (*s 328(2A)*);

(b)   gains or losses recognised in OCI arising from a debtor or creditor loan relationship or from translating profits and losses from one part of the company's business (*s 328(3)*); or

(c)   gains or losses on loan relationships being of a description specified by Treasury regulations, ie where matching is applied under the Disregard Regulations (*s 328(4)*).

10.65   As regards (a), the exchange movements relating to loan relationships and related income that arise from the consolidation of the branch results into the entity sterling accounts are disregarded.

10.66   As regards (b) and (c), exchange gains and losses recognised in the company's OCI (ie not going to profit and loss) are disregarded. This is most likely to arise when a company following IAS 21 has foreign currency debt hedging investments in the shares of foreign subsidiaries, when 'matching' will apply and the exchange movements are brought back into account on the disposal of the shares. Therefore, only exchange movements taken to profit and loss are recognised for tax purposes as they arise. In certain circumstances, exchange movements on liabilities taken to profit and loss are 'matched' with other assets such as shares, and therefore disregarded, under *reg 3* of the *Disregard Regulations* (introduced under *s 328(4)*). In other, limited, circumstances, exchange movements on loan assets are 'matched' with the exchange movements on foreign currency shares issued by the company (regarded as liabilities under IAS 32) and are therefore disregarded under *reg 3(6)* of the Disregard Regulations.

10.67   Special rules apply where fair value accounting is used: *Loan Relationship and Derivative Contracts (Exchange Gains and Losses Using Fair Value Accounting) Regulations 2005, SI 2005/3422*. By and large, exchange differences will be automatically incorporated into the fair values.

10.68   Accordingly, if debt securities are issued in a currency other than sterling, such as US dollar or euro, foreign exchange gains or losses will be separately brought into the computation of loan relationship credits and debits.

Where foreign exchange gains and losses are put through the profit and loss account:

income	=	increase in the sterling value of an asset or decrease in the sterling value of a liability
expenditure	=	decrease in the sterling value of an asset or increase in the sterling value of a liability

The accounting entries will be:

Event	Cause	Accounting entry	Profit and loss
Increase in asset	Debt increases in value (creditor)	DR	CR
Increase in liability	Debt increases in value (debtor)	CR	DR
Decrease in asset	Debt falls in value (creditor)	CR	DR
Decrease in liability	Debt falls in value (debtor)	DR	CR

Controlled foreign companies

10.69   A controlled foreign company (CFC) is a company which is (*TIOPA 2010, s 371AA(3), (6)*):

(a)   resident outside the UK; and

(b)   'controlled' by persons resident in the UK.

10.70   The basic rule in *CTA 2010, s 5* is that companies must compute and express their taxable profits in sterling, subject to special rules in *CTA 2010, ss 6–8* for profits and losses that fall to be computed in accordance with generally accepted accounting practice (GAAP), which is most items of significance except dividends and chargeable gains.

10.71   Looking at *ss 6* and *7*, a CFC will not fall within either of these sections unless it identified a functional currency in its accounts which differs from the currency in which the accounts are prepared. While this might be the case if the CFC is resident in an EU territory and accounts under IFRS, in many cases it will not be. If neither *s 6* nor *7* applies, *s 8* does, and simply says that the profits or losses should be computed in the accounts currency and the result translated into sterling. The average rate of exchange for the accounting period must be used (*s 10*).

Partnerships including companies

10.72   For the purpose of applying *CTA 2009, s 1259* to a UK resident corporate member of a UK or foreign partnership, it is necessary to compute the profits or losses of the partnership business in the relevant foreign currency if:

(a)   the partnership prepares its accounts as a whole in a currency other than sterling in accordance with generally accepted accounting practice; or

(b)   the partnership prepares its accounts as a whole in sterling but, insofar as an individual part of the business is concerned, the accounts are prepared using the closing rate method in financial statements and records prepared in a currency other than sterling.

10.73   For the purpose of applying *CTA 2009, s 1259* to a non-UK resident corporate member of a partnership, it is necessary to compute the profits and losses of the partnership business in the relevant foreign currency if:

(a)   the partnership prepares its accounts as a whole in a currency other than sterling and uses that (or another) foreign currency in whatever accounts may be required in respect of the UK business;

(b)   the partnership prepares its accounts as a whole in sterling but, insofar as they relate to the relevant part of the business, the accounts are prepared using the closing rate method from financial statements and records prepared in a currency other than sterling; or

(c)   the accounts supporting the partnership return are in sterling but, insofar as they relate to the relevant UK business, the accounts are prepared using the closing rate/net investment method from financial statements and records prepared in a currency other than sterling.

Translation

10.74   Where a company lends or borrows in a foreign currency, has a loss or profits measured in a foreign currency, enters into transactions priced in a foreign currency, and carries forward or carries back a foreign currency loss, it is necessary to translate the resultant foreign currency item.

10.75   Both IAS 21/FRS 102 require transactions denominated in a foreign currency to be translated at the exchange rate ruling on the date of the transaction. On initial recognition, foreign currency transactions are translated into the functional currency using the exchange rate between the foreign currency and the functional currency on the date of the transaction. If the transaction is settled in the same accounting period as that in which it occurred, all the exchange differences are recognised in that period.

10.76   Where translation is necessary for calculating the equivalent profits or losses of a company, whether from sterling into another currency or from another currency into sterling, *CTA 2010, ss 10, 11* require the use of the average rate for the period or, in the case of a single transaction, the spot rate or 'a just and reasonable' rate.

10.77   There are special rules for the translation of carried-forward or carried-back losses: *CTA 2010, ss 12–17*. When the transaction is settled in a subsequent accounting period, or a loss computed in a foreign currency is carried forward or back, then exchange differences recognised in each period between initial recognition and the date of settlement are determined by the exchange rates during each period.

10.78   The translation date will be (a) the transaction date; (b) the balance sheet date; or (c) the valuation date (if different from the balance sheet date). At each balance sheet date:

- foreign currency monetary items are translated using the closing rate;

- non-monetary items are measured at historic cost; and

- non-monetary items measured at fair value are recorded at their most recent fair value valuations.

Example 10.3

A UK entity sells goods to a Belgian entity for €140,000 on 31 August 2016, when the exchange rate is £1: €1.40. It records a sale and corresponding receivable of £100,000. On balance sheet date, 31 December 2016, the rate of exchange is 1:1.10. It records a foreign exchange gain of £(127,272 − 100,000) = £27,272. When payment is received on 31 July 2017, the exchange rate is 1:1.20 and the amount received is £116,667. The company records an exchange loss of £(116,667 − 127,272) = £(10,605). In practice, the company would invariably hedge the transaction.

10.79   Interest, discounts and accruals continue to be computed under the loan relationship rules, whether they are expressed in sterling or in a foreign currency. Interest is an item distinct from the debt. Foreign currency interest is translated at the spot rate when it accrues, so no gain or loss arises. An accrual of discount or premium is treated as an alteration in the amount of a debt of varying size.

10.80   Translation dates are T_1, T_2 etc. In the case of a liability or asset, at the later translation date, the sterling equivalent of the item will be measured, and the sterling equivalent at the immediately preceding translation date deducted. In the case of a forward exchange contract, which is an asset plus a liability, the 'first currency amount' (amount to be received) and the 'second currency amount' (amount to be paid) will be measured in sterling at the later translation time, and the difference ascertained (= A). The 'first currency amount' (amount to be received) and the 'second currency amount' (amount to be paid) will be measured in sterling at the immediately preceding translation time, and the difference ascertained (=B). The exchange difference is A − B.

Example 10.4

A company borrows $1,300 on 30 June 2016 when post-Brexit the spot rate is 1:1.30. It records the loan in its books at £1,000. Its year end is 31 December. The closing rate at 31 December 2016 is 1:1. It retranslates the loan at £1,300. The exchange loss is £1,000 – £1,300 = £(300).

Example 10.5

X is an investment company. On 1 April 2016, X Co pays Y Co $500 by way of premium for a currency option. X issues a loan note with a face value of $600, redeemable on 31 March 2019, to pay the premium. X's accounting period ends on 31 March. The loan note carries interest at 2% of the face value, due at 31 March. X uses amortised cost accounting. Exchange rates are:

01.04.2016	1:1.50
01.04.2017	1:1
01.04.2018	1:10

Once the foreign exchange gain has been worked out, the sterling equivalent of the discount and interest is accounted for as a loan relationship debit.

Taxable exchange differences y/e 31.03.17

	$
Basic valuation 01.04.16	500
Basic valuation 31.03.17	550
Interest	12
	£
Liability at 31.3.17 ($550 @ 1:1)	550
Liability at 01.04.16 ($500 @ 1:5)	(333)
Less: Discount ($50 @ 1:1)	(50)
FX loss (LR debit)	167
Discount	50
Interest $12 @ 1:1	12
Non-trading debit	62
Total loan relationship debits	229

Taxable exchange differences y/e 31.03.18

	$
Basic valuation 01.04.17	550
Basic valuation 31.3.18	600
Interest	12
	£
Liability at 31.03.18 $600 @ 1:1.10	545
Liability at 01.04.17 $550 @ 1:1	(550)
Less: Discount ($50 @ 1:1.10)	(45)
FX gain (LR credit)	(50)
Discount	45
Interest $12 @ 1:1.10	11
Non-trading debit	6
Total loan relationship credits	(44)

Example 10.6

A UK company, whose presentation currency is sterling, borrows $70 on 1 January 2016, repayable at $100 after three years. The company's accounting reference date is 31 December. The effective rate of interest is 12.62%. Assume the closing rate of exchange between sterling and the US dollar is:

Date	£:$
01.01.16	1:1.5
31.12.16	1:1.20
31.12.17	1:1
31.12.18	1:1.10

Year	Opening balance $	Finance cost $	C/f $	Finance cost £	FX difference*	Loan rel debit**
1	70	8.9	78.9	(7.4)	(19.08)	(26.48)
2	78.9	9.9	88.8	(9.9)	(22.83)	(32.73)
3	88.8	11.2	100	(10.18)	(2.1)	(12.28)
		30				

* Year 1 – (65.75 – 46.67)
  Year 2 – (88.8 – 65.97)
  Year 3 – (90.9 – 88.8)
** amortised cost basis

Chapter 11

Reorganisations, Acquisitions and Disposals

Overview

11.1 This chapter deals with:

- Debt for equity swaps
- Reorganisations
- Exchanges
- Reconstructions
- Intra-group asset transfers
- Earn-outs
- Novations

Structure of the legislation

11.2 Individual investors are subject to income tax on income receipts and capital gains tax on gains which are not subject to income tax. Similarly, companies pay corporation tax on income and capital gains. The value ingrained in shares or debt assets may be realised by (a) the payment of income in the form of distributions or interest, or (b) by disposal of the underlying security. Where a security is disposed of in return for another security, the policy of the legislation is to defer any charge to tax which would otherwise arise until disposal of the replacement instrument for cash.

11.3 The fundamental concepts are derived from the capital gains tax legislation. The basic concept is that of 'reorganisation' as defined in *TCGA 1992, ss 126, 127*. This is a transaction between a company and its shareholders. A transaction which is a reorganisation may also be a 'conversion' within *s 132*. A conversion in turn brings in the application of *TCGA 1992, s 116*, if a chargeable asset is converted into an exempt asset (share-for-debt exchange), or vice versa (debt-for-share, ie debt-equity swap). The concept of reorganisation is extended to transactions which bring in a third party, such as 'share-for-share exchanges' (*s 135*) and reconstructions (*ss 136, 139, Sch 5AA*). These are deemed reorganisations.

11.4   The common feature of all these arrangements is that, so long as no money passes from the company or a third party to the investor, any charge to tax is deferred until an occasion when money does change hands.

Reorganisations

11.5   'Reorganisation' means 'reorganisation of a company's share capital' (*TCGA 1992, s 126(1)*). This is a transaction between the company and its shareholders. The concept is extended, for tax purposes, to apply to a wide range of corporate transactions involving a third party, in which one form of share or security is replaced by another form of share or security. These transactions are: conversion (*s 132*); share exchanges (*s 135*); reconstructions and amalgamations involving the issue of securities (*s 136*); and reconstructions and amalgamations involving the transfer of a business (*s 139*). These are also treated as reorganisations for tax purposes, subject to appropriate modifications of the basic rule for reorganisations in *s 127*. A debt-equity swap is a conversion within *s 132*. For the purposes of *s 136*, 'scheme of reconstruction' is defined in *Sch 5AA*. The Court has said:

> '"Reorganisation of a company's share capital" is not a term of art. It derives colour from its context.' (Per Balcombe LJ, *Dunstan v Young, Austen & Young* [1989] STC 69 at 74)

11.6   Reorganisation includes:

- issuing of new securities ('new holding') 'in respect of and in proportion to' an existing holding ('original shares') (*TCGA 1992, s 126(1), (2)*);

- indirect demergers (*CTA 2009, s 1076*);

- reduction of capital (other than by paying off redeemable preference shares) (*TCGA 1992, s 126(3)*);

- rights issue;

- bonus issue; and

- any transaction in which new shares are acquired by existing shareholders in proportion to their existing beneficial holdings.

The payment of stock dividends does not constitute a reorganisation: *TCGA 1992, s 142(2); ITTOIA 2005, ss 410–414; CTA 2010, ss 1049–1050*.

11.7   The basic rule on reorganisations depends upon two fictions: the 'no disposal' fiction; and the 'same asset' fiction. This rule is contained in *TCGA 1992, s 127*. This is the centrepiece of the UK's tax law relating to the reconstruction of corporate groups:

> 'a reorganisation shall not be treated as involving any disposal of the original shares or any acquisition of the new holding or any part of it, but the original shares (taken as a single asset) and the new holding (taken as a single asset) shall be treated as the same asset acquired as the original shares were acquired.'

11.8   In other words, (a) there has been no disposal, and (b) the original shares are still present in the form of the new holding, which is treated as having been acquired at the same time and at the same price as the original shares.

These rules as to reorganisations apply also on share-for-share exchanges and reconstructions (*TCGA 1992, ss 132, 135, 136*).

11.9   Under the capital gains tax reorganisation rules, where shares are exchanged for paper rather than sold for cash, the 'new holding' (shares or securities) is deemed to be the same asset as the original shares (*TCGA 1992, s 126*). The 'original shares' are the 'shares held before and concerned in the reorganisation' (*s 126(1)(a)*). The 'new holding' means 'in relation to any original shares, the shares in and debentures of the company which as a result of the organisation represent the original shares' (*s 126(1)(b)*). The new holding results from the reorganisation. On a reorganisation which does not involve the issue of qualifying corporate bonds (QCBs), the new holding is treated as the same asset as the original shares. The reorganisation does not involve a disposal of the original shares, and any gain is effectively carried into the new holding.

11.10   It is a fundamental rule that 'any asset representing a loan relationship of a company' is a QCB (*TCGA 1992, s 117(A1)*). Gains on QCBs are not 'chargeable gains' and so not subject to 'corporation tax in respect of chargeable gains' in the case of companies, or 'capital gains tax in respect of chargeable gains' in the case of persons other than companies (*TCGA 1992, ss 1(2), 2(1), 115(1)*). In general, all profits and losses on loan relationships, ie QCBs, come under the loan relationship rules (*CTA 2009, s 306A(1)*).

11.11   In *Dunstan v Young, Austen & Young* [1989] STC 69 the Court of Appeal held that an increase in share capital could constitute a reorganisation, even though the legislation only refers to a reduction in share capital. The Court observed at 75 that the policy of the Act was that:

> 'there shall not be a disposal … where the shareholders remain the same and they now hold their shares in the same proportions.'

11.12   The reorganisation rules cannot apply, without modification, where the original holding falls within one tax regime and the new holding falls within a different one. Companies' gains on shares are taxed under the capital gains tax rules, while profits on QCBs held by companies fall under the loan relationship rules. Individuals' gains on shares fall under the capital gains tax rules, while QCBs are exempt assets.

11.13   If the reorganisation involves shares for shares (or shares for non-QCBs), the transaction stays within the capital gains tax reorganisation rules. However, if the conversion involves QCBs at either or both ends of the transaction, the reorganisation rules are modified. As QCBs are outside the charge to capital gains, a gain on shares could be eliminated by exchanging the shares for a QCB, if no provision was made for freezing the gain inherent in the shares. Instead, the rules in *TCGA 1992, s 116* take precedence over both *TCGA 1992, ss 126–130* and the loan relationship rules (*TCGA 1992, s 116(5), (16)*). This is because *s 116(2)* says:

> '(2)   In this section references to a transaction include references to any conversion of securities … within the meaning of section 132'

11.14   Hence, under *TCGA 1992, s 116* the general 'new for old' reorganisation rules do not apply where QCBs are replaced by shares, or shares by QCBs (*s 116(5)*). A transaction which – apart from *TCGA 1992, s 116(5)* – would fall within the reorganisation rules is a 'relevant transaction' within *TCGA 1992, s 116* (*s 116(2)*). In place of the terms defined in *s 126* – 'original shares' and 'new holding' – the terms 'the old asset' and 'the new asset' respectively are used (*s 116(3), (4)*). Where QCBs are exchanged for shares, or QCBs for QCBs, the rule in *s 116(9)* will apply. Where shares are exchanged for QCBs, the rule in *s 116(10)* will apply.

11.15   Accordingly, as QCBs are outside the charge to capital gains, the reorganisation rules are modified, where either (a) a QCB/loan relationship is exchanged for shares, or (b) shares are exchanged for QCBs/a loan relationship. Otherwise:

(a)   in the case of an individual, a gain on shares could be eliminated by exchanging shares for a QCB, the subsequent disposal of which would give rise to neither a chargeable gain nor an allowable loss;

(b)   in the case of a company, a gain or loss on a loan relationship could be switched from the loan relationships to the capital gains regime.

In these situations, *s 116(1)* disapplies *ss 127–130* and applies instead the provision of *s 116* to the reorganisation or other transaction.

11.16 The reorganisation regime has accordingly separate rules for two situations which arise on a paper-for-paper exchange:

(a)   where a chargeable asset is exchanged for another chargeable asset (rollover, *ss 127, 135*); and

(b)   where either a chargeable asset is exchanged for an exempt asset (frozen gains, *s 116*), or an exempt asset is exchanged for a chargeable asset (immediate disposal).

11.17 The two regimes work quite differently. The *s 116* regime applies both to individuals (who hold QCBs) and to companies (for whom all QCBs are loan relationships). In the case of companies, the provisions of *TCGA 1992, s 116* take precedence over the loan relationship rules: *TCGA 1992, s 116(16)*.

11.18 *TCGA 1992, s 116* applies where, in the course of a reorganisation, conversion or reconstruction, a person acquires or transfers QCBs in exchange for other shares or securities.

11.19 *Section 116*:

(a)   treats QCBs as a deferred payment of cash;

(b)   allows gains on shares to be deferred where the shares are replaced by QCBs;

(c)   brings such deferred gains into charge to capital gains tax only when the QCB/loan relationship is disposed of (*s 116(10)*); but

(d)   bring gains and losses on QCBs into immediate charge to tax (or relief) under the loan relationship rules (*s 116(8A)*).

11.20 *TCGA 1992, s 116* only applies to shares and QCBs which a company holds as investments. If the assets are held as trading stock, all profits will enter into the computation of trading profits, and not constitute 'chargeable gains'.

11.21 The transactions in question which involve loan relationships (QCBs) and fall under *TCGA 1992, s 116* are the replacement in the course of a reorganisation (*s 127*), conversion (*s 132*), exchange (*s 135*) or reconstruction (*s 136*) of:

● shares with QCBs;

● QCBs with shares;

● QCBs with QCBs;

● other assets with QCBs; or

● shares with non-QCBs.

In these transactions, both the capital gains tax reorganisation rules (*TCGA 1992, ss 126–140*) and the capital gains QCB rules (*TCGA 1992, ss 115–117B*) fall to be applied.

11.22   Where a chargeable asset is replaced by a chargeable asset (eg on a share exchange under *s 135*), there is a rollover of tax. The new asset completely replaces the old asset, so that they are regarded as a single asset. The effect is that the shareholders in the target company, ie the company being taken over, are neutral, so that shareholders in the target company are treated as respects the new shares which they acquire in the acquiring company, as if those new shares had been acquired at the time of their original acquisition of shares in Target Co and the base cost simply flows through. Where a chargeable asset is replaced by an exempt asset, there is a holdover of tax. The gain arising at that stage is put in a box and taken out later. The distinction arises because debentures are nearer to cash than to shares. The issue of a debenture is really deferred cash consideration and treated for tax as if it were cash.

11.23   The mere cancellation of a particular class of shares is not a reorganisation: *Unilever (UK) Holdings Ltd v Smith* [2003] STC 15. A reorganisation requires (a) something which would, but for *s 127*, involve a disposal, or (b) where there is more than one class of shares, an alteration of the rights attaching to the shares of any class. The substantial shareholding exemption (SSE) takes precedence over the reorganisation rules: *TCGA 1992, Sch 7AC, para 4(1)*.

Debt-equity swaps

11.24   A very common form of debt restructuring is the debt-equity swap. A QCB (loan relationship in the case of a corporate creditor) is replaced by shares. Debt for equity transactions are a means by which a company replaces a liability to a creditor with a liability to a shareholder, by transferring the amount of the money debt to share capital or share premium, thereby strengthening its balance sheet and conserving cash. The basic principle involved in all debt-equity swaps is that the subscription money for new shares can be paid by using a debt asset for the purpose. The creditor sets off the amount owed to him on the debt against the subscription monies which he owes to the issuing company. A debt-equity swap is a conversion within *TCGA 1992, s 132*, but not a share exchange within *TCGA 1992, s 135*, because that involves exchanging securities of one company (Company A) for securities of another company (Company B). A debt-equity swap involves exchanging debentures of a company for shares of the same company.

11.25   This swap typically occurs in three situations:

1   where a highly geared and debt-laden company cannot service or redeem its borrowings;

2   where the bond is convertible and the share price has risen since the borrowing was incurred, leading to the conversion of the bond into shares under a term in the bond; and

3   where, in a group situation, a company with a trade debt applies the debt to pay up shares in the debtor company.

11.26   Situations (1) and (2) fall within the term 'reorganisation' in *TCGA 1992, s 126* and 'conversion' within *s 132*, because *s 132* applies both to conversions 'occurring in consequence of the operation of the terms of any security or of any debenture which is not a security', and to exchanges 'effected by a transaction'. However, situation (3) falls outside *s 132*, because it does not involve 'securities'. Trade debt does not come within the definition of 'securities' within *s 132(3)(b)*, which says:

'(b)   "security" includes any loan stock or similar security whether of the Government of the United Kingdom or any other government, or of any public or local authority in the United Kingdom or elsewhere, or of any company, and whether secured or unsecured.'

Trade debt is a 'relevant non-lending relationship' within *CTA 2009, s 478*, and, where impairment losses occur, this will fall under the loan relationship rules.

11.27   Convertibles falling within *CTA 2009, s 585* are bifurcated into a deeply discounted security and an equity option. The deeply discounted security comes within the loan relationship rules. The equity option is, in the hands of the investor, a derivative contract falling within *CTA 2009, s 584*. These are dealt with in **Chapter 13**.

Company law position

11.28   The basis of the company law analysis is that the issuing of shares by a company costs the company nothing and does not constitute payment in any legal sense. The company issues bits of paper, in return for money or money's worth contributed to the company. The bits of paper, according to their terms, entitle the holders to participate in the company's profits and share in its assets. This entitlement is conferred not at the expense of the company, but at the expense of existing shareholders, insofar as the reduction in their proportionate interest in the company is not matched by a corresponding increase in its assets. Indeed, debt-equity swaps often wipe out the value of existing shareholders, because their shares will be subordinated to the rights attached to the new shares. Under company law, new shares issued by a company:

(a)   must have a nominal value (*CA 2006, s 542*);

(b)   must not be issued at a discount (*s 580*); and

(c)   must be paid up in money or money's worth (*s 582(1)*).

'Payment in cash' includes 'a release of a liability of the company for a liquidated sum' (*s 583(3)(c)*). Requirement (b) is of key importance in relation to debt-equity swaps.

11.29 While, therefore, shares can be issued at a premium, and for the subscription of the nominal value, they cannot be issued for less than the nominal value. In *Shearer (Inspector of Taxes) v Bercain Ltd* [1980] STC 359 at 375, Walton J observed:

> 'In general, it is the duty of the directors to issue shares in their company for the best equivalent they can obtain, and in a very large number of cases that will mean that they will be able to issue them at a premium, and consequently must do so.'

11.30 That premium must be taken to share premium account. Hence, any excess of the amount of the debt released over the nominal value of the shares issued will be taken to share premium account by the debtor.

11.31 *Companies Act 2006, ss 611–613* set out the circumstances in which either a share premium account is not required or only limited amounts must be transferred to it. The exceptions are:

(a) a merger by share exchange where a company secures 90% of the equity shares of another company in exchange for the issue of its own shares; and

(b) a group reconstruction whereby a wholly-owned subsidiary receives assets other than cash in return for the issue of its shares to its parent or a wholly-owned subsidiary of its parent.

11.32 Where a creditor undertakes to subscribe in cash for new shares in a company, he can set off an amount owed by the company to him against his liability to pay subscription moneys, and the shares will be issued for a consideration equal to the part of the debt thereby discharged. The amount of the debt released will equal the amount credited to share capital (called-up share capital and share premium account). The amount of debt discharged will be debited to liabilities over assets, and a corresponding amount will be credited to share capital.

11.33 In company law terms, it is of central importance that a conversion, or debt-equity swap, does not involve the 'release' of a debt. Instead, the debt is discharged by the issue of shares. A debt release is an exoneration of the debtor. It is a gratuitous transaction. The creditor gets nothing in return. A debt-equity swap is quite different. There is no 'release' of the debt. Instead, 'in consideration of ... shares ... the creditor company treats the liability as discharged': *CTA 2009, s 356*. If shares are issued in full satisfaction of a debt which constitutes a loan relationship, there is not a release, there is discharge by performance.

11.34 As regards the issuing company, a debt-equity swap is, in company law terms, purely a balance sheet transaction. Accordingly, it is common to account for debt-equity swaps without bringing in a credit to the profit and loss account.

Example 11.1

B has an authorised capital of £10,000, of which 5,000 £1 shares have been issued. Z Bank has lent B £1,000.

(a)   Z releases £900 of the debt and B issues 400 £1 shares to Z. The market value of the new shares is £100. Z writes the debt down to £100 because it carries the new shares as debt in its books. Z gets impairment relief of £900. B credits share capital with £400 and share premium account with £600. This is debited to liabilities, and so the debt is reduced to nil.

(b)   As above, but the 400 shares issued to Z are worth £800. Z only gets £200 impairment relief. B's position is unaltered.

(c)   As in (a), but the new shares are worthless. Z gets impairment relief of £1,000. B's position is unaltered.

Example 11.2

A Ltd wishes to borrow £1,000 from the bank. The bank will only agree if B Ltd (an unconnected investment company) guarantees the loan and provides security to the value of £1,000 to back the guarantee. B Ltd agrees to do this, provided that A Ltd issues to B ten new £1 shares as fully paid. The market value of the new shares is £500. A Ltd values the services provided by B Ltd at £500. B Ltd subscribes £10, and A Ltd issues ten £1 ordinary shares to B Ltd as fully paid. The share issue is treated as follows:

1   A Ltd credits share capital with £10 and share premium account with £490;

2   A Ltd debits £10 to cash;

3   A Ltd charges £490 to profit and loss account as a loan relationship debit under *CTA 2009, s 307(4)(a)*, being the cost of bringing the loan relationship into existence.

11.35 Thus, in company law terms, 'consideration' for the issue of new shares has a legal meaning. The market value of the new shares issued is irrelevant. By contrast, accounting rules and, in practice, tax law may give 'consideration' a commercial meaning, and take into account the market value of the shares exchanged for debt.

Accounting position – creditor

11.36 There is an accounting consensus that the creditor is required to recognise the equity instruments issued to it at their fair value. The difference between the carrying value of the debt, and the fair value of the equity instruments received in its place, is recognised in the profit and loss account of the creditor. Thus, the creditor must recognise any profit or loss arising on the transaction.

Accounting position – debtor

11.37 As regards the debtor, there are two possible accounting treatments:

(a) On the first analysis, the debtor – following the company law position – is not required to bring a credit into the profit and loss account. This is a balance sheet transaction, which does not produce a profit or loss.

Example 11.3

X Ltd owes B Bank £6,000. B Bank agrees to subscribe for 4,000 new £1 ordinary shares. X Ltd does not show a profit on the transaction.

	Before		*After*		*A/c entries*
Assets	5,000		5,000		
Debt liabilities	(6,000)		(2,000)		DR 3,000
Net assets		(1,000)		3,000	
Share capital	1,000		5,000		CR 3,000
Profit and loss	(2,000)		(2,000)		
		(1,000)		3,000	

(b) On the second analysis, the debtor is required to bring a credit into the profit and loss account, in respect of the excess of the debt extinguished over the fair value of the new shares issued, which corresponds to the debit brought in by the creditor.

11.38 UITF 47 (IFRIC 19) applies for accounting periods beginning on or after 1 July 2010, and deals with 'Extinguishing Financial Liabilities with Equity Instruments', ie debt-equity swaps. It applies to UK companies under FRS 102. It only applies to the debtor company. It requires the debtor company to bring in a credit corresponding to the difference between the carrying value of the liability and the fair value of the equity instruments issued to extinguish it. It does not apply where the creditor is a shareholder in the debtor. If only part of the liability is extinguished, the consideration received has to be apportioned. The basis of the IFRIC (UITF) is that the issue of equity instruments to extinguish all or part of the financial liability of the issuer constitutes 'consideration paid' in accordance with IAS 39, para 41. This says:

> 'The difference between the carrying amount of a financial liability (or part of a financial liability) extinguished or transferred to another party and the consideration paid, including any non-cash assets transferred or liabilities assumed, shall be recognised in the profit and loss.'

It follows that the issuing entity should measure the equity instruments issued in extinguishment of the financial liability not at their *nominal* value but at their *fair* value, recognising the difference in the income statement.

11.39 The issue is considered in Deloitte, *iGAAP 2016,* Vol C, 553–564. This says at 554:

> 'it is not acceptable simply to reclassify the carrying amount of the financial liability to equity (unless the fair value of the equity instruments issued happens to equal the carrying amount of the financial liability at the date of extinguishment).

11.40 Under UK company law, shares cannot be issued at a discount. As *CA 2006, s 580(1)* states:

> '(1) A company's shares must not be allotted at a discount.'

Nor can capital be reduced, except by the means provided by company law, which require either a reduction of capital approved by the court (*CA 2006, s 645*) or a reduction of capital following the solvency resolution procedure: *CA 2006, s 642*. In the UK the amount to be credited to share capital and to share premium on issue of shares is a matter of law and does not depend on the accounting for the transaction. The amount which the accounting treatment would take to profit and loss (as a release of a liability), company law takes to share premium account. Any apparent conflict between the accounting treatment and legal analysis can be resolved by transfers between components of equity.

11.41 The result is that debt for equity swap transactions are recorded so that the difference between the liquidated debt amount and the fair value of equity issued is recognised in full in the share premium account rather than through the income statement.

Example 11.4

X plc has debt of £1,000,000. The bank agrees to subscribe for 100,000 new £1 ordinary shares at a premium of £9 a share. The fair value of the new shares issued is £100,000.

	Before		*After*	
Assets	1,000,000		1,000,000	
Debt liabilities	(1,000,000)		0	
Net assets		0		1,000,000
Share capital	1,000,000		1,100,000	
Share premium			900,000	
Profit and loss	(1,000,000)		(1,000,000)	
		0		1,000,000

11.42   In other words, the end result in accounting terms is exactly the same whether or not UITF 47 applies. UITF 47 can only make a practical difference in systems whose corporate law allows the issue of shares at a discount. This is one of the difficulties of having a straight read through from IAS to new UK GAAP.

Debt-equity swaps – tax treatment

11.43   Where the debtor takes the credit to share premium account, the tax problems which formerly arose are resolved by *CTA 2009, s 308(1)* (as amended for accounting periods beginning on or after 1 January 2016 by *F(No 2) A 2015, Sch 7, para 5(2)*), which confines tax charges and reliefs in regard to loan relationships to amounts passing through the income statement. Hence the tax treatment broadly follows the company law position, and does not follow the UITF 47 treatment, in so far as the latter may require a credit to profit and loss.

11.44   There are four provisions which specifically deal with debt-equity swaps:

● *TCGA 1992, s 116(8A)* deals with the non-connected creditor;

● *CTA 2009, s 322(4)* deals with the non-connected debtor;

- *CTA 2009, s 356* deals with the unconnected creditor who becomes connected as a result of a debt-equity swap; and

- *CTA 2009, s 358* deals with the connected debtor.

11.45 The first point to note is that the debt-equity swap will be a disposal of the debt in a 'related transaction' under *CTA 2009, s 304(1)*. The tax issue is, then, what profit or loss will be recognised for tax purposes.

Position of the non-connected creditor

11.46 If a company is unable to service or repay its loans, a bank will, if it holds a debenture, appoint an administrative receiver to realise its security and collect the sums owed. Alternatively, a bank may consider a debt-equity swap, ie exchanging its loans for an equity stake, so that it can recover its money on a subsequent recovery of the company. The mechanism of debt-equity swaps is that the company issues to the bank a new class of shares. Existing shares are usually reduced to nil value by the issue of the new shares. The bank, in turn, uses its debt to subscribe for the new shares at their nominal value, and takes its chance of enjoying future growth as a shareholder. A company's gearing ratios alter dramatically, debt being reduced and share capital increased, albeit by a smaller amount, to reflect adjustments in asset values.

11.47 Under what is called the Massey-Ferguson rule, loan-equivalent treatment applies. The bank limits the write-off by reference to an estimated value of the new equity and continues to treat the quasi-debt as a loan in its books. The debt (a current asset) only needs to be reclassified as a fixed asset if there is a long-term intention to retain the shares. Dividends paid by the company will constitute dividends, not interest.

11.48 If (as is likely) the new shares held by a bank will be of very little value, the bank will hold the loans as stock in trade and can obtain impairment relief on a trading loan relationship.

11.49 In the case of an investment company creditor, because the qualifying corporate bond (QCB) is a loan relationship, there will also be a disposal of the debt, and gains and losses then arising will be recognised for tax purposes under *TCGA 1992, s 116(8A)*. Thus, if a debt is treated as discharged in return for the issue of valueless shares, or shares worth less than the nominal value of the debt disposed of, the lender will obtain a loan relationship debit for the loss under *s 116(8A)*. If there is a built-in gain or unrealised loss on the loan relationship, it will be recognised at this point, subject to the exclusion of connected-party gains and losses.

Example 11.5

X Ltd issues a debenture to A Ltd in return for a loan of £100. X Ltd gets into difficulties. When the market value of the debt is £5, A Ltd agrees to exchange the debt for 100 £1 ordinary shares in X Ltd. The consideration received by X Ltd is £100. The acquisition cost of A Ltd's shares is £5. A Ltd has a loan relationship debit of $(100 - 5) = £95$.

11.50   *TCGA 1992, s 116(8A)* provides that, if a QCB is exchanged for a non-QCB, the transaction is deemed to be a disposal of the loan relationship at its market value on the date of the disposal (ie the exchange). This means that, for the purpose of calculating the relevant credit or debit in the hands of the disponor, the calculation assumes that he has received an amount equal to the market value of the loan relationship at the date of the exchange. In addition, any chargeable gain or allowable loss which has previously been rolled over into the QCB will crystallise on the exchange: see **11.69–11.70**.

11.51   Thus, if debt is treated as discharged in return for the issue of valueless shares, or shares worth less than the nominal value of the debt disposed of, the lender will obtain non-trading loan relationship debits for the loss under *TCGA 1992, s 116(8A)*, unless the companies are connected prior to the transaction. If there is a built-in gain or unrealised loss on the loan relationship, it will be recognised at this point, subject to the exclusion of connected-party gains and losses.

Position of connected company creditor

11.52   If the creditor and debtor have a connected companies relationship, no impairment relief for the debt will be available, if the impairment is recognised when the debt-equity swap occurs: *CTA 2009, s 354*.

11.53   If the companies become connected only as a result of a debt-equity swap, and prior to this transaction they were not connected, then the creditor company's impairment loss will be recognised for tax purposes. This is the single most important departure from the rule in *CTA 2009, s 354*, and is contained in *s 356*:

'(1)   An impairment loss or release debit in relation to a liability to pay any amount to a company ("the creditor company") under its creditor relationship is not prevented from being brought into account by section 354 if conditions A, B and C are met.

(2)   Condition A: the creditor company treats the liability as discharged.

(3)   Condition B: it does so in consideration of –

    (a)   any shares forming part of the ordinary share capital of the company on which the liability would otherwise have fallen, or

    (b)   any entitlement to such shares.

(4)   Condition C: there would be no connection between the two companies for the accounting period in which the consideration is given if the question whether there is such a connection were determined by reference only to times before the creditor company –

    (a)   acquired possession of the shares, or

    (b)   acquired any entitlement to them.'

11.54   What is striking about this provision is that it (correctly) refers to the 'discharge' rather than the 'release' of the debt in these circumstances, ie it uses the language of company law, rather than accountancy. This makes use of the term 'release' in other contexts doubly confusing.

Example 11.6

Debtor Ltd has 100 issued ordinary shares. Debtor Ltd owes Creditor Ltd £900. Creditor Ltd agrees to subscribe for 900 new £1 shares in Debtor. It uses its asset of 900 to settle its liability to pay £900 of subscription moneys to Debtor. The market value of the new shares is £10. Creditor obtains impairment loss of (900 – 10) = £890, notwithstanding that it now controls Debtor.

11.55   This statutory relaxation of the connected persons rule applies only in the accounting period of the swap and in respect of loans or the part of loans treated as discharged in return for the issue of a controlling shareholding in consideration of the issue of shares. The relief applies to the transaction which produces the change from unconnected to connected status, but subsequent debt-equity swaps will not attract bad debt relief.

Example 11.7

Finance plc has an accounting date of 31 December. It has lent £1,000 to Ramicon Ltd. Ramicon has an issued share capital of 100 £1 ordinary shares, owned by Mr and Mrs Jones.

Ramicon cannot repay its loan. In the accounting period ending 31 December 2012, Finance plc writes off £800 of the loan and uses the balance of £200 to subscribe for 200 new £1 ordinary shares.

In 2012, Finance plc gets bad debt relief of 800.

Position of connected company debtor

11.56   The connected company does not have to bring in any credit for the discharge of the debt (even if he might otherwise have to do so): *CTA 2009, s 358(1)*. However, this rule does not apply to deemed releases: *s 358(2)*. A debt-equity swap will not, in general, produce a credit to profit and loss account, and is not brought into account in determining a company's profits or losses for that accounting period: *s 307(2)*. There is no release because the transaction in which the debt is derecognised is payment for an asset. However, it will increase share capital. The part of the debt which is used to pay for the new shares is treated as discharged.

Position of unconnected debtor

11.57   The key rule is in *CTA 2009, s 322(4)*. This tax treatment does not depend upon the accounting treatment, but follows instead the company law position. It operates to prevent a credit being brought into account under the loan relationship rules by the unconnected debtor in the debt-equity swap, whether or not a profit might be recognised for accounting purposes.

11.58   *CTA 2009, s 322* deals with the position of the debtor company in debt-equity swaps. Debt-equity swaps potentially within *s 322(4)* may take one of three forms:

1   Debtor Ltd owes Creditor Ltd £100. Creditor Ltd releases £80 of the debt, and converts the balance of £20 into ordinary shares in Debtor. In this case, there is no credit for tax purposes in Debtor, because the release is 'in consideration of, or of any entitlement to shares forming part of the ordinary capital' of Debtor.

2   Debtor Ltd owes Creditor Ltd £100. Creditor Ltd agrees to subscribe for 100 £1 shares in Debtor. It uses its asset of £100 to settle its liability to pay 100 of subscription moneys to Debtor. Here there is no release, simply a discharge.

3   Debtor Ltd owes Creditor Ltd £100. Creditor Ltd agrees to subscribe for 100 £1 shares in Debtor. It uses its asset of £100 to settle its liability to pay 100 of subscription moneys to Debtor. It immediately sells on the new shares to the existing shareholders for £1.

11.59 *Section 322* deals generally with the circumstances in which a release is not taxed in the debtor company. It says (with effect for accounting periods beginning on or after 1 January 2016):

'(1) This section applies if –

  (a) a liability to pay an amount under a company's loan relationship is released, and

  (b) the release takes place in an accounting period an amortised cost basis of accounting is used in respect of that relationship.

(2) The company is not required to bring into account a credit in respect of the release for the purposes of this Part if any of condition A to E is met.

(3) Condition A is that the release is part of a statutory insolvency arrangement.

(4) Condition B is that the release is not a release of relevant rights and is –

  (a) in consideration of shares forming part of the ordinary share capital of the debtor company, or

  (b) in consideration of any entitlement to such shares.

(5) Condition C is that –

  (a) the debtor company meets one of the insolvency conditions (see subsection (6)), and

  (b) the debtor relationship is not a connected companies relationship (see section 348).

(5A) Condition D is that the liability is released in consequence of the making of a mandatory reduction instrument or a third country instrument or the exercise of a stabilisation power under Part I of the Banking Act 2009.

(5B) Condition E is that –

  (a) the release is neither a deemed release, as defined by section 358(3), nor a release of relevant rights, and

  (b) immediately before the release, it is reasonable to assume that, without the release and any arrangements of which the release forms part, there would be a material risk that at some time within the next 12 month the company would be unable to pay its debts.'

11.60   *CTA 2009, s 476(1)* says that for the purposes of the loan relationship rules 'share' means a share on which distributions may be payable. The term used in *s 322(4)* is 'ordinary share capital'. Ordinary share capital is defined in *CTA 2009, s 1319, Sch 4* and *CTA 2010, s 1119* as all shares other than fixed rate non-participating preference shares. Hence, zero coupon preference shares are ordinary share capital under the latter definition, but not shares forming part of ordinary share capital under the *s 476(1)* definition. The question is therefore, whether the definition of 'ordinary share capital' in *s 322(4)* is modified by *s 476*, before going to *CTA 2010, s 1119*, or whether the definition in *s 1119* applies for the purposes of *s 322(4)*. There is no discernible policy reason for importing the *s 476* definition into *s 322(4)*, when the *CTA 2010* definition has already been imported into the 2009 Act as a whole.

11.61   If, later, the shares are cancelled on a reduction of capital, that does not produce a credit to the income statement, and so does not give rise to a credit under the loan relationship rules: *CTA 2009, s 308(1)*.

Example 11.8

X Ltd has share capital of £10,000, but cannot pay dividends because of a deficit of £5,000 on the profit and loss account. The company decides to reduce its share capital by £6,000:

	Before	*After*	*A/c entries*
Assets	10,000	10,000	
Liabilities	(5,000)	(5,000)	
Net assets	5,000	5,000	
Share capital	10,000	4,000	DR 6,000
Profit and loss	(5,000)	1,000	CR 6,000
	5,000	5,000	

11.62   It is common for a debt-equity swap to be accompanied by a release, eg debtor company owes bank £5,000; bank agrees to subscribe for 1,000 new £1 ordinary shares and to release £4,000 of the loan. In that case, there will be a credit recognised in profit and loss, but it will not give rise to a charge to tax: *CTA 2009, s 322(4)*.

HMRC's view

11.63   The ex-creditor will not normally want to retain his shares, but will sell them to the other shareholders for a nominal amount. HMRC have sought to limit the scope of *CTA 2009, s 322(4)* or to extend the charge to tax in these circumstances. HMRC's stance is that the creditor must take a commercial and economic interest in the company. The shares must be held for some time, on this view, in order for *s 322(4)* to apply. However, there is nothing in the legislation which requires this, and the legislation does not provide any time frame. All that it demands is that the legal requirements for the holding and issue of shares are fulfilled. The only question is, has the creditor subscribed for shares in cash as a matter of company law?

11.64   The HMRC view is set out in these terms in the Corporate Finance Manual at CFM33200–33202. HMRC focus on the words 'in consideration of' and say that the company is paying consideration, and consideration has a commercial meaning. They also rely on *Carreras Group Ltd v Stamp Commissioner* [2004] STC 1377 to amalgamate the debt-equity swap and disposal of the shares into a release of the debt for nominal consideration. However, in that case the shares held by A ended up being held by B in return for a payment of cash by B to A. In the case of a debt-equity swap, the end result is an actual increase in share capital, paid for by a reduction in external indebtedness.

11.65   A new version of CFM33202 appeared on 7 October 2011. While not law, it embodies HMRC's understanding of the law. The general tenor of the changes is towards the formal, company law position, namely, that a debt-equity swap involves a discharge of debt, not a release of debt. The revised version provides as follows:

1   It restates the view that 'it is not enough for a release of debt merely to be accompanied by an issue of shares' to come within *CTA 2009, s 322(4)*. This, however, begs the question whether there is a release or a discharge of the debt.

2   To decide whether or not relief is due, it is necessary to take a realistic view of the transaction. This does not tell us whether a 'realistic' view is the accounting treatment or the company law analysis, assuming that they differ.

3   In the majority of cases, an arm's-length transaction will fall within the exemption. Critically, there is no requirement for the shares issued by the debtor company to be held for any particular length of time. It is here that the more liberal approach emerges, though this is not consistent with the other statements noted above.

4   If, prior to the debt-equity swap, there are contractual or other arrangements in place for the new shares to be sold on for a nominal consideration, this may indicate that the creditor has received cash, not shares:

> 'the release of the shares may be entirely gratuitous and a realistic view of the transaction may be that the shares are issued merely to obtain a tax advantage for the debtor company.'

This is quite inconsistent with the company law position, which is that there has been payment for the shares.

11.66 HMRC provide a 'white list' of cases which, in their view, will not give rise to a tax charge in the debtor (CFM33202):

> '• the debt may be transferred, by novation or otherwise, to other companies in the same group;
>
> • the debt may be split into tranches and the seniority changed;
>
> • there may be arrangements to allow one party to exit a joint venture, or for one party in such a venture to become the controlling shareholder of the debtor company or its group;
>
> • a newco may be set up to hold the shares issued in exchange for debt;
>
> • the shares issued in exchange for the debt may have different rights to other shares issued by the debtor company;
>
> • derivative contracts hedging the debt may be closed out;
>
> • the release may include part of the debt, and accrued interest on the debt;
>
> • interest may be released that has been disallowed under the late interest provisions or transfer pricing rules …;
>
> • where the shares are sold on to a third party, this may be on deferred terms so that the lender benefits from a future increase in their value.'

11.67 HMRC give three examples in CFM33203:

- *Example 1*: bank accepts shares worth £500 in consideration for release of £80m debt. Shares are non-voting with limited dividend rights. Bank accepts shares in hope their value increases but sells them after a subsequent review. Debt-for-equity treatment not prevented from applying just because bank does not hold the shares long term.

- *Example 2*: as Example 1, but borrower is a joint venture and, under the terms of a wider rescue, one joint venture party buys out the other and the shares issued to the bank in consideration for the release. Debt-for-equity treatment applies.

- *Example 3*: as Example 1, but contractual arrangements are put in place for the bank to sell the shares to the existing shareholders for £500 immediately after they are issued. HMRC say it is unlikely they would provide clearance that debt-for-equity treatment applies.

11.68 The general lesson to be taken from these changes is that, in most cases, where the new shares are held for a time (say six months), there are no arrangements in place prior to the transaction for their immediate onward sale, and the correct company law procedures are followed, the transaction can safely be treated as falling within the exemption from charge in *CTA 2009, s 322(4)*. What HMRC appear to object to is sales of the new shares to existing members. As, in most cases, they will be the people most interested, or the only people interested, in taking over the new shares, the new version may not offer any greater certainty than its predecessor.

11.69   The rule in *TCGA 1992, s 116(9)* applies if the relevant transaction involves the replacement of QCBs by QCBs, or QCBs by shares. The 'no disposal' and 'same asset' fictions in *s 127* are both excluded: *s 116(1), (5)*. The relevant transaction is treated as a disposal of the old asset and acquisition of the new asset (*s 116(9)*). Gains and losses then arising will be recognised for tax purposes. This is achieved by an express modification of the loan relationship rules by *s 116(4A), (8A)*. Where the reorganisation provisions would have applied but for *s 116(5)*, the provisions of *s 116* will apply to the exchange. In that case, the loan relationship is deemed to be disposed of at its market value at the date of the reorganisation, and the replacement shares are deemed to be acquired at that value: *s 116(5), (6), (8A)*. This means that, for the purpose of calculating the relevant credit or debit in the hands of the creditor, the calculation assumes that he has received an amount equal to the market value of the loan relationship at the date of the exchange. In addition, any chargeable gain or allowable loss which has previously been rolled over into the QCB will crystallise on the exchange. The profit or loss on the disposal of the old asset is brought into charge as a loan relationship credit or debit: *s 116(5)–(8A)*. Where no cash element is payable, the new asset (shares or securities) is deemed to be acquired at the time of the reorganisation or other event (ie at the time of the relevant transaction) for a sum equal to the market value of the old asset at the time of the reorganisation: *s 116(5), (6), (9)*.

11.70   The key rule in *s 116(8A)* states:

'(8A) Where subsection (6) above applies for the purposes of corporation tax in a case where the old asset consists of a qualifying corporate bond, the loan relationship rules shall have effect so as to require such debits and credits to be brought into account for the purposes of that Chapter in relation to the relevant transaction as would have been brought into account if the transaction has been a disposal of the old asset at the market value immediately before that time.'

Shares replaced by QCBs (loan relationship)

11.71   In the opposite case, if the relevant transaction involves the replacement of shares by QCBs, the 'no disposal' rule applies, but the 'same asset' rule does not. The transaction is not treated as a disposal, but any gain or loss on the old asset is calculated at that moment and held over until the bond is disposed of: *TCGA 1992, s 116(10)*. *Section 116(10)* applies where, on a reorganisation, chargeable assets (shares) are replaced by non-chargeable assets (QCBs), and it is a general rule which applies 'except in a case falling within' *s 116(9)*. *Section 116(10)* provides:

'(10) Except in a case falling within subsection (9) above, so far as it relates to the old asset and the new asset, the relevant transaction shall be treated for the purposes of this Act as not involving any disposal of the old asset but –

(a) there shall be calculated the chargeable gain or allowable loss that would have accrued if, at the time of the relevant transaction, the old asset had been disposed of for a consideration equal to its market value immediately before that transaction; and

(b) subject to subsections (12) to (14) below, the whole or a corresponding part of the chargeable gain or allowable loss mentioned in paragraph (a) above shall be deemed to accrue on a subsequent disposal of the whole or part of the new asset (in addition to any gain or loss that actually accrues on that disposal); and

(c) on that subsequent disposal, section 115 shall have effect only in relation to any gain or loss that actually accrues and not in relation to any gain or loss which is deemed to accrue by virtue of paragraph (b) above.'

Example 11.9

Invest Co plc acquired all the shares in A Ltd for £1,000 in April 2012. A Ltd is an investment company. In April 2017, it sells the A Ltd shares for £10,000. The price is payable in $5 \times £2,000$ loan notes, redeemable at one-yearly intervals from April 2018 onwards. Invest Co's accounting reference date is 31 December.

Frozen gain:	Proceeds of sale	10,000
	Acquisition price	(1,000)
	Indexation allowance: $(1,000 \times 0.10)$	(100)
	Gain	8,900
	Taxable in accounting period ending 31 December 2018:	
	$8,900/5 =$	1,180

11.72   Accordingly, where shares are exchanged for a QCB, this is not treated as a disposal of the shares, but the gain or loss is calculated as if a disposal at market value had occurred (*s 116(5), (10)*). Thus, any gain or loss held over into the QCB under *TCGA 1992, s 116(10)* will become chargeable. This deferred gain becomes chargeable under *s 116(10)(b)*, ie is crystallised, on a subsequent disposal of the QCB. This means that indexation allowance for companies is not available on any gain on the shares for the period after the exchange.

11.73   Where shares are replaced by QCBs and a deferred gain on the shares arises, but the QCB subsequently loses its value because the issuer becomes insolvent, in the case of an individual it is not possible, in the case of loans made on or after 17 March 1998, to set the loss against the deferred gain on the shares.

11.74   Where, following a replacement of shares by QCBs and calculation of the deferred gain or loss under *s 116(10)(a)*, the QCB is transferred on a no gain/no loss basis, the transferee inherits the acquisition cost and deferred gain of the transferor. This rule is given by *s 116(11)*, which states:

'(11) Subsection (10)(b) and (c) above shall not apply to any disposal falling within section 58(1), 62(4), 139, 140A, 171(1) or 172, but a person who has acquired the new asset on a disposal falling within any of those sections (and without there having been a previous disposal not falling within any of those sections or a devolution on death) shall be treated for the purposes of subsection (10)(b) and (c) above as if the new asset had been acquired by him at the same time and for the same consideration as, having regard to subsections (5) to (8) above, it was acquired by the person making the disposal.'

11.75   The situations to which this rule applies are (as the subsection indicates):

- transfers between spouses (*s 58*);

- transfer by personal representatives to a legatee (*s 62(4)*);

- transfer on a reconstruction of a business (*s 139*);

- transfer by a company resident in one EU Member State of a UK branch to a company resident in another Member State wholly in consideration of shares in the transferee company (*s 140A*);

- transfers between group companies, including a transfer between a UK resident company and a UK branch of a non-resident company (*s 171*); and

- transfer by a non-UK company of a UK branch to a UK subsidiary (*s 172*).

Example 11.10

Investor Co plc owns 90 shares in Loamshire United FC plc (L), which it acquired for £20 per share when the club was floated in March 1991. Indexation allowance is 0.722. In January 2016, M Corporation plc makes an offer for all the shares in Loamshire, with the following alternatives:

(a)   10 M shares (value £1,000) for each L share;

(b)   M plc £1,000 9% fixed rate loan stock (market value £1,000) for each share in L, redeemable in equal amounts over five years, or earlier at the option of the holder; or

(c)   cash of £1,000 per share.

Investor accepts each of these offers in respect of 30 of its shares.

Additionally, Investor holds £2,000 15% Loamshire loan stock, now worth £4,000. M plc offers for every £100 of L loan stock either:

(i)   £200 M plc 9% loan stock; or

(ii)   £200 cash.

Investor accepts each of these offers in respect of half of its loan stock.

In September 2016, Investor has lost £50,000 (including exchange differences) on corporate bonds (loan relationship deficit). Investor's financial year is the calendar year.

Tax treatment of each of these transactions is:

(a)   *Share for share exchange*

Held-over gain on Loamshire FC shares:

£30,000 − £1,033 (30 × £20 × 1.722) = £28,967

M plc shares are regarded as same asset as Loamshire shares.

(b)   *Share for loan stock exchange*

By December 2016 the new asset (M loan stock) has increased in value to £35,000 and Investor opts to redeem it.

Redemption proceeds	£35,000
Taxable amounts	
Capital gain (*TCGA 1992, s 116(10)*)	£28,967
Loan relationship credit:	
(£35,000 – £30,000)	£5,000

The corporate bond loss can be set against the loan relationship credit of £5,000. It can also be set against the capital gain as a non-trading deficit on loan relationships.

(c)   *Shares sold for cash*

There is an immediate capital gain of £28,967. The non-trading deficit on loan relationships (Russian bond loss) can be set off against this profit.

(d)   *QCB for QCB exchange*

New asset	£2,000
Acquisition cost	£1,000
Loan relationship credit (*TCGA 1992, s 116(9)*)	£1,000

(e)   *Loan stock for cash*

Loan relationship credit	£1,000

In the case of (d) and (e) also, the corporate bond loss can be set off against the gain.

Summary

Profits realised	(b)	£28,967
		£5,000
	(c)	£28,967
	(d)	£1,000
	(e)	£1,000
		£64,934
Corporate bond loss		£(50,000)
Chargeable		£14,934

Tax treatment of creditors who are individuals

11.76   If the debt is a QCB held by an individual, no gain or loss will arise (other than held-over gains or losses). In this case, *TCGA 1992, s 116(9)* provides that there will be a disposal of the debt. The 'same asset' fiction is also excluded. By reason of *s 115*, no gain or loss will arise on the debt disposal. The shares are treated as acquired for the market value of the bond immediately prior to the relevant transaction: *s 116(6)*. Thus, in the case of an individual, neither a gain nor a loss arising on a debt-equity swap involving a QCB will be recognised.

Example 11.11

X Ltd issues a QCB to Mr A in return for a loan of £100. X Ltd gets into difficulties. When the market value of the debt is £5, Mr A agrees to exchange the debt for 100 £1 ordinary shares in X Ltd. The consideration received by X Ltd is £100. The acquisition cost of Mr A's X Ltd shares is £5. Mr A cannot claim relief for the loss unless he purchased the QCB before 17 March 1998.

11.77   Where shares are exchanged for non-QCBs, the shares and loan notes are treated as the same asset for capital gains tax purposes. The effect of this is that the base cost of the shareholder in the shares is carried forward to the loan notes: *TCGA 1992, s 135*. An exchange of shares for cash or debt instruments is also treated as a conversion within *s 132*.

11.78   Where, for commercial reasons, an acquisition is made by a subsidiary of the acquiring company, a 'double rollover' is required if the shareholders of the target company are to hold over their gain. First, the shares in the target are swapped for loan notes in the takeover vehicle; then, the loan notes are exchanged for shares in the acquiring company. In the case of individuals, the loan notes must be non-QCBs, otherwise on their disposal the deferred gain on the shares will be brought into charge under *TCGA 1992, s 116(10)*.

Loan note alternatives

11.79   These rules fundamentally determine the shape and structure of transactions. The type of paper to be offered by a purchaser to a vendor will depend upon the circumstances and objectives of both sides. The issuing of paper saves the purchaser an immediate cash cost, which he may be unable to raise or pay. Equally, it spares the vendor an immediate capital gains tax charge on the inherent capital gain in his shares.

11.80   If the deal is essentially a merger, and the shareholders of the acquired company wish to remain shareholders of the merged company, they will exchange their shares in the target company for shares in the acquiring company, ie an asset whose value fluctuates.

11.81   If the transaction is essentially a sale, but both sides wish to defer a payment or receipt of cash, the acquiring company will issue loan notes to the vendor shareholders to pay for the shares in the target company. The acquiring company can finance the purchase more easily, by spreading the cost. Loan note alternatives allow shareholders in the target company to receive loan notes in the bidder in exchange for their shares, instead of receiving cash, with the result that the capital gain on the disposal of the shares is deferred until the loan notes are sold or redeemed, and the charge under *TCGA 1992, s 116(10)* is crystallised. If the loan note is primarily for the benefit of the vendor shareholders, the interest rate payable on the loan notes will be slightly below market rates and a number of redemption dates will be offered. This structure has been popular with individual shareholders, who can redeem a tranche of loan notes each year, setting the deferred capital gain on the shares which the loan notes represent against their annual capital gains tax exemption.

11.82   Where the vendor shareholder qualifies for entrepreneurs' relief under *TCGA 1992, ss 169H–169S*, different considerations arise. Post-disposal is it unlikely that he will be able to claim entrepreneurs' relief when the held-over gain comes into charge on the redemption of the loan notes, because the company will no longer meet the requirement for the relief that it is his 'personal company' within *s 169S(3)*, ie he has a 5% interest in the company. Accordingly, *s 169R* gives the vendor shareholder an option to elect out of *TCGA 1992, s 116(10)*, so that the gain becomes immediately chargeable at the 10% rate of tax provided for by entrepreneurs' relief. He thus has a choice between paying tax on the disposal at a lower rate of tax, or paying tax in the future at a higher rate of tax.

11.83   The new securities will generally be loan notes, which must have a minimum term of six months. Otherwise, they will be treated as cash, because they lack 'a structure of permanence': *Taylor Walker International Ltd v Lewis* [1997] STC 499; *Carreras Group Ltd v Stamp Comr* [2004] STC 1377.

11.84   Another factor favouring loan note alternatives on takeovers is the fact that, if the purchaser is not the parent company in a UK tax group, the issuing of ordinary shares may lead to the degrouping of the purchaser, which will cease to be a 75% subsidiary of the parent. This problem does not arise if the paper issued is fixed rate preference shares or loan notes which are normal commercial loans.

Section 136 and 139 reconstructions

11.85   A statutory definition of 'scheme of reconstruction', contained in *TCGA 1992, Sch 5AA*, applies for the purposes of *TCGA 1992, ss 136, 139*. These provisions embody the case law definition of 'reconstruction' that post-reconstruction 'substantially the same business shall be carried on and substantially the same persons shall carry it on': per Buckley J, *Re South African Supply and Cold Storage Co* [1904] 2 Ch 208. The definition also allows partitions to be classified as reconstructions: *TCGA, Sch 5AA, para 4(2)*.

11.86   'Scheme of reconstruction' means a 'scheme of merger, division or other restructuring', which meets three conditions. The conditions are:

1   the scheme involves the issue of ordinary capital by one or more companies (the 'successor company' or 'successor companies') to the holders of ordinary share capital of another company or companies (the 'original company' or 'original companies') and to no-one else; and

2   all shareholders holding ordinary shares of the original company or a particular class of shares of ordinary shares are entitled to ordinary shares of the successor company; and *either*

3A   the whole business or substantially the whole of the business of the original company is carried on by the successor company; *or*

3B   the scheme is carried out pursuant to a *CA 2006, ss 895, 899* reconstruction (or under an equivalent foreign legal procedure) and no part of the business of the original company is transferred to any other person.

11.87   A business carried on by a company controlled by another company ('control' being defined in *CTA 2010, s 1124*) is 'treated as carried on by the controlling company as well as the controlled company': *TCGA 1992, Sch 5AA, para 4(3)*. 'Ordinary share capital' is defined as in *CTA 2010, s 1119*.

11.88   The rules for share exchanges and reconstructions under *TCGA 1992, ss 135, 136, 139* include cases where the acquiring company has no share capital, eg:

• a US limited liability company (LLC) which only has participation rights;

• exchanges of units in an authorised unit trust; or

• acquisition of a business by a company limited by guarantee.

11.89   A reconstruction involves the transfer of the whole or part of the 'business' of one company to another unrelated company, without an intermediate transfer to the shareholders of the transferor company, as illustrated below.

Example 11.12

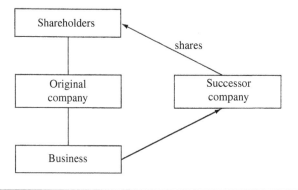

Example 11.13

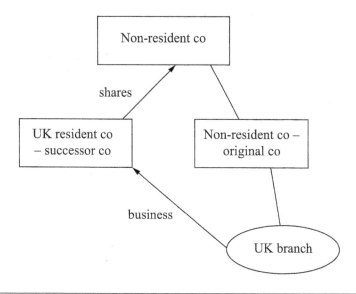

11.90   Relief is given at two levels:

(a)   if shareholders of one company are issued shares in another company, in proportion to their existing shareholdings, the original shares are treated as not having been disposed of;

(b) there is no disposal by the transferor company of the business transferred to the successor company.

11.91 *Section 139* reconstructions allow a business to be transferred on a tax-free basis where a UK transferor (original company) transfers its business to another company, in consideration solely for the assumption by the transferee (successor company) of all or part of the liabilities of the business. The relief is available where both the original company and the successor company are either a company resident in the UK at the time of the acquisition, or a UK trading branch or agency of a non-resident company: *TCGA 1992, s 139(1A)*. If, in consideration of the acquisition of the business, the successor company issues shares to the shareholders of the original company, *TCGA 1992, ss 135(3)* and *136* take effect so as to exclude any disposal by the shareholders of the original company. The 'no disposal' and 'same asset' fictions apply, so that the shareholders are not regarded as having disposed of their shares in the original company (whether those shares are retained or cancelled). The new shares issued to them by the successor company, together with their shares in the original company (if retained rather than cancelled), are, taken together, regarded as a single asset acquired at the time of the acquisition of the original shares.

11.92 *Section 136* also applies to holders of debentures and to issues of debentures, so that, in the case of corporate investors, there is no loan relationship credit under *TCGA 1992, s 116(8A), (9)*.

11.93 Typically, the transaction will take the form of one of the following:

(a) reconstruction under *Insolvency Act 1986, s 110*;

(b) a scheme under *CA 2006, ss 895, 899*;

(c) a liquidation agreement;

(d) a distribution on a demerger under *CTA 2010, s 1075*; or

(e) a purchase of own shares under *CA 2006, ss 690–723*.

11.94 An *Insolvency Act 1986, s 110* reconstruction requires the agreement of 75% of the shareholders, as does a *Companies Act, Part 26* reconstruction. The need for winding up the original company in a *TCGA 1992, s 139* reconstruction normally arises from the fact that, while the transfer of the business to the successor company will not be a 'distribution' by the original company (not being a transfer of assets by the original company 'to its members'), the issuing of shares by the successor company to the shareholders of the original company will be 'at the cost of' the original company and therefore treated as a distribution by the original company 'out of assets in respect of shares' within *CTA 2010, s 1000(1)B*. In effect, the original company is paying the successor company to make a distribution on its behalf. If, however, it is a capital distribution on a winding up, it will not be income in the hands of the original company's shareholders.

11.95 If the benefit of *TCGA 1992, s 139* is to be obtained, the original company must receive 'no part of the consideration for the transfer (otherwise than by the other company taking over the whole or part of the liabilities of the business)': *s 139(1)(c)*. The transferor's liabilities will include its debtor loan relationships. The difficulty is that they cannot be assigned, because, while a creditor can assign the benefit of an obligation, the debtor cannot force his creditor to accept someone else as debtor. The simplest course is for the successor company to put the original company in funds to pay off its liabilities.

Clearance procedure

11.96 In the case of a *TCGA 1992, s 135* share exchange, or a *s 136* reconstruction, an exchange of shares for shares or, in the case of an individual, an exchange of shares for non-QCB loan notes (which is treated as a share for share exchange) will *not* qualify for rollover relief under *s 135* 'unless the exchange or scheme of reconstruction in question is effected for bona fide commercial reasons and does not form part of a scheme or arrangements of which the main purpose or one of the main purposes, is avoidance of liability to capital gains tax or corporation tax': *s 137(1)*.

11.97 It follows that, where non-QCBs are issued to an individual in exchange for shares, it is essential to be able to demonstrate that (a) the purchaser wanted to employ loan notes to effect the purchase, and (b) there was a commercial reason for doing this, besides the advantage of tax deferral for the vendor. Where, on the evidence, it was held that the vendor or one of the vendors had an intention to take non-QCB loan notes in order to have the opportunity of redeeming them when non-resident, relief under *s 135* was not available: *Snell v R & C Comrs* [2007] STC 1279; *Coll v R & C Comrs* [2010] STC 1849. Where different vendors have different intentions, it appears that it is not possible to look at vendors separately, though that is questionable.

11.98 It follows that in order to secure rollover treatment within *TCGA 1992, s 135* (share exchange) it is normally essential to be table to demonstrate that there is no alternative means by which the transaction could be structured or that there is a commercial (non-fiscal) reason for structuring the deal in this way. *TCGA 1992, s 137* (which imposes the 'no tax avoidance' condition for qualification for the rollover treatment) does not apply if shareholders in the target company own less than 5% of the shares in it.

11.99 A clearance procedure is available under *s 138*, which should ordinarily be utilised, although in some cases time pressures and the need to seal a deal do not permit this. The clearance will be ineffective if there has not been full disclosure in the clearance application: *s 138(5)*; see *Harding v R & C Comrs* [2007] STC (SCD) 553 at [100]. An appeal to the First-tier Tribunal may be made against a refusal to grant a clearance: *s 138(4)*.

Intra-group transactions

11.100 As far as intra-group transactions are concerned:

(a) *TCGA 1992, s 18(1), (2)* provides that transactions between connected persons shall be treated as transactions made 'otherwise than by way of a bargain at arm's length' if and only if there is an acquisition and a corresponding disposal.

(b) *TCGA 1992, s 17(1)* substitutes market value as the consideration in a transaction made otherwise than by way of a bargain at arm's length.

(c) *TCGA 1992, s 17(2)* says that the market value rule is disapplied in relation to the acquisition of an asset if (but only if) both:

(i) there is no corresponding disposal of the asset; and

(ii) there is no consideration in money or money's worth or the consideration is inadequate;

eg an issue of new shares at discount to market value.

(d) *TCGA 1992, s 171(1)* says that an intra-group transfer of capital assets will be on a no gain/no loss basis, and this rule overrides *ss 17 and 18*.

(e) *TCGA 1992, s 171(3)* says that the no gain/no loss transfer rule in groups (*s 171(1)*) does not apply to a transaction falling within *ss 127–135* (but therefore will apply to a transaction falling under *s 116(9), (10)*).

(f) If a company ceases to be a member of a group and has in the previous six years acquired an asset on an intra-group disposal within *TCGA 1992, s 171(1)*, the company leaving the group, ie the transferee company, is deemed to have sold the asset for market value immediately after acquiring it, and the consequent gain or loss accrues at the later of the commencement of the accounting period during which the company leaves the group, and the time immediately after the intra-group transfer (*s 179*): see *Dunlop International AG v Pardoe (Inspector of Taxes)* [1999] STC 909.

(g) Where the transferee company leaves its group, two additional forms of relief from the degrouping charge are available: under *TCGA 1992, s 179A* the chargeable gain (or loss) can be reallocated to another company in the group; and, under *s 179B* and *Sch 7AC* the transferee company can roll over the gain in accordance with *s 152.*

(h) Disposals of substantial shareholdings (10% of ordinary share capital held for 12 months) are exempt from capital gains tax, if numerous qualifying conditions are satisfied: *TCGA 1992, s 192A, Sch 7AC.*

Example 11.14

The interlocking of these provisions can be illustrated by considering the making of a direct subsidiary into a sub-subsidiary, by the parent's (P) transferring the shares in S2 to S1 in consideration of both an issue of shares, and an issue of securities by S1 to P (*Westcott (Inspector of Taxes) v Woolcombers Ltd* [1987] STC 600 and *NAP Holdings UK Ltd v Whittles (Inspector of Taxes)* [1994] STC 979).

Two situations are envisaged:

(a) Before the transaction

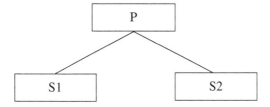

(b) After the transaction

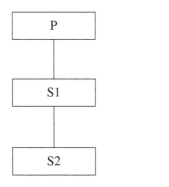

11.101   Nothing is transferred intra-group to P, so *TCGA 1992, s 171(3)* does not apply to P. P is treated as if it had never disposed of its S2 shares (original shares), which it continues to own in the form of the new S1 shares (new holding). Thus, there are two assets (the new S1 shares held by P, and the S2 shares held by S1) which, as far as P is concerned, are regarded as the same asset. The question is whether the base cost of the new S1 shares held by P is the same as the base cost of the S2 shares held by S1. *Section 171(3)* – designed to reverse *Woolcombers* – has two effects:

(a)   it prevents doubling up of gains/losses where there is a reorganisation; and

(b)   it allows deferral of taxation of the gain on the disposal of the shares in S2 outside the group until the disposal by P of its shares in S1 (in which case, under the post-2002 law, the substantial shareholdings exemption may apply).

11.102   Accordingly, where shares are transferred in exchange for the issue of shares by the acquiring company under *s 135*, the vendor-shareholder is treated as not having disposed of the shares for capital gains tax purposes under the reorganisation rule (*s 127*), the new shares acquired by the vendor in exchange for shares being deemed to have been purchased at the same time and at the original base cost of the 'original shares'. Where the share exchange is undertaken for commercial reasons, *s 171(3)* prevents the normal intra-group transfer rules applying to transfers, where share for share relief under the reorganisation rule is available. This means that:

•   P (the transferor company) is treated as exchanging shares under the reorganisation rule, so that it acquires the new S1 shares (the transferee company) for the acquisition cost of the S2 shares when those shares were acquired; and

•   S1 (the transferee company) is treated as acquiring the S2 shares at market value, thereby securing a tax-free uplift in their value.

11.103   Where no clearance is given, on the grounds that the transaction does not satisfy the *bona fide* commercial purpose test of *TCGA 1992, s 137*, the normal no gain/no loss intra-group transfer rule will apply to the transfer of shares to S1, which will therefore acquire the S2 shares at P's base cost plus indexation. The issue of S1 shares to P may still constitute a reorganisation. In that case, P acquires the shares at the base cost of the S2 shares. Otherwise, the base cost of the consideration shares to P will be the lower of the market value of the new shares and the consideration given by the transferor, ie the market value of the transferred subsidiary S2: *s 17(2)*.

11.104 If P owns S1 and S2, and P transfers its shares in S2 to S1 in consideration for an issue of loan notes by S1, the loan notes will be QCBs within *TCGA 1992, s 116*. The reorganisation rules therefore do not apply: *s 116(5)*. There is no disposal of the S2 shares (the old asset): *s 116(10)*. The deferred gain will be brought into charge on the disposal of P's S1 loan notes. As far as S1 is concerned, *ss 127–130* are excluded: *s 116(5)*. S1's acquisition of the shares in S2 is at a market value, not on a no gain/no loss basis. *Section 116(10)* says that the transaction does not involve any disposal of the shares, and this applies for all the purposes of capital gains tax, including S1's acquisition of the S2 shares, since *s 171(1)* requires both an acquisition and a corresponding disposal. Accordingly, there is no disposal of shares to which *s 171(1)* could apply (*Tax Bulletin*, Issue 26, December 1996, 372).

11.105 The operation of these rules can be further illustrated in a case where a principal company of a capital gains tax group transfers an asset with a built-in capital gain to a subsidiary.

Example 11.15

J Ltd owns land worth £10m which it acquired for £1m. J owns all the shares in K Ltd, an investment company. K has issued 2 £1 shares for £2. Indexation allowance on the land is £100,000.

J transfers the land to K:

(i)   for free;

(ii)   for the issue of 98 £1 shares in K to J issued as fully paid; or

(iii)   for the issue of an interest-free loan note by J for £7.3m.

In each case, following the transfer, either:

(a)   J sells all its K securities to an unrelated purchaser; or

(b)   K sells the land to an unrelated purchaser (P) for £10m.

In all three cases, the land will pass to K under *TCGA 1992, s 171(1)*, with the result that K's acquisition cost is £1.1m. In all three cases also, if J sells all its K securities, there will be a degrouping charge on K on the amount of £10m − £1.1m = £8.9m. Assume that the tax payable by K on the degrouping charge is £2.7m. The degrouping charge will give K an acquisition cost for the land of £10m.

(i) Free transfer

The transfer of the land from J to K is a depreciatory transaction within *TCGA 1992, s 176* (see *Whitehall Electric Investments Ltd v Owen* [2002] STC (SCD) 229).

On the sale of the K shares, J would realise a capital gain, but the amount which the purchaser would be willing to pay would be reduced to take account of the degrouping charge on K. Alternatively, if K sells the land for £10m, it realises a capital gain of £8.9m (tax payable, say £2.7m), ie its post-tax profit is £7.3m. If J sells the K shares for £7.3m, it also makes a capital gain of this amount. P's acquisition cost for the shares would be £7.3m. In consequence of the degrouping charge, K's acquisition cost for the land is £10m and the degrouping charge of £2.7m can be paid by K, financed either by a loan from P, who will have paid a reduced amount for the shares for this reason, or by selling the land to P.

(ii) Transfer to K for 98 shares

The issue of new shares by K does not involve a disposal. However, K receives consideration in money or money's worth, namely, the transfer of the land. J will acquire the shares at market value under *TCGA 1992, s 17(1)*. The principle in *Stanton (Inspector of Taxes) v Drayton Commercial Investment Co Ltd* [1982] STC 585 will not apply in an intra-group context, the principle being that where a company issues shares as fully paid, for consideration which the company agrees to accept as representing in money's worth the nominal value of the shares, the consideration given for the new shares will be the price at which the shares are issued, namely, their par value plus any amount credited to share premium account. J can sell the K shares without realising a capital gain, but this will trigger a degrouping charge in K.

(iii) Transfer to K for £7.3m interest-free loan note

J's acquisition cost for the loan notes will be £7.3m. Assuming that the sale consideration for the shares and loan notes is attributed entirely to the loan notes, J will make no capital gain on the shares and incur no loan relationship credit on the assignment of the loan notes. P's acquisition cost for the shares is £2 and for the loan notes £7.3m. If J does not sell the K securities, but instead K sells the land for £10m, it makes a taxable gain of £8.9m (post-tax proceeds £7.3m, with which it can repay the J loan note).

Earn-outs

11.106 It is often the case that, on a company acquisition, part of the purchase price is an earn-out right, ie it is payable in the future by reference to the financial performance of the acquired company subsequent to the acquisition. If the amount of the additional payment is certain, and the only question is whether or not it will in fact become payable, this constitutes additional consideration for the shares, and must be treated as received on the disposal under *TCGA 1992, s 48*, without any discount for postponement. If the additional amount does not become payable or is irrecoverable, an adjustment will be made to the calculation of the gain on the original disposal: *Goodbrand (Inspector of Taxes) v Loffland Bros North Sea Inc* [1998] STC 930.

11.107 In the more usual case, the earn-out is contingent both as to amount and as to payment: *Marson (Inspector of Taxes) v Marriage* [1980] STC 177. In those circumstances, *Marren v Ingles* [1980] STC 500 establishes that, on a disposal of shares, an earn-out element is a separate chargeable asset, which has to be valued at the date of the disposal of the shares. When payments are received in respect of the separate earn-out asset, this constitutes a disposal or part disposal of that asset. This disposal does not qualify for entrepreneurs' relief.

11.108 An earn-out must be distinguished from consideration which is contingent. If consideration is ascertainable but contingent, it is taxed as if immediately receivable under *TCGA 1992, s 48*, with provision for later adjustment if it is not in fact received. If consideration is both contingent and unascertainable, it constitutes the receipt of a new asset, a *Marren v Ingles* right. The distinction between the two situations is considered in HMRC Capital Gains Manual at CG14880. Earn-outs will generally be calculated by reference to future profits. The presence of a maximum amount, an upper limit, will not necessarily cause the potential receipt to be ascertainable. If the earn-out consideration is both contingent and unascertainable, a base cost will need to be allocated to the new *chose in action* which the vendor obtains. This may be nil. If the earn-out is to be paid in cash, there will be a disposal or part disposal of the *chose in action* each time a payment is received. If a loss arises, relief is available against the earlier gain under *ss 279A–279D*.

11.109 'Earn-out right' is defined in *TCGA 1992, s 138A(1)* and this definition only applies to additional consideration which is 'unascertainable at the time when the right is conferred'. 'Unascertainable' is, in turn, defined in *s 138A(7)* as meaning 'made referable to matters relating to any business or assets' of a company and those matters are uncertain on account of future business or assets being included in them.

11.110 Where the earn-out right is consideration for the transfer of shares or securities (the old securities), and can only be satisfied by the issue to the transferor of shares or securities in another company (the new securities), *TCGA 1992, s 138A* provides that the earn-out right itself is treated as a security, and the gain rolled into that security can in turn be rolled into the shares or debentures received in satisfaction of that right. The securities will generally be loan notes, which must have a minimum term of six months. Otherwise, they will be treated as cash, because they lack 'a structure of permanence': see **11.83**. The earn-out right is a 'security' within *s 132* which 'is incapable of being a qualifying corporate bond' (*s 138A(3)*). The earn-out right becomes a notional security, and there is then a double conversion. The original shares are converted into the new holding (earn-out right, deemed to be a non-QCB security); on payment, the notional security is then converted into a security.

11.111   Since *TCGA 1992, s 138A* deems the earn-out right to represent a non-QCB security, the rules in *s 135* on share exchanges are brought into play, with the deemed security being exchanged as part of the consideration for the vendor's shares. The relevant part of the base cost of the vendor's original shares (as apportioned for the initial consideration) becomes the base value of the deemed security acquired at the same time as the original shares under the reorganisation rule in *s 127*. The deemed non-QCB security is treated in the same way as shares. The discharge of an earn-out right by the issue of new securities is treated as a conversion within *s 132*.

11.112   Securities obtained through the exercise of an earn-out right are unlikely to qualify for entrepreneurs' relief, because they will not be securities in the holder's 'personal' company: *TCGA 1992, s 169S(3)*. The effect of the relief (where, and to the extent, applicable) is to reduce the rate of capital gains tax from 20% (2016/2017) to 10%.

11.113   The *TCGA 1992, s 138A* treatment is automatic, unless an election is made to disapply it. The election must be made by the first anniversary of the 31 January following the tax year in which the earn-out right was conferred. This can be advantageous in any of the following situations:

• disposals prior to 6 April 2008 of assets qualifying for business asset taper relief; or

• to individuals whose shares qualified for entrepreneurs' relief prior to the initial disposal but not post-deal; or

• where the old securities are standing at a loss; or

• where the vendor has current year losses or an annual exemption.

11.114   In drafting share sale agreements the level of earn-out must be geared to the business or assets to which the right relates. It cannot be geared to an external index, such as the FTSE 100. An option to choose between cash and securities does not make the amount of consideration unascertainable. If the holder has an option to choose between cash and securities when the earn-out right becomes payable, he can bring himself within the earn-out rules by making an irrevocable election to take securities at the time of the share sale.

11.115 The amendment of an earn-out after it has been acquired can be treated as a disposal of the original earn-out right for a new *chose in action*. This, in turn, may be an earn-out right, falling within *TCGA 1992, s 138A*.

Example 11.16

Mr A sells his shares in a trading company, X Ltd (acquisition cost £150 in April 2004), for £5,000 in 2016/2017, plus the right to receive loan notes in 2013/2014, which are valued at £10,000. In 2017/2018, the value of loan notes received is £15,000.

2016/2017

Cash received	5,000
Base cost: 5,000/15,000 × 150	(50)
Capital gain	4,950
Entrepreneurs' relief: tax at 10%	495

2017/2018

Loan notes received	15,000
Acquisition cost: 150 – 50	(100)
Capital gain	14,900
Tax @ 20%	2,980

11.116 Earn-outs may also have income tax implications if the earn-out represents not just an additional element of sale proceeds but an element of reward for services in the performance period. *ITEPA 2003, s 408(8)* defines 'securities option' as 'a right to acquire securities'. Where the earn-out right is acquired by reason of employment or prospective employment (as defined by *ITEPA 2003, s 471*), the gain may be liable to income tax rather than capital gains tax. The earn-out right will, however, be regarded as further consideration for the share sale rather than remuneration if the sale agreement makes this clear, and (where the seller continues to work for the company) the earn-out targets relate to the performance of the acquired company rather than the satisfaction of any personal targets by the seller.

11.117 HMRC may seek to treat consideration received on an earn-out as employment earnings, ie earnings from current employment, not a gain from a previous disposal of an asset. The approach is set out in the HMRC Employment

Related Securities Manual at ERSM110940. The matters to which HMRC will have regard are as follows:

(a)   The sale agreement demonstrates that the earn-out is part of the valuable consideration given for the securities of the company.

(b)   The value received from the earn-out reflects the value of the securities sold.

(c)   When the vendor continues to work for the target company, he is fully remunerated and the earn-out amounts do not constitute payment for employment.

(d)   When the vendor continues to be employed, the earn-out is not conditional on future employment beyond a reasonable requirement to protect the value of the business being sold.

(e)   When the vendor continues to work in the business being sold, there are no personal performance targets incorporated in the earn-out right.

(f)   Those not continuing in employment receive the earn-out on the same terms as those continuing.

(g)   Evidence as to the negotiations on the level of earn-out.

(h)   Any clearances under *TCGA 1992, s 138* or *ITA 2007, s 701.*

Novation

11.118   While rights can be transferred by assignment under the *Law of Property Act 1925, s 136*, liabilities can only be transferred with the consent of the creditor. This involves the making of a new contract, a process called novation. When a contract is novated, the original agreement is discharged and replaced by a new agreement between different parties. Novation acts as a mechanism whereby the burden of a contract can be transferred to another party. This is in contrast to assignment, which can be used to transfer rights but not liabilities. An assignment is a bipartite transaction; a novation is a tripartite transaction: *Collins v Addies* [1991] STC 445 at 453. The benefit of a contract can be assigned, but the burden of a contract can only be novated. Where the creditor assigns his right of payment, the loan relationship remains undisturbed. Sometimes, one debtor is substituted for another, eg a loan agreement provides for one group company to be substituted for another. Such a transaction can only be effected by novation, ie a new contract in which the creditor agrees to accept the substituted debtor. Novation releases the original liability, and replaces it with a new liability owed by a different lender. Novation of debt comprises two elements: (a) the annulment of one debt; and (b) the creation of a substituted debt in its place. This is stated in *Re United Railways of Havana and Regla Warehouses Ltd* [1960] Ch 52 at 58. Hence the discharge of one borrower and the substitution of a new borrower involves the redemption of the original debt and creation of a new one. Has the liability been transferred or discharged? In many cases, this will make no practical difference, eg intra-group transactions, where the loan relationship is transferred between companies in the same capital gains tax group on a no gain/no loss basis: *CTA 2009, s 336*.

11.119 A contractual novation (the substitution of one party to a contract by another) will normally involve the discharge of one debtor and the creation of a new, replacement loan relationship.

Example 11.17

Mr Jones holds 100 ordinary shares in Jones Ltd, which have a base cost of £100. Mr Jones sells his shares to Acquirer Ltd for non-QCB loan notes with a nominal value of £5,000 redeemable after five years. After two years, Mr Jones agrees that a related company, Acquirer Holdings Ltd, may be substituted as debtor. At that point, Mr Jones is treated as selling his shares for £5,000, and the rolled-over gain is brought into charge.

11.120 In some cases, it is possible to substitute a different debtor without falling over the edge into a novation, with its attendant tax consequences. HMRC Capital Gains Manual at CG53535 accordingly states:

'Sometimes the original debtor under a debt agreement is replaced by a substitute debtor, who takes on the original debtor's liabilities.

If this takes place in accordance with a "substitution of debtor" clause which was included in the terms of the debt instrument *at the time it was originally issued*, you may accept the substitution simply as performance of the original terms. Essentially, in these cases, the debt continues. The person holding the debt (the creditor) does not make any disposal of the debt at the time of substitution.

If there was no such clause in the debt as originally issued, or the substitution was outside the terms of the clause, a change of debtor may amount to a novation – that is, the creation of a new debt at the time of the change. In such cases the creditor would be treated as having disposed of the original debt asset at that time.' (emphasis supplied)

11.121 The statement in the Capital Gains Manual reflects the law as outlined in *Greene King No 1 Ltd v Adie* [2005] STC (SCD) 398:

(a)   GK Ltd created two secured debentures to external lenders which paid fixed interest above market rates, and whose fair value (£53.3m) exceeded their book value (£42m).

(b)   GK plc became the parent of GK Ltd and it was decided to transfer GK Ltd's debt liabilities to GK plc. For accounting purposes, GK plc took over the debentures at their fair value. In the novation agreement, GK Ltd became indebted to GK plc in the sum of £53.3m.

(c)   GK Ltd claimed a non-trading loan relationship debit of £11.3m (ie the excess of the fair value over the book value of the liabilities).

(d)   The law at the time (*FA 1996, Sch 9, para 12(2)*) provided that, on an intra-group transfer of a loan relationship, credits and debts arising from the transaction would be disregarded, if the transferee was substituted for the debtor.

11.122   The appellant's arguments were summarised in these terms:

'[GL plc] did not replace the appellant as a party to a loan relationship within para 12 either directly or indirectly. The novation released the liability of the appellant, extinguishing its debts … there was not an acquisition by [GK plc] of liabilities "under" the existing loan relationship.'

It was held that this provision could not apply, because the debt was cancelled and replaced. Novation involved the cancellation of one debt and the creation of a new debt, not a transfer of indebtedness.

11.123   The tribunal held at [51] that GK plc was not substituted for GK Ltd:

'We hold that since novation results in a new and distinct legal relationship there was no replacement of the appellant by [GK plc] as a party to the prior loan relationships.'

11.124   Under the version of *FA 1996, Sch 9, para 12* as it applied in 1999/2000, in order for GK plc to acquire the debt at its value in GK Ltd's books, it had to replace GK Ltd as debtor. Accordingly, it was successfully argued that this provision could not apply, because novation involved the cancellation of one debt and creation of a new debt, not a transfer of indebtedness. *FA 1996, Sch 9, para 12* was amended with effect from 31 March 2000 to apply not only to 'related transactions' between companies in the same group (eg a transfer of a loan asset) but also to 'a series of transactions having the same effect as a related transaction' (eg a novation of a liability). The corresponding provision is now *CTA 2009, s 336(3)*.

Chapter 12

Special Companies

Overview

12.1   This chapter deals with:

- Investment companies

- Approved investment trusts

- Venture capital trusts

- Venture capital limited partnerships

- Authorised unit trusts

- Open-ended investment companies

- Offshore funds

- Insurance companies

- Controlled foreign companies

- Corporate partnerships

- Industrial and provident societies

Investment companies

12.2   Interest payable by or to investment companies is brought within the scope of *CTA 2010, ss 677–692* which prevent carry-forward of excess management expenses in certain cases following a change of ownership. These measures apply to deny relief for losses arising from interest accrued in periods prior to the change of ownership for accrued but unpaid interest.

12.3   *Section 677* applies where, following a change of ownership, there is:

(a)   a significant increase in the company's capital;

(b)   a major change in the nature or conduct of the business carried on by the company within a six-year period commencing three years before the change of ownership; or

(c)   a considerable revival in the business where it had previously become small or negligible.

12.4   *Section 692* applies where, after the change of ownership, an asset is transferred on a no gain/no loss basis intra-group and then sold.

12.5   The effect of these rules is to restrict the available loan relationship debits brought forward in respect of the company's loan relationships arising pre-change of ownership. This possibility arises because *s 679(1)* says:

> 'This section shall have effect for the purpose of restricting the debits to be brought into account for the purposes of Part 5 of CTA 2009 (loan relationships) in respect of the company's loan relationships.'

12.6   Where *s 679* applies, the accounting period in which the change of ownership occurs is divided into two notional accounting periods, one running from the start of the period to the date of the change of ownership, the other from that date to the normal end of the accounting period. Loan relationship debits accruing for the accounting period are apportioned between the two notional accounting periods on a time basis. Loan relationship debits accruing before the change of ownership cannot be deducted in accounting periods following the change of ownership to the extent that they exceed profits for the accounting period ending in the change of ownership.

Approved investment trusts

12.7   Investment trusts are a long-established form of investment vehicle. Confusingly, they are not trusts but companies. The investor buys shares in the investment trust, which is a listed company. The investment trust in turn uses the funds raised to hold a diversified range of securities. The value of the shares held by the investor is governed by the market price of the shares, rather than the value of the underlying assets. Tax law uses the term 'investment trust' where company law uses the term 'investment company': *CA 2006, s 833*. This is because 'investment company' has a much wider meaning for tax law purposes than it has for company law purposes.

12.8   Approved investment trusts (*CTA 2010, ss 1158–1159*) are approved under the *Investment Trust (Approved Company) (Tax) Regulations 2011, SI 2011/2999*. An approved investment trust (AIT) cannot be a close company. AITs, being companies, come within the derivative contracts rules and the loan relationship rules, but on a special accounting basis: *CTA 2010, s 1160*.

For tax purposes, investment trusts must follow the 'main method', set out in the SORP: Financial Statements of Investment Trust Companies and Venture Capital Trusts ('AIC SORP') of January 2015: *Investment Trusts (Approval of Accounting Methods for Creditor Relationships) Order 2001, SI 2001/391.* As companies, investment trusts are within the charge to corporation tax but are exempt from corporation tax on capital gains: *TCGA 1992, s 100(1).* As a condition of exemption from corporation tax on capital gains, approved investment trusts may not retain more than 15% of their income in an accounting period: *SI 2011/2999, reg 19.* Income from creditor loan relationships is determined without a deduction for debits on debtor relationships: *reg 20.*

12.9   The SORP requires a single statement of total comprehensive income, in accordance with FRS 102, para 5.2 ('single statement approach'). The income statement is divided into three columns:

Revenue   Capital   Total

12.10   The former rule that capital profits are non-distributable has been abolished. Realised capital profits may be distributed by way of dividend. 'Realised' is defined in ICAEW Tech 02/10. Changes in fair values may be realised profits for these purposes. Profits and losses of a capital nature on loan relationships are not brought into charge: *CTA 2009, s 395.* 'Profits or losses of a capital nature' means profits or losses accounted for through the capital column of the statement of comprehensive income.

12.11   For derivatives contracts, *CTA 2009, s 637* provides a similar rule. Sums arising from reduction of share capital do not appear in the comprehensive income statement. The investment trusts SORP requires that the effective yield on debt securities should be recognised as income and accrued over the life of the instrument, on the assumption that it will be held to maturity. Thus, purchased premiums and discounts will be amortised to income account over the life of the security on an effective yield basis. Actual returns in excess of the expected yield will be capital profits and not subject to tax in the fund.

Example 12.1

Investment trust buys a bond for £90 with ten years to maturity. After three years, the bond is sold for £95.

Year	Accrued/taxable income	Value at year end (£)	Capital profit (£)
1	1	91	
2	1	92	
3	1	93	2

As above, but the bond is purchased for £110, and sold after two years for £106.

Year	Accrued/taxable income	Value at year end (£)	Capital profit (£)
1	(1)	109	
2	(1)	108	(2)

Venture capital trusts

12.12   The venture capital trust (VCT) regime largely follows the tax law and company law rules for investment trusts: *CTA 2009, ss 396, 638*. The AIC SORP also covers VCTs. Investment trusts can only hold listed shares and securities. VCTs were introduced by *FA 1995* (a) to allow individuals to invest in unlisted UK companies on a diversified basis, and so (b) to facilitate the raising of capital by such companies.

Venture capital limited partnerships

12.13   Venture capital limited partnerships are associations of passive investors (the limited partners) and an investment manager (the general partner) set up under the *Limited Partnerships Act 1907*, which are used as vehicles for raising funds wholly or partly for investment in unquoted companies. In a limited partnership, so long as one partner has unlimited liability, the other partners may have their liability limited to the extent of the sums severally contributed to the firm's capital. The partner with unlimited liability is called the general partner, but the general partner is invariably a limited liability company, so his liability is also limited. The limited partners are often individuals. Most venture capital limited partnerships will be collective investment schemes ('CIS limited partnership') within the *Financial Services and Markets Act 2000, s 235*.

12.14   The tax treatment of these groups of persons was agreed in a statement approved by the Inland Revenue and Department of Trade and Industry, and issued by the British Venture Capital Association on 26 May 1987. The 1987 Guidelines were modified by a revised statement of 22 July 2003 ([2003] STI 1364–1369). This was to take account of *ITEPA 2003, s 421B(3)*, which deems securities to be employment related if the right to acquire them is made available by the employer or a person connected with the employer. 'Carried interest' means an interest in a venture capital partnership which entitles the holder to participate in 'super profits' made by the fund which are allocated to employees and directors of the general partner ('carried interest holders'). Where the payment represents a return on investments, rather than a reward for services, the security acquired by a carried interest holder will be regarded as a unit in a collective investment scheme, under *ITEPA 2003, s 420(1)(c)*. The tax treatment of carried interest is regulated by *ITA 2007, ss 809EZA–809FZZ* (extensively amended by *FA 2016, ss 36, 37*). These provisions impose an income tax charge on disguised management fees or management fees, unless the amounts constitute a return on investment-based carried interest (IBCI). Carried interest is subject to capital gains tax in its entirety if the average holding period for an investment is 40 months.

12.15 Debt financing provided by venture capital limited partnerships to the companies which they finance will generally fall within the transfer pricing rules. These rules require adjustments to make provisions between connected enterprises conform to an arm's-length standard where (*TIOPA 2010, ss 161, 162*):

(a) the lender and the other persons acted together in relation to such arrangements; and

(b) the requisite degree of connection would be satisfied if all the rights and powers of the other persons were attributed to the lender.

12.16 'Acting together' involves shareholders or partners participating 'in collective or co-ordinated transactions which may also involve third parties such as lenders'. 'Acting together' only matters if the result differs from an arm's-length standard, but the legislation establishes a presumption that, where the parties have 'acted together', the result will differ from an arm's-length standard. P and other persons who 'acted together' in relation to financing arrangements of A are all regarded as indirectly participating in the management, control or capital of A. Likewise, Q and other persons acting together with him in relation to financing arrangements of B are all regarded as indirectly participating in the management, control or capital of each of B and another affected person, if Q and the other persons acting together would have controlled both B and the other affected person. Accordingly, the interests of venture capital partners will be aggregated for transfer pricing purposes.

12.17 No compensating adjustment is available in respect of borrowing caught by *TIOPA 2010, ss 161, 162* if the debt is guaranteed by a person with whom the borrower has a 'participatory relationship'. A participatory relationship exists between two parties if one is indirectly participating in the management, control or capital of the other. In any case, if the investor is not resident in the UK, no compensating adjustments are available.

Authorised unit trusts/OEICs

12.18 The taxation of authorised unit trusts and open-ended investment companies is mainly governed by the *Authorised Investment Funds (Tax) Regulations 2006, SI 2006/964* (the '*AIF Regulations*'). 'Authorised investment funds' are defined as:

● open-ended investment companies (OEICs), and

● authorised unit trusts (AUTs).

12.19   Both are open-ended investment companies, in that the fund issues shares (OEICs) or units (AUTs) which represent the value of its assets, which the investor can redeem at any time. The fund therefore has to maintain sufficient cash and highly liquid assets in order to meet redemptions. Payment difficulties may arise if the fund is insufficiently liquid, or experiences an abnormal number of redemptions.

12.20   'Unit trust scheme' is defined in *FSMA 2000, s 237*. The trustees of an AUT are treated as a company, and unit holders as shareholders: *CTA 2010, ss 610, 617*. AUTs have now largely been replaced by OEICs, whose investors are actual shareholders, albeit in a company of a special kind: *CTA 2009, s 488; CTA 2010, ss 613–615*. An OEIC is a collective investment scheme (within the undertakings for collective investment in transferable securities (UCITS) Directive 2009/65/EC ('UCITS V') and *FSMA 2000, s 235*) which has a variable share capital, ie shareholders can freely redeem their shares and the company can issue new shares without limit. Uniquely within UK company law, it can issue shares without a par value. In principle, OEICs can only invest in transferable securities (ie listed securities). The investors hold shares in the company rather than units in a unit trust. The company will, on application, redeem or buy back these shares. OEICs are particularly adapted to serve as umbrella funds (ie a single collective investment scheme with several sub-funds, each of which concentrates on a different type of underlying investment), because different classes of shares relating to different sub-funds can be issued. Shareholders can then exchange shares in one sub-fund for shares in another.

12.21   OEICs are treated on the same basis as authorised unit trusts for corporation, income and capital gains tax purposes. AUTs and OEICs are within the loan relationship and derivative contracts rules; but, as with AITs, their 'capital profits and losses' are excluded from both the loan relationship and the derivative contracts rules: *CTA 2009, s 490; AIF Regulations, regs 10, 12*. These are identified by reference to the accounts of the fund drawn up in accordance with the SORP for AUTs and OEICs respectively. 'Capital profits and losses' fall under the headings:

- net gains/losses on investments; and

- other gains/losses.

12.22   Accordingly, the 'all income' treatment does not apply. This is because gains on disposals of OEIC shares or AUIT units are subject to capital gains tax. The rules for loan relationships and derivative contracts within AUTs and OEICs are explained in *Tax Bulletin*, Issue 60, August 2002, 948–950.

12.23   Accordingly:

- OEICs are liable to corporation tax at the basic rate of income tax (*ITA 2007, s 6; CTA 2010, ss 614, 618*).

- OEICs are exempt from corporation tax on capital gains (*TCGA 1992, s 100*).

- Distributions to shareholders can be in the form of dividends or interest distributions.

12.24 AUTs and OEICs remain liable to a special rate of corporation tax equal to the basic rate of income tax (20%): *CTA 2010, ss 614, 618*. They are exempt from corporation tax on capital gains. All income in the authorised unit trust is taxed and then distributed. There are two types of distribution by authorised unit trusts:

(a) dividends; and

(b) interest.

12.25 Gilt and bond funds can only pay interest distributions. The unit trust SORP limits the ability of authorised unit trusts to use derivatives to produce returns equivalent to interest; see Inland Revenue Press Release, 12 July 1996. Private investors are taxed as if they were paid a dividend by a company. There is capital gains tax on disposals of units or shares. Gilt and bond unit trusts retain the disadvantage that, whereas gilts and bonds held directly by individuals and trustees are exempt from capital gains tax (*TCGA 1992, s 115*), units in collective investment schemes are treated as shares and so liable to capital gains tax on disposal.

12.26 Where a company holds:

(a) units in an AUT;

(b) shares in an OEIC; or

(c) an interest in an offshore fund (as defined in *TIOPA 2010, ss 355–363*);

and the investment fund fails at any time in the year the 'qualifying investments test', the investment is treated as a creditor loan relationship: *CTA 2009, s 490*.

12.27 'Qualifying investments' are gilts, bonds and cash: *CTA 2009, s 494*. The 'qualifying investments test' requires that the fund in question should not hold qualifying investments whose market value exceeds 60% of the fund's investments: *s 493*. The purpose of this provision is to prevent corporate investors disguising interest as dividends via an investment fund holding. Life insurance companies holding an authorised unit trust which passes the non-qualifying investments test are subject to an annual deemed disposal, but within the capital gains tax rules, with net gains and losses being spread over seven years.

12.28 Where a relevant holding fails the qualifying investments test in one accounting period but not in another, the rules apply in the former period but not in the latter. For capital gains tax purposes, there is a disposal of the relevant holding by the company at the end of the first accounting period, and any profit or loss is immediately chargeable, except to the extent to which it constitutes a QCB (which it almost invariably will), in which case the gain is exempt. The base cost of the holding to be carried forward for capital gains tax purposes is the market value of the holding at the end of the previous accounting period.

12.29   When a relevant holding fails the test in the first accounting period, but passes it in the second, for companies other than life insurance companies the rule in *TCGA 1992, s 116(10)* will apply, ie there is a deemed disposal at the end of the first accounting period, but it is treated as not involving a disposal, and the frozen gain or loss is held over and carried forward until the new holding is disposed of. Again, the market value at the end of the first accounting period is the opening valuation for the fair value basis. If the investor is a life insurance company, there is a deemed disposal at the end of the first accounting period under *TCGA 1992, s 212*, and the market value becomes the opening fair value.

12.30   Where a company is party to a 'relevant contract' (as defined by *CTA 2009, s 577*) which is not a 'derivative contract' (as defined by *s 576*), and the underlying subject matter of the contract is (a) rights under an AUT, (b) shares in an OEIC, or (c) a 'relevant interest' in an offshore fund, the relevant contract is treated as a derivative contract and must be accounted for on a fair value basis: *CTA 2009, s 587*.

Offshore funds

12.31   'Offshore fund' is defined in *TIOPA 2010, ss 354–363*. The basic concept is that of a fund which would be a 'collective investment scheme' as defined by *FSMA 2000, s 235* if resident in the UK, but which is not resident in the UK. *TIOPA 2010* instead adopts a separate definition of 'mutual fund'. The essential attributes of a mutual fund are as follows (*TIOPA 2010, ss 355, 356*):

(a)   it is constituted as a non-resident company;

(b)   the contributions of the investors are pooled;

(c)   the investors do not have day-to-day control of the management of the property;

(d)   the investments acquired with the pooled contributions are managed as a whole by the operator of the scheme; and

(e)   an investor can realise his investments by reference to the net asset value of the fund (or sub-fund) as a whole.

12.32   The concern of HMRC is that an offshore fund may roll up untaxed income, thereby enabling the UK investors to escape income tax on such returns, only paying capital gains tax on the disposal of units. The tax policy is to tax such gains as income. Offshore funds are divided into two categories: reporting; and non-reporting. A reporting fund is a fund which meets the conditions set out in the *Offshore Funds (Tax) Regulations 2009, SI 2009/3001*. A non-reporting fund is any offshore fund which is not a reporting fund. In the case of reporting funds, income is taxed on the participants as it accrues in the fund, whether or not it is distributed. In the case of a non-reporting fund, all distributions and disposals of units are taxed as income. No liability arises under these provisions if the participant is required to treat his interest in the fund as a loan relationship or derivative contract: *reg 25*.

Insurance companies

12.33   Insurance companies provide many different types of insurance, but carry on a single trade of insurance. The income of life insurance companies largely arises from the return on investments. Accordingly, since 1915, such companies have been taxed either as investment companies or as trading companies. General insurance and life insurance are separate trades for tax purposes. The history of the taxation of life insurance companies is set out by Lord Walker in *Scottish Widows plc v R & C Comrs* [2011] STC 2171 at [40]–[48].

12.34   Insurance companies may be proprietary (shareholder owned) or mutual (member owned). Companies normally carry on different categories of insurance business, subject to different computational rules. Proprietary insurance companies are taxed on the 'I minus E' basis (gross investment income [I] less management expenses [E], hence 'I minus E basis').

12.35   *Finance Act 2012, ss 55–149* contain a comprehensive regime for the taxation of life insurance companies. *Sections 68, 69* give precedence to the I – E charge for profits of the basic life assurance and general annuity business (BLAGAB) carried on by an insurance company over the general charge to corporation tax on trade profits. Under *s 71* non-BLAGAB long-term business is subject to the general charge to corporation tax on trade profits minus E basis.

12.36   UK insurance companies and mutuals are subject to the loan relationship and derivative contracts rules. However, special rules apply to insurance companies under *CTA 2009, ss 386–394*, to take account of the particular features of insurance business. *Finance Act 2012, s 88* ensures that for the purposes of the I – E calculation the rules on non-trading loan relationships and derivative contracts apply. The following activities are treated as non-trading (*CTA 2009, s 298(3)*):

- mutual insurance;

- mutual business other than life assurance business; or

- basic life assurance and general annuity business.

12.37   There are special provisions for a non-trading deficit on loan relationships for BLAGAB and general annuity business: *CTA 2009, ss 387–391*. For the purposes of the I – E basis, credits and debits from loan relationships are to be included in the calculation as non-trading items. Any deficit will, in the first instance, be set against any net income and gains of the deficit period referable to the relevant category of insurance business. Subject thereto, carry-back is allowed on a last in/first out (LIFO) basis of net deficits against the company's three previous accounting periods' adjusted net profits arising from its loan relationships. The offset in the previous accounting periods is restricted to the adjusted eligible profit for that period, namely the non-trading profits and gains arising from the company's loan relationships and attributable to the category of business concerned, as reduced by the management expenses and charges attributable to that category to the extent that they are not covered by other income and gains. Claims for a set-off against profits of the same accounting period must be made within two years of the end of the accounting period in question. Unrelieved profits are otherwise carried forward as 'expenses' (E). Where a company is required to compute its profits on a trading basis, either for the company as a whole or for a particular category of business, in the case of debtor relationships, credits will be treated as receipts of the trade and debits as expenses.

12.38   For the purpose of calculating exchange gains and losses, in the case of a company carrying on insurance business, deferred acquisition costs (within the *Large and Medium-sized Companies and Groups (Accounts and Reports) Regulations 2008, SI 2008/410, Sch 3, Part 1, para 13*) and provisions for unearned premiums or unexpired risks are treated as money debts: *CTA 2009, s 483(6)*.

12.39   An insurance company, whether life or general, may fair value investments in its balance sheet, without having to take changes in fair values into its income statement: *SI 2008/410, Sch 3, Part 2, paras 18, 32–35*. In these circumstances, the company may use the amortised cost basis for its creditor loan relationships, as well as its debtor loan relationships. Insurance companies have an option to elect irrevocably for amortised cost basis for debt assets linked to BLAGAB and for assets of the long-term business fund not linked to a particular category of insurance.

12.40   Where an insurance company is carrying on BLAGAB business, and is a party to a creditor loan relationship with a connected company linked to that business, the connection is ignored, so that it need not use amortised cost accounting: *CTA 2009, ss 468–471*. The asset must be either listed on a recognised stock exchange or redeemable within 12 months of issue. It must be available to other investors, and not more than 30% of the debt security must be in the ownership of a connected person for more than three months in a year.

12.41 The 'continuity of treatment' rules (*CTA 2009, ss 335–337*) apply where an insurance company transfers the whole or part of its long-term business to another insurance company or there is a 'qualifying overseas transfer', ie where one of the companies is an overseas life insurance company: *s 337*. The no gain/no loss treatment on intra-group transfers of assets does not apply where an asset is transferred into or from the long-term business fund of an insurance company, or where an asset is held by the transferor for one class of business and by the transferee for another class of business.

12.42 The loan relationship rules do not apply to assets and liabilities of Lloyd's corporate members' premium trust funds: *CTA 2009, s 392*.

Non-corporates

12.43 *ITTOIA 2005, ss 427–460* apply to individuals, trustees and personal representatives, and trustees of an unauthorised unit trust, who acquire deeply discounted securities. Persons to whom these rules apply are only taxed on discounts on a realisations basis. Where a person realises a profit on a deeply discounted security, he is charged to income tax as savings and investment income. A profit is realised if the amount paid to the holder on redemption or transfer of the security exceeds his acquisition cost: *s 439*. When a transfer takes place between connected persons, or in certain other circumstances, it is treated as taking place for market value: *s 440*. 'Connection' is defined in accordance with *ITA 2007, s 993* (ie the narrower test of connection).

12.44 Where a loss arises on a transfer of a deeply discounted security to a connected person, under *ITTOIA 2005, s 456*, that loss is not allowable for tax purposes where:

(a)   the transferor has held the security since issue;

(b)   the amount paid to acquire the security on issue exceeded its market value; and

(c)   the issuer was connected with the transferor, a close company or controlled by the transferor and other persons who also subscribe for such securities.

12.45 Under the rules as originally enacted in *FA 1996, Sch 13*, relief could be claimed against income in respect of a loss sustained on the disposal of a deeply discounted security. This gave rise to a number of avoidance schemes. In *Campbell v IRC* [2004] STC (SCD) 396:

1   Mr C formed a company, C Ltd;

2   Mr C borrowed £3.75m which he used to subscribe for deeply discounted securities issued by C Ltd; C Ltd then invested these funds;

3   Mr C gifted the loan notes to Mrs C, the market value of the loan notes being £2.5m;

4   Mr C claimed loss relief of £(3.75m – 2.5m) = 1.25m, which he set against his taxable income; and

5   C Ltd redeemed loan notes to the value of £368,150.

12.46   The Special Commissioners held that the main purpose of the formation of the company and issue of loan notes was to secure a tax advantage, and that the gift to Mrs C was wholly tax-motivated. They further held that 'loss' in the legislation was an artificial, legal concept and that Mr C had sustained a loss within the meaning of the Act:

> '89. Here, the amount paid by the Appellant in respect of the Loan Notes exceeded the amount which he was treated as obtaining on the transfer to his wife. It follows that by the express words of para 2(2) he sustained a loss for the purpose of Sch 13.'

12.47   Such schemes were countered by introducing *FA 1996, Sch 13, para 9A* with effect from 26 March 2002 (now *ITTOIA 2005, s 456*). This says that a loss which arises on a transfer to a connected person is not allowable for income tax purposes.

Controlled foreign companies

12.48   See **10.69–10.71**. A controlled foreign company (CFC) is a non-resident company controlled by UK resident participators, and which is subject to 'a lower level of taxation', ie the local tax is less than three-quarters of the UK tax on equivalent profits: *TIOPA 2010, ss 371AA–371VJ*. Under corporation tax self-assessment, UK controllers are required to include the whole or part of the profits of the CFC in their own profits for corporation tax purposes. No such attribution is required if, *inter alia*, the CFC is pursuing an 'acceptable distribution policy' (ADP). A CFC must distribute 90% of its 'net chargeable profits' to meet the ADP test. The derivative contracts and loan relationships rules have to be applied to the profits of the CFC to establish whether or not the ADP standard is reached. As far as the loan relationships rules are concerned, there are no special rules, and the normal 'connected party' provisions apply.

12.49 *TIOPA 2010, s 371AA(3)* defines a CFC as a non-resident company which is controlled by a UK person or persons. *Section 371BB* contains a 'gateway' test, to determine:

(a)   the assets, risks and profits of a CFC;

(b)   the identification of significant people functions (SPFs) to determine cases where there is an artificial separation of assets and risks from people functions; and

(c)   a profit attribution to a deemed UK permanent establishment.

12.50 The specific exemptions are:

●   low profit exemption (£500,000, of which not more than £50,000 can be non-trading income);

●   low profit margin exemption (< 10% of relevant operating expenditure);

●   excluded territories exemption; and

●   low rate of tax exemption.

The finance company partial exemption (FCPE) gives a special regime for financing activities involving 'qualifying loan relationships'.

Corporate partnerships

12.51 If a partnership contains one or more corporate partners ('company partnership'), each company partner determines separately its credits and debits on loan relationships and derivative contracts. The profits of the partnership are worked out as if the partnership were a UK resident company. If the company partnership includes at least one non-resident company, the partnership profits are computed as if the partnership were a non-resident company. The partnership profits so ascertained are then apportioned between the company partners in accordance with their profit-sharing ratios: *CTA 2009, ss 1256–1260*. Where there is a company partner, and the partnership is a party to a loan relationship or derivatives contract, that company partner stands in the shoes of a partner in the partnership.

Industrial and provident societies

12.52 Industrial and provident societies are incorporated under statute and registered under the *Industrial and Provident Societies Act 1965*. They are not companies under the Companies Act (*Re Devon and Somerset Farmers Ltd* [1993] BCC 410 at 419). Share interest or loan interest paid by a society to its members is not treated as a distribution but as interest paid under a loan relationship of the society: *CTA 2009, s 499*.

Chapter 13

Derivative Contracts – Definition and Scope

Overview

13.1   This chapter deals with:

- Definition of derivative contract

- Accounting conditions

- Contracts which do not satisfy the accounting conditions

- Embedded derivatives

- Excluded contracts

- Basis of taxation

- Intra-group transfers

- Anti-avoidance rules

- Cases involving taxation of derivatives

Introduction

13.2   The central principle which now governs the subject is the principle introduced by IAS that all derivative contracts must be recognised at fair value on inception and taken to balance sheet. Accountants both construct reality and picture it. The tax regime for derivative contracts is largely the result of the accounting principle that all such contracts must be fair valued. This is intended to mirror economic reality but also creates it by producing profits and losses which would not exist but for the accounting treatment.

13.3   All profits arising to a company from its 'derivative contracts' are chargeable to UK corporation tax in accordance with the provisions of *CTA 2009, Part 7*. The rules are broad in their scope, encompassing both 'real' derivatives and embedded derivatives. The regime applies to all derivatives other than the futures and options relating to intangible fixed assets which are not contracts for differences. The derivative contracts rules follow the pattern of the loan relationships rules, but with the major distinction that all derivative contracts are fair valued, whereas most loan relationships will be accounted for on an amortised cost basis. Where the rules apply, most of the transactions of a company in derivative contracts are treated as income, but certain contracts are taxed on a capital gains basis.

13.4   The amounts taxed or relieved in any accounting period follow the amounts recognised in the accounts for the same period. In general, the amounts taxed or relieved are treated as income. However, in the case of futures and options whose value is derived from an asset which would be a chargeable asset for capital gains purposes, the regime treats profits and losses as chargeable gains and allowable losses recognised on an annual basis.

13.5   The tax rules establish two regimes:

1   an income regime based on fair values for derivative contracts whose underlying subject matter is not a chargeable asset; and

2   an annual capital gains regime for relevant contracts and deemed relevant contracts arising from the bifurcation of instruments containing an embedded derivative, whose underlying subject matter is a chargeable asset, where the contract is not held by a bank, financial trader or CIS.

Capital gains calculated on an annual, accounts basis are merged with capital gains calculated on a realisations basis. The special capital gains regime is dealt with under embedded derivatives in **Chapter 15**.

13.6   'Underlying subject matter' is defined in *CTA 2009, s 583* as the subject matter to which the contract relates, which may be an index, an exchange rate and, in the case of a contract for differences, interest rates, weather conditions or creditworthiness. Accordingly, the particular volatility by reference to whose value changes amounts payable under the contract are generated is the underlying subject matter. Hence, the underlying subject matter of a share option is the particular share; the underlying subject matter of an interest rate future is the interest rate; the underlying subject matter of a currency contract is the currency. If the value of the excluded subject matter is small in relation to the contract as a whole or subordinate, the contract will not be an excluded contract because it will be characterised by reference to its predominant subject matter: *s 590*. As a matter of HMRC practice, 'small' means 5% or less of the value of the contract. In a case where a relevant contract has excluded and non-excluded underlying subject matter, and neither constitutes the predominant element, the contract will be treated as two notional contracts, one with excluded underlying subject matter and the other without such.

13.7   The history of the legislation is set out in full in earlier editions of this book. A brief reference to the development of these rules is helpful to explain them.

13.8   An Inland Revenue Consultative Document was issued in August 1991 on the tax treatment of financial instruments for managing interest rate risk. The proposals considered three possible approaches:

• a hedging approach,

• an analytic approach,

• an assimilation to income approach.

13.9   A hedging approach would characterise transactions by reference to related transactions; this was rejected as too subjective. An analytic approach would characterise transactions as income or as capital by reference to their intrinsic nature, ie transactions would be assimilated to existing legal categories as income, capital, loans or debts on a security; this was rejected as too complex. The assimilation to income approach would put all payments and receipts in an income pot, and only distinguish trading from non-trading use of the instruments. Equity and commodity-linked instruments were to be excluded from the special rules because they were 'not thought appropriate for the management of interest rate risk' (para 4.19). 'Mark to market' accounting for financial instruments held for trading purposes had been introduced in the 1980s. On the question of income recognition, an 'as paid basis' was rejected in favour of an accruals basis. On the question of mark to market, the Document observed (para 5.33): 'it might be felt that "mark to market" would move the tax system too far away from the normal principle that profits or losses are only taxed when they are realised'.

This last observation suggested a note of caution which has since been rejected as over-timid.

13.10   The adoption of IFRS led to a wholesale revision of the rules:

(a) all derivative contracts had to be fair valued; and

(b) new and more restrictive hedging rules were introduced for accounting purposes.

13.11   Both of these changes rendered obsolete the former distinction based on the economic purpose for which derivatives were held, being either trading or hedging. The fair valuing of contracts included the fair valuing of liabilities. This is because IAS 47 provides:

> 'After initial recognition, an entity shall measure all financial liabilities at amortised cost using the effective interest method, except for:
>
> (a)   financial liabilities at fair value through profit or loss. Such liabilities, including derivatives that are liabilities, shall be measured at fair value'

This produces very odd results. For example, a bank can realise large profits if its derivative liabilities are written down because of the risk of its own default.

Definition of 'derivative contract'

13.12   Under *CTA 2009, s 576*, in relation to a company subject to UK corporation tax, a 'derivative contract' is a 'relevant contract' which either:

(a)   satisfies the accounting test; or

(b)   though it does not satisfy the accounting test, is nevertheless classified as a derivative contract.

13.13   The first requirement is a contract entered into by a company. The normal legal requirements of a contract must be fulfilled. There must be:

- agreement;

- contractual intention; and

- consideration.

13.14   The company must enter into the agreement in a way binding on the company. Any formal requirements for a particular type of contract (eg a contract relating to land, a guarantee) must be satisfied. There must be sufficient evidence of the contract.

13.15   The next requirement is that the contract should be a 'relevant contract'. A 'relevant contract' is stated by *s 577* to be:

- an option,

- a future, or

- a contract for differences.

These are, in turn, defined in *ss 580–582*.

13.16   In *s 580* an 'option' is given its commercial meaning as a contract which gives the holder the ability to buy from the writer of the option the property to which the agreement relates, or to sell to the writer of the option the property to which the agreement relates. This includes exchange traded and over-the-counter options as well as options that can be cash settled or run to delivery. Contracts which are cash settled (as opposed to performed by delivery) are not options within this definition, unless they are currency options. Exchange traded options are options intended to be bought and sold in a traded options market and are listed on a recognised stock or futures exchange. Over the counter options are prepared by financial institutions for particular customers. Warrants, ie securitised options, are included in this category: *s 580(1)*. It is immaterial whether the shares or securities to which the holder of the warrant is entitled to subscribe exist or are identifiable.

13.17   In *s 581* a 'future' is defined as a contract to sell property with delivery at a later date, with the date of delivery and the price agreed at the time of the contract. The price will be agreed if it relates to a market (eg a contract to deliver a specified amount of US dollars entered into on 1 February can specify a contract price by reference to the spot rate on 1 August) or could be adjusted by reference to a certain level or quantity or quality of the property delivered. The latter is of particular relevance to futures relating to commodities. Futures thus include:

(a)   contracts for the future delivery of shares, securities, foreign currency or other financial instruments;

(b)   contracts that are settled by delivery and contracts that are settled by payment or cash differences determined by movements in the price of such instruments which include contracts where settlement is based on the application or an interest rate or a financial index to a notional principal amount; and

(c)   exchange traded and over-the-counter contracts.

13.18   Exchange traded futures are standard form contracts which can be bought or sold in a futures market or exchange. Such contracts are usually closed out by buying another future with reciprocal obligations. Over-the-counter futures are forward contracts created by financial institutions for particular customers. There is no established market in them. They will often run to maturity unless they can be settled by payment. A cash-settled option or future is a 'contract for differences'.

13.19   *Section 582* says that a 'contract for differences' is a contract:

'the purpose or pretended purpose of which is to make a profit or avoid a loss by reference to fluctuations in –

(a)   the value or price of property described in the contract, or

(b)   an index or other factor designated in the contract.'

13.20   This wording is borrowed from the *FSMA 2000 (Regulated Activities) Order 2001, SI 2001/544, reg 85*. However, only part of that definition is used. This truncated definition is then cut down by *s 582(2)*, which says that none of the following shall be a contract for differences:

(a)   a future,

(b)   an option,

(c)   a contract of insurance,

(d)   a capital redemption policy,

(e)   a contract of indemnity,

(f)   a guarantee,

(g)   a warranty, or

(h)   a loan relationship.

13.21   A contract for differences accordingly is a contract whose purpose is to make a profit or avoid a loss by reference to fluctuations in (a) the value or price of property described in the contract, or (b) an index or other factor designated in the contract. An index could include an existing index, eg the FTSE 100, while 'other factors' include creditworthiness, interest rates and weather conditions. *Section 582(2)* lists a number of exceptions from the definition, including futures, options, contracts of insurances, capital redemption policies. contracts of indemnity, guarantees, warranties and loan relationships. *Section 582(2)* makes it clear that 'contract for differences' is thus a residual category.

13.22   Inland Revenue SP 3/02, 'Tax Treatment of Transactions in Financial Futures and Options' gives guidance on when a taxpayer will be regarded as trading in these instruments. It is mainly concerned with financial futures and options held by individuals, charities and non-corporates. It does not apply to companies within the *CTA 2009* rules, unless the underlying subject matter of financial futures and options consists in shares, a holding in an AUT or convertibles.

The accounting conditions

13.23   A relevant contract is only a derivative contract for tax purposes if it meets the accounting test: *CTA 2009, s 579(1)(a)*. The accounting definition of a 'derivative financial instrument' in FRS 102, Appendix 1 (IFRS 9, Appendix A; IAS 39, para 9) has three features:

●   the underlying subject matter is a volatility, ie something which changes;

- the cost of entering into the contract is nil or small compared with the sums contingently payable under the contract; and

- the contract is to be performed at a future date.

13.24   Because relevant contracts are widely defined, and might encompass contracts which are not derivatives, the 'accounting conditions' excludes contracts which are not treated as 'derivative financial instruments' in accordance with IAS 39 and FRS 102. FRS 102, paras 12.4–12.5 distinguish between (a) options, forwards and swaps which are to be settled by delivery, and (b) contracts where no delivery is intended. The former are not financial instruments. Hence, options and forwards which are intended to result in delivery of the underlying subject matter will be outside FRS 102, Section 12 and so will not be derivative contracts, unless they are relevant contracts which, although not classified as derivative financial instruments for accounting purposes, are, by way of exception to the general rule, brought within the derivative contracts rules. A warrant is a financial instrument within FRS 102, whether it is traded or intended to be exercised.

13.25   FRS 102, para 12.3(e) takes equity instruments out of the scope of financial instrument treatment as regards the issuer but not as regards the holder. This is not intended to exclude equity options from derivative financial instrument treatment.

Contracts which do not satisfy the accounting conditions

13.26   Certain contracts which do not satisfy the accounting conditions are nevertheless treated as derivative contracts. Some instruments fail the 'derivative' test because they are pre-paid (so the initial investment is not small or nil), and so they are scoped out of the definition of derivative contract. They are nevertheless regarded as derivatives for tax purposes. The principal contracts falling within this group are pre-paid forward contracts, deep in the money swaps, equity futures and options and credit: *CTA 2009, s 579(1)(b)*. In such a situation *CTA 2009, s 600* requires fair value accounting to be used.

13.27   If a contract does not pass the accounting test in *s 579(1)(a)* or *(b)*, *s 579(2)* brings additional contracts within the derivative contracts rules as follows:

'(2)   A relevant contract falls within this subsection if –

   (a)   its underlying subject matter is commodities, or

   (b)   it is a contract for differences whose underlying subject matter is –

(i)   land (wherever situated),

(ii)   tangible movable property, other than commodities which are tangible assets,

(iii) intangible fixed assets,

(iv)   weather conditions, and

(v)   creditworthiness.'

13.28   Hence, as well as options, futures and contracts for differences (as defined), most derivative transactions also satisfy the condition in *s 579*, which is that the transaction either:

(a)   is classified as a derivative under FRA 102;

(b)   has commodities as its underlying subject matter;

(c)   qualifies as a contract for differences the underlying subject matter of which consists of–

   - land,

   - tangible movable property (other than commodities which are intangible assets),

   - intangible fixed assets,

   - weather conditions,

   - creditworthiness.

Categories (b) and (c) do not require the derivative transaction to qualify as a derivative under FRS 102.

Embedded derivatives

13.29   Like Russian dolls, a conventional financial instrument may contain within it a derivative contract (embedded derivative), and a derivative contract may itself contain within it another derivative contract (hybrid derivative). Accounting rules may require that a conventional contract is bifurcated into a non-derivative element ('host contract') and an 'embedded derivative' (see Chapter 15). This is to ensure that a derivative contract is not accruals accounted. Accounting rules do not require the further analysis of a contract which is itself a derivative contract. A number of special rules determine whether the embedded derivative falls within or outside the derivative contracts rules.

13.30   The main rule is that embedded derivatives which are separated out from a loan relationship (eg a convertible bond which is bifurcated into a loan relationship and embedded derivative) come within the derivative contracts legislation: *CTA 2009, s 585*. In most other cases, embedded derivatives are excluded from the derivative contracts rules by *ss 586* and *616*, even if they meet the accounting conditions in *s 579(1)(a)–(c)*. These provisions are considered in **Chapter 15**.

Excluded contracts

13.31 Contracts excluded by reason of underlying subject matter are dealt with in *CTA 2009, ss 589–593*. The first exclusion is for those relevant contracts which are physically settled futures and options over intangible fixed assets: *s 589(2)(a), (4)*.

13.32 A relevant contract other than an embedded derivative is excluded from the derivative contracts rules where its underlying subject matter consists of shares, but only in a narrow range of circumstances set out in *s 591(2)–(6)*:

(a)   plain vanilla contracts held by a life assurance company which are approved derivatives for the purposes of Rule 3.2.5 of the Insurance Prudential Sourcebook;

(b)   equity derivatives held for non-trading purposes which are in a hedging relationship;

(c)   quoted warrants entered into or acquired for non-trading purposes;

(d)   equity derivatives acquired or held for non-trading purposes which are options or futures to acquire shares in a company, and the shares to be acquired or delivered constitute a substantial shareholding within *TCGA 1992, Sch 7AC, para 8* (ie 10% or more);

(e)   there is a hedging relationship between the relevant contract and a loan relationship with an embedded derivative.

13.33 Relevant contracts whose underlying subject matter is units in an AUT or shares in an OEIC *other than* holdings which are treated as creditor relationships under *CTA 2009, s 490* (offshore funds) are also excluded from the derivative contracts rules: *s 589(2)(c), (3)(b)*.

13.34 'Hedging relationship' is defined in *CTA 2009, ss 475A, 707*. First, the hedge must be a designated hedge. Second, the hedge must be a fair value hedge.

13.35 'Plain vanilla contract' is defined in *CTA 2009, s 708* as a relevant contract other than (a) hybrid derivatives, (b) convertible bonds, and (c) other contracts with embedded derivatives falling within *s 586*, ie bifurcated contracts not falling within (a) or (b).

13.36   Except where the excluded contract relates to intangible fixed assets, the effect of excluding a contract from the derivative contracts is to make it a chargeable asset for the purpose of the charge to corporation tax on chargeable gains: *CTA 2009, ss 661, 662*.

13.37   If a derivative contract whose underlying subject matter is shares is designed to produce a return which equates in substance to interest ('disguised interest') that return is taxable under the loan relationship rules: *CTA 2009, s 589(5)*.

Basis of taxation

13.38   FRS 102, Section 12 requires all derivatives to be regarded as held for trading and measured at fair value, with changes in carrying amount being taken to income. One of the difficulties in applying the legislation is whether to record profits on a contract-by-contract or a cumulative basis. Companies will normally run books of derivatives on a portfolio basis. The book is split into constituent cash flows and managed as one pool. As the court has observed:

> 'Companies hold portfolios of instruments whose risks are often mutually off-setting and value them on an aggregate basis.' (*South Tyneside Metropolitan Borough Council v Svenska International Handelsbank* [1995] 1 All ER 545 at 552)

and

> 'Hedging transactions cannot be looked at in isolation from one another and without having regard to the overall position of the bank. Hedging transactions involve a complex of decisions on an on-going basis.' (*Kleinwort Benson Ltd v South Tyneside Metropolitan Borough Council* [1994] 4 All ER 972 at 983)

13.39   The use of fair value accounting means that an accounting event does not require a transaction with third parties. Valuation changes will, of themselves, be recognised for accounting purposes. A derivative will have value zero on trade date. As it acquires a positive value – 'in the money' (ITM) – or negative value – 'out of the money' (OTM) – profits and losses will be realised. In most cases, collateral will have to be posted when a derivative goes OTM. The posting of collateral may, in turn, have to be funded. Collateralised positions will be netted by counterparty according to collateral support agreements (CSAs). Confronted with these complex cash flows, the tax legislation, for all its detail, has to take a broad brush approach.

13.40   Profits arising from derivative contracts are chargeable to corporation tax as income (*CTA 2009, s 571(1)*), unless they are chargeable to corporation tax as chargeable gains (*s 571(2)*). Profits and losses are charged to tax as credits and debits (*s 572*). They are brought into charge as trading items (*s 573*) or non-trading items (*s 574*). The computational rules largely follow the loan relationships rules, save that only fair value accounting can be used (subject to the hedge accounting rules). Non-trading on derivative contracts are merged with non-trading deficits on loan relationships.

13.41   If there is a change in accounting standards, the Treasury has power to amend the law by regulation: *s 701A*.

13.42   Credits are the aggregate of:

(a)   payments becoming due and payable to the company; and

(b)   any increase in the value of derivative contracts during the period for which they are held.

Debits are the aggregate of:

(a)   payments becoming due and payable *by* the company; and

(b)   any fall in the value of contracts during the period for which they are held.

13.43   Fair value adjustments to the carrying value of derivative contracts will be bilateral counterparty valuation adjustments (CVAs). Where the contract as a whole, and so liabilities under the contract, are fair valued, a creditor valuation adjustment paradoxically will lead to an increase in earnings as the credit standing of the obligor deteriorates.

13.44   Expenses are only deductible for the purposes of the derivative contracts rules if they are incurred:

●   in bringing the derivative contract into existence (eg fees, commission, option premiums);

●   in entering into or giving effect to related transactions;

●   in making payments pursuant to the contracts; or

●   in taking steps to ensure the receipt of payments under the transactions.

13.45   Under FRS 102 it is not possible for a company to take exchange movements on a derivative contract used to hedge an asset to reserves in its accounts, but *reg 4* of the Disregard Regulations permits exchange movements arising on a derivative contract used to hedge an investment in shares, ships or aircraft to be left out of account for tax purposes. Exchange gains and losses on derivative contracts whose underlying subject matter is a currency and which arise from the translation of amounts from the functional currency and are not taken to the profit and loss account but are instead recognised in OCI, are excluded from the derivative contracts rules: *CTA 2009, s 606(3)*. This will apply where, for example, the accounts of an overseas branch are in one currency and the company's presentation currency is another.

13.46   Where a company continues to recognise items of profit or loss in respect of a derivative contract to which it has ceased to be a party, or recognises items of profit or loss in respect of a derivative contract to which it is not and has never been a party, those amounts are taken into account for tax purposes: *CTA 2009, s 607A*. This is subject to restrictions for debits, and rules to prevent double counting: *ss 607B, 607C*.

13.47   There is an exit charge if a company holding derivative contracts ceases to be UK resident: *s 609*. This is modelled on the capital gains tax exit charge under *TCGA 1992, s 185*. The exit charge takes the form of a deemed disposal and reacquisition for fair value. If the contracts become part of the assets of a UK permanent establishment, there is no exit charge.

Partnerships involving companies

13.48   As in the case of similar provisions under the loan relationships rules, where a partnership contains corporate partners and the partnership is a party to derivative contracts, gains or losses on the derivative contracts are allocated to company partners in accordance with their profit-sharing ratios: *CTA 2009, s 619*.

Changes of accounting policy

13.49   Where a change in accounting policy produces a prior year adjustment, or a change in comparative figures for the previous financial year, the amount of the adjustment will be brought into charge under *CTA 2009, ss 597, 613*. For accounting periods beginning on or after 1 January 2016, amounts will only be brought into charge to the extent that they are recognised in a company's accounts as an item or profit or loss. This includes amounts recycled from OCI.

Payments to non-residents

13.50   Under *CTA 2009, s 696* and *697*, where the derivative contract is with a non-resident, payments of notional interest are to be left out of account (ie the paying company does not get a debit) in respect of notional interest payments to the extent that, on a cumulative basis, these exceed the notional interest receivable.

13.51 Under *s 697*, there are three exceptions, where the payments are made to the non-resident party in one of three circumstances:

(a) the payer is a bank, building society, financial trader or recognised clearing house, acting as principal, and the contract is held solely for the purposes of its UK trade;

(b) the non-resident payee holds the contract as principal solely for the purposes of a trade carried on by it through its UK branch or agency; or

(c) the non-resident payee is resident in a country which has a double taxation agreement with the UK and the double taxation agreement contains an interest article.

Intra-group transfers

13.52 As with loan relationships, derivative contracts may be transferred on a tax neutral basis between companies which belong to the same capital gains tax group, and one company replaces the other as party to the contract: *CTA 2009, ss 624–632*. However, these provisions are of limited application, because they do not apply where the transferor uses fair value accounting for the contract: *s 628*. As companies using FRS 102 or IFRS will fair value all their derivative contracts (subject to *Loan Relationships and Derivative Contracts (Disregard and Bringing into Account) Regulations 2004, SI 2004/3256* (the 'Disregard Regulations'), *regs 7–9*), the group continuity rules are of limited application.

13.53 As futures and contracts for differences involve both obligations to make and entitlements to receive payments, they will normally have to be transferred by novation, rather than assignment.

13.54 In cases where *s 625* does apply (group continuity rule) but the transferee company leaves the group within six years of the intra-group transfer, there is a degrouping charge under *ss 630–632*. The transferee company is deemed to dispose of the contract for its fair value immediately before leaving the group, unless this would produce a loss. There is no degrouping charge if the derivative contract is a hedging instrument and was transferred at the same time as the loan relationship with which it had a hedging relationship.

There is also no degrouping charge in the case of exempt distributions on demergers.

13.55 Under *CTA 2009, s 695*, where:

● a company (A), which is within the charge to corporation tax, holds an option granted by

- a connected company (B), which is not within the charge to corporation tax, and

- the option is in the money (ITM), and

- A transfers value to B by allowing the option to lapse, and

- had the companies not been connected, the option would have been exercised in full,

A must bring in a credit of the 'appropriate amount' for the profit forgone.

Anti-avoidance provisions

13.56   In numerous instances, if a company is a party to 'tax avoidance arrangements', the normal rule which would otherwise apply is set aside. 'Tax avoidance arrangement' is defined as an arrangement whose main purpose or one of whose main purposes is to obtain a 'tax advantage'. 'Tax advantage' is, in turn, defined as a saving of the tax which would otherwise be payable, if there were no tax avoidance arrangements. Thus, all the definitions are entirely circular. A company is seeking to gain a tax advantage if it is a party to tax avoidance arrangements, and it is a party to tax avoidance arrangements if it is seeking to gain a tax advantage. The only exclusion is where the main purpose can be shown to be other than that of gaining a tax advantage. However, as any corporate debt produces a tax advantage for the debtor, in the form of a finance deduction, any loan relationship can be said to produce a tax advantage. The courts have proved unwilling or unable to distinguish the purpose of a transaction from the consequence of a transaction. As a result, these provisions are simply a form of executive enabling provision. They have no specific meaning, save than to allow HMRC to tax a transaction on a different basis than that which would apply if the ordinary rules applied, but whose effects can be suspended by invoking the notion of 'tax avoidance'.

13.57   Debits are disallowed where a derivative contract or a related contract is entered into for an unallowable purpose: *CTA 2009, ss 690, 691*. 'Unallowable purpose' has the same meaning as in the loan relationships rules: *s 441*. 'Tax advantage' is defined in accordance with *CTA 2010, s 1139*.

13.58   Where a company enters into a derivative contract on non-arm's length terms and the pricing would be adjusted under transfer pricing rules, the transfer pricing rules will apply to adjust the terms of an arm's-length standard, whether or not they would otherwise have applied: *CTA 2009, ss 693, 694*. Foreign exchange gains and losses are left out of account in making such adjustments: *s 694(3)*.

13.59   Where a company 'with the relevant avoidance intention' disposes of a derivative contract, and under GAAP the full disposal consideration is not recognised for accounts purposes, the whole of the consideration will be recognised for tax purposes: *s 698*.

13.60   A company may write a derivative on its own shares, liabilities or assets, or enter into a matching loan relationship. In that case, the hedging contract and hedged item may be matched, and the derivative or loan relationship derecognised. In that case a profit or loss on the derivative contract will not be recognised for accounting purposes. Such credits or debits on the derecognised derivative contract or loan relationship will, however, be recognised for tax purposes where (a) a company is party to 'tax avoidance arrangements', and (b) the derivative contract held by a company is derecognised because it is matched with a capital contribution received by a company, or the company's shares or similar securities in another company or partnership interest: *ss 599A, 599B*.

Chapter 14

Derivative Contracts – Measurement of Profits

Overview

14.1   This chapter deals with:

- Margining
- Interest rate agreements
- Interest rate futures
- Forward rate agreements
- Interest rate swaps
- Interest rate options, floors and collars
- Valuation of swaps
- Breakage payments
- Currency contracts and options
- Cross currency swaps
- Currency options
- Credit derivatives
- Credit risks
- Acquisition of shares in a foreign corporation

Margining

14.2   In the case of exchange-traded instruments, price movements on individual contracts are measured by ticks, ie the unit of price movement. Tick value is the cash value of one tick. In the case of an interest rate contract, 1 tick = 0.01% of notional principal, eg:

for a 3 months' deposit of €1m, a tick is:

$0.01\% \times €1m \times 3/12 = €25.$

14.3 Where instruments are exchange traded, initial and variation margins have to be paid, which are calculated by reference to ticks. Ticks record the daily movement in value paid or received. The use of margining means that the instrument is, in effect, sold and reacquired each day, producing a credit or debit to profit and loss. The overall profit or loss will be spread over the period for which the instrument is held. Margin payments will reflect fluctuations in value. The daily mark to market by the exchange resulting in a receipt or payment of margin will constitute a credit or debit.

Example 14.1

The spot price of interest rate futures is $(100 - I)$, where I = current rate of interest. If interest rates fall, the price of interest rate futures rises. If interest rates rise, interest rate futures fall in price.

(a)   C needs to borrow £1m for three months in six months' time (July) at 7%.

(b)   He sells, for settlement in July, two three-month sterling interest rate futures of £500,000 for $93 \times 100 = 9,300$.

(c)   In July, interest rates are 9% and interest rate futures have fallen to 91.

(d)   C buys two interest rate futures at 91 which he sells for 93, making a profit of:

$(9,300 - 9,100) \times 12.50 \times 2 = £5,000.$

(Tick size is $0.01\% \times 500,000 \times 3/12 = 12.50$.)

(e)   This exactly equals his extra cost of borrowing, ie $2\% \times £1m \times 3/12 = £5,000$.

(f)   The interest paid will be a loan relationships debit, while the profit on the interest rate contract will be an amount A credit under the derivative contracts rules. Provided that the receipts and payments produce corresponding but opposite tax results, the hedge will be perfect both pre- and post-tax.

14.4 A similar result can be obtained by buying an interest rate put option with July expiry for 93, paying a premium of 0.2. If interest rates in July are

9%, the option can be exercised, selling it for 93 and buying the future back at 91. Because of the premium which has to be paid, the effective rate of interest is now 7.02%.

14.5   If, in the above example, interest rates had fallen to 5% instead of rising to 9%, C would have to sell for 93 contracts now worth 95. The loss would equal the saving on borrowing costs. C would have fixed his cost of borrowing at the expense of losing the advantage of the interest rate fall.

Example 14.2

T buys, on 1 March, four three-month sterling interest rate futures of £500,000 at 84. Tick size is $0.01\% \times 500,000 \times 3/12 = 12.50$. Initial margin is price times tick size.

	£
Initial margin posted: $84 \times 12.50 \times 4$	(4,200)
On 14 May, price is 86.50. Variation margin received is $(8,650 - 8,400) \times 12.50 \times 4$	12,500
Sell contracts and recover initial margin	4,200
Profit	12,500

14.6   The derivative contracts rules do not recognise the netting of obligations, only of settlement.

Example 14.3

(a)   M plc's financial year ends on 31 December. On 1 December, it will have to renew for a further three months a loan of £10m, on which it currently pays interest at 8%. The price of December sterling three-month interest rate futures is 91, reflecting an inherent interest rate of 9%.

(b)   In September, M sells 20 sterling £500,000 three-month interest rate futures at 91.

(c)   In December, interest rates are 10% and the price of three-month interest rate futures is 90. M sells the interest rate futures at 91 and buys replacement futures at 90. The loan is rolled over at 10%.

			£
(d) Interest costs are:	Sept–Nov $£10m \times 8\% \times 3/12$		200,000
	Dec–Feb $£10m \times 10\% \times 3/12$		250,000

(e) Derivatives transactions are:

Sept: Sell 20 sterling three-month interest rate futures @ 91

Initial margin: $91 \times 20 \times 12.50$	(22,750)
1 Dec: Variation margin received	
$(9,100 - 9,000) \times 20 \times 12.50$	25,000
Initial margin returned	22,750

Because of the difference in basis between the cash market and the futures market, the hedge is only 50% successful (£50,000 extra interest; £25,000 gain on futures transaction). The interest rate inherent in the interest rate future, and actual interest rates, have not coincided.

Master agreements

14.7 The bulk of derivative transactions are conducted in standardised form through the use of master agreements. The standard pattern is:

(a) A deal is documented by a deal ticket.

(b) This will be followed by a confirmation, setting out the terms of the transaction, and incorporating a number of definitions ('Definitions').

(c) Both will incorporate the terms of a master agreement, setting out the general conditions, governing a range of transactions between the parties, and containing a customised form of schedule, recording special terms of a particular transaction. Under the master agreement's terms, a legally binding contract is established at the moment that the deal ticket is completed. Confirmations are only evidence of the particulars of an already established contract and do not constitute the contract itself.

Exchange-traded transactions employ the exchange's own documentation and rules.

14.8 Master agreements commonly provide that the deal ticket and all confirmations which govern the transactions between the parties are to form a single agreement, and all reciprocal payments can be netted, either as such or on the basis that the transactions may be regarded as involving constructive payments of the gross amounts. While the master agreement will link settlement obligations, so that a net sum can be paid, payment obligations are not as such linked. Each payment essentially derives from a separate contract, though the contracts are capable of off-setting.

14.9   Common examples of master agreements are:

(a)   2002 International Swaps and Derivatives Association (ISDA) Master Agreement;

(b)   International Foreign Exchange and Options Master Agreement (FEOMA);

(c)   International Foreign Exchange Master Agreement (IFEMA);

(d)   International Currency Options Master Agreement (ICOM);

(e)   Loan Market Association Standard Terms and Conditions for Par and Distressed Trade Transactions (Bank/Debt Claims).

Interest rate agreements

14.10   An interest rate contract provides for a company to pay or receive at least one variable rate payment in exchange for one or more variable rate payments, fixed rate payments or fixed payments. The payment may only be contingently payable, as under a cap. The notional principal or variable rate payment can be established by reference to a formula, eg a swap can be made by reference to a reducing balance (amortising notional principal) or by reference to two different interest rates (a basis swap). The category covers any contract for a variable rate payment, eg swaps, forward rate agreements, caps, collars, interest rate futures. Interest rate agreements comprise:

- interest rate futures;
- forward rate agreements;
- interest rate swaps; and
- interest rate options.

Interest rate futures

14.11   An interest rate future is an exchange traded agreement to buy or sell a standard amount of a specified financial instrument at a fixed price at a fixed future date. On the London International Financial Futures and Options Exchange (LIFFE), the terms of the three-month sterling interest rate future contract are as follows:

Unit of trading	£500,000
Delivery/expiry months	March/June/September/December
Last trading day	11.00 on third Wednesday of delivery month
Delivery/expiry/exercise day	First business day after last trading day
Tick (minimum price movement)	0.01 (£12.50)

Forward rate agreements

14.12 The general rule in *CTA 2009, s 595(1)* is applied to foreign exchange contracts by *s 606(1)*, subject to the exclusions provided for in that section and the Disregard Regulations.

14.13 A forward rate agreement (FRA) is an interest rate contract for differences under which a buyer (who wants protection against a future rise in interest rates) and seller (who wants protection against a future fall in interest rates) agree to exchange the difference between the current interest rate and a pre-agreed fixed rate. If rates have risen, at maturity the buyer receives a compensation payment from the seller. If rates have fallen, the seller receives a compensation payment from the buyer. Under a forward rate agreement, the difference between one interest rate and another applied to a notional principal for a fixed period is payable by one party to the other.

14.14 The difference between the spot rate and the forward rate (reflecting different interests rates between the two currencies) gives rise to a forward premium or discount.

14.15 Exchange gains and losses will be disregarded for the purposes of the derivative contracts legislation where they arise from the translation of the results of part of the company's business and in accordance with GAAP the differences are taken to the company's SOCIE: *CTA 2009, s 606(3)*.

14.16 The master contract for forward rate agreements (FRAs) is the forward rate agreement published by the British Bankers' Association (FRABBA). A forward rate agreement is an agreement which fixes interest rates on a specified principal amount for a fixed period. The contract is settled by a single compensation payment representing the difference between the market rate of interest and the contractual rate of interest, applied to the specified principal for the specified period. The payment is made at the start of the period, and is discounted to take account of the fact that it can be invested at the market rate for the period in question.

Example 14.4

(a) A borrows £1m for three months in six months' time.

(b) A buys an FRA from B to lock into 6% for three months, six months hence.

(c) On settlement day a compensation payment is made by B to A (if rates are above 6%), or by A to B (if interest rates are below 6%).

(d)   For example, if the interest rate is 7% on settlement day, the compensation payment which B pays to A is:

	£
£1m × (7 – 6%) × 3/12	2,500
Discount 2.500 × $\dfrac{1}{1 + (7\% \times 3/12)}$	2,457

(e)   Applying fair value accounting, the contract will be regularly revalued at the replacement rate, ie the amount which would be received on a close-out. The revaluations will be posted direct to profit and loss.

Example 14.5 – Forward rate agreement valuation

Assume the following terms:

Fixed rate payer	Party A
Nominal	€25,000,000
Rate	8.79%
Trade date	6 February 2017
Start date	6 August 2017
Period covered	184 days

The market valuation as at 6 July 2017 for Party A, given a market rate of 9.62% for a six-month FRA starting in August 2017, will be:

Interest differential:

- 25,000,000 × 184/365 × (9.62 – 8.79%) = €104,602.

The net present value of the interest differential, which represents the fair value, is therefore:

- €104,602 × 1/(1 + 184/365) × 9.62%) = €99,675.

Party A has made a profit on the FRA due to the rise in interest rates.

Interest rate swaps

14.17   FRAs are the building blocks from which swaps are constructed. An interest rate swap is two FRAs.

14.18 *Derivative Contracts – Measurement of Profits*

14.18 The Bank for International Settlements (BIS) defines a swap as:

'a financial transaction in which two counterparties agree to exchange streams of payments over time.'

14.19 An interest rate swap is defined as a swap where:

'no actual principal is exchanged either initially or at maturity, but interest payment streams of differing character are exchanged according to predetermined rules and based on an underlying notional principal amount'.

14.20 The three main types of interest swap are:

(a)   coupon swaps (one fixed rate to a floating rate in the same currency);

(b)   basis swaps (one floating rate index to another floating rate index in the same currency); and

(c)   cross currency interest rate swaps (fixed rate in one currency to a floating rate in another currency).

Interest rate swaps typically have a maturity of around three years.

14.21 The standard master agreement for interest rate swaps is BBAIRS. Swaps can be deconstructed into a series of cash inflows and outflows. Swaps cover the following exchanges:

- floating to fixed;
- fixed to floating;
- LIBOR to prime; and
- prime to LIBOR.

14.22 The components of amounts A and B for tax purposes will be:

- arrangement fee;
- periodic payments;
- return on credit risk; and
- return on operating costs of servicing the transaction.

14.23 The accounting entries for swaps are similar to FRAs. Gains and losses will be mirrored by an entry to a revaluation account as other assets/

liabilities. This account will be offset periodically by receipts or payments of cash. The total profit or loss will be:

Movement in unrealised surplus (loss) between valuation dates	x
Movement in interest accruals	x
Cash received/paid	x
Profit or loss for period	x

14.24   The payments flows involved can be shown in two examples.

Example 14.6

One company has an AAA credit rating, while another company has a BBB credit rating. The rates at which they can borrow money are as follows:

	Fixed	*Floating*
AAA	9%	LIBOR + 0.5%
BBB	12%	LIBOR + 2%
AAA's advantage	3%	LIBOR + 1.5%

AAA and BBB can cut financing costs, if each borrows at his most favourable rate and then swaps obligations with the other.

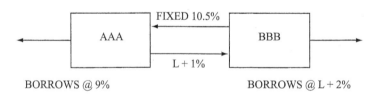

BORROWS @ 9%   BORROWS @ L + 2%

Cash flows:	AAA	BBB
Debt	(9.0)%	(L + 2)%
Swap payment	(L + 1)%	(10.5)%
Swap receipt	10.5%	L + 1%
Effective loan cost	L – 0.5%	11.5%
Without swap	L + 0.5%	12%
Saving	1.0%	0.5%

Example 14.7

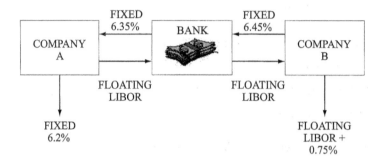

Company A can borrow fixed at 6.2%, floating at LIBOR.

Company B can borrow fixed at 7.35%, floating at LIBOR + 0.75%.

A bank arranges a swap between A and B, so that each reduces its borrowing costs by 0.15%, and the bank makes a turn of 0.1%.

B pays the bank 6.45% fixed and the bank pays 6.35% fixed to A. A pays the bank LIBOR, which the bank passes on to B. B has fixed rate borrowing of (6.45 + 0.75 = 7.2%). A has a floating rate borrowing of (LIBOR – 0.15%).

Interest rate options, caps and floors

14.25   An interest rate option is an option to enter into an interest rate contract, or an option to enter into such an option, eg a swaption. In many cases, an interest rate contract and an interest rate option will be difficult to distinguish, eg a two-year interest cap may consist of eight three-month interest rate options. As each option settles automatically, this is better regarded as an interest rate contract. A cap provides an automatic option for a borrower if interest rates exceed a prescribed level. A floor provides an automatic option for a lender if interest rates fall below a prescribed level.

14.26   Options display a one-sided pattern of risks and rewards. The writer's profits are confined to premiums received, but potential losses are unlimited, subject to hedging strategies. The option holder's losses are limited to the premiums paid, but the potential gains are unlimited. Credits and debits will be:

(a)   premiums;

(b)   cash differences on exercise of 'in the money' (ITM) options;

(c)   margin payments; and

(d)   valuation changes.

14.27   The value of an option can be split into the intrinsic value and the time value:

(a)   The intrinsic value of an option is the benefit to the purchaser if he were to exercise the option immediately. Where the option has an intrinsic value, it is ITM. Where the option is not worth exercising, it is out of the money (OTM) and has an intrinsic value of zero.

(b)   The time value of an option is the difference between the market value of the option and its intrinsic value. The time value reflects the fact that, as long as the option has some time life before the expiry date, there is a chance that the intrinsic value will increase, in some cases meaning that the option will move into the money.

An option premium will be held as an asset (purchased option) or liability (written option) until maturity.

14.28   In the case of interest rate caps, the seller pays the buyer the excess of the prevailing market rate over the cap rate on an agreed notional principal amount for an agreed period. Credits and debits will be:

(a)   for the buyer, initial and regular premiums;

(b)   for the seller, compensation payments; and

(c)   valuation changes.

Example 14.8

G has issued a floating rate loan of £1m for three months at LIBOR + 2%, interest payable six monthly in arrears. G wishes to cap its interest obligations. The premium for the interest rate cap will be 1.02%, ie £10,200. Interest rates are:

Loan note rate	6%
Cap rate	6%
3 months' LIBOR	4%

If rates rise to 6% for the three months of the loan, the result is:

Loan note rate	8%
Cap rate	6%

Excess rate	2%
Excess rate for three-month period	0.5%
Notional principal	£1m
Compensation payment	£1m × 0.5% = £5,000

The net result for the buyer is A = £5,000, B = £10,200, ie loss of (£5,200).

14.29   In practice, derivatives are often incorporated into debt instruments, ie conditions are written into the bond which protect the borrower from increases, or the lender from falls, in the interest rate. In these instances, accounting rules will not require bifurcation; so, for accounting and tax purposes, the bond is treated as a single instrument.

Example 14.9

Zippy Co is a trading company which wishes to raise £100m in the bond market to fund major capital expenditure. It intends to cap its finance costs, and can do this by embedding a cap into the bonds or by taking a stand-alone cap.

Summary of indicative terms – bond

Issuer:	Zippy Co
Principal:	£100m
Coupon:	Six-month LIBOR + 1.5% (semi-annual basis)
Term:	Five years
Redemption amount:	Par
Form:	Eurobond
Status:	The guarantee will rank *pari passu* with all other senior obligations of the guarantor
Covenants:	Standard Euromarket covenants
Redemption:	There will be no early redemption. In the event of imposition of withholding tax, or on the occasion of an event of default, investors will have the right to put the bonds to the issuer
Arranger:	Technical Bank
Arrangement fees:	£250,000

Summary of indicative terms – bond with embedded interest option

Issuer:	Zippy Co
Principal:	£100m
Coupon:	Six-month LIBOR + 2% (semi-annual basis) subject to a maximum LIBOR of 7%
Term:	Five years
Redemption amount:	Par
Form:	Eurobond
Status:	The guarantee will rank *pari passu* with all other senior obligations of the guarantor
Covenants:	Standard Euromarket covenants
Redemption:	There will be no early redemption. In the event of imposition of withholding tax, or on the occasion of an event of default, investors will have the right to put the bonds to the issuer
Arranger:	Technical Bank
Arrangement fees:	£250,000

Summary of indicative terms – interest rate cap on six-month LIBOR

Purchaser:	Zippy Co
Underlying nominal principal:	£100m
Cap rate:	7% (LIBOR)
Term:	Five years
Documentation:	ISDA
Seller:	Technical Bank
Premium:	2% (£2,000,000)

Commercial considerations

14.30

- Using the bond with the embedded cap allows the cost of the cap to be spread over five years. The separate cap requires an upfront payment for the cap premium, and thus has a cash flow disadvantage.

- There is less flexibility if the option is embedded; if it is a separate transaction, the cap can be retained if the loan is repaid, or the cap assigned and the bond retained.

The accounting treatment of holding the combined product or the separate products for a year is set out below:

Bond with embedded cap

14.31

(a)   LIBOR < 7%:

- Bond interest payable 100,000,000 × (LIBOR + 2%).

(b)   LIBOR > 7%:

- Bond interest payable 100,000,000 × 9%.

Separate cap and bond

14.32

(a)   LIBOR < 7%:

- Bond interest payable 100,000,000 × (LIBOR + 1.5%)
- Cap premium 2,000,000.

(b)   LIBOR > 7%:

- Bond interest payable 100,000,000 × (LIBOR + 1.5%)
- Cap receipt receivable (LIBOR- 7%) × 100,000,000
- Cap premium 2,000,000.

Comparison

14.33

(a)   If LIBOR < 7%:

- The annum cost of the embedded bond held is 100,000,000 × LIBOR + 2,000,000

- If the two separate products are held, the cost will be 100,000,000 × LIBOR + 1,900,000.

(b)   If LIBOR > 7%:

- The annual cost of embedded bond held is 100,000,000 × 9% = 9,000,000

- If the two separate products are held, the annual cost will be 100,000,000 × 8.50% + 400,000 = 8,900,000.

In both cases, the cap can be treated as a cash flow hedge, because it restricts Zippy's exposure to a rise in interest rates above 9%.

Bond with embedded interest option

14.34

- If the bond is a quoted Eurobond, there is no withholding tax on interest payments.

- Interest is allowable on an accounts basis under the loan relationships rules.

- Arrangement fees are allowable on the basis adopted for accounts.

Interest rate cap on six-month LIBOR

14.35

- The upfront premium is tax deductible.

- Any payments received under the agreement will be taken to balance sheet.

- Arrangement fees will be tax deductible on an accounts basis (whether or not they are transferred to the share premium account).

Bond with embedded cap

14.36   Assumptions:

- LIBOR 7% Year 1, 8% Years 2 to 5

- Corporation tax rate 19%, and tax is paid 9 months after year end

Accounting treatment	£	£	£	£	£
	Year 1	Year 2	Year 3	Year 4	Year 5
Interest @ 9%	9,000,000	9,000,000	9,000,000	9,000,000	9,000,000
Arrangement fee 250,000	9,250,000	9,000,000	9,000,000	9,000,000	9,000,000

Less CT @ 19%	(1,757,500)	(1,710,000)	(1,710,000)	(1,710,000) (1,710,000)
After tax effect	7,492,500	7,290,000	7.290,000	7.290,000 7,290,000
Total				36,652,500
Net present value of cash flows				29.753,905

Plain vanilla bond and cap

14.37   Assumptions:

* LIBOR 7% Year 1, 8% Years 2 to 5
* Corporation tax rate 19%, and tax is paid 9 months after year end

Item	£	£	£	£	£
	Year 1	*Year 2*	*Year 3*	*Year 4*	*Year 5*
Interest	9,000,000	10,000,000	10,000,000	1 0,000,000	10,000,000
Arrangement fee	250,000				
Proportion of premium cap	400,000	400,000	400,000	400,000	400,000
Cap receipt		(1,000,000)	(1,000,000)	(1,000,000)	(1,000,000)
Total	9,650,000	9,400,000	9,400,000	9,400,000	9,400,000
Less CT @ 19%	(1,833,500)	(1,786,000)	(1,786,000)	(1,786,000)	(1,786,000)
After tax effect	7,816,500	7,614,000	7,614,000	7, 614,000	7, 614,000

Total	38,272,905
Net present value of cash flows	31,166,992

Comparison:

	Net accounting expense	Net present value
Bond with embedded cap	36,652,500	29,753,905
Plain vanilla bond and cap	38,272,905	31,166,992

Bond with embedded option

14.38   Zippy Co again wishes to raise £100m in the bond market, this time giving the investor some protection against falling interest rates. Zippy Co could issue the bond with an embedded option or it could break it down into its component parts.

Summary of indicative terms – bond with investor interest option

Issuer:	Zippy Co
Principal:	£100m
Coupon:	Years 1 and 2, six-month LIBOR + 1.25% or 6.25% (subject to a minimum coupon of 6.25%, semi-annual basis); Years 3 to 5, six-month LIBOR + 1.25%, or 6.25% fixed rate (semi-annual) at the investors' option

Term:	Five years
Redemption amount:	Par
Form:	Eurobond
Status:	The guarantee will rank *pari passu* with all other senior obligations of the guarantor
Covenants:	Standard Euromarket covenants
Investor option:	On any interest payment due from the second anniversary of the issuance of the bond, the investors will have a right to fix the coupon on the bond at 6.25% (semi-annual basis) for the remaining life of the bond. This right expires after two years
Redemption:	There will be no early redemption. In the event of imposition of withholding tax, or on the occasion of an event of default, investors will have the right to put the bonds to the issuer
Arranger:	Technical Bank
Arrangement fees:	£250,000

Summary of indicative terms – bond

Issuer:	Zippy Co
Principal:	£100m
Coupon:	Six-month LIBOR + 1.5% (semi-annual basis)
Term:	Five years
Redemption amount:	Par
Form:	Eurobond
Status:	The guarantee will rank *pari passu* with all other senior obligations of the guarantor
Covenants:	Standard Euromarket covenants

Redemption:	There will be no early redemption. In the event of imposition of withholding tax, or on the occasion of an event of default, investors will have the right to put the bonds to the issuer
Arranger:	Technical Bank
Arrangement fees:	£250,000

Summary of indicative terms – interest rate floor on six-month LIBOR

Purchaser:	Technical Bank
Underlying nominal principal:	£100m
Floor LIBOR rate:	6.25%
Term:	Two years
Documentation:	ISDA
Seller:	Zippy Co
Premium:	0.35% (£350,000)

Summary of indicative terms – interest rate swaption on six-month LIBOR

Purchaser:	Technical Bank
Underlying nominal principal:	£100m
Swaption rate:	The purchaser has the right to receive a fixed rate of 6.25% against payment of six-month sterling LIBOR
Swaption maturity:	Five years
Style:	American
Exercise period:	Two years
Documentation:	ISDA
Seller:	Zippy Co
Premium:	1.0% (£1,000,000)

Treatment of bond with embedded floor and swaption

14.39　The bond can be analysed as follows:

- Straight five-year bond £100m at LIBOR + 1.25%.

- Written two-year floor at 5% LIBOR with principal of £100m.

- Written swaption for a three-year £100m swap at LIBOR versus 6.25% starting in two years' time.

14.40 The interest margin on the bond has been reduced because the treasury have written two options as part of the bond agreement. The bond is not hedged by these written options, as they have not restricted the issuer's exposures to adverse price movements.

Interest will be accrued at the contracted rate, and liabilities arising under the option agreements will be fair valued.

Separate floor, swaption and bond

14.41 The individual products which are economically equivalent to the embedded bond would create the following costs if they were accounted for on an accruals basis, as set out above:

14.42 For Years 1 and 2:

(a) If LIBOR < 6.25%:

- Annual cost of bond 100,000,000 × (LIBOR + 1.5%)
- Annual cost of interest rate floor 100,000,000 × (6.25% – LIBOR)
- Amortisation of floor premium income 350,000 × 1/2.

(b) If LIBOR> 6.25%:

- Annual cost of bond 100,000,000 × (LIBOR + 1.5%)
- Annual cost of interest rate floor is zero, as option will not be exercised
- Amortisation of floor premium income 350,000 × 1/2.

14.43 For Years 3 to 5:

(a) If swaption exercised by investor:

- Annual cost of bond 100,000,000 × (LIBOR + 1.5%)
- Amortisation of premium income 1,000,000 × 1/3
- Cash flows on swaps 100,000,000 × (6.25% – LIBOR).

(b) If swaption is not exercised by investor:

- Annual cost of bond 100,000,000 × (LIBOR + 1.5%)
- Amortisation of swaption premium income 1,000,000 × 1/3.

Comparison

14.44   For Years 1 and 2:

(a)   If LIBOR < 6.25%:

- The embedded bond total annual accounting cost is £6,250,000

- The separate products total annual accounting cost is £6,325,000.

(b)   If LIBOR > 6.25%:

- The embedded bond annual accounting cost is LIBOR × 100,000,000 + 1,250,000

- The separate products annual accounting cost is LIBOR × 100,000,000 + 1,325,000.

14.45   For Years 3 to 5:

(a)   If the option exercised by investor:

- The embedded bond annual accounting cost is £6,250,000

- The separate products annual accounting cost is £6,166,667.

(b)   If the option is not exercised by the investor:

- The embedded bond annual accounting cost is 100,000,000 × (LIBOR + 1.25%)

- The separate products annual accounting cost is 100,000,000 × (LIBOR + 1.5%) – 333,333.

Valuation of swaps

14.46   As a swap is simply a stream of cash flows, the fair value is computed as the present value of the future cash flows expected to arise from the swap at current market rates. A zero coupon yield curve is used to determine the discount factor for the payments on the floating leg of the swap.

Example 14.10 – Valuation of a plain vanilla swap

Assume a plain vanilla interest rate swap between Party A (fixed rate payer) and Party B (floating rate payer).

Terms	Notional principal	£15,000,000
	Start date	2 January 2015
	Maturity	2 January 2019
Fixed	Fixed coupon	11%
	Payment frequency	annual
Date count	30/360	
Floating	Index	Six-month LIBOR
	First LIBOR rate	10.5%
	Payment frequency	Semi-annual
	Day count	actual/365
	Reset frequency	Semi-annual
Zero coupon yield curve	Month 6	10.7%
('ZC rate'):	Year 1	11.0
	Year 2	11.1
	Year 3	11.2
	Year 4	11.2

Opening value for Party A (fixed rate payer)

Receive (Pay)	*Cash flow*	*ZC Rate*	*Discount factor*	*Value £*	*Value £*
Receive	15,787,500	10.7	0.9504		15,004,440
Pay	(1,650,000)	11.0	0.9009	(1,486,485)	
	(1,650,000)	11.1	0.8102	(1,336,830)	
	(1,650,000)	11.2	0.7273	(1,200,045)	
	(16,650,000)	11.2	0.6540	(10,889,100)	
					(14,912,460)
Fair value					91,980

At the end of Year 1, on 31 December 2015, if LIBOR rates were 10.8% on 1 July 2015 and 11.1% on 1 January 2016, the value of the swap will be:

Receive (Pay)	*Cash flow*	*ZC Rate*	*Discount factor*	*Value £*	*Value £*
Receive	15,832,500	11.1	0.9484		15,015,543
Pay	(1,650,000)	11.1	0.9001	(1,485,165)	

(1,650,000)	11.2	0.8087	(1,334,355)
(16,650,000)	11.2	0.7273	(11,109,545)

	(14,929,065)
Fair value	86,478

The profit for Year 1 is:

Opening fair value	91,980
Change in fair value (91,980 – 86,478)	(5,502)
Change in cash:	
(1,597,500 – 1,650,000)	(52,500)
Profit	33,978

The accounting entries are:

DR	Debtor	33,978	CR Profit and loss	33,978

Breakage payments

14.47 If a contract is closed out before its contractual termination is reached, a breakage payment will arise. In the case of exchange traded contracts, a contract is closed out by entering into an equal and opposite contract. In the case of OTC contracts, it is necessary to calculate a breakage payment. The breakage payment is a debit or credit arising on a related transaction. When a contract is closed out by entering into a reciprocal contract (ie an equal and opposite contract), the market value of the original contract is treated as nil, and any payment made or received on termination is a credit or debit. If a contract is discharged by making an actual exchange of currencies, the actual market value of the currency paid and received prior to termination, and not a nil value, will be used to calculate the credits and debits.

Example 14.11

In Year 1 when LIBOR is 9.75%, A Co enters into an interest rate swap with B Co, to pay interest of 11% fixed and receive LIBOR + 1.25% for six years on a notional amount of £30m. LIBOR rises to 11.5% by the start of Year 3, so that A Co can be paid the difference between $(12.75 – 11\%) \times £30m = £525,000$. B Co terminates the swap by making a payment of the net present value (NPV) of the interest differential. Assuming that the zero coupon rate is 12% for the remainder of the swap term, the breakage payment is:

Year	Cash Receipt – £	NPV – £
1	525,000	468,750
2	525,000	418,527
3	525,000	373,684
		1,260,961

A Co will have recognised fair values profits on the swap each year, taking the cash receipt to balance sheet. The balance of profit will be recognised on termination.

Currency contracts and options

14.48   A currency contract requires the exchange of a specified amount of one currency (the first currency) for a specified amount of another currency (the second currency) at the same time and at a given rate of exchange. A currency contract is analysed into two sums of money: a deposit (the amount of the currency to be received, the 'first currency amount'); and a borrowing (the second currency which is to be delivered, the 'second currency amount'). Thus it comprises two legs: an asset (purchase) leg, the right to receive currency B; and a liability (sale) leg, the obligation to pay currency A. The definition embraces currency forwards, currency futures and currency swaps. The definition includes net payment contracts, ie contract for differences. Each leg is translated separately. So long as the local currency equivalent of each amount does not alter between translation times, there is no exchange gain or loss. Thus, if the second currency amount is valued at the rate implied in the contract at T_1, no gain or loss will arise at that stage.

14.49   The forward sale by one party will be the forward purchase of the counterparty. The notion of currency contract covers fixed to fixed, and fixed to floating, currency swaps. Where only the net difference is payable, as will almost invariably be the case, exchange of periodic payments will be simultaneous. The requirement for exchange of currencies will, in most cases, take this form of payment of net differences by reference to the sterling equivalent, or the relevant foreign currency equivalent.

14.50   A contract will normally be for a fixed period from the date of the contract, eg one month, six months, one year. Forward rates are a function of the difference between spot rates and interest rates, ie the rate under the contract is a function of:

(a)   the spot rate at the date the contract is taken out; and

(b)   the interest rate differential between the two currencies.

14.51   This is because the amount of foreign currency which the purchaser will receive, and the amount of sterling which he has to pay for it, are calculated by discounting the amounts payable back to the NPV by reference to the prevailing interest rates.

Example 14.12

On 31 March 2017, X plc contracts to buy €1,400 from its bank in a year's time. The spot rate is 1:1.4. UK interest rates are 4.5%. Euro interest rates are 3.5%. The rate under the contract is calculated as if the bank had, on 31 March 2012:

(a)   sold the company at the spot rate the amount of Euros which would produce €1,400 in a year's time, ie $1/(1 – 0.035) \times 1 = 0.965 \times 1,400 =$ €1,351;

(b)   placed €1,351 on deposit for X plc; and

(c)   lent X plc the sterling equivalent of €1,351, ie 1,351/1.4 = £965 repayable with interest at 4.5% in a year's time, ie £1,008.43.

Hence, the contract rate is 1,400/1,008.43 = 1.39. The forward rate is below the spot rate because sterling interest rates are higher. In other words, a forward exchange contract will always be a synthetic sterling loan.

Example 14.13

On 1 July 2017, A plc agrees to buy 180,000 yen six months forward for £1,000 (rate implied in the contract, 1:180). On 31 December 2017, the spot rate is £1 = 170 yen.

31 December 2017

Receive (first currency amount)	T_2	180,000 @ 1:170	1,059
Pay (second currency amount)			1,000
			59

1 July 2017

Receive (first currency amount)	T_1	180,000 @ 1:180	1,000	
Pay (second currency amount)			1,000	–
Foreign currency gain				59
(increase in amount receivable)				

14.52 Differences in forward rates reflect differences in interest rates:

Example 14.14

One year £ interest	7.64%
One year € interest	4.04%
Spot rate £1 =	€1.5678
£100 + year's interest (A)	107.64
€156.78 + year's interest (B)	€163.11
Forward rate B/A	1.5154
Forward points: 1.5678 – 1.5154	524

The higher interest rate on the sterling deposit is needed to maintain its value, because it is expected to decline against the euro.

14.53 An implied forward discount or premium arises if a company values a currency contract at a spot rate rather than a forward rate. Forward premiums and discounts are calculated by applying the difference between the two rates of exchange to the principal amount of the currency specified in the contract. The forward premium is a finance cost to be spread over the life of the contract.

Example 14.15

At T_1 (the start of its financial year), B plc contracts to buy \$100 two years forward for £88. It values the contract at the spot rate. The spot and forward rates are as follows:

Date	Spot £	Forward £
T_1	100	
T_2	83	85
T_3	91	88

The overall gain is the sterling equivalent of the amount received at T_3, less the amount payable, ie $91 - 88 = 3$. This is computed as follows:

Gain as per accounts		
Year 1	$83 - 100 =$	(17)
Year 2	$91 - 83 =$	8
		(9)
Forward discount		
Spot at T_1	100	
Forward at T_3	88	
Forward discount		12
		3
Allocate		
Year 1	$6^* - 17 =$	(11)
Year 2	$6^* + 8 =$	14
Overall profit		3

* The forward discount accrued over the two years.

14.54 The difference between the exchange rate in the forward contract (forward rate) and the current rate (spot rate) is the forward discount or premium, and reflects differences in interest rates between the two currencies. The only payment is the exchange of currencies at the end of the contract (or payment of differences), but accounting treatment may give rise to a payment or receipt.

14.55 If forward contracts are valued using spot rates at the time of entering into the contract (T_1), the forward discount or premium will be reflected in taxable exchange differences. Accounting treatment may deem this to be payable on the maturity of the contract, with any difference between the local currency equivalent of the two currency amounts specified in the currency contract being calculated at the time the contract is concluded. There will be no difference if the accounts use the rate implied in the contract, or forward rate of exchange, to calculate the second currency amount (ie amount payable) at T_1.

14.56 Accordingly, an implied forward discount or premium will only arise where a company uses spot rates. In such cases, the company will be undertaking to buy (or sell) for $£y$ something which is, at the date of the contract, worth $£x$. If the company is the purchaser, and $x > y$, there will be an immediate profit, ie an implied forward premium. If the company is the purchaser, and $y > x$, there will be an immediate loss, ie an implied forward discount. An implied forward difference is essentially a payment of interest. It reflects the difference in interest rates between two currencies over a period of time. The forward premium or discount is measured in 'forward points', ie the difference between the spot rate and the forward rate.

Example 14.16

If UK interest rates are 8%, euro interest rates are 4% and the spot rate of exchange between sterling and the euro is 1:1.5, then:

	£
(A) £100 @ 8% for one year	108
(B) €150 @ 4% for one year	156
Forward rate (B/A)	1.44
Forward difference 1.50 – 1.44	0.06

14.57 The effect of the interest differential is to give a higher return over a year for a given amount of sterling, compared with the equivalent amount of euros using the spot rates.

Example 14.17

Company X sells €5,000 one year forward against sterling. The contract comprises:

(a) a liability to deliver €5,000 (cost £3,333 at spot rate);

(b) a right to receive £3,472 (at forward rate); and

(c) a forward exchange premium of £3,472 – £3,333 = £139.

The amortisation of the foreign exchange difference (being akin to interest) has to be taken through the profit and loss account. If, when the contract comes to be performed, the spot rate is 1:1.40, the accounting entries for tax purposes are:

Fwd liability	Fwd asset	Fwd difference	Profit
£	£	£	£
3,333	3,472	139	139
3,571	3,472		(99)

Example 14.18

Investor plc has £3,333 to invest for one year. Euro interest rates are 4%. Sterling interest rates are 8%. The company's financial year is the calendar year. The company values currency contracts on inception at spot rates. Spot rates are:

1 January 2017	£1 = €1.5
31 December 2017	£1 = €1.444

The company treasurer has three financial strategies:

(a)   invest in sterling;

(b)   invest in euros; and

(c)   buy euros forward.

Tax treatment of the three strategies is as follows:

Strategy (a)
Loan relationship credit:

£3,333 × 8%	£267
Strategy (b)	£
Loan relationship credit:	
€5,000 @ 4% = 200 @ 1.444	138

Exchange gain

First currency amount (T_2)		
€5,000 @ 1.444	3,462	
Second currency amount (T_1)		
€5,000 @ 1.5	3,333	
Foreign exchange gain		129
Amount taxable		£267

Strategy (c)

It is normal to sell forward not just the original amount invested but also the interest that will be received. In this way, the overall profit is locked in. Therefore, buy €5,200 12 months forward for £3,600 (rate 1:1.444).

		£
Loan relationship credit (as in (a))		267
Exchange gain		
First currency amount (T$_2$) – no change		
Second currency amount (T$_2$)		
€5,200 @ 1.444	3,600	
Second currency amount (T$_1$)		
€5,200 @ 1.5	3,466	
Increase in amount payable		(134)
Forward discount		
Forward value of contract at T$_1$ (A)	3,600	
Spot value of contract at T$_1$ (B)	3,466	
Derivative contract profit		134
Amount taxable		£267

14.58   When a company has non-matched foreign currency debts, exchange differences will fall exclusively under the loan relationship rules.

Example 14.19

A UK company has a US$ loan on 1 January 2017 of $150,000. Interest at 4% is charged to the company at the end of each quarter. On 31 October 2017, the company repays $25,000, which is allocated first to the interest and secondly to the capital. The exchange difference for the company's year ending 31 December 2017 is calculated as follows:

Date	Amount US$	Exchange rate $:£	Interest accrual US$	Cash movement $	LCE £
01.01.17	150,000	1:2	–	–	75,000
31.03.17	151,500	1:1.65	1,500	–	909
30.06.17	153,015	1:1.70	1,515	–	891
30.09.17	154,545	1:1.60	1,530	–	956
31.10.17	138,416	1:1.55	–	(25,000)	(16,129)
31.12.17	139,854	1:1.50	1,438	–	959
			5,983		

Debt outstanding at 31.12.17 (139,854/1.50)		93,236
Debt at 1.1.17		75,000
Add: interest accruals	909	
	891	
	956	
	959	
	3,715	
	78,715	
Less: payment of interest on 31.10.17		
((1,500 + 1,515 + 1,530) @ 1.55)	(2,932)	
Payment of capital (£16,129 – £2,932)	(13,197)	
		(62,586)
Exchange loss (increase in liability)		30,650

Cross currency swaps

14.59 Plain vanilla currency swaps are equivalent to spot purchases and forward sales of foreign currencies. A currency swap involves two currency contracts, in which counterparty A undertakes:

(a)   at T_1 a spot sale of one currency for another, combined with

(b)   a simultaneous forward contract to repurchase at T_2 the agreed currency amounts at the spot rate at T_1 and

(c)   an agreement between the counterparties to exchange interest payments on their swapped currencies at periodic intervals.

14.60 Currency amounts are normally notional, ie no actual exchange of currencies or repayment takes place, but cash differences are paid. The major accounting issue is what rate (forward or spot) should be used to value the re-exchange of principal at maturity.

Example 14.20

X plc enters into a three-year swap agreement on 1 January 2017. The terms are:

Fees	£90
Initial exchange	X receives €1,670
	X pays £1,000

440

Periodic payments: 31 December
Pay €-LIBOR @ 5% on €1,670
Receive sterling-LIBOR @ 10% on £1,000
Final exchange 31.12.2015 –   X receives £1,000
                                                X pays €1,670

Spot exchange rates in Year 1 are: 01.01.17 – 1: 1.67
                                      31.12.17 – 1: 1.80
Interest rates do not change in the first year.

31 December 2017
Sterling receivable   1,000
€ payable 1,670 @ 1.80   (928)
                                                            72

Less: difference at 01.01.17
Sterling receivable   1,000
€ payable 1,670 @ 1.67   (1,000)
                                                             0
Foreign exchange gain   72
Interest receivable – 1,000 @ 10%   100
Interest payable – 1,670 × 5% @ 1.80   (46)
Fee 90/3   (30)
Profit/credit   96

14.61   A currency swap is similar to an interest rate swap and a long-dated currency forward. Interest rate differentials between two currencies are recognised through periodic payments rather than by payment of a lump sum on maturity. Profits and losses will be calculated on a fair value basis and taxed under the derivative contracts rules. If a currency contract runs to maturity, and is settled by either:

(a)   delivery of foreign currency,

(b)   gross payment in sterling, or

(c)   netting of the two amounts,

the sterling leg of a currency swap will not alter over the term of the agreement. However, if neither of the currencies used in the contract is sterling, and the company does not use a non-sterling local currency for one of the currencies, the exchange gains and losses on each leg of the contract will have to be calculated and translated into sterling.

Example 14.21

Amounts payable in foreign currency are valued at the year end spot rates. X enters into a three-year currency swap of notional £10m for notional €16.4m. Details are:

Arrangement fee to broker	£10,000
Fee to swap counterparty	£50,000
Initial exchange of principal	notional
Periodic payments	30 June and 31 December
X to pay six-month € LIBOR on €16.4m	
X to receive £ LIBOR on £10m	
Initial exchange 1 October 2017	
Re-exchange 30 September 2020	
X's accounting year ends on 31 December	

Spot exchange rates are:

1 October 2017	£1 = €1.64
31 December 2017	£1 = €1.54
1 January 2020	£1 = €1.50
30 September 2020	£1 = €1.60

Interest rates are:

Six-month LIBOR	£6.5%
Six-month LIBOR	€5.5%

Year ended 31 December 2017

£ receivable	10,000,000	
€ payable 16.4m @ 1.54	(10,649,350)	
Exchange difference		(649,350)

£ receivable – 10m × 6.5% × 3/12	162,500	
€ payable – 16.4m × 5.5% × 3/12 @ 1.54	(146,428)	
		16,072
Broker's fee £10,000		(10,000)
Initial fee £50,000		(50,000)
Carry to p/l account		(693,278)
Year ended 31 December 2020		
30 September 2020		
£ received	10,000,000	
€ paid 16.4m @ 1.60	(10,250,000)	
		(250,000)
31 December 2019		
£ receivable	10,000,000	
€ payable 16.4m @ 1.50	(10,933,333)	
		(933,333)
Exchange difference		683,333
£ receivable – 10m × 6.5% × 9/12	487,500	
€ payable – 16.4m × 5.5% × 9/12 @ 1.60	(422,812)	
		64,688
Carry to p/l account		748,021

Currency options

14.62 A currency option is:

(a) an option to enter into a currency contract or an option to enter into such an option;

(b) an option to buy or sell specified amounts of currency within any specified period or at a specified time, the exercise of which gives rise to the immediate exchange of currencies; or

(c) a conditional contract giving rise to an immediate exchange of specified amounts of two currencies upon fulfilment of the condition; this applies to options which automatically settle in cash if it is valuable to the holder on termination.

Credit derivatives

14.63   Credit derivatives are particular types of derivative contracts, such as swaps and options, designed to transfer credit risk on loans or other assets from one party (the protection buyer) to another party (the protection seller). The seller will receive a premium, interest-related or yield-related payment in return for the undertaking to make payments to the buyer linked to the credit standing or a reference asset or assets such as a loan or other obligations. Credit risk may be transferred for the duration of the reference asset or for a short period, and either to effect full cover or only part.

14.64   *CTA 2009, s 579(2)(b)(v)* states that a relevant contract will be a derivative contract if it is a 'contract for differences', whose 'underlying subject matter' is 'creditworthiness'.

14.65   Credit derivatives are generally:

- credit default products;
- total return swaps;
- credit link notes; or
- credit spread options.

In the case of a bank or financial trader, these will be held in the trading book if they are financial instruments, and otherwise in the banking book. Most credit derivatives will be either interest rate contracts, currency contracts or debt contracts.

14.66   The important distinction is between partial and complete transfer of credit risk. The two most common types of credit derivative are credit default swaps (or options) and total return swaps (see below).

14.67   In a credit default swap, a seller of risk (V) contracts with a purchaser of risk (P) that, should a specified credit default occur to the detriment of V, P will – in consideration of periodical payments by V – pay to V the difference between what V would have received, had the default not occurred, and what V is expected to receive, the default having occurred.

Example 14.22

V acquires a sterling bond paying interest at 4% for three years, with a nominal and market value of £1,000. At that time, LIBOR is 5.5%. V agrees to pay P interest at 0.5% on £1,000, on condition that, if LIBOR rises to 6%, P will pay him the difference between £1,000 and the market value of a notional security with the characteristics of V's bond. After two years (by which time V has paid P £10), LIBOR rises to 6%, and the market value of a bond similar to V's falls to £980. P pays V £20.

In a total value return swap the seller of risk (V) substitutes a buyer of risk (P) for an actual debtor (X). P pays to V what X has agreed to pay to V, less an interest margin. V pays to P what X actually pays to V. Periodic and settlement payments are netted. Total return swaps pass the whole of the credit risk in a specific asset. The asset will remain with the owner, so there is no transfer or assignment. What is transferred is the right to payments under the loan agreement, in exchange for the payments calculated by reference to a different loan agreement, actual or notional. In either case, if a defined circumstance occurs, the seller of protection will pay to the buyer of protection an amount calculated by reference to the notional amount of the swap and any concomitant drop in value of one or more of the debt obligations. The buyer of protection will, for his part, pay the seller a combination of an up-front fee and periodic payments.

The seller of credit risk could in turn sell on his new credit risk against P, and could sell on his new credit risk against X. Should this happen, a situation analogous to spiral reinsurance would arise.

14.68   There are three basic documentation structures for credit derivatives: note form; bespoke agreement; and master agreement. For most credit derivatives, the master agreement used is the ISDA Annex for Credit Derivatives. A seller of risk is a 'fixed rate payer'. The buyer of risk is the 'floating rate payer'. A third party borrower is the 'reference entity', and the debts which he owes are the 'reference obligations'. A default by the reference entity in respect of his reference obligation is a 'credit event'. The 'cash settlement amount' is the amount payable on the occurrence of a credit event. The 'reference entity' is defined as 'entity or entities whose credit risk is being transferred or traded'. 'Reference obligations' are 'specified obligations or a basket of obligations … issued or guaranteed by the reference entity or entities, which may be a loan, security or other type of obligation and which (a) are used to price the payout on Cash Settlement … [and] (b) may be used as a reference to determine existence of a Credit Event'.

14.69   'Credit events' are defined as:

- failure to pay;
- repudiation;
- downgrade;
- restructuring;

- bankruptcy;

- credit event upon merger; and

- cross acceleration.

14.70   Materiality tests are designed to provide an objective way of determining whether one of the more subjective default events has occurred. A calculation agent may be appointed to calculate the value of reference obligations and the amount and value of payments due or made under the agreement.

Credit risk

14.71   Forwards are largely OTC and lack the margin requirements which exchange trading requires. Accordingly, forwards carry the greatest credit risk, because the value of the contract only passes on maturity or when it is closed out. Exchange traded options are fair valued, and require margin payments, so that, as with futures, default risk is controlled. Swaps represent a half-way house as far as credit risk is concerned. Part of the value passes each time a periodic payment is due, but a residuum of value only passes when principal or notional principal is re-exchanged on termination of the swap.

14.72   When a collateralised trade is out of the money, additional collateral (usually cash) must be posted and hence funded. This will often take the form of a counterparty valuation adjustment (CVA). A CVA may be used to profit from increased credit default swap spreads, ie a party makes a paper profit on its own risk of default.

Example – acquisition of shares in foreign currency

Stage 1 – the bid

14.73   XYZ plc, the holding company of a UK trading group, is looking to expand overseas. It intends to make a competitive sealed bid for Target Inc and its subsidiaries, a cocoa trading division of a large US multinational corporation.

14.74   Target Inc has net assets of US$150m and the Board of XYZ plc has decided to make a bid of US$300m plus a contingent deferred payment equal to movements in the cocoa price over a specified period based on US$50m principal (which reflects Target's current cocoa stocks).

14.75   The bid has to be submitted within the next six weeks and the successful bidder will be announced two weeks later. Completion will take place five weeks after the successful bid is accepted.

14.76   The current rate of exchange is £1 = US$1.50. The funding for the acquisition will be drawn in equal proportions from:

- a recent sterling rights issue; and

- a five-year sterling revolving credit facility.

14.77   The board of XYZ plc would like to hedge the currency exposure in respect of the bid, the interest risk associated with the potential funding costs and the exposure to movements in the price of cocoa associated with the contingent element of the bid.

Hedging the bid

14.78   A currency option is the most obvious instrument to use purely to hedge the bid cost during the tender period. Options are ideally suited to tender situations where the outcome is unknown, as the cost is limited to the premium paid, compared to a forward foreign exchange contract where the exposure is unlimited if the bid does not succeed. In addition, options would allow XYZ plc to profit from any favourable move in the £:$ rate. XYZ plc could sell the option if it were exchange traded should the bid lapse and may be able to terminate or exercise an OTC option to release positive cashflow.

14.79   A compound currency has some of the advantages of a currency option, in that the maximum cost is known, whatever the outcome of the bid. A compound currency option will be cheaper initially, so if the bid fails, this will be a cheaper choice than a currency option. However, if the bid succeeds and the option is exercised, this will prove more expensive than a currency option (around 1.5 to 1.75 times as expensive).

14.80   The break forward contract has the advantage that the upfront premium is payable, and the contract can therefore be broken if the bid fails. However, economically, a break forward is similar to a standard currency option, with the premium payable as part of the achieved exchange rate or as the break cost. Commercially, break forwards are generally more expensive than standard currency options.

14.81   Exchange traded cocoa options are available from the London Commodities Exchange but the market is unlikely to be very liquid as total daily volume for cocoa futures is of the order of 4,000 contracts (for 10 tonnes each at some £16,000 a tonne) and this option would be over more than 3,000 contracts. Alternatively, OTC options could be acquired; however, the price of these would reflect the difficulty the provider would have in hedging the exposure.

Hedging the funding costs

14.82 The various options to hedge the funding costs are all commercially available. The main pros and cons of each are summarised below:

Caption: As an option on an option, the spread on this is likely to be higher than that for a basic cap. The purchase of a caption would not eat into bank lines.

Option on gilt future: These are exchange traded and readily available in a liquid market.

Interest rate swap: The swaption market is more liquid than that for a caption and a swaption could be purchased at reasonable spread. Purchasing a swaption would use up bank lines.

Hedging the bid price

14.83 XYZ plc will be exposed to movements in the £:$ exchange rate if the bid is successful.

(a) If the success of the bid is considered probable, any transactions entered into to reduce this expected exchange rate exposure could be accounted for as hedges, with any profits or losses arising on these transactions carried to equity.

(b) If the success of the bid is not considered probable, any transaction entered into should not be classified as a hedge for accounting purposes, and fair value changes should be passed through the income statement.

Currency option

14.84 A £:$ currency option can be purchased to eliminate any downside exchange rate risk. The premium payable for the currency options will depend on the strike price in the option.

14.85 Currency options are fair value hedges, as they reduce XYZ's potential exposure to adverse exchange rate movements in relation to the bid. If the option is exercised, the exercise price should be used to compute the sterling cost of Target Inc.

14.86 If the bid is not successful, all costs incurred in purchasing the option should be recognised immediately; any profits should be recognised on a fair value basis.

Compound currency option

14.87   The accounting treatment of a compound option will be the same as that for a currency option if the option purchased will reduce the expected currency exposure if the bid succeeds. Hedge accounting would be appropriate, and the same accounting treatment as that described above will be relevant, except in the following circumstances.

Break forward currency contracts

14.88   A break forward contract, that reduces the currency exposure, would be accounted for in a consistent way to a currency option, except:

- No premium would be payable upfront.

- If the bid succeeds, the rate under the break forward contract would be used to determine the sterling cost of the acquisition.

- If the break forward contract is not exercised, the break payment should be incorporated in the bid costs and treated appropriately.

- If the bid fails, the break forward contract would have to be revalued to compute what loss should be recognised in the accounting records, as XYZ plc would be committed to paying the difference between the break price and the market price if the company did not wish to make the currency exchange.

Cocoa option

14.89   The cocoa option could again be treated as a hedge. The premium cost should be treated in the same way as for the currency option, and the rate used to fix the provision for deferred consideration.

Hedging the funding costs – the bid

14.90   If the bid is successful, XYZ plc will be exposed to movements in the funding rates for the acquisition finance:

(a)   If the success of the bid is considered probable, any transactions entered to reduce this exposure could be accounted for as a hedge of a net investment in a foreign operation, with any profits or losses arising on these transactions recognised in equity until the outcome of the bid.

(b)   If the success of the bid is not considered probable, any hedging transaction entered into should not be classified as a hedge for accounting purposes and should be accounted for in the income statement.

14.91   Purchasing the appropriate caption would reduce the exposure of XYZ plc to adverse interest rate movements if the bid is successful, and so this could be treated as a hedge. The accounting treatment will be as follows.

Option on gilt futures

14.92   An option on gilt futures would reduce the treasury's exposure to interest rate movements, but would not perfectly hedge the interest rate exposures, as the gilts market does not always move in line with LIBOR.

Interest rate swaption

14.93   Purchasing an appropriate interest rate swaption could eliminate the exposure of XYZ plc to interest rate movements on the revolving credit facility if the bid is successful. Therefore, this would classify as a cash flow hedge. If the bid is not successful, the swaption will be either exercised, or terminated for a receipt, or it will expire worthless. If it is exercised, the fair value gain or loss will be recognised in the income statement.

Currency swaption

14.94   The appropriate currency swaption would reduce the exposure to both currency fluctuations and potential interest rate exposures incurred in financing the acquisition.

Hedging the bid price

14.95   Currency option:

- The currency option is a derivative contract: all receipts and payments under the contract are therefore taxable or relievable on a fair value basis.

- Payments and receipts are aggregated with non-trading interest and other non-trading gains/losses of the period taxable under loan relationship rules.

- Net profits will be brought into account as investment income for the accounting period.

- Net losses can be offset against other income of the accounting period, surrendered as group relief, carried forward or carried back against similar profits in the previous year.

Compound currency option

14.96   The compound currency option will be a derivative contract, and all receipts and payments under the contract are therefore taxable or relievable on a fair value basis.

Break forward currency option

14.97   Although, in substance, this is equivalent to a dollar call sterling put option with a deferred premium, it is structured as a combination of a forward purchase of dollar for sterling and a dollar put sterling call option. As the agreement provides for XYZ plc to purchase US$300m at the forward rate specified, but also gives it the right to sell $300m at the break rate, this should be regarded as a currency contract plus a dollar put sterling call currency option, both of which are derivative contracts. Accordingly, all receipts and payments are taxable or relievable on a fair value basis.

Cocoa future

14.98   The cocoa future contract will be a derivative contract: *CTA 2009, s 579(2).*

Stage 2 – the bid succeeds

14.99   XYZ plc's bid is accepted, sterling has strengthened and interest rates have fallen, so any options entered into at the time of the bid are abandoned. XYZ plc will amortise the goodwill acquired, but wishes to protect its balance sheet from the effect of exchange rate movements on the value of Target Inc's US$150m net asset value. It therefore proposes to enter into a $:£ currency swap to convert the sterling facility into a synthetic floating rate dollar loan. It would also like to hedge its interest rate risk, and is considering using one of the following:

- interest rate swap;
- zero cost collar; or
- 'diff' swap (differential swap).

14.100   The currency swap qualifies as a fair value hedge because it reduces XYZ plc's potential exposure to currency fluctuations. The appropriate currency swap would be where XYZ plc paid sterling and received dollars. Thus the cashflows payable on the sterling borrowing would be offset by the sterling cashflows receivable on the swap, and the net payments would be dollar payments on the swap and thus equivalent to dollar denominated debt.

14.101   At the swap's maturity, XYZ plc would receive back the sterling principal, with which it could pay off its sterling loan, and pay back the dollars, with any currency movement in dollars against sterling offset by the movement in the dollar investment's value.

14.102   The appropriate interest rate swap would qualify as a cash flow hedge, as it reduces the exposure to interest rate fluctuations. A zero cost collar is a combination of a purchased cap and written floor on which the premium payable on the cap is offset by the premium receivable on the floor. Although a zero cost collar includes a written option, it can be treated as a hedge because:

- The exposure to interest rate fluctuations is reduced by purchasing the collar.

- The treatment of the collar on a 'pay as you go' basis is consistent with the accounting treatment for fixed rate borrowing where losses due to adverse movements of interest rates are not provided for.

14.103   A 'diff' swap would not represent a hedge and therefore would have to be accounted for through the income statement. This is because a 'diff' swap would not reduce XYZ plc's exposure to interest rate movements.

After tax currency hedging

14.104   If the sterling loan that is used to acquire the shares is swapped into a dollar loan, this will provide a pre-tax hedge against movements in the value of the shares caused by exchange rate fluctuations. However, this is not an efficient after tax hedge, as there is a mismatch in the tax treatment of the liability and the asset that is being hedged. That is, gains and losses on the foreign currency liability are brought to account for tax on an ongoing basis, but movements in the value of the shares (ie the asset that is being hedged) are not taxed until the asset is disposed of. In recognition of this, a matching treatment allows foreign exchange movements on a foreign currency liability used to hedge a net investment in an overseas operation to be deferred for accounting and tax purposes until the asset being hedged is disposed of.

Stage 3 – early disposal

14.105   Twelve months after acquiring Target Inc, the Board of XYZ plc decides to concentrate on its core activities, and sells Target Inc for US$350m. It therefore wishes to repay its borrowing and unwind the five-year interest rate and currency swaps it has entered into. Sterling has weakened and interest rates have fallen, with the result that the termination fees which must be paid to cancel the two swaps are:

Interest rate swap	US$3,000,000
Currency swap	£10,000,000

Swap termination payments

14.106 The termination payments on the swaps should be accounted immediately with any profits or losses on the sale of Target Inc and repayment of the borrowing.

14.107 The underlying transaction, the investment in Target Inc, has been sold, and therefore any profit or loss from repaying the borrowings which were hedging this investment should be recognised immediately. These profits or losses would usually be rolled up with the profit or loss on the sale of Target Inc to give the aggregate profit or loss on the sale. This would generally be a write off through the income statement. Under IAS 39, para 39, profits or losses on the repurchase of own debt should be taken through the profit and loss account at the time the debt is repaid.

Possible alternative actions

14.108 Matching swaps could be taken out to hedge the existing swaps at current market rates. In these cases, the floating flows on the respective swaps would net out and XYZ plc would lock into a fixed series of repayments over the remaining lives of the swaps.

14.109 The company could also consider entering into a reciprocal swap at market rates with the same maturity date as the original, ie receive US dollar floating rate interest on US$150m and pay sterling floating rate interest on sterling equivalent of US$150m at current spot rate (say £110m).

Chapter 15

Embedded Derivatives

Outline

15.1   This chapter deals with:

- Accounting treatment
- Convertibles
- Tax treatment – individual investors
- Tax treatment – companies
- Convertible, exchangeable and asset linked debt

Hybrid contracts

15.2   A financial liability is an obligation to deliver cash or another financial instrument to the holder. An equity instrument is a contract which evidences a residual interest in the assets of an entity, after deduction of all its liabilities. Where an instrument contains both a liability component and an equity component, it is known as a compound financial instrument, and the two components may have to be separately accounted for.

Example 15.1

X plc issues, and Y plc purchases, a five-year equity-linked note for £100. At maturity, X plc will pay the holder £100 plus the percentage increase in the FTSE index over the period of the note. If the FTSE index after five years has fallen as compared with its level when the note was issued, no additional amount is payable on redemption. The equity index feature is an embedded derivative and, assuming the instrument is not already accounted for at fair value through profit and loss account, must be bifurcated for accounting purposes. The £100 payable on issue must be allocated between the host debt and derivative financial instrument. The host debt is treated as a zero coupon bond and is amortised from its fair value at initial recognition to £100 over the five years using the effective interest method.

Accounting treatment

15.3   Most derivatives stand alone. But some financial instruments (for example, a convertible bond held by a company) are *hybrid instruments* that combine a non-derivative *host contract* with an *embedded derivative*. Embedded derivatives are components of hybrid contracts that cause some of the cash flows of the hybrid to vary in a similar way to a stand-alone derivative. According to IFRS 9, para 4.3, and FRS 102, paras 22.11–22.13 and Appendix, the issuer must recognise the derivative elements at fair value, separately from the non-derivative host contract, when they have economic characteristics and risks that are not 'closely related' to those of the host contract. The standards contain detailed rules which must be applied on a case-by-case basis to determine whether or not a particular derivative is closely related to its host contract. IAS 39 required the investor also to bifurcate the instrument in this way. IFRS 9 and FRS 102 allow the investor to account for the whole instrument on a non-separated basis.

15.4   A derivative is defined as a financial instrument which meets the following conditions:

- its value changes in response to changes in an 'underlying' price or index;

- it requires no initial net investment, or an initial net investment that is smaller than would be required to purchase the underlying instrument; and

- it is settled at a future date.

15.5   IFRS requires that all derivatives are recognised at fair value, with movements in value recognised in the profit and loss account, except derivatives that are designated as hedging instruments. The purpose of the embedded derivative rules is to prevent derivatives being 'hidden' in the terms of non-derivative contracts that are not accounted for at fair value, thus avoiding the volatility to the income statement that arises from recording changes in the fair value of derivatives. Effectively, the rules for embedded derivatives are a form of accounting anti-avoidance rule.

15.6   IFRS 9 achieves this object by requiring the contract to be disaggregated, for accounting purposes, into a notional non-derivative contract ('the host contract') and a separate instrument (the 'embedded derivative') embedded in the host contract. The splitting of a single instrument into two separate components for accounting purposes is known as 'bifurcation'.

15.7 *Embedded Derivatives*

15.7   As regards the issuer, IFRS 9, para 4.3.3 [IAS 39.11] requires that an embedded derivative be separated from its host contract and accounted for as a derivative when:

- the economic risks and characteristics of the embedded derivative are *not closely related* to those of the host contract;

- a separate instrument with the same terms as the embedded derivative would meet the definition of a derivative; and

- the entire instrument is not measured at fair value with changes in fair value recognised in the income statement.

15.8   If an embedded derivative is separated/bifurcated, the host contract is accounted for under the appropriate standard, and an embedded derivative must be accounted for at fair value. The host contract is itself a financial instrument, but embedded derivatives can be found within other types of contract, such as leases or sale or purchase contracts.

15.9   An embedded derivative is defined as a feature that sits within another contract (the 'host contract') and causes some or all of the cash flows of the host contract to change, according to a specified index or other variable. No definition is given of 'closely related', but IFRS 9 [IAS 39] explains the term by the use of a number of rule-based examples. Broadly, an embedded derivative is considered to be closely related to the host contract where it modifies an instrument's inherent risk but leaves the instrument substantially unaltered. For example, a fixed to floating interest rate swap embedded in a debt instrument would usually be considered closely related, but an option to convert into equity shares of the issuer would not be closely related.

15.10   Embedded derivatives can arise in any contract and are not confined to contracts that are financial instruments. Examples of contracts which may include embedded derivatives considered in IAS 39 include lease contracts (eg index-linked rent) and supply contracts (eg contracts to purchase goods in a foreign currency). The identification of embedded derivatives and determination as to whether or not they should be bifurcated is a complex area.

15.11   As regards the issuer, the instrument carved out of the loan relationship does not meet the definition of a derivative, and so is an equity instrument. Because, not being a derivative, fair value accounting is not required, it is kept at a fixed amount in the balance sheet of the issuer. If conversion occurs, it is transferred to share capital. Under IAS 39, the separated out instrument held by the investor – the share option – is an embedded derivative and so has to be fair valued, with changes in fair value going to the income statement pending redemption or conversion.

15.12   Not all convertible bonds are considered part debt and part equity for accounting purposes, however. Examples where the embedded derivative is considered to be a derivative financial instrument, as opposed to an equity instrument, include:

(a)   where the shares into which the convertible converts are themselves considered a financial liability of the issuer (for example, redeemable preference shares);

(b)   where the shares into which the convertible converts are shares in another entity (ie an exchangeable);

(c)   where the instrument confers a right to subscribe for a variable number of shares with a fixed value;

(d)   where the instrument confers the right on the issuer to pay cash instead of issuing shares; and

(e)   where the convertible bond is in a currency other than the functional currency of the issuer.

Convertibles

15.13   A convertible bond is a common form of hybrid contract containing an embedded derivative. The underlying loan is the host contract, and the option to exchange or convert into shares is the embedded derivative. If the nature of the conversion option is not closely related to the loan, the overall arrangement must be 'bifurcated' (ie split in two) and the two component parts must be shown separately in the accounts of both the issuer and the holder. The value of the liability element is determined first, and the residual amount – by reference to the issue price less the amount attributable to the liability – is allocated to the derivative (equity instrument). The derivative will itself be classified as either a derivative financial instrument or an equity instrument, a distinction which has a significant impact on the resultant tax treatment.

15.14   A convertible contains an obligation of the issuer to pay the redemption price, but is also contingent equity. It is neither wholly debt, nor wholly equity, but partakes of both. Until redemption or conversion occurs, its character is ambiguous. An investor who holds a convertible bond has, in substance, two instruments: he has a simple debt instrument which promises him the return of his principal after a time and may in addition offer an interest coupon; and he holds a share option, ie typically a right to acquire a certain number of shares in the issuer at a fixed price (the redemption price of the bond) at a determinate date in the future. The interest payable on the bond is reduced, compared with plain vanilla debt of the issuer, to take account of the equity element. If the market value of the shares receivable on conversion rises above the price payable for them, the investor will make a profit on the share option.

15.15   A convertible security is, in commercial terms, contingent equity. The conversion price can be expressed either at a rate (eg 10 shares per £100 nominal of debt) or as a price (eg £10 per share). The normal practice is to fix the conversion price at a premium to the market price of the shares then prevailing. It is usual, and in the case of listed securities required, for the price to be adjusted for any event which would dilute the holder's potential stake in the company, eg a rights issue or bonus issue. The gamble which the investor takes is that the increase in share value prior to conversion will exceed the loss of the interest which would have been payable on a conventional security.

15.16   In the case of a company investor, if the convertible meets the conditions of *CTA 2009, s 585*, the notional loan relationship ('host contract') will be used to acquire or subscribe for new shares. Accordingly, if the convertible security held by the corporate investor will fall within *TCGA 1992, s 116(1)(b), (9)*, the disposal of the bond will be a 'related transaction' within *CTA 2009, s 304*. The investor's base cost in the shares will be the original subscription price for the host contract adjusted for any net credits and debits already brought into account on the embedded derivative.

15.17   Where a compound financial instrument is bifurcated, the equity element (eg the conversion option in the case of a convertible bond) is accounted for as an equity instrument of the issuer, as opposed to a derivative financial instrument, and is therefore not subject to the requirement to account for the embedded derivative at fair value. In fact, the amount allocated to equity on issue of the bond is not subsequently revalued at all for accounting purposes. Thus, most issuers of convertible bonds will not be subject to volatility in their profit and loss account due to fair value movements in the embedded derivative, but will suffer an increased finance cost due to the additional amortisation on the host contract.

Example 15.2

D Ltd can borrow money at 8%. Its shares trade at 45. It issues a two-year bond for £1,000, paying interest at 1% and convertible at the end of two years into 20 D Ltd shares (ie £50 per share).

The fair value of cash flows on the host contract, discounted at 8%, is £875. The part of the subscription price allocated to the equity component is the difference between the issue price and the fair value of the host contract, ie £125 (1,000 – 875).

From the investor's point of view, the price paid (interest forgone) for the equity call option is:

$$\frac{(8\% - 1\%) \times 1,000}{1.08} + \frac{(8\% - 1\%) \times 1,000}{1.08^2} = 125$$

Hence the bond is bifurcated into a discounted bond issued at £875 and accreting to £1,000 over two years, and (for the issuer) an equity instrument of £125. The effective interest rate on the bond including the interest coupon is 8%. Finance costs will be debited on this basis.

15.18   Where the conversion option is considered to be a derivative financial instrument, rather than an equity instrument, the normal rules for embedded derivatives apply – the embedded derivative will be required to be separately accounted for at fair value through profit and loss account where it is not closely related to the host contract.

Tax treatment – individual investors

15.19   *TCGA 1992, s 251(1)* states that a 'debt on a security' is a chargeable asset for capital gains tax purposes. In the case of an individual, a convertible is not a qualifying corporate bond (QCB), because a QCB must be a 'normal commercial loan', and a normal commercial loan does not include convertibles, unless the security is only convertible into fixed rate preference shares (*CTA 2010, s 162; TCGA 1992, s 117(1)(a)*).

15.20   In the case of an individual who holds securities convertible directly or indirectly into shares in the company and carrying any right to receive shares in or securities of the company, *CTA 2010, ss 1000(1)F and 1015* provide that interest paid on securities prior to conversion will be treated as a dividend unless the interest does not exceed a reasonable commercial return and the securities are listed on a recognised stock exchange or, not being securities listed on a recognised stock exchange, are issued on terms which are reasonably comparable with the terms of listed securities. In the case of a corporate investor, provided that both the paying and recipient company are within the charge to corporation tax, payments received in respect of the bonds will be interest and will not be liable to treatment in part as dividends (*CTA 2010, s 1032(1)*).

15.21   Conversion is treated as a reorganisation (*TCGA 1992, s 132*). Because they are not QCBs, convertibles in the hands of individuals will be regarded as shares from the beginning, other than as regards income. On conversion, there will be no disposal, and the new shares will be treated as having been acquired at the time of, and for the cost of, the convertible bonds (*TCGA 1992, s 127*).

Tax treatment – companies

15.22   The tax consequences of embedded derivatives mirror the accounting position set out in IAS 39, para 11. The tax regime for embedded derivatives is designed to broadly mirror the accounting regime by respecting the separate components of the single contract, but with a number of specific rules for particular circumstances.

15.23   The essence of the tax approach for convertible, exchangeable and asset-linked debt, subject to a number of detailed provisions and various exceptions, is:

(a)   to follow the accounting treatment which bifurcates hybrid debt into plain vanilla debt and an asset-linked derivative or other instrument;

(b)   for investors, where bifurcations adopted under IAS 39, in the case of non-traders to treat gains or losses on the separated-out element on a 'modified capital gains', rather than an 'all income', basis; and

(c)   for issuers, to treat gains or losses on the separated-out element as a tax nothing.

Bifurcation of loan relationships is dealt with in *CTA 2009, ss 415, 585.*

15.24   *Section 415* states that, if, in its accounts, a company treats rights and liabilities under a loan relationship as divided between (a) a loan relationship ('the host contract') and (b) an equity instrument or derivative financial instrument, the company is treated as party to a loan relationship which comprises only the host contract.

15.25   *Section 415* provides:

'(1)   This section applies if in accordance with generally accepted accounting practice a company treats the rights and liabilities under a loan relationship to which it is party as divided between –

(a)   rights and liabilities under a loan relationship (the "host contract") and

(b)   rights and liabilities under one or more derivative financial instruments or equity instruments.

(2)   The company is treated for the purposes of this Part as a party to a loan relationship whose rights and liabilities consist only of those of the host contract.

(3)   For the corresponding treatment of the rights and liabilities within subsection (1)(b), see section 585 (loan relationships with embedded derivatives).'

15.26   *Section 585* is the counterpart of *s 415* and states that, where *s 415* applies, the company will be treated as party to an embedded derivative, which may be an equity instrument (in the case of the issuer) or a derivative contract.

15.27   *Section 585* provides:

'(1)   This section applies if in accordance with generally accepted accounting practice a company treats the rights and liabilities under a loan relationship to which it is party as divided between –

(a)   rights and liabilities under a loan relationship, and

(b)   rights and liabilities under one or more derivative financial instruments or equity instruments ("embedded derivatives").

(2)   The company shall be treated for the purposes of this Part –

(a)   as a party to a relevant contract whose rights and liabilities consist only of those of the embedded derivative, or

(b)   if there is more than one embedded derivative, as a part to relevant contracts each of whose rights and liabilities consist only of those of one of the embedded derivatives.

(3)   Each relevant contract to which a company is treated as a party under subsection (2) is treated for the purposes of this Part as an option, a future or a contract for differences – depending on what the character of a separate contract containing the rights and liabilities of the embedded derivative would be.'

15.28   In addition, a company could, subject to old UK GAAP, elect in certain circumstances that it should be treated for tax purposes as bifurcating an asset, even though it does not actually do so for accounting purposes: *CTA 2009, ss 416, 417*.

15.29   Embedded derivatives not embedded in loan relationships are also treated as relevant contracts by *CTA 2009, s 577*. Subject to satisfying the remaining requirements of *Part 7 (ss 570–710)*, these embedded derivatives also fall to be taxed as derivative contracts. This is, however, subject to the rule in *CTA 2009, s 616* that derivatives which are embedded in contracts which are themselves neither loan relationships nor derivative contracts should be treated for tax purposes as if the original contract had not been bifurcated for accounting purposes.

Convertible, exchangeable and asset linked debt

15.30   Where a company is not party to the debt for the purposes of its trade and is not an authorised unit trust, the tax position for such hybrid debt is broadly as follows:

1   Pending redemption, the tax rules follow the bifurcated accounting treatment. The investor will be taxed under the loan relationship provisions in *CTA 2009, Part 5* in respect of the host contract and under the derivative contract rules in *Part 7* in respect of the embedded derivative. The issuer will also adopt the bifurcated treatment for tax purposes.

2   The effect of bifurcation is to make all host contracts into discounted bonds, and so to increase the effective finance cost. Issuer and investor are taxed and relieved on the discount accordingly as income under the loan relationships regime.

3   If, as will normally be the case, the investor has to treat the embedded derivative as a derivative for accounting purposes, he will realise gains and losses on the embedded derivative on a fair value basis, but these gains and losses will be treated as capital gains for tax purposes on an annual basis.

4   Depending on whether the embedded derivative in the issuer is accounted for as an equity instrument or as a derivative financial instrument, there will either be no ongoing revaluations or the embedded derivative will be accounted for on a fair value basis. In the first case, the deemed relevant contract fails the accounting test in *s 579* and hence is not strictly a derivative contract (although a capital loss can arise in certain circumstances). In the latter case, whilst the deemed relevant contract is a derivative contract, the annual fair value movements are ignored for tax purposes.

5   If the investor assigns the instrument, he will realise a gain or loss at that point, allocating the disposal proceeds between the debt asset and the derivative contract.

6   If the instrument is redeemed for cash, both issuer and investor will then realise a profit or loss by reference to the carrying values at that time of the two components of the instrument. Depending on the nature of the embedded derivative in the issuer, a capital gain or loss may potentially arise at this point.

7   If the instrument is converted into shares, *CTA 2009, ss 652–653* apply, to bring in *TCGA 1992, s 144(2)* and the reorganisation rules in *TCGA 1992, ss 127–132*. Accordingly, (a) the grant of the option and its exercise are treated as a single transaction, and (b) the subscription price of the shares will be the original issue price of the instrument, that being the amount of cash received by the company as an addition to its capital. Conversion will be a 'conversion' within *TCGA 1992, s 132,* and the

investor's base cost in the shares will be the original subscription price adjusted for any net credits and debits already brought into account on the embedded derivative. In determining the allowable gain or loss on the exercise of the option, the market value rule of *TCGA 1992, s 17(1)* is disapplied, so that the actual consideration paid is used for tax purposes.

8   Under *CTA 2009, s 670*, gains and losses on the embedded derivative arising before conversion are incorporated into the subsequent sale price of the shares acquired to avoid double-counting. This applies where the bond is converted, or the company disposes of a convertible security otherwise than in exchange for shares.

Example 15.3

(a)   Convertible bond is issued at 100 and bifurcated into 90 (host contract) and 10 (price of share option). Prior to conversion, gains of 10 arise on the share option. The host contract is converted into shares. The shares are then sold for 120.

(b)   The gain on the shares is:

Proceeds of sale	120
Cost: 90 + 10	(100)
Gains on share option	(10)
Gain	10

15.31   Where either the investor or issuer accounts for the entire bond at fair value through profit and loss account and there is no requirement to bifurcate the bond, the normal loan relationship rules apply. Except in the case of connected party loan relationships, where an amortised cost basis is required to be followed for tax purposes, the fair value movements give rise to loan relationship debits and credits.

15.32   It is relatively common for listed convertible bonds to be issued by a special purpose vehicle (SPV) of the group, with the bond convertible (often in two stages) into ordinary shares of the parent. In these circumstances, it is necessary to examine the contractual relationships in detail to determine the appropriate accounting treatment in each of the parties. Typically, in addition to the convertible bond instrument in the issuer, there may exist one or more derivatives in the listed parent relating to the obligation to issue its own shares. The tax position in respect of such convertible instruments can only be determined once the detailed accounting position is known.

Example 15.4 – Accounting for convertible debt

Initial recognition

On initial recognition of a compound instrument such as a convertible bond, IAS 32 requires the issuer to:

(a) identify the various components of the instrument;

(b) determine the fair value of the liability component (see below); and

(c) determine the equity component as a residual amount, essentially the issue proceeds of the instrument less the liability component determined in (b) above.

Thereafter the liability component (and any identified financial asset component) is accounted for in accordance with the rules for measurement of financial liabilities (and, if relevant, financial assets) in IAS 39.

The liability component of a convertible bond should be measured first, at the fair value of a similar liability, including any embedded non-equity derivative features (eg an issuer's or holder's right to require early redemption of the bond) of a similar liability that does not have an associated equity conversion feature.

In practical terms, this will be done by determining the net present value of all potential contractually determined future cash flows under the instrument, discounted at the rate of interest applied by the market at the time of issue to instruments of comparable credit status and providing substantially the same cash flows, on the same terms, but without the conversion option. The fair value of any embedded non-equity derivative features is then determined and included in the liability component.

This treatment is illustrated below:

An entity issues 2,000 convertible bonds. The bonds have a three-year term, and are issued at par with a face value of €1,000 per bond, giving total proceeds of €2,000,000. Interest is payable annually in arrears at a nominal annual interest rate of 6% (ie €120,000 per annum). Each bond is convertible at any time up to maturity into 250 ordinary shares. When the bonds are issued, the prevailing market interest rate for similar debt without conversion options is 9% per annum. The entity incurs issue costs of €100,000.

The economic components of this instrument are:

● a liability component, being a discounted fixed rate debt, perhaps with an imputed holder's put option (due to the holder's right to convert at any time), and

● an equity component, representing the holder's right to convert at any time before maturity. In effect, this is a written call option (from the issuer's perspective) on American terms (ie it can be exercised at any time until maturity of the bond).

The liability component is measured first, at the net present value of the maximum potential cash payments that the issuer could be required to make, and the difference between the proceeds of the bond issue and this calculated fair value of the liability is assigned to the equity component. The net present value (NPV) of the liability component is calculated as €1,848,122, using a discount rate of 9%, the market interest rate for similar bonds having no conversion rights, as shown:

Year	Cash flow	€	Discount factor (at 9%)	NPV of cash flow €
1	Interest	120,000	1/1.09	110,092
2	Interest	120,000	1/1.09²	101,001
3	Interest and principal	2,120,000	1/1.09³	1,637,029
	Total liability component			1,848,122
	Total equity component (balance)			151,878
	Total proceeds			2,000,000

It is next necessary to deal with the issue costs of €100,000. In accordance with the requirements of IAS 32 for such costs, these would be allocated to the liability and equity components on a pro-rata basis. This would give the following allocation of the net issue proceeds:

	Liability component €	Equity component €	Total €
Gross proceeds (allocated as above)	1,848,122	151,878	2,000,000
Issue costs (allocated pro-rata to gross proceeds)	(92,406)	(7,594)	(100,000)
Net proceeds	1,755,716	144,284	1,900,000

In double entry terms, the initial entries are:

DR	Cash	€1,900,000
CR	Liability	€1,755,716
CR	Equity	€144,284

Accounting during the life of the convertible

Accounting for the liability component

On the assumption that the liability is not classified as at fair value through profit and loss, the €1,755,716 liability component would be accounted for under the effective interest rate method. It should be borne in mind that, after taking account of the issue costs, the effective interest rate is not the 9% used to determine the gross value of the liability component, but 10.998%, as shown below:

Year	Liability b/f	Interest at 10.998%	Cash paid	Liability c/f
	€	€	€	€
1	1,755,716	193,094	(120,000)	1,828,810
2	1,828,810	201,134	(120,000)	1,909,944
3	1,909,943	210,056	(2,120,000)	
Total finance cost		604,284		

The total finance cost can be proved as follows:

- cash interest: 360,000
- gross issue proceeds originally allocated to equity component: 151,878
- issue costs allocated to liability component: 92,406.

In double entry terms:

Taking as an example the interest costs for the liability component during Year 1:

DR	P&L interest expense	€193,094
CR	Cash	€120,000
CR	Liability	€73,094

Accounting for the equity component

On initial recognition of a compound financial instrument, the equity component (eg the €144,284 identified above) is credited direct to equity. IAS 32 does not prescribe:

- whether the credit should be to a separate component of equity; or

- if the entity chooses to treat it as such, how it should be described. The €144,284 credited to equity is not subsequently re-measured.

After initial recognition, the classification of the liability and equity components of a convertible instrument is not revised, for example as a result of a change in the likelihood that a conversion option will be exercised.

The amount originally credited to equity is not subsequently recycled to the income statement. Thus, as illustrated above, the effective interest rate shown in the income statement for a simple convertible bond will be equivalent to the rate that would have been paid for non-convertible debt. In effect, the dilution of shareholder value represented by the embedded conversion right is shown as an interest expense.

Conversion at maturity

On conversion of a convertible instrument at maturity, IAS 32 requires the entity to derecognise the liability component and recognise it as equity. There is no gain or loss on conversion at maturity.

Thus, if the bond in the example above were converted at maturity, the accounting entry required by IAS 32 is:

| DR | Liability | €2,000,000 |
| CR | Equity | €2,000,000 |

The precise allocation of the credit to equity (eg as between share capital, additional paid-in capital, share premium, other reserves and so on) would be a matter of local legislation.

Capital gains tax treatment in relation to derivative contracts

15.33   In a range of situations, profits and losses on certain derivative contracts are taken out of the derivative contracts rules (all income treatment) and instead are treated as chargeable gains and losses: *CTA 2009, s 641(1)*. The fundamental rule is contained in *CTA 2009, s 640*, which provides that, in the case of deemed relevant contracts resulting from a bifurcation and which fall under *ss 643, 645, 648* and *650*, profits and losses will not be treated as 'income' for corporation tax purposes, but as chargeable gains. The underlying subject matter of a deemed relevant contract which brings an instrument within *s 640* are:

CTA 2009	Underlying subject matter
s 643	Contracts relating to land and tangible movable property
s 645	Share options in creditor loan relationships relating to qualifying ordinary shares and mandatorily convertible preference shares
s 648	Creditor relationship embedded derivatives which are exactly tracking contracts for differences
s 650	Property-based total return swaps

15.34   The principal rules covering the tax treatment of embedded derivatives described above are contained in *CTA 2009, ss 640–659*. As noted above, for non-trading investors, who are not insurance companies or collective investment schemes, the credits and debits representing the fair value movements in the equity element in certain convertibles, and the land or equity element in asset-linked contracts, are brought into account as capital gains and not as income in relation to the holders. These rules apply to convertibles (as regards the investor) and asset-linked securities (as regards both debtor and creditor).

15.35   The contracts must not be held for trading purposes. The creditor must not be an AUT, OEIC, approved investment trust (AIT) or VCT. *TCGA 1992, ss 143–148* do not apply to such derivatives when held by companies.

15.36   Where *CTA 2009, s 640* applies, the normal all income treatment is excluded by *s 640(1)* and the tax treatment specified by *s 641* is substituted instead. In *s 641(4)*, credits for an accounting period are 'C' and debits for an accounting period are 'D':

> '(4) For the purposes of corporation tax on chargeable gains –
>
> (a)   if C exceeds D, a chargeable gain equal to the amount of the excess is treated as accruing to the company in the accounting period, and
>
> (b)   if D exceeds C, a loss equal to the amount of the excess is treated as accruing to the company in the accounting period.'

Losses arising under *s 641* can be carried back 24 months (*s 663*).

15.37   The rules apply to exclude, from the charge to corporation tax on income, (a) deemed derivative contracts arising as a result of bifurcation, and (b) stand-alone derivative contracts whose underlying subject matter is land or tangible movable property. Unlike the normal form of chargeable gains or allowable losses, these do not arise from a disposal and thus are not charged to tax on a realisations basis. They are instead assessed on an accounts basis. Allowable losses arising under the derivative contracts rules can be carried back for two years prior to the beginning of the loss period, to be offset against gains from the same source, to prevent such losses from becoming stranded.

15.38   In the case of deemed share options, the substantial shareholding exemption in *TCGA 1992, Sch 7AC* takes precedence, so that, if the investor sold a stand-alone option which had the same terms as the embedded derivative in circumstances where the substantial shareholding exemption would apply, no chargeable gain arises: *CTA 2009, s 642.*

15.39   *CTA 2009, s 645* imposes conditions which apply to obtain the capital gains treatment for equity options. In the case of convertible and exchangeable debt instruments, the shares into which the instrument converts must be qualifying ordinary shares or mandatorily convertible preference shares. The extent to which shares are acquired must not be determined using a cash value specified in the terms of the instrument. There is no exclusion of deeply discounted securities or requirement that there is no connection between the issuer and the investor. Conversion will constitute a reorganisation within *TCGA 1992, ss 127, 132(3),* and so will not give rise to a disposal. The shares thereby acquired will inherit the base cost of the non-bifurcated convertible security. Under *CTA 2009, s 670* the acquisition cost is adjusted to take account of fair value gains or losses on the embedded derivative, being increased for gains and decreased for losses. This avoids double-counting of gains or double allowance for losses.

15.40   In summary, the conditions are:

- the contract is not held for the purposes of a trade;

- the investor is not an AUT or OEIC;

- the option relates to qualifying ordinary shares or mandatorily convertible preference shares;

- the option is not exercisable using a cash value for shares specified in the original contract; and

- the company is not entitled or obliged to receive a payment instead of shares which are the subject matter of the contract which differs by a more than insignificant amount from the value of the shares which the company would be entitled to acquire at the time it became entitled or obliged to receive the payment.

15.41 'Qualifying ordinary shares' are the issued shares of a company which:

(a) are not fixed rate non-participating preference shares;

(b) are not non-participating shares; and

(c) are listed on a recognised stock exchange or shares in an unlisted holding or trading company.

15.42 'Holding company' is defined in *TCGA 1992, Sch A1, para 22(1)* and is not restricted just to a holding company of a trading group.

15.43 'Mandatorily convertible preference shares' are shares issued in exchange for debt which are within 24 hours automatically convertible into qualifying ordinary shares. Such shares are commonly issued when a share exchange has to take place in two stages.

15.44 In the case of asset-linked instruments, the conditions for capital gains treatment include a requirement that the embedded derivative is an exactly tracking contract for differences: *CTA 2009, s 648*. The amount to discharge the contract is determined by applying the relevant percentage change in the value of assets that form the underlying subject matter of the contract (being land or ordinary shares) to the initial cost of the asset which represents the non-bifurcated creditor relationship.

15.45 There is a 'relevant disposal' if shares are issued or transferred in fulfilment of the obligations under the option: *s 653. Section 653(1)(b)* refers to the issue of new shares as a 'relevant disposal', although an issue of shares is not a disposal for capital gains tax purposes. Where the option is satisfied by the issue of new shares or the transfer of existing shares, the whole transaction, comprising the grant of the option and the transaction entered into by the grantor to fulfil his obligation under the option, is treated as a single transaction within *TCGA 1992, s 144(2)*.

15.46 If the option is cash settled, a capital gain or loss can arise: *CTA 2009, s 654*. If the issuer has to pay 20 to satisfy a conversion right which he initially recognised as an embedded derivative at 15, a loan relationship debit of 5 will arise. If the issuer ceases to be party to the debtor relationship in circumstances where the option has not been exercised (ie a redemption), a capital gain is deemed to arise to the issuer equal to the initial carrying value of the option. This is equivalent to the position in respect of a free-standing option over its own shares which falls outside the derivative contracts rules (eg a quoted option to subscribe for shares), although here the gain arises under *TCGA 1992, s 144* at the point of the issue of the option and is subsequently cancelled if the option is exercised.

15.47 Where the embedded derivative is treated as an equity instrument of the issuer, the deemed relevant contract is not a derivative contract since it does not satisfy the accounting requirements in *CTA 2009, s 579* to be treated for accounting purposes as a derivative financial instrument. As a result, debits and credits on the equity instrument, to the extent they arise, are effectively tax nothings. The derivative contracts regime does, however, deem a capital loss to arise where an amount is paid to the investor in discharge of the issuer's obligations under the bond. The amount of the capital loss is the amount treated for accounting purposes as relating to the discharge of its obligations under the embedded derivative, less the carrying value of the embedded derivative on issue. It is not possible for a capital gain to arise in these circumstances.

15.48 The embedded derivative in the issuer of asset linked debt falling within *CTA 2009, s 656* (issuers of securities with embedded derivatives deemed contracts for differences) is subject to a similar rule. Movements in the fair value of the embedded derivative are not brought into account for tax purposes; instead, a chargeable gain arises equal to the difference between the proceeds of the issue of the security and the amount paid to discharge the company's obligations: *CTA 2009, s 658*.

15.49 Index-linked gilts have to be fair valued for tax purposes: *CTA 2009, s 399*. The index-linked element in index-linked gilts is exempt from tax. In many cases, the embedded derivative will be considered closely related to the host contract and will not need to be separately accounted for. Where the embedded derivative does have to be bifurcated, the credits and debits are not required to be brought into account for tax purposes: *CTA 2009, s 623*.

Example 15.5

A company issues a convertible bond for 100. It is bifurcated into 85 (host contract) and 15 (embedded derivative/equity instrument). After two years, the bond can be converted into 10 fully paid ordinary shares of the issuer at the option of the holder. At the end of Year 1, the shares are standing at 11. The fair value of the derivative is 10. At the end of Year 2, the shares are trading at 12.50. The FV of the derivative is 25. The holder exercises the option to convert.

The accounting entries are:

Issuer

	Issue of bond			*Year 1*		*Year 2*
DR	Cash	100		Expenses	7	8
CR	Liabilities		85			
CR	Equity instrument		15	Creditors	7	8

Investor

	Issue of bond		Year 1		Year 2	
DR	Debt assets	85	Debtors 7		8	
DR	Other assets	15		5 [P/L]	15 [Other assets]	
CR	Cash		100	Interest	7	8
CR	Cash	100			5 [Other assets]	15 [P/L]

Conversion

	Issuer				Investor	
DR	Liabilities	85			Share assets	125
DR	Liabilities	15	85			
DR	Equity instrument	15				
CR	Share capital		115		Debt assets	85
CR					Debtors	15
CR					Other assets	25

In summary:

1   The shares are subscribed for at a premium of 15.

2   The 10 on which the investor is taxed pending conversion is added to his acquisition cost.

Derivatives embedded in contracts other than loan relationships

15.50   A hybrid contract may be bifurcated into a derivative financial instrument, and a rump contract (host contract): *CTA 2009, s 584(1)(b)(ii)*. In that case, both may come within the derivative contracts rules, so that for tax purposes the instrument can be treated as non-bifurcated. Where a relevant contract which meets the accounting conditions in *s 579(1)(b), (c)* (pre-paid instruments) itself falls to be bifurcated ('a hybrid derivative'), and one separated-out part does and another separated-out part does not pass the accounting test, that part which passes the accounting test is a derivative contract for tax purposes: *ss 584, 586*. Besides the special rules for hybrid derivatives (*s 584*), there are also special rules for:

● other contracts (*s 586*); and

● interest rate contracts used as hedging instruments (*ss 586, 616(1)(d)*).

15.51 Where a company is party to other contracts containing embedded derivatives, which are neither loan relationships nor hybrid derivatives, the company is treated as being party to a relevant contract: *s 586*. However, the profits and losses are disregarded: *s 616(2)*.

15.52 Embedded derivatives other than those separated out from a convertible bond will not generally come within the derivative contracts rules: *CTA 2009, s 616*. Profits on both the host contract and any separated-out instrument will be accounted for on an amortised cost basis. A company can elect into fair value accounting, unless the contract is a contract of long-term insurance, or the underlying subject matter of the embedded derivative is or includes commodities: *s 617*. Where a *s 617* election is made by one company within a group, which transfers the contract to another company in the group, the election applies to both contracts: *s 618*.

15.53 Accordingly, under *s 616*, where a derivative is not embedded in a loan relationship, profits and losses will not come within the derivative contracts rules and are accounted for as if the contract had not been bifurcated and fair value accounting does not apply, unless *s 592* or *Loan Relationships and Derivative Contracts (Disregard and Bringing into Account of Profits and Losses) Regulations 2004, SI 2004/3256* (the 'Disregard Regulations'), *reg 9* applies.

15.54 A further specific exception to the general treatment of derivatives embedded in contracts other than loan relationships applies where the underlying subject matter of the embedded derivative consists, or is treated as consisting, wholly of shares in a company or rights of a unit holder under a unit trust scheme, and the host contract is treated for accounting purposes as, or forming part of, a financial asset: *CTA 2009, s 592*. Where this section applies, the host contract is treated as a creditor loan relationship of the company, and the embedded derivative is treated as having excluded underlying subject matter and therefore falling outside the derivative contracts regime.

15.55 In the case of non-monetary assets (stocks, fixed assets, equity investments), balances are not retranslated. For monetary assets and liabilities, the carrying amount will be translated at balance sheet date unless a forward rate has been agreed. For this reason, hedging can generally only be used for current assets, with the result that matching can only be undertaken with a currency contract or the liability leg of a currency swap. Where monetary assets are hedged with a derivative, the rate implied in the contract (hedge accounting) may be used to value the asset for accounts purposes, so that no foreign exchange movements are recognised.

15.56 *CTA 2009, s 650* applies where a company is party to a contract for differences and at least one index, designated in the contract, is an index of changes in the value of land and the underlying subject matter also includes interest rates. This provision is effective for contracts entered into on or after 1 August 2004 in an accounting period ending after 16 September 2004.

15.57   If a free standing share option is exercised realising a profit (eg shares with market value of 130 acquired at 110), but a loss later arises on the disposal of the shares (eg shares acquired at 130 sold for 90), the base cost of the shares acquired by exercise of the option will be increased by the gain on the option (130 + 20), so that the loss recognised (90 – 150 = (60)) will reverse the earlier gain: *ss 667, 669.*

Chapter 16

Hedging and Deferral

Overview

16.1   This chapter deals with:

- Purpose of hedging

- History of the legislation

- Hedge accounting

- Three types of hedge

- Tax hedging

- The Disregard Regulations

- The BAGL Regulations

- One-way exchange effects

- Over-hedging

- Group mismatch schemes

Purpose of hedging

16.2   Quite apart from ordinary commercial risks, multinational groups and small companies alike are exposed to the risk of:

- currency fluctuations; and

- interest rate fluctuations.

16.3   Business margins are normally very fine and precisely calculated. Changes in these rates can make the difference between profit and loss, survival and liquidation. Hence, even in small companies, it is not simply good practice to hedge these risks; it is essential. This may be conducted at entity or at group level.

16.4   Hedging is taking one risk to offset another. If a company borrows money at a floating rate, it will fix the interest rate by entering into a floating to fixed swap. The question is whether, for accounting purposes, the company should treat the combination of the floating rate debt plus interest rate swap as a synthetic fixed rate loan, and report its interest charge on a net basis. Hedge accounting is an accruals/historic cost concept – hence the lack of favour with which it is regarded under IAS. The aim of hedge accounting is to match any profit or loss which arises due to movements in the hedged item (as a result of the hedged risk) with corresponding (but opposite) movements in the hedge.

16.5   'Hedging' refers to seeking to reduce or eliminate a damaging business risk by entering into a transaction which produces an equal and opposite risk, so neutralising the damaging risk.

16.6   The accounting difficulty arises because hedging normally involves the use of a derivative, and the first rule of IFRS is that all derivative financial instruments must be recognised at fair value and taken to balance sheet. Accordingly, a derivative cannot be recognised as part of a synthetic financial instrument. Hedging allows recognition of accounting changes in fair value to be deferred until it affects the economic performance of a business.

16.7   Under IFRS 9 and FRS 102, all derivative contracts must be carried on the balance sheet at fair value, and any subsequent movements taken through the income statement. The items which they are hedging may fall into any one of a number of categories that are accounted for on a different basis, and if the hedge is taken out on a prospective basis, the underlying item may not yet be recognised in the accounts. In these circumstances, there will be a mismatch between the accounting for the hedge and the hedged item. The increased use of fair value accounting can give rise to additional volatility in a company's results, something which the hedging policy is itself intended to minimise. Moreover, the accounting mismatch will generally flow through to the tax result, causing corresponding volatility in the company's cash tax position. Hedge accounting provides an alternative method of accounting for derivatives and/or the hedged item in certain circumstances and is intended to minimise this volatility.

16.8   The aim of hedging is to match changes in the value of one item with equal and opposite changes in the value of a related item, or to eliminate negative and positive changes in cash flow. The hedging contract may be a loan relationship but will more commonly be a derivative contract. Hedge accounting allows recognition of changes in the value of both the hedged item and the hedging instrument to be deferred, until changes in the value of the hedged item enter the profit and loss account. At that point, changes in the value of the hedging instrument are recycled to profit and loss, where – if the hedging is fully effective – the two will cancel each other out.

16.9 Hedging involves a 'hedging relationship' between the 'hedged item' (eg a loan) and the 'hedging instrument' (eg an interest rate swap). In the absence of hedge accounting, a company risks a mismatch in accounting (amortised cost basis for the hedged item and fair value accounting for the derivative) which will be productive of income and so tax volatility. There is an economic relationship if the values of the hedged items and hedging instrument move in opposite directions in response to the hedged risk

---

Example 16.1

When £1 = $1.50, a UK exporter sells goods to a US purchaser for $15,000, payable in 12 months' time. A Ltd debits sales with £10,000. He sells $15,000 forward 12 months for £10,000. In 12 months' time, £1 = $1. He debits cash £15,000, and credits sales £10,000 (profit £5,000). He buys $15,000 for £15,000, and then sells them under the forward contract for £10,000 (loss £5,000).

This illustrates that, to hedge a currency asset, you sell the currency forward. To hedge a currency liability, you purchase the currency forward.

Example 16.2

The finance director wants to borrow £500,000 in two months' time for a term of three months. The current interest rate is 6.5%, and the price of a three months interest rate forward is $(100 - 6.5) = 93.5$. He sells forward two months a three months interest rate contract with a notional principal of £500,000 for $(500,000 \times 93.5/100 \times 0.25) = £116,875$.

In two months' time, the interest rate is 8% (additional interest, £1,875). The price of a three months interest rate forward is $(500,000 \times 92/100 \times 0.25) = 115,000$. He buys back his contract (profit £1,875).

This illustrates that, to hedge an interest rate liability, you sell the interest rate forward. To hedge an interest entitlement, you buy the interest rate forward.

In both cases, the company fixes its receipt or expenditure, forgoing a possible profit and limiting a possible additional cost.

Example 16.3

Parent plc (UK resident) borrows $10m to buy a US company. It has a monetary liability (the loan) and a non-monetary asset (the shares). Both have to be translated into sterling. The liability will be revalued as currency rates change, but the shares will be kept at their acquisition cost.

16.10   Multinational groups invariably use foreign currency borrowing and other derivative contracts to hedge against the risk of currency fluctuations reducing the value of their overseas assets or increasing their non-sterling liabilities. For example, as in **Example 16.3**, a UK company with subsidiaries in the US may choose to denominate some of its borrowings in US dollars in order to protect the US dollar proportion of its group balance sheet from fluctuations in the US$/£ exchange rate. If the liability can be matched to the amount of the asset, no net exchange gain or loss would be recognised (either in the group or in the entity accounts) and no net exchange gain or loss would arise.

16.11   Where companies do not use hedge accounting, they have to account for hedged transactions at the exchange rate ruling on the date of the transaction, and record all subsequent exchange differences in the income statement.

History of the legislation

16.12   When the foreign exchange tax regime was introduced by *FA 1993*, exchange movements on the US$ borrowing became taxable, or were relieved, as they accrued in each accounting period, whether they were taken to the profit and loss account or directly to reserves. The shares in the subsidiary remained subject to the rules for the taxation of capital gains, so that no exchange gain or loss was recognised for tax purposes until there was a taxable disposal of the shares. This created a fundamental mismatch between the tax and accounting treatment, which could leave the UK company with a substantial tax liability on an unrealised exchange gain (on the liability) that did not appear in the consolidated group accounts.

16.13   In order to mitigate this problem, the 1993 rules made provision for a formal 'matching election'. Where a matching election was made in respect of a qualifying asset, exchange gains and losses on corresponding liabilities were not taxed on an accruals basis but were held over pending ultimate disposal of the asset. At the time of disposal, the deferred gain or loss on the liabilities was recognised as a chargeable gain or allowable loss, thereby eliminating an equal and opposite proportion of the loss or gain on the shares.

16.14   *FA 2002* introduced compulsory matching, ie if matching was used for accounting purposes, it also had to be used for tax purposes. *FA 2002* also made fundamental changes to the regime for taxing capital gains, by introducing the exemption for 'substantial shareholdings': *TCGA 1992, Sch 7AC*. Foreign exchange movements on liabilities hedging shares in an overseas subsidiary give rise to a permanent, rather than a timing, difference for tax purposes, if the shares constitute a substantial shareholding. This caused a new anomaly.

16.15   In this situation, *TCGA 1992, Sch 7AC, para 39* provided that the movements on the liabilities should be initially disregarded and then themselves exempt where the asset proved to be exempt from tax on capital gains on disposal.

16.16   The introduction of IFRS-based accounts, requiring a quite different approach to hedging, in turn necessitated a fundamental recasting of the tax rules. FRS 102 marked the long-delayed demise of SSAP 20.

Hedge accounting

16.17   The general accounting standard dealing with hedging is IFRS 9 (which replaces IAS 39, with effect from 1 January 2017). This is followed by FRS 102, paras 12.15–12.25. A hedging strategy requires consistency with risk management objectives, ie an identification of damaging risks and a plan to neutralise them. A hedging relationship consists of a hedging instrument and a hedged item. Hedge accounting can be applied if certain qualifying conditions are met.

16.18   The conditions for hedge accounting are:

- There must be an eligible hedged item and hedging instrument.

- It must be consistent with management objectives.

- There must be an economic relationship between the hedged item and the hedging instrument.

- There must be documentation of the hedging instrument, the hedged item, the hedged risk and the causes of ineffectiveness.

16.19   IFRS 9 [IAS 39] contains detailed conditions which must be met before a company can adopt hedge accounting. These must generally be done on an item-by-item basis and include:

- designation;

- documentation; and

- effectiveness testing.

16.20   Management should formally designate and document the hedging relationship. This includes identifying the hedging instrument, the hedged item or transaction, the nature of the hedged risk, and how the entity will assess the hedge's effectiveness, and recording them together with details of the entity's risk management objective and strategy for undertaking the hedge.

16.21   Accordingly, in order for a derivative contract to qualify for a hedging treatment under IFRS 9 [IAS 39], the following conditions must be satisfied:

(a)   formal designation and documentation at inception;

(b)   hedge expectation is highly effective (80–125%);

(c)   in case of cash flow hedges, a forecast transaction must be highly probable;

(d)   effectiveness of hedge can be reliably measured; and

(e)   hedge is assessed on an on-going basis.

16.22   The entity must be able to measure and track the hedging instrument's effectiveness, both at inception and over the life of the transaction. The standard does not require the hedge to be perfectly effective, but it is expected to be 'highly' effective throughout the designated period. It must be highly effective (a prospective test) and be demonstrated to have actually been highly effective (a retrospective test). 'Highly effective' is defined as a bright line quantitative test of 80–125%. Thus a hedge is regarded as 'highly' effective if, at inception and in subsequent periods, it is *expected* to be highly effective in achieving offsetting changes in fair value or cash flows attributable to the hedged risk during the designated period, and it is *actually* between 80% and 125% effective. By contrast FRS 102 does not contain prescriptive effectiveness requirements for hedging relationships.

16.23   The question for accounting and tax purposes is: two transactions or one? Can the hedged item and the hedging contract be combined to produce a synthetic asset or liability? To the accounting purist, any form of deferral of recognition is anathema. This smacks of concealing gains and losses in the balance sheet, of the cardinal sin of smoothing the accounts. It also goes against the central tenet of IAS that all derivative financial instruments must be fair valued. Accordingly, IFRS is much more restrictive in the use of hedge accounting than old UK GAAP (SSAP 20).

16.24   As a consequence of this mixed measurement model adopted by IFRS, it is often the case that, where one instrument economically hedges another instrument, there may be a mismatch, as one will be measured at fair value (the derivative in the hedging relationship) and the other (generally the hedged item) at amortised cost. Because of the central requirement of IFRS that all derivatives should be brought on balance sheet and fair valued, derivative transactions will be evaluated according to their components, rather than as entire transactions. IFRS and consequently FRS 102 allow limited scope for hedge accounting.

The three types of hedge

16.25   IFRS 9 [IAS 39] only permit three types of hedging relationship:

- Fair value hedge, hedging the risk of the exposure to changes in the fair value of an asset or liability recognised on the balance sheet, or that of an unrecognised firm commitment, which are attributable to a certain risk.

- Cash flow hedge, hedging the exposure to changes in cash flow of an asset or liability recognised on balance sheet, or that of a forecast transaction which are attributable to a certain risk.

- Hedge of net investment in a foreign operation.

16.26   A fair value hedge is designed to reduce exposure to changes in fair value. A cash flow hedge is designed to reduce exposure to variability in cash flows. A hedge of a net investment hedge in a foreign operation (as defined by IAS 21) is designed to reduce exposure to foreign exchange differences on translation of a foreign operation on consolidation. Net investment hedges can only be recognised in consolidated accounts.

16.27   A hedge of a foreign currency risk (other than a net investment in a foreign operation) may be accounted for as a fair value hedge or a cash flow hedge. Hedge accounting is optional. IFRS 9 allows either deferral of gains and losses in the equity section of the balance sheet, for release when the hedged item impacts on profit and loss (a cash flow hedge), or adjusting the way in which the hedged item is measured so as to create an offsetting movement to the hedging instrument in the income statement.

Fair value hedge

16.28   A fair value hedge is a hedge of the exposure to changes in the fair value of a recognised asset, liability or unrecognised firm commitment, that is attributable to a particular risk and could affect profit or loss (IAS 39, para 86(a)). An interest rate swap hedging a fixed rate borrowing would be an example of a fair value hedge.

16.29   Assuming the hedging instrument comprises a derivative contract, a company must record a fair value hedge as follows:

- The derivative contract is measured at fair value.

- The carrying value of the hedged item is adjusted for the hedged risk only, ie if it is normally carried at amortised cost, the hedged item is not adjusted to its full fair value but simply adjusted in respect of the risk that has been hedged.

- Gains and losses on both the hedging instrument and the hedged item are taken to the income statement so that there is little, if any, net profit and loss effect other than any hedged ineffectiveness.

Cash flow hedge

16.30   A cash flow hedge is a hedge of the exposure to variability in the cash flows that is attributable to particular risk associated with a recognised asset or liability, or a highly probable forecast transaction, and could affect profit and loss. An interest rate swap hedging a variable rate borrowing would be an example of a cash flow hedge.

16.31   Assuming the hedging instrument comprises a derivative contract, to the extent that it is effective, a company must record a cash flow hedge as follows:

- The hedging instrument is measured at fair value.

- Gains and losses on the hedging instrument are taken to a separate component of equity.

- For hedges of highly probable forecast transactions that give rise to recognition of a financial asset/liability, the gains or losses on the hedging instrument previously recognised in equity are recycled (ie transferred) to the income statement in the same period as the asset/liability affects profit or loss.

- For hedges of highly probable forecast transactions that give rise to a non-financial asset/liability, the entity must adopt either of the following approaches as its accounting policy and apply that policy consistently–

  - reclassify gains and losses previously recognised in equity to the income statement in the same period as the non-financial asset/liability affects profit or loss (eg in the periods in which a tangible fixed asset is depreciated or when inventory is written off as part of cost of sales); or

  - remove the gains and losses previously recognised in equity and include in the initial cost or other carrying amount of the asset or liability.

Net investment hedge

16.32   Net investment hedging is covered in IFRS 9 and FRS 102 but is only permitted on consolidation, ie in the group accounts. There is therefore no mechanism in the new standards to support the legislative basis of 'tax matching' at an entity level. A hedge of a net investment in a foreign operation is the hedge of the reporting entity's share of the net assets in that operation. This type of hedge can therefore only be used in consolidated financial statements.

16.33   In the consolidated financial statements, the foreign operations net assets are retranslated, with gains and losses being taken to equity. The hedging instrument is accounted for similarly to a cash flow hedge (whether or not it is a derivative contract), ie it is retranslated at the closing exchange rate, and any gain or loss on the effective portion is taken to equity and offset against gains or losses on the corresponding net assets. The movement on any ineffective portion must be recognised in the income statement. Any net gain or loss that has been recognised in equity must be transferred to profit and loss on disposal of the foreign operation. Where a monetary item for which settlement is neither planned nor likely to occur in the foreseeable future is part of a reporting entity's net investment in its foreign operation, it should be accounted for as part of the net investment. This treatment applies to long-term receivables and loans but not trade debtors or creditors.

The hedged item

16.34   A hedged item can be a single:

- recognised asset or liability;
- unrecognised firm commitment;
- a highly probable forecast transaction; or
- net investment in a foreign operation;

or it can be a group of assets, liabilities, firm commitments, highly probable forecast transactions, or net investments in foreign operations with similar risk characteristics.

16.35   The hedged contract or arrangements must be with a party external to the reporting entity. Where groups of items are hedged they must be:

- individually eligible,
- share same risk,
- managed together,
- not net positions.

16.36   Components of these permitted items must be:

- separately identifiable and measurable,
- one or more selected cash flows,
- specified part of nominal amount.

Hedging instruments

16.37 Permitted hedging instruments are:

- financial instruments measured at FVTPL, or a proportion;

- with a party external to the reporting entity;

- which is not a written option (because speculative and trading);

- the FX component of a foreign currency loan, which can hedge a FX risk.

Summary of accounting treatment

16.38

Type of hedge	Hedging instrument	Hedged item
Fair value	No change – FVTPL	FVTPL (ie adjust carrying amount)
Cash flow	Take fair value changes to equity and recycle	No change – amortised cost
Net investment	Take fair value changes to equity and recycle	No change – amortised cost

16.39 This gives rise to the following treatment:

Item	Fair value hedge	Cash flow hedge	Net investment hedge
Hedging instrument	Gain or loss recognised in profit and loss	Separate component of equity (cash flow hedge reserve) adjusted to the lower of the cumulative gain or loss on the hedging instrument or fair value changes to expected cash flows of hedged item	Gain or loss on effective portion of hedging instrument recognised in OCI, ineffective portion in profit and loss

Item	Fair value hedge	Cash flow hedge	Net investment hedge
Hedged item	Carrying amount of hedged item adjusted for fair values movements attributed to hedged risk and recognised in profit and loss For firm commitments initial carrying amount is adjusted Amortisation of adjustments reflecting the effective interest rate (EIR) for instruments measured at amortised cost	Recognised through OCI Ineffectiveness recognised in profit and loss For non-financial assets/liabilities or firm commitments initial carrying amounts are adjusted For others reclassification to profit and loss	No recycling on disposal of foreign operation – stay in cash flow hedge reserve
Summary	Changes in hedging instrument/ hedged item go to profit and loss	Deferral of recognition of profit or loss - Changes in hedging instrument/ hedged item go to equity	Changes in hedging instrument/ hedged item go to equity

Hedging breaks

16.40   If the hedging instrument is expired, sold, terminated or exercised, or conditions for hedging no long met, then the following treatment applies:

Fair value hedge	Amortise fair value adjustment
Cash flow hedge	If cash flows no longer expected to occur, recycle
	If cash flows expected to occur, release from cash flow hedge reserve as normal
	If hedging instrument retained, fair value through profit and loss
Net investment hedge	No recycling

Tax problems arising from IFRS

16.41 Companies adopting IFRS, FRS 101 or FRS 102 in place of old UK GAAP (which included SSAP 20) face a number of difficulties concerning the tax treatment of hedge arrangements.

16.42 IFRS 9 and FRS 102 change the way in which derivative contracts are accounted for, and take a much more restrictive approach to hedging. Tax rules predicated on 'old' UK GAAP accounting would not always produce an acceptable commercial result for companies adopting new accounting principles. Difficulties include the following:

1 The main problem is the undesignated hedge. Under IFRS hedges must meet strict criteria as to–

- designation;
- documentation; and
- effectiveness testing.

FRS 102 does not contain prescriptive effectiveness tests.

In many cases a company will be economically hedged but does not hedge account, either because the accounting requirements are not fulfilled or by reason of business choice. In such cases the company will account for the hedged item at amortised cost and the hedging instrument at fair value. This will produce an accounting and tax mismatch.

2 In accounting periods prior to the accounting period beginning on or after 1 January 2016 there was also a cash flow hedge problem. This was because the derivative contracts legislation taxed amounts taken to reserves as well as credits and debits taken to profit and loss. Under IFRS 9 and FRS 102 all derivative contracts have to be fair valued and value changes taken to profit and loss. Accordingly, it is not possible to use synthetic accounting, whereby the hedged item and the hedging contract are treated as a single item. However, for periods of account beginning on or after 1 January 2016 only amounts taken to profit and loss are taxed: *CTA 2009, s 594A*. Hence if both the cash flow volatility and the hedging gains or losses on the hedging instrument recycled from equity pass through profit and loss, they should cancel each other out.

3 It is not permitted to tax exchange movements on a loan to hedge an investment in shares or a joint venture to reserves in entity accounts. Net investment hedging is only possible at the consolidated level, because such exchange movements may only be taken to reserves in consolidated accounts.

4   Exchange movements on loans to hedge investment in a ship or aircraft may not be taken to reserves. Instead, IFRS 9 and FRS 102 will apply to exchange movements on a loan which is a hedge.

5   SSAP 20 permitted the use of the exchange rate specified in a related or matching forward contract, while IFRS 9 and FRS 102 do not.

6   Hedging of future transactions may not be recognised. In particular, forward contracts cannot be valued using the forward rate.

7   Shares may not be revalued on the basis of the net asset value underlying the shares.

16.43   For these reasons, without special rules, many hedge relationships would not be effective for tax purposes, whether designated or undesignated. The *Loan Relationships and Derivative Contracts (Disregard and Bringing into Account of Profits and Losses) Regulations, SI 2004/3256* (the 'Disregard Regulations') were introduced to take account of this problem. Broadly speaking, where a derivative is part of a hedging relationship, the rules operate to allow economic hedging to apply for tax purposes, where it is not or cannot be used for accounting purposes. Where the rules apply, the tax position for hedging is largely in accord with old UK GAAP (SSAP 20).

16.44   As a result since the mid-1990s, under the tax rules governing loan relationships and derivative contracts, companies have been generally able to carry out tax-efficient financing and hedging transactions even after the introduction of a more restrictive approach to hedging under IFRS. Where companies have hedging relationships, which satisfy the conditions, the Disregard Regulations mean that the amounts recognised in the accounts are ignored in their entirety and instead an accruals or realisations basis is imposed from a tax perspective. The tax authorities have sought to replicate old UK GAAP, in order to eliminate tax volatility. However, this creates a compliance burden of having commercial accounts and tax accounts. Under the redrafted rules, a company has to elect from the commercial accounts into the alternative tax regime, rather than (as previously) elect out of the alternative tax regime and into the commercial accounts. Companies have to determine which is more important to them: minimising tax cash volatility or avoiding compliance complexity.

Tax rules – general

16.45   As the tax rules governing derivative contracts closely follow the accounting treatment, the changes introduced by IFRS have a substantial effect on the taxation of hedging transactions. The ability to follow the hedge accounting rules is therefore critical. HMRC's general approach prior to the introduction of IFRS accounts was set out in:

•   SP 2/02 Exchange rate fluctuations;

- SP 3/02 Tax treatment of transactions in financial futures and options; and

- SP 4/02 Definition of financial trader for the purposes of *FA 2002, Sch 26, para 31.*

16.46   Because, as explained below, the tax treatment seeks to preserve the pre-IFRS position, by allowing tax hedging in a wider range of circumstances than is permissible under accounting hedging rules, these Statements of Practice are of continuing importance.

16.47   *CTA 2009, s 328(1),(3)–(3C)* brings foreign exchange gains and losses on loan relationships into the loan relationships rules, if the exchange gain or loss is recognised in the income statement. This rule does not apply to exchange gains and losses on loan relationships of a description specified in Treasury regulations: *s 328(4)*. The regulations in question are the Disregard Regulations.

16.48   *CTA 2009, s 597* provides that for the purposes of the derivatives contracts rules the amounts recognised in the company's accounts as an item of profit or loss are the amounts recognised for tax purposes. *Section 598* then says that this rule does not apply to amounts specified in Treasury regulations (meaning the Disregard Regulations).

16.49   Investment in overseas subsidiaries may be by way of shares or capital contribution (ie a 'permanent as equity' loan). Only in the case of net investment hedges – borrowings (or derivative contracts) taken out in currency to hedge the foreign exchange exposure in the consolidated value of overseas net assets – did the group have to take any particular action under SSAP 20 to ensure the tax position was effective. In these circumstances, the non-sterling loan (or derivative contract) had to be pushed down to the UK water's edge company which held the shares in the first tier overseas subsidiary, so that the company could adopt para 51 of SSAP 20 and take foreign exchange movements on both the loan (or derivative contract) and the shares through reserves. Once this accounting treatment was adopted, the UK tax rules followed to provide automatic relief from tax on the foreign exchange differences on the hedging instrument. This technique was referred to as 'matching'.

The Disregard Regulations

16.50   The Disregard Regulations came into effect for accounting periods beginning on or after 1 January 2005. This was to take account of the widespread adoption of IAS following the IAS Regulation. The Disregard Regulations automatically applied where the relevant conditions were fulfilled, unless a company opted out of the Regulations under *reg 9A*.

16.51   For accounting periods beginning on or after 1 January 2015 the position is reversed. The commercial accounts apply for tax purposes unless a company makes an election under *reg 6A* for *regs 7, 8 and 9* to apply: *Loan Relationships and Derivative Contracts (Disregard and Bringing into Account of Profits and Losses) (Amendment) Regulations 2014, SI 2014/3188, regs 2, 6.* Where there is no such election there is no deferral of tax on hedged transactions, unless the hedge accounting is recognised under IFRS. This was designed to reflect the situation that many more companies would be within the IFRS/FRS 102 hedging regime. Under the transitional regulations (*SI 2014/3188*), where a company had not elected out of *reg 8*, it is automatically deemed to have elected into *reg 8* under the revised rules.

16.52   For companies within the Senior Accounting Officer Regime (ie 'large' companies') such elections have to be made within six months of the start of the accounting period in which IFRS 9/FRS 101/FRS 102 is adopted. In other cases (non-large companies) the election has to be made within 12 months from the end of the first relevant period (*reg 6A*). Where a company has previously applied *regs 7, 8 or 9* for periods of account prior to 1 January 2015, the company must make an election to apply them before the date of entering into a derivative contract to which the election is to apply (*reg 6A*). Where a company has at the time of the accounting change a designated cash flow hedge, and has no *reg 9A* election in place, *reg 9A* automatically applies to ensure that only amounts recognised in profit and loss go into the tax computation.

16.53   The 2015 changes were effected by:

- *Loan Relationships and Derivative Contracts (Disregard and Bringing into Account of Profits and Losses) (Amendment) Regulations 2014, SI 2014/3188;*

- *Exchange Gains and Losses (Bringing into Account Gains or Losses) (Amendment) Regulations 2015, SI 2015/1960;*

- *Loan Relationships and Derivative Contracts (Disregard and Bringing into Account of Profits and Losses) (Amendment) Regulations 2015, SI 2015/1961.*

- *Loan Relationships and Derivative Contracts (Change of Accounting Practice) (Amendment No 2) Disregard and Bringing into Account of Profits and Losses) (Amendment) Regulations 2015, SI 2015/1962;*

- *Loan Relationships and Derivative Contracts (Exchange Gains and Losses using Fair Value Accounting) (Amendment) Regulations 2015, SI 2015/1963.*

16.54   Crucially, the Regulations apply to both 'designated' and non-designated hedges: *reg 2(5)*. A designated hedge is any hedge designated as such in accordance with IFRS. A non-designated hedge is any other case where the hedging instrument is intended to act as a hedge against:

- the exposure to changes in the fair value of the hedged item which is a recognised asset or liability or unrecognised firm commitment (or portion thereof);

- the exposure to cash flow variability attributable to a particular risk associated with the hedged item that is a recognised asset or liability or forecast transaction; or

- a net investment in a foreign operation.

16.55   The Disregard Reguations are in essence the solution to the problem of the undesignated hedge (**16.42**(1)). Under *reg 3(3)* the underlying subject matter of the derivative contract must be such that the company intends by entering into or continuing to be a party to that contract to eliminate or substantially reduce the economic risk of holding the asset in question, to the extent that it is attributable to exchange rate risk.

16.56   Thus, non-designated hedges rest upon that anathema of IFRS – subjective management intention. No guidance is given as to how a company demonstrates its 'intention' (or lack of it) to ensure it is within (or outside) the second situation. Contemporaneous documentation by the company of such intentions is highly desirable. Where the conditions are met, the effect of claiming the relief is identical to traditional 'matching' under SSAP 20.

16.57   Accordingly, tax matching can be achieved provided that one of two conditions is satisfied:

- Condition 1 – designated hedge (*reg 2(5)(a)*).

- Condition 2 – intention to be hedge of –

    - fair value of recognised asset or liability or unrecognised firm commitment (or part) attributable to particular risk that could affect profit or loss;

    - cash flow variability associated with recognised asset or liability or unrecognised firm commitment (or part) attributable to particular risk that could affect profit or loss

    (*reg 2(5)(b)*).

16.58   While no election is required for *regs 3* and *4*, for accounting periods beginning on or after 1 January 2016 it is necessary to election into *regs 7, 8* and *9*. If moving from old UK GAAP to new UK GAAP, the election had to be made within six or 12 months of the first accounting period adopting FRS 102. If a company was using fair value accounting prior to the adoption of FRS 102, there is no transition to the new accounting framework. Fair value changes which are deferred to equity fall outside the tax calculation, and there is no need to apply the Disregard Regulations. If the Disregard Regulations do not apply, then accounting changes on the adoption of FRS 102 fall within the *Loan Relationships and Derivative Contracts (Change of Accounting Practice) Regulations, SI 2004/3271.* The main effect of these rules is to spread the tax effect of changes arising from the adoption of IFRS when restating comparatives over ten years. Under the 2015 amendments, valuation changes relating to own credit risk are spread over five years.

16.59   There are numerous carve-outs from the elections. *Regulation 6(5A)* sets out categories of derivative instruments which cannot fall within the scope of the election into *reg 9*.

16.60   The Disregard Regulations apply in four situations:

1   net investment hedging, ie FX hedging relationship between a loan relationship or derivative contract of a company and an investment in shares, ships or aircraft (*regs 3, 4*);

2   hedging of prospective transactions using currency contracts, ie company has a loan relationship or derivative contract which hedges FX risk in respect of a forecast transaction, firm commitment or future share issue (*reg 7*);

3   hedging of prospective transactions using commodity contracts and debt contracts, ie company had an economic hedging relationship between a commodity or debt contract and a forecast transaction or firm commitment (*reg 8*); and

4   hedging of creditor and debtor loan relationships using interest rate contracts, ie there is an economic hedging relationship between a loan and an interest rate contract (*reg 9*).

For accounting periods beginning on or after 1 January 2015, a company must opt into *regs 7, 8* and *9* under *reg 6A*.

16.61   The Regulations are set out as follows:

Regulation	*Topic*	*Purpose*
1	Introduction	Scope and effective date
2	Definition of terms	Includes non-designated hedges
3–5	Net investment hedging at consolidated level	Allow tax hedging at entity level

Regulation	Topic	Purpose
3, 4	Net investment hedging with loans (*reg 3*) or derivative contracts (*reg 4*) matched with shares, ships or aircraft	*Regs 3, 4* allow exchange movements on a derivative contract entered into to hedge an investment in shares, ships and aircraft to be left out of account in computing a company's profits for the purposes of the derivative contracts legislation
4	Hedging only possible in consolidated accounts	*Reg 4* allows exchange gains or losses to be left out of account for tax purposes, where matching is only permitted on a consolidated basis under IAS 21/FRS 102
4A–4C	Allows shares to be valued by net asset value, and review periods	Enables companies to match higher of accounts value of shares and the value of the net assets underlying the shareholding
5	Ancillary rules for foreign exchange net investment hedging	Determines order of matching
5A	Ancillary rules for foreign exchange net investment hedging	For purposes of *CTA 2009, s 328(4)* and *606(4)* (as amended by *F (No2) A 2015, Sch 7, para 20(5)*) makes designated hedges of loan relationships and derivative contracts hedging a net investment in a foreign operation a prescribed exchange gain or loss
6, 6A	Two separate elections, for *regs* *7* and *8* contracts and *reg 9* contracts respectively	Allows companies to choose whether the alternative hedging tax treatments apply to contracts of the type concerned
6B, 6C, 6D	Intra-group transfers	Restrict application of regulations where a derivative contract is transferred to a group company within *CTA 2009, s 625*
7	Apply to currency contracts which are hedges of future transactions (forecast transaction or firm commitment)	*Reg 7* addresses hedges of currency risk arising from hedges of firm commitments and forecast transactions, provided that the hedged item is not itself subject to fair value accounting for tax purposes. Such hedges for tax purposes are brought back into account when hedged transaction occurs (*reg 10*)

Regulation	Topic	Purpose
7A, 10A, 13	Rights issue or open offer for shares in currency other than functional currency	*Regs 7A, 10A* and *13* allow a company to fix the proceeds of a rights issue or open offer to shareholders to subscribe for new shares in the company, where the subscription monies are to be paid in a currency other than the company's functional currency, by hedging the anticipated capital raised to be received with a forward currency contract
		Excluded exchange gains may be brought into account when they are distributed to shareholders
		Reg 7A contains special rules where *reg 7, 8* or *9* contracts are transferred within groups
8, 10	Hedges of commodity price risk on forecast transactions or firm commitments by commodity contracts or debt contracts	*Reg 8* only applies to commodity contracts. Deferred gain or loss will be brought into charge under *reg 10*
9	Hedges of interest rate and foreign exchange risk by interest rate contracts	*Reg 9* addresses interest rate hedging and applies where an amortised cost basis is applied to the hedged item for tax purposes, and the hedging instrument is an interest rate contract. Because the periodic payments under interest rate swaps are determined by reference to interest rates, they are classified as interest rate contracts. Indices that refer to income or retail prices count as interest rates. *Reg 9* disregards for tax purposes the fair value profits and losses arising in respect of interest rate contracts. They are instead taxed on an 'appropriate accruals basis'. In applying an appropriate accruals basis it is necessary to have regard to the real facts of the hedging relationship
		This is the key regulation applying to undesignated interest rate swaps which are cash flow hedges. The fair value profit is parked in a cash flow hedge reserve. It is not subsequently brought into charge under *reg 10*. 'Appropriate accruals basis' means treating a hedged floating rate loan as a synthetic fixed rate loan

Regulation	Topic	Purpose
10	Bringing back into account deferred gains and losses	Where fair value profits and losses are disregarded under *regs 7, 7A* and *8* they are subsequently brought back into charge by *reg 10* when the hedged item affects profit and loss. The disregarded profits or loss are taxed at the earlier of the time when the hedged item begins to affect profit or loss, or when the company ceases to be party to the contract. Where the hedged item is expenditure falling to be taken into account in computing the profits of a trade or property business for tax purposes, the disregarded profits or losses are taxed in the accounting period in which the expenditure would fall to be deducted. Special rules apply in the case of capital expenditure which has been hedged

Types of hedging arrangement addressed by the Disregard Regulations

16.62   As set out in the previous paragraph, the Regulations address four types of hedging arrangement:

(a)   net investment hedges;

(b)   hedging of prospective transactions using currency contracts;

(c)   hedging using commodity contracts – prospective transactions;

(d)   hedging using interest rate contracts.

Net investment hedges ('foreign exchange matching')

16.63   Currency risk hedge accounting is covered IFRS 9 and FRS 102, which allow net investment hedging to be done only in consolidated accounts. On consolidation, the foreign exchange movements on the hedging instrument – whether a loan or derivative contract – may be offset against the foreign exchange movements arising on consolidation of the underlying overseas assets of foreign operations. The consolidated position is irrelevant for tax.

16.64   Under these standards, individual UK companies must carry shares in an overseas company at a sterling value and recognise foreign exchange movements on any non-sterling borrowings, and fair value movements on currency derivatives, through the income statement. Offsetting in reserves movements on the loan or derivative against equivalent movements on the currency value of the shares is not permitted. Accordingly, companies following IFRS 9 or FRS 102 will have a one-sided foreign exchange movement in their entity income statement. The movement is inherently taxable or relievable under *CTA 2009*, impacts cash tax, and reduces the effectiveness of the hedge on consolidation.

16.65 *Regulations 3* and *4* of the *Disregard Regulations* extend the scope of 'matching' relief to situations where the loan or derivative contract is:

(a)   accounted for under IFRS 9 or FRS 102 as a fair value hedge of the currency risk in an investment in shares; or

(b)   intended to hedge (part of) the economic risk in foreign shareholdings.

16.66 Where *regs 3 and 4* apply, exchange gains and losses are disregarded, and brought into account when there is a disposal of the shares, ship or aircraft. Exchange gains and losses falling within *reg 3* are disregarded in computing the company's loan relationships profits and losses. They are taken to equity and recycled to profit and loss for tax purposes in the accounting period in which the company ceases to be a party to the matched asset. *Regulation 4* deals with derivative contracts matched with a non-financial asset.

16.67 Shares, ships and aircraft are matched (*reg 4(3)*):

●   first, with designated hedges; and

●   second, with undesignated hedges, where the company enters into the debtor relationship to eliminate or substantially reduce the economic risk of holding the asset or part of the asset which is attributable to fluctuations in exchange rates.

16.68 Where IAS 32 applies to treat preference shares as a liability, and the share capital is non-sterling denominated, exchange gains and losses may be matched with the share capital: *reg 3(6)*. In the case of shares, there is an election which may be made to match the higher of the carrying value of the shares and the underlying net asset value: *regs 3(7), 4A(1)*.

16.69 The option must be exercised within 30 days of the end of the accounting period in which the shares were matched with a loan relationship.

16.70 *Regulation 5* supplements *regs 3 and 4* by prescribing the order of priority for matching assets and liabilities. Where a company holds more than one asset which qualifies for matching under *regs 3* and *4*, the extent to which the asset is matched is determined as follows:

- debtor loan relationships and currency contracts are matched to the greatest possible extent with ships or aircraft;

- then with chargeable assets generally; and

- then with shares qualifying for substantial shareholding exemption (SSE).

Example 16.4

A UK company with sterling presentation currency buys shares in a United States subsidiary for $10m by means of a dollar loan for that amount. The loan is matched with the shares. If the dollar weakens, the fall in value of the shares is counterbalanced by the decrease in the sterling equivalent of the loan liability. If the dollar strengthens, the situation is reversed. Exchange gains and losses on the loan are not brought into account until the shares are sold.

Example 16.5

A UK company with sterling presentation currency buys shares in a United States subsidiary for $10m using its own funds. The company acquires a put option over $10m from a third party bank. The option is matched with the shares. If the dollar weakens, the put option will be exercised, so that the fall in value of the shares is counterbalanced by the increase in the value of the option. The exchange gain on the option is not brought into account for tax purposes. If the dollar strengthens, the put option will not be exercised and no taxable exchange differences would arise.

Hedging using currency contracts – prospective transactions

16.71 Companies frequently enter into forward purchases or sales of currency to fix the (sterling) value of their commercial sales, cost of sales, and so forth. However, hedges are not only taken in respect of *actual* sales and purchases (ie over debtors and creditors), but also over *future expected* (ie contracted and budgeted) sales and purchases, where no transaction has yet been recorded in the accounts. Under SSAP 20, off-balance sheet accounting for hedging transactions was common, where a company entered into a forward contract to hedge the value of particular debtors or creditors.

16.72   One of the most important changes introduced by FRS 102 is that this type of off-balance sheet hedging is no longer permitted. Under IFRS 9 [IAS 39] and FRS 102, companies are required to bring *all* derivative contracts on to the balance sheet at their fair value and recognise any subsequent movements in that fair value in the income statement. Similarly, sales and purchases must generally be booked at the spot rate on the date of the transaction, and foreign exchange movements must be recognised on retranslation and/or settlement of the resultant debtors and creditors. Both the fair value adjustments and the foreign exchange movements are taxable/relievable under *CTA 2009*. Where a company enters into a forward contract to hedge the value of a particular debtor or creditor, the fair value movements on the contract should net out against equivalent foreign exchange movements on the underlying debtors/ creditors, and the tax position will similarly net out to zero. The Disregard Regulations do not apply to hedges of debtors and creditors that are recognised in the accounts, which are taxed in accordance with the accounting entries.

16.73   When hedging forecast transactions or firm commitments, however, the company must recognise fair value movements on the contract in their accounts at a time when there is no debtor or creditor in the accounts. Absent the Disregard Regulations, such movements would be taxable/relievable and impact the company's cash tax position.

16.74   *Regulation 7* of the Disregard Regulations deals with currency contracts which are a hedge of a forecast transaction of future commitment. *Regulation 7* excludes fair value profits on currency contracts where there is a hedging relationship between a currency contract and a forecast transaction or firm commitment. It requires a company to disregard fair value movements on a currency contract if:

- it is hedging a forecast transaction or firm commitment *of the same company*; and

- no fair value movements are brought into tax in respect of the hedged item.

16.75   While a forward purchase of currency comes within *reg 7*, an exchange of notional principals in two different currencies to be followed by a re-exchange, does not. Such transactions are likely to come within *reg 9*. In other words, as *reg 7* only applies to currency contracts, and *reg 8* only applies to commodities, an interest rate cross currency swap cannot fall into either *reg 7* or *reg 8*.

16.76   *Regulation 10* contains detailed instructions about how and when to bring these movements back into the charge to tax and are dictated by the nature of the underlying income or expenditure. Credits and debits which are excluded by *regs 7 and 8* are brought back into account wherever there is a termination event, ie:

- the company ceases to be party to a contract; and
- the transaction affects the profit and loss account.

Hedging using commodity contracts – prospective transactions

16.77   Some companies enter into forward purchases or sales of commodities in much the same way that they enter into forward purchases or sales of currency. *Regulation 8* deals with commodity contracts and debt contracts used as hedges of forecast transactions or firm commitments. *Regulation 8* contains parallel provisions for commodity hedges that require a company to disregard the fair value movements on commodity contracts that are hedges of *forecast transactions* or *firm commitments* of the same company, if no fair value movements are brought into tax on the hedged item.

16.78   A company may elect into *regs 7* and *8* and be taxed on its derivative contracts on a hedged basis: *reg 6(1)(a), 6A*.

Hedging using interest rate contracts

16.79   Under IFRS 9 [IAS 39] or FRS 102 all derivative contracts must be brought on to the balance sheet at their fair value. Any movement in that value must then be booked to the income statement (ie profit and loss account). An interest rate contract is frequently entered into as a hedge. Nevertheless, the basic accounting treatment will apply unless the company is able to adopt the 'hedge accounting' rules.

16.80   Unless the company is a financial trader, it is likely to be accounting for the hedged loans at their nominal value, recognising interest and foreign exchange movements as they accrue but no fair value movements. Absent any hedge accounting treatment, the company's income statement will therefore be imbalanced – it will reflect fair value movements on the derivative contract but not on the hedged item. As the tax rules governing loans and derivatives require all debits and credits in the accounts to be taxed as they arise (whether in the income statement or in equity, ie reserves), unless the Disregard Regulations apply, the company's cash tax will be susceptible to volatility as a result of these one-sided fair value movements.

16.81   IFRS 9 [IAS 39] and FRS 102 permit two types of hedge for interest rate risk at entity level: a fair value hedge and a cash flow hedge.

16.82   Under a fair value hedge, which applies when hedging fixed rate interest into floating rate, the company will revalue the hedged loan for the effect of interest rate movements. As a result, the income statement will reflect equal and opposite fair value movements on the hedge and the loan, so that the accounting position is symmetrical and the tax will automatically follow suit.

16.83   Under a cash flow hedge, which applies when hedging floating rate interest into fixed rate, the company will take fair value movements on the interest rate contract to equity (ie reserves) and recycle (ie transfer) part to the income statement, to produce a fixed finance charge in respect of the hedged loan. Without specific relieving provisions for cash flow hedges, the derivative contract rules would require the company to tax the fair value movements taken to reserves.

Example 16.6

A company borrows £1m at fixed rate reset every three months. Current interest rate is 6%. At next reset date, rates will increase or decrease. To protect himself against increase on 15 June, treasurer sells forward for delivery on 15 September a £1m three-month sterling interest rate for 94. At next reset date interest rates are 7.5%. He buys a contract for $(100 - 7.5) = 92.5$, which he then sells for 94.

Profit on futures contract $= £1m \times 0.01\% \times (9,400 - 9,250) \times ¼ = 3,750$

Extra borrowing cost $= £1m \times (7.5 - 6\%) \times ¼ = 3,750$

The loss in the cash market is matched by the gain in the futures market. The company cannot offset the two entries for accounting or tax purposes. Variation margin will be held in the balance sheet and amortised over the period of the arrangement.

Accounting entries will be:

Initial margin account	2,000
Variation margin account	(3,750)
Deferred gains/losses account	3,750

Example 16.7

Enterprises Ltd has a floating rate loan for £1m repayable in four years' time. The finance director wishes to fix his interest costs at 8%. The company enters into a floating-to-fixed swap under which it will pay a fixed rate of 8% (the floating rate at the time of the swap). Periodic payments are to be made in arrears at annual intervals on a net basis. Interest rates in the four years in question are:

Year	Loan-floating	Swap-fixed leg	Swap-floating leg
1	8%	8%	8%
2	10%	8%	10%
3	9%	8%	9%
4	7%	8%	7%

Cash payments will be as follows:

Year	Interest	Payment received	Payment made	Receipts (payments) under swap
1	(80,000)	80,000	(80,000)	(0)
2	(100,000)	100,000	(80,000)	20,000
3	(90,000)	90,000	(80,000)	10,000
4	70,000	70,000	(80,000)	(10,000)

Thus, economically, the transaction is flat in each of the four years. For hedging to be adopted where a company uses a derivative contract to reduce interest rate exposure, the instrument must be related to actual assets or liabilities or a probable commitment, and must change the nature of the interest rate by converting a fixed rate to a variable rate, or vice versa.

16.84   In these circumstances, IFRS 9 [IAS 39] or FRS 102 allows four possibilities:

1   *Apply ordinary accounting rules*

The loan is held at amortised cost (£1m, adjusted for accrued interest less amounts paid/received).

The swap is treated within the category of financial assets or financial liabilities at fair value through profit and loss, with fair value movements going to the income statement.

The fair value of the swap is ascertained, at any point in time, by:

(a)   computing the present value (PV) of payments receivable; and

(b)   deducting the PV of amounts payable.

The PV of the swap payments is ascertained by discounting future cash flows by the applicable interest rate, the discount factor being $1/(1 + i)$. Payments received are *deducted* from movements in fair value. Payments made are *added* to changes in fair value. Assuming that the interest rate changes at the year end, the gains and losses on the swap for Enterprises Ltd are:

Year	FV b/f	FV gain/ loss	FV realised by receipt/ payment	FV c/f	Movement between periods
1	0	49,735	0	49,735	49,735
2	49,735	(11,876)	20,000	17,860	(31,876)
3	17,859	(8,124)	10,000	(265)	(18,124)
4	(265)	(9,735)	(10,000)	0	265
Total		20,000	(20,000)		0

The accounting and tax deductions are:

Year	Loan relationship	Derivative	Trading profit
1	(80,000)	49,735	(30,265)
2	(100,000)	(11,876)	(111,876)
3	(90,000)	(8,124)	(98,124)
4	(70,000)	(9,735)	(79,735)
Total			(320,000)

Thus, the finance director has economically fixed his interest costs at 8%, but at the cost of accounting and tax fluctuations.

2   *Cash flow hedge accounting*

The swap (hedging instrument) is designated as a cash flow hedge of the variable interest rate payments (the hedged item).

The interest payments on the loan are unaffected.

The fair value variations are taken to equity and recycled to the income statement in the period in which the hedged transaction affects the profit and loss.

The result is:

Year	Loan relationship	Derivative to equity	Recycled	Balance	Trading profit
1	(80,000)	49,735	0	49,735	(80,000)
2	(100,000)	(11,876)	20,000	17,859	(80,000)
3	(90,000)	(8,124)	9,735	0	(80,265)
4	(70,000)		(9,735)		(79,735)
Total	(340,000)		20,000		(320,000)

Accounting and tax fluctuations are substantially eliminated, but hedging can only be achieved to the extent that there are reserves in equity available for recycling.

3   *Fair value hedge accounting*

Under cash flow hedge accounting, the treatment of the derivative contract changes. Under fair value hedge accounting, the treatment of the hedged item changes. The swap would be designated as a fair value hedge of the variable rate interest liability. The hedged item would then be fair valued. However, in this case the fair value of a variable rate loan liability would be constant. Hence, fair value hedge accounting would not be possible.

4   *Fair value option*

The company can elect for the non-derivative financial asset or liability to be fair valued through profit and loss account. In that case, the fair value movements of the derivative and the non-derivative instruments should achieve a natural offset, though separately recorded.

16.85 *Regulation 9* of the *Disregard Regulations* provides relief from tax where the interest rate contract is a designated cash flow hedge for accounting purposes, or the company intends the interest rate contract to be a hedge (whether of fixed or floating rate interest) but does not fulfil the detailed accounting requirements. Where *reg 9* applies, for tax purposes the company must substitute an 'appropriate accruals basis' of accounting for the contract. This is equivalent to following 'old' UK GAAP for tax. Fair value changes will not be taxed when taken to equity, but will be taxed when recycled to profit and loss. 'Interest rate contract' is defined so as to include swap contracts: *reg 9(4)*. Where *reg 9* applies, credits and debits are not disregarded in the way prescribed by *regs 7* and *8*. Instead the 'appropriate accruals basis' as defined in *reg 9(4)* is used in relation to the contract rather than fair value accounting, ie synthetic instrument accounting is used, and for tax purposes a floating rate loan hedged by a fixed to floating swap is accounted for as fixed rate debt.

Permanent equity

16.86   Companies frequently suffer exposure to tax on foreign exchange differences on quasi-equity loans to subsidiaries (capital contributions). Under the rules, the foreign exchange movements are deferred for tax purposes if the loan is accounted for as part of the long-term investment in the subsidiary, and foreign exchange movements arising on the loan asset are taken to reserves. Where there is a disposal of an asset representing a loan relationship on which foreign exchange gains or losses have been deferred, an amount equal to any net gain or loss is brought into account as a loan relationship credit or debit (respectively) in the period in which the disposal takes place.

Derivative contracts

16.87   The derivative contracts rules contain corresponding provisions to ensure that foreign exchange gains and losses on currency contracts used to hedge assets are similarly left out of account (*CTA 2009, s 606(3)*). Exchange movements that are taken to OCI as a result of the translation of the results of all or part of the company's business from the functional currency are left out of account for tax purposes, eg the results of an overseas branch. There is no requirement for such amounts to be subsequently recycled. No exchange gains and losses of an investment company are to be brought into account as a result of the change of the functional currency, unless the company has elected for a designated currency under *CTA 2010, s 9A*. The section also allows the Treasury to prescribe an alternative basis for bringing into account exchange gains and losses on derivative contracts of a prescribed description.

Bringing deferred amounts back into charge

16.88   Where exchange movements on loan relationship liabilities and on assets are offset in the same reserve, the rules for recognising initially disregarded exchange movements on 'matched' liabilities at the time of disposal of the relevant asset are contained in the *Exchange Gains and Losses (Bringing into Account Gains or Losses) Regulations 2002, SI 2002/1970* (the 'BAGL Regulations'). This brings the exchange movements on the liability into tax at the time of disposal of the asset by virtue of *regs 3(1A)(b)(i), (3), (4)*.

16.89   There is an exception where the asset is a 'foreign business asset', ie 'an asset … which for accounting purposes is a foreign operation consisting of a branch': *reg 2(1)*. So, even if the matching rules apply (which they will if the results of retranslating net branch assets are taken to reserves using the closing rate/net investment method of accounting), exchange movements on branch liabilities that are taken to reserves and offset exchange movements on branch assets are not brought back into tax. The same applies where exchange movements on a company's own share capital treated as a liability for accounting purposes are hedged.

16.90   In the case of chargeable assets, the general rule is that the consideration received on a disposal of a chargeable asset is increased by deferred gains and reduced by deferred losses. These amounts must be brought back into charge to tax when the company disposes of the underlying chargeable asset: *BAGL Regulations, regs 4, 5*.

16.91   No gain or loss is brought back into charge to tax where the asset comprises:

(a)   a foreign business asset; or

(b)   shares (or an asset related to shares) on which no chargeable gain accrues by virtue of *TCGA 1992, Sch 7AC, Part I* (the substantial shareholding exemption): *BAGL Regulations, reg 4(4)*.

16.92   If the asset comprises:

(a)   a loan relationship of the company; or

(b)   a ship or aircraft,

the deferred amount is brought back into charge as a loan relationship credit or debit rather than as a capital item: *BAGL Regulations, reg 6(1), (2)*.

Order of set off

16.93   Where a company holds more than one asset which qualifies for matching treatment under *regs 3* and *4*, the order of matching rules apply. Liabilities are matched with assets in a prescribed order. Understanding and applying these rules becomes important when determining the amount of deferred gains and losses that must be brought back into charge to tax on disposal of an asset. Assets or liabilities may be 'fully matched' or 'partly matched': *BAGL Regulations, reg 7(5A)*. Where liabilities are 'matched' against more than one asset, it is necessary to determine the order in which the assets are utilised: *reg 7(7)*. There are three rules which prescribe that liabilities are deemed to be matched with assets in the following order:

Rule 1   loan relationships,

            or

            ships and aircraft;

Rule 2   assets (other than foreign business assets) on which a chargeable gain would accrue on disposal;

Rule 3   assets on which no chargeable gain accrues on disposal by virtue of *TCGA 1992, Sch 7AC, Part I* (substantial shareholding relief),

or

assets on which no chargeable gain would accrue by virtue of *TCGA 1992, Sch 7AC, Part I* (substantial shareholding relief) if they were held for the relevant time (ie 12 months) but excluding assets which are not ultimately held for that time,

or

foreign business assets held at the time of the relevant disposal.

16.94   At the time of disposing of one asset that is hedged, a company may hold another hedged asset that it expects to be exempt from tax on capital gains on the basis that it is a qualifying shareholding and is likely to be held for more than 12 months. Such an asset would fall within Rule 3. If, however, that asset is not ultimately held for 12 months as originally anticipated, it will become a Rule 2 asset. The company would have to recognise the effect of such a reclassification retroactively, ie when determining the order of offset applicable to the original disposal. As a company has 12 months in which to file its corporation tax return, there should be sufficient time to finalise the computation on the correct basis, but some uncertainty may arise in the interim period.

Assets subject to capital gains reorganisation provisions

16.95   The regulations also make specific provision for the treatment of deferred amounts where assets are disposed of in circumstances which are affected by capital gains reorganisation provisions. In particular:

1   *No gain/no loss disposals*

    Where the disposal of an asset is at no gain/no loss, foreign exchange gains or losses deferred on liabilities under the matching provisions are further deferred and brought into account on the first subsequent disposal which is not a no gain/no loss disposal: *BAGL Regulations, reg 8.*

2   *No disposal of the asset by virtue of TCGA 1992, s 116(10)*

    The gain or loss which would, but for *TCGA 1992, s 116(10)*, be brought in as a chargeable gain or allowable loss increases or decreases the market value of the asset for the purpose of *s 116(10)(a)*. If the amount of any loss exceeds the market value, an allowable loss equal to the excess is brought in on subsequent disposal of the new asset: *BAGL Regulations, reg 9.*

3   *No disposal of the asset by virtue of TCGA 1992, s 127*

The gain or loss which would, but for *TCGA 1992, s 127*, be brought in as a chargeable gain or allowable loss increases or decreases the consideration received on the subsequent disposal of the new holding. If the amount of any loss exceeds the consideration received, an allowable loss equal to the excess is treated as accruing on that subsequent disposal: *BAGL Regulations, regs 11, 12*.

One-way exchange effect

16.96   The 'one way exchange effect' (prior to repeal, *CTA 2009, ss 328A–328H*) is repealed for accounting periods beginning on or after 1 January 2016, because under the revised rules it would be caught by *CTA 2009, s 455B*. 'One-way hedging effects' arose if hedging arrangements were so structured that recognition of profits was deferred, but recognition of losses was not. This was only possible on a group basis where the hedging instrument contains an option or contingent payment obligation, ie on hedging relationship between connected companies.

Over-hedging ('risk transfer schemes')

16.97   *CTA 2010* contains a number of 'generic' rules, ie rules which apply to both loan relationships and derivative contracts, and are therefore not included in *CTA 2009*, where they might more logically be found. The first set of rules is found in *CTA 2010, ss 937A–937O*, dealing with what are called 'risk transfer schemes', but more commonly 'over-hedging'.

16.98   In a group situation, it is often the case that a hedged item is held in Company A and the hedging contract is held by Company B. In that case, hedging is only possible in the consolidated accounts. Where, in a group situation, exchange movements on a cross currency swap are not recognised for accounting purposes, groups over-hedge, ie the hedge is grossed up by the company's corporation tax rate, so that the after-tax amount of any profit on the hedge corresponds to the loss on the hedged item and the hedge is fully effective on an after-tax basis.

16.99   'Risk transfer schemes' are defined in *CTA 2010, s 937C* by reference to four conditions:

- The purpose of the scheme is to obtain a financial advantage of the relevant group in relation to a relevant risk by arranging for the payment profile to exceed the hedged risk.

- The relevant risk is a risk of economic loss by reason of a change in the exchange rate, the RPI or any other price or index.

- As a result of the scheme, the relevant risk is substantially eliminated.

- The relevant risk would not be eliminated if the Corporation Tax Acts did not allow losses to be offset against profits.

16.100 These conditions are applied on the assumption that the losses on the hedged item can be fully relieved ('tax capacity assumption' – *s 937J*). It is this factor which confines the application of these provisions to 'over'-hedging.

16.101 If the loss on the hedging contract is an allowable loss, the debit is restricted to 'the relevant proportion' of the group's 'pre-tax economic loss', and unrelieved losses can only be carried forward against future gains on such contracts: *ss 937A–937O*.

16.102 Relief for exchange losses on the hedging contract or loan relationship is restricted to the economic loss to the company or group. The disallowed losses are ring-fenced and carried forward against future profits on the hedging contract.

Group mismatch schemes

16.103 The second set of rules is in *CTA 2010, ss 938A–938N* and deal with 'group mismatch schemes'. A group mismatch scheme means a scheme by which members of a group of companies seek to gain a tax advantage of at least £2m. This is essentially an extension of the over-hedging rules

16.104 In certain cases, over-matching may bring a deferral of tax liabilities on loan relationships and derivative contracts. If the economic value of the deferral (having regard to the time value of money) exceeds £2m, and there is no practical likelihood that this result will not be obtained, this constitutes a 'relevant tax advantage', which is liable to counteraction under the 'group mismatch scheme' rules.

16.105 These rules only apply to groups of companies, as defined in *CTA 2010, s 938E*. A 'group' is Company A and any companies with which it is associated. A company ('Company B') is associated with Company A if:

- Company A and Company B have consolidated accounts;

- Company A and Company B are connected under the control test in *CTA 2009, s 466*;

- Company A has a major interest in Company B, or vice versa, major interest being defined as a 40% shareholding (where another company also has a 40% shareholding) in accordance with *CTA 2009, ss 473, 474*;

- a third company with which the Company A accounts are consolidated has a major interest in Company B; or

- a third company with which Company A is connected has a major interest in Company B.

16.106 'Group mismatch scheme' is defined in *CTA 2010, ss 938B, 938C* as a scheme:

- which involves a group;

- where there is no practical likelihood that a tax advantage of less than £2m will be obtained;

- where the tax advantage comprises an economic profit to the group over the scheme period;

- where the scheme is entered into for the purpose of securing that tax advantage;

- where there is little chance that the scheme will result in a tax disadvantage;

- where the profit or loss on the scheme would otherwise be brought into account under the loan relationship or derivative contracts rules; and

- where that profit or loss meets one of two asymmetry conditions.

16.107 The asymmetry conditions are (*s 938C*):

- the profit or loss affects the relevant tax advantage, or

- the profit or loss might have arisen from a transaction which would have affected the relevant tax advantage.

16.108 Where the rules apply, the scheme profit or loss is not brought into account under the loan relationship or derivative contracts rules, or under any other provisions of the Corporation Tax Acts.

16.109 Transactions with non-UK resident counterparties are excluded, but transactions with controlled foreign companies (CFCs) are included: *ss 938L, 938M*.

Chapter 17

Case Law

17.1   There have now been a large number of cases involving the loan relationship and derivative contracts legislation, but mostly concerned with detailed provisions which have since been amended. It is not always possible to include these at an appropriate place in the text, either because of publishing constraints, or because – as often the case in tax – cases have multiple points of reference. This chapter is an unsystematic attempt to put together relevant cases which, for reasons good or bad, have not been integrated into the substantive text.

Bank of Scotland v Dunedin Property Investment Co

17.2   In *Bank of Scotland v Dunedin Property Investment Co Ltd* 1998 SC 657:

(a)   a borrower (D) borrowed £10m from a bank (BOS) for a fixed term of ten years at a fixed rate of interest;

(b)   D issued a debenture to BOS;

(c)   BOS entered into a fixed to floating interest rate swap with C as a specific hedge for its contract with D;

(d)   condition 3 of the debenture gave D the right to redeem the security on giving six months' notice 'subject to the bank being fully reimbursed for all costs, charges and expenses incurred by it in connection with the stock';

(e)   because the cost of borrowing had fallen, D gave notice to redeem and BOS incurred a breakage fee of £1.25m payable to C. BOS claimed this sum from D under condition 3. The Inner House of the Court of Session held that the breakage cost fell within condition 3.

Citibank Investments Ltd v Griffin

17.3   The relationship between derivatives and lending transactions was considered in *Citibank Investments Ltd v Griffin* [2000] STC (SCD) 92. An investment company in the Citibank group, Citibank Investments Ltd ('Invest Co'), wanted to place £150m for 16 months with the banking division of the group, Citibank International plc ('Bank Co'). Invest Co wanted its return on the fund to be in the form of a capital gain, rather than income. This was because it could then set the capital gain against capital losses. The transactions in question pre-dated the introduction of *ICTA 1988, Sch 5AA* (which charged to income tax transactions producing guaranteed returns on futures and options). Being equity options, the contracts also fell outside *FA 1994*. Accordingly, Invest Co and Bank Co entered into an 'equity box structure', comprising a matching set of call and put options on the same index, which would produce a pre-determined return.

17.4   The arrangement took this form:

1   The item which was the subject of the call and put options was the FTSE All Shares Index future. Suppose the spot price of the index level at time T_2 is £I.

2   The exercise date (T_2) for both sets of options was 29 April 1996. The contracts were to be cash-settled.

3   On 29 December 1994 (T_1), Invest Co paid a premium of £70m to Bank Co to buy 330,181 call options at an exercise price of £3,000, with cash settlement for each option of $£(I - 3,000)$ or £500, whichever was the lesser. Hence, the maximum payable by Bank Co to Invest Co in respect of each call option was £500, which would be the case where $I > 3,500$. The premium for each option was £212.

4   On 29 December 1994, Invest Co paid a premium of £80m to Bank Co to buy 330,181 put options at an exercise price of $£(3,500 - I)$ or £500, whichever was the lesser. Hence, the maximum payable by Bank Co to Invest Co in respect of each put option was £500, which would be the case where $I < 3,000$. The premium for each option was £212.

The amount payable by Bank Co to Invest Co after 16 months was determined according to whether either set of options was exercised singly or both were exercised together. The case of not exercising either is impossible, as can be seen from the diagram below.

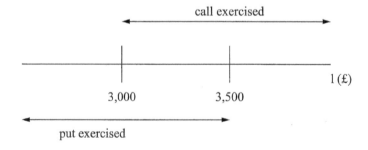

17.5

1   If, on 29 April 1996, I > 3,500, Invest Co would exercise the call options only and abandon the put options, realising £500 × 330,181 = £165m, profit £15m.

2   If, on 29 April 1996, I < 3,000, Invest Co would exercise the put options only and abandon the call options, realising £500 × 330,181 = £165m, profit £15m.

3   If, on 29 April 1996, I was between 3,000 and 3,500, Invest Co would exercise both the call and put options. However, the combined payback on both sets of contracts would always be £165m, profit £15m. This was because, if I was in the range 3,500 to 3,000, the call options paid $(I - 3,000)$, while the put options paid $(3,500 - I)$. The sum of these two amounts was necessarily 500.

17.6   On the assumption that $3,000 < I < 3,500$, the payback on both sets of options is calculated as follows:

$$
\begin{aligned}
\text{payback} &= \text{payback on call options} + \text{payback on put options} \\
&= £(330,181 \times (I - 3,000) + 330,181 \times (3,500 - I)) \\
&= £(330,181 \times (I - 3,000 + 3500 - I)) \\
&= £165m
\end{aligned}
$$

In other words, I automatically cancelled itself out; in the range 3,500 – 3,000, for every extra £1 which the call options paid, the put options paid £1 less, and vice versa; and the only real figure was the difference between 3,500 and 3,000.

17.7   The question was, how was the difference between £165m and £150m to be characterised for tax purposes? Did the sum of £15m constitute (as Invest Co claimed) a gain on qualifying options, chargeable to capital gains tax? Or was it (as the Revenue claimed) equivalent to a return on a zero-coupon bond and so taxable on an accruals basis as income? Were the premiums what they held themselves out to be (a premium payable under an options contract) or did they constitute a deposit, ie a loan?

17.8   The transactions were effected by means of the 1992 ISDA master agreement. The evidence was that the master agreement was apt to effect a derivatives transaction, but not a lending transaction. 'The legal analysis of the transactions,' the Commissioners concluded, 'reveals that they were options and not loans ... The options were purchased under an ISDA master agreement, which was an agreement to purchase options and not an agreement for a loan' (at 103–104 (paras 53–54)).

17.9   Moreover, there was evidence that the options were granted on commercial terms and, while it was unlikely, Invest Co could have dealt in each separately, assigning one and keeping the other. Each set of options had a separate legal existence, because they were capable of separate assignment.

17.10   This decision was upheld in the High Court: *Griffin (Inspector of Taxes) v Citibank Investments Ltd* [2000] STC 1010. Because of the findings by the Special Commissioners, the Revenue had to rely on a 'two-tier' *Ramsay* argument, to argue that the transaction should be recharacterised as a fixed-term deposit with rolled-up interest. The first-tier argument was that the call and put options, together acquired for £150m and together offering a fixed payback of £165m after 16 months, were both 'part of a single composite transaction', and that composite transaction was not a transaction involving 'financial options' within *TCGA 1992, ss 143(2), 144(8)(c)*. That contention, the judge held, was inconsistent with the findings of the Special Commissioners. Even if the steps constituted a composite transaction in this sense, the judge held that none of the steps were artificial steps 'inserted without any commercial or business purpose apart from a tax advantage':

> 'True it is that the purpose of the equity box structure was to allow investment in a form which produced a capital gain rather than an income profit. But that is no more than the choice which faces any investor. There seems to me to be a real difference between the taxpayer who sets out to utilise a tax avoidance scheme in order to reduce or eliminate an already existing tax liability and one who makes a legitimate choice between investment options having regard to his own fiscal and financial position.' (Patten J at 1039)

The judge concluded (at 1042):

> 'in the absence of such inserted steps the *Ramsay* principle does not permit the court to treat the transactions under consideration other than as they in fact are.'

17.11   The second-tier *Ramsay* argument was that there was a wider, residual rule which enabled transactions with a tax avoidance purpose to be recharacterised. The judge observed that this would be to confuse the result of applying the *Ramsay* principle with the conditions necessary for its application.

HSBC Life (UK) Ltd v Stubbs

17.12   In *HSBC Life (UK) Ltd v Stubbs* [2002] STC (SCD) 9, the issue was whether equity derivatives purchased by insurance companies to back guaranteed investment bonds sold to investors fell to be taxed under the capital gains tax rules in *TCGA 1992* or under the loan relationship provisions of *FA 1996*. As noted, the policy of the financial instruments legislation in *FA 1994*, and the loan relationships legislation in *FA 1996*, was to bring into income taxation profits on debt and debt-based products, while leaving gains on shares and equity-linked instruments within the capital gains rules. In *HSBC* the gain in question was on an equity-linked instrument. As in *Citibank*, the Revenue raised the argument that, because the financial return mirrored that on a zero-coupon bond, taxation was imposed by the loan relationships rules.

17.13   The Special Commissioners held that profits arising to an insurance company from transactions in financial futures were not profits on loan relationships. Accordingly, the profits were not taxed on an accruals basis under the loan relationships rules, but on a realisations basis under the capital gains tax rules.

17.14   Guaranteed investment bonds are a familiar retail investment product. A saver may invest £1,000 at 5%, giving a return of £50 after one year. Instead, he may pay the insurance company £1,000 for a guaranteed investment bond, and the insurance company will use the £50 which would otherwise have been paid in interest to buy a call option on a financial market option, such as the FTSE 100. Typically, the bond will last for five years. At the end of the five years the investor is guaranteed to recover his £1,000, plus any increase on the FTSE index which the call option bought for £50 will realise. The bond will often provide for regular payments (typically, quarterly or annual) during the life of the bond, which will be credited against the amount finally paid on the bond. The different elements of payment obtainable under the bond will be described as 'monthly income', 'quarterly income', 'annual income' and 'growth'. Thus, a bond might offer a guaranteed annual income of 5% and a final maturity value linked to the FTSE 100 Index. Thus, with guaranteed equity bonds, the return to the investor is linked to an index such as the FTSE 100, but periodic payments and repayment of a minimum amount are guaranteed, so setting a floor to the downside risk ('FTSE growth with a floor').

17.15   In order to provide these products, insurance companies had to back the bond which they issued with derivatives. Typically, arrangements included the following elements:

1   *Equity forward transaction.* Insurance company pays £1,050 under a contract written under the terms of the ISDA master agreement, whereby a bank agrees to deliver in five years' time a number of shares, whose value will be the sum of (a) £1,000 and (b) an amount related to the growth of the share index over the period. The settlement amount will be a percentage of the initial share price/final share price. Settlement date will be five years from the date of the contract. This is an over-the-counter (OTC) derivative.

2   *Equity put option.* Also under the ISDA master agreement, the bank grants the insurance company, for a small premium, a put option to sell the shares to the bank for their market value at settlement date.

3   *Deposit transaction.* In connection with the equity forward transaction, the bank deposits cash at regular intervals with the insurance company, the amounts of the deposits totalling some £1,000. The times of the deposits will coincide with the dates of the periodic payments to investors. The deposit is repayable on the settlement date under the equity forward transaction. Interest is rolled up on the deposits, and becomes payable on settlement date.

4   *Netting agreement.* This may be incorporated in the deposit transaction, or be a separate agreement. Amounts which the insurance company owes to the bank under the deposit transaction can be netted against amounts owed by the bank to the insurance company under the equity forward transaction.

17.16   The regular deposits enable the insurance company to make periodic payments to the investors. The deposit arrangement as a whole serves as security for the performance of the bank's obligations under the equity forward transaction. The insurance company's aim was to receive a sum on maturity which would meet its obligations to the bond holders and its own tax liabilities. The insurance company's analysis was that:

(a)   the profit on the equity forward transaction was taxable on a capital gains basis in Year 5;

(b)   interest payments under the deposit transaction were deductible on an accruals basis in Years 1 to 5;

(c)   thus, the insurance company was able to defer taxation until the time when it had to pay out to the investors.

17.17   As regards (a), the essential feature of the equity forward transaction was that it involved an equity-linked instrument, which fell outside the categories of financial instrument to which *FA 1994* applied. The Revenue argued that, as the instrument was cash-settled, it was economically equivalent to a loan. A loan relationship exists where there is (a) a money debt, which arises (b) from a transaction which is or is treated as a transaction for the lending of money. The two requirements are cumulative. For the accounting periods in question, 'money debt' was defined by *FA 1996, s 81(2)* as one which 'falls to be settled (a) by the payment of money'. The insurance company argued that 'falls to be settled' meant 'requires to be settled'. The Crown argued that the form of settlement had to be looked at in each accounting period, to see whether a legal obligation constituted a loan relationship in that particular accounting period. The Special Commissioners found that what mattered was the way in which it was intended to settle the obligation at the outset: if for cash, there was a money debt; if for shares, but with an option to take cash, no money debt was created until the option was exercised.

17.18   The Revenue argued that the equity forward transaction and deposit transaction had to be looked at together. The deposit by the bank with the insurance company eliminated the equity risk. *FA 1996, s 103* said:

'"debt" includes a debt the amount of which falls to be ascertained by reference to matters which vary from time to time'

17.19   Having regard to this definition, it was said, what the insurance company received was variable rate interest, rather than an equity return. The insurance company knew from the start that it would get back a certain sum of money (the guaranteed payments to the investors on maturity) plus a variable return, which would be the profit element for the investors. It could not therefore be said that the insurance company would get back 'an unascertainable amount of money at an unknown date' (*Marren v Ingles* 54 TC 76 at 98). The insurance company's asset as regards the bank was a debt, not a payment under a derivatives contract.

17.20   Much weight was attached to the fact that none of the witnesses 'was prepared to recognise any of the derivatives purchases transactions as loans' (para 72). The Special Commissioners quoted, with approval, the evidence of one of the witnesses, where he stated:

'the documentation used for the index-linked transactions would not be used, and would not be suitable to be used, for loan transactions, even though the cash flows or the economic effect of a given loan and a particular derivatives transaction may turn out to be similar.'

17.21   As the Special Commissioners concluded at para 71:

'It emerges clearly … that the mere economic equivalence of a transaction to a loan does not show that it is a loan … by specifically referring to "a transaction for the lending of money", section 81(1)(b) [FA 1996] evidently intends to confine a concept whose extent may otherwise be uncertain within well-known and ascertainable bounds.'

IRC v Scottish Provident

17.22   *IRC v Scottish Provident Institution* [2002] STC 252 involved a cross-option scheme implemented using the ISDA agreement. In 1995 an insurance company wrote an option for a premium of £30m under which Citibank could, on exercise, buy £104m (nominal £100m) of gilts for £70m (Option A). The insurance company also paid £10m for the right to buy £104m (£100m nominal) of gilts for £90m (Option B). Both were exercisable on 1 April 1996 after 'debt options' had been introduced as 'qualifying contracts' under *FA*

1994, s 147A. The premium which the insurance company *received* for writing Option A (£30m) was not taxable under the pre-1996 rules, but the loss arising from *performing* the option (£30m) was a deductible expense under the post-1 April 1996 rules. If a fair value basis was used, the result on each contract was equal to qualifying payments received less qualifying payments made: *FA 1994, s 155(4)*. For Option A the result was £34m (70 – 104). For Option B the result was £14m (104 – 90). The aggregate result for the insurance company was thus (it was argued) a loss of £20m for tax purposes, allowable under *FA 1994, s 155(2)*.

17.23   Because the arrangement involved the bank paying £30m to the insurance company but only receiving £10m until the exercise of the options, the insurance company also made an interest-free loan of £20m to the bank, until the bank exercised Option A. On 20 March 1996, it was agreed that, if both options were exercised together, payments and stock deliveries could be netted off.

17.24   Essentially, the question was whether for business purposes, and so for tax purposes, the two transactions should be regarded separately or together. The Special Commissioners found ([2002] STC 252 at 266):

'there was a genuine practical likelihood or a genuine commercial possibility that the taxpayer company would not exercise Option B … while it is near the limit, the degree of uncertainty saves the transaction from being ignored for tax purposes … They were genuine transactions under which the parties could make a profit or loss even though the expectation was that they would not. Transactions A and B were entered into by taxpayer company and Citibank acting at arm's length … There was a genuine commercial possibility and real practical likelihood that the two options would be dealt with separately.'

17.25   In the House of Lords, Lord Nicholls regarded this as a finding of fact which could not be disturbed on appeal, but said that this did not conclude the question of how the statute was to be applied to the transactions ([2005] STC 15 at [16]):

'The Special Commissioners thus made a finding of fact, which a court hearing an appeal on a question of law is not entitled to disturb, that there was an outside but a commercially real possibility that circumstances might occur in which the two options would not be exercised so as to cancel each other out. The question of law is whether … the existence of this contingency prevented the Commissioners from applying the statute to the scheme as it was intended to operate.'

17.26 The question was whether the grant and exercise of the two options should be regarded as a single composite transaction (at [19]):

'The question depends upon what the statute means by "entitlement" … if the [Citibank] option formed part of a larger scheme by which Citibank's right to the gilts was bound to be cancelled by SPI's right to the same gilts, then it could be said that in a practical sense Citibank had no entitlement to gilts.'

17.27 The remote possibility that SPI's option might not be exercised arose from the strike price chosen. As the court said:

'[22] There was no commercial reason for choosing a strike price of 90 … the contingency upon which SPI rely for saying that there was no composite transaction was a part of that composite transaction, chosen not for any commercial reason but solely to enable SPI to claim that there was no composite transaction …

[23] … it would destroy the value of the *Ramsay* principle of construing provisions such as s 150A(1) of the 1994 Act as referring to the effect of composite transactions if their composite effect had to be disregarded simply because the parties had included a commercially irrelevant contingency, creating an acceptable risk that the scheme might not work as planned …

[24] … the Special Commissioners erred in law in concluding that their finding that there was a realistic possibility of the options not being exercised simultaneously meant, without more, that the scheme could not be regarded as a single composite transaction …'

17.28 Accordingly, the premium received by SPI before the change of law was regarded as forming part of a composite transaction which took place after the change of law, in which the debits and credits produced a flat result.

HBOS Treasury Services plc v R & C Comrs

17.29 In *HBOS Treasury Services plc v R & C Comrs* [2010] SFTD 134:

(a) a bank held ITM fixed-rate legs of a fixed to floating swap, which hedged its own fixed-rate borrowings, the value of the excess payments being £180m; the potential tax liability on the profit was £54m;

(b) to reduce its credit exposure to the counterparty, the bank wished to close out, ie monetise and recoupon, the swaps;

(c) this was a standard commercial transaction but the bank sought to carry it out in a tax-advantaged manner;

(d)   the bank capitalised a new subsidiary D with £180m, and then novated the swaps to D for a payment of £180m, in the expectation that this would be a no gain/no loss intra-group transfer (*FA 2002, Sch 26, para 28*; now *CTA 2009, ss 625–627*); a fee of £2.2m was paid to the counterparty;

(e)   the theory was, that, while D would inherit the latent tax liability, the bank would not be taxed on the £180m;

(f)   the bank sold the D shares to a third party for £150m (loss of £30m); this was odd because the third party was clearly paying more than the shares were worth, taking account of the latent tax liability;

(g)   the bank then entered into replacement swaps with its original counterparty to continue the hedging relationship;

(h)   if the bank was correct on the assumption of a tax-free intra-group transfer, HMRC argued that a claimed loss of £30m on the sale of the D shares was to be disregarded under the value-shifting rule in *TCGA 1992, s 30*.

17.30   The Tribunal held that there was a tax avoidance scheme, aimed at avoiding the tax which would have been payable on a recouponing with third parties, by rolling the potential tax liability into D, and disposing of the D shares at a loss – in other words, by turning an income receipt into a capital receipt.

17.31   The basic issue was whether D replaced the bank as a party to the novation swaps. Under the novation, the counterparty had a contingent right to terminate the swap which did not exist under the original contract. In this circumstance, the Tribunal held that the rights and liabilities under the novation were not 'equivalent' to those under the original agreement, and accordingly the requirements of *FA 2002, Sch 26, para 28* for a no gain/no loss intra-group transfer were not fulfilled. The Tribunal concluded at [84]:

'the rights and liabilities of [D] immediately after the novation were not "equivalent" to those of [the bank] immediately before the novation'

17.32   The judge thus held that 'equivalent rights and liabilities' meant semi-identical rights and liabilities, and the inclusion of new contingent termination events in the novated swap prevented the group continuity rules from applying.

The fee of £2.2m paid to the counterparty was held to be deductible under *FA 2002, Sch 26, para 15*.

Klincke v R & C Comrs

17.33   In *Harding v R & C Comrs* [2008] STC 3499 the Court of Appeal held that the word 'provision' for currency conversion applied to any provision in the bond, irrespective of whether it was currently exercisable. The bond did not become a QCB when the currency conversion clause lapsed. A literal and purposive construction gave the same result

17.34 In *Klincke v R & C Comrs* [2010] STC 2032 the Upper Tribunal held that an amendment to a bond to remove the provision for currency conversion was effective to convert a non-QCB into a QCB. However, the rolled over gain was frozen at the point when the non-QCB became a QCB and became chargeable to tax when the gain was realised.

This was followed in *Blumenthal v R & C Comrs* [2012] SFTD 1264.

Abbey National Treasury Services plc v R & C Comrs

17.35 In *Abbey National Treasury Services plc v R & C Comrs* [2015] SFTD 929, Treasury Services (TS) was a party to in the money gross paying interest rate swaps with its parent (P). TS issued tracker shares to P entitling P to receive dividends equivalent to the cash flows on the swaps. The swaps giving rise to the cash flows were derecognised in TS's accounts on the grounds that the risks and rewards had been transferred to P, and claimed a debit for 'swap recognition taken to equity' under *FA 2002, Sch 26, para 15(1)(a)*. Two issues arose:

(a)   whether the debit was deductible for tax purposes;

(b)   if so, whether the transfer pricing rules required an adjustment to be made to TS's taxable profits.

17.36 The Revenue argued that the derecognition should be taken to the statement of changes in equity and not to the income statement. This was a transaction with shareholders, not with a third party. The debit did not arise from the derivative contracts (the same argument that was to be used in *Stagecoach* - see below at **17.45**). *Paragraph 15(1)(a)* contained the 'fairly represent' override.

17.37 The FTT considered whether the derecognition deduction was deductible as a payment arising from derivative contracts. The Tribunal considered the phrase 'fairly represent' as a restraint on accounting treatment. While rejecting an 'economic substance over form' approach, the FTT held that the debit should be regarded as a distribution of profits, a dividend, ie non-deductible: [91]. The Tribunal also concluded that the debit did not derive directly from the derivative contracts: [96]. As the Tribunal put it at [97]:

'The debit arose … because of the contractual obligation to pay on the Swap Cash Flows under the Tracker Shares, which had no legal impact on the Swaps at all. This debit might be economically connected to, or related to, the derivative contracts, but it does not arise from those contracts as required by paragraph 15.'

17.38 The Tribunal also held that the issue of shares for £1,000 which had a market value of £161m was a 'provision' for transfer pricing purposes. The FTT was prepared to apply the transfer pricing provisions to the share issue, but then to disregard the share issue, applying para 1.37 of the 1995 OECD Transfer Pricing Guidelines, as a step which was not 'commercially rational' and which 'impeded the tax administration from determining the appropriate transfer price', to arrive at a comparator situation in which shares had not been issued at all.

Pike v R & C Comrs

17.39 In *Pike v R & C Comrs* [2014] STC 2549, a company issued loan stock to an individual. The redemption amount was the issue amount plus interest at 7.25% per annum. He transferred the loan stock to a trust, claiming that he suffered a loss on a relevant discounted security. The Court of Appeal held that the additional amount was interest and not a premium. The loan stock was not therefore a relevant discounted security. The interest was not denatured by being aggregated with another payment: *Chevron Petroleum UK Ltd v BP Petroleum Development Ltd* [1981] STC 689 at 694. As Lord Fraser observed in *Willingale v International Commercial Bank Ltd* [1978] STC 75 at 81, 'Interest accrues from day to day or at other fixed intervals but discount does not.'

Biffa (Jersey) Ltd v R & C Comrs

17.40 *Biffa (Jersey) Ltd v R & C Comrs* [2015] SFTD 163 was concerned with a sale and repurchase of securities. *ICTA 1988, s 730A* required that the price differential on a repo should be regarded as a deductible expense in the original holder and a chargeable receipt in the interim holder. B Ltd (as original holder) sold shares in A Ltd for £200m to A Ltd (as interim holder), against A Ltd's undertaking to issue replacement shares for £214m in 12 months' time.

17.41 B Ltd claimed a loan relationship debit of £14m. A Ltd claimed that it did not have to bring in a corresponding credit, because *FA 2003, s 195* enabled a company to buy back its shares without cancelling them or acquiring an asset, but instead to hold them as treasury shares. Hence A Ltd had not acquired the shares as interim holder. The FTT held that, while *s 195(2)* provided that the buy-back of shares should not be regarded as an acquisition of an asset, it did constitute an acquisition of shares. Hence *s 730A(1)* applied to produce a symmetrical tax treatment.

Bristol & West plc v R & C Comrs

17.42 In *Bristol & West plc v R & C Comrs* [2016] STC 1491, in the money interest rate swaps novated from one group company to another on 29 August 2003 for a payment of £91m. The transferor company fell within new rules for accounting periods beginning on or after 1 Oct 2002, under which intra-group transfers of derivatives were disregarded (group neutrality rule: *FA 2006, Sch 26, para 28*). The transferee company was by contrast within new rules, under which on an intra-group transfer of derivatives the transferee company acquired at market value. Hence, on the group's analysis, the acquisition cost of the transferee company was raised to market value, without any corresponding charge on the transferor company.

17.43 On the substantive issue the Upper Tribunal held that the transitional rules could not operate unless both transferor and transferee companies were within the new rules. The Court of Appeal upheld this conclusion.

17.44 There was also a procedural issue. The Revenue had by mistake issued a closure notice under *FA 1998, Sch 18, para 32* stating that no additional tax was payable by the transferor company. The Court of Appeal held that, in the context, the purported closure notice could not be interpreted to mean that the Revenue had closed their enquiry: [34].

Stagecoach Group plc v R & C Comrs

17.45 In *Stagecoach Group plc v R & C Comrs* [2016] UKFTT 120 (TC), the structure was:

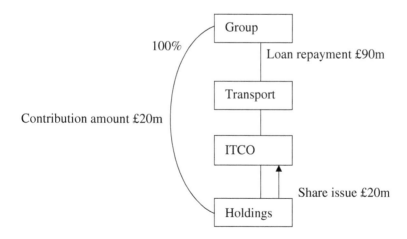

1   ITCO and Holdings required recapitalisation.

2   Transport owed Group £90m.

3   Holdings agreed to issue to ITCO 20,000 new shares, in return for payment of 22.4% of Transport's loan repayment to Group up to a maximum of £20m (a forward subscription agreement (FSA)).

4   On the issue of the new shares Group derecognised £20m of the Transport loan. The accounting entries were DR Investments CR Loan.

5   Group paid £20m to Holdings, and Holdings issued 20,000 new shares to ITCO.

6   In computing its loan relationship profits Group claimed a 'derecognition debit' of £40m, deductible for tax purposes under *CTA 2009, s 320* (capitalisation of debt: DR to fixed assets, CR to liabilities). This was on the basis that there was a relievable debit in Group, with no corresponding tax charge in Holdings or ICTO.

17.46   The Revenue:

(a)   issued a closure notice disallowing the loan relationships debit in Group; and alternatively

(b)   issued a receipt (arbitrage) notice to Holdings and Services under *TIOPA 2010, s 249*, the effect of which was to tax the subscription proceeds received by Holdings (see **20.33**).

17.47   The oddity in the case is that no-one appears to have suggested that the loan relationship debit was non-deductible by reason of *CTA 2009, s 354* (connected company loan relationships). The reason appears to have been that the Revenue argued that the debit was not '*in respect of a company's loan relationship*' within *CTA 2009, s 320(1)* (for accounting periods beginning on or after 1 January 2016, *s 320(1)(a)*), but in respect of the forward subscription agreement. The debit was not 'in respect of' Group's loan relationship with Transport. The only references by the Tribunal to *s 354* were at [52] and [106].

17.48   The Tribunal started from the principle that the loan relationships legislation was based on the principle of symmetry, derived from the principles of double entry bookkeeping. For every loan relationship debit there should be a corresponding loan relationship credit: [99]. There was '*a general principle of tax symmetry*': [176]. That is true as far as it goes (see **5.2**) but it does not take us very far, because there are many instances in the legislation where it does not produce symmetry in this sense, eg impairment relief for non-connected company debt.

17.49   The Tribunal then donned the mantle of philosophy, by asking whether there was a causative relationship between the debit to fixed assets and the credit to loans: 'the phrase "in respect of" has a causative flavour but is not a but for test' ([84]). After a long excursus the Tribunal concluded that the requisite causal relationship did not exist:

> '116 … the debit is not in respect of a loan relationship. The existence of the debit is entirely attributable to the FSA'

17.50 The requirement for the causal link cannot be derived from the legislation. This is an unacceptable gloss on the legislation and appears to derive from the illusory search for the *ignis fatuus* of principles in tax legislation. This appears to be what is meant by 'purposive interpretation'. As the Tribunal said, 'do the basic facts, realistically assessed, fall within the scope of the statutory provision, purposively construed?': [84].

17.51 The Tribunal also held that, if it was wrong on the main issue, Holdings would be required to recompute its profits to eliminate the mismatch under the arbitrage rules: [188].

Trigg v R & C Comrs

17.52 In *Trigg v R & C Comrs* [2016] STC 1310, an individual bought bonds at a discount, which he later sold at a profit. He claimed that the profit was tax free, because the bonds were QCBs and so exempt assets for capital gains tax.

17.53 The QCBs contained a clause that the sterling amounts payable under the bond were to be converted into euros if the UK joined the EMU. The Revenue argued that the bonds thereby ceased to be QCBs within *TCGA 1992, s 117(1)(b)* because they contained a provision for conversion into another currency, and hence were not 'sterling bonds'. The FTT held that any conversion would be at the spot rate prevailing at the time of redemption following the adoption of the euro, and therefore would be at the spot rate prevailing at the time of redemption under *s 117(2)(b)*. *Section 117(2)(b)* thus applied a limited exception to the otherwise wider provision of that sub-clause.

17.54 The Upper Tribunal conducted an extensive review of the relevant case-law and principles of interpretation. 'Sterling' in *TCGA 1992, s 117* could only mean the lawful currency of the UK. It could not include any other currency which might replace sterling. The clause providing for conversion into euros was a conversion clause, which as such placed the bonds outside the definition of QCB.

17.55 It is submitted that this conclusion was plainly wrong, and is an example of adopting a literal construction where a purposive interpretation should have been used, as opposed to the more common mistake of adopting a purposive construction where a literal construction should have been adopted.

Greene King plc v R & C Comrs

17.56   *Greene King plc v R & C Comrs* [2016] EWCA Civ 782 has already been considered at **5.89–5.91** and **6.144**. It concerns a scheme to secure asymmetric tax treatment in a group (deduction for debt in one group company, with no corresponding taxation of credit in another group company).

Union Castle Mail Steamship Company Ltd v R & C Comrs

17.57   *Union Castle Mail Steamship Company Ltd v R & C Comrs* [2016] UKFTT 0256 (TC) is very similar to *Abbey National Treasury Services* (see **17.35–17.38**). However, the Tribunal distinguished the reasoning in *Abbey National*: [47], [52].

17.58   The case concerned an arrangement to turn taxable profits on derivatives into tax-free capital gains:

1   A subsidiary (Union Castle) of an AIT (Caledonian) held in the money derivatives (put options used to hedge the investment trust's share investments against a fall in prices). It transferred the benefit of the derivatives to its parent (Caledonia) by issuing a special class of shares (A shares) which carried the right to 95% of the profits on the derivatives on close out. The subscription price of the A shares was £5,200 and the market value £39.1m.

2   Both parent and subsidiary used IAS. Union Castle derecognised 95% of the fair value of the derivatives (£39.1m) (IAS 39, paras 17–20, 'where an entity retains the contractual rights to receive the cash flows of a financial asset but assumes a contractual obligation to pay the cash flows to one or more recipients').

3   Union Castle debited the £39.1m in computing its profits on derivatives: *FA 2002, Sch 26, para 15.*

4   Union Castle claimed a tax loss of £39.1m: *FA 2002, Sch 26, para 25A.*

5   The parent recognised the acquisition of the new shares at FVTPL, but did not recognise a profit in its income statement. This was because Caledonian, being an AIT, was not chargeable to tax on capital transactions.

17.59   HMRC argued that the transaction did not involve a financial liability, but a shareholder event. The Tribunal accepted accountancy evidence that the subsidiary correctly recognised the debit in its income statement: [28]. However, it held that Union Castle had not suffered a tax loss, because it chose to give away the cash proceeds of the derivatives: [49]. However, the issue was not whether the transfer of benefits was gratuitous. The issue was whether the transaction gave rise to an allowable loss in Union Castle.

17.60   The Tribunal considered the transfer pricing issue at [68]–[87], correctly rejecting the FTT's reasoning in *Abbey National Treasury Services* and holding that the transfer pricing rules do not apply to equity transactions.

Chapter 18

Islamic Finance

Overview

18.1   This chapter deals with:

* Islamic financing arrangements
* Shari'a-compliant financing
* UK tax treatment

Islamic financing arrangements

18.2   Western societies have adopted a secular view of the human condition and regard religion only as acceptable if confined within the limits of human reason. Globalisation has brought Western financial practice into conflict with restrictions imposed by different systems of society. Muslim societies place a central emphasis on religious tenets of Shari'a-law. Islam is a way of life, which does not contemplate a sharp divide between the secular and the religious sphere. These impose restrictions upon the ways in which business can be conducted and finance raised. These restrictions seek also to ensure that business is conducted on a sustainable basis, by reliance on co-operation and fair dealing rather than competition. Islamic financing consists of arrangements devised and approved by Islamic scholars to enable Muslims to engage in modern commerce without having to resort to the often speculative nature of Western financial tools. The UK has taken account of these constraints by providing for taxation of 'alternative financial arrangements'.

18.3   Use of Islamic financial arrangements is not confined to Muslims. Hence the availability of an alternative form of taxation makes available choices which may be taken purely for tax reasons without regard to other commercial reasons.

18.4   Islamic law prohibits a number of common Western financial transactions. It seeks to exclude interest, speculative transactions and gambling. This leads to prohibitions on riba, gharar and maysir.

18.5   In particular, payment or receipt of interest (riba) is broadly prohibited. It is permissible to obtain a return on funds which has been earned as a profit derived from a commercial risk which the provider of funds has incurred. However, speculation which does not involve productive effort is also prohibited. A charge on a property as security for a loan is prohibited.

18.6   Gharar refers to excessive or avoidable risk geared to a future event. Highly leveraged and derivative transactions will fall under this prohibition.

18.7   Maysir prohibits extreme uncertainty in the form of gambling, and is not relevant to the business sphere.

18.8   What Islamic law seeks to do is avoid the prohibitions of riba, gharar and maysir, using tools which correspond to social and commercial reality and which it would be wrong to see as simply formalistic disguises. Like Western models, they break down into equity-based and debt-based models.

18.9   A further aspect is that Islamic law does not widely recognise the corporation as an independent juristic person which serves as a vehicle for the conduct of commerce. Instead Islamic law relies exclusively on the concept of the partnership. Hence business transactions are analysed as joint ventures between parties with shared interests, rather than as agreements between parties with conflicting interests.

18.10   A wide spread difficulty of applying UK legal concepts not only to Muslim arrangements but also to particular ethnic groups (eg Indians, Pakistanis) is that, whereas Western legal systems are based on the concept of exclusive individual ownership of property, in some communities property is regarded as family property, which is placed at the disposal of individuals as they require it, but is not in any sense their exclusive property. For example, one might have 30 properties registered in the name of one individual, but he is not in any sense the beneficial owner and identifying beneficial ownership in a UK laws sense is an unreal if not impossible exercise.

18.11   In summary, therefore, Islamic financing is consensus based rather than conflict based and is risk averse. There is a widespread recognition of family and community property, rather than exclusive individual ownership. The emphasis is on risk avoidance and risk prevention. The economic model is that of an equilibrium fundamentally different to that produced by the interaction of supply and demand, beloved by classical economists. This approach can afford valuable correctives to Western models.

18.12   The Court of Appeal considered these issues in *Project Blue Ltd v R & C Comrs* [2016] EWCA Civ 485. In this case:

1   The State of Qatar sovereign wealth fund (PBL) wished to purchase a large development site for £959m. It needed to raise finance to do so.

A conventional loan at interest secured by a charge on the property would not have been Shari'a-law compliant.

2   The vendor undertook to sell on the property to MAR, a Qatari bank, for £1.25bn, and MAR undertook to lease the property back to PBL for 999 years. PBL undertook to make payments to MAR during the rental period, which could be terminated earlier.

3   This was a form of Shari'a-compliant financing, comprising a lease plus an option (Ijara). It was explained in detail by Patten LJ at [7]:

'It respects the Islamic prohibition on usury by providing for the property in question to be acquired by the financial institution as its property and then leased to the person seeking the finance in exchange for agreed rental payments giving the institution a return on its money.'

The financial institution must be the outright purchaser of the property.

4   The contracts under (1)–(2) were simultaneously completed on 31 January 2008.

5   *FA 2003, s 45(3)* (which applies to sub-sales) had the effect of displacing the conveyance by V to PBL so that the transaction for SDLT purposes was the conveyance from V to MAR. This was 'the only possible acquisition of a chargeable interest': [17].

6   *FA 2003, ss 71A, 72, 73* were introduced to accommodate Ijara-financing, provided that MAR (the financial institution) became the owner of the property on purchase from the vendor, and the vendor was the beneficiary of the Ijara-financing. This did not apply here because MAR acquired the property from V, not PBL (effect of *s 71A(2)*, following from (5)).

7   The court held that MAR was liable to SDLT as purchaser by reference to the sum of £1.25bn. However, it was too late for the Revenue to assess this liability on MAR. The state's claim for tax was extinguished, because it was unenforceable.

8   The Revenue relied on the argument that *s 75A* (which would otherwise have been excluded by *s 71A*) imposed a charge in the same amount on PBL on a notional land transaction between V and MAR.

9   The court regarded this as 'a particularly inapt and harsh result' because it would charge SDLT on the finance cost ([28]), rather than limit SDLT to the consideration paid to the third party vendor. It was rejected because *s 75A(1)(c)* excluded from *s 75A* cases where the SDLT payable on the scheme transactions was the same as more than the SDLT payable on the notional transaction.

10   The amendment of *FA 2003, s 45(3)* with effect from 24 March 2011 removed the difficulty for subsequent transactions, by removing the disregard of the original contract (V to PBL) in cases where the secondary contract (PBL to MAR) was exempt by virtue of *s 73*.

18.13   The case is also important for the review of Islamic financing by Lewison LJ at [47]–[48]. He referred there to the alternatives of Musharaka and diminishing Musharaka.

18.14   Types of Shari'a-compliant financing are:

1   *Equity-based arrangements*

  (a)   *Sukuk*: a bond entitling the holder to an economic return on an asset or portfolio of assets ('investment bond arrangement').

  (b)   *Musharaka* ('sharing' or 'partnership'): this provides a return based on a joint ownership interest, under which the value of the holder's ownership interest diminishes as he receives payments from the eventual owner ('diminishing shared ownership arrangements/ profit share agency arrangements'). Distribution of profits (and losses) has to be based on profits, not capital contributed.

  (c)   *Mudaraba or dimihsing musharaka*: one party provides the capital, and another party carries on the business, his share of ownership increasing in proportion to profits.

  (d)   *Takaful*: mutual risk sharing.

  (e)   *Wakala*: profit share agency.

2   *Debt-based arrangements*

  (a)   *Ijara* ('to give something on rent'): acquisition by financial institution, with leaseback to real purchaser and option to end lease early).

  (b)   *Murabaha*: purchase of asset specified by client by financier and onwards sale to client at higher price ('purchase and resale arrangement', 'mark-up arrangements). This is similar to Ijarah, as used in *Project Blue*.

  (c)   *Tawarruq of reverse murabaha:* purchase of asset by financier for deferred payment by client, followed by sale for original purchase price to third party.

  (d)   *Modaraba*: contribution of money to a fund with entitlement to profit and loss on the fund ('deposit arrangement').

  (e)   *Salam and Istisna'a*: financier pays in advance for product, eg sale of crop, to enable producer to finance production costs; a forward contract for commodities, designed to finance production, not to speculate in future prices.

18.15   The legal incidents of these arrangements may be governed by any chosen system of law. Participation in Islamic finance arrangements is not confined to persons subject or allegiant to Islamic law. However, the financial aspects must be certified as conforming with Islamic law.

UK tax treatment

18.16   The problem for the UK tax system is that it makes a fundamental distinction between debt returns and equity returns. An investor return based on the results of the business will ordinarily be a distribution. On the other hand, there is a policy objective of treating economically equivalent transactions as subject to the same tax charge. It would also be incompatible with the secular basis of the system, and indeed a multi-cultural society, to vary tax liability in accordance with religious tenets.

18.17   Where a company is a party to an Islamic finance arrangement, the loan relationship rules have a number of special rules which deal with some of these situations. The loan relationship rules apply as if the alternative financial arrangements were loan relationships (*CTA 2009, ss 509, 510*):

- Murabaha is dealt with in *s 503* ('purchase and resale arrangements').

- Musharaka is dealt with under *s 504* ('diminishing shared ownership arrangements').

- Modaraba is dealt with under *s 505* ('deposit arrangement').

- Wakala is dealt with under *s 506* ('profit share agency arrangements').

- Sukuk is dealt with under *s 507* ('investment bond arrangement').

18.18   Where these provisions apply, the 'alternative finance return' or 'profit share return' is treated as (in the case of an individual) interest or (in the case of a company) a credit on a loan relationship, unless the transaction is not at arm's length: *s 508*.

18.19   The general rule is that a company which is party to such arrangements is treated as if it were party to a loan relationship: *s 509*. There are more detailed rules on how this is to be achieved under *ss 510–520*. However, there is no guidance on how these tax rules are related to accounting treatment in cases where what is treated for tax purposes as a liability will, for accounting purposes (to be Shari'a-law compliant), be treated as an investment.

18.20   The special rules all require that one of the parties to the transaction should be a 'financial institution'. This is defined in *CTA 2009, s 502* as a person holding a banking licence, a consumer credit licence or an insurance company. There is a similar definition for SDLT purposes in *FA 2003, s 71A(8)*; *ITA 2007, s 546B*.

18.21   Alternative Finance Investment Bonds (AFIBs) fall under CTA 2009, s 507. Sukuk means 'certificate'. The Sukuk must be issued on a recognised stock exchange, as widely defined in *ITA 2007, s 1005(2A)*. The Sukuk issuer will declare a trust over the assets to be acquired with the funds raised by the Sukuk issuance. The assets or activities must be Shari'a-law compliant. The holders of Sukuk certificates thus obtain an entitlement to the return produced by the assets or activities. For tax purposes the Sukuk issuer is regarded as entitled to the yield on the assets (taxable under *s 518*), while the holders of the certificates are treated as receiving income distributions taxable under *s 510(5)* as interest on loan relationships (if companies) and otherwise liable to income tax.

18.22   The capital gains tax rules which apply to alternative finance arrangements are in *TCGA 1992, ss 151H–151Y*, and follow the pattern of *CTA 2009, ss 501–521*.

18.23   There is no requirement that either (a) the financial arrangements should be certified as being Shari'a-compliant; or (b) the tax outcome should be comparable with that which would result from conventional financing designed to produce the same commercial outcome. The alternative taxation of financing arrangements is thus generally available, and may in some cases offer a less taxed outcome that conventional financing.

18.24   The transfer pricing rules do not apply where the alternative finance rules apply. The payer of the return does not obtain a deduction for his finance costs.

18.25   Where Islamic financing is adopted, this places considerable restrictions on intra-group finance arrangements, which cannot be by the conventional means of intra-group loans and cash pools. The OECD Model Convention does not take account of Islamic financing. Hence the interest article cannot be applied. The application of transfer pricing rules to Islamic financing is the subject of important current research, in particular: Niko Sievert, 'International Corporate Taxation of MNEs in the Middle East and North Africa: the Challenges of Modernisation and Integration' (PhD thesis, Queen Mary, University of London).

Chapter 19

Stock Lending and Repos

Overview

19.1   This chapter deals with:

- Introduction to stock lending and repos
- Stock lending – legal and accounting
- Tax treatment of stock lending
- Repos – outline
- Gilt repos
- Repos – accounting treatment
- Repos – legislation
- Repos – tax treatment
- Manufactured payments
- Stamp duty
- Euro-conversion

Introduction

19.2   Stock lending and repos are a key feature of how financial markets work. The transactions which fall under these headings are:

(a)   stock lending;

(b)   repurchase agreements ('repos');

(c)   buy-sell agreements (a form of repo); and

(d)   the provision of collateral to secure counterparty and credit exposures under a stock lending or repo.

19.3   A stock loan is a temporary transfer of fungible securities from an investor to a securities trader, so that the trader can meet an order to sell such securities. Besides paying a fee, the trader undertakes to retransfer equivalent securities at an agreed future date.

19.4   A repo is an agreement whereby a company obtains finance by selling its property (securities) subject to an obligation or option to re-acquire it later at a fixed price. In economic substance, such an arrangement is the same as borrowing from a financier and using the assets as security for the loan. This can, alternatively, be called a sale and repurchase agreement.

All are transactions designed to promote liquidity of securities (stock lending) or cash (repos).

19.5   Securities lending enhances trading in securities, because it enables share-dealers to settle a transaction without affecting their own short position. At the same time, the lenders of the securities can improve their investment returns by obtaining stock lending fees, while retaining the collateral value of the lent securities in support of secured credit facilities.

19.6   Stock lending can also serve speculative purposes, as where a borrower sells the borrowed stock, intending to buy replacement stock at a lower price. Repos are a means of borrowing money rather than avoiding delivery risk. The transaction takes the form of a sale of the securities with a simultaneous agreement to repurchase them at a specified future date.

19.7   Thus, stock lending is an arrangement whereby holders of securities (banks, insurance companies, custodians, pension funds, charities) transfer them to market makers and other dealers in securities, to enable them to complete 'short' sales. The borrower undertakes:

(a)   to retransfer securities of the same kind and amount; and

(b)   to pay manufactured dividends and interest to the lender, to replace the real dividends and interest, which go to the stock borrower during the period of the stock lending.

19.8   Although called 'lending', the process involves in law an actual transfer of ownership of the securities, rather in the way that a legal mortgage of land by way of security prior to 1925 required an actual conveyance of the land to the lender, subject to a promise to re-convey, on payment of the mortgage debt.

19.9   For accounting purposes (IAS 39, IFRS 9, FRS 102), the payment of manufactured dividends on the borrowed stock and the borrower's redelivery obligation mean that the lender retains substantially all the risks and rewards of ownership, so that the assets are not derecognised in the lender or recognised in the borrower. Accordingly, both the transfer of securities and the transfer of income rights are derecognised. Where shares and securities are fair valued by the lender, fair value profits and losses will continue to be recognised during the transfer of ownership. In other words, accounting ignores the legal position and adopts the economic substance.

19.10   In an electronic system, securities are transferred by credit and debit entries in the accounts of account holders, as in a banking system. In a banking system, a customer has no title to money as a chattel, but simply a contractual claim in debt against the bank. The reduction of securities transactions to pure banking transactions has been thought to involve a risk to the original owners of the transferred securities who wish to retain a proprietary interest in specific securities. In general, there are three approaches to the legal status of securities held by an intermediary:

(a)   *Contractual relationship*: The original owner is treated as having a general contractual claim against the intermediary.

(b)   *Traceable property rights*: The original owner is treated as retaining a proprietary interest in the transferred securities.

(c)   *Pro rata interest in a pool of securities*: The original owner has a proprietary interest in a pro rata fraction of a pool of securities held by the interim holder.

19.11   While (b) and (c) are thought to offer the transferor a greater degree of security against intermediary insolvency than (a), neither fits the circumstances of a book entry system. However, the legal and tax analysis of these transactions is essentially conducted on the basis of the fiction that the dematerialised securities exist in physical form.

19.12   The key to these arrangements is fungibility. Fungible assets are assets which lend themselves to substitution. Securities are fungible if they have exactly the same terms, eg as to interest, redemption, covenants, events of default and voting rights. Securities of the same issue are usually fungible even if they are numbered. Securities deposited within the Euroclear system are fungible with other Euroclear securities of the same issue. Securities placed with depositaries on behalf of Euroclear are held on a segregated basis, so that Euroclear securities held by that depositary are not fungible with securities held by that depositary for other clients.

19.13   There is a statutory definition of fungibility in *TCGA 1992, s 263B(5), (6)*. *Section 263B(5)* says that references to the transfer and transfer back of securities are references to securities 'of the same description'. *Section 263B(6)* says that:

> 'securities shall not be taken to be of the same description as other securities unless they are in the same quantities, give the same rights against the same persons and are of the same type and nominal value as the other securities.'

This provision does not cover cases of sub-division or consolidation of shares during the term of the arrangement.

19.14   In the case of stock lending, the provision of cash collateral by the transferee of the securities is necessary:

(a)   to reduce risks arising from different settlement times in different markets, eg where the settlement of collateral occurs at a different time to the settlement of the loan of securities, or to minimise risk of settlement failures; and

(b)   to enable investment returns to be enhanced by investment management of the cash collateral.

The holder of the collateral will rebate interest to the provider of the collateral (ie the stock lender will make payments representing interest to the stock borrower).

19.15   The growth of the scale and frequency of these transactions has been driven by the reduction of settlement intervals, ie the interval between the date of a securities trade (T) and the date of its final settlement (normally T + 3). Securities transactions involve a number of stages: matching of trades; the calculation of resultant obligations (clearing); transfer of securities (delivery); and transfer of funds (payment) to discharge the obligations (settlement). Acceleration of settlement is part of a general trend towards real time gross settlement (RTGS), under which the gap between trade and settlement is reduced to a minimum. One of the problems is linking delivery of the securities with payment for them, the general issue being delivery versus payment (DVP). DVP and RTGS place great strains on stock and cash liquidity, which are alleviated by stock lending and repos. The transfer of the securities or deposit of collateral will carry with it income arising during the course of the arrangement.

19.16   The heightened need for liquidity requires the ability to make rapid, secure and temporary transfers of securities and cash between parties. For reasons of practicality, economy and security, these transactions will generally be conducted through custodians who act as intermediaries. The transfer of shares and debt securities will normally be made not by the physical transfer of securities, but by book-entry transfers in an electronic system, eg CREST (for UK equities) and CGO (for UK gilts). The principal international central securities depository (ICSD) which holds and settles trades in Eurobonds is Euroclear. Bearer securities or global certificates are immobilised within the network of the custodian and sub-custodians, and subsequent transfers made by book-entry.

19.17   Manufactured payments are payable in two sets of circumstances:

(a)   After the record date but before payment date, A transfers or sells securities cum div to B. As registered owner of the securities at the record date, A will receive the dividend or interest, so he will make a payment 'representative' of the dividend to B. Thus, when a cum div short sale is settled with ex div stock, a payment will be made by the vendor to compensate the purchaser for not receiving the real dividend.

(b)   A holds securities which he transfers to B by way of loan, so that – if the arrangement crosses a record date – B receives dividends or interest while the stock lending or repo arrangement subsists. B agrees that A will have the benefit of the income. In both repos and stock lending, normal practice is for the interim holder to pass back the benefit of real dividends and interest to the original owner by means of manufactured dividends.

19.18   The legal right to receive a coupon or a dividend on a security rests with the legal owner. Transfer of the legal title to securities in the form of securities lending or a repo carries with it the right to receive the dividend or coupon for the lifetime of the transaction. The stock borrower (or interim holder) needs to compensate the stock lender (or seller) for the economic loss of not receiving the dividend or interest. A compensation payment is made from the borrower (buyer) to the lender (seller). Hence the interim holder will make payments to the original owner representative of the real dividends and interest which he receives. The term 'manufactured payments' reflects the fact that payments representative of real dividends or interest received by the manufacturer are not actual dividends or interest, any more than periodic payments under a swap are real interest. Strictly, one should speak of 'a manufactured payment representative of a real dividend', and 'a manufactured payment representative of real interest'. Manufactured payments must be made separately or built into the repurchase price.

19.19   Manufactured payments are payments received by the stock borrower or interim holder which are representative of payments due to the stock lender or original holder. Manufactured payments are actual cash payments. Deemed manufactured payments are notional payments.

Example 19.1

When the shares in X plc stand at 200, A sells forward 1,000 shares at £200 for delivery in a month's time. He anticipates that the price of the shares will fall. On completion date, he borrows 1,000 X shares from Z (an insurance company) for a fee of 100, undertaking to redeliver equivalent stock in a month's time. As security, he deposits with Z the sum of 1,000 × 200. By the date of redelivery, the price of X shares has fallen to 190. A buys 1,000 X shares in the market and delivers them to Z, who retransfers the cash deposit to A. A's profit is:

$$[(200 - 190) \times 1,000] - 100 = 9,900.$$

While the stock loan lasts:

Z (the stock lender)

- receives real interest on the deposit;

- receives manufactured dividends on the shares; and

- pays rebate interest to A.

A (the stock borrower)

- receives real dividends on the shares;

- receives rebate interest on the deposit; and

- pays manufactured dividends on the shares to Z.

Example 19.2

B owns fixed interest bonds issued by D plc with a market value of £1m. B requires cash of £1m, but anticipates that the bond price will rise. He transfers the bonds to F for one month, undertaking to repurchase them for £1,008,333. F pays £1m to B, on which it is currently earning interest at 8% (£6,666 per month). At the end of the month, the value of the bonds has risen to £1.05m. B repays £1,008,333 to F, who retransfers equivalent bonds to B.

B's profit is £50,000 – £8,333 = £41,667

F's profit is £8,333 – £6,666 = £1,667

During the term of the repo:

F (the purchaser)

- receives real interest from D; and
- pays manufactured interest to B to represent the bond coupons.

B (the repurchaser)

- has use of £1m; and
- receives manufactured interest from F.

Stock lending – legal and accounting

19.20   As in related areas, these transactions are now carried out on the basis of market standard documentation. The global master securities lending agreement (GMSLA) of 2000 is generally used. The essence of these agreements is the absolute transfer of securities and collateral, even though the transfer is only made for temporary purposes. The reason for insisting on absolute transfer is to ensure that the holder of the securities or collateral does not have a mere security interest, which could be defeated by non-registration or on the insolvency of a counterparty. Because of the absolute nature of the transfer, the transferee is entitled to real payments of dividends and interest during the duration of the arrangement, and the transferor is correspondingly entitled to payments from the transferee representing the real interest and dividends ('manufactured dividends'). In the event of default, redelivery obligations are accelerated, obligations are valued in money terms, all transactions between the same counterparties are closed out and set off, and one party will prove for any outstanding balance in his favour.

19.21   Under most systems of law, a beneficiary loses his legal rights of ownership in an asset if he transfers it to someone who can use the property as his own, even if the transferee must substitute equivalent securities and replace in cash any loss of value or income. Stock lending involves a real, if temporary, transfer of ownership.

Tax treatment of stock lending

19.22   A definition of 'stock lending arrangement' for share purposes is contained in *TCGA 1992, s 263B(1)*. 'Stock lending arrangement' is defined as:

> 'so much of any arrangements between two persons ("the borrower" and "the lender") as are arrangements under which–

(a) the lender transfers securities to the borrower otherwise than by way of sale; and

(b) a requirement is imposed on the borrower to transfer those securities back to the lender otherwise than by way of sale.'

There is a similar definition for loan relationship purposes in *CTA 2010, s 805*.

19.23 The transfer of securities from the stock lender to the stock borrower, or the retransfer on the termination of the arrangement, does not constitute a disposal.

19.24 The basic tax rule is contained in *TCGA 1992, s 263B(2)*:

'the disposals and acquisitions made in pursuance of any stock lending arrangement shall be disregarded for the purposes of capital gains tax.'

19.25 In the case of a stock loan (or repo) of debt securities, *CTA 2009, s 330A* provides that where a company recognises in its accounts credits and debits in respect of a loan relationship to which it is not, or no longer is (be it temporarily) a party, the company is required to include within its accounts those amounts in computing its loan relationship profits and losses. Hence:

(a) a stock loan (repo) will not be regarded as a disposal or acquisition for tax purposes;

(b) subsequent reacquisition will not be a disposal or acquisition;

(c) to the extent recognised in GAAP-compliant accounts, manufactured payments will be taxable on the stock borrower/interim holder;

(d) to the extent recognised in GAAP-compliant accounts, manufactured payments will be correspondingly deductible in the stock lender/original holder.

19.26 Stock lending fees will be liable to corporation tax either as trading income or other income.

Repos – outline

19.27 A repo consists of a spot leg and a forward leg, ie a spot sale and a forward purchase of the same parcel of securities, the price differential being treated as interest. Because the original owner receives back the same securities, he continues to be exposed to the economic risk of holding them. Where the repo is in respect of overseas equities, the payment of a manufactured dividend is a manufactured overseas dividend. The spot leg occurs at T_1 and the forward leg is executed at T_2.

Example 19.3

Spot leg – T_1

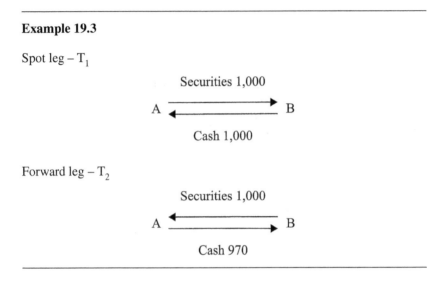

Forward leg – T_2

19.28   Under a repo, a holder of securities borrows money short-term. A repo is a form of secured lending. Borrowing rates are correspondingly lower. In a repo, one party to the repo (the original holder/seller/borrower) sells shares or securities (the repoed securities) to another party (the interim holder/buyer/lender). The repo buyer agrees to sell the shares or securities back to the repo seller at the end of the term of the repo for a price agreed at the outset. The transferred securities are actually sold, so the money paid upon delivery of the securities represents the sales price, rather than collateral. As the repurchase price is fixed, the risks and rewards of ownership of the securities, in terms of movements in their value, remain with the original holder. The price differential between the sale price and the repurchase price normally equates to the finance return for the repo buyer. The price differential, when expressed as a percentage, is the 'repo rate' and represents the cost of the borrowing. The repo rate can be positive or negative. It will be negative if the repoed bonds pass a coupon date and the interim holder keeps the interest payment rather than paying a manufactured dividend. In this case, the original holder will reduce the resale price by a corresponding amount.

19.29   Where income arises on the repoed securities during the term of the repo, the interim holder will usually be required to make manufactured payments to the original holder. A transaction in which income arises on the repoed securities during the term of the repo where there is no manufactured payment obligation, and instead the interim holder retains the income in return for a corresponding reduction of the repurchase price, is often referred to as a buy/sell transaction.

19.30   Repos are of three kinds:

(a)   general collateral repo (non-specific stock);

(b)   special repo (specific stock); and

(c)   market value repo.

19.31   In a general collateral repo, the interim holder lends money to the original owner, and becomes interim holder of a bundle of bonds as security, undertaking to retransfer equivalent securities to the original owner at the end of the repo. The original owner pays interest at the 'repo rate', ie the interest rate implied by the difference between the sale price and the repurchase price. In a special repo the original owner undertakes to pay the market value of the specified securities at repayment date. In a market value repo, the original owner undertakes to pay the market value of the equivalent securities at repayment date.

19.32   In practice, the distinction between the different types of repo, and between repos and stock lending, may be eroded. The repo buyer will often also be able to use the securities to establish a short position or fulfil a delivery obligation during the term of the repo. The repo seller may also be given a right of substitution enabling it to retrieve the repoed securities and to replace them with alternative securities.

19.33   In some cases, the repurchase obligation may take the form of a sale and repurchase agreement, an option, a put option granted to the interim holder, or a cross option. In the case of the borrower, these arrangements are called 'debtor quasi-repos' in the legislation, as defined in *CTA 2009, s 549*.

Gilt repos

Example 19.4 – gilt repo

A seller/borrower raises finance by a sale of Treasury stock to a lender/buyer, the transaction being reversed after 60 days.

Amount	£1m
Security	Treasury 6% 2028

Term	60 days 5 April–4 June
Clean price	95
Repo rate	4.95%
Coupon dates	31 January, 31 July

All in/dirty price:

	£
Nominal £1m × 0.95	950,000
Accrued interest, 54 days	8,876
Consideration (loan)	958,876

Consideration is payable by interim holder on opening leg

Repurchase price	= consideration + price differential
Price differential	= consideration × repo rate × number of days
	= 958,876 × 4.95% × 60/365 = £7,802

Settling the closing leg:

	£
Original owner pays (958,876 + 7,802) =	966,678
Interim holder transfers stock worth	958,876

19.34   In the case of gilt repos, gilts are delivered and redelivered through electronic transfer (book entry transfer) between Central Gilts Office (CGO) accounts. Gilts can be delivered to 1p of nominal stock. A delivery-by-value (DBV) transaction allows stock to a given aggregate value (rather than specific securities) to be delivered to another CGO member on an overnight basis, usually to provide collateral. The second leg of a repo is typically settled at the repurchase price agreed at the outset, with any variation margin in the form of stock being retransferred on a free-of-value delivery basis.

19.35   Standard documentation in repo markets is the PSA/ISMA (Public Securities Association/International Securities Market Association) global master repurchase agreements and annexes.

Repos – accounting treatment

19.36   IFRS 9/IAS 39 applies derecognition principles to stock lending, repos and sale and repurchase agreements. FRS 102, paras 11.33–11.38 provides that the transfer of legal ownership is ignored for accounting purposes, so that the transferor retains the securities as assets in its balance sheet. In order to preserve economic ownership, the transactions provide for any dividend or interest arising during the currency of the temporary transfer to be passed on to the original owner. A market value repo, ie where the repurchaser undertakes to pay the market value of the equivalent securities at repurchase date, is regarded as a sale and the transfer is not derecognised. In the case of a bank, a repo is derecognised, ie the assets are kept on balance sheet, notwithstanding their absolute transfer.

19.37 The accounting treatment of repos reflects the economic substance of these transactions. A repo transaction is accounted for as a loan to the repo seller/borrower, and the securities sold to the repo buyer/lender remain on the balance sheet of the repo seller because the repo buyer has agreed to transfer them back to the repo seller at the end of the arrangements for a fixed price, so that the risks and rewards arising from changes in the value of the securities remain with the repo seller. In other words, the accounting treatment is much the same as for finance leasing.

19.38 The repo seller/borrower will continue to recognise the repoed securities on its balance sheet, on the basis that it retains the risks and rewards of price fluctuations in respect of those repoed securities. The proceeds of sale of the repoed securities will be recorded as a liability which will increase at a constant rate to reflect the effective rate of interest. The repo seller will continue to recognise the income arising from the repoed securities in its accounts as if the transaction had not taken place, and does not separately recognise any manufactured payment which the repo buyer makes to it in respect of the income.

19.39 The repo buyer/lender will not recognise the repoed securities on its balance sheet. The advance to the repo seller in the form of the purchase price will be recognised as a financial asset which will increase at a constant rate to reflect the effective rate of interest. Where the repo buyer receives the real income and makes a manufactured payment representative of that income, it will not recognise either receipt or payment in its profit and loss account or income statement.

Repos – the legislation

19.40 The applicable legislation is in:

- *TCGA 1992, ss 261F–261H, 263A;*
- *ITA 2007, ss 614ZA–614ZD;*
- *CTA 2009, ss 517, 539–559, 599A, 599B;* and
- *CTA 2010, ss 780–814D.*

19.41 These rules apply to sales of securities 'which equate, in substance, to a transaction for the lending of money at interest from or to a company, with the securities which were sold as collateral for the loan': *CTA 2009, s 542(1)*. The general aim is to tax repos in accordance with their accounting treatment, ie in substance a loan, so that the transfer of the securities does not give rise to corporation tax consequences. The primary condition to be satisfied before a transaction falls within these rules is that it is accounted for as a financial liability (borrower/repo seller) or financial asset (lender/repo buyer).

19.42   The following terminology is used in the legislation:

Term	Legislation	Subject of definition
Creditor repo	CTA 2009, s 543	Sale of securities for an advance and repurchase of securities which are derecognised under GAAP
Creditor quasi-repo	CTA 2009, s 544	A creditor repo in which the rights or obligations of the borrower may be performed by another person
Debtor repo	CTA 2009, s 548	A creditor repo from the borrower's point of view
Debtor quasi-repo	CTA 2009, s 549	A creditor quasi-repo from the debtor's point of view

19.43   Five conditions contained in *CTA 2009, s 543* (creditor repos) and *s 548* (debtor repos) have to be met for an arrangement to come within the statutory definitions:

- Condition A: under an arrangement, a company, referred to in these conditions as the borrower, received from another person any money or other asset (the 'advance').

- Condition B: in accordance with GAAP, the accounts of the borrower for the period in which the advance is received record a financial liability in respect of the advance, and the accounts of the lender record a financial asset.

- Condition C: under the arrangement, the borrower sells any securities at any time to the lender.

- Condition D: the arrangement makes provision conferring a right or imposing an obligation on the borrower to buy those or similar securities at any subsequent time.

- Condition E: in accordance with GAAP, the subsequent buying of those or similar securities would extinguish the financial liability in respect of the advance recorded in the accounts of the borrower.

19.44   Quasi-repos arise in the context of tri-partite and multi-party repos. For example:

- where the original repo seller/borrower's rights and obligations under a repo are novated to another company or where the original arrangement itself provides for a debtor substitution; or

- where the original repo buyer/lender's rights and obligations under a repo are novated to another company.

19.45   For tax purposes, the treatment of quasi-repos is normally the same as for actual repos. However, a transfer of shares by a company under a creditor quasi-repo is a disposal for the purposes of corporation tax and may give rise to a chargeable gain (or allowable loss).

Repos – tax treatment

19.46   For capital gains tax and loan relationship purposes, the accounting treatment is followed, so that the disposal or related transaction is also not regarded as taking place for tax purposes. The consequence of ignoring the sale, and following the accounting treatment which treats the seller/borrower as retaining the repoed securities on its balance sheet, is that manufactured payments are also ignored. The seller/borrower is treated as retaining the securities. The seller/borrower is simply taxable on the income on the repoed securities which is recognised in his accounts for accounting purposes, and obtains a debit for the finance cost. The buyer/lender is taxed on the finance return recorded in his accounts.

19.47   *TCGA 1992, s 263A* defines repos and states that the acquisition of the securities by the interim holder, and the disposal of those securities to the repurchaser, are to be disregarded for capital gains tax purposes. As far as the capital gains tax rules are concerned, if the intention to retransfer securities ceases to apply, the lender makes a disposal of the securities at that point (*TCGA 1992, s 263B(4)*). If the cash value of the securities is paid, the lender likewise makes a capital gains tax disposal (*s 263C*). *TCGA 1992, ss 263B* and *263C* apply equally to a chain of lenders and replacement loans, because each transaction will be a distinct stock lending arrangement.

19.48   The seller/borrower is treated as still holding the securities: *CTA 2009, ss 330A, 550*. The seller/borrower will accordingly be taxable on the interest in accordance with his accounts, even though the buyer/lender holds the securities and may receive the actual interest (though not recognised as such in his accounts). Under *CTA 2009, s 545*, the sale of securities, the receipt of real income or dividends by the buyer/lender, and the payment of manufactured interest by the buyer/lender are ignored. The finance return is taxable on the buyer/lender under *s 546*. The repo seller/borrower is treated, for corporation tax purposes, as if it did not receive manufactured payments in respect of the repoed securities. By the same token, the repo buyer/lender is treated for corporation tax purposes as if it does not make any manufactured payments in respect of the repoed securities, except to the extent that such payments are recognised in accordance with GAAP: *s 551*. These principles also apply to quasi-repos. Any finance charges which the seller/borrower records or finance income which the buyer/lender records in GAAP-compliant accounts enters into the calculation of loan relationship profits and losses.

19.49   In a buy/sell transaction, there are usually no manufactured payment obligations. The repurchase price will be reduced to reflect the absence of the manufactured payment obligations. The tax treatment of buy/sell transactions will usually be similar to the tax treatment of gross paying repo transactions.

19.50   There is an anti-avoidance rule in *CTA 2009, s 550* (ignoring the effect on the borrower of the sale of securities). This applies only to repos and states that, where a seller/borrower has a debtor repo or debtor quasi-repo or a liability under a 'relevant arrangement', and the main purpose or one of the main purposes of the arrangement is obtaining a tax advantage, the debtor is treated as retaining ownership of the securities which are the subject of the arrangement, unless under GAAP he is treated as receiving manufactured payments.

Manufactured payments

19.51   For both stock lending and repos, tax rules on the treatment of manufactured payments are contained in *ITA 2007, ss 572–611* and *CTA 2010, ss 780–814D*. The legislation recognises four types of manufactured payments:

(a)   manufactured interest (*CTA 2009, s 539*);

(b)   manufactured dividends (*CTA 2010, s 782*);

(c)   manufactured overseas dividends, which comprise both dividend and interest payments (*CTA 2010, s 790*); and

(d)   deemed manufactured payments (*CTA 2010, s 812*).

Manufactured interest

19.52   For loan relationship purposes, there is a deemed loan from the stock lender to the stock borrower. Manufactured interest is interest payable by the borrower and taxable on the lender: *CTA 2009, s 540*. The only credits and debits brought into account for tax purposes are those actually recognised for accounting purposes: *s 540(3)*. The borrower cannot bring in a debit for the manufactured interest which he pays, and is not taxable on the real interest which he receives. This will leave the borrower flat in tax terms. *Section 540* was enacted to counter the scheme used in *DCC Holdings (UK) Ltd v R & C Comrs* [2011] STC 326, which was ultimately held not to work.

19.53   If the stock loan or repo is capable of lasting for at least a year (so that the deemed interest is annual interest) and the payment has a UK source, the stock borrower or repo buyer/lender would be required to withhold on account of UK income tax under *ITA 2007, s 874*, subject to the normal exemptions which allow interest to be paid gross.

19.54   If the stock borrower or repo buyer/lender is UK resident or pays the manufactured interest in the course of a trade carried on in the UK through a permanent establishment, it is required to withhold tax at the savings rate from the gross amount of this deemed manufactured interest: *ITA 2007, s 919*. However, if the person making the manufactured payment of interest under *s 919* would not have been required to withhold tax, the stock lender or repo seller/borrower is not required to account for and pay any income tax under *s 920*. There is an exemption from the withholding obligation under *s 921* where the manufactured interest is paid in respect of gross-paying securities.

19.55   The stock lender or repo seller/borrower can claim the tax credit for UK tax withheld under the *Manufactured Interest (Tax) Regulations 2007, SI 2007/2488*, provided that the arrangements require the payment of manufactured interest.

Manufactured dividends

19.56   A company has a 'manufactured dividend relationship' if (*CTA 2010, s 814B*):

- Condition A: an amount is payable to the company or any other benefit is given by or to the company.

- Condition B: the arrangements relate to the transfer of shares in a company.

- Condition C: the amount of value of the other benefit is represented by a dividend on the shares or is representative of a dividend on the shares.

19.57   A company is unable to obtain a deduction for the payment of a manufactured dividend in calculating its income for corporation tax purposes, unless the company is carrying on a trade and the payment forms an expense of the trade or relates to the BLAGAB business of an insurance company: *CTA 2010, s 814C*.

19.58   Dividends received by borrowers during the term of the stock loan will generally be exempt under *CTA 2009, Part 9A*. Where the dividend receipt is taxable, manufactured dividends are deductible from the profits of the borrower if the manufactured dividend relates to a trade investment or life insurance business: *CTA 2010, s 783*. The stock borrower is not entitled to a tax credit: *CTA 2010, s 808*. If the dividends are not taxable on the lender, he will be treated as receiving dividends on actual shares: *CTA 2010, s 784*.

19.59   Where the stock loan or repoed securities are UK shares and the payer is a UK resident company, the manufactured dividend is treated for income tax purposes as an actual dividend of the paying company. There are special rules dealing with manufactured payments in respect of shares in a real estate investment trust (REIT): *ITA 2007, ss 576, 918*.

19.60   Where a person pays a manufactured dividend in connection with the transfer of shares or securities, the payer is similarly not entitled to a deduction for income tax purposes, other than under the rules for calculating the profits of a trade: *ITA 2007, s 614ZC*. In the hands of the recipient, the manufactured payment is treated as a real interest or dividend payment: *ITA 2007, s 614ZD*.

Manufactured overseas dividends

19.61   If tax free, these are simply passed through the books of the borrower on to the lender. If taxable, they are deductible in the borrower and taxable in the lender, if the manufactured dividend relates to a trade or investment of life insurance business of the borrower: *CTA 2010, s 791*. Any foreign tax credit is attributable to the lender: *ITA 2007, s 590*; *CTA 2010, ss 792–795*. If the manufactured dividend plus tax credit is less than the gross amount of the overseas dividend, the recipient of the overseas dividend is required to account for tax on the gross amount of the dividend: *CTA 2010, s 798*. If a person who pays a manufactured overseas dividend is UK resident or makes the payments in the course of a trade carried on in the UK through a permanent establishment, the payer must deduct and account for income tax at the savings rate: *ITA 2007, s 922*.

19.62   A 'reverse charge' requirement applies to manufactured interest under *ITA 2007, s 920* and to manufactured overseas dividends under *s 923* where the stock borrower or repo buyer/lender is non-resident and pays the manufactured payments otherwise than in the course of a trade carried on through a permanent establishment in the UK. Where either tax is withheld by a UK resident dividend manufacturer under *ITA 2007, s 922* or accounted for and paid by the recipient under the 'reverse charge' rules in *ITA 2007, ss 920, 923*, the stock lender or repo seller/borrower is treated as receiving an actual overseas dividend equal to the gross amount of the manufactured overseas dividend paid after the withholding tax. The amount deducted or accounted for and paid is treated as an amount withheld on account of overseas tax instead of an amount on account of income tax. The stock lender or repo seller/borrower will be able to claim a credit in respect of any such relevant withholding tax accounted for and paid.

Deemed manufactured payments

19.63   If there is a stock lending arrangement which makes no provision for manufactured payments, and a person other than the lender receives a manufactured payment, the stock borrower is treated as required to make manufactured payments, and discharges that obligation on receipt of the real dividends or interest: *CTA 2010, s 812*.

Anti-avoidance rules

19.64   There are anti-avoidance rules in *CTA 2010, ss 799–801*, which apply where the arrangement has an 'unallowable purpose'. An unallowable purpose is a purpose which is not among the business or other commercial purposes of a company: *s 800(2)*. A tax avoidance purpose is not an unallowable purpose if it is not amongst the main purpose or one of the main purposes of the company: *s 800(7)*. Where the arrangements have an unallowable purpose, the stock borrower is denied a tax deduction for manufactured payments.

Stamp duty

19.65   Stock lending and repos benefit from exemption from stamp duty and SDRT under *FA 1986, ss 79, 80C, 82* and *89AA*.

Euroconversion

19.66   *The European Single Currency (Tax) Regulations 1998, SI 1998/3177* deal with the consequences of the adoption of the euro (euroconversion) while a stock lending or repo is outstanding. Because, under stock lending and repos, economic ownership stays with the original owner, the consequences of euroconversion fall on him. For repos, the International Securities Market Association (ISMA) also introduced an EMU Annex in June 1998. This provides that the redenomination of a security is not regarded as making that security into a different security from that which formed the subject-matter of the agreement. *Regulations 14* and *19* provide that, where securities are the subject of euroconversion, the new euro securities will be regarded as 'similar' securities to the securities in their former denomination. If the interim holder receives a capital payment in respect of which he is not required to make a payment representing it to the original owner, that payment will be disregarded if it does not exceed €500. If it exceeds this amount, the interim holder is regarded as receiving a capital distribution arising from a part disposal of the securities: *reg 15*. If the payment is passed on to the original holder, it will normally increase the price differential on repurchase (*reg 16*) or, failing that, be treated as a capital distribution: *reg 18*.

19.67 Where, because of renominalisation, the interim holder cannot return to the original holder exactly the equivalent amount of securities (ie the aggregate nominal value of the securities to be sold back is not – as a result of renominalisation – a whole multiple of the new minimum denomination), the interim holder sells back as many units as he can, and makes a compensation payment to the original holder for the difference. That payment will be ignored if it does not exceed €500, and the arrangement does not require it to be paid. Otherwise, it goes to increase the repurchase price: *reg 17*. The rules for stock lending arrangements which become subject to euroconversion replicate those for repos: *regs 21–23*.

19.68 As regards the worldwide debt cap (**Chapter 21**), when determining whether the gateway test is passed, a repo which lasts for longer than a year qualifies as a 'relevant asset' or 'relevant liability'.

Chapter 20

International Aspects

Overview

20.1   This chapter deals with:

- Non-resident companies

- Double taxation agreements

- Interaction of double tax relief and loan relationships rules

- Arbitrage rules

- Attribution of profits to permanent establishments

- EU Mergers Directive

BEPS

20.2   The effective taxation of multi-national enterprises (MNEs) requires a significant degree of integration into the international tax system. The Base Erosion Profit-Shifting (BEPS) initiative of the OECD, with the support of the EU and G20, seeks to achieve a deeper integration at worldwide level to cope with the reality of the global market.

20.3   Developing and developed states alike face similar problems in achieving an acceptable ratio of tax to GDP, attracting foreign direct investment, keeping existing investment, administering and collecting taxes, creating comprehensive national tax systems and integrating that national system into an international one, to the extent that it exists.

20.4   This means that in tax terms states have a relationship of competition as well as co-operation. The economic necessity to raise taxes conflicts with the economic necessity to attract and retain businesses to pay taxes, create employment and provide investment. Within a state, tax collection may kill enterprise and internationally it is a considerable challenge to strike a balance between shared interests and competing interests. Ultimately it is a question of how national interest is defined. The dispute between the Irish government and the European Commission about whether illegitimate state aids have been granted to the Apple Group illustrates the real dilemmas which exist. National benefits are concrete and measureable. Benefits to the international community are abstract and remote. Clarity is not aided by repeating slogans about tax avoidance and fair taxation, which are largely self-righteous humbug.

20.5   The OECD has sought to stimulate and organise an internationally co-ordinated approach. On 12 February 2013 it published its report on 'Addressing Base Erosion and Profit Shifting (BEPS)'. The Final Report was published on 5 October 2015. This contains 15 Action Points (one more than Woodrow Wilson's Fourteen Points).

20.6   The UK has responded quickly by:

(a)   proposing general restrictions on tax allowable debt interest deductions by reference to Fixed ratio rule or Group ratio rule from 2017 onwards (see **9.95–9.98**), implementing Action 4; and

(b)   introducing extensive provisions in *TIOPA 2010, ss 259A–259NE* which apply to counteract tax advantages arising from hybrid mismatches (Action 2), implementing the Final Report on 'Neutralising the Effects of Hybrid Mismatch Arrangements' of 5 October 2015. The hybrid mismatch rules are regarded as the key output from the BEPS project [**20.58–20.70**].

However, if post-Brexit the UK government needs to turn the UK into a tax haven, different priorities would apply.

Non-resident companies

20.7   Resident and non-resident companies alike have loan relationships and, for the purposes of establishing whether companies are connected, resident and non-resident companies are treated identically. Accordingly, if a non-resident parent lends money to its UK subsidiary, and the debt is released, there is no charge to corporation tax on the UK subsidiary. By the same token, if a UK parent writes off a debt owed by a non-resident subsidiary, the UK company obtains no impairment relief.

20.8   Non-resident companies are only chargeable to corporation tax in respect of loan relationships if they carry on a trade in the UK through a permanent establishment (PE): *CTA 2009, s 5(2)*. In that case, loan relationships of the non-resident company are attributed to the UK PE if it is held or used for the purposes of the PE: *CTA 2009, s 334(1)*.

20.9   If the loan relationship ceases to be held for the purposes of the PE other than as a result of a related transaction (ie a disposal), a charge to tax arises as if the loan relationship had been disposed of for market value and immediately reacquired: *s 334(2)*.

20.10 There is no charge under this provision if the group continuity rules allow a transfer on a no gain, no loss basis: *ss 334(3), 344*.

There is no deemed disposal if the non-resident company goes into liquidation.

20.11 If a company ceases to be UK resident, it is deemed to dispose of all its loan relationships for fair value under *CTA 2009, s 333*. This does not apply if there is an intra-group transfer of such assets and liabilities: *s 340*. The rule in *s 333* also applies if loan relationship ceases to be held for the purposes of a UK PE.

Double taxation agreements

20.12 There are two methods of conferring relief from double taxation of cross-border payments:

- the exemption method; and
- the credit method.

These two methods are provided for in alternative versions of *art 23* of the *OECD Model Tax Convention on Income and Capital*.

20.13 Under rules of international taxation, a payment may be taxed:

(a) primarily in the country of source; and

(b) secondarily in the country of residence of the payee.

It is thus for the country of residence to relieve double taxation, either by exemption or by credit.

20.14 Under the exemption method, the country of residence exempts the foreign income in question from taxation (*OECD Model Convention, art 23A*). There is no requirement that the state of source should actually impose any tax for the exemption to apply. Thus, where the exemption method is used, cross-border payments will be either:

(a) subject to tax only in the state of source; or

(b) free of tax.

20.15 The source state has the exclusive right to tax. The exemption method applies in eg France and Germany. Domestic tax can be repaid to foreign residents, but subject to withholding tax of 5% (strategic investor) or 15% (portfolio investor).

20.16 Under the credit method, if tax is imposed in the state of source, the state of residence of the recipient gives credit for the source state tax against tax imposed by the state of residence of the recipient (*OECD Model Convention, art 23B*). Both the source state and the residence state can tax the income.

20.17 Where loan relationship credits are subject to foreign tax, and double taxation relief is available either under a double taxation agreement (DTA) or in the form of unilateral relief, the foreign tax credits may be set against UK tax on the same income: *TIOPA 2010, s 18(2)*. Two principles operate:

(a) foreign income and gains are kept separate from UK income and gains, where this is necessary to preserve for tax credits (*TIOPA 2010, s 50*); and

(b) double tax relief on foreign income and gains is limited to the amount of UK corporation tax payable on those profits (*TIOPA 2010, s 42*).

20.18 *TIOPA 2010, s 42* limits foreign tax credits to the amount of the corporation tax chargeable on the foreign income or gains, the foreign income or gains being reduced by general deductions and deficits or debits on loan relationships, which are separately dealt with under *ss 52–56*.

20.19 Where a company has no foreign source loan relationship credits in respect of which relief for foreign tax is available, non-trading deficits on loan relationships will be set against non-trading credits and other income and gains as set out in the claim: *TIOPA 2010, s 42*. In other words, UK-source income and foreign source income will be blended. Where a company has non-trading loan relationship credits which carry foreign tax credits, *s 50(2)* requires the non-trading credits to be reanalysed into UK-source and non-UK source income. This enables losses to be set against the UK source income alone, thereby preserving the integrity of foreign tax credits in relation to the non-UK source income. The aim of the provisions is to preserve the gross character of foreign interest, in order to allow full utilisation of foreign tax credits; and to enable non-trading deficits on loan relationships to be set against profits as if they were charges.

20.20 Under *TIOPA 2010, s 52*, general deductions may be allocated in the way that is most beneficial to the company. A company can allocate general deductions between domestic and overseas profits in such manner as it chooses. If charges are offset against UK profits in priority to foreign income and gains, a higher amount of foreign profits is left to absorb double tax credits.

Example 20.1

A plc pays corporation tax at 19%, pays royalties of £15,000, has UK trading profits of £100,000, and has foreign income of £30,000 taxed at 25%.

1   Allocate charges to foreign profits:

	UK	*Foreign*	*Total*
	£	£	£
Profits	100,000	30,000	130,000
Royalties	–	(15,000)	(15,000)
	100,000	15,000	115,000
UK tax	19,000	2,850	21,850
Double tax relief	–	(2,850)*	(2,850)
Tax payable	24,000	–	19, 000

* Foreign tax of £7,500 restricted to UK tax payable on foreign income.

2   As above, but allocate charges to UK profits:

Profits	100,000	30,000	130,000
Royalties	(15,000)	–	(15,000)
	85,000	30,000	115,000
UK tax	16,150	5,700	21,850
Double tax relief	–	(5,700)	(5,700)
Tax payable	20,400	0	16,150

20.21   Under *TIOPA 2010, s 54*, if a company has non-trading loan relationship credits which carry a foreign tax credit, non-trading deficits on loan relationships may be allocated in the way that is most beneficial, the claim being limited to:

Total non-trading deficit – (carry back claim + carry forward claim + group relief claim).

Example 20.2

X plc has both UK interest of 1,000, taxed foreign interest of 500 and a current year loan relationship deficit of 700. Hence, *TIOPA 2010, s 54(1)* applies. Its loan relationship credits are reanalysed as follows:

UK interest	1,000	
Non-UK interest	500	[foreign tax credit – 125]

X plc is taxed as follows:

	UK interest	Non-UK interest
	1,000	500
Sideways relief – current year	(700)	
Profit	300	500
UK tax @19%	57	95
DTC		(95)
	57	0

Example 20.3

X plc has both UK and taxed foreign interest. Group company Y plc has profits of 500. X plc's profits and losses are as follows:

UK interest	1,000	
Loan relationship debit	(3,000)	
Profits of property business	1,000	
Non-UK interest	500	[foreign tax credit – 125]

X plc is taxed as follows:

	UK interest	Property business	Non-UK interest	Group relief	Carry forward
	1,000	1,000	500	500	
Allocate non-trading LR deficit	(1,000)	(1,000)	(38)	(500)	462
Profits	0	0	462*	0	
UK tax @ 19%	0	0	88	0	
Double tax credit			(88)		

*Gross up net of tax foreign profits by UK rate to find maximum amount of foreign tax credit available.

20.22   Where a foreign tax payment is made in connection with a loan asset which is in a hedging relationship with a derivative contract, only the net amount of income is brought into charge for UK tax: *TIOPA 2010, s 46*. A tax deduction can be obtained for the financial expenditure incurred in earning the foreign interest or dividends, in particular for loan relationships debits, ie the costs of borrowing funds in order to on-lend them: *s 44(3)*.

20.23   Where a UK company sells to another UK company the benefit of a debt with accrued interest, which is later paid with foreign tax deducted from the interest, foreign tax which, on a 'just and reasonable apportionment', is not attributable to the taxpayer's period of ownership is excluded. The benefit of the foreign tax credit is given to the transferor of the loan, on the grounds that he will have had to bring in the accrued interest as a loan relationship receipt: *TIOPA 2010, ss 107, 108*. This does not apply where foreign securities are transferred under repo or stock lending arrangements. The transferor (stock lender) will continue to account for the interest or dividends which it may not receive during the term of the arrangement, and may claim relief for the proportion of foreign tax attributable to the amount of interest on which it is taxed: *ss 109, 110*. The use of any foreign tax credits thus remains throughout with the party who both originally and ultimately owns the securities.

20.24   Double tax relief on debt securities is restricted to the amount of double tax relief which accrues in the period of ownership, ie if a security is owned for 30 days, 30/365 of the double tax relief available in that year in respect of foreign tax on the income of that security can be claimed.

20.25   The foreign resident has to make a treaty claim. Tax can be deducted at the treaty rate (or the payments made gross) only after HMRC have approved an application by the lender to this effect under *Double Tax Relief (Taxes on Income) (General) Regulations 1970, SI 1970/488, reg 2*. However, there is a provisional authorisation scheme: see *Tax Bulletin Issue 12, August 1994, 153–154*; *Issue 41, June 1999, 668–670*. If a non-resident company which is treaty protected is involved as the lender, the parties may still wish to structure the return as a discount, in order to save the need for HMRC authorisation.

Example 20.4

A US company obtained authority for a UK company to make royalty payments gross, under *art 12(2)* of the UK-USA DTA. The contractual arrangements were modified. HMRC claim that the authorisation had lapsed. However, it is the commercial substance of the arrangement that matters.

20.26   Where the amount of an obligation is reduced in the year by an impairment provision, it will be treated as a debt whose amount varies in an accrual period. If the provision is made at year end, but the deterioration in creditworthiness is regarded as taking place throughout the year, the average rate should be used.

20.27 If loan relationship losses are set against profits which have suffered foreign taxation, this will lead to displacement of foreign tax credits. The ability to make partial claims allows companies to maximise use of double tax relief, by restricting the amount of the deficit to be set against profits which carry foreign tax credits. A company can allocate non-trading deficits against particular categories of income to ensure that double taxation relief is not wasted.

20.28 In the case of a foreign trade, an interest debit will reduce foreign source profit and so restrict the availability of double tax relief. The result is that foreign withholding tax (ie foreign tax on overseas income) may be expensed. This is only an issue if non-trading losses exceed taxable income.

20.29 The identification of costs relating to the receipt rule reduces the amount of foreign income available for tax credit. Other overseas income, such as royalties, is not subject to this restriction. However, in reliance on *GCA International v Yates* [1991] STC 157, HMRC will seek to limit foreign tax credit to the net return in other areas. Venezuelan withholding tax was imposed on contractual payments due to GCA. Unilateral relief was claimed against UK corporation tax. It was held that only a proportion of the payments related to 'income arising in' Venezuela, and accordingly only a corresponding proportion of the foreign tax was creditable.

20.30 Where a double taxation agreement is in force, the interest article (*OECD Model Convention, art 11*) will generally limit foreign withholding tax on interest to 10% and often there will be no withholding. If no withholding is involved, the bank is not required to identify the interest separately in its corporation tax computations.

Interaction of foreign tax credits and loan relationships rules

20.31 The examples below show how the loan relationship rules allow for the availability of double tax relief to be maximised.

Example 20.5

X plc, an investment company, has the following results:

	FX gains (losses)	UK interest	Property income	Taxed foreign income (25%)	Other group companies
	£	£	£	£	£
Year 1	(10,000)	2,000	1,000	3,000	2,000
Year 2	(5,000)	2,000	500	4,000	1,500
Year 3	4,000	1,500	(1,500)	3,500	(2,500)

Under the loan relationship rules, there is one pot of non-trading debits (NTD). This has to be calculated first:

	Year 1	Year 2	Year 3
	£	£	£
FX (loss)/gain	(10,000)	(5,000)	4,000
Interest	2,000	2,000	1,500
Non-trading LR credit (deficit)	(8,000)	(3,000)	5,500
Relieved as follows:			
Loss b/f	–	–	(1,500)
Property income	1,000	500	(1,500)
Group relief surrender	2,000	1,500	(2,500)
Loss c/f	(5,000)	(1,000)	–
Foreign income	3,000	4,000	3,500
Available tax credits	750	1,000	875

Example 20.6

	UK trading	Taxed foreign income (20%)	Non-trading deficit
	£	£	£
	1,000,000	600,000	(1,400,000)
Relief	(1,000,000)	(120,000)	(1,200,000)
		480,000	
Tax payable @ 19%		91,200	
Foreign tax credit (600,000 @ 20%)		(91,200)	
Non-trading deficit c/fwd		200.000	

Note:

1   Foreign tax credits are grossed up at the applicable rate of corporation tax to calculate the amount of the non-trading deficit to be set against foreign income.

2   The balance of £300,000 of the deficit is available for surrender as group relief or for carry-back, or will be carried forward as a carried-forward deficit.

Example 20.7

B Ltd (an investment company) has a UK-located US$10m deposit. Foreign tax at 25% is paid on foreign income. FX gains and losses, and other income, are:

Year	£:$	FX difference	Interest	Foreign income	Property income	Other group companies
		£	£	£	£	£
0	1.5	–	–	–	–	–
1	1.6	(189,393)	500,000	50,000	50,000	100,000
2	1.5	416,667	400,000	70,000	40,000	(200,000)
3	1.7	(784,314)	700,000	40,000	70,000	150,000

First, calculate the non-trading credit/deficit:

	Year 1	Year 2	Year 3
	£	£	£
Non-trading credits	500,000	816,667	700,000
Non-trading debits	(189,393)	–	(784,314)
	310,607	816,667	(84,314)

In Year 2, losses of £200,000 can be surrendered to B by other group companies.

In Year 3, the non-trading deficit can be utilised as follows:

	£
Property income	70,000
Sideways relief	(70,000)
Carry back to non-trading profit of previous accounting period	(4,314)

By making a carry-back claim, foreign tax can be offset against UK corporation tax.

Example 20.8

When £1 = $1.60, B plc lends US$50m by way of debenture to G Inc, its US subsidiary, at 7% fixed payable annually in arrears.

Exchange rates and market value of the debenture are as follows:

	Year 1	Year 2	Year 3
Exchange rate (year end)	1.65	1.70	1.60
Exchange rate (average)	1.62	1.65	1.62
Market value ($)	45	40	50

Average rates must be used for interest to reflect accruals. Interest and exchange gains and losses are aggregated.

Year	Interest	FX differences	Income
	£	£	£
1	2,160,493	(946,969)	1,213,524
2	2,121,212	(891,265)	1,229,947
3	2,160,493	1,838,235	3,998,728

On 1 July 2017 a company agrees to buy 100,000 roubles 12 months forward for £100. On 31 December 2017, its accounting date, 800 roubles = £1.

T_2 (31.12.17)

First currency amount (receive)	125	
Second currency amount (pay)	100	
		25

T_1 (01.7.17)

First currency amount (receive)	100	
Second currency amount (pay)	100	
		0
Exchange difference		25

Arbitrage rules

20.32   There are overlapping sets of rules in *CTA 2009* and *TIOPA 2010* which all seek to disallow finance deductions or tax dividend receipts as interest. More than one set of these rules may apply to the same situation.

20.33   'Deduction scheme cases' are dealt with in *TIOPA 2010, ss 231–259*. The rules apply to cases where a 'deduction scheme' generates a tax deduction in the UK, if certain conditions are fulfilled.

20.34 'Scheme' means any type of arrangement or understanding, including cases where it would have been reasonable to assume that one or more of the transactions would not have been entered into independently of the other: *s 258*.

20.35 These are concerned with cases in which a UK company seeks to gain a UK tax advantage (as defined in *s 234*) because a transaction or instrument enjoys a different legal classification in a foreign jurisdiction and in the UK respectively. The rules are expected and intended to apply in cross-border contexts. However, they can apply in exclusively UK contexts and HMRC sought to rely on them as an alternative base of charge in *Stagecoach Group plc v R & C Comrs* [2016] UKFTT 120 (TC): see **17.45–17.51**.

20.36 The rules apply to six types of 'deduction scheme' which generate a tax deduction in the UK, where one of the main purposes of the scheme is to achieve a UK tax advantage (defined in *s 234*) of more than a minimal amount.

- The first type involves hybrid entities, ie an institution that is transparent in one jurisdiction but has entity status in another: *TIOPA 2010, s 236*.

- The second type looks at instruments which have hybrid effects so that they may alter their tax characteristics, eg convertibles: *s 237*.

- The third type looks to the issue of convertible shares, where there is a reasonable expectation at issue that the shares will be converted into securities: *s 238*.

- The fourth type applies to the issue of convertible securities, where there is a reasonable expectation at issue that the securities will be converted into shares: *s 239*.

- The fifth type is where a company issues debt instruments which may be treated as equity under GAAP: *s 240*.

- The sixth type is concerned with the issue of shares (other than ordinary shares) to a connected person or a transfer of rights under a security to a connected person.

20.37 'Connection' is defined in terms of *CTA 2010, ss 1122–1124* (ie the 'control' definition): *TIOPA 2010, ss 241, 242, 259(2)*. 'Equity holder' is defined in accordance with *CTA 2010, s 158*.

Example 20.9

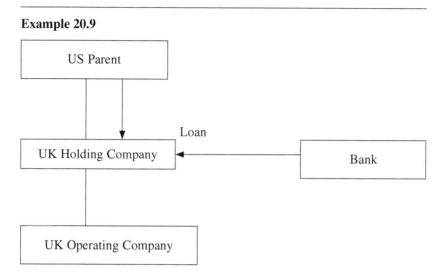

US Parent 'checks the box' so that UK Holding Company is disregarded, but US Parent obtains a US tax deduction for the interest payable to Bank. UK Holding Company claims a deduction for the interest payable to US Parent and Bank, surrendering any loss by group relief. If HMRC so direct by issuing a 'deduction notice' under *TIOPA 2010, s 232*, the company has to recalculate its tax liability, and a deduction for interest under either loan may be denied under *ss 243–245*.

20.38   Where the scheme conditions apply, HMRC may issue a 'deductions notice'. The effect of the deduction notice is to deny a deduction in computing profits for corporation tax purposes where:

(a)   there would otherwise be a double deduction in respect of amounts paid under the scheme, because the amount in question would be otherwise allowable or deductible (*s 244*); or

(b)   where a payment qualifies for a tax deduction but the payee is not taxable on the receipt, ie rule against deduction for 'untaxable amounts' (*s 255*).

20.39   *TIOPA 2010, ss 249–254* deal with 'receipts cases' (deferred subscription), whereby a UK company receives a 'qualifying payment', ie a payment which constitutes a contribution to the capital of the company, the standard example being unpaid subscription monies for shares. Where the section applies, the UK company is treated as receiving disguised interest within *CTA 2010, s 486A*, ie as a profit on an RNLR. An HMRC direction under *s 249* is necessary for these provisions to apply.

20.40 Where there are reasonable grounds for considering that *TIOPA 2010, s 250* applies, HMRC may issue a 'receipts notice' under *s 249*, which charges the receipt in question to corporation tax as additional income.

Attribution of profits to permanent establishments

20.41 For tax purposes, a permanent establishment (PE) is treated as a 'distinct and separate enterprise'. The fundamental hypothesis set out in *OECD Model Convention, art 7(2)*:

> 'where an enterprise of a Contracting State carries on business in the other Contracting State through a permanent establishment situated therein, there shall be attributed to that permanent establishment the profits which it might be expected to make if it were a distinct and separate enterprise engaged in the same or similar activities under the same or similar conditions and dealing wholly independently with the enterprise of which it is a permanent establishment.'

20.42 The purpose of this hypothesis is not to achieve equality of outcome between a branch and a subsidiary in terms of profit. It is recognised that the choice of business medium has real economic effects.

20.43 The rule that home state taxation is limited to the profits attributable to the PE is essentially a restriction on source state taxation. This derives from *art 7(2)* of the *OECD Model Convention*. The alternative view is that the global profits of the enterprise are considered, and a fraction of these is attributed to the PE. This is based on *art 7(1)*. The difference between the two approaches turns on internal dealings between different parts of the business as a source of profits for tax purposes, though no profit is realised at enterprise level, eg closing stock of a branch may be treated as sold to head office at year end. On the 'limited independence' view of the PE, internal interest will not be recognised except in the case of banks.

20.44 If a permanent enterprise is treated as a legally separate company, the OECD Transfer Pricing Guidelines can be applied by analogy in computing the attributable profits of a PE.

20.45 International banks normally operate through branches (PEs) in order to use capital efficiently. Otherwise, each branch would have to be separately capitalised, with capital divided into separate pots and assigned to each individual operation. Hence, for tax purposes, a PE may hold branch assets, borrow funds and pay interest. If a branch 'borrows' funds from parts of the bank in other jurisdictions, and pays interest, it may eliminate its taxable profits in the jurisdiction in which it carries on business. To safeguard its tax base, host states require a PE to be allocated a certain amount of 'free capital' (imputed equity), sufficient to enable it to carry on its banking business, and interest costs attributable to that free capital are non-deductible in computing branch profits.

20.46 In March 2003 the OECD released two papers dealing with the attribution of profits to PEs of (a) banks carrying on traditional banking business in one jurisdiction, and (b) PEs engaged in global trading in financial instruments. As regards PEs carrying on traditional banking business, the activities carried on in a banking enterprise are to be identified by the 'people functions'. Assets and risks are to be attributed to a PE where those functions are carried out, not where loans are booked. In order to satisfy the 'same or similar conditions' hypothesis, the branch is given the same credit rating as the bank of which it is a part. The global trading paper follows the 1998 OECD Paper 'The Taxation of Global Trading of Financial Instruments'. This identified three trading and risk management models: integrated trading; centralised product management; and separate enterprise.

20.47 Under *CTA 2009, s 5*, a company not resident in the UK is not liable to corporation tax unless it carries on a trade in the UK through a PE, as defined in *CTA 2010, s 1119*. Under *CTA 2009, s 5(1)* and *TCGA 1992, s 10B*, corporation tax is imposed on 'all profits, wherever arising, that are attributable to its permanent establishment in the United Kingdom', and chargeable gains arising from the disposal of assets situated in the UK and used for the purposes of the trade of the PE. The UK PE is required to keep separate accounts for its UK activities based upon generally accepted accounting practice.

20.48 Attribution and quantification of profits is dealt with by *CTA 2009, ss 20–33*. Where there is a double taxation agreement in force with a business profits article, that will apply in priority to these provisions. In practice, this will not make a great difference, because these provisions seek to incorporate OECD principles into UK law. *Section 21* embodies the 'separate enterprise principle'. *Section 21(2)* is specifically directed at branches of foreign banks operating in the UK, and says that (a) the branch is regarded as having the same credit rating as the bank of which it is a part, and (b) the separate enterprise principle will be applied on the basis of this assumption. However, no provision is made for payment of notional guarantee fees to the notional parent.

20.49 HMRC have published Guidance Notes ('Guidance on Capital Attribution to Banks') which envisage five stages in the 'capital attribution tax adjustment'. The fundamental question is: what regulatory capital would a branch have if it were a separate enterprise?

1   *Step One*. Construct the branch balance sheet. The Notes envisage that the level of branch capital will, in general, be 9–15% of risk-weighted

assets, ie in excess of Basel Committee requirements. The assets which 'belong' to a branch have to be identified, using the 'booking' rather than the 'people functions' principle. The fundamental issue is therefore where a financial asset 'belongs' for tax purposes. Conflict of laws rules provide a number of approaches to this question.

2   *Step Two.* The assets which 'belong' to the branch then have to be 'risk-weighted' using FSA regulatory principles, which will in turn be based on Basel principles, to give the 'risk-weighted assets' (RWA). However, the starting point may be home state regulatory rules. Netting of assets and liabilities within the entity will be allowed, where this is consistent with regulatory principles.

3   *Step Three.* Calculation of the amount of equity capital. It is recognised that there is a tension between the separate enterprise principle (no link with head office) and the 'same activities under the same conditions' principle (which presupposes a connection with head office).

4   *Step Four.* Calculation of the amount of loan capital, whether Tier 1, Tier 2 or Tier 3. It is also necessary to assume what would be the market rate of interest to raise this capital.

5   *Step Five.* Calculation of the 'capital attribution tax adjustment'. The disallowance of interest and related costs, and foreign exchange losses, will increase the taxable UK branch profit. Hence the actual interest expense, less any additional interest which would have been payable on non-connected party debt, will be reduced by the capital attribution tax adjustment, ie the interest attributable to the imputed equity.

20.50   Various examples are given in the Guidance Notes. A simplified example may be given as follows. UK branches of foreign banks will characteristically be financed by deposits from other parts of the bank, which are credited with interest for the deposit. The UK branch then on-lends these funds. Hence, if a branch has taken in deposits of 1,000 for one year from head office, for which it is notionally charged interest at 7%, and it on-lends these funds at 10%, the branch accounts will show:

Interest received	100
Interest paid	70
Gross profit	30

Step One

The branch balance sheet is:

Assets	1,000
Capital	1,000

Step Two

Risk weight assets. If risk-weighting is 100%, RWA = 1,000.

Step Three

Assume Tier 1 equity capital of 8% of RWA = 80. Disallowable interest expense is $80/1000 \times 70 = 5.6$.

Step Four

Assume Tier 2 loan capital of 4% of RWA = 40, paying interest at 5%. Disallowable interest expense is $(7\% - 5\%) \times 40/1000 \times 70 = 0.06$.

Step Five

Capital attribution tax adjustment is $(5.6 + 0.06) = 5.66$.

Gross branch profit:	Interest received:	100.00
	Interest paid (70 – 5.66)	(64.34)
	Gross profit	35.66

Interest ($2m)	1.33
Provision ($4m)	(2.67)
Net loss	(1.34)
Para 9(2) credit ($4m × 80%)	2.14
Exchange loss	(0.45)
	0.35
Year to 31 March 2017	
Interest ($2m)	1.29
Provision ($4m)	(2.58)
Exchange loss	(0.59)
	(1.88)
Loss on sale: 5.00 – (10.67 – 2.58)	(3.09)
Net loss	(4.97)

EU Mergers Directive

20.51 The EU Mergers Directive (2009/133/EC) requires Member States to enact legislation which provides for tax neutral treatment of cross-border mergers, divisions, partial divisions, transfers of assets and share exchanges. All these transactions are defined in *art 2*. The Directive applies where:

(a)   there is a merger, division, partial division, transfer of asset or share exchange involving a company resident in the UK and a company resident in another Member State;

(b)   there is a transfer by a UK resident company of a permanent establishment located in another Member State to a company resident in another Member State;

(c)   the transferee is, immediately after the transfer, within the charge to corporation tax;

(d)   the transaction is wholly for shares or debentures issued by the transferee to the transferor; and

(e)   the transaction is undertaken for genuine commercial reasons and the main purpose or one of the main purposes of the transaction is not avoidance of liability to UK tax.

20.52   The loan relationship and derivatives contracts legislation contains parallel sets of provisions designed to ensure compliance with the Directive. *TIOPA 2010* in turn has a set of rules in the same form governing double taxation relief.

20.53   Where the Directive applies, then in the case of loan relationships (*CTA 2009, ss 421–430*):

(a)   on a transfer of assets, loan relationships are transferred at their notional carrying value, ie what would have been the carrying value if the transferor had ceased to be party to the loan relationship immediately before the transfer: *s 422*;

(b)   on a transfer of assets, loan relationships are transferred at their fair value if fair value accounting is used: *s 423*;

(c)   on a reorganisation within *TCGA 1992, ss 127–130* or *s 116*, the reorganisation is treated as giving rise to a disposal of the loan relationship for an amount equal to its notional carrying value or fair value: *CTA 2009, ss 424, 425*;

(d)   where there is a merger, being–

•   a European Company (Societas Europaea, SE) formed by the merger of two or more companies;

•   a European Co-operative Society (SCE) formed by the merger of two or more co-operative societies; or

- the transfer by two or more companies resident in different Member States of all their existing assets and liabilities to a single existing company resident in a Member State,

the merger is treated as giving rise to a disposal of the loan relationship for an amount equal to its notional carrying value or fair value (*ss 424–436*).

20.54 Where the Directive applies, then in the case of derivative contracts:

(a) where the transferor accounts for derivative contracts other than on a fair value basis, derivatives are to be transferred at their notional carrying value, ie the value it would have had in the accounts of the transferor if its accounting period had ended immediately before the transfer: *CTA 2009, s 675*;

(b) where (as will be normal) the transferor accounts for derivative contracts on a fair value basis, and the transferor is not a transparent entity, the derivative contract will be transferred at a fair value basis: *s 676*;

(c) where there is a merger comprising:

- a European Company (Societas Europaea, SE) formed by the merger of two or more companies;

- a European Co-operative Society (SCE) formed by the merger of two or more co-operative societies; or

- the transfer by two or more companies resident in different Member States of all their existing assets and liabilities to a single existing company resident in a Member State,

derivative contracts are transferred at their notional carrying value or fair value (*ss 682, 684, 685*).

20.55 These rules do not apply if the transferor or transferee is a 'transparent entity', ie a company without ordinary share capital: *CTA 2009, ss 429, 687*.

20.56 Where, on a transaction falling within these provisions, tax would have been chargeable in another Member State apart from the Mergers Directive ('tax notionally chargeable'), double taxation relief remains available as if the tax notionally chargeable had been actually chargeable: *TIOPA 2010, ss 118–125*.

20.57 A clearance procedure is available: *CTA 2009, ss 427, 428, 679; TIOPA 2010, s 118(4)*.

Hybrid mismatches

20.58 *FA 2016* introduced measures effective from 1 January 2017 designed to counter 'hybrid mismatch' arrangements. These are arrangements which give rise to a deduction for one party without a corresponding charge in the other party or that give rise to double deductions for both parties. Where these rules apply, the deduction will be automatically disallowed, ie without reference to motive. These rules were inserted into *TIOPA 2010* as 14 Chapters – *ss 259A–259NE* – as the key measure implementing BEPS Action 2. The Final Report of the OECD on 'Neutralising the Effects of Hybrid Mismatch Arrangements' is referred to in *TIOPA 2010, s 259BA(2)*. The rules are of particular application to regulatory capital instruments, falling within the *Taxation of Regulatory Capital Securities Regulations 2013, SI 2013/3209*. The rules take effect subject to related UK legislation such as the arbitrage rules.

20.59   The rules are designed to counteract cases in respect of which 'it is reasonable to suppose' that the arrangements would give rise to:

- a 'deduction/non-inclusion mismatch' (D/NI – *s 259A(2)*); or
- a double deduction mismatch (DD – *s 259A(3)*).

To know whether there is in fact a mismatch, it will usually be for the payer to know how the payee will treat the payment in his tax jurisdiction.

20.60   While displaying all the traditional virtues of parliamentary counsel, the legislation is a very large nut to crack a relatively small nut. All the chapters cover much the same ground, and in the manner of the Tax Law Rewrite there is a very high degree of repetition amongst the different Chapters of the legislation, the same rule or concept being repeated each time it appears, instead of being stated once and then made applicable in other cases.

20.61   For its application the legislation relies to a large extent on 'reasonable supposition'. The formula 'it is reasonable to suppose' does not tell us who has to suppose what is reasonable. Presumably it means 'it would be reasonable for HMRC to suppose', but is intended to impose some objective test to limit executive discretion: *TIOPA 2010, s 259A(1)*. *Section 259L* deals with what happens if a reasonable supposition is made which 'turns out to be mistaken or otherwise ceases to be reasonable'. In such cases, such consequential adjustments will be made as are 'just and reasonable'.

20.62   The legislation targets payments under mismatch arrangements that are deductible under the rules of the payer jurisdiction and are not included in ordinary income of the payee or related party jurisdiction, ie funding arrangements that are regarded as debt in the borrower jurisdiction but as equity for the lender/investor.

Example 20.10

1   A Subco issues preference shares to Parent (both resident in jurisdiction A).

2   P repoes the Subco prefs to unrelated interim holder (H) in jurisdiction B.

3   Subco pays a dividend to H and H is not required to make a substitute payment to P.

4   P accounts for the transaction as a borrowing, the finance cost being the Subco dividend, and claims a deduction for the finance cost.

5   H treats the repo as giving rise to a gain or loss on the repurchase and is not liable for tax on the pref dividend.

The rules apply both to 'payments' and 'quasi-payments'. Quasi-payments are transactions where no payment is involved but which give rise to a deduction. The finance deduction claimed by P here would be a 'quasi-payment'.

Example 20.11

1   A non-UK tax exempt fund makes a stock loan of debt securities to a UK bank.

2   The UK bank receives a coupon and makes a substitute payment to the stock lender.

3   The non-UK fund is not liable to tax on the substitute payment.

20.63   The scope of the legislation can be summarised in tabular form:

Chapter	Sections	Mismatch	Sphere of application
3	259C–259CD	D/NI	Financial instruments
4	259D–259DF	D/NI	Repos and stock lending
5	259E–259ED	D/NI	Payers which are hybrid entities
6	259F–259FC	D/NI	Permanent establishments
7	259G–259GE	D/NI	Payees which are hybrid entities
8	259H–259HD	D/NI	Payee is a company which is part of an MNE
9	259I–259IC	DD	Company is a hybrid entity
10	259J–259JC	DD	Hybrid entity is a dual resident company of a multi-national company
11	259K–259KB		Imported mismatches

20.64 Counteraction will normally take the form of a disallowance of the deduction in the payer (primary counteraction). Secondary disallowance involves a charge to tax on the payer.

20.65 *Chapter 3 (TIOPA 2010, ss 259C–259CD)* is concerned with 'impermissible deduction/non-inclusion mismatches. The conditions for its application are:

- Condition A: there is a payment or quasi-payment made under or in connection with a financial instrument.

- Condition B: the payer or payee is within the charge to UK corporation tax.

- Condition C: the 'reasonable to suppose' condition is satisfied, disregarding *Chapters 5–10 (ss 259E–259JC)*.

- Condition D: the payer and payee are related at any time in the specified period or the financial instrument is a structured arrangement or (in the case of quasi-payments) the payer is also the payee.

20.66 A 'structured arrangement' exists if (a) it is reasonable to suppose that the hybrid transfer arrangement is designed to secure a hybrid transfer deduction/non-inclusion mismatch, or (b) the terms of the hybrid transfer arrangement share the economic benefit of the mismatch between the parties: *s 259CA(6), (7)*.

20.67 *Chapter 4 (TIOPA 2010, ss 259DA–259DF)* is concerned with deduction/non-inclusion mismatches. The conditions for its application follow that of *s 259C*, with the additional condition that there must be a hybrid transfer arrangement in relation to the underlying instrument.

20.68 A hybrid transfer arrangement is defined in *s 259DB*. It is a repo, stock lending or similar arrangement, which is equivalent to the lending of money at interest, and in relation to which either (a) one party treats it as a loan and the other does not ('the dual payment condition'), or (b) a payment or quasi-payment is made that is representative of the underlying return and is paid to someone other than the person to whom the underlying return arises ('the substitute payment condition').

20.69 There is a financial trader exemption (*s 259DD*) which applies under the following conditions:

- Condition A: the mismatch arises because the payment or quasi-payment is a substitute payment which the financial trader brings into account for corporation tax purposes.

- Condition B: the financial trader also brings any associated payments into account.

- Condition C: if the underlying return arose directly to the payee neither *Chapter 3* nor the equivalent non-UK law would apply and the hybrid transfer arrangement is not a structured arrangement.

20.70   The remaining Chapters follow the same model, and there are additional definitions in *ss 259N–259NE*.

Chapter 21

Worldwide Debt Cap

Overview

21.1   This chapter deals with:

- Purpose of the legislation
- Scheme of the legislation
- Worldwide groups
- Key definitions
- Gateway test
- Financial service groups
- Group treasury companies
- Other exclusions
- The disallowance
- Tested expense amount
- Available amount
- Exemptions
- Giving effect to the disallowance
- Financing income exemption
- Intra-group financing exemption
- Anti-avoidance rules
- Administration

Future of the legislation

21.2   The UK government has stated that, if general restrictions on interest deductibility are introduced, the worldwide debt cap legislation is likely to become largely redundant and will be replaced by a much simplified Chapter of *TIOPA 2010*: see **9.95–9.98**. As it is, the legislation produces major compliance costs and complication, without achieving significant additional tax revenues.

Purpose of the legislation

21.3   See **3.65**. The distributions exemption in *CTA 2009, ss 931A–931W* assimilates foreign dividends to distributions made by UK companies, and makes them exempt from corporation tax. The concern of HMRC was that, if debt investment in foreign subsidiaries was made free of tax, and equity returns on foreign investments were also made free of tax, the Exchequer would lose at both ends. The UK profits would be reduced by the finance cost of debt raised to make share investments in foreign subsidiaries. When the product of the investment was returned in the form of dividends, those profits would be exempt. The logical consequence of exempting foreign profits was to restrict UK finance cost deductions.

21.4   The legislation on the worldwide debt cap is contained in *TIOPA 2010, ss 260–353B, Sch 9, Part 7*.

21.5   *CTA 2009, ss 931B(1)(a), 931C* exempt from UK corporation tax dividends paid to UK companies by companies resident in a 'qualifying territory', ie a territory with which the UK has a double taxation agreement containing a non-discrimination article. The purpose of the legislation is to meet the cost of the exemption for foreign distributions income conferred by *CTA 2009, ss 931B(1)(a), 931C* by restricting the interest deduction which UK companies belonging to international groups could otherwise obtain. Tax relief on UK finance costs is to be restricted by reference to global finance costs. The limit is by reference to the external finance cost of the worldwide group. In a case of cross-border financing, the aim of the legislation is to limit the UK tax deduction for intra-group finance expense to the external gross interest expense.

21.6   *TIOPA 2010, s 286* does this by limiting the deduction available for finance expenses of international groups of companies, which rely on loans into the UK to UK companies (either upstream from related companies or from external lenders) to finance acquisitions in the UK. In other words, it is a measure directed against highly leveraged UK buy-outs, where the interest is paid by someone in the UK to someone outside the UK, so sheltering UK profits from corporation tax. The form of the limitation is that a financing deduction is disallowed to the extent that the 'tested expense amount' exceeds the 'available amount': *TIOPA 2010, s 274*.

21.7   The effect is to limit the aggregate UK tax deduction for UK members of the group to the consolidated gross finance expense of the group.

21.8 *Worldwide Debt Cap*

The legislation is only applicable if the net UK debt is > £3m and > 75% of the gross debt of the worldwide group.

21.8   Because of the need to construct the legislation in a way which is compliant with EU law, a worldwide group can consist solely of UK resident companies.

21.9   The legislation applies for accounting periods of the worldwide group beginning on or after 1 January 2010. A 'period of account' is the period for which financial statements are drawn up. An 'accounting period' is the period for which a UK resident company must file a CTSA return.

Scheme of the legislation

21.10   There are seven stages in applying the legislation:

1   Is there a worldwide group?

2   Is the gateway test failed? This is purely a balance sheet test.

3   Find the net financing expense from the UK entity accounts, to establish the tested expense amount (T).

4   Identify the worldwide finance expense, being the figure given by the worldwide consolidated accounts, to establish the available amount (A).

5   Deduct A from T to find the total disallowed amount (TDA), so capping the net financing expense by reference to the available amount, ie $(T - A)$ = TDA.

6   Calculate the tested income amount (TIA) of UK group companies to find the financing income exemption (FIE), which is limited to the lower of TIA and TDA.

7   Allocate TDA and FIE amongst UK group companies.

21.11   Net disallowance of deductions for UK corporation tax purposes is accordingly:

$$T - (A + FIE), \text{ where } FIE \leq (TIA - A).$$

The worldwide group

21.12   The legislation applies to:

- UK group companies, and
- relevant group companies

which are members of worldwide groups. There are two definitions of worldwide groups. First, for the purpose of disallowing finance expenses, a group consists of an ultimate parent and relevant group companies (definition A): *TIOPA 2010, s 337*. For the purpose of applying the gateway test and the financing income exemption, a worldwide group consists of an ultimate parent, UK group companies and members of the group resident in an EEA country, provided that one or more of those companies is a relevant group company (definition B). In other words, A is the narrower definition (ultimate parent + relevant group companies); B is the broader definition (ultimate parent + UK group companies + EEA residents); and so A is a subset of B:

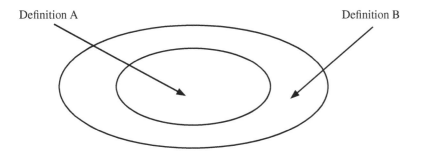

21.13 The ultimate parent is the entity at the summit of the worldwide group, which is not a direct or indirect subsidiary of any other entity: *s 339*. 'Subsidiary' is defined by reference to a 51% shareholding or control: *s 351*. The ultimate parent may be a non-corporate, provided that shares or other interests in the entity are listed on a recognised stock exchange, and those interests are widely held (no one person holds more than 10% by value). The purpose of this carve-out is to exclude collective investment schemes. A company which would not be a 'relevant subsidiary of the ultimate parent of the worldwide group' is to be treated as such if arrangements are in place whose main purpose is to ensure that the company should not be classified as a relevant subsidiary.

21.14 A group is defined by reference to IAS 21, ie by reference to control. The control test looks to all rights and powers, as well as voting rights. A group is large if no member of the group is an SME, as defined in the Annex to Commission Recommendation 2003/361/EC of 6 May 2003: *TIOPA 2010, s 344* (see **2.168–2.183**). Stapled entities are treated as a single entity: *s 342*. Corporate entities which are treated under IAS as a contractual business combination are also treated as a single entity: see IAS 22, para 43. A worldwide group must contain one or more 'relevant group companies'. Where a group contains more than one ultimate parent, each of the parents is treated as heading a separate group: *TIOPA 2010, s 338(2)*.

Key definitions

21.15   Many of the key concepts in the legislation are defined in terms of each other. The key definitions are:

- 'relevant subsidiary';
- 'relevant group company'; and
- 'UK group company'.

21.16   A 'relevant subsidiary' is defined by reference to a 75% shareholding of the ultimate parent: *TIOPA 2010, s 345(6)*. A relevant subsidiary may be resident anywhere. The normal threefold test of group membership for group relief purposes applies.

21.17   A 'relevant group company' is (*s 345*):

(a)   a UK resident company, or

(b)   a non-resident company carrying on a trade in the UK through a permanent establishment,

which is either:

(c)   an ultimate parent, or

(d)   a relevant subsidiary,

and is not:

(e)   a securitisation company within *TIOPA 2010, s 273A* and *CTA 2010, s 623*.

A relevant group company can only belong to one worldwide group.

21.18   A 'UK group company' is (*s 345(2)*):

(a)   a member of the worldwide group,

which is either:

(b)   a UK resident company, or

(c)   a non-resident company carrying on a trade in the UK through a permanent establishment, and is not:

(d)   a relevant subsidiary.

21.19   It is therefore a wider concept than 'relevant group company': s 345(2). In effect, a relevant group company (other than an ultimate parent) is a 75% subsidiary, and a UK group company is a 51% subsidiary.

21.20   The key rule is that the disallowance applies to any company which is a 'relevant group company' at any time during the 'relevant period of account'.

21.21   It follows from these definitions that either the ultimate parent or a relevant subsidiary must be UK resident in order for a worldwide group to exist, ie it must be a 'UK group company'. A 'large' group comprising a UK parent and its 100% subsidiary constitutes a 'worldwide group'. In other words, while a UK tax residence is necessary to come within the legislation, a foreign tax residence is not required to form a worldwide group.

Example 21.1

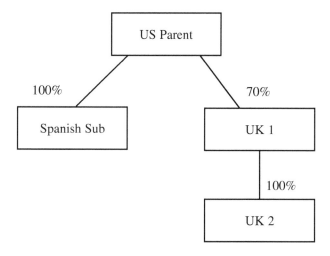

1   UK 1 and UK 2 are not relevant subsidiaries and so do not form part of a worldwide group, because 75% shareholding is required.

2   UK 1 and UK 2 do not themselves form a worldwide group because ultimate parent cannot itself be a subsidiary.

3   Therefore UK 1 and UK 2 are outside the regime.

The gateway test

21.22   The legislation does not apply at all if (*TIOPA 2010, s 262*):

$$U:W \leq 0.75:1$$

where:

- U = net UK debt, and
- W = gross worldwide debt.

In other words, UK net debt must not exceed 25% of gross worldwide debt.

21.23   This is a balance sheet test and is called the gateway test. For this purpose, the B definition is used.

21.24   UK companies with net debt of < £3m are excluded from the calculation: *s 262(3)*. Net debt is found by subtracting relevant assets from relevant liabilities. 'Relevant assets' includes 'cash and cash receivables'. This will include trade debtors; ie trade debts are relevant assets.

21.25   Dormant companies within *Companies Act 2006, s 1169* have a net debt of nil: *TIOPA 2010, s 262(4)*.

21.26   The legislation becomes applicable if the worldwide group contains one UK company, and the UK net debt of the group (= U) exceeds 75% of the worldwide gross debt (= W). The 'UK net debt' of a worldwide group of companies is the 'net debt' of each company, taking the average of the net debt at the start of the accounting period and the end of the accounting period: *s 262(1), (2)*. 'Net debt' is defined as (relevant liabilities – relevant assets): *s 263*. 'Relevant liabilities' are borrowings plus finance income payable in respect of finance leases. 'Relevant assets' are debt assets, and finance income receivable in respect of finance leases.

21.27   'Worldwide gross debt' is defined in *s 264* as the average of the relevant liabilities of the group at the start and end of the accounts period as disclosed in the consolidated accounts.

21.28   The accounts of the worldwide group are defined as the consolidated accounts drawn up in accordance with IAS: *TIOPA 2010, s 347*.

21.29   Where a UK resident company has made an election under *CTA 2009, s 18A* to exclude the profits of an overseas permanent establishment from its taxable profits, this election also applies for the gateway test: *TIOPA 2010, s 317A*.

21.30   As the disallowed amount has to be calculated in sterling, foreign currency amounts have to be translated into sterling.

21.31   For the purposes of the gateway test, where the worldwide consolidated balance sheet is expressed in a currency other than sterling, that amount is translated into sterling at the spot rate. If all the entity and consolidated accounts are expressed in the same non-sterling currency, the non-sterling amounts are used for all the purposes of the gateway test. In other words, there is no need to translate foreign currency amounts into sterling.

21.32   This means that foreign exchange rates may determine whether or not a group passes the gateway test.

21.33   For all other purposes, foreign currency amounts are translated into sterling at the average rate for the period.

21.34   Foreign exchange gains and losses are not included in the 'financing expense amounts' or 'financing income amounts' as defined in *ss 313, 314*. Hence, if a UK company has foreign currency debt, and the exchange rate of sterling against the currency of the debt deteriorates, that will not increase the UK net debt.

21.35   For UK corporation tax purposes, the entity accounts are used. The disallowance deriving from the consolidated accounts thus has to be allocated to companies on the basis of their entity accounts. The UK intra-group interest expense will be computed on the basis of the UK entity accounts.

21.36   For the worldwide debt, the consolidated accounts are used, or a number of national GAAPs, including UK GAAP.

21.37   However, the transfer pricing rules are applied *before*, while gains and losses on fair value and cash flow hedges which hedge debt liabilities and assets are taken into account *after*, the worldwide debt cap rules. Hence the 'accounts' used by the worldwide debt rules are a significantly modified versions of the commercial accounts, whether entity or consolidated.

21.38   Where company-level relevant liabilities are calculated on a different basis to group-level relevant liabilities, the latter figure is taken: *s 265A*.

Example 21.2 – Gateway test failed

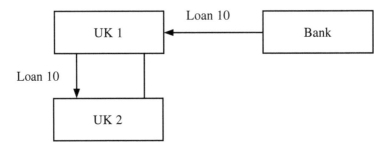

1   UK 1 and UK 2 are 'relevant companies', and UK 1 is parent of a worldwide group.

2   UK debt is 10. Worldwide group debt is 10 (75% = 7.50).

3   UK net debt 10 > 75% of worldwide gross debt.

4   UK 1 and UK 2 are within the regime.

Example 21.3 – Gateway test failed

U = UK debt

W = worldwide group debt

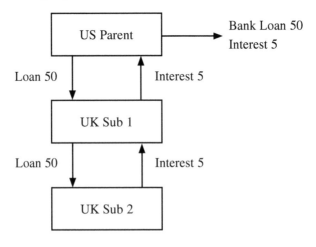

U = 50

W = 50

U:W is 100% of W

Gateway test is failed.

Example 21.4 – Gateway test passed

Position start of year

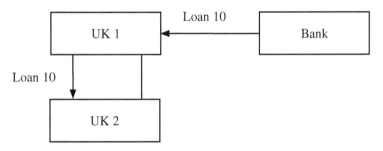

Position end of year

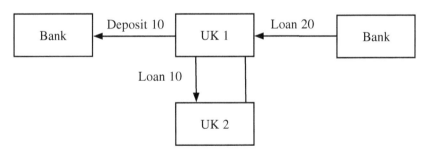

1   UK net debt $(20 - 10) = 10$

2   Worldwide gross debt $(10 + 20) / 2 = 15 \times 75\% = 11.25$

3   UK net debt $10 < 75\%$ of worldwide gross debt.

4   Regime does not apply.

Financial services group

21.39   Debt is an integral part of the trade of groups in the financial services sector. Qualifying financial services groups are exempted from the legislation: *TIOPA 2010, ss 261(2), 266–273A*. The excluded activities are: lending; insurance; and trading in financial instruments on own account. 'Qualifying financial services group' is defined in *s 266*. Insurance activities are defined in *s 269*. Dealing in financial instruments is defined in *s 270*. Calculation of trading income is dealt with in *ss 271–273*.

21.40   A worldwide group is a 'qualifying financial services group' in a period of account if it either meets the 'UK trading income' condition or would have met it but for trading losses. To meet this condition, either the whole or substantially the whole of the 'UK trading income' or the 'worldwide trading income' must derive from 'qualifying activities', as defined in *s 267*, ie lending, insurance or trading in financial instruments.

Group treasury companies

21.41   Having exempted financial services groups, it was logical to exempt group treasury companies on the same basis: *TIOPA 2010, s 316*. In calculating financing expense amounts and financing income amounts, amounts payable to and received by group treasury companies may be excluded by election. 'Group treasury company' is defined in *s 316(5)–(12)* as a company:

- which is a member of the worldwide group;
- which undertakes treasury activities for the worldwide group; and
- where 90% of its relevant income is group treasury revenue.

21.42   The group treasury election in many cases has the effect of leaving a group with a full interest deduction. However, the effect of the election may be to deny relief for the financing income exemption, where the treasury company has significant finance income. If there is more than one group treasury company, they are looked at separately.

Other exclusions

21.43   External finance costs are ignored insofar as they are taken into account in calculating the profits of:

(a)   a company carrying on a ring fence trade within *CTA 2010, s 277* (ie oil extraction), and the finance costs form part of the ring fence profits: *TIOPA 2010, s 333*;

(b)   a shipping company which is in the tonnage tax regime in *FA 2000, Sch 22: TIOPA 2010, s 334*; or

(c)   a UK real estate investment trust (REIT) within *CTA 2010, s 541: TIOPA 2010, s 335*.

The disallowance

21.44   Where the legislation applies, there is no disallowance if:

$$T{:}A \le 1{:}1$$

where:

- T = tested expense amount; and
- A = available amount.

If, on the other hand, T > A, there is a disallowance of the excess. For this purpose, the A definition of worldwide group is used.

21.45   The basic rule is that the interest deduction of the relevant group companies is restricted if the 'tested expense amount' (T) exceeds the 'available amount' (A).

'Tested expense amount' is defined in *TIOPA 2010, s 329* and 'available amount' in *s 332*.

21.46   The tested expense amount is calculated by subtracting 'financing income amounts' (defined in *s 314*) from 'financing expense amounts' (defined in *s 313*).

21.47   The total of the amounts disallowed for corporation tax purposes is the amount by which the tested expense amount exceeds the available amount. The disallowed deduction is accordingly (T – A). The disallowed amount is allocated amongst the relevant group companies and UK group companies.

21.48   The disallowance applies to any company which is a relevant group company at any time in the accounting period.

21.49   The total net intra-group finance expense of the UK members of the group (T) is compared with the net external finance expense of the worldwide group (A). If the UK interest deduction exceeds non-UK external borrowing costs, the excess of the UK interest deduction over the non-UK external borrowing costs is disallowed as a deduction for UK corporation tax purposes.

Tested expense amount

21.50   The tested expense amount (T) is the net finance costs of the relevant group companies ('the net financing deductions of each relevant group company'). The 'net financing deduction' is the 'sum of financing expense amounts' less 'the sum of financing income amounts': *TIOPA 2010, s 329(2).* This is compared with the available amount, ie the worldwide non-UK group consolidated external financing costs.

21.51   Financing deductions and financing income are 'small' if less than £500,000: *ss 329(5), 330(2), 331.* Small amounts are disregarded in calculating T. This creates anomalies where UK group companies have net financing income below £500,000 (which is treated as = 0) but other UK group companies have net financing deductions in excess of £500,000.

21.52   T is found for each 'relevant group company', ie the ultimate parent if UK resident and UK resident relevant subsidiaries. The tested expense amount comprises the sum of the individual UK companies' net finance costs, being:

- each relevant group company's 'financing expense amounts' for the period of account of the worldwide group (F1), less

- each relevant group company's 'financing income amounts' (F2).

In other words, (F1 – F2) = T.

21.53   The 'financing expense amount' (defined in *s 313*) comprises:

- Condition A: Loan relationship debits, other than 'excluded debits', which are (a) an impairment loss, (b) an exchange loss, and (c) a loss on a related transaction;

- Condition B: Financing costs implicit in finance leases; and

- Condition C: Financing costs payable in respect of debt factoring.

Where accounting periods do not coincide, time apportionment is made.

21.54   The 'financing income amount' (defined in *s 314*) comprises:

- Condition A: Loan relationship credits, other than 'excluded credits', which are (a) the reversal of an impairment loss, (b) an exchange gain, and (c) a gain on a related transaction;

- Condition B: Income implicit in amounts received under finance leases;

- Condition C: Income receivable on debt factoring; and

- Condition D: Guarantee fees.

21.55 If F2 > F1, the result is nil: *s 329(4)*. If (F1– F2) < 500,000, the result is also nil.

21.56 In calculating the tested expense amount, transitional adjustments arising on the adoption of IAS and spread over ten years, in accordance with *Loan Relationships and Derivative Contracts (Change of Accounting Practice) Regulations 2004, SI 2004/3271, reg 3A*, are disregarded, so that amounts which would otherwise have been deductible in accounting periods beginning before 1 January 2010 do not affect the calculation: *TIOPA 2010, Sch 9, para 32*.

21.57 As noted above, in calculating the finance expense amount, and the finance income amount, exchange gains and losses, impairment losses and profits and losses arising from related transactions are excluded: *TIOPA s 315*.

Available amount

21.58 The available amount is the gross finance expense of the worldwide group, and is defined in *TIOPA 2010, s 332* as the sum of the worldwide group's finance costs as disclosed in its consolidated accounts. As intra-group payments and loans are eliminated on consolidation, the available amount is only concerned with external debt. The finance costs do not include dividends payable on preference shares treated as debt under IAS 32. The accounts of the worldwide group are defined as the consolidated accounts drawn up in accordance with IAS.

Capitalised finance costs can be included in the available amount.

21.59 The available amount additionally includes such amounts as are specified in the *Tax Treatment of Costs and Income (Available Amount) Regulations 2010, SI 2010/2929*, eg:

- interest on relevant non-lending relationships,
- manufactured interest,
- payments under alternative finance arrangements.

21.60 Where a company makes a fair value or hedge adjustment to a finance cost which enters into the Available Amount, so that the payment in question in the accounts of the worldwide group (= A) is different from the corresponding loan relationship debit in the accounts of the relevant group company (ie the UK resident company) (= B), the Available Amount is decreased if A > B, and increased if B > A: *Tax Treatment of Financing Costs and Income (Correction of*

Mismatches) Regulations 2010, SI 2010/3025. The regulations have particular importance in relation to debt restructurings: *reg 15.*

21.61 It may be observed that in terms of casuistic specificity these regulations come from the same stable as the Disregard Regulations.

Example 21.5

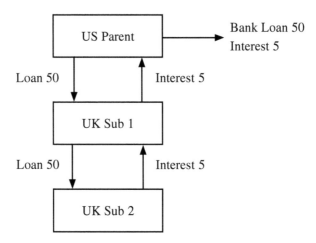

F1 = financing expense amount [loan relationship debits (other than excluded debits) and other finance expenses]

F2 = financing income amount [loan relationship credits (other than excluded credits) and other finance income]

T = tested expense amount [net amount of UK companies' finance expenses, being > 500,000]

A = available amount [consolidated finance costs of worldwide group]

The question is: does the tested expense amount exceed available amount?

$(F1 - F2) = T = (10 - 5) = 5$

$A = 5$

T:A = 1:1 – therefore, no disallowance.

Example 21.6

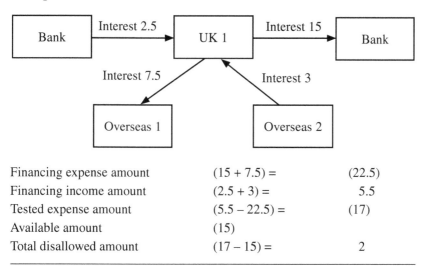

Financing expense amount	(15 + 7.5) =	(22.5)
Financing income amount	(2.5 + 3) =	5.5
Tested expense amount	(5.5 – 22.5) =	(17)
Available amount	(15)	
Total disallowed amount	(17 – 15) =	2

Example 21.7

FRS 102/IFRS: financing expense is dollar interest; swap accounted for as derivative financial instrument (DFI).

Fair value: FV movements on loan are financing expense amount but do not form part of available amount.

Exemptions

21.62 Stranded non-trading loan relationship deficits under *CTA 2009, s 457* may arise in periods where a group does not have sufficient current-year capacity to group relieve all of its external interest expense. If both the payer and recipient companies are members of the same worldwide group and are resident in the UK, both companies can elect that the amount in question should be excluded from the calculation of the financing expense amount: *TIOPA 2010, ss 322, 323*. The joint election must be made within 36 months of the end of the period of account of the worldwide group to which the amount in question relates.

21.63 The consequence of such an election is that the paying company does not have a financing expense and the payee company does not have financing income.

21.64 In the case of stranded deficits on management expenses, a similar election may be made: *TIOPA 2010, ss 324, 325*.

21.65 Short-term intra-group finance expenses on loan relationships can, on election, be excluded from amounts T and A. Cash pooling is a major concern. Many groups have short-term facilities that roll over on a regular basis. Cash pooling is taken out of the debt cap. 'Short-term' means less than 12 months and repayable on demand. If the debt is renewed within six months of repayment, it does not count as short-term: *s 321*.

21.66 To come within this provision the debt must comply with the conditions set out in the *Corporation Tax (Exclusion of Short-Term Loan Relationships) Regulations 2009, SI 2009/3313*. These exclude: (a) long-term funding purposes (indebtedness will not be discharged within 12 months); (b) long-term aggregated loan relationships (short-term funding which is rolled over).

Giving effect to the disallowance

21.67 If T > A, the balance – known as the 'total disallowed amount' (TDA) – is disallowed as a finance cost in computing the profits of the relevant group companies: *TIOPA 2010, s 274*. The TDA is defined in *ss 274, 286*. This gives:

$$T - A = TDA$$

21.68 A group must produce a statement of the TDA, which is allocated amongst the relevant group companies. One company may be appointed to be the 'reporting body' (defined in *s 277*) for all relevant group companies: *s 276*. The reporting company produces a statement of the TDA, and a statement of how the TDA is allocated amongst the relevant group companies. These statements must be produced within 12 months of the end of the period of account in question: *ss 278–281*. Where a CTSA has already been submitted, it is deemed to be amended by the statement of the TDA and allocations.

21.69 The TDA relates to the period of account of the worldwide group, which may not coincide with the accounting period of the UK company.

21.70   If there is a disallowance, relief may be given to group companies which are UK group companies but not relevant group companies. This is because UK group companies can benefit from the financing income exemption.

21.71   Groups may allocate the TDA in any way they see fit, provided that the disallowance does not exceed a company's financing expense amount.

21.72   If groups make no allocation, there is a default allocation, which is (*s 284*):

$$\frac{NFD \times TDA}{T}$$

where NFD = net financing deduction.

Financing income exemption

21.73   Where a group has a TDA, the net financing income of UK group companies is treated as exempt from corporation tax, up to the lower of TDA and the tested income amount (TIA): *TIOPA 2010, ss 286, 287, 292*. Parallel with the TDA procedure, a group must also calculate its financing income exemption (FIE). This reduces the group's charge to UK tax. FIE is not netted off against the TDA, as might have been thought sensible. Instead, a group has one set of disallowances and another set of disallowances of the disallowance.

21.74   The key concept is the TIA, which is defined in *TIOPA 2010, s 330*. This is the sum of the net financing incomes of UK group companies. Again, if the net financing income is < 500,000, it is treated as nil. Part of this financing income of UK group companies is exempted from corporation tax, up to the lower of the tested income amount and the TDA: *s 292(6)*.

21.75   The FIE arises for two reasons:

1   a relevant group company with no financing expense may have financing income but does not feature in the calculation of tested expense amount; or

2   a UK group company which is not a relevant group company may have net finance income which is subject to UK tax.

21.76   As with the TDA, a reporting company in a group has to produce a 'statement of allocated exemptions': *s 292*.

21.77   'Financing income amounts' (loan relationship credits) are defined in *s 314* (ie the same definition which is used in calculating the tested expense amount). The amounts specified in the statement of allocated exemptions are not brought into account for corporation tax purposes. The rule is in *s 293*:

> 'A financing income amount of a company to which this Chapter applies [UK group companies] that is specified in a statement of allocated exemptions under section 292(4)(b) is not to be brought into account by the company for the purposes of corporation tax.'

Example 21.8

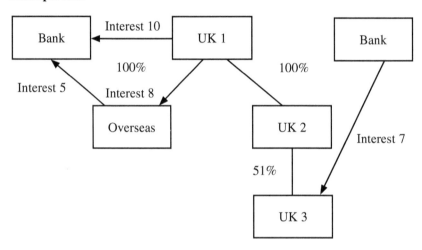

Tested expense amount (10 + 8) = (18)

Available amount (10 + 5) = (15)

Total disallowable amount = (18 – 15) = 3

Finance income exemption = 3

UK tax deduction: (–18 + 3) + (7 – 3) = (11), i.e UK 1's loan relationships debits (18) + UK 3's loan relationship credit of 7

Intra-group financing income

21.78 Under *TIOPA 2010, ss 288–305*, intra-group financing income received from a company resident in the EEA, excluding the UK, may be exempt from corporation tax.

21.79   Where a UK company:

- receives finance income from an EEA territory company,

- both companies are members of the same worldwide group,

- the payer and recipient are 'relevant associates', and

- the payer does not receive tax relief for the payment in the country of residence,

the recipient company can elect that the income should not be included in the calculation of its financing income amount.

21.80   Two companies are 'relevant associates' if there is 75% common ownership: *TIOPA 2010, s 300*.

21.81   The purpose of this provision is to ensure that the tax treatment between UK members of a worldwide group, and other members resident in another EEA state, is non-discriminatory.

Anti-avoidance rules

21.82   The legislation would not be complete without the usual battery of anti-avoidance rules of studied and deliberate vagueness. If a scheme is entered into whose main purpose or one of whose main purposes is:

1   to enable a group to pass the gateway test, the scheme is ineffective for that purpose;

2   to increase T or A or decrease TDA, it is ineffective: *TIOPA 2010, ss 307–310*;

3   is to exploit the intra-group funding exemption in *s 299*, the conditions in *s 299* are deemed not to have been met;

4   to exclude the definition of a worldwide group in *TIOPA s 337*, that rule is applied as if the scheme had not been entered into.

21.83   An 'excluded scheme' (which is to be defined in regulations which have not been issued) is outside these provisions: *ss 306, 312*.

Controlled foreign company

21.84   One of the situations which the debt cap rules are intended to target is a UK multi-national enterprise (MNE) which establishes a non-resident finance subsidiary which is a controlled foreign company (CFC), and the finance subsidiary lends money back to the UK; the finance expense is likely to be disallowed in the UK company; but, in apportioning the profits of the CFC to the UK controller, the profits so apportioned will include the payments from the UK company.

Administration

21.85   Two returns feature in the legislation:

- statement of allocated disallowances; and

- statement of allocated exemptions.

21.86   A group must return:

- tested expense amount;

- allowable amount;

- disallowance;

- allocation of disallowance; and

- financing income exemption.

The legislation in practice

21.87   If the transfer pricing rules are applied before the worldwide debt cap rules, the transfer pricing rules may introduce a financing expense which is then disallowed under the worldwide debt rules.

21.88   The way to keep out of the rules is to minimise amounts of UK debt (U) and tested expense amount (T), and maximise amounts of worldwide gross debt (W) and available amount (A). If, say, a US parent has a UK and a German subsidiary, external borrowing by the German subsidiary will reduce the interest disallowance in the UK subsidiary. If the intended effect of the legislation to drive debt and therefore investment out of the UK, the legislation is likely to succeed in its objective.

21.89   Further, the rules would appear to favour equity investment into the UK and debt investment outside the UK.

Appendix

Loan Relationships and Derivative Contracts (Disregard and Bringing into Account of Profits and Losses) Regulations 2004, SI 2004/3256

The Treasury, in exercise of the powers conferred upon them by sections 84A(3A), 85B(3)(a) and 85B(5)(b) of the Finance Act 1996 and paragraphs 16(3A), 17C(1) and 17C(3)(b) of Schedule 26 to the Finance Act 2002 make the following Regulations:

1 Citation, commencement and effect

(1) These Regulations may be cited as the Loan Relationships and Derivative Contracts (Disregard and Bringing into Account of Profits and Losses) Regulations 2004 and shall come into force on 1st January 2005.

(2) These Regulations have effect in relation to periods of account beginning on or after 1st January 2005.

2 Interpretation

(1) In these Regulations–

[…]¹

['CTA 2009' means the Corporation Tax Act 2009;

'CTA 2010' means the Corporation Tax Act 2010;]²

'deferred shares' has the same meaning as in the Building Societies Act 1986;]³

'derivative contract' has the same meaning as in [Part 7 of CTA 2009]⁴;

['exchange gain or loss' has the same meaning as in [section 475 of CTA 2009]⁴;]⁵

…⁶

['fair value profit or loss' means the profit or loss brought into account in relation to a derivative contract or an asset or liability representing a loan relationship where for the period in question—

(a) the derivative contract or asset or liability representing a loan relationship is measured at fair value, or

      (b)   the derivative contract or asset or liability representing a loan relationship is a hedged item in a designated fair value hedge and the carrying value of the hedged item is adjusted for changes in fair value attributable to the hedged risk;][7]

['loan relationship' has the same meaning as in [section 302 of CTA 2009][4];

['a section 614 or 615 credit or debit'][4] means the credit or debit to be brought into account in accordance with [section 614 or 615 of CTA 2009][4];

'a prior period adjustment credit or debit' means so much of any credit or debit as represents a prior period adjustment taken into account by virtue of [section 597(1)(b) of CTA 2009][4] as a result of a change of accounting basis;][8]

['regulatory capital security' has the meaning given in regulation 2 of the Taxation of Regulatory Capital Securities Regulations 2013;][9]

'underlying subject matter' has the same meaning as in [Part 7 of CTA 2009][4].

(2)   In these Regulations–

'for accounting purposes' means for the purposes of accounts drawn up in accordance with generally accepted accounting practice;

'generally accepted accounting practice' has the meaning given in [section 1127 of CTA 2010][4]; and

'amortised cost', [consolidated accounts,][10] 'designated', 'effective hedge', 'effective interest method', ['fair value hedge'][11] 'firm commitment', 'forecast transaction', 'foreign operation'[, 'fair value, items of other comprehensive income'][12] and 'net investment in a foreign operation' have the same meaning as for accounting purposes.

(3)   In these Regulations any reference to an asset which is a ship or aircraft includes a reference to a contract–

      (a)   to which section 67 of the Capital Allowances Act 2001 applies; and

      (b)   which relates to plant or machinery which is a ship or aircraft.

[(3A) For the purposes of these Regulations, a liability representing a loan relationship or a derivative contract is treated as matched with shares, ships or aircraft from the date that, and to the extent that, either condition 1 or 2 of regulations 3(3) or 4(3) are satisfied.][13]

(4)   In these Regulations–

      (a)   any reference to a hedging instrument includes a reference to part of an instrument; and

      (b)   any reference to a hedged item includes a reference to part of a hedged item.

(5)   For the purposes of these Regulations, a company has a hedging relationship between a derivative contract or a liability representing a loan relationship on the

one hand ('the hedging instrument') and an asset, liability, receipt or expense on the other ('the hedged item') if and to the extent that–

(a)   the hedging instrument and the hedged item are designated by the company as a hedge; or

(b)   in any other case the hedging instrument is intended to act as a hedge of–

(i)   the exposure to changes in fair value of a hedged item which is a recognised asset or liability or an unrecognised firm commitment or an identified portion of such an asset, liability or commitment that is attributable to a particular risk and could affect profit or loss of the company;

(ii)   the exposure to variability in cash flows that is attributable to a particular risk associated with a hedged item that is a recognised asset or liability or a forecast transaction and could affect profit or loss of the company; or

(iii)   a net investment in a foreign operation of the company.

[(6)   For the purposes of regulations 3 to 5, where an asset referred to is shares in a company, the asset comprises all the shares held in that company whenever acquired.][10]

---

1   Revoked by the Taxation of Regulatory Capital Securities Regulations 2013, SI 2013/3209, reg 10(1), (2)(a).
2   Inserted by the Loan Relationships and Derivative Contracts (Disregard and Bringing into Account of Profits and Losses) (Amendment) Regulations 2014, SI 2014/3188, regs 2, 8(1)(a).
3   Inserted by the Loan Relationships and Derivative Contracts (Disregard and Bringing into Account of Profits and Losses) (Amendment) Regulations 2013, SI 2013/2781, reg 2(1), (2).
4   Substituted by the Loan Relationships and Derivative Contracts (Disregard and Bringing into Account of Profits and Losses) (Amendment) Regulations 2014, SI 2014/3188, regs 2, 8(1)(b), (c), (e)-(h), (2)(a).
5   Substituted by the Loan Relationships and Derivative Contracts (Disregard and Bringing into Account of Profits and Losses) (Amendment) Regulations 2005, SI 2005/2012, regs 2, 3(a).
6   Revoked by the Loan Relationships and Derivative Contracts (Disregard and Bringing into Account of Profits and Losses) (Amendment) Regulations 2015, SI 2015/1961, regs 2, 3(a).
7   Substituted by the Loan Relationships and Derivative Contracts (Disregard and Bringing into Account of Profits and Losses) (Amendment) Regulations 2015, SI 2015/1961, regs 2, 3(b).
8   Inserted by the Loan Relationships and Derivative Contracts (Disregard and Bringing into Account of Profits and Losses) (Amendment) Regulations 2005, SI 2005/2012, regs 2, 3(b).
9   Inserted by the Taxation of Regulatory Capital Securities Regulations 2013, SI 2013/3209, reg 10(1), (2)(b).
10   Inserted by the Loan Relationships and Derivative Contracts (Disregard and Bringing into Account of Profits and Losses) (Amendment No. 2) Regulations 2007, SI 2007/3431, reg 2(1), (2).
11   Inserted by the Loan Relationships and Derivative Contracts (Disregard and Bringing into Account of Profits and Losses) (Amendment) Regulations 2014, SI 2014/3188, regs 2, 8(2)(b).
12   Inserted by the Loan Relationships and Derivative Contracts (Disregard and Bringing into Account of Profits and Losses) (Amendment) Regulations 2015, SI 2015/1961, regs 2, 3(c).
13   Inserted by the Loan Relationships and Derivative Contracts (Disregard and Bringing into Account of Profits and Losses) (Amendment No. 2) Regulations 2011, SI 2011/2912, regs 2, 3.

3 Exchange gains or losses arising from liabilities or assets hedging shares etc.

(1) For the purposes of [section 328(4) of CTA 2009][1] there is prescribed an exchange gain or loss arising to a company in an accounting period in relation to a liability representing a loan relationship of the company which is matched with the whole or part of any shares, ships or aircraft.

[(1ZA) But where the matched shares, ships or aircraft are matched after the company became party to the loan relationship, paragraph (1) only applies to a just and reasonable proportion of any exchange gain or loss having regard to—

    (a) the fraction of the accounting period for which the shares, ships or aircraft are matched with the loan relationship,

    (b) the fraction of the accounting period for which the company was party to the loan relationship, and

    (c) fluctuations in exchange rates during the accounting period.][2]

[(1A) ...[3]][4]

(2) This regulation does not apply if movements in the fair value[, or profits or losses arising on the disposal,][4] of any shares, ships or aircraft which are an asset falling within regulation 3(1) are brought into account by the company in computing, for the purposes of corporation tax, the profits of a trade carried on by it which consists of or includes dealing in shares, ships or aircraft.

(3) [Shares, ships or aircraft are matched to the greatest possible extent with—

    (a) the liability representing the loan relationship designated as a hedge if condition 1 is satisfied;

    (b) subject to paragraph (a), the liability representing the loan relationship referred to in condition 2 if that condition is satisfied.][5]

    ...[6]

[Condition 1][5]

The condition is that ...[7] the shares, ships or aircraft are a hedged item under a designated hedge of exchange rate risk in which the liability is the hedging instrument.

[Condition 2][5]

The condition is that the currency in which the liability is expressed is such that the company [intends][5], by entering into [[or][8] continuing to be subject to][4] that liability, ...[6] to eliminate or substantially reduce the economic risk of holding the asset, or part of the asset, which is attributable to fluctuations in exchange rates.

(4) If [condition 2][5] applies, a liability is matched with an asset only to the extent that the carrying value of the liability ...[9] [...[9]][4] does not exceed the unmatched carrying value of the asset at [the relevant time][10].

(5) For the purposes of [section 328(4) of CTA 2009][1] there is prescribed an exchange gain or loss arising to a company in an accounting period in relation to

an asset representing a loan relationship of the company which is matched with the whole or part [of—

(a)   any share capital of the company,

(b)   in relation to a building society, any deferred shares issued by the building society to the extent that they are accounted for as equity instruments in accordance with generally accepted accounting practice, or

(c)   [a regulatory capital security][11] issued by the company to the extent that it is accounted for as an equity instrument in accordance with generally accepted accounting practice.][12]

(6)   An asset is matched with share capital [in particular where][13] for the accounting period of the company immediately preceding the first accounting period to which these Regulations apply–

(a)   exchange gains and losses on the asset were taken to a reserve; and

(b)   set off there against exchange gains and losses on the share capital.

(7)   In this regulation–

'carrying value' means, in relation to a liability, the value as shown in the company's accounts of that liability; and

'unmatched carrying value' means, in relation to an asset, an amount equal to the [relevant value][13] to the extent that that amount has not previously been matched in accordance with this regulation or regulation 4.

---

1   Substituted by the Loan Relationships and Derivative Contracts (Disregard and Bringing into Account of Profits and Losses) (Amendment) Regulations 2014, SI 2014/3188, regs 2, 8(3).

2   Inserted by the Loan Relationships and Derivative Contracts (Disregard and Bringing into Account of Profits and Losses) (Amendment No. 2) Regulations 2011, SI 2011/2912, regs 2, 4(1).

3   Revoked by the Loan Relationships and Derivative Contracts (Disregard and Bringing into Account of Profits and Losses) (Amendment) Regulations 2014, SI 2014/3188, regs 2, 3.

4   Inserted by the Loan Relationships and Derivative Contracts (Disregard and Bringing into Account of Profits and Losses) (Amendment) Regulations 2005, SI 2005/2012, regs 2, 4(1)-(3), (4)(c)(ii), (5)(b).

5   Substituted by the Loan Relationships and Derivative Contracts (Disregard and Bringing into Account of Profits and Losses) (Amendment) Regulations 2005, SI 2005/2012, regs 2, 4(1), (4)(a), (c)(i), (d), (5)(a).

6   Revoked by the Loan Relationships and Derivative Contracts (Disregard and Bringing into Account of Profits and Losses) (Amendment) Regulations 2005, SI 2005/2012, regs 2, 4(1), (4)(b), (c)(iii).

7   Revoked by the Loan Relationships and Derivative Contracts (Disregard and Bringing into Account of Profits and Losses) (Amendment No. 2) Regulations 2011, SI 2011/2912, regs 2, 4(2).

8   Substituted by the Loan Relationships and Derivative Contracts (Disregard and Bringing into Account of Profits and Losses) (Amendment) Regulations 2011, SI 2011/698, regs 2, 3.

9   Revoked by the Loan Relationships and Derivative Contracts (Disregard and Bringing into Account of Profits and Losses) (Amendment No. 2) Regulations 2007, SI 2007/3431, reg 2(1), (3)(a).

10 Substituted by the Loan Relationships and Derivative Contracts (Disregard and Bringing into Account of Profits and Losses) (Amendment No. 2) Regulations 2007, SI 2007/3431, reg 2(1), (3)(b).

11 Substituted by the Taxation of Regulatory Capital Securities Regulations 2013, SI 2013/3209, reg 10(1), (3).

12 Substituted by the Loan Relationships and Derivative Contracts (Disregard and Bringing into Account of Profits and Losses) (Amendment) Regulations 2013, SI 2013/2781, reg 2(1), (3).

13 Substituted by the Loan Relationships and Derivative Contracts (Disregard and Bringing into Account of Profits and Losses) (Amendment No. 2) Regulations 2005, SI 2005/3374, regs 2–4.

---

4 Exchange gains or losses arising from derivative contracts hedging shares etc.

(1)   For the purposes of [section 606(4) and 598(1)(a) of CTA 2009][1] there is prescribed an exchange gain or loss arising to a company in an accounting period in relation to a derivative contract of the company which is matched with the whole or part of any shares, ships or aircraft.

[(1A) But where the matched shares, ships or aircraft are matched after the company became party to the derivative contract, paragraph (1) only applies to a just and reasonable proportion of any exchange gain or loss having regard to—

(a)   the fraction of the accounting period for which the shares, ships or aircraft are matched with the derivative contract,

(b)   the fraction of the accounting period for which the company was party to the derivative contract, and

(c)   fluctuations in exchange rates during the period.][2]

(2)   This regulation does not apply if movements in the fair value[, or profits or losses arising on the disposal,][3] of any shares, ships or aircraft which are an asset falling within regulation 4(1) are brought into account by the company in computing, for the purposes of corporation tax, the profits of a trade carried on by it which consists of or includes dealing in shares, ships or aircraft.

(3)   [Shares, ships or aircraft are matched to the greatest possible extent with—

(a)   the derivative contract designated as a hedge if condition 1 is satisfied;

(b)   subject to paragraph (a), the derivative contract referred to in condition 2 if that condition is satisfied.][4]

      ...[5]

[Condition 1][4]

The condition is that ...[6] the shares, ships or aircraft are a hedged item under a designated hedge of exchange rate risk in which the derivative contract is the hedging instrument.

[Condition 2][4]

The condition is that the underlying subject matter of the derivative contract is such that the company [intends][4], by entering into [[or][7] continuing to be party to][3] that contract, ...[5] to eliminate or substantially reduce the economic risk of holding the asset, or part of the asset, which is attributable to fluctuations in exchange rates.

(4) If [condition 2]^4 applies, a derivative contract is matched with an asset only to the extent that the [value of the obligation under]^4 the derivative contract ...^{8} [...^{8}]^3 does not exceed the unmatched carrying value of the asset at [the relevant time]^9.

[(4A) For the purposes of [section 606(4) of CTA 2009]^1 there is prescribed an exchange gain or loss arising to a company in an accounting period in relation to a derivative contract of the company which is matched with the whole or part [of—

(a) any share capital of the company,

(b) in relation to a building society, any deferred shares issued by the building society to the extent that they are accounted for as equity instruments in accordance with generally accepted accounting practice, or

(c) [a regulatory capital security]^{10} issued by the company to the extent that it is accounted for as an equity instrument in accordance with generally accepted accounting practice.]^{11}

(4B) A derivative contract is matched with share capital in particular where for the accounting period of the company immediately preceding the first accounting period beginning on or after 1st January 2005—

(a) exchange gains and losses on the derivative contract were taken to a reserve; and

(b) set off there against exchange gains and losses on the share capital.]^{12}

(5) In this regulation–

['the value of the obligation under the derivative contract' means the value of the obligation of the company to pay in exchange for one currency an amount of a second currency and includes any notional obligation to pay an amount of currency in respect of a contract for differences;]^3

...^{5}

'unmatched carrying value' means, in relation to an asset, an amount equal to the [relevant value]^{13} to the extent that that amount has not previously been matched in accordance with this regulation or regulation 3.

---

1 Substituted by the Loan Relationships and Derivative Contracts (Disregard and Bringing into Account of Profits and Losses) (Amendment) Regulations 2014, SI 2014/3188, regs 2, 8(4), (5).
2 Inserted by the Loan Relationships and Derivative Contracts (Disregard and Bringing into Account of Profits and Losses) (Amendment No. 2) Regulations 2011, SI 2011/2912, regs 2, 5(1).
3 Inserted by the Loan Relationships and Derivative Contracts (Disregard and Bringing into Account of Profits and Losses) (Amendment) Regulations 2005, SI 2005/2012, regs 2, 5(1), (2), (3)(c)(ii), (4)(c), (5)(b).
4 Substituted by the Loan Relationships and Derivative Contracts (Disregard and Bringing into Account of Profits and Losses) (Amendment) Regulations 2005, SI 2005/2012, regs 2, 5(1), (3)(a), (c)(i), (4)(a), (b).
5 Revoked by the Loan Relationships and Derivative Contracts (Disregard and Bringing into Account of Profits and Losses) (Amendment) Regulations 2005, SI 2005/2012, regs 2, 5(1), (3)(b), (c)(iii), (5)(a).
6 Revoked by the Loan Relationships and Derivative Contracts (Disregard and Bringing into Account of Profits and Losses) (Amendment No. 2) Regulations 2011, SI 2011/2912, regs 2, 5(2).

7   Substituted by the Loan Relationships and Derivative Contracts (Disregard and Bringing into Account of Profits and Losses) (Amendment) Regulations 2011, SI 2011/698, regs 2, 4.
8   Revoked by the Loan Relationships and Derivative Contracts (Disregard and Bringing into Account of Profits and Losses) (Amendment No. 2) Regulations 2007, SI 2007/3431, reg 2(1), (4)(a).
9   Substituted by the Loan Relationships and Derivative Contracts (Disregard and Bringing into Account of Profits and Losses) (Amendment No. 2) Regulations 2007, SI 2007/3431, reg 2(1), (4)(b).
10 Substituted by the Taxation of Regulatory Capital Securities Regulations 2013, SI 2013/3209, reg 10(1), (3).
11 Substituted by the Loan Relationships and Derivative Contracts (Disregard and Bringing into Account of Profits and Losses) (Amendment) Regulations 2013, SI 2013/2781, reg 2(1), (3).
12 Inserted by the Loan Relationships and Derivative Contracts (Disregard and Bringing into Account of Profits and Losses) (Amendment No. 2) Regulations 2005, SI 2005/3374, regs 2, 5.
13 Substituted by the Loan Relationships and Derivative Contracts (Disregard and Bringing into Account of Profits and Losses) (Amendment No. 2) Regulations 2005, SI 2005/3374, regs 2, 3.

[[4A   Relevant value

(1)   For the purposes of regulations 3(7) and 4(5), 'relevant value' means—

   (a)   in relation to shares held by the company in another company ('Company A'), where the company elects, the higher of—

      (i)   the net asset value underlying the shares in Company A, and

      (ii)   the value shown in the accounts of the company; and

   (b)   in any other case, the value shown in the accounts of the company.

(2)   In paragraph (1)(a)(i) the net asset value underlying the shares in Company A is an amount equal to—

   (a)   the value of the assets, less

   (b)   the value of the liabilities

   of Company A and any direct or indirect subsidiary of Company A denominated in the relevant currency.

   This is subject to paragraph (6).

(3)   The value of assets and liabilities referred to in paragraph (2) is the value at the relevant time shown in—

   (a)   a balance sheet of Company A, or

   (b)   where Company A has a direct or indirect subsidiary, a notional consolidated balance sheet of Company A prepared in the relevant currency.

(4)   For the purposes of paragraph (3) in determining whether an asset or liability would be recognised in the balance sheet or notional consolidated balance sheet and, if so recognised the value that would be accorded to it, regard shall be had to the accounting treatment of the asset or liability—

   (a)   in any consolidated accounts prepared by the company, or

    (b)   where the company does not prepare consolidated accounts, in any consolidated accounts prepared by a company that directly or indirectly controls the company.

(5)   Nothing in paragraphs (3) or (4) shall prevent an asset or liability, which might be eliminated in the preparation of any consolidated accounts, from being taken into account in paragraph (2).

(6)   If the company does not directly hold the entire issued share capital in Company A, the net asset value underlying the shares in Company A shall be reduced by such amount as is just and reasonable having regard to—

    (a)   the proportion of the issued shares held by the company, and

    (b)   where there is more than one class of share, the rights attached to the shares held by the company.

[(7)   An election under paragraph (1)—

    (a)   must be made by the company by notice in writing to an officer of Revenue and Customs, and

    (b)   must specify the review period.

(7A) An election—

    (a)   applies to all the shareholdings held by the company which are matched in accordance with regulation 3(3)(b) or 4(3)(b), and

    (b)   has effect from a date specified in the notice which must be later than the date the notice is given.

(7B) An election may be amended or revoked by notice in writing to an officer of Revenue and Customs—

    (a)   before the election has effect, or

    (b)   with effect from a date specified in the notice which must be—

        (i)   later than the date the notice is given, and

        (ii)   at least 12 months after the election was made.

(7C) Where the date specified in a notice under paragraph (7) or (7B) is not the first day of an accounting period so much of the period as falls before that date and so much of the period as falls on or after that date are treated as separate accounting periods.][1]

(8)   ...[2]

[(8A) ...[2]

(8B) ...[2]][3]

[(9)][4] In this regulation—

    'relevant currency' means the currency which, as a result of exchange rate fluctuations, gives rise to the economic risk referred to in regulations 3(3) and 4(3);

    'control' has the meaning given in [section 1124 of CTA 2010][5].][6][7]

1 Substituted by the Loan Relationships and Derivative Contracts (Disregard and Bringing into Account of Profits and Losses) (Amendment) Regulations 2014, SI 2014/3188, regs 2, 4(1), (2).
2 Revoked by the Loan Relationships and Derivative Contracts (Disregard and Bringing into Account of Profits and Losses) (Amendment) Regulations 2014, SI 2014/3188, regs 2, 4(1), (3).
3 Inserted by the Loan Relationships and Derivative Contracts (Disregard and Bringing into Account of Profits and Losses) (Amendment) Regulations 2011, SI 2011/698, regs 2, 5(1), (3).
4 Substituted by the Loan Relationships and Derivative Contracts (Disregard and Bringing into Account of Profits and Losses) (Amendment) Regulations 2011, SI 2011/698, regs 2, 5(1), (4).
5 Substituted by the Loan Relationships and Derivative Contracts (Disregard and Bringing into Account of Profits and Losses) (Amendment) Regulations 2014, SI 2014/3188, regs 2, 8(6).
6 Substituted by the Loan Relationships and Derivative Contracts (Disregard and Bringing into Account of Profits and Losses) (Amendment No. 2) Regulations 2007, SI 2007/3431, reg 2(1), (5).
7 Inserted by the Loan Relationships and Derivative Contracts (Disregard and Bringing into Account of Profits and Losses) (Amendment No. 2) Regulations 2005, SI 2005/3374, regs 2, 6.

[4B   Relevant time

(1)   For the purposes of regulations 3(4), 4(4) and 4A('relevant time' is determined as follows.

(2)   In a case within regulation 4A(1)(a) (relevant value determined by net asset value) the relevant time is the start of each review period in an accounting period.

(3)   In a case within regulation 4A(1)(b) (relevant value determined by accounts value), the relevant time is the time when the liability or contract is entered into or, if later, when the asset is acquired.]¹

[[4C   Review period

(1)   For the purposes of [regulations 4A(7)(b)]¹ and 4B(2), a review period is a period, or one of a series of successive periods, of a length specified by a company making an election in accordance with regulation 4A(1)(a).

This is subject to the provisions of this regulation.

(2)   A review period, or where more than one in an accounting period the first review period in that accounting period, begins on the first day of the accounting period or, if later, the date that a liability or derivative contract first becomes matched with shares in accordance with regulation 3(3)(b) or 4(3)(b).

(3)   A review period, or where more than one in an accounting period the last review period in that accounting period, must end on the last day of the accounting period.

(4)   If a company has matched shares in accordance with regulation 3(3)(b) or 4(3)(b) ('the first asset'), the first review period in relation to shares which are subsequently matched—

(a)   begins when the subsequent matching occurs, and

(b)   ends at the same time as the review period which is current in relation to the first asset when the subsequent matching occurs.

(5)   If during a review period ('the current period') there is a significant variation in the net asset value underlying shares which have been matched in accordance with regulation 3(3)(b) or 4(3)(b), there shall be a new review period in relation to those shares which—

(a)   begins on the day that any variation in the net asset value becomes a significant variation, and

(b)   ends at the same time as the current period.

(6)   In paragraph (5) 'significant variation' means an increase or decrease of 10% in the net asset value underlying the matched shares.

(7)   In this regulation the net asset value underlying shares shall be determined in accordance with regulation 4A(2).][2][3

---

1 Substituted by the Loan Relationships and Derivative Contracts (Disregard and Bringing into Account of Profits and Losses) (Amendment) Regulations 2014, SI 2014/3188, regs 2, 5.
2 Substituted by the Loan Relationships and Derivative Contracts (Disregard and Bringing into Account of Profits and Losses) (Amendment) Regulations 2011, SI 2011/698, regs 2, 6.
3 Substituted by the Loan Relationships and Derivative Contracts (Disregard and Bringing into Account of Profits and Losses) (Amendment No. 2) Regulations 2007, SI 2007/3431, reg 2(1), (5).

---

5   Regulations 3 and 4: supplementary

(1)   Where in any accounting period–

(a)   a company holds more than one asset in relation to which there are amounts of exchange gains and losses falling within regulations 3 or 4; and

(b)   the currency–

(i)   in which the assets are denominated and the liability [mentioned in regulation 3(1)][1] expressed; or

(ii)   which is the underlying subject matter of the derivative contract [mentioned in regulation 4(1)][1],

is the same currency …[2] [the extent to which an asset is matched is determined in accordance with the following rules][1].

[Rule 1

Liabilities and contracts are regarded as matched to the greatest possible extent with assets which are ships or aircraft.][3]

Rule 2

Subject to Rule 1, liabilities and contracts are regarded as matched to the greatest possible extent with assets on the disposal of which a chargeable gain would accrue [if the disposal were made on a date falling more than 12 months after the date of acquisition of the asset][1].

Rule 3

Subject to Rules 1 and 2, liabilities [and contracts][1] are regarded as matched with assets on a disposal of which no chargeable gain would be treated as accruing by virtue of Part 1 of Schedule 7AC to the Taxation of Chargeable Gains Act 1992 ...[2].

(2)   If–

    (a)   part only of a liability falling within the [condition 2][4] in regulation 3, or

    (b)   part only of a contract falling within the [condition 2][4] in regulation 4,

could reasonably be expected to eliminate or substantially reduce the economic risk of holding the asset which is attributable to fluctuations in exchange rates, the liability or contract is to be treated as being matched with a corresponding amount of value of an asset.

(3)   For the purposes of paragraph (1), a currency in which a liability is expressed or which is the underlying subject matter of a derivative contract, is to be treated, if it is not the case, as the same currency in which an asset is denominated if–

    (a)   borrowing in that currency, or

    (b)   the obligation to deliver that currency,

could reasonably be expected to eliminate or substantially reduce the economic risk of holding the asset, or part of the asset, which is attributable to fluctuations in exchange rates.

(4)   Where regulation 3 or [section 328(3) of CTA 2009][5] applies to a company in an accounting period in relation to a liability representing a loan relationship there is prescribed, for the purposes of regulation 3 or [section 328(4)][5] of that Act, an exchange gain or loss treated by virtue of [section 192(1) of the Taxation (International and Other Provisions) Act 2010][5] as arising in that accounting period to another company in relation to the same loan relationship.

---

1 Inserted by the Loan Relationships and Derivative Contracts (Disregard and Bringing into Account of Profits and Losses) (Amendment) Regulations 2005, SI 2005/2012, regs 2, 6(1), (2)(a), (b), (3), (5), (6)(a).
2 Revoked by the Loan Relationships and Derivative Contracts (Disregard and Bringing into Account of Profits and Losses) (Amendment) Regulations 2005, SI 2005/2012, regs 2, 6(1), (2)(c), (6)(b).

3 Substituted by the Loan Relationships and Derivative Contracts (Disregard and Bringing into Account of Profits and Losses) (Amendment) Regulations 2005, SI 2005/2012, regs 2, 6(1), (4).
4 Substituted by the Loan Relationships and Derivative Contracts (Disregard and Bringing into Account of Profits and Losses) (Amendment) Regulations 2007, SI 2007/948, regs 2, 4.
5 Substituted by the Loan Relationships and Derivative Contracts (Disregard and Bringing into Account of Profits and Losses) (Amendment) Regulations 2014, SI 2014/3188, regs 2, 8(7).

[5A   Net investment hedge of foreign operations

(1)   For the purposes of sections 328(4) and 606(4) of CTA 2009 there is prescribed an exchange gain or loss arising to a company in an accounting period in relation to a liability representing a loan relationship or derivative contract of the company where—

   (a)   the loan relationship or derivative contract is a designated hedge of a net investment in a foreign operation of the company, and

   (b)   amounts representing exchange gains or losses in respect of the loan relationship or derivative contract have, in accordance with generally accepted accounting practice, been recognised in the company's accounts as items of other comprehensive income.

(2)   In determining what amounts fall within paragraph (1)(b) at any time in an accounting period, it is to be assumed that the accounting policy applied in drawing up the company's accounts for the period was also applied in previous accounting periods.

(3)   But if the company's accounts for the period are, in accordance with generally accepted accounting practice, drawn up on an assumption as to the accounting policy in previous accounting periods which differs from that mentioned in paragraph (2), that different assumption applies in determining what amounts fall within paragraph (1)(b) at the time in question.][1]

1 Inserted by the Loan Relationships and Derivative Contracts (Disregard and Bringing into Account of Profits and Losses) (Amendment) Regulations 2015, SI 2015/1961, regs 2, 4.

[6   Application of regulations 7, 8 and 9 in relation to derivative contracts where fair value accounting applies

(1)   Regulation 7, 8 or 9 apply in relation to a derivative contract (which satisfies the conditions in regulation 7(1)(a), 8(1)(a) or 9(1), as the case may be) if—

   (a)   an election under regulation 6A has effect in relation to the contract,

   (b)   the contract or part of the contract is a designated fair value hedge,

   (c)   the hedged item is a loan relationship in relation to which the company uses fair value accounting, or

    (d)   the contract forms part of an arrangement the main purpose, or one of the main purposes, of which is to obtain a tax advantage in relation to that contract that would not arise if regulation 7, 8 or 9 applies.

(2)   In paragraph (1)(d)—

'arrangement' includes any agreement, understanding, scheme, transaction or series of transactions (whether or not legally enforceable);

'tax advantage' has the meaning given in section 1139 of CTA 2010.]¹

---

1 Substituted by the Loan Relationships and Derivative Contracts (Disregard and Bringing into Account of Profits and Losses) (Amendment) Regulations 2014, SI 2014/3188, regs 2, 6.

[6A   Election to apply regulations 7, 8 or 9

(1)   An election for the purposes of regulation 6(1)(a) must be made by a company by notice in writing to an officer of Revenue and Customs and applies regulations 7, 8 and 9 unless the notice states which of those regulations apply to the company's derivative contracts.

(2)   The election has effect—

    (a)   in the case of a new adopter where the election is made on or before the later of the dates set out in paragraph (3), in relation to derivative contracts held in the first relevant period and any subsequent period, and

    (b)   in any other case, in relation to derivative contracts entered into on or after a date specified in the election which must be later than the date the election is made, and in the case of a new adopter cannot be before two years after the end of the first relevant period.

(3)   The dates referred to in paragraph (2)(a) are—

    (a)   the date six months after the start of the first relevant period,

    (b)   the date six months after the date the company first enters into a relevant derivative contract [which the company measures at fair value]¹, and

    (c)   in the case of a company which is not a qualifying company for the purposes of Schedule 46 to the Finance Act 2009, the date 12 months after the end of the first relevant period.

(4)   An election may be amended or revoked by notice in writing to an officer of Revenue and Customs—

    (a)   in the case of an election made by a new adopter within paragraph (2)(a), before the later of the applicable dates set out in paragraph (3), or

    (b)   [either]¹—

        (i)   before the election has effect, or

        (ii)   after the election has effect, in relation to derivative contracts entered into on or after a date specified in the notice which must be later than the date the notice is given, and in the case of a new adopter cannot be before two years after the end of the first relevant period.

(5)   For the purposes of this regulation—

(a)   a 'new adopter' is a company which [measures a relevant derivative contract at fair value for the first time on or after 1st January 2015][1],

(b)   'the first relevant period' is the first accounting period in which a company [measures a relevant derivative contract at fair value][1],

(c)   a 'relevant derivative contract' is a derivative contract which satisfies the conditions in regulation 7(1)(a), 8(1)(a) or 9(1).][2]

---

1 Substituted by the Loan Relationships and Derivative Contracts (Disregard and Bringing into Account of Profits and Losses) (Amendment) Regulations 2015, SI 2015/1961, regs 2, 5.
2 Substituted by the Loan Relationships and Derivative Contracts (Disregard and Bringing into Account of Profits and Losses) (Amendment) Regulations 2014, SI 2014/3188, regs 2, 6.

[[6B   Effect of elections on group member replacing another as party to derivative contract: regulations 7 and 8

(1)   This regulation applies if—

(a)   one company replaces another as party to a derivative contract in relation to which regulation 7 or 8 applies, in circumstances in which section 625 of CTA 2009 applies or would apply but for section 628 of that Act,

(b)   the transferee (within the meaning of section 625 of CTA 2009) meets the conditions in regulation 7(1)(a)(i) and (ii) or 8(1)(a)(i) and (ii), as the case may be, in relation to the contract, and

(c)   the hedged item in relation to the derivative contract remains the same before and after the change of party.

(2)   Where this regulation applies—

(a)   section 628 applies (and accordingly section 625 does not apply),

(b)   regulation 7 or 8, as the case may be, applies in respect of the contract in relation to the transferee, and

(c)   regulation 10(9) applies.][1]][2]

---

1 Substituted by the Loan Relationships and Derivative Contracts (Disregard and Bringing into Account of Profits and Losses) (Amendment) Regulations 2015, SI 2015/1961, regs 2, 6.
2 Substituted by the Loan Relationships and Derivative Contracts (Disregard and Bringing into Account of Profits and Losses) (Amendment) Regulations 2014, SI 2014/3188, regs 2, 6.

[6C   Effect of elections on transfers within groups: regulation 9

(1)   This regulation applies if—

(a)   one company replaces another as party to a derivative contract in relation to which regulation 9 applies, in circumstances in which section 625 of CTA 2009 applies or would apply but for section 628 of that Act,

(b)   the transferee (within the meaning of section 625 of CTA 2009) meets the conditions in regulation 9(1)(a) and (b) in relation to the contract, and

(c)   the hedged item in relation to the derivative contract is the same before and after the change of party.

(2)   Where this regulation applies—

(a)   section 628 does not apply (and accordingly section 625 applies),

(b)   regulation 9 applies for the purposes of determining the carrying value of the contract for the purposes of section 702 of CTA 2009 as that regulation applies for the purposes of determining the debits and credits to be brought into account under Part 7 of that Act, and

(c)   regulation 9 applies in respect of the contract in relation to the transferee.][1]

---

1 Substituted by the Loan Relationships and Derivative Contracts (Disregard and Bringing into Account of Profits and Losses) (Amendment) Regulations 2015, SI 2015/1961, regs 2, 6.

[6D   Transfers within groups where no election under regulation 6A

(1)   This regulation applies if—

(a)   one company replaces another as party to a derivative contract in relation to which no election under regulation 6A has effect in circumstances in which section 625 of CTA 2009 applies or would apply but for section 628 of that Act,

(b)   the transferee (within the meaning of section 625 of CTA 2009) meets the conditions in regulation 7(1)(a)(i) and (ii), 8(1)(a)(i) and (ii) or 9(1)(a) and (b), as the case may be, in relation to the contract, and

(c)   the hedged item in relation to the derivative contract is the same before and after the change of party.

(2)   Where this regulation applies, any election made by the transferee under regulation 6A has no effect in relation to the contract.][1]

---

1 Substituted by the Loan Relationships and Derivative Contracts (Disregard and Bringing into Account of Profits and Losses) (Amendment) Regulations 2015, SI 2015/1961, regs 2, 6.

---

7 Fair value profits or losses arising from derivative contracts which are currency contracts

[(1)   For the purposes of [section 598(1)(a) of CTA 2009]¹ there is prescribed in relation to a derivative contract whose underlying subject matter consists wholly of currency—

   (a)   all credits and debits representing the whole or part of a company's fair value profit or loss in an accounting period if—

      (i)   there is a hedging relationship between the contract or part of the contract and a forecast transaction or a firm commitment ('the hedged item') of the company; and

      (ii)   the hedged item is not one [for which fair value profits or losses are brought into account for the purposes of corporation tax]²;

   (b)   a company's [section 614 or 615 credit or debit]¹ in relation to such a contract, if for the accounting period in which the [section 614 or 615 credit or debit]¹ falls to be brought into account sub-paragraph (a) applies to the contract; and

   (c)   a company's prior period adjustment credit or debit in relation to such a contract, if for the accounting period in which the prior period adjustment credit or debit falls to be brought into account sub-paragraph (a) applies to the contract,

and the credits and debits mentioned in sub-paragraphs (a) to (c) together make up the regulation 7 fair value profits or losses.]³

(2)   …⁴

(3)   Where there is a hedging relationship between part of a currency contract and a hedged item, the part of the [regulation 7]⁵ fair value profit or loss that is prescribed is the part which bears to the whole the proportion which the value of that part of the contract which is in the hedging relationship bears to the value of the whole of the contract.

[(4)   …⁶]⁵

[(5)   Where regulation 4 applies to a contract to which this regulation applies, nothing in this regulation or regulation 10 is to require any exchange gains or losses in relation to that contract to be brought into account.]⁷

---

1 Substituted by the Loan Relationships and Derivative Contracts (Disregard and Bringing into Account of Profits and Losses) (Amendment) Regulations 2014, SI 2014/3188, regs 2, 8(8)(a), (9), (10).
2 Substituted by the Loan Relationships and Derivative Contracts (Disregard and Bringing into Account of Profits and Losses) (Amendment No. 2) Regulations 2005, SI 2005/3374, regs 2, 8.
3 Substituted by the Loan Relationships and Derivative Contracts (Disregard and Bringing into Account of Profits and Losses) (Amendment) Regulations 2005, SI 2005/2012, regs 2, 8(1), (2).
4 Revoked by the Loan Relationships and Derivative Contracts (Disregard and Bringing into Account of Profits and Losses) (Amendment) Regulations 2005, SI 2005/2012, regs 2, 8(1), (3).

5 Inserted by the Loan Relationships and Derivative Contracts (Disregard and Bringing into Account of Profits and Losses) (Amendment) Regulations 2005, SI 2005/2012, regs 2, 8(1), (4), (5).
6 Revoked by the Loan Relationships and Derivative Contracts (Disregard and Bringing into Account of Profits and Losses) (Amendment) Regulations 2015, SI 2015/1961, regs 2, 7(a).
7 Inserted by the Loan Relationships and Derivative Contracts (Disregard and Bringing into Account of Profits and Losses) (Amendment) Regulations 2015, SI 2015/1961, regs 2, 7(b).

[7A Exchange gains or losses arising from derivative contracts hedging anticipated or future proceeds from certain issues of shares

(1)　For the purposes of section 598(1)(a) of the Corporation Tax Act 2009, an exchange gain or loss arising to a company is an excluded amount in an accounting period in relation to a derivative contract if—

　　(a)　the underlying subject matter of the contract consists wholly of currency; and

　　(b)　there is a relevant hedging relationship within the meaning of paragraph (2).

(2)　There is a relevant hedging relationship between a derivative contract (or part of a derivative contract) and the anticipated or future proceeds of an announced or proposed rights issue or open offer of shares ('relevant share issue') if, and to the extent that—

　　(a)　the contract (or part of the contract) is intended to hedge the economic risk to future capital raised under the relevant share issue ('the hedged item'); and

　　(b)　the economic risk is attributable to fluctuations in exchange rates between the currency in which the relevant share issue is denominated and the company's functional currency.

(3)　If there is a hedging relationship between part of a currency contract and a hedged item, the part of the fair value profit or loss that is an excluded amount is the part which bears to the whole the proportion which the value of that part of the contract which is in the hedging relationship bears to the value of the whole contract.

(4)　Paragraph (1) shall not apply to a derivative contract which is entered into with a person ('person A') to whom the company is connected unless—

　　(a)　a person who is connected to the company enters into a derivative contract with a person who is not connected with the company; and

　　(b)　that contract confers rights or imposes liabilities which are equivalent to those of A under the contract which A entered with the company.

(5)　Section 466 of the Corporation Tax Act 2009 (companies connected for an accounting period) applies for the purposes of paragraph (4).

(6)　A derivative contract to which this regulation applies may act as a hedge of the anticipated or future proceeds from a relevant share issue only to the extent that the value of the obligation under the derivative contract (within the meaning of regulation 4(5)) does not exceed the anticipated or future proceeds from the relevant share issue which, but for the derivative contract, would not be hedged.

(7) Subsections (3) and (4) of section 606 of the Corporation Tax Act 2009 do not apply to any exchange gain or loss which is an excluded amount by virtue of paragraph (1).

(8) In this regulation—

(a) 'functional currency', in relation to a company, means the currency of the primary economic environment in which the company operates; and

(b) 'rights issue or open offer of shares' means an offer or invitation to existing shareholders to subscribe for or purchase further shares in proportion to (or as nearly as may be in proportion to) their current holdings.][1]

---

1 Inserted by the Loan Relationships and Derivative Contracts (Disregard and Bringing into Account of Profits and Losses) (Amendment) Regulations 2009, SI 2009/1886, regs 3, 5.

---

8   Profits or losses arising from derivative contracts which are commodity contracts or debt contracts

[(1) For the purposes of [section 598(1)(a) of CTA 2009][1] there is prescribed in relation to a commodity contract or debt contract—

(a) all credits and debits representing the whole or part of a company's fair value profit or loss arising in an accounting period if—

(i) there is a hedging relationship between the contract or part of the contract and a forecast transaction or a firm commitment ('the hedged item') of the company; and

(ii) the hedged item is not one [for which fair value profits or losses are brought into account for the purposes of corporation tax][2];

(b) a company's [section 614 or 615 credit or debit][1], if for the accounting period in which the [section 614 or 615 credit or debit][1] falls to be brought into account, sub-paragraph (a) applies to the contract; and

(c) a company's prior period adjustment credit or debit, if for the accounting period in which the prior period adjustment credit or debit falls to be brought into account, sub-paragraph (a) applies to the contract,

and the credits and debits mentioned in sub-paragraphs (a) to (c) together make up the regulation 8 fair value profits or losses.][3]

(2) In this regulation–

'a commodity contract' means a derivative contract whose underlying subject matter is commodities unless the contract is an interest rate contract within the meaning of regulation 9(4); and 'a debt contract' means a derivative contract whose underlying subject matter is an asset or liability representing a loan relationship unless the contract is an interest rate contract within the meaning of regulation 9(4).

(3)   Where there is a hedging relationship between part of a commodity contract or part of a debt contract as the case may be and a hedged item, the part of the fair value profit or loss that is prescribed is the part which bears to the whole the proportion which the value of that part of the [regulation 8][4] contract which is in the hedging relationship bears to the value of the whole of the contract.

---

1 Substituted by the Loan Relationships and Derivative Contracts (Disregard and Bringing into Account of Profits and Losses) (Amendment) Regulations 2014, SI 2014/3188, regs 2, 8(8)(b), (9).
2 Substituted by the Loan Relationships and Derivative Contracts (Disregard and Bringing into Account of Profits and Losses) (Amendment No. 2) Regulations 2005, SI 2005/3374, regs 2, 8.
3 Substituted by the Loan Relationships and Derivative Contracts (Disregard and Bringing into Account of Profits and Losses) (Amendment) Regulations 2005, SI 2005/2012, regs 2, 9(1), (2).
4 Inserted by the Loan Relationships and Derivative Contracts (Disregard and Bringing into Account of Profits and Losses) (Amendment) Regulations 2005, SI 2005/2012, regs 2, 9(1), (3).

---

9 Profits or losses arising from derivative contracts which are interest rate contracts

(1)   For the purposes of [section 598(1)(a) of CTA 2009][1] there is prescribed all credits and debits representing the whole or part of the fair value profit or loss arising to a company in relation to its interest rate contracts in an accounting period if–

(a)   there is a hedging relationship between the contract or a portion of the contract and any of the risks arising in respect of an asset, liability, receipt or expense ('the hedged item'); and

(b)   fair value profits or losses arising on the hedged item or in relation to any of the risks[, in relation to which the contract was intended to act as a hedge,][2] arising in respect of the hedged item, or any portion of the hedged item, are not brought into account for the purposes of corporation tax for that period.

(2)   Where paragraph (1) applies, credits and debits shall be brought into account for the purposes of [section 598(1)(b) of CTA 2009][1] on the assumption that an appropriate accruals basis had been used in relation to the contract for that accounting period.

[(2A) Where an interest rate contract—

(a)   becomes a contract to which paragraph (1) applies, or

(b)   ceases to be a contract to which paragraph (1) applies,

the amount to be brought into account for the purposes of [section 598(1)(b) of CTA 2009][1] is such amount as is just and reasonable in the circumstances and with regard to whether as a result of the change any amounts cease to be brought into account or are brought into account more than once [and to the unexpired term of the hedged item]^3.]^4

(3) Where [regulation 4 or 5A]^5 apply to a contract to which this regulation applies nothing in this regulation is to require any exchange gains or losses in relation to that contract to be brought into account.

(4) In this regulation–

'an appropriate accruals basis' in relation to a derivative contract is one where–

(a) the contract is shown in the company's accounts at cost (which may be nil), and the cost is adjusted for any cumulative amortisation of any premium or other amount falling to be recognised in arriving at the cost of the contract;

(b) the aggregate of–

(i) the amount of periodical payments under the contract, or in the case of a swap contract under which only a single payment is to be made, the value of the payment and

(ii) the credits or debits representing interest arising, on the assumption that an effective interest method is used, in respect of the asset or liability representing a loan relationship which is the hedged item,

represent the credits or debits that would be given by generally accepted accounting practice in relation to an asset or liability representing a loan relationship whose terms include those of both the hedged item and the interest rate contract;

(c) exchange gains and losses are recognised as a result of the translation of the contract at the balance-sheet date; and

(d) profits and losses which arise as a result of the contract coming to an end before its stated date of maturity are amortised and brought into account over the unexpired term of the hedged item.

'an interest rate contract' means–

(i) a derivative contract whose underlying subject matter is, or includes, interest rates, or

(ii) if not falling within paragraph (i), a swap contract in which payments fall to be made by reference to a rate of interest or to an index determined by reference to income or retail prices.

(5) ...^{6}

(6) ...^{6}

(7) ...^{7}

---

1 Substituted by the Loan Relationships and Derivative Contracts (Disregard and Bringing into Account of Profits and Losses) (Amendment) Regulations 2014, SI 2014/3188, regs 2, 8(8)(c), (11).
2 Inserted by the Loan Relationships and Derivative Contracts (Disregard and Bringing into Account of Profits and Losses) (Amendment) Regulations 2006, SI 2006/3236, regs 2, 4.

3 Inserted by the Loan Relationships and Derivative Contracts (Disregard and Bringing into Account of Profits and Losses) (Amendment) Regulations 2015, SI 2015/1961, regs 2, 8(a).
4 Inserted by the Loan Relationships and Derivative Contracts (Disregard and Bringing into Account of Profits and Losses) (Amendment No. 2) Regulations 2005, SI 2005/3374, regs 2, 9.
5 Substituted by the Loan Relationships and Derivative Contracts (Disregard and Bringing into Account of Profits and Losses) (Amendment) Regulations 2015, SI 2015/1961, regs 2, 8(b).
6 Revoked by the Loan Relationships and Derivative Contracts (Disregard and Bringing into Account of Profits and Losses) (Amendment) Regulations 2015, SI 2015/1961, regs 2, 8(c).
7 Revoked by the Loan Relationships and Derivative Contracts (Disregard and Bringing into Account of Profits and Losses) (Amendment) Regulations 2014, SI 2014/3188, regs 2, 8(12).

[9A   ...[1]

...[1]][2]

1 Revoked by the Loan Relationships and Derivative Contracts (Disregard and Bringing into Account of Profits and Losses) (Amendment) Regulations 2015, SI 2015/1961, regs 2, 9.
2 Inserted by the Loan Relationships and Derivative Contracts (Disregard and Bringing into Account of Profits and Losses) (Amendment No. 2) Regulations 2005, SI 2005/3374, regs 2, 10.

10   Bringing fair value profits or losses into account on currency and commodity contracts

(1)   For the purposes of [section 598(1)(c) of CTA 2009][1]–

    (a)   there is prescribed the aggregate of the credits and debits representing any [regulation 7 or 8][2] fair value profits or losses excluded in relation to a derivative contract of a company ...[3]; and

    (b)   the amount of that aggregate is brought into account for the period in which a termination event occurs.

This is subject to paragraphs (3), (5), (7) [and (9)][4].

(2)   In paragraph (1) a 'termination event' occurs–

    (a)   on the company ceasing to be a party to the contract; or

    (b)   if earlier, when the hedged item begins to affect the company's profit or loss.

(3)   If the forecast transaction or firm commitment which is the hedged item mentioned in regulation 7 or regulation 8 is a forecast transaction of, or a firm commitment to a purchase of, anything the expenditure in relation to which–

    (a)   falls to be taken into account in computing the profits of a trade or property business carried on by the company, or

    (b)   would fall to be deducted but for any provision of the Corporation Tax Acts prohibiting the deduction of capital expenditure in respect of depreciation of an asset, then the aggregate mentioned in paragraph (1)(a) in relation to the contract is[, subject to paragraph (3A),]² to be brought into account in the accounting period in which the expenditure falls or would fall to be deducted.

[(3A) [Subject to paragraph (3B),]⁵ if paragraph (3)(b) applies—

(a) the amount to be brought into account in an accounting period is the product of

DA/E × FVP,

where—

DA is the amount of depreciation recognised in the profit and loss account or income statement in relation to the hedged item in the accounting period,

E is the total expenditure on the hedged item, and

FVP is the aggregate amount of regulation 7 or 8 fair value profit;

(b) where the hedged item is disposed of, the balance of the aggregate amount mentioned in paragraph (1)(a) which has not been brought into account under sub-paragraph (a) of this paragraph shall be brought into account in the accounting period in which the disposal takes place.]²

[(3B) Where the disposal mentioned in paragraph (3A)(b) is to a company ('the transferee') which is a member of the same group of companies, in applying paragraph (3A)(a) to the transferee FVP shall be treated as meaning the fair value profits and losses of the transferor.

(3C) In paragraph (3B), 'group of companies' has the meaning given in [section 624(3) of CTA 2009]¹.]⁵

(4) In paragraph (3) 'property business' has the meaning given in [section 748(4) of CTA 2009]¹ (gains and losses of a company from intangible fixed assets).

(5) Where–

(a) part of a contract to which this regulation applies terminates without the company ceasing to be a party to the contract, or

(b) part only of the hedged item begins to be recognised in determining the company's profit and loss,

paragraph (1)(b) [or paragraph (3)]² is to apply to a proportionate amount of the aggregate.

(6) In paragraph (5) 'proportionate amount' means that proportion of the relevant aggregate amount which is–

(a) in a case where it is part of the contract which matures, the [proportion]⁶ which the fair value of the part of the contract maturing bears to the fair value of the whole of the contract at that time, and

(b) in any other case the proportion which the fair value of the hedged item [which begins]⁶ to be recognised bears to the fair value of the whole of the hedged item at that time.

617

(7)   Where immediately on ceasing to be a party to the contract ('the old contract'), the company enters into another contract ('the new contract') which meets the conditions in regulation 7 or regulation 8 in relation to the same hedged item as was the hedged item in relation to the old contract–

    (a)   paragraph (1)(b) shall not apply in relation to the old contract, and

    (b)   the aggregate prescribed in paragraph (1)(a) in relation to the old contract shall be treated for the purposes of the application of this regulation to the new contract as included in the aggregate prescribed in relation to the new contract.

(8)   ...[7]

[(9)   Where regulation 6B applies—

    (a)   paragraph (1)(b) does not apply to the transferor, and

    (b)   the aggregate prescribed in paragraph (1)(a) in relation to the contract held by the transferor is treated as included in the aggregate prescribed in relation to the contract held by the transferee.

In this paragraph 'the transferor' and 'the transferee' have the same meaning as in section 625 of CTA 2009.][4]

(10)   ...[7]

(11)   ...[7]

---

1   Substituted by the Loan Relationships and Derivative Contracts (Disregard and Bringing into Account of Profits and Losses) (Amendment) Regulations 2014, SI 2014/3188, regs 2, 8(13)-(15).

2   Inserted by the Loan Relationships and Derivative Contracts (Disregard and Bringing into Account of Profits and Losses) (Amendment) Regulations 2005, SI 2005/2012, regs 2, 10(1), (2)(a), (3)-(5).

3   Revoked by the Loan Relationships and Derivative Contracts (Disregard and Bringing into Account of Profits and Losses) (Amendment) Regulations 2005, SI 2005/2012, regs 2, 10(1), (2)(b).

4   Substituted by the Loan Relationships and Derivative Contracts (Disregard and Bringing into Account of Profits and Losses) (Amendment) Regulations 2015, SI 2015/1961, regs 2, 10(a), (b).

5   Inserted by the Loan Relationships and Derivative Contracts (Disregard and Bringing into Account of Profits and Losses) (Amendment No. 2) Regulations 2005, SI 2005/3374, regs 2, 11(1)-(3).

6   Substituted by the Loan Relationships and Derivative Contracts (Disregard and Bringing into Account of Profits and Losses) (Amendment) Regulations 2005, SI 2005/2012, regs 2, 10(1), (6).

7   Revoked by the Loan Relationships and Derivative Contracts (Disregard and Bringing into Account of Profits and Losses) (Amendment) Regulations 2015, SI 2015/1961, regs 2, 10(c).

[10A Bringing exchange gains into account on contracts to which regulation 7A applies

(1) For the purposes of section 598(1)(c) of the Corporation Tax Act 2009 there is an amount to be brought into account which is equivalent to the amount of any exchange gain specified in paragraph (2).

(2) The exchange gain specified is any exchange gain—

(a) arising to a company in relation to a derivative contract to which regulation 7A applies or applied, and

(b) which has been distributed to the shareholders of the company.

(3) The amount to be brought into account by paragraph (1) is to be brought into account for the accounting period in which the distribution is made.]¹

---

1 Inserted by the Loan Relationships and Derivative Contracts (Disregard and Bringing into Account of Profits and Losses) (Amendment) Regulations 2009, SI 2009/1886, regs 3, 6.

[11 Profits and losses arising from loan relationships with embedded derivatives

[(1) For the purposes of [section 310(1) of CTA 2009]¹ (amounts recognised in determining company's profits and loss) the amounts described in paragraph (2) are prescribed in relation to a company which is party to a creditor relationship to which—

(a) either—

(i) section 92 (convertible securities etc: creditor relationships), or

(ii) section 93 (relationships linked to the value of chargeable assets),

of the Finance Act 1996 applied immediately before the start of the first accounting period of the company to begin on or after 1st January 2005, and

(b) section 94A of the Finance Act 1996 (loan relationships with embedded derivatives) applies in the first accounting period of the company to begin on or after 1st January 2005.

(1A) Where paragraph (1) does not apply, for the purposes of [section 310(1) of CTA 2009]¹ the amounts described in paragraph (3) are prescribed in relation to a company which is party to a creditor relationship to which—

(a) section 92, or

(b) section 93,

of the Finance Act 1996 applies immediately before the start of the first accounting period of the company to begin on or after 1st January 2005.]²

(2) The prescribed amounts are all credits and debits in respect of the host contract save for—

(a) credits in relation to interest accruing in respect of the creditor relationship without regard to the amounts given by the effective interest method; and

    (b)   [where paragraph (1)(a)(i) applies,]³ credits and debits in respect of exchange gains and losses.

(3)   The prescribed amounts are all credits and debits save for—

    (a)   credits in relation to interest, and

    (b)   [where paragraph (1A)(a) applies,]³ credits and debits in respect of exchange gains and losses.

[(4)   Where there is a change of accounting policy in drawing up a company's accounts from one period of account to the next affecting the amounts to be brought into account for accounting purposes in respect of the company's loan relationships, the amounts prescribed in paragraphs (1) to (3) that would otherwise be brought into account for the purposes of [Part 5 of the Corporation Tax 2009]¹ shall not be brought into account.]⁴]⁵

---

1 Substituted by the Loan Relationships and Derivative Contracts (Disregard and Bringing into Account of Profits and Losses) (Amendment) Regulations 2014, SI 2014/3188, regs 2, 8(17) (a), (18).
2 Substituted by the Loan Relationships and Derivative Contracts (Disregard and Bringing into Account of Profits and Losses) (Amendment) Regulations 2006, SI 2006/3236, regs 2, 6(1), (2).
3 Inserted by the Loan Relationships and Derivative Contracts (Disregard and Bringing into Account of Profits and Losses) (Amendment) Regulations 2006, SI 2006/3236, regs 2, 6(1), (3), (4).
4 Inserted by the Loan Relationships and Derivative Contracts (Disregard and Bringing into Account of Profits and Losses) (Amendment No. 2) Regulations 2005, SI 2005/3374, regs 2, 12.
5 Inserted by the Loan Relationships and Derivative Contracts (Disregard and Bringing into Account of Profits and Losses) (Amendment) Regulations 2005, SI 2005/2012, regs 2, 11.

[12

[(1)   For the purposes of [section 310(1) of CTA 2009]¹ the amounts described in paragraph (2) are prescribed in relation to a company which is party to a debtor relationship to which—

    (a)   either—

        (i)   section 92A (convertible securities etc: debtor relationships), or

        (ii)   section 93,

        of the Finance Act 1996 applies immediately before the start of the first accounting period of the company to begin on or after 1st January 2005, and

    (b)   section 94A of the Finance Act 1996 applies in the first accounting period of the company to begin on or after 1st January 2005.

    This is subject to paragraph (4).

(1A)   Where paragraph (1) does not apply, for the purposes of [section 310(1) of CTA 2009]¹ the amounts described in paragraph (2A) are prescribed in relation to a company which is party to a debtor relationship to which—

    (a)   section 92A, or

    (b)   section 93,

of the Finance Act 1996 applies immediately before the start of the first accounting period of the company to begin on or after 1st January 2005.

This is subject to paragraph (4).

(2)   The prescribed amounts are—

    (a)   where paragraph (1)(a)(i) applies, [all debits and credits in respect of the host contract save for—

        (i)   debits in relation to interest accruing in respect of the debtor relationship,

        (ii)   credits and debits in respect of discounts, premiums, fees and other incidental costs to the extent that these amounts are not within section 92A(3) of the Finance Act 1996, and

        (iii)   debits and credits in respect of exchange gains and losses,

        without regard to the amounts given by the effective interest method, and][2]

    (b)   where paragraph (1)(a)(ii) applies, all debits and credits in respect of the host contract save for debits in relation to interest accruing in respect of the debtor relationship without regard to the amounts given by the effective interest method.

(2A)   The prescribed amounts are—

    (a)   where paragraph (1A)(a) applies, debits to the extent that they are within section 92A(3) of the Finance Act 1996;

    (b)   where paragraph (1A)(b) applies, all debits and credits in respect of the host contract save for debits in relation to interest.][3]

[(3)   Where there is a change of accounting policy in drawing up a company's accounts from one period of account to the next affecting the amounts to be brought into account for accounting purposes in respect of the company's loan relationships, the amounts prescribed in paragraphs (1) and (2) that would otherwise be brought into account for the purposes of [Part 5 of the Corporation Tax 2009][1] shall not be brought into account.

(4)   This regulation does not apply to a company which is a party to a debtor relationship in a case where—

    (a)   the company is carrying on a banking business or a business consisting wholly or partly in dealing in securities, and

    (b)   it entered into the debtor relationship in the ordinary course of that business.][4][5]

---

1 Substituted by the Loan Relationships and Derivative Contracts (Disregard and Bringing into Account of Profits and Losses) (Amendment) Regulations 2014, SI 2014/3188, regs 2, 8(17)(b), (18).

2 Substituted by the Loan Relationships and Derivative Contracts (Disregard and Bringing into Account of Profits and Losses) (Amendment) Regulations 2007, SI 2007/948, regs 2, 6.

3 Substituted by the Loan Relationships and Derivative Contracts (Disregard and Bringing into Account of Profits and Losses) (Amendment) Regulations 2006, SI 2006/3236, regs 2, 7.

4 Inserted by the Loan Relationships and Derivative Contracts (Disregard and Bringing into Account of Profits and Losses) (Amendment No. 2) Regulations 2005, SI 2005/3374, regs 2, 13(1), (4).

5 Inserted by the Loan Relationships and Derivative Contracts (Disregard and Bringing into Account of Profits and Losses) (Amendment) Regulations 2005, SI 2005/2012, regs 2, 11.

[12A   Loan relationships as permanent as equity

(1)   The amounts described in paragraph (3) are not brought into account for the purposes of Part 5 of the Corporation Tax Act 2009 in relation an asset representing a loan relationship of a company which is denominated in a currency which is not, or was not, the company's functional currency, if there is a relevant change of accounting policy.

(2)   A relevant change of accounting policy is a change of accounting policy in drawing up a company's accounts from one period of account to the next where in accordance with generally accepted accounting practice—

   (a)   in the earlier period the loan relationship is treated (in accordance with SSAP 20) as permanent as equity and either—

      (i)   the loan relationship was brought into account at an historic rate, or

      (ii)   debits and credits in relation to the loan relationship were not brought into account by virtue of section 328(3) of the Corporation Tax Act 2009, and

   (b)   in the later period the loan relationship was brought into account at a spot rate of exchange.

(3)   The amounts are—

   (a)   debits and credits representing the difference between the carrying value of the loan relationship recognised for accounting purposes at the end of the earlier period and the value recognised at the beginning of the later period to the extent the debits or credits are attributable to the different rates of exchange, and

   (b)   debits and credits representing exchange gains and losses arising in the later period and subsequent accounting periods in relation to the loan relationship.

(4)   But an amount is not within paragraph (3)(b) to the extent that in any period—

   (a)   the loan relationship is a hedged item under a hedging relationship where the hedging instrument is a liability representing a loan relationship of the company or an obligation of the company under a derivative contract to pay in exchange for one currency an amount in a second currency, or

   (b)   regulation 3(5) applies in relation to the loan relationship.

(5) For the purposes of this regulation—

    (a) where there is a change of accounting policy in drawing up a company's accounts from one period of account to the next, the 'earlier period' is the first of those periods of account and the 'later period' is the next period;

    (b) 'functional currency' means the currency of the primary economic environment in which a company operates;

    (c) 'historic rate' and 'as permanent as equity' have the same meaning as for accounting purposes;

    (d) 'SSAP 20' means Statement of Standard Accounting Practice No.20 on Foreign Currency Translation, issued by the Accounting Standards Board on 1st April 1983.][1]

---

1 Inserted by the Changes in Accounting Standards (Loan Relationships and Derivative Contracts) Regulations 2014, SI 2014/3325, reg 3.

[13 Transitional provision: exchange losses arising from contracts to which regulation 7A applies

(1) This regulation applies to a derivative contract to which regulation 7A applies—

    (a) which was entered into on or after 1st January 2009;

    (b) which formed part of a relevant hedging relationship (within the meaning of regulation 7A) up to and including 10th March 2009; and

    (c) in respect of which an exchange loss would have arisen to the company had an accounting period ended on 9th March 2009.

(2) For the purposes of section 598(1)(c) of the Corporation Tax Act 2009 the amount to be brought into account is the lower of—

    (a) the exchange loss arising to the company which is incurred on the termination of the derivative contract; or

    (b) the exchange loss which would have arisen to the company in relation to the derivative contract had an accounting period ended on 9th March 2009.

(3) Paragraph (4) applies if there is more than one derivative contract to which regulation 7A applies in relation to the same hedged item.

(4) The total amount of the exchange loss in relation to those contracts which is to be brought into account under this regulation shall not exceed the aggregate net exchange losses (if any) which—

    (a) arose to the company on the termination of those contracts, or

    (b) would have arisen to the company in relation to those contracts had an accounting period ended on 9 March 2009.

(5)   Where paragraph (4) applies, the amount of loss to be brought into account is to be apportioned between each of the contracts on a just and reasonable basis.

(6)   For the purposes of this regulation, the termination of a derivative contract shall be regarded as having occurred on the earlier of—

    (a)   the day on which the contract is terminated, or

    (b)   the last day of the first accounting period which ends on or after 10th March 2009.

(7)   The amount to be brought into account for the purposes of section 598(1)(c) of the Corporation Tax Act 2009 is nil in a case where—

    (a)   no exchange loss arises to the company on the termination of the derivative contract;

    (b)   there is more than one derivative contract to which regulation 7A applies in relation to the same hedged item and no aggregate net exchange loss arises to the companion the termination of those contracts; or

    (c)   there is more than one derivative contract to which regulation 7A applies in relation to the same hedged item and no aggregate net exchange loss would have arisen to the company in relation to those contracts had an accounting period ended on 9th March 2009.][1]

---

1 Inserted by the Loan Relationships and Derivative Contracts (Disregard and Bringing into Account of Profits and Losses) (Amendment) Regulations 2009, SI 2009/1886, regs 3, 7.

Index

Milton Keynes UK
Ingram Content Group UK Ltd.
UKHW021452210324
439693UK00009B/2